BRIDGING THE GAP

COLLEGE READING

NINTH EDITION

Annotated Instructor's Edition

Brenda D. Smith

Emerita, Georgia State University

PEARSON

Longman

New York   Boston   San Francisco
London Toronto Sydney Tokyo Singapore Madrid
Mexico City Munich Paris Cape Town Hong Kong Montreal

To my mother and in honor of my father

Acquisitions Editor: Melanie Craig
Director of Development: Mary Ellen Curley
Development Editor: Janice Wiggins-Clarke
Marketing Manager: Thomas DeMarco
Supplements Editor: Donna Campion
Media Supplements Editor: Jenna Egan
Production Manager: Donna DeBenedictis
Project Coordination, Text Design, and Electronic Page Makeup: Nesbitt Graphics, Inc.
Cover Designer/Manager: John Callahan
Cover Photo: BigStockPhoto, Inc.
Photo Researcher: Julie Tesser
Manufacturing Buyer: Lucy Hebard
Printer and Binder: Courier Corporation/Kendallville
Cover Printer: Moore Langen

Please visit us at http://www.ablongman.com/smith

ISBN-13: 978-0-321-44602-2   ISBN-10: 0-321-44602-X (Student Edition)
ISBN-13: 978-0-205-53315-2   ISBN-10: 0-205-53315-9 (Annotated Instructor's Edition)

2 3 4 5 6 7 8 9 10—CRK—10 09 08

Brief Contents

Detailed Contents

Chapter 2   Vocabulary   57

Chapter 4   Main Idea   149

Chapter 7   Inference   351

Chapter 8   Point of View   419

Preface

Even before I wrote the first word of the first edition of *Bridging the Gap*, the title was somehow in my mind. In many ways, the title describes my reasons for writing the book. I initially wanted students to have a textbook that would fill in the gaps between successful high school reading and what is needed for the more independent and challenging task of college reading and learning.

Little did I know that the title would become even more relevant as reading theory evolved. Not only are we bridging the demands of the two institutional settings, but we are also bridging concept development by creating schemata for college content courses with academic readings. We are forming strong learning links by bridging new knowledge with prior knowledge. In accordance with evolving reading theory, this new ninth edition emphasizes the importance of three deliberate, but not totally new, bridges that are necessary for successful reading and learning: (1) connecting the text and your own personal experiences, (2) connecting the new text and other written material, and (3) connecting with bigger issues, events, and societal concerns. Needless to say, I still like the title and remain committed to helping students actively learn and consequently succeed in the academic courses required for graduation.

New to the Ninth Edition

The ninth edition of *Bridging the Gap* has been improved by the addition of 15 new longer reading selections. With this new material there are now three longer reading selections for most chapters. Returning to the three-selection format of the first edition should offer more than enough material to meet individual student interests and provide maximum flexibility for teachers.

The ninth edition has also been updated with 26 new Contemporary Focus articles from current newspapers and magazines. Paired with the longer reading selections, this feature makes connections, generates curiosity, enhances schema, and expands thinking.

Additional practice exercises on main idea, patterns of organization, and annotating, outlining, and mapping have also been added.

Many new vocabulary items have been created in Chapter 2 and in the ten Vocabulary Booster exercises at the ends of chapters. The focus is on linking and learning words through word parts or word families. The Vocabulary Booster features offer an opportunity for weekly vocabulary expansion and reinforcement.

Content and Organization

The ninth edition continues the tradition of previous editions by using actual college textbook material for teaching and practice. Designed for an upper-level course in college reading, each chapter introduces a new skill, provides short practice exercises to teach the skill, and then offers practice through longer textbook selections.

Presentation of skills in the text moves from the general to the specific. Initial chapters discuss active learning (Chapter 1), vocabulary (Chapter 2), study strategies (Chapter 3), main idea (Chapter 4), and patterns of organization (Chapter 5), while later chapters teach inference (Chapter 7), point of view (Chapter 8), critical thinking (Chapter 9), graphic illustrations (Chapter 10), rate flexibility (Chapter 11), and test-taking skills (Chapter 12). The reading and study skills discussions in the first portion of the book stress the need to construct the main idea of a passage and to select significant supporting details. Exercises encourage "engaged thinking" before reading, while reading, and after reading. Four different methods of organizing textbook information for later study are explained.

Special Features of the Ninth Edition

- In **Concept Prep**, a popular feature carried over from the eighth edition, key concepts in a variety of academic disciplines are matched with the subjects in many of the longer reading selections. These selected concepts, reflecting common knowledge that lies at the core of each academic area, are also an important part of the shared cultural heritage of educated thinkers.

  The purpose of this innovative feature is to develop schema and prior knowledge for students' later academic success. For example, the first Concept Prep for Psychology discusses people and ideas at the heart of every introductory psychology course, including Sigmund Freud's and Carl Jung's theories, Ivan Pavlov's discovery of and experiments with classical conditioning, and B. F. Skinner's behaviorism.

- **Establish a Purpose for Reading** preview activities have been enriched to connect text-to-self by recalling prior knowledge and experiences, to encourage predictions, and to state a purpose.

- Twenty-seven **Contemporary Focus** articles paired with the longer textbook readings are included to activate schemata, enrich content knowledge, connect text-to-text, and to promote group discussion. Each article is drawn from a popular source, such as a magazine or newspaper, to demonstrate the textbook reading's relevance to the "real world."

- **Write About the Selection** questions encourage text-to-self and text-to-world connections by asking students to make a personal link to the text book selection or to link to the larger global issues.

- **Contemporary Link** questions promote text-to-text and critical thinking by demonstrating the relevance of the introductory articles to the textbook selections that they accompany. A list of textbook readings, along with their accompanying **Contemporary Focus** features, follows the Preface.

- **Vocabulary Booster** activities focus on linking and learning words through word parts or word families. The lessons can be assigned weekly, and student progress can be measured using the assessment quizzes in the Instructor's Manual. In addition, this edition includes more than 160 vocabulary words in context after the longer reading selections.

- **Fifteen new longer reading selections** balance out the chapters so that most chapters now include three readings each.

- **Many new photos** have been carefully chosen to amplify the exposition.
- Improved **Search the Net** activities after the longer textbook reading selections encourage students to amplify textbook study through Internet research. Because electronic reading skills are now essential for college students, the first Search the Net activity in Chapter 1 begins with a general explanation of how to plan and conduct an effective Internet search.

  Subsequent activities encourage students to find suggestions on the text's Web site (http://www.ablongman. com/smith) to connect Internet exploration with the textbook topics in each longer reading selection.
- **Making Sense of Figurative Language and Idioms** (Appendix) presents updated idiomatic expressions that will be of particular value to ESL students seeking practice opportunities with English similes, metaphors, and idioms.
- A **Progress Chart** is located on the inside back cover so students can record their progress in understanding the longer reading selections.
- Chapter-by-chapter **Reader's Journal** activities now appear on the text's Web site. With these reflective activities, students can learn about themselves, consider their strengths and weaknesses, and monitor their progress. After these activities are completed, they can either be e-mailed to the instructor or printed out and handed in.

Continuing Features

Other classroom-tested features of the book include the following:

- Actual **textbook selections** are used for practice exercises.
- **Many academic disciplines** are represented throughout, including psychology, history, communications, economics, business, health, sociology, criminal justice, and literature—including essay, short story, poetry, and narrative nonfiction forms.
- **Vocabulary is presented in context;** and vocabulary exercises follow each of the longer textbook reading selections. In addition to the end-of-chapter **Vocabulary Booster** lessons, a broad range of **vocabulary development** topics and corresponding exercises is presented in Chapter 2.
- **Reader's Tip** boxes give easy-to-access advice for readers, condensing strategies for improving reading into practical hints for quick reference.
- Each longer textbook selection has both **explicit and inferential questions**. Multiple-choice items are labeled as *main idea, inference,* or *detail questions*.
- Some selections include essay questions that elicit an organized **written response**.
- Although skills build and overlap, **each chapter can be taught as a separate unit** to fit individual class or student needs.
- **Pages are perforated** so that students can tear out and hand in assignments.
- Discussion and practice **exercises on barriers to critical thinking**—including cultural conditioning, self-deception, and oversimplification—appear throughout the book.
- Practice is offered in **identifying fallacies** in critical thinking and in **evaluating arguments**.

The Teaching and Learning Package

Text-Specific Ancillaries

Annotated Instructor's Edition (0-205-53315-9). This is an exact replica of the student edition but includes all answers printed directly on the fill-in lines provided in the text.

Instructor's Manual (0-205-53526-7). This manual contains overhead transparency masters and additional vocabulary and comprehension questions for each reading selection. The true-false, vocabulary, and comprehension quizzes can be used as prereading quizzes to stimulate interest or as evaluation quizzes after reading. Vocabulary-in-context exercises are also included to reinforce the words in the longer textbook selections. In addition, a true-false quiz is provided for each of the Concept Prep sections.

Test Bank (0-205-53569-0). This test bank includes additional reading selections, chapter tests, and vocabulary tests.

Computerized Test Bank (0-205-53175-X). This electronic test bank includes chapter tests and vocabulary tests in TestGen format.

Bridging the Gap **Companion Website** (www.ablongman.com/smith). For a wealth of additional materials, including online chapter summaries, quizzes, and Internet activities, be sure to visit the Companion Website.

To receive an examination copy of the any text-specific ancillaries, please contact your Longman sales representative. You may also request an examination copy by calling 1-800-552-2499 or by sending your request via e-mail to exam@ablongman.com.

In addition to these text-specific supplements, many other skills-based supplements and testing packages are available for both instructors and students.

The Longman Developmental English Package

Longman is pleased to offer a variety of support materials to help make teaching reading easier on teachers and to help students excel in their coursework. Contact your local Longman sales representative for more information on pricing and how to create a package.

For Reading and Study Skills Instructors

Printed Test Bank for Developmental Reading (0-321-08596-5). This test bank offers more than 3,000 questions in all areas of reading, including vocabulary, main idea, supporting details, patterns of organization, critical thinking, analytical reasoning, inference, point of view, visual aides, and textbook reading.

Electronic Test Bank for Developmental Reading (0-321-08179-X). This electronic test bank offers more than 3,000 questions in all areas of reading, including vocabulary, main idea, supporting details, patterns of organization, critical thinking, analytical reasoning, inference, point of view, visual aides, and textbook reading. Instructors simply choose questions, then print out the completed test for distribution OR offer the test online.

The Longman Guide to Classroom Management (0-321-09246-5). This guide is designed as a helpful resource for instructors who have classroom management problems. It includes helpful strategies for dealing with disruptive students in the classroom and the "do's and don'ts" of discipline.

The Longman Guide to Community Service-Learning in the English Classroom and Beyond (0-321-12749-8). Written by Elizabeth Rodriguez Kessler of California State University–Northridge, this monograph provides a definition and history of service-learning, as well as an overview of how service-learning can be integrated effectively into the college classroom.

The Longman Instructor's Planner (0-321-09247-3). This planner includes weekly and monthly calendars, student attendance and grading rosters, space for contact information, Web references, an almanac, and blank pages for notes.

For Students

Vocabulary Skills Study Cards (0-321-31802-1). Colorful, affordable, and packed with useful information, Longman's Vocabulary Study Card is a concise, eight-page reference guide to developing key vocabulary skills, such as learning to recognize context clues, reading a dictionary entry, and recognizing key root words, suffixes, and prefixes. Laminated for durability, students can keep this Study Card for years to come and pull it out whenever they need a quick review.

Reading Skills Study Card (0-321-33833-2). Colorful, affordable, and packed with useful information, Longman's Reading Skills Study Card is a concise, eight-page reference guide to developing basic reading skills, such as concept skills, structural skills, language skills, and reasoning skills. Laminated for durability, students can keep this Study Card for years to come and pull it out whenever they need a quick review.

The Longman Textbook Reader, Second Edition (with answers 0-321-48629-3; without answers 0-205-51924-5). This collection of five complete chapters from textbooks across disciplines gives students practice with authentic college material. Each chapter includes additional comprehension quizzes, critical thinking questions, and group activities.

The Longman Reader's Portfolio and Student Planner (0-321-29610-9). This unique supplement provides students with a space to plan, think about, and present their work. The portfolio includes a diagnostic area (including a learning style questionnaire), a working area (including calendars, vocabulary logs, reading response sheets, book club tips, and other valuable materials), and a display area (including a progress chart, a final table of contents, and a final assessment), as well as a daily planner for students including daily, weekly, and monthly calendars.

The Longman Reader's Journal, by Kathleen McWhorter (0-321-08843-3). The first journal for readers, the Longman Reader's Journal, offers a place for students to record their reactions to and questions about any reading.

10 Practices of Highly Effective Students (0-205-30769-8). This study skills supplement includes topics such as time management, test taking, reading critically, stress, and motivation.

Newsweek **Discount Subscription Coupon (12 weeks)** (0-321-08895-6). *Newsweek* gets students reading, writing, and thinking about what's going on in the world around them. The price of the subscription is added to the cost of the book. Instructors receive weekly lesson plans, quizzes, and curriculum guides as well as a complimentary *Newsweek* subscription. The price of the subscription is 59 cents per issue (a total of $7.08 for the subscription). *Package item only.*

Interactive Guide to *Newsweek* (0-321-05528-4). Available with the 12-week subscription to *Newsweek*, this guide serves as a workbook for students who are using the magazine.

Research Navigator Guide for English, H. Eric Branscomb & Doug Gotthoffer (0-321-20277-5). Designed to teach students how to conduct high-quality online research and to document it properly, Research Navigator guides provide discipline-specific academic resources, in addition to helpful tips on the writing process, online research, and finding and citing valid sources. Research Navigator guides, which include an access code to Research Navigator™, provide access to thousands of academic journals and periodicals, the New York Times Search-by-Subject Archive, Link Library, Library Guides, and more.

Penguin Discount Novel Program. In cooperation with Penguin Putnam, Inc., Longman is proud to offer a variety of Penguin paperbacks at a significant discount when packaged with any Longman title. Excellent additions to any developmental reading course, Penguin titles give students the opportunity to explore contemporary and classical fiction and drama. The available titles include works by authors as diverse as Toni Morrison, Julia Alvarez, Mary Shelley, and Shakespeare. To review the complete list of titles available, visit the Longman-Penguin-Putnam website: http://www.ablongman.com/penguin.

Oxford American College Dictionary (0-399-14415-3). Drawing on Oxford's unparalleled language resources, including a 200-million-word database, this college dictionary contains more than 175,000 entries and more than 1000 illustrations, including line drawings, photographs and maps. *Available at a significant discount when packaged with a Longman textbook—only $15.*

The New American Webster Handy College Dictionary (0-451-18166-2). This paperback reference text has more than 100,000 entries.

Multimedia Offerings

Interested in incorporating online materials into your course? Longman is happy to help. Our regional technology specialists provide training on all of our multimedia offerings.

MyReadingLab (www.myreadinglab.com). The MyReadingLab Web site provides unparalleled reading practice and assessment for college reading courses. A combination of the best-selling Reading Road Trip skill tutorial and the Lexile Framework® for Reading by MetaMetrics, MyReadingLab gives the unprecedented ability to diagnose both reading skills and reading levels and track student progress during the course.

MyReadingLab complements textbook learning and improves reading ability with these features:

- **Thoroughly revised and redesigned Reading Road Trip.** New questions have been written for each location, including open ended questions, and a new bank of combined skills tests.
- **Accurate assessment of students' reading levels.** Students are offered a unique set of exercises designed to help them improve their reading level through mastery-based practice.
- **Personalized student study plans.** Generated based on results of the diagnostic tests, individualized study plans direct students to the skills they need to work through to improve reading ability.
- **Progress-tracking gradebook.** Available for students and instructors, the gradebook shows individual student's progress or the performance of an entire class.
- **Access to Study Skills, Vocabulary, and Research Navigator Web sites.** Subscriptions to these popular sites are included with MyReadingLab.

State-Specific Supplements

For Florida Adopters

Thinking Through the Test: A Study Guide for the Florida College Basic Skills Exit Test, by D.J. Henry. This workbook helps students strengthen their reading skills in preparation for the Florida College Basic Skills Exit Test. It features both diagnostic tests to help assess areas that may need improvement and exit tests to help test skill mastery. Detailed explanatory answers have been provided for almost all of the questions. *Package item only—not available for sale.*

Available Versions:

Thinking Through the Test:
A Study Guide for the Florida College Basic Skills Exit Tests:
Reading and Writing, Second Edition   0-321-27660-4

Thinking Through the Test:
A Study Guide for the Florida College Basic Skills Exit Tests:
Reading and Writing, with Answers, Second Edition   0-321-27756-2

Thinking Through the Test:
A Study Guide for the Florida College Basic Skills Exit Tests:
Reading   0-321-27746-5

Thinking Through the Test:
A Study Guide for the Florida College Basic Skills Exit Tests:
Reading, with Answers   0-321-27751-1

Reading Skills Summary for the Florida State Exit Exam, by D. J. Henry (0-321-08478-0). An excellent study tool for students preparing to take Florida College Basic Skills Exit Test for Reading, this laminated reading grid summarizes all the skills tested on the Exit Exam. *Package item only—not available for sale.*

CLAST Test Package, Fourth Edition (Instructor/Print ISBN 0-321-01950-4). These two, 40-item objective tests evaluate students' readiness for the Florida CLAST exams. Strategies for teaching CLAST preparedness are included.

For Texas Adopters

The Longman THEA Study Guide, by Jeannette Harris (0-321-27240-0). Created specifically for students in Texas, this study guide includes straightforward explanations and numerous practice exercises to help students prepare for the reading and writing sections of THEA Test. *Package item only—not available for sale.*

TASP Test Package, Third Edition (Instructor/Print 0-321-01959-8). These 12 practice pre-tests and post-tests assess the same reading and writing skills covered in the Texas TASP examination.

For New York/CUNY Adopters

Preparing for the CUNY-ACT Reading and Writing Test, edited by Patricia Licklider (0-321-19608-2). This booklet, prepared by reading and writing faculty from across the CUNY system, is designed to help students prepare for the CUNY-ACT exit test. It includes test-taking tips, reading passages, typical exam questions, and sample writing prompts to help students become familiar with each portion of the test.

Acknowledgments

I would like to thank my Basic Skills Editor, Melanie Craig. My developmental editor, Janice Wiggins-Clarke, has worked with me on several projects, and I admire her skills. I appreciate her tireless efforts, encouraging words, organizational skills, and attention to detail. Janice has been an essential factor in the coordination and development of the ninth edition. I want to thank Rochelle Favale for her research, careful proofing, and many contributions to this book. I would also like to thank Sharon Swallwood, Jim Rogge, Staci Carroll, and Kessea Weiser for their contributions to this edition.

Lisa Moore, my researcher, located many of the Contemporary Focus articles. Lisa has been prompt, responsive, and clever in offering many interesting possibilities to match with our longer reading selections.

I feel extremely privileged to have received advice from so many learned colleagues in the college reading profession for this and previous editions of *Bridging the Gap*. Special thanks go to those reviewers of the eighth edition of *Bridging the Gap* whose thoughtful commentary strengthened this ninth edition:

Edith Alderson
Joliet Junior College

Anna Apple
Cy-Fair College

Hilda Barrow
Pitt Community College

Linda Black
St. John's River College

Carlos Blanco
St. Louis Community College

Kathleen Colarusso
College of Southern Maryland

Marlys Cordoba
College of the Siskiyous

Kathy Daily
Tulsa Community College

Barbara Doyle
Arkansas State University

Mary Dubbe
Thomas Nelson Community College

Rochelle Favale
College of DuPage

Margaret Hampson
Caldwell Community College and Technical Institute

Beth Healander
Lexington Community College

Wei Lei
North Harris College

Luanne Lundberg
Clark College

Cathy Moran
College of the Mainland

Pamela Price
Greenville Technical College

Rick Richards
St. Petersburg College

Roberta Sampere
Brevard Community College

John Sandin
Tacoma Community College

Melinda Schomaker
Georgia Perimeter College

Sharette Simpkins
Florida Community College

Peggy Strickland
Gainesville College

Sharon Swallwood
St. Petersburg College

Roberta Ziegler
Palo Alto College

—Brenda D. Smith

An Overview of *Bridging the Gap*

The ninth edition of *Bridging the Gap* features triple readings at the end of most chapters, in many cases followed by a Concept Prep for a particular academic discipline. Each reading selection begins with a Contemporary Focus article drawn from a popular source, such as a newspaper or magazine, that introduces the subject and promotes learning by connecting the academic selection to current issues. The Concept Prep feature continues to highlight academic knowledge expected of educated thinkers.

Discipline/Genre of Reading Selection	Textbook or Academic Selection	Accompanying Contemporary Focus Article	Accompanying Concept Prep
Chapter 1: Active Learning			
Education	"The Joy of Reading"	"Kid Doesn't Want to Read"	
Psychology	"Critical-Period Hypothesis"	"Early Pup Separation Leads to Aggression"	Psychology
Health	"Steroids"	"Keeping Kids Off the Juice"	Health
Chapter 3: Strategic Reading and Study			
History	"Madame C. J. Walker"	"Entrepreneur Draws Inspiration from Cosmetics Industry Pioneer"	History
Sociology	"Unity in Diversity"	"Culture Clash: Closing Gaps between Different Worlds Is Crucial to Building Team Trust"	Anthropology
Business	"On the Front Lines of the Service Sector"	"Watch How People Treat Staff"	
Chapter 4: Main Idea			
Psychology	"Monkey Love"	"Mother's Love Works Like Opiate"	Psychology
Short Story	"On the Sidewalk, Bleeding"	"A Chance for a Clean Start"	Literature
Criminal Justice	"Female Police Officers"	"Arresting Development"	
Chapter 5: Patterns of Organization			
Narrative	"What I Did for Love"	"So Many Men, So Few Women"	
History	"Women in History"	"What Makes Condi Run"	Art History
Business	"Why Is Papa John's Rolling in the Dough?"	"Investors Hope for Slice of Pizza Box Business"	Business

Discipline/Genre of Reading Selection	Textbook or Academic Selection	Accompanying Contemporary Focus Article	Accompanying Concept Prep
Chapter 6: Organizing Textbook Information			
Communications	"Influence of Magazines"	"Snuffing Out Magazines"	Communications and Language
Health	"Nutrition, Health, and Stress"	"Drink and Be Wary"	Health
Criminal Justice	"Electronic Monitoring"	"Can I Cut Off My Electronic Monitoring Bracelet?"	
Chapter 7: Inference			
Short Story	"A Dip in the Poole"	"Short in Length But Large in Stature"	Philosophy and Literature
Short Story	"Witches' Loaves"	"Today in History: O. Henry"	
Narrative Nonfiction	"Learning to Read: Malcolm X"	"Remembering a Civil Rights Hero"	Political Science
Chapter 8: Point of View			
Essay	"What is the Quarterlife Crisis?"	"Growing Up Is Taking Longer Than It Used To"	
Communications	"Gender Gap in Cyberspace"	"Study Reveals Gender Divide in Use of News Media"	
Sociology	"The Big Win: Life After the Lottery"	"Obtain Professional Advice If You Win Big"	
Chapter 9: Critical Thinking			
Essay	"The Importance of Being Beautiful"	"The Beauty Premium"	
Essay	"Study Links Cell Phones to Brain Damage"	"Mobile Phones Affect DNA"	
Essay	"How Boys Become Men"	"Boys' Perceptions of the Male Role"	
Chapter 10: Graphic Illustrations			
Economics	"The Principality of Monaco"	"Monaco Cleans Up Its Act"	
Science	"Effects of Earthquakes"	"Shock Tactic That Could Save a City"	
Sociology	"Technology and the Environment"	"Water Crisis Will Worsen Plight"	

1 Active Learning

- What is active learning?
- How does the brain "pay attention"?
- Can you do two things at once?
- What are multiple intelligences?
- How can you improve your concentration?
- What are common internal and external distractors and cures?
- Why is your syllabus important?

Fernand Leger (1881–1955), *The Reading*, 1924. Oil on canvas. Photo Bertrand Prevos.

What Is Active Learning?

Active learning is not just a single task; it is a *project with multiple components*. You, your instructor, your textbook, and your classmates are all parts of the project. Learn to use all four effectively, and you are on the road to success.

As a starting point, active learning requires concentration and attention to details beyond academics. You must manage yourself, manage the assignment or learning task, and manage others who can contribute to or detract from your success. In this chapter, we discuss many factors that contribute to your ability to become an effective active learner. First, however, let's consider what psychologists have to say about focusing your attention, thinking, and learning. Understanding these cognitive aspects is a part of managing yourself.

What Is Cognitive Psychology?

Cognitive psychology is the body of knowledge that describes how the mind works, or at least how experts think the mind works. Fortunately or unfortunately, the activity of the brain when concentrating, reading, and remembering cannot be observed directly. These cognitive processes are invisible, as are thinking and problem solving.

Because so little is actually known about thinking, the ideas of cognitive psychologists are frequently described as *models*, or comparisons with something else we understand. For more than thirty years, for example, the central processing unit of a computer has been a popular model for describing how the brain processes information. The human brain is more complex than a computer, but the analogy provides a comparison that can help us understand.

How Does the Brain Screen Messages?

Cognitive psychologists use the word **attention** to describe a student's uninterrupted mental focus. Thinking and learning, they say, begin with attention. During every minute of the day, the brain is bombarded with millions of sensory messages. How does the brain decide which messages to pay attention to and which to overlook? At this moment, are you thinking about the temperature of the room, outdoor noises, or what you are reading? With all this information available to you at the same time, how can your brain choose what's most important?

The brain relies on a dual command center to screen out one message and attend to another. According to a researcher at UCLA, receptor cells send millions of messages per minute to your brain.[1] Your reticular activating system (RAS)—a network of cells at the top of the spinal cord that runs to the brain— tells the cortex of the brain—the wrinkled outer layer that handles sensory processing, motor control, and memory storage—not to bother with most of the sensory input. Your RAS knows that most sensory inputs do not need attention. For example, you are probably not aware at this moment of your back pressing

---

[1]H. W. Magoun, *The Waking Brain*, 2nd ed. (Springfield, IL: Charles C. Thomas, 1963).

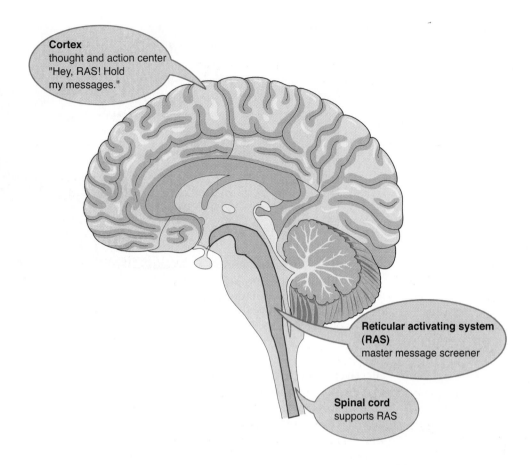

against your chair or your clothes pulling on your body. Your RAS has decided not to clutter your brain with such irrelevant information and to alert the cortex only when there is an extreme problem, such as your foot going to sleep because you have been sitting on it.

The cortex can also make attention decisions and tells your RAS to hold some messages while you concentrate on others. How well are your RAS and cortex cooperating in blocking out distractions so you can concentrate on learning?

Is Divided Attention Effective?

Is it possible to do two things at once, such as watching television and doing homework? Is it safe to drive and talk on a cell phone? In a 2002 study, researchers Rodriguez, Valdes-Sosa, and Freiwald found that dividing your attention usually has a cost.[2] You are more likely to perform one or both tasks less efficiently than if you were to concentrate on a single task. This corroborated, or made more certain, the earlier findings of two other scientists who tested the

---

[2]V. Rodriguez, M. Valdes-Sosa, and W. Freiwald, "Dividing Attention Between Form and Motion During Transparent Surface Perception," *Cognitive Brain Research* 13 (2002): 187–93.

David Young-Wolff/Stone/Getty Images

Dividing your attention can have a cost. Researchers have found that the auto accident rate among people who drive while talking on the phone (including those using headsets) is four times that of drivers who do not use the phone as they drive.[3]

effectiveness of divided attention.[4] These researchers asked participants questions as they watched two televised sports events with one superimposed over the other. When participants were instructed to watch only one of the games, they successfully screened out the other and answered questions accurately. When asked to attend to both games simultaneously, however, the participants made eight times more mistakes than when focusing on only one game. Thus, this research seems to confirm the old adage "You can't do two things at once and do them well."

Can Tasks Become Automatic?

Can you walk and chew gum at the same time? Does every simple activity require your undivided attention? Many tasks—walking, tying shoelaces, and driving a car, for example—begin under controlled processing, which means that they are deliberate and require concentrated mental effort to learn. After much practice, however, such tasks become automatic. Driving a car, for example, is a learned behavior that researchers would say becomes an automatic process after thousands of hours of experience. You can probably drive and listen to the radio at the same time, but it may not be a good idea to drive and talk on a cell phone. Similarly, a skilled athlete can dribble a basketball automatically while also attending to strategy and position. Attention is actually not divided because it can shift away from tasks that have become automatic.

---

[3]D. A. Redelmeier and R. J. Tibshiramni, "Association Between Cellular-Telephone Calls and Motor Vehicle Collisions," *New England Journal of Medicine* 336 (1997): 453–58.

[4]U. Neisser and R. Becklen, "Selective Looking: Attending to Visually Significant Events," *Cognitive Psychology* 7 (1975): 480–94.

Automatic Aspects of Reading

The idea of doing certain things automatically is especially significant in reading. As a first-grade reader, you had to concentrate on recognizing letters, words, and sentences, as well as trying to construct meaning. After years of practice and over-learning, much of the recognition aspect of reading has become automatic. You no longer stop laboriously to decode each word or each letter. For example, when you look at the word *child*, you automatically think the meaning. Thus, you can focus your mental resources on understanding the *message* in which the word appears, rather than on understanding the word itself.

College reading can be frustrating because it is not as automatic as everyday reading. College textbooks often contain many unfamiliar words and complex concepts that the brain cannot automatically process. Your attention to a book's message can be interrupted by the need to attend to unknown words, creating the dilemma of trying to do two things at once—trying to figure out word meaning as well as trying to understand the message. After the break, you can regain your concentration, and little harm is done if such breaks are infrequent. However, frequent interruptions in the automatic aspect of reading can undermine your ability to concentrate on the message. Thus, mastering the jargon or vocabulary of a new course early on can improve your concentration.

Cognitive Styles

Do you learn easily by reading or do you prefer a demonstration or a diagram? Do you like to work with details or do you prefer broad generalizations? Many psychologists believe that people develop a preference for a particular style or manner of learning at an early age and that these preferences affect concentration and learning. Cognitive style theorists focus on strengths and assert that there is no right or wrong way. These researchers believe that instruction is best when it matches the learner's particular preference.

Although knowing your preferences may not affect how your classes are taught, such knowledge can improve your attitude about yourself as a learner and enable you to build on your strengths.

Cognitive Style Preferences

One popular inventory that can be used to determine individual cognitive style preferences is the Myers-Briggs Type Indicator (MBTI). Based on psychologist Carl Jung's theory of personality types, it measures personality traits in four categories. The results are used as indicators for learning styles, teaching styles, management styles, career planning, team building, organizational development, and even marriage counseling. The inventory must be administered by a licensed specialist and is frequently given to entering college freshmen. The following descriptions of the four MBTI categories give an idea of the issues its proponents consider significant:

1. **Extroverted—introverted.** Extroverts prefer to talk with others and learn through experience, whereas introverts prefer to think alone about ideas.

2. **Sensing—intuitive.** Sensing types prefer working with concrete details and tend to be patient, practical, and realistic. Intuitive types like abstractions and are creative, impatient, and theory oriented.
3. **Thinking—feeling.** Thinking types tend to base decisions on objective criteria and logical principles. Feeling types are subjective and consider the impact of the decision on other people.
4. **Judging—perceiving.** Judging types are time oriented and structured, whereas perceivers are spontaneous and flexible.

Another test that uses the same type indicators as the MBTI is the Keirsey Temperament Sorter II. You can take this seventy-item personality inventory online and receive an extensive printout. However, experts do not consider it to have passed the same rigorous standards for validation and reliability as the MBTI. The Keirsey Web site (http://www.keirsey.com) provides background information about the test. It begins with a brief questionnaire and then provides a link to the longer Keirsey Temperament Sorter II.

Right- Versus Left-Brain Dominance

Another popular cognitive style theory is concerned with right- or left-brain dominance. Proponents of this theory believe that left-brain dominant people are analytical and logical and excel in verbal skills. Right-brain people, on the other hand, are intuitive, creative, and emotional, and tend to think in symbols. Albert Einstein, for example, said that he rarely thought in words but that his concepts appeared in symbols and images.

If you are "turned off" by an assignment, try to translate it into activities and ideas that are more compatible with your learning preferences. For example, if you prefer right-brain activities, use maps, charts, and drawings to help you concentrate while studying. Acknowledge your strengths and use them to enhance your concentration.

Multiple Intelligences: There Is More Than One Way to Be Smart

Has our culture put too much emphasis on verbal and logical thinking? How did we start thinking of intelligence as a single score? Let's take a closer look at the way this all evolved.

In early-twentieth-century France, the government enacted universal elementary education and wanted to identify public school children who might need extra help to be successful. In response, French psychologist Alfred Binet and his collaborator, Theodore Simon, invented an IQ (intelligence quotient) test—an intelligence test—that quickly caught on. Adapted for use in the United States by professors at Stanford University, it was renamed the Stanford-Binet Intelligence Scale. During World War I, its popularity increased as the test was given to more than a million U.S. military recruits. Although criticized for measuring only *schoolhouse giftedness*, it nevertheless remained the standard for assessing abilities for many years.

However, in 1983, Harvard professor Howard Gardner changed the way many people think about being smart. Taking a much broader, more inclusive view of abilities, he developed a **theory of multiple intelligences.** According to this theory, there are eight different ways to be intelligent, and some people develop certain ways of being intelligent to a greater extent than they do others.

The following list describes Gardner's eight ways to be smart, with possible career choices for each. In which areas do you excel?

1. **Word smart.** *Linguistic* thinkers like reading, writing, and speaking. They become journalists, teachers, executives, and comedians.
2. **Picture smart.** *Spatial* thinkers like pictures, charts, and maps. They become architects, artists, and surgeons.

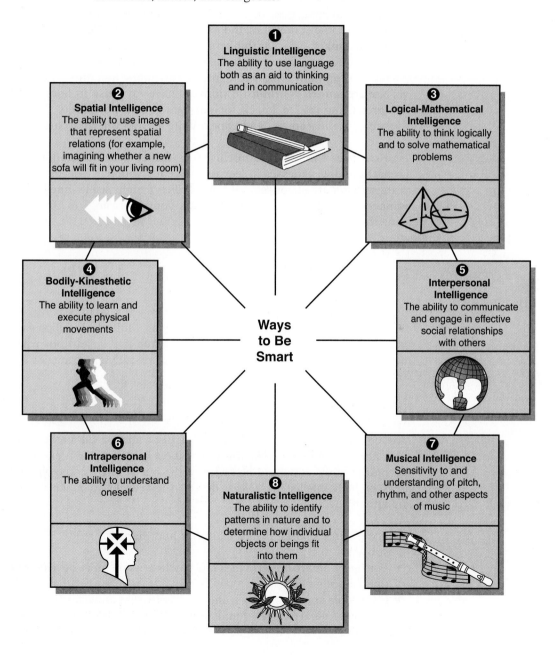

3. **Logical smart.** *Logical-mathematical* thinkers like to reason, sequence, and think in terms of cause and effect. They become scientists, accountants, bankers, and computer programmers.

4. **Body smart.** *Bodily-kinesthetic* thinkers like to control body movements and handle objects skillfully. They become athletes, dancers, craftspeople, mechanics, and surgeons.

5. **People smart.** *Interpersonal* thinkers who work well with people can perceive the moods, intentions, and desires of others. They become networkers, negotiators, social service professionals, and teachers.

6. **Self smart.** *Intrapersonal* thinkers are introspective and meditative or can be self-disciplined, goal directed independents who understand the inner self. They become counselors, theologians, and self-employed businesspeople.

7. **Music smart.** *Musical* thinkers with a "good ear" can sing and play in tune, keep time, and listen with discernment. They become musical audio engineers, symphony conductors, music educators, and musicians.

8. **Nature smart.** *Naturalistic* thinkers have expertise in flora and fauna, have "green thumbs," a knack for gardening, and an affinity for animals. They become landscapers, landscape architects, and veterinarians.

How does the multiple intelligences theory provide another way to look at strengths and weaknesses in learning? See for yourself. You may excel in several of these eight intelligences. Match Gardner's eight listed intelligences with the numbers listed below and honestly rank yourself from 1 to 10 on each (with 10 being the highest agreement):

1. _____ 2. _____ 3. _____ 4. _____

5. _____ 6. _____ 7. _____ 8. _____

For a more scientific evaluation of your strengths, go to http://www.mitest. com/ o7inte~1.htm and respond to a quick-scoring Multiple Intelligence Test (which includes only seven intelligences). Use the Web site to find out what your score means and to get suggestions for learning and studying strategies to match your strongest intelligences.

What If I'm Not a Verbal or Logical Learner?

Most college teaching is geared toward linguistic and logical-mathematical smarts. If those are not your strengths, how can you compensate? First, and most important, recognize the dilemma and be happy with your strengths, knowing that you have areas of high intelligence. Next, devise a few tricks to make the most of your strengths.

- For picture smarts, create diagrams and maps for study. Watch films on the subject.
- For music smarts, use rhymes and rhythms as memory devices, or *mnemonics,* to enhance memory.
- For people smarts, network and study with classmates.
- For body smarts, seek hands-on experiences to complement your tactile sensitivity.

- For self smarts, reflect for self-understanding to enrich and guide your life.
- For nature smarts, relate learning to environmental issues.

In summary, cognitive psychologists offer many ways of looking at attention and learning by encouraging us to recognize our strengths and weaknesses. Use your strengths and be proud of them.

What Is Concentration?

Regardless of your intelligences and the way you learn, knowing how to concentrate is critical to college success. Concentration is a skill that is developed through self-discipline and practice. It is a **habit** that requires time and effort to develop for consistent success. Athletes have it, surgeons have it, and successful college students must have it. *Concentration is essential for active learning.*

Concentration can be defined as the process of *paying attention*—that is, focusing full attention on the task at hand. Someone once said that the mark of a genius is the ability to concentrate completely on one thing at a time. This is easy if the task is fun and exciting, but it becomes more difficult when you are required to read something that is not very interesting to you. In such cases, you may find yourself looking from word to word and spacing out.

Poor Concentration: Causes and Cures

The type of intense concentration that forces the RAS and cortex to close out the rest of the world is the state we would all like to achieve each time we sit down with a textbook. Most of the time, however, lots of thoughts compete for attention.

Students frequently ask, *How can I keep my mind on what I'm doing?* or they say, *I finished the assignment, but I don't understand a thing I read.* The best way to increase concentration is not by using some simple mental trick to fool the brain; rather, it involves a series of practical short- and long-range planning strategies targeted at reducing external and internal distractions.

External Distractions.

External distractions are the temptations of the physical world that divert your attention away from your work. They are the people in the room, the noise in the background, the time of day, or your place for studying. To control these external distractions, you must create an environment that says, "Now this is the place and the time for me to get my work done."

Create a Place for Studying. Start by establishing your own private study cubicle; it may be in the library, on the dining room table, or in your bedroom. Wherever your study place is, choose a straight chair and face the wall. Get rid of gadgets, magazines, and other temptations that trigger the mind to think of *play.* Stay away from your bed because it triggers *sleep.* Spread out your papers, books, and other symbols of studying, and create an atmosphere in which the visual stimuli signal *work.* Be consistent by trying to study in the same place at the same time.

Use a Pocket Calendar, Assignment Book, or Personal Digital Assistant. At the beginning of the quarter or semester, record dates for tests, term papers, and special projects on some kind of planner, such as a calendar or personal digital assistant (PDA). Use your planner to organize all course assignments. The mere sight of your planner will remind you of the need for both short- and long-term planning. Assigned tests, papers, and projects will be due whether you are ready or not. Your first job is to devise a plan for being ready.

Schedule Weekly Activities. Successful people do not let their time slip away; they manage time, rather than letting time manage them. Plan realistically and then follow your plan.

Use the weekly activity chart shown here. First, write your fixed activities—including class hours, work time, mealtime, and bedtime. Next, estimate how much

WEEKLY ACTIVITY CHART

Time	Monday	Tuesday	Wednesday	Thursday	Friday	Saturday	Sunday
7:00–8:00							
8:00–9:00							
9:00–10:00							
10:00–11:00							
11:00–12:00							
12:00–1:00							
1:00–2:00							
2:00–3:00							
3:00–4:00							
4:00–5:00							
5:00–6:00							
6:00–7:00							
7:00–8:00							
8:00–9:00							
9:00–10:00							
10:00–11:00							
11:00–12:00							

time you plan to spend on studying and how much on recreation. Plug those estimates into the chart. For studying, indicate the specific subject and exact place involved.

Make a fresh chart at the beginning of each week because responsibilities and assignments vary. Learn to estimate the time you usually need for typical assignments. Always include time for a regular review of lecture notes.

Examinations require special planning. Many students do not realize how much time it takes to study for a major exam. Spread out your studying over several days, and avoid last-minute cramming sessions late at night. Plan additional time for special projects and term papers to avoid deadline crises.

Take Short Breaks. Even though it is not necessary to write this on the chart, remember that you need short breaks. Few students can study uninterrupted for two hours without becoming fatigued and losing concentration. In fact, research shows that studying in chunks rather than long spans is most efficient.[5] Try the *50:10 ratio*—study hard for fifty minutes, take a ten-minute break, and then promptly go back to the books for another fifty minutes.

Internal Distractions.

Internal distractions are the concerns that come repeatedly into your mind as you try to keep your attention focused on an assignment. You have to run errands, do laundry, make telephone calls, and pay bills. How do you stop worrying about getting an inspection sticker for the car or about picking up tickets for Saturday's ball game when you need to be concentrating completely on your class assignment?

Make a List. To gain control over mental disruptions, make a list of what is on your mind and keeping you from concentrating on your studies. Jot down on paper your mental distractions, and then analyze each to determine if immediate action is possible. If you decide you can do something right away, get up and do it. Make that phone call, write that e-mail, or finish that chore. Maybe it will take a few minutes or maybe half an hour, but the investment will have been worthwhile if the quality of your study time—your concentration power—has improved. Taking action is the first step in getting something off your mind.

For a big problem that you can't tackle immediately, ask yourself, "Is it worth the amount of brain time I'm dedicating to it?" Take a few minutes to think and make notes on possible solutions. Jotting down necessary future action and forming a plan of attack will help relieve the worry and clear your mind for studying.

Right now, list five things that are on your mind that you need to remember to do. Alan Lakein, a pioneer specialist in time management, calls this a **to do list.** In his book, *How to Get Control of Your Time and Your Life,* Lakein claims that successful business executives start each day with such a list.[6] Rank the activities on your list in order of priority, and then do the most important things first. Some people even make a list before they go to sleep at night.

---

[5]H. P. Bahrick, L. E. Bahrick, A. S. Bahrick, and P. E. Bahrick, "Maintenance of Foreign Language Vocabulary and the Spacing Effect," *Psychological Science 4,* no. 5 (September 1993): 316–21.

[6]A. Lakein, *How to Get Control of Your Time and Your Life* (New York: Signet,1974).

To Do List	Sample
1.	1. Get hair cut
2.	2. Do my book report
3.	3. Buy stamps
4.	4. Call power co.
5.	5. Pay phone bill

Increase Your Self-Confidence. Saying "I'll never pass this course" or "I can't get in the mood to study" is the first step to failure. Concentration requires self-confidence. Getting a college degree is not a short-term goal. Your enrollment indicates that you have made a commitment to a long-term goal. Ask yourself, "Who do I want to be in five years?" In the following space, describe how you view yourself, both professionally and personally, five years from now:

Five years from now I hope to be _____

_____

_____

_____

Sometimes, identifying the traits you admire in others can give you insight into your own values and desires. Think about the traits you respect in others and your own definition of success. Answer the two questions that follow, and consider how your responses mirror your own aspirations and goals:

Who is the person that you admire the most? _____

Why do you admire this person? _____

_____

_____

Improve Your Self-Concept. Have faith in yourself and in your ability to be what you want to be. How many people do you know who have passed the particular course that is worrying you? Are they smarter than you? Probably not. Can you do as well as they did? Turn your negative feeling into a positive attitude. What are some of your positive traits? Are you a hard worker, an honest person, a loyal friend? Take a few minutes to pat yourself on the back. Think about your good points, and in the following spaces, list five positive traits that you believe you possess:

Positive Traits

1. _____

2. _____

3. _____

4. _____

5. _____

What have you already accomplished? Did you participate in athletics in high school, win any contests, or master any difficult skills? Recall your previous achievements, and in the following spaces, list three accomplishments that you view with pride:

Accomplishments

1. _____

2. _____

3. _____

Reduce Anxiety. Have you ever heard people say, "I work better under pressure"? This statement contains a degree of truth. A small amount of tension can help you direct your full attention on an immediate task. For example, concentrated study for an exam is usually more intense two nights before, rather than two weeks before, the test.

Yet too much anxiety can cause nervous tension and discomfort, which interfere with the ability to concentrate. Students operating under excessive tension sometimes "freeze up" mentally and experience nervous physical reactions. The causes of high anxiety can range from fear of failure to lack of organization and preparation; the problem is not easily solved. Some people like to go for a run or a brisk walk when they feel overly stressed. Sustained physical activity can change the blood chemistry and improve mood, increasing the odds of focusing successfully on what needs to be done.

Another immediate, short-term fix for tension is muscle relaxation exercises and visualization. For example, if you are reading a particularly difficult section in a chemistry book and are becoming frustrated to the point that you can no longer concentrate, stop your reading and take several deep breaths. Use your imagination to visualize a peaceful setting in which you are calm and relaxed. Imagine yourself rocking back and forth in a hammock or lying on a beach listening to the surf; then focus on this image as you breathe deeply to help relax your muscles and regain control. Take several deep breaths, and allow your body to release the tension so you can resume reading and concentrate on your work. Try that right now.

As a long-term solution to tension, nothing works better than success. Just as failure fuels tension, success tends to weaken it. Each successful experience helps to diminish feelings of inadequacy. Early success in a course—passing the first exam, for instance—can make a big psychological difference and replace anxiety with confidence.

Spark an Interest. Make a conscious effort to stimulate your curiosity before reading, even if it feels contrived. Make yourself want to learn something. First, look over the assigned reading for words or phrases that attract your attention, glance at the pictures, check the number of pages, and then ask yourself the following questions: "What do I already know about this topic?" and "What do I want to learn about it?"

With practice, this method of thinking before reading can create a spark of enthusiasm that will make the actual reading more purposeful and make concentration more direct and intense. We will cover this in greater depth in Chapter 3.

Set a Time Goal. An additional trick to spark your enthusiasm is to set a time goal. Study time is not infinite; and short-term goals create a self-imposed pressure to pay attention, speed up, and get the job done. After looking over the material, predict the amount of time you will need to finish it. Estimate a reasonable completion time, and then push yourself to meet the goal. The purpose of a time goal is not to "speed read" the assignment but to be realistic about the amount of time to spend on a task and to learn how to estimate future study time. The Reader's Tip summarizes how you can raise your level of concentration while studying.

Reader's *Tip* —— Improving Concentration

- Create an environment that says, "Study."
- Use a calendar, assignment book, or PDA for short- and long-term planning.
- Keep a daily to do list.
- Take short breaks.
- Visualize yourself as a successful college graduate.
- Reduce anxiety by passing the first test.
- Spark an interest.
- Set time goals for completing daily assignments.

Successful Academic Behaviors

Good concentration geared toward college success involves more than the ability to comprehend reading assignments. College success demands concentrated study, self-discipline, and the demonstration of learning. If the "focused athlete" can be successful, so can the "focused student." Begin to evaluate and eliminate behaviors that waste your time and divert you from your goals. Direct your energy toward activities that will enhance your chances for success. Adopt the following behaviors of successful students.

Attend Class. At the beginning of the course, college professors distribute an outline of what they plan to cover during each class period. Although they may not always check class attendance, the organization of the daily course work assumes perfect attendance. College professors *expect* students to attend class; and they usually do not repeat lecture notes or give makeup lessons for those who are absent, although some post lecture notes on a course Web site. Be responsible and set yourself up for success by coming to class. You paid for it!

Be on Time. Professors usually present an overview of the day's work at the beginning of each class, as well as answer questions and clarify assignments. Arriving late puts you at an immediate disadvantage. You are likely to miss important "class business" information. In addition, tardy students distract both the professor and other students. Put on a watch and get yourself moving.

Recognize Essential Class Sessions. Every class session is important, but the last class before a major test is the most critical of all. Usually, students will ask questions about the exam that will stimulate your thinking. In reviewing, answering questions, and rushing to finish uncovered material, the professor will often drop important clues to exam items. Unless you are critically ill, take tests on time because makeups are usually more difficult. In addition, be in class when the exams are returned to hear the professor's description of an excellent answer.

Read Assignments Before Class. Activate your knowledge on the subject before class by reading homework assignments. Look at the illustrations and read the captions. Jot down several questions that you would like to ask the professor about the reading. Then the lecture and class discussion can enhance your newly created knowledge network.

Review Lecture Notes Before Class. Always, always, always review your lecture notes before the next class period, preferably within twenty-four hours after the class. Review them with a classmate during a break or on the phone. Fill in gaps and make notations to ask questions to resolve confusion.

Consider Using a Tape Recorder. If you are having difficulty concentrating or are a strong audio or linguistic learner, with the professor's permission, tape-record the lecture. Take notes as you record, and you can later review your notes while listening to the recording.

Predict the Exam Questions. Never go to an exam without first predicting test items. Turn chapter titles, subheadings, and boldface print into questions, and then brainstorm the answers. Outline possible answers on paper. Preparation boosts self-confidence.

Pass the First Test. Stress interferes with concentration. Do yourself a favor and overstudy for the first exam. Passing the first exam will help you avoid a lot of tension while studying for the second one.

Network with Other Students. You are not in this alone; you have lots of potential buddies who can offer support. Collect the names, phone numbers, and e-mail addresses of two classmates who are willing to help you if you do not understand the homework, miss a day of class, or need help on an assignment. Be prepared to help your classmates in return for their support.

Classmate _____ Phone _____ E-mail _____

Classmate _____ Phone _____ E-mail _____

Form a Study Group. Research involving college students has shown that study groups can be very effective. Studying with others is not cheating; it is making a wise use of available resources. Many professors assist networking efforts by posting the class roll with e-mail addresses. A junior on the dean's list explained, "I e-mail my study buddy when I have a problem. One time I asked about an English paper because I couldn't think of my thesis. She asked what it was about. I told her and she wrote back, 'That's your thesis.' I just couldn't see it as clearly as she did." Use the Internet to create an academic support group to lighten your workload and boost your grades. Manage e-mail efficiently, as indicated in this Reader's Tip.

Learn from Other Students' Papers. Talking about an excellent paper is one thing, but actually reading one is another. In each discipline, we need models of excellence. Find an A paper to read. Don't be shy. Ask the A students (who should

---

Reader's *Tip* ──── Managing E-mail Efficiently

- Always fill in an appropriate subject header to guide your reader.
- Don't recycle the same subject header over and over. Unless it is important to see the thread of e-mail exchanges, write a new one to get your reader's attention.
- Keep your message short and to the point. People are busy.
- Use correct grammar, spelling, and punctuation. Your message represents you.
- Use consecutive uppercase letters sparingly. They YELL, which is called "flaming."
- In formal messages, avoid emoticons—combinations of keyboard characters that represent emotions, such as smileys :-).
- Use an autoreply if you are away for a week or longer.
- If appropriate, save time by using the same message for several individual replies.
- Don't feel you have to reply to everything.
- If pressed for time, save your message as "new" and reply later.
- Delete unwanted advertisements without reading them after reporting them as spam.
- Do not reply to an entire group when an individual reply is more appropriate.
- Know your group before sending humor.
- If you are unsure about a group member, seek permission before forwarding a message. If sending humor, cut and paste as a new message rather than forwarding with many group member names.
- When sending a single message to many people, mail the message to yourself and list other recipients as blind copies (bcc) to protect their e-mail address privacy.
- Monitor how much time you spend on e-mail.

be proud and flattered to share their brilliance) or ask the professor. Don't miss this important step in becoming a successful student.

Collaborate. When participating in group learning activities, set expectations for group study so that each member contributes, and try to keep the studying on target. As a group activity, ask several classmates to join you in discovering some campus resources by answering the questions in Exercise 1.1. First, brainstorm with the group to record answers that are known to be true. Next, divide responsibilities among group members to seek information to answer unknown items. Finally, reconvene the group in person or on the Internet to share responses.

exercise 1.1   **Campus Facts**

Form a collaborative study group to answer the following questions.

1. What does a student need in order to obtain a library card? Is there a fee?
   Answers will vary.
   _____

2. If your instructor is an adjunct faculty member, how can you reach him or her? Is there a part-time faculty office? Where is it located, and what are the hours? Answers will vary.
   _____
   _____

3. Does your school have an academic support center? Where is it located? What must you do to schedule an appointment? Answers will vary.
   _____
   _____

4. If you accidentally leave your materials in your car, are there convenient places on campus at which you can purchase pens, pencils, or paper? Where are they located? Answers will vary.
   _____

5. Suppose you begin to feel unwell during class. Is there a nurse or health aide available? Where is the health services office? What are the staff able to provide students? Do they offer evening and weekend hours? Answers will vary.
   _____
   _____

6. After the term begins, you realize that money is tight. Is there a career services office that helps students find jobs? Where must you go to find out about student employment? Answers will vary.

   _____

7. You were able to afford your tuition, but the cost of books is another story. Does your financial aid office provide textbook scholarships? What must you do to apply? What other types of scholarships or grants are available through this department? Answers will vary.

   _____

8. In a rush to get to class, you inadvertently lock your keys in your car. Where can you go to get help? Answers will vary.

   _____

9. You realize that you left some of your books underneath the seat in a previous class. However, when you return to collect them, the books are not there. Where would you go to locate missing items or to report them as missing? Answers will vary.

   _____

10. Your car is on its last legs. You need to find another way to get to campus while the mechanic takes a look. Is there public transportation to campus? Where are the stops? Where can you go to find out about a possible ride share? Answers will vary.

    _____

Use the Syllabus. A syllabus is a general outline of the goals, objectives, and assignments for the entire course. Typically, a syllabus includes examination dates, course requirements, and an explanation of the grading system. Most professors distribute and explain the syllabus on the first day of class.

Ask questions to help you understand the "rules and regulations" in the syllabus. Keep it handy as a ready reference, and use it as a plan for learning. Three-hole-punch it for your binder or staple it to your lecture notes; tape a second copy to your wall or door. Devise your own daily calendar for completing weekly reading and writing assignments.

The following is a syllabus for Psychology 101. Study the course syllabus and answer the questions that follow.

INTRODUCTION TO PSYCHOLOGY

Class: 9:00–10:00 a.m. daily
10-week quarter
Office hours: 10:00–12:00 daily

Dr. Julie Wakefield
Office: 718 Park Place
Telephone: 555–651–3361
E-mail: JuWakeABC.edu

Required Texts
Psychology: An Introduction, by Josh R. Gerow
Paperback: Select one book from the attached list for a report.

Course Content
The purpose of Psychology 101 is to overview the general areas of study in the field of psychology. An understanding of psychology gives valuable insights into your choices and behaviors and those of others. The course will also give you a foundation for later psychology courses.

Methods of Teaching
Thematic lectures will follow the topics listed in the textbook assignments. You are expected to read and master the factual material in the text as well as take careful notes in class. Tests will cover both class lectures and textbook readings.

Research Participation
All students are required to participate in one psychological experiment. Details and dates are listed on a separate handout.

Grading
Grades will be determined in the following manner:

Tests (4 tests at 15% each)	60%
Final exam	25%
Written report	10%
Research participation	5%

Tests
Tests will consist of both multiple-choice and identification items as well as two essay questions.

Important Dates
Test 1: 1/13
Test 2: 1/29
Test 3: 2/10
Test 4: 2/24
Written report: 3/5
Final exam: 3/16

(continued)

Written Report

Your written report should answer one of three designated questions and reflect your reading of a book from the list. Each book is approximately 200 pages long. Your report should be at least eight typed pages. More information to follow.

Assignments

Week 1: Ch. 1 (pp. 1–37), Ch. 2 (pp. 41–75)

Week 2: Ch. 3 (pp. 79–116)

    TEST 1: Chapters 1–3

Week 3: Ch. 4 (pp. 121–162), Ch. 5 (pp. 165–181)

Week 4: Ch. 5 (pp. 184–207), Ch. 6 (pp. 211–246)

    TEST 2: Chapters 4–6

Week 5: Ch. 7 (pp. 253–288), Ch. 8 (pp. 293–339)

Week 6: Ch. 9 (pp. 345–393)

    TEST 3: Chapters 7–9

Week 7: Ch. 10 (pp. 339–441), Ch. 11 (pp. 447–471)

Week 8: Ch. 11 (pp. 476–491), Ch. 12 (pp. 497–533)

    TEST 4: Chapters 10–12

Week 9: Ch. 13 (pp. 539–577), Ch. 14 (pp. 581–598)

    WRITTEN REPORT

Week 10: Ch. 14 (pp. 602–618), Ch. 15 (pp. 621–658)

    FINAL EXAM: Chapters 1–15

---

exercise 1.2   **Review the Syllabus**

Refer to the syllabus to answer the following items with *T* (true), *F* (false), or *CT* (can't tell).

_____F_____   1. This professor is available for student conferences in the afternoon.

_____T_____   2. Tests will be based on both classroom lectures and assigned readings.

_____F_____   3. The written report counts for the same percent of a student's final grade as one test.

_____CT_____   4. The final counts for more points than the midterm exam.

_____T_____   5. The syllabus does not provide a due date for the research participation project.

exercise 1.3   **Review Your Own Course Syllabus**

Examine your syllabus for this college reading course, and answer the following questions.

1. Will you have weekly or daily quizzes or tests in this course? _____

_____

_____

2. Does the instructor penalize students for poor attendance? _____

_____

_____

3. What is your instructor's policy regarding late work? _____

_____

_____

4. Does your instructor allow makeup tests, quizzes, or assignments? _____

_____

_____

5. Are tardies penalized?_____

_____

6. Will you be having both a midterm and a final exam in this class? _____

_____

_____

7. Does your instructor require any special projects or reports? Are due dates
given for these?_____

_____

8. Are any other materials required for this class, aside from your reading textbook?_____

_____

9. Does your instructor require any outside reading, such as a novel, during the
term?_____

_____

10. Do you have any questions that do not appear to be addressed within the syllabus? Write them on the following lines._____

_____

_____

Summary *Points*

➤ **What is active learning?**
Active learning is your own intellectual involvement with the teacher, the textbook, and fellow learners in the process of aggressively accumulating, interpreting, assimilating, and retaining new information.

➤ **How does the brain "pay attention"?**
Research indicates that the brain has two cooperating systems, the RAS and the cortex, that allow it to selectively attend to certain inputs and to block out others.

➤ **Can you do two things at once?**
The ability to do several tasks at once depends on the amount of cognitive resources required for each.

➤ **What are multiple intelligences?**
Gardner's theory of multiple intelligences changed the way many people view intelligence. According to his theory, there are eight types of abilities or intelligences for problem solving and understanding complex materials.

➤ **What are common internal and external distractors?**
External distractions are physical temptations that divert your attention. Internal distractions are mental wanderings that vie for your attention.

➤ **How can you improve your concentration?**
Concentration requires self-confidence, self-discipline, persistence, and focus. You can manipulate your study area to remove external distractions. You can learn to control internal distractions by organizing your daily activities, planning for academic success, and striving to meet your goals for the completion of assignments.

➤ **What academic behaviors can lead to college success?**
Adopt successful academic behaviors, including networking with other students and collaborating on assignments, to focus your energy and enhance your chances for success. Use your syllabus as a guide for learning.

➤ **Why is your syllabus important?**
Your syllabus is the learning guide designed by the instructor to document the goals and requirements of the course.

selection 1   Education

Contemporary *Focus*

According to an article in The Clarion-Ledger, *"Only five percent of children learn to read effortlessly, and twenty to thirty percent learn to read relatively easily once exposed to formal instruction." What, then, can we assume about the other 65 percent? What can parents do to help children learn to read, and what will good reading skills mean to the child in the long run?*

Kid Doesn't Want to Read

By Billy Watkins
The Clarion-Ledger, January 20, 2005

The benefits of reading spread further than the classroom.

"Reading builds knowledge and power," says Lucy Hansford, Communications Specialist with Jackson Public Schools and a longtime teacher. "Everybody wants to be able to contribute to a conversation or understand what's being talked about. If a student isn't reading, it's a good chance he or she will feel left out."

Pointers for parents who would like to see their middle school or high school student increase his or her reading interests and skills:

Make sure your child sees you reading.

Spend 10 or 15 minutes a day reading aloud to your child. Yes, even those in high school.

"When kids hear someone read, usually it's a fluent reader," says Katie Tonore, Director of Volunteer Programs and Grad Schools Coordinator at the Barksdale Reading Institute in Jackson. "That's important because the child can hear how a sentence is supposed to sound—the emphasis on a certain word, things like that. That helps with comprehension."

Never demand that your child read a certain book. Instead, allow the child to pick something of interest.

COLLABORATE   Collaborate on responses to the following questions:

➤ Did your parents read aloud to you?

➤ As a child, what was your favorite book?

➤ What do your parents read?

Skill Development: Active Learning

Before reading the following selection, take a few minutes to analyze your active learning potential and answer the following questions.

1. **Physical Environment**   Where are you and what time is it? _____

_____

_____

What are your external distractions? _____

_____

2. **Internal Distractions**   What is popping into your mind and interfering with your concentration? _____

_____

3. **Spark Interest**   Glance at the selection and predict what it will cover. What do you already know about this topic? What about the selection will be of interest to you? _____

_____

4. **Set Time Goals**   How long will it take you to read the selection? _____ minutes. To answer the questions? _____ minutes.

Increase Word Knowledge

What do you know about these words?

avid	clarity	prodigy	oddity	ridiculed
subverted	appropriately	arrogant	desperation	sullen

Your instructor may give a true-false vocabulary review before or after reading.

Time Goal

Record your starting time for reading. _____:_____

SUPERMAN AND ME

I learned to read with a Superman comic book. Simple enough, I suppose. I cannot recall which particular Superman comic book I read, nor can I remember which villain he fought in that issue. I cannot remember the plot, nor the means by which I obtained the comic book. What I can remember is this: I was 3 years old, a Spokane
5   Indian boy living with his family on the Spokane Indian Reservation in eastern Washington state. We were poor by most standards, but one of my parents usually managed to find some minimum-wage job or another, which made us middle-class by reservation standards. I had a brother and three sisters. We lived on a combination of irregular paychecks, hope, fear and government surplus food.
10   My father, who is one of the few Indians who went to Catholic school on purpose, was an avid reader of westerns, spy thrillers, murder mysteries, gangster epics, basketball player biographies and anything else he could find. He bought his books by the pound at Dutch's Pawn Shop, Goodwill, The Salvation Army and Value Village. When he had extra money, he bought new novels at supermarkets, convenience stores and
15   hospital gift shops. Our house was filled with books. They were stacked in crazy piles

Rob Casey

Sherman Alexie, the author, has written extensively on
Native American culture.

in the bathroom, bedrooms and living room. In a fit of unemployment-inspired
creative energy, my father built a set of bookshelves and soon filled them with a random assortment of books about the Kennedy assassination, Watergate, the Vietnam
War and the entire 23-book series of the Apache westerns. My father loved books,
20   and since I loved my father with an aching devotion, I decided to love books as well.

      I can remember picking up my father's books before I could read. The words
themselves were mostly foreign, but I still remember the exact moment when I first
understood, with a sudden clarity, the purpose of a paragraph. I didn't have the
vocabulary to say "paragraph," but I realized that a paragraph was a fence that held
25   words. The words inside a paragraph worked together for a common purpose. They
had some specific reason for being inside the same fence. This knowledge delighted
me. I began to think of everything in terms of paragraphs. Our reservation was a
small paragraph within the United States. My family's house was a paragraph; distinct from the other paragraphs of the LeBrets to the north, the Fords to our south
30   and the Tribal School to the west. Inside our house, each family member existed as
a separate paragraph but still had genetics and common experiences to link us.
Now, using this logic, I can see my changed family as an essay of seven paragraphs:
mother, father, older brother, the deceased sister, my younger twin sisters and our
adopted little brother.

35   At the same time I was seeing the world in paragraphs, I also picked up that
Superman comic book. Each panel, complete with picture, dialogue and narrative
was a three-dimensional paragraph. In one panel, Superman breaks through a door.

His suit is red, blue and yellow. The brown door shatters into many pieces. I look at the narrative above the picture. I cannot read the words, but I assume it tells me
40 that "Superman is breaking down the door." Aloud, I pretend to read the words and say, "Superman is breaking down the door." Words, dialogue, also float out of Superman's mouth. Because he is breaking down the door, I assume he says, "I am breaking down the door." Once again, I pretend to read the words and say aloud, "I am breaking down the door." In this way, I learned to read.

45   This might be an interesting story all by itself. A little Indian boy teaches himself to read at an early age and advances quickly. He reads "Grapes of Wrath" in kindergarten when other children are struggling through "Dick and Jane." If he'd been anything but an Indian boy living on the reservation, he might have been called a prodigy. But he is an Indian boy living on the reservation and is simply an
50 oddity. He grows into a man who often speaks of his childhood in the third-person, as if it will somehow dull the pain and make him sound more modest about his talents.

A smart Indian is a dangerous person, widely feared and ridiculed by Indians and non-Indians alike. I fought with my classmates on a daily basis. They wanted me to stay quiet when the non-Indian teacher asked for answers, for volunteers, for
55 help. We were Indian children who were expected to be stupid. Most lived up to those expectations inside the classroom but subverted them on the outside. They struggled with basic reading in school but could remember how to sing a few dozen powwow songs. They were monosyllabic in front of their non-Indian teachers but could tell complicated stories and jokes at the dinner table. They submissively
60 ducked their heads when confronted by a non-Indian adult but would slug it out with the Indian bully who was 10 years older. As Indian children, we were expected to fail in the non-Indian world. Those who failed were ceremonially accepted by other Indians and appropriately pitied by non-Indians.
     I refused to fail. I was smart. I was arrogant. I was lucky. I read books late into
65 the night, until I could barely keep my eyes open. I read books at recess, then during lunch, and in the few minutes left after I had finished my classroom assignments. I read books in the car when my family traveled to powwows or basketball games. In shopping malls, I ran to the bookstores and read bits and pieces of as many books as I could. I read the books my father brought home from the pawnshops and second-
70 hand. I read the books I borrowed from the library. I read the backs of cereal boxes. I read the newspaper. I read the bulletins posted on the walls of the school, the clinic, the tribal offices, the post office. I read junk mail. I read auto-repair manuals. I read magazines. I read anything that had words and paragraphs. I read with equal parts joy and desperation. I loved those books, but I also knew that love had only
75 one purpose. I was trying to save my life.
     Despite all the books I read, I am still surprised I became a writer. I was going to be a pediatrician. These days, I write novels, short stories, and poems. I visit schools and teach creative writing to Indian kids. In all my years in the reservation school system, I was never taught how to write poetry, short stories or novels. I was
80 certainly never taught that Indians wrote poetry, short stories and novels. Writing was something beyond Indians. I cannot recall a single time that a guest teacher visited the reservation. There must have been visiting teachers. Who were they? Where are they now? Do they exist? I visit the schools as often as possible. The Indian kids crowd the classroom. Many are writing their own poems, short stories
85 and novels. They have read my books. They have read many other books. They look at me with bright eyes and arrogant wonder. They are trying to save their lives. Then there are the sullen and already defeated Indian kids who sit in the back rows and

ignore me with theatrical precision. The pages of their notebooks are empty. They
carry neither pencil nor pen. They stare out the window. They refuse and resist.
90 "Books," I say to them. "Books," I say. I throw my weight against their locked doors.
The door holds. I am smart. I am arrogant. I am lucky. I am trying to save our lives.

(1,290 words)

—By Sherman Alexie

Time Goals

Record your finishing time: _____:_____

Calculate your total reading time: _____

Rate your concentration as high _____ medium _____ or low _____.

Recall what you have read, and review what you have learned.

Your instructor may choose to give a true-false comprehension review.

Write About the Selection

What does the author mean by the statements "I was trying to save my life" and "I
am trying to save our lives"? What does he see as the difficulties of growing up on
an Indian reservation?

Response Suggestion: Explain what the author sees as the expectations for
Indian children, how he broke away, and what he is doing to effect change.

Contemporary *Link*

*How are the tips for parents in the Mississippi newspaper article exemplified in the
reality of the Spokane Indian boy's experience?*

Check Your Comprehension

After reading the selection, answer the following questions with *a, b, c,* or *d*. In order to help you analyze your strengths and weaknesses, the question types are indicated.

Main Idea   __d__   1. Which is the best statement of the main idea of this selection?
- a. Storytelling rather than reading is valued in Indian culture.
- b. Life on an Indian reservation is viewed negatively by the non-Indian world.
- c. Comic books should be used to introduce children to reading.
- d. Books can be a salvation.

Inference   __b__   2. The author's love of books developed primarily because
- a. the teachers at his school encouraged reading.
- b. his father loved books.
- c. he was often bored and not allowed to play.
- d. his brothers and sisters read to him.

Detail   __d__   3. The author's father read
- a. only fiction.
- b. only nonfiction.
- c. mostly comic books.
- d. both fiction and nonfiction.

Detail   __a__   4. The author equates a paragraph to
- a. a fence, house, and sister.
- b. a fence and a sentence.
- c. letters that make words.
- d. the United States.

Inference   __a__   5. The reader can assume that being a prodigy is something
- a. positive.
- b. negative.
- c. unwanted.
- d. not unusual.

Inference   __a__   6. The reader can conclude that the author does not approve of
- a. Indians who praise other Indians who do poorly in the non-Indian world.
- b. Indians who work for minimum wage.
- c. schools.
- d. Indians who live on the reservation.

Inference _____b_____ 7. From his classroom visits, the author concludes that

    a. most Indians are not interested in his visits.
    b. many Indian students are reading and saving their lives.
    c. most teachers do not welcome his visits.
    d. his visits serve little purpose.

Inference _____a_____ 8. In the last paragraph, the author says that the defeated Indian students ignored him with "theatrical precision," and thus implies that those students

    a. intended to be rude.
    b. did not intend to be noticed.
    c. are not smart enough to understand.
    d. have been held back by poor teachers.

Inference _____c_____ 9. In the last paragraph, "locked doors" means

    a. unwilling teachers.
    b. families without money.
    c. closed minds of students.
    d. lives that are saved.

Inference _____c_____ 10. The author says at the end of the story, "I am smart. I am arrogant. I am lucky." to suggest that

    a. he is confused.
    b. it is always best to be optimistic.
    c. he refused to be a "dumb," victimized stereotype.
    d. he is a difficult person.

Answer the following with *T* (true) or *F* (false).

Inference _____F_____ 11. The author's father had a government job as a supervisor on the reservation.

Inference _____T_____ 12. The author condemns Indians for accepting failure.

Inference _____T_____ 13. The author argued with classmates because he would not play stupid.

Inference _____T_____ 14. Many Indian children "played dumb" in school but were quite capable outside of school.

Detail _____F_____ 15. The author states that non-Indians do not pity Indians who fail.

Build Your Vocabulary

According to the way the italicized word was used in the selection, select *a, b, c,* or *d* for the word or phrase that gives the best definition. The number in parentheses indicates the line of the passage in which the word is located.

___b___ 1. *"avid* reader" (11)
　　a. extremely slow
　　b. enthusiastic
　　c. careful
　　d. fast

___a___ 2. "sudden *clarity"* (23)
　　a. clearness
　　b. cleanness
　　c. vagueness
　　d. eagerness

___d___ 3. "a *prodigy"* (49)
　　a. uncertain child
　　b. slow child
　　c. child of normal
　　　development
　　d. child genius

___d___ 4. "an *oddity"* (50)
　　a. event
　　b. extra
　　c. routine
　　d. abnormality

___b___ 5. "feared and *ridiculed"*
　　　(52)
　　a. looked up to
　　b. made fun of
　　c. accepted
　　d. appreciated

___a___ 6. *"subverted* them" (56)
　　a. ruined
　　b. created
　　c. kept
　　d. covered

___d___ 7. *"appropriately* pitied" (63)
　　a. happily
　　b. sadly
　　c. sometimes
　　d. fittingly

___b___ 8. "was *arrogant"* (64)
　　a. scared
　　b. conceited
　　c. happy
　　d. eager

___d___ 9. "joy and *desperation"* (74)
　　a. misery
　　b. gladness
　　c. confusion
　　d. hopelessness

___b___ 10. *"sullen* and already
　　　defeated" (87)
　　a. good-natured
　　b. bad-tempered
　　c. ignorant
　　d. poor

Time Goals

Record your time for answering the questions: _____:_____

Calculate your total time for reading and answering the questions:

_____

_____

What changes would you make to enhance your concentration on the new selection?

_____

_____

Search the Net

To challenge your computer skills, research skills, and critical thinking skills, most of the reading selections in this book will be accompanied by an Internet exercise. You will use the Internet, also known as the World Wide Web (WWW) or the Web, to research a question and find information at different Web sites. You can conduct your own search or use sites suggested on this textbook's companion Web site, http://www.ablongman.com/smith/. You will then blend the new information with your own thoughts to produce a written response. These Internet exercises can be done individually or as group activities. To help you get started, read the following suggestions for successful Internet searches.

SECRETS OF A SUCCESSFUL SEARCH

Searching for information on the Internet can be both rewarding and frustrating. The key to avoiding frustration, or at least minimizing it, is organization. Organization requires a plan, an ongoing search strategy, and good record keeping. A successful Internet search consists of the following five steps:

1. Make a plan.
2. Search and search again.
3. Read selectively.
4. Record as you go.
5. Consider the source.

1. Make a Plan

Locating information on the Web requires the use of a search engine such as Google, Yahoo, Ask.com, AltaVista, Excite, Dogpile, or Lycos. Once you have selected a search engine, enter a search term or phrase, which may consist of one or more words, a phrase, or a name. The search engine will comb the Internet for sites that contain your term or phrase, count them, and display the best ten to twenty-five sites (called "hits") on your computer screen. A successful search depends on the wording of your chosen terms and the way you enter them.

For serious research, experts recommend using a notebook to organize your search strategy. Begin by writing down your general research topic and related questions. Next, jot down all the key terms you can think of that relate to your topic, and create additional questions if necessary. At this beginning point, prior knowledge of the topic is extremely helpful. If your knowledge of the topic is limited, however, you can familiarize yourself with related terminology, names, and events by performing a quick search to select and read a few sites on the topic.

SAMPLE SEARCH NOTEBOOK PAGES

Research Topic	Indian Reservations
Research questions	Why were Indian Reservations created?
	Where are Indian Reservations located?
	How are Indian Reservations governed?
	What is life like on an Indian Reservation?
What I already know	There are Indian Reservations throughout the United States.
	There are laws and treaties that established the Indian Reservations.
	The idea and establishment of Indian Reservations can be controversial.

Search Terms	**Notes and Web sites**
➤ Indian Reservation and Law	Facts about Native Americans today **http://www.infoplease.com/ipa/A0192524.html**
➤ Trail of Tears	Information about Cherokee Indians forcibly removed from North Georgia **http://ngeorgia.com/history/nghisttt.html**
	Trail of Tears Map **http://ngeorgia.com/history/trailoftearsmap.html**
➤ Indian Removal	Treaties signed by different Native American Tribes **http://www.pbs.org/wgbh/aia/part4/4p2959.html**
	Historical background of Indian Removal Act **http://www.mcps.k12.md.us/schools/springbrookhs/rights/AI/historical_background.html**

Research topic	Maternal instincts of birds
Research questions	What are some unusual maternal instincts of birds?
	How do these instincts aid in the survival of the species?
What I already know	Birds and other animals have some unusual instincts such as imprinting. Imprinting is the process whereby young birds and other young animals form an attachment to the first social objects they encounter. Konrad Lorenz led the research on imprinting, using goslings.

Search Terms	**Notes and Web sites**
➤ Bird behavior	Poor results—sites are related to pet bird behaviors
➤ Maternal instincts	Only found instincts on cows, pigs, and sheep
➤ Bird instincts	Host-parasite conflict **http://birding.miningco.com/library/weekly/aa060797.htm**
➤ Maternal instincts of birds	Killdeer mother feigns broken wing **http://www.birdwatching.com/stories/killdeer.html**
	Personal report **http://www.newton.dep.anl.gov/natbltn/400-499/nb482.htm**
	Very brief description **http://www.baylink.org/wpc/killdeer.html**

Research Topic	Steroids
Research Questions	Who is most likely to use steroids?
	How are the effects of steroid use different for teenagers and adults?
	What other supplements act like steroids? What are their health consequences?
What I already know	There has been an increase in steroid use among high school students.
	Steroid abuse is growing rapidly among young women.
	Supplements may also cause health problems.
Search Terms	**Notes and Web sites**
➤ Steroids and teenagers	Information on steroids. Specific information about teens. http://www.aap.org/family/steroids.htm
	Tips for teens. http://www.ncadi.samhsa.gov/govpubs/phd726/
➤ Steroids and health	Overview http://teens.drugabuse.gov/mom/mom_ster1.asp
	Overview. Specific information about teens. http://www.whitehousedrugpolicy.gov/drugfacts/steroids/index.html
➤ Steroids and supplements	Health consequences and other supplements http://www.coolnurse.com/steroids.htm

Decide on a few key words that you believe will help you locate the information you want, and use them as search terms. Using a two-column format in your notebook, list each search term on the left side of the paper and allow room on the right side for writing the locations of Web sites and comments about the site. For example, if your research topic is Indian Reservations, your list of search terms may include Native American or Indian persecution, Native American or Indian culture, and treatment of Native Americans. Sample search notebook pages are illustrated above.

Check with your college library on how to gain access to online databases containing online journals, collections, and other resources that can provide a wealth of information. Some of the most commonly used databases are listed in the Reader's Tip on page 34.

2. Search and Search Again

One of the most important tasks in conducting a successful search is to enter search terms that will produce the information that you want. Search terms that are too *wide* may bring thousands of hits. Some researchers suggest beginning with a *broad* search (a single term) and then narrowing the search, whereas others suggest beginning with a *narrow* search (multiple terms) and broadening it later. Both methods are acceptable, and you can experiment to discover which works

---

Reader's *Tip* ── Popular College Databases ────────────────

- Galileo
- Periodical abstracts
- Newspaper abstracts
- LexisNexis Academic Universe
- MLA Bibliography
- ABI Inform
- PsycFIRST
- Social Science abstracts
- ERIC
- Medline

---

best for you. Be flexible in trying new terms and different combinations. In the previous example, searching for Indians, reservations, or culture alone will bring a multitude of hits. Narrowing your search by typing in Native American culture should produce sites more attuned to your research. Entering too many terms, however, may result in no hits or only limited information. Searches also provide additional terms to pursue. More search suggestions are offered in the Reader's Tip below.

Reader's *Tip* ── Manipulating the Search ────────────────

In our first sample search case (see page 32), entering Indian Reservations in the search term box will give you all sites that contain the term Indian, reservations, or Indian Reservations. Placing quotation marks around a phrase or the term—that is, "Indian Reservations"— will pull up only those sites containing the full term. Another way to find suitable sites is to add an AND, +, OR, or NOT in the phrase.

At some point, you may need to find the home page of a particular company—for example, Harley-Davidson. If your search does not produce the home page of the company, try to guess or work out the company's Uniform Resource Locator (URL). Remember that a simple URL is composed of four or five parts. The first part is usually *http://*. *Http* is a protocol or mechanism used by browsers to communicate with Web sites. The second part is *www* for the World Wide Web. The third part is usually the name or abbreviation of a company, product, or institution. The fourth part is the site's designation. The three-letter designation at the end of the URL, sometimes called the **domain**, depends on the type of site. For example, *gov* is for government, *org* is for organization, *com* is for commercial site, and *edu* is for education. Some URLs have a fifth part; they end in a two-letter code to signify a country. For example, *uk* means *United*

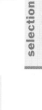

Kingdom in the Web site for the British monarchy, http://www. royal.gov.uk (see the diagram).

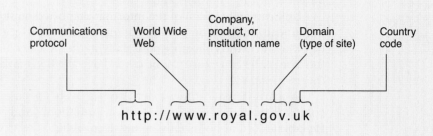

3. Read Selectively

The amount of information on the Internet can be overwhelming. Rarely, however, is it desirable or practical to read all the available information on a subject. Read selectively to narrow the scope of your research. After entering a search term and receiving a list of possible sites, scan the list of hits to look for key words relating to your search needs. The sites that contain the most information are usually listed first. Some search engines, such as Excite and Infoseek, will place a percentage value next to the site link, indicating the likelihood that the information sought is located at that site. In addition, a summary of the site may also be included.

After selecting a Web site or link that appears to have the information you need, study the table of contents or outline and move around the site to determine its layout or structure. Check secondary links that look promising. Skim definitions, statements, quotes, and other text while asking yourself, "Is this the information I am looking for?" Web pages present information in some uniform patterns, but styles vary because there is no standard format. Most Web sites, however, contain a title, subtitles, links, a table of contents, and an outline or introductory paragraph.

4. Record As You Go

As you discover sites, make sure to record them in your notebook. Once you have searched a term, check it off on your term list and note the results of the search next to the term. This will help you avoid searching for the same term a second time. Include the site location (the URL), particularly if you would like to return to the site or include it as a reference. If you are trying to locate a specific URL, such as a Web site listed in this textbook, do not be surprised if the URL has changed. Unfortunately, site locations often change without notice, thus making mastery of the steps in the search process even more important.

There are three ways of noting the site: (1) by recording the URL in your notebook next to the term; (2) by printing out the site material, since the URL is usually listed at the top of the printout; or (3) by **bookmarking** or saving the site so you can return to it at a later date. If you are using a computer in a location that you may not again have access to, save your bookmarks on a disk.

5. Consider the Source

Information on the Internet, although abundant, may not necessarily be accurate. In 1998, a U.S. congressman saw an obituary for a prominent entertainer posted on the Web and announced the death to Congress. As it turned out, the obituary had been posted by accident, and the entertainer, comedian Bob Hope, was quite alive and hitting golf balls at the time.

Unfortunately, much of the information posted on the Web can be misleading, unfounded, or based on personal opinions and beliefs rather than facts. One of the best ways to avoid collecting poor data on the Internet is to use good judgment. In the case of the congressman, he could have avoided embarrassment by confirming the information.

When reviewing information from a Web site, ask yourself, "What person, company, or agency is providing the information?" and "Is this a reliable source?" Reliable information usually comes from reliable sources. Information gathered from sites such as news stations, libraries, city newspapers, and government databases is probably more reliable than that from obscure sites with no obvious signs of credibility. Finally, when you are doing a research paper, do not rely entirely on Internet sources. Use books, journals, and other reliable print sources as well.

Search the Net

Use a search engine such as Google, AltaVista, Excite, Infoseek, Dogpile, Yahoo, or Lycos to find information on the history of Indian reservations. Discuss how and why they were created and the decisions about where they are located. Are there different laws governing Indian reservations? Explain three social and health-related issues that are more common on Indian reservations and reasons they may exist. For suggested Web sites and other research activities, go to http://www.ablongman. com/smith/.

selection 2   Psychology

Contemporary *Focus*

An unfortunate new trend—bringing home adorable little puppies at earlier than eight weeks of age—robs the animals of critical time needed to imprint. During the first eight to sixteen weeks of life, a puppy learns socialization skills from its parents and siblings. If separated from them before eight weeks, the puppy is more likely to be fearful, run away, bite, and bark.

Early Pup Separation Leads to Aggression

By Joan Klucha
North Shore News (British Columbia), October 23, 2005

New dog owners may see nothing wrong with this, but the reality of the situation is a puppy brought home before eight weeks of age is almost doomed to develop behavioral problems regarding aggression and self-control.

Acclaimed animal behaviorist Roger Abrantes says that the first signs of aggression are shown at around four to five weeks of age, and this is a normal stage of development at this time as the puppies seek and engage in conflicts and begin to become more assertive. These conflicts with their litter mates and parents are necessary for them to become social animals by developing methods of compromise. They may challenge one another, and that challenge is either met with success or failure. In either case, they still remain a part of the social group, so they understand that failure doesn't have a negative consequence. As a result, they develop confidence. Thus, you can imagine what happens when puppies are then removed during this period to be on their own or are born into litters without siblings. They never learn how to initiate conflict without aggression or to end conflict with compromise instead of aggression. As a result they have little or no ability to resolve issues and harbor aggression long after a conflict is over.

Not only do pups have less confidence when removed from the litter earlier than eight weeks, they also have less or no bite inhibition. Bite inhibition is a skill a pup learns from its parents and siblings (how much or little to bite is necessary to resolve an issue). This means that young pups never learn that it is okay to walk away from conflict instead of biting to get their way. Even at eight weeks bite inhibition is limited. They often have issues with being selfish and have a higher than normal level of resource guarding—threatening behavior such as growling, snapping and biting to prevent a valuable item from being taken away.

COLLABORATE Collaborate on responses to the following questions:

➤ Why are puppies being separated from their litters before eight weeks of age?

➤ How would you try to socialize a four-week-old abandoned puppy?

➤ Is it just a stereotype, or do you think only children are more selfish than children raised with siblings? Why or why not?

Skill Development: Active Learning

Before reading the following selection, take a few minutes to analyze your active learning potential and answer the following questions.

1. **Physical Environment**   Where are you and what time is it? _____

_____

What are your external distractions? _____

_____

2. **Internal Distractions**   What is popping into your mind and interfering with

your concentration?_____

3. **Spark Interest**   Glance at the selection and predict what it will cover. What

do you already know about the topic? What about the selection will be of

interest to you? _____

4. **Set Time Goals**   How long will it take you to read the selection? _____

minutes. To answer the questions? _____ minutes.

Increase Word Knowledge

What do you know about these words?

hypothesis	incubator	genetic	instinctive	sustain
restrained	inseminate	disrupted	irreversible	coax

Your instructor may give a true-false vocabulary review before or after reading.

Time Goal

Record your starting time for reading. _____:_____

CRITICAL-PERIOD HYPOTHESIS

There is some evidence that the best time for a child to learn a given skill is at the time the child's body is just mature enough to allow mastery of the behavior in question. This belief is often called the *critical-period hypothesis*—that is, the belief that an organism must have certain experiences at a *particular time* in its develop-
5 mental sequence if it is to reach its mature state.

There are many studies from animal literature supporting the critical-period hypothesis. For instance, German scientist Konrad Lorenz discovered many years ago that birds, such as ducks and geese, will follow the first moving object they see after they are hatched. Usually the first thing they see is their mother, of course, who has been sitting on the eggs when they are hatched. However, Lorenz showed
10 that if he took goose eggs away from the mother and hatched them in an incubator, the fresh-hatched *goslings* would follow him around instead.

Nina Leen/Time Life Pictures/Getty Images

Lorenz swims with the goslings who have imprinted on him.

After the goslings had waddled along behind Lorenz for a few hours, they acted as if they thought he was their mother and that they were humans, not geese. When Lorenz returned the goslings to their real mother, they ignored her. Whenever Lorenz appeared, however, they became very excited and flocked to him for protection and affection. It was as if the visual image of the first object they saw moving had become so strongly *imprinted* on their consciousness that, forever after, that object was "mother."

During the past 20 years or so, scientists have spent a great deal of time studying *imprinting* as it now is called. The effect occurs in many but not in all types of birds, and it also seems to occur in mammals such as sheep and seals. Whether it occurs in humans is a matter for debate. Imprinting is very strong in ducks and geese, however, and they have most often been the subjects for study.

The urge to imprint typically reaches its strongest peak 16 to 24 hours after the baby goose is hatched. During this period, the baby bird has an innate tendency to follow anything that moves, and will chase after its mother (if she is around), or a human, a bouncing football or a brightly painted tin can that the experimenter dangles in front of the gosling. The more the baby bird struggles to follow after this moving object, the more strongly the young animal becomes imprinted to the object. Once the goose has been imprinted, this very special form of learning cannot easily be reversed. For example, the geese that first followed Lorenz could not readily be trained to follow their mother instead; indeed, when these geese were grown and sexually mature, they showed no romantic interest in other geese. Instead, they attempted to court and mate with humans.

If a goose is hatched in a dark incubator and is not allowed to see the world until two or three days later, imprinting often does not occur. At first it was thought that the "critical period" had passed and hence the bird could never become imprinted to anything. Now we know differently. The innate urge to follow moving objects does appear to reach a peak in geese 24 hours after they are hatched, but it does not decline thereafter. Rather, a second innate urge—that of fearing and avoiding new objects—begins to develop, and within 48 hours after hatching typically overwhelms the prior tendency the bird had to follow after anything that moves. To use a human term, the goose's *attitude* toward strange things is controlled by its genetic blueprint—at first it is attracted to, then it becomes afraid of, new objects in its environment. As we will see in a moment, these conflicting "attitudes" may explain much of the data on "critical periods" in both animals and humans.

How might these two apparently conflicting behavioral tendencies help a baby goose survive in its usual or natural environment?

50   In other experiments, baby chickens have been hatched and raised in the dark for the first several days of their lives. Chicks have an innate tendency to peck at small objects soon after they are hatched—an instinctive behavior pattern that helps them get food as soon as they are born. In the dark, of course, they cannot see grain lying on the ground and hence do not peck (they must be hand-fed in the dark during this period of time). Once brought into the light, these chicks do begin to peck, but they
55   do so clumsily and ineffectively, as if their "critical period" for learning the pecking skill had passed. Birds such as robins and blue jays learn to fly at about the time their wings are mature enough to sustain flight (their parents often push them from the nest as a means of encouraging them to take off on their own). If these young birds are restrained and not allowed to fly until much later, their flight patterns are often
60   clumsy, and they do not usually gain the necessary skills to become good fliers.

THE "MATERNAL INSTINCT" IN RATS

Suppose we take a baby female rat from its mother at the moment of its birth and raise the rat pup "by bottle" until it is sexually mature. Since it has never seen other rats during its entire life (its eyes do not open until several days after birth), any sexual or maternal behavior that it shows will presumably be due to the natural un-
65   folding of its genetic blueprint—and not due to learning or imitation. Now, suppose we inseminate this hand-raised female rat artificially—to make certain that she continues to have no contact with other rats. Will she build a nest for her babies before they are born, following the usual pattern of female rats, and will she clean and take care of them during and after the birth itself?

70   The answer to that question is yes—*if*. If, when the young female rat was growing up, there were objects such as sticks and sawdust and string and small blocks of wood in her cage, and which she played with. Then, when inseminated, the pregnant rat will use these "toys" to build a nest. If the rat grows up in a bare cage, she won't build a nest *even though we give her the materials to do so once she is impreg-*
75   *nated*. If this same rat is forced to wear a stiff rubber collar around her neck when she is growing up—so that she cannot clean her sex organs, as rats normally do—she will not usually lick her newborn babies clean *even though we take off the rubber collar a day or so before she gives birth*. The genetic blueprint always operates best within a particular environmental setting. If an organism's early environment is
80   abnormal or particularly unusual, later "innate" behavior patterns may be disrupted.

OVERCOMING THE "CRITICAL PERIOD"

All of these examples may appear to support the "critical-period" hypothesis—that there is one time in an organism's life when it is best suited to learn a particular skill. These studies might also seem to violate the general rule that an organism can "catch up" if its development has been delayed. However, the truth is more compli-
85   cated (as always) than it might seem from the experiments we have cited so far.

Baby geese will normally not imprint if we restrict their visual experiences for the first 48 hours of their lives—their fear of strange objects is by then too great. However, if we give the geese tranquilizing drugs to help overcome their fear, they can be imprinted a week or more after hatching. Once imprinting has taken place, it
90   may seem to be irreversible. But we can occasionally get a bird imprinted on a human to accept a goose as its mother, if we coax it enough and give it massive rewards for

approaching or following its natural mother. Chicks raised in darkness become clumsy eaters—but what do you think would happen if we gave them special training in how to peck, rather than simply leaving the matter to chance? Birds restrained in the nest
95　too long apparently learn other ways of getting along and soon come to fear heights; what do you think would happen if we gave these birds tranquilizers and rewarded each tiny approximation to flapping their wings properly?

There is not much scientific evidence that human infants have the same types of "critical periods" that birds and rats do. By being born without strong innate be-
100　havior patterns (such as imprinting), we seem to be better able to adjust and survive in the wide variety of social environments human babies are born into. Like many other organisms, however, children do appear to have an inborn tendency to imitate the behavior of other organisms around them. A young rat will learn to press a lever in a Skinner box much faster if it is first allowed to watch an adult rat
105　get food by pressing the lever. This learning is even quicker if the adult rat happens to be the young animal's mother. Different species of birds have characteristic songs or calls. A European thrush, for example, has a song pattern fairly similar to a thrush in the United States, but both sound quite different from blue jays. There are *local dialects* among songbirds, however, and these are learned through imitation. If a
110　baby thrush is isolated from its parents and exposed to blue jay calls when it is very young, the thrush will sound a little like a blue jay but a lot like other thrushes when it grows up. And parrots, of course, pick up very human-sounding speech patterns if they are raised with humans rather than with other parrots.

(1,631 words)

—by James V. McConnell, *Understanding Human Behavior*, Copyright © 1974.
Reprinted with permission of Wadsworth, a division of Thomson Learning.

Time Goals

Record your finishing time: _____:_____

Calculate your total reading time: _____

Rate your concentration as high _____ medium _____ or low _____.

Recall what you have read, and review what you have learned.

Your instructor may choose to give you a true-false comprehension review.

Write About the Selection

Provide proof that a critical period exists during which an organism must have certain experiences to reach its normal mature state.

Response Suggestion: Review the selection and number the experiments that provide proof of the hypothesis. Define the hypothesis and describe three to five suporting examples from the text.

Contemporary *Link*

Using the studies on the critical period for the development of instinctive behaviors in chicks, rats, and birds, explain why you think there should or should not be a law forbidding professional dog breeders from selling puppies prior to eight weeks of age.

Check Your Comprehension

After reading the selection, answer the following questions with *a, b, c,* or *d.* In order to help you analyze your strengths and weaknesses, the question types are indicated.

Main Idea ___b___ 1. Which is the best statement of the main idea of this selection?

   a. Studies show that goslings can imprint on humans.
   b. A particular few days of an animal's life can be a crucial time for developing long-lasting "natural" behavior.
   c. Imprinting seems to occur in mammals but is very strong in ducks and geese.
   d. The "crucial period" of imprinting is important but can be overcome with drugs.

Detail ___a___ 2. The critical-period hypothesis is the belief that

   a. there is a "prime time" to develop certain skills.
   b. most learning occurs during the first few days of life.
   c. fear can inhibit early learning.
   d. the "maternal instinct" is not innate but is learned.

Detail ___c___ 3. In Lorenz's studies, after the goslings imprinted on him, they would do all of the following *except*

   a. follow him around.
   b. flock to him for protection.
   c. return to their real mother for affection.
   d. become excited when Lorenz appeared.

Detail ___c___ 4. The author points out that in Lorenz's studies, the early imprinting of geese with humans

   a. was easily reversed with training.
   b. caused the geese to be poor mothers.
   c. later produced sexually abnormal behavior in the geese.
   d. made it difficult for the goslings to learn to feed themselves.

Inference ___c___ 5. The author suggests that by 48 hours, the innate urge to imprint in geese is

   a. decreased significantly.
   b. increased.
   c. overwhelmed by the avoidance urge.
   d. none of the above.

Inference ___d___ 6. In a small gosling's natural environment, the purpose of the avoidance urge that develops within 48 hours of hatching might primarily be to help it

   a. learn only the behavior of its species.
   b. follow only one mother.
   c. escape its genetic blueprint.
   d. stay away from predators.

Inference _____a_____ 7. The author suggests that there is a critical period for developing all the following *except*

    a. the desire to eat.
    b. pecking.
    c. flying.
    d. cleaning the young.

Inference _____c_____ 8. The studies with rats suggest that nest-building and cleaning behaviors are

    a. totally innate behaviors.
    b. totally learned behaviors.
    c. a combination of innate and learned behaviors.
    d. neither innate nor learned behaviors.

Detail _____b_____ 9. Abnormal imprinting during the critical period can later be overcome by using all of the following *except*

    a. tranquilizing drugs.
    b. natural tendencies.
    c. special training.
    d. massive reward.

Inference _____a_____ 10. Because humans do not seem to have strong innate behavior patterns, the author suggests that humans

    a. are better able to adapt to changing environments.
    b. have more difficulty learning early motor skills.
    c. find adjustment to change more difficult than animals do.
    d. need more mothering than animals.

Answer the following with *T* (true) or *F* (false).

Detail _____T_____ 11. The author states that whether imprinting occurs in humans is a matter of debate.

Inference _____T_____ 12. The author implies that a goose can be imprinted on a painted tin can.

Inference _____F_____ 13. In the author's opinion, studies show that organisms can catch up adequately without special training when skill development has been delayed past the critical period.

Inference _____T_____ 14. If an abandoned bird egg is hatched and raised solely by a human, the author suggests that the bird will be abnormal.

Inference _____T_____ 15. The author suggests that the urge to imitate is innate in both humans and animals.

Build Your Vocabulary

According to the way the italicized word was used in the selection, select *a, b, c,* or *d* for the word or phrase that gives the best definition. The number in parentheses indicates the line of the passage in which the word is located.

_____b_____ 1. "The critical-period
hypothesis" (3)
a. association
b. tentative assumption
c. law
d. dilemma

_____d_____ 2. "in an *incubator*" (11)
a. cage
b. electric enlarger
c. nest
d. artificial hatching
apparatus

_____c_____ 3. "its *genetic* blueprint" (44)
a. sexual
b. emotional
c. hereditary
d. earned

_____b_____ 4. "an *instinctive* behavior
pattern" (51)
a. desirable
b. innate
c. early
d. newly acquired

_____a_____ 5. "to *sustain* flight" (57)
a. support
b. imitate
c. begin
d. imagine

_____c_____ 6. "birds are *restrained*" (59)
a. pressured
b. pushed
c. held back
d. attacked

_____b_____ 7. "suppose we *inseminate*"
(66)
a. imprison
b. artificially impregnate
c. injure
d. frighten

_____a_____ 8. "may be *disrupted*" (80)
a. thrown into disorder
b. repeated
c. lost
d. destroyed

_____d_____ 9. "seem to be *irreversible*"
(90)
a. temporary
b. changeable
c. frequent
d. permanent

_____a_____ 10. "*coax* it enough" (91)
a. encourage fondly
b. punish
c. feed
d. drill

Time Goal

Record your time for answering the questions: _____:_____

Calculate your total time for reading and answering the questions: _____

What changes would you make to enhance your concentration on the new selection?

_____

_____

Search the Net

Use a search engine such as Google, AltaVista, Excite, Infoseek, Dogpile, or Lycos to find autobiographical information on Konrad Lorenz. Describe the experiences that led to his interest in imprinting. For suggested Web sites and other research activities, go to http://www.ablongman.com/smith/.

selection 2

Concept Prep for Psychology

What does psychology cover?

Psychology is the scientific study of behavior and the mind. Behavior is observed, studied, and measured with the ultimate objective of explaining why people act and think as they do. Special areas that you will study in psychology include the following:

Biological psychology: How do your genes, brain, and hormones affect your behavior?

Behavioral psychology: What stimulus in the environment triggers your response?

Cognitive psychology: How do you think and remember?

Humanistic psychology: Can you be anything you want to be? Do you control your destiny?

Life span psychology: How do thoughts, desires, and actions differ in infancy, childhood, adolescence, adulthood, and old age?

Cross-cultural psychology: How do cultural differences affect your behavior and sense of self?

Why is Freud so important?

Sigmund Freud was a physician in Vienna, Austria, who formulated a theory of personality and a form of psychotherapy called **psychoanalysis.** Freud emerged as a leader in modern psychology and wrote twenty-four books popularizing his theories. After Freud's death in 1939, psychologists questioned many of his ideas and criticized him because of his focus on sexual desires. Still, Freud has contributed many ideas to our culture and words to our vocabulary.

Freud's theories evolved from observing and treating patients who suffered ailments without any visible physical basis but who responded favorably to hypnosis. He believed in treating their problems by tracing difficulties back to childhood experiences. Freud also believed in **dream interpretation,** a process in which the unconscious mind provides clues to psychological problems.

akg-images

Sigmund Freud theorized that mundane behavior has underlying psychological causes.

Freud's basic theories suggest that people are driven from early childhood by three principal unconscious forces: the **id** (an animal instinct and desire for pleasure), the **ego** (the sense of self that fights the id for reasonable compromises), and the **superego** (the social feeling of right and wrong and community values). Other terms that Freud established include **pleasure principle,** which refers to an instinctive need to satisfy the id regardless of the consequences; **libido,** which refers to sexual drive; and **egotism,** which refers to a sense of self-importance and conceit.

Other words we use today emerge from Freud's five stages of personality development: *oral, anal, phallic, latency,* and *genital.* An **oral personality** is fixated in the first stage of sucking and is satisfied by the pleasures of the mouth—for example, talking, smoking, eating, and chewing gum excessively. An **anal personality** is associated with the childhood period that involves bowel control and toilet training and as an adult is excessively focused on details and orderliness. Another term Freud popularized is *Oedipus complex,* which suggests that a young boy has a sexual desire for his mother. Finally, Freud was the originator of the

Freudian slip, which is a misspoken word—such as *sex* for *six*—that reveals unconscious thoughts.

Who was Carl Jung?

Carl Jung was a Swiss psychologist who classified people as **introverts** (shy) or **extroverts** (outgoing). Jung was one of the original followers of Freud but later broke with him. Adding to Freud's theory of repressed personal experiences, Jung believed that we also inherit the memories and symbols of ancestors in an **inherited collective unconscious.** He believed this was exhibited in an inborn fear of snakes or spiders. Jung also developed theories about concrete and abstract learning stages. Many of his theories are used as a basis for the Myers-Briggs Type Indicator.

Review Questions

After studying the material, answer the following questions:

1. Using visual images on note cards to improve memory of vocabulary words suggests what area of psychology? cognitive

2. Desiring a rocky road ice cream cone after passing a Baskin-Robbins store suggests what area of psychology? behavioral

3. Mapping physical activity in different areas of the brain as people read or listen to music suggests what area of psychology? biological

4. Attending a motivational seminar to become salesperson of the year suggests what area of psychology? humanistic

5. What is psychoanalysis? It is a form of therapy, originated by Freud, that seeks causes for behavior in the unconscious.

6. What are the goals of the id, ego, and superego? The id wants pleasure, the ego seeks protection of self, and the superego wants to abide by the ethical rules of society.

7 How does Freud relate dreams to reality? Dreams give unconscious clues to real problems.

8. Why did some psychologists break with Freud? They disagreed with his emphasis on sexual drives.

9. How do the theories of Jung and Freud differ? Jung added the inherited collective unconscious.

10. What is Jung's inherited collective unconscious? It is innate knowledge inherited from ancestors.

Your instructor may choose to give a true-false review of these psychology concepts.

selection 3   Health

selection 3

Contemporary *Focus*

One high school in South Carolina reported that 7 percent of the boys were using anabolic steroids. This figure is twice the national average. What factors in the environment foster steroid use? What personal dangers does a young athlete risk by taking steroids?

Keeping Kids Off the Juice

By Anne M. Peterson

Associated Press State & Local Wire, April 23, 2006.

Used with permission of the *Associated Press*; copyright © 2006. All rights reserved.

The police officer investigating Taylor Hooton's suicide emerged from the bedroom where the 17-year-old baseball player hanged himself and pointedly asked the teen's father if he knew anything about steroids.

Sure. Taylor had experimented with steroids, but his flirtation had passed, Donald Hooton thought, up until that moment.

Suddenly, the insidiousness of the drug became clear.

"I needed to understand, what happened to this kid? We're a good family. Taylor had everything he needed," Donald Hooton said. "I needed to know what in the heck happened here."

Taylor Hooton wanted to be a baseball player like Mark McGwire and Sammy Sosa. But along the way a misguided coach told him that to reach the next level, he needed to get bigger. So he turned to the juice.

COLLABORATE   Collaborate on responses to the following questions:

➤ At $50 to $150 a test, should high school athletes be randomly tested for steroid use? Why or why not?

➤ How do professional athletes manipulate the thinking of teen wannabees?

➤ What is the responsibility of a gifted athlete to be a role model?

➤ What is the responsibility of a coach regarding steroid use among team players?

Skill Development: Active Learning

Before reading the following selection, take a few minutes to analyze your active learning potential and answer the following questions.

1. **Physical Environment**   Where are you, and what time is it? _____

What are your external distractions? _____

_____

_____

2. **Internal Distractions** What is popping into your mind and interfering with your concentration? _____

_____

3. **Spark Interest** Glance at the selection, and predict what it will cover. What do you already know about the topic? What about the selection will be of interest to you? _____

_____

4. **Set Time Goals** How long will it take you to read the selection? _____ minutes. To answer the questions? _____ minutes.

Increase Word Knowledge

What do you know about these words?

heightened	promote	extent	euphoria	adverse
atrophy	alternatives	alleged	OTC	disclose

Your instructor may give a true-false vocabulary review before or after reading.

Time Goal

Record your starting time for reading. _____:_____

STEROIDS

Public awareness of anabolic steroids recently has been heightened by media stories about their use by amateur and professional athletes, including Arnold Schwarzenegger during his competitive bodybuilding days. Anabolic steroids are artificial forms of the male hormone testosterone that promote muscle growth
5 and strength. These ergogenic drugs are used primarily by young men who believe the drugs will increase their strength, power, bulk (weight), speed, and athletic performance.

EXTENT OF ABUSE

Most steroids are obtained through the black market. It once was estimated that approximately 17 to 20 percent of college athletes used them. Now that stricter
10 drug-testing policies have been instituted by the National College Athletic Association (NCAA), reported use of anabolic steroids among intercollegiate athletics has dropped to 1.1 percent. However, a recent survey among high school students found a significant increase in the use of anabolic steroids since 1991. Little data exist on the extent of steroid abuse by adults. It has been esti-
15 mated that hundreds of thousands of people age 18 and older abuse anabolic steroids at least once a year. Among both adolescents and adults, steroid abuse is

Roy Madhur/Reuters/Landov

The use of anabolic steroids has increased in recent years.

higher among males than among females. However, steroid abuse is growing most rapidly among young women.

TWO AVAILABLE FORMS

Steroids are available in two forms: injectable solution and pills. Anabolic steroids
20 produce a state of euphoria, diminished fatigue, and increased bulk and power in both sexes. These qualities give steroids an addictive quality. When users stop, they can experience psychological withdrawal and sometimes severe depression that in some cases leads to suicide attempts. If untreated, such depression associated with steroid withdrawal has been known to last for a year or more after steroid use stops.

EFFECTS

25 Adverse effects occur in both men and women who use steroids. These drugs cause mood swings (aggression and violence) sometimes known as "roid rage," acne, liver tumors, elevated cholesterol levels, hypertension, kidney disease, and immune system disturbances. There is also a danger of transmitting AIDS through shared needles. In women, large doses of anabolic steroids may trigger the development of
30 masculine attributes such as lowered voice, increased facial and body hair, and male pattern baldness; they also may result in an enlarged clitoris, smaller breasts, and changes in or absence of menstruation. When taken by healthy males, anabolic steroids shut down the body's production of testosterone, which causes men's breasts to grow and testicles to atrophy.

PENALTIES

35 To combat the growing problem of steroid use, Congress passed the Anabolic Steroids Control Act of 1990. This law makes it a crime to possess, prescribe, or dis-

tribute anabolic steroids for any use other than the treatment of specific diseases. Anabolic steroids are now classified as a Schedule III drug. Penalties for their illegal use include up to five years' imprisonment and a $250,000 fine for the first offense,
40 and up to ten years' imprisonment and a $500,000 fine for subsequent offenses.

TRENDS

A new and alarming trend is the use of other drugs to achieve the supposed performance-enhancing effects of steroids. The two most common steroid alternatives are gamma hydroxybutyrate (GHB) and clenbuterol. GHB is a deadly, illegal drug that is a primary ingredient in many performance-enhancing formulas. GHB does not
45 produce a high. However, it does cause headaches, nausea, vomiting, diarrhea, seizures and other central nervous system disorders, and possibly death. Clenbuterol is used in some countries for veterinary treatments, but it is not approved for any use—in animals or humans—in the United States.

New attention was drawn to the issue of steroids and related substances when
50 St. Louis Cardinals slugger Mark McGwire admitted to using a supplement containing androstenedione (andro), an adrenal hormone that is produced naturally in both men and women. Andro raises levels of the male hormone testosterone, which helps build lean muscle mass and promotes quicker recovery after injury. McGwire had done nothing illegal, since the supplement can be purchased OTC (with esti-
55 mated sales of up to $800 million a year). Also, its use is legal in baseball, although it is banned by the National Football League, the NCAA, and the International Olympic Committee. A recent study found that when men take 100 mg of andro three times daily, it increases estrogen levels up to 80 percent, enlarges the prostate gland, and increases heart disease risk by 10 to 15 percent. This finding may or may
60 not affect its use in major league baseball—no decision has yet been made.

Although andro has been banned by many sports organizations, visits to the locker rooms of many teams belonging to these organizations would disclose large containers of other alleged muscle-building supplements, such as creatine. Although they are legal, questions remain whether enough research has been done
65 concerning the safety of these supplements. Some people worry that they may bring consequences similar to those of steroids, such as liver damage and heart problems.

(805 words)

—by Rebecca J. Donatelle,
Health: The Basics,
4th edition

Time Goals

Record your finishing time: _____:_____

Calculate your total reading time: _____

Rate your concentration as high _____ medium _____ or low _____.

Recall what you have read, and review what you have learned.

Your instructor may choose to give you a true-false comprehension review.

Write About the Selection

Describe the effects and danger of steroids and the newer performance-enhancing alternatives.

Response Suggestion: Describe the available forms with their effects and dangers, and then do the same for GHB, clenbuterol, and andro.

Contemporary *Link*

What mentality accepts steroid use? Why do some competitive athletes believe that steroid use is not a sign of poor sportsmanship? Why do they endanger their bodies for enhanced short-term performance?

Check Your Comprehension

After reading the selection, answer the following questions with *a*, *b*, *c*, or *d*. In order to help you analyze your strengths and weaknesses, the question types are indicated.

Main Idea _____c_____ 1. Which is the best statement of the main idea of this selection?

   a. Readers should push for harsher legal penalties for the use of steroids and related drugs.
   b. Those contemplating the use of steroids and related drugs should be careful to learn the laws concerning their use.
   c. Although steroids and related drugs offer short-term advantages to athletes, serious medical risks are associated with their use.
   d. Although some medical dangers exist, media coverage of celebrities' use of steroids and other drugs has greatly exaggerated these dangers.

Detail _____b_____ 2. Anabolic steroids can be defined as

   a. having no ergogenic characteristics.
   b. artificial forms of the male hormone testosterone.
   c. drugs that contain high levels of GHB.
   d. drugs that contain estrogen, which stimulates breast development.

Detail _____a_____ 3. According to the passage, the use of steroids has been most effectively decreased in college athletes by

   a. stricter policies of drug testing by college athletic associations.
   b. the increased availability of other less dangerous drugs.
   c. increased public awareness of health dangers of steroid use.
   d. reluctance on the part of college athletes to use a drug popular with high school students.

Inference _____c_____ 4. The author suggests that AIDS can be contracted by steroid users who

   a. use the drug for a prolonged period of time.
   b. experience psychological withdrawal symptoms.
   c. share needles with other users.
   d. have already experienced hypertension or kidney disease.

Detail _____c_____ 5. According to the passage, the Anabolic Steroids Control Act of 1990 does all of the following *except*

   a. criminalize prescribing steroids to enhance athletic performance.
   b. increase the penalty for repeat offenses.
   c. remove steroids from the Schedule III drug category.
   d. allow steroids to be used for the treatment of specific diseases.

Inference _____a_____ 6. U.S. policy regarding the use of clenbuterol might best be defined as

   a. more stringent than that of some other countries.
   b. acceptable for treatment of animals but not for treatment of humans.
   c. likely to permit legalization for most uses in the near future.
   d. allowing its use by athletes as long as they have been warned of the possible dangers.

selection 3

Detail _____d_____ 7. Androstenedione (andro) can most accurately be defined as

   a. a drug that decreases testosterone.
   b. a hormone that strengthens bones.
   c. a drug that can be obtained only by prescription.
   d. an adrenal hormone produced by men and women.

Inference _____b_____ 8. The reader can conclude that if Mark McGwire had been a football player at the time he used andro

   a. his use of the drug would have been considered legal.
   b. his use of the drug would have been considered illegal.
   c. the supplements would have been provided free by the OTC.
   d. the legality of his drug use would have been determined by the St. Louis Cardinals.

Inference _____d_____ 9. The passage implies that steroid use may cause

   a. a decrease in breast size for both men and women.
   b. an increase in breast size for both men and women.
   c. no changes in sexual characteristics for men or for women.
   d. the growth of some male sex characteristics in women and the growth of some female sexual characteristics in men.

Detail _____b_____ 10. Of the drugs mentioned in the passage, the only one explicitly cited as promoting faster recovery after injury is

   a. creatine.
   b. andro.
   c. GHB.
   d. clenbuterol.

Answer the following with *T* (true) or *F* (false).

Detail _____F_____ 11. The slang term "roid rage" refers to the enhanced sense of athletic competitiveness caused by the use of steroids.

Inference _____T_____ 12. Steroids produce euphoria (a high) among users, but GHB does not.

Detail _____T_____ 13. According to the passage, the rate of increase in abuse of steroids is highest among young women.

Inference _____F_____ 14. The reader can conclude that creatine is also a steroid.

Detail _____F_____ 15. The most dangerous symptom associated with steroid withdrawal is physical exhaustion.

Build Your Vocabulary

According to the way the italicized word was used in the selection, select *a*, *b*, *c*, or *d* for the word or phrase that gives the best definition. The number in the parentheses indicates the line of the passage in which the word is located.

___a___ 1. "Has been *heightened*" (1)
   a. intensified
   b. examined
   c. rubbed
   d. lessened

___c___ 2. "*promote* muscle growth" (4)
   a. graduate
   b. discredit
   c. encourage
   d. idealize

___c___ 3. "*extent* of steroid abuse" (14)
   a. exit
   b. discussion
   c. amount
   d. decline

___d___ 4. "state of *euphoria*" (20)
   a. gloom
   b. depression
   c. sleepiness
   d. bliss

___c___ 5. "*adverse* effects" (25)
   a. reverse
   b. wonderful
   c. negative
   d. positive

___a___ 6. "to *atrophy*"(34)
   a. shrink
   b. enlarge
   c. hurt
   d. change

___b___ 7. "steroid *alternatives*" (42)
   a. difficulties
   b. choices
   c. medications
   d. disorders

___d___ 8. "purchased *OTC*" (54)
   a. or through contracts
   b. only the cheapest
   c. openly through countries
   d. over the counter

___d___ 9. "would *disclose*" (62)
   a. negate
   b. withhold
   c. cover
   d. expose

___a___ 10. "*alleged* muscle building supplements" (63)
   a. supposed
   b. illegal
   c. dangerous
   d. hidden

Time Goal

Record your time for answering the questions: _____:_____

Calculate your total time for reading and answering the questions: _____

What changes would you make to enhance your concentration on the new selection?

_____

_____

Search the Net

Use a search engine such as Google, AltaVista, Excite, Infoseek, Dogpile, Yahoo, or Lycos to find information about substances banned by professional sports. List the substances banned by football, baseball, basketball, and hockey organizations, and determine if there are differences among their steroid policies. For suggested Web sites and other research activities, go to http://www.ablongman.com/smith/.

2 Vocabulary

- How do you remember new words?
- What are context clues?
- Why learn prefixes, roots, and suffixes?
- What will you find in a dictionary?
- What is a glossary?
- What is a thesaurus?
- What are analogies?
- What are acronyms?
- How are transitional words used?

Stuart Davis (1894–1964) *International Surface No. 1.* 1960. oil on canvas. Gift of S.C. Johnson & Son. Inc. Courtesy of VAGA, New York.

Remembering New Words

Have you ever made lists of unknown words that you wanted to remember? Did you dutifully write down the word, a colon, and a definition, and promise to review the list at night before going to bed? Did it work? Probably not! Memorization can be an effective cramming strategy, but it does not seem to produce long-term results. Recording only the word and definition does not establish the associations necessary for long-term memory.

Instead, use clever memory techniques to expand your vocabulary. With these tricks, or **mnemonic devices,** you visualize and organize units into new relationships. You can also use rhymes to tie words together. For example, to remember the word *mnemonics*, think of Nem-on-ic as in remembering by putting a name on it. To remember that *suppression* means to force out bad thoughts, visualize SUPerman PRESSing evil thoughts away. A noted speaker, John Berthoud, usually begins a speech by explaining how to pronounce his last name, which is French. He tells audiences to think, "Not one *bear*, but *two*," or "You are naked, and I am *bare, too*." The following suggestions can help you associate and organize.

Associate Words in Phrases

Never record a word in isolation. Rather, think of the word and record it in a phrase that suggests its meaning. The phrase may be part of the sentence in which you first encountered the word or one you imagine yourself. Such a phrase provides a setting for the word and enriches the links to your long-term memory link.

For example, the word *caravel* means a small sailing ship. Record the word in a phrase that creates a memorable setting, such as "a caravan of gliding caravels on the horizon of the sea."

Associate Words with Rhymes or Sounds

Link the sound of a new word with a rhyming word or phrase. The brain appreciates connections and patterns. For example, the word *hoard*, which means to accumulate or stockpile, can be linked with *stored*, as in "He stored his hoard of Halloween candy in the closet."

Associate Words with Images

Expand the phrase chosen for learning the word into a vivid mental image. Create a situation or an episode for the word. Further, enrich your memory link by drawing a picture of your mental image.

For example, the word *candid* means frank and truthful. Imagine a friend asking your opinion on an unattractive outfit. A suggestive phrase for learning the word might be "My candid reply might have hurt her feelings."

Associate Words in Families

Words, like people, have families that share the same names. In the case of words, the names are called *prefixes, roots, and suffixes*. A basic knowledge of word parts can help you unlock the meaning to thousands of associated family members.

For example, the prefix *ambi-* means both, as in the word *ambivert*, which means "being both introverted and extroverted." You can apply your knowledge of *ambi-* to new words such as *ambidextrous*, *ambiguous*, and *ambivalence* to help determine and remember their meanings.

Seek Reinforcement

Look and listen for your new words. You will probably discover that they are used more frequently than you thought. Notice them, welcome them, and congratulate yourself on your newfound word knowledge.

Create Concept Cards

Many students use index cards to record information on new words. As illustrated below, one good system is to write the word in a phrase on the front of the card, also noting where the word was encountered. On the back of the card, write an appropriate definition, use the word in a new sentence, and draw an image illustrating the word. Review the cards, quiz yourself, and watch your vocabulary grow.

Front   Back

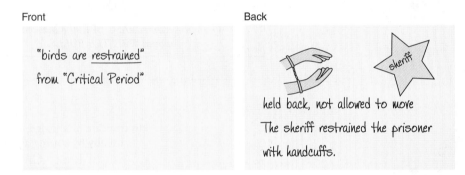

The concept card is elevated to a new level in *Vocabulary Cartoons*, a series of inventive books by a father-son team in which humor is skillfully combined with the techniques of association.[1] The idea for the books came from the son's inability to remember the definition of *aloof*. His father asked him for a rhyming word, and they envisioned the family cat being "so aloof that she hid on the roof." To illustrate, the father drew a cartoon with an accompanying word link and playful sentence, and his son never forgot the definition. The rhyme, the image, and the humor all became mnemonics. When the authors tested their cartoons on 500 Florida students, they found that students who had been given definitions and cartoons learned 72 percent more words than those who had been given definitions only.

Try adding rhyme and other sound associations to your own concept cards. The illustration on page 60 shows how cleverly the authors use sound and images to form memory links for the words *irascible* and *curtail*.

---

[1]S. Burchers, M. Burchers, and B. Burchers, *Vocabulary Cartoons I* and *Vocabulary Cartoons II* (Punta Gorda, FL: New Monic Books, 1997 and 2000).

IRASCIBLE
(i RAS uh bul)
easily angered, irritable
Link: **WRESTLE BULLS**

"When he became IRASCIBLE, the Masked Marvel would WRESTLE BULLS."

CURTAIL
(ker TALE)
to truncate or abridge; to lessen,
usually by cutting away from
Link: **CAT TAIL**

"Rex readies himself to CURTAIL the CAT'S TAIL."

Courtesy of New Monic Books, publisher of *Vocabulary Cartoons SAT Word Power*.

exercise 2.1   **Creating Mnemonics to Associate Meaning**

Pair up with a classmate to create your own mnemonics for the following words. For each item, use rhyme and imagery to create a word link, a playful sentence, and a cartoon.

1. *scrutinize:* to look very carefully; to examine

2. *dormant:* asleep or inactive

3. *entreat:* to ask earnestly; to implore, plead, beg

4. Make up a mnemonic to help people remember your name.

Using Context Clues

What strategies can you use to figure out the meaning of a new word? Using **context clues** is the most common method of unlocking the meanings of unknown words. The *context* of a word refers to the sentence or paragraph in which it appears. Readers use several types of context clues. In some cases, words are defined directly in the sentences in which they apear; in other instances, the sentence offers clues or hints that enable the reader to arrive indirectly at the meaning of the word. The following examples show how each type of clue can be used to figure out word meanings in textbooks.

Definition or Synonym

Complex material, particularly scientific material, has a heavy load of specialized vocabulary. Fortunately, new words are often directly defined as they are introduced in the text. Often, **synonyms**—words with the same or a similar meaning as the unknown word—are given. Do you know the meaning of *erythrocytes* and *oxyhemoglobin?* Read the following textbook sentence in which these two words appear, and then select the correct definition for each word.

EXAMPLE   When oxygen diffuses into the blood in external respiration, most of it enters the red blood cells, or erythrocytes, and unites with the hemoglobin in these cells, forming a compound called oxyhemoglobin.

—Willis H. Johnson et al.,
Essentials of Biology

_____ *Erythrocytes* means

    a. diffused oxygen.
    b. red blood cells.
    c. the respiration process.

_____ *Oxyhemoglobin* means

a. hemoglobin without oxygen.
b. dominant oxygen cells.
c. a combination of oxygen and hemoglobin.

> **EXPLANATION** The answers are *b* and *c*. Notice that the first word, *erythrocytes*, is used as a synonym. Sometimes a signal word for a synonym is *or*. Other signal words that will help you discover meaning through the use of definition are *is, that is, in other words, for example,* and *is defined as.* The second word, *oxyhemoglobin*, is part of the explanation of the sentence.

Elaborating Details

Terms are not always directly defined in the text. Instead, an author may give descriptive details that illustrate meaning. In political science texts, for example, you may come across the term *confederation*. Keep reading and see if you can figure out the meaning from the hints in the following paragraph.

> **EXAMPLE** There is a third form of governmental structure, a *confederation*. The United States began as such, under the Articles of Confederation. In a confederation, the national government is weak and most or all the power is in the hands of its components, for example, the individual states. Today, confederations are rare except in international organizations such as the United Nations.
>
> —Robert Lineberry,
> *Government in America*

_____ A *confederation* is a governmental structure with

a. strong federal power.
b. weak federal power.
c. weak state power.
d. equal federal and state power.

> **EXPLANATION** The answer is *b* and can be figured out from the details in the third sentence.

Examples

At other times, examples will be given to clarify meaning. In psychology courses, for example, you will frequently encounter a complicated word describing something you have often thought about but not named. Read the following paragraph to find out what *psychokinesis* means.

> **EXAMPLE** Another psychic phenomenon is psychokinesis, the ability to affect physical events without physical intervention. You can test your powers of psychokinesis by trying to

influence the fall of dice from a mechanical shaker. Are you able to have the dice come up a certain number with a greater frequency than would occur by chance?

—Douglas W. Matheson,
Introductory Psychology: The Modern View

_____ *Psychokinesis* means

    a. extrasensory perception.
    b. an influence on happenings without physical tampering.
    c. physical intervention affecting physical change.

EXPLANATION The answer is *b*. Here the word is first directly defined in a complicated manner, and then the definition is clarified by a simple example.

Comparison

In certain cases, complex concepts are best understood when compared with something else. Economics texts, for example, include many concepts that are difficult to understand. The use of a familiar term in a comparison can help the reader relate to a new idea. Can you explain a *trade deficit?* The following comparison will help.

EXAMPLE When the United States imports more than it exports, we have a *trade deficit* rather than a trade balance or surplus. Similarly, a store manager who buys more than she sells will create a financial deficit for the company.

_____ A *trade deficit* means that a nation

    a. sells more than it buys.
    b. buys more than it sells.
    c. sells what it buys.

EXPLANATION The answer is *b*. The comparison explains the definition by creating a more understandable situation.

Contrast

In other cases, a contrast is made to help you read between the lines and infer word meaning. Can you explain what *transsexuals* are and how they differ from *homosexuals?* The following paragraph gives some clues.

EXAMPLE *Transsexuals* are people (usually males) who feel that they were born into the wrong body. They are not homosexuals in the usual sense. Most homosexuals are satisfied with their anatomy and think of themselves as appropriately male or female; they simply prefer members of their own sex. Transsexuals, in contrast, think of themselves as members of the opposite sex (often from early childhood) and may be so desperately unhappy with their physical appearance that they request hormonal and surgical treatment to change their genitals and secondary sex characteristics.

—Rita Atkinson et al.,
Introduction to Psychology

_____ A *transsexual* is a person who thinks of himself or herself as a

a. homosexual.
b. heterosexual.
c. member of the opposite sex.
d. person without sex drive.

EXPLANATION The answer is *c*. By contrasting homosexuals and transsexuals, the reader is better able to infer the difference between the two. Signal words that indicate contrast are *but, yet, however,* and *in contrast*.

Antonyms

Finally, the context clue may be an **antonym,** or a word that means the opposite of the unknown word. Antonyms are signaled by words and phrases such as *however, but, yet, in contrast,* or *on the other hand*. Using the following context, is *nonconfrontational* behavior violent?

EXAMPLE   Some passive belief systems call for *nonconfrontational* behavior; yet others call for rebellion.

—Adapted from Daniel G. Bates and Elliot M. Franklin,
Cultural Anthropology, 3rd ed.

_____ A *nonconfrontational* behavior is

a. violent.
b. rebellious.
c. not openly rebellious.
d. sympathetic.

EXPLANATION The signal word *yet* suggests that *nonconfrontational* is the opposite of violent and rebellious, so *c* is correct. The word *passive* is also a clue to the meaning.

Limitations of Context Clues

Although the clues in the sentence in which an unknown word appears are certainly helpful in deriving the meaning of the word, these clues will not always give a complete and accurate definition. To understand totally the meaning of a word, take some time after completing your reading to look up the word in a glossary or dictionary. Context clues operate just as the name suggests: they are hints, not necessarily definitions.

exercise 2.2   **The Power of Context Clues**

How can context clues assist you in unlocking the meaning of unknown words? For each of the following items, make two responses. First, without reading the sentence containing the unknown word, select *a, b, c,* or *d* for the definition that you feel best fits each italicized word. Then read the material in which the word is used in context and answer again.

    Compare your answers. Did reading the word in context help? Were you initially uncertain of any word but then able to figure out the meaning after reading it in a sentence?

____d____   1. *usurped*

    a. shortened
    b. acknowledged
    c. aggravated
    d. seized

    ____d____ Henry, to the end of his life, thought of himself as a pious and orthodox Catholic who had restored the independent authority of the Church of England *usurped* centuries before by the Bishop of Rome.

              —Shepard B. Clough et al.,
              A History of the Western World

____a____   2. *assimilationist*

    a. one who adopts the habits of a larger cultural group
    b. a machinist
    c. a typist
    d. one who files correspondence

    ____a____ When members of a minority group wish to give up what is distinctive about them and become just like the majority, they take an *assimilationist* position. An example is the Urban League.

              —Reece McGee et al.,
              Sociology: An Introduction

____b____   3. *dyad*

    a. star
    b. two-member group
    c. opposing factor
    d. leader

    ____b____ George Simmel was one of the first sociologists to suggest that the number of members in a group radically transforms its properties. He began with an analysis of what happens when a *dyad,* a two-member group, becomes a triad, a three-member group.

              —Ibid.

_____b_____ 4. *hyperthermophiles*

    a. animals
    b. heat lovers
    c. birds
    d. winter plants

    _____b_____ Another group of archaea, the *hyperthermophiles,* thrive in very hot waters; some even live near deep-ocean vents where temperatures are above 100°C, the boiling point of water at sea level.

                  —Neil Campbell et al.,
                  Biology: Concepts & Connections, 3rd ed.

_____a_____ 5. *expropriated*

    a. took from its owners
    b. industrialized
    c. approximated
    d. increased in size

    _____a_____ Under a decree of September 1952, the government *expropriated* several hundred thousand acres from large landholders and redistributed this land among the peasants.

                  —Jesse H. Wheeler, Jr., et al.,
                  Regional Geography of the World

_____b_____ 6. *adherents*

    a. children
    b. followers
    c. instigators
    d. detractors

    _____b_____ One of the fundamental features of Hinduism has been the division of its *adherents* into the most elaborate caste system ever known.

                  —Ibid.

_____c_____ 7. *stimulus*

    a. writing implement
    b. distinguishing mark
    c. something that incites action
    d. result

    _____c_____ While we are sleeping, for example, we are hardly aware of what is happening around us, but we are aware to some degree. Any loud noise or other abrupt *stimulus* will almost certainly awaken us.

                  —Gardner Lindzey et al.,
                  Psychology

_____a_____ 8. *debilitating*

> a. weakening
> b. reinforcing
> c. exciting
> d. enjoyable

_____a_____ However, anyone who has passed through several time zones while flying east or west knows how difficult it can be to change from one sleep schedule to another. This "jet lag" can be so *debilitating* that many corporations will not allow their executives to enter negotiations for at least two days after such a trip.

—Ibid.

_____d_____ 9. *autocratic*

> a. automatic
> b. democratic
> c. self-starting
> d. dictatorial

_____d_____ Autocratic leadership can be extremely effective if the people wielding it have enough power to enforce their decisions and if their followers know that they have it. It is especially useful in military situations where speed of decision is critical. Among its disadvantages are the lack of objectivity and the disregard for opinions of subordinates.

—David J. Rachman and Michael Mescon,
Business Today

_____c_____ 10. *ice page*

> a. Web page that wiggles to center itself
> b. Web page anchored to the right of the screen
> c. Web page anchored to the left of the screen
> d. Web page that flows to fit any size screen

_____c_____ Ice, jello, and liquid are related terms describing three approaches to controlling content placement on a Web page. An ice page is one in which the primary content has a fixed width and is "frozen" to the left margin.

—H. L. Capron,
Computers: Tools for an Information Age, 6th ed.

exercise 2.3 **Context Clues in Academic Reading**

Use the context clues of the sentence to write the meaning of each of the following italicized words.

1. Some psychologists suspect that negative emotions—especially depression and anxiety—may be the most *infectious* of all. "Stress and depression are like emotional germs—they jump from one person to the next," notes psychologist Ellen McGrath.

—Adapted from Stacy Colino,
"Happiness Is Catching: Why Emotions Are Contagious,"
Family Circle, March 12, 1996

Infectious means contagious or capable of rapidly spreading to others
_____.

2. Robbery, which should not be confused with burglary, is a personal crime and involves a face-to-face confrontation between victim and *perpetrator*.

—Frank Schmalleger,
Criminal Justice Today, 8th ed.

A *perpetrator* is one who commits a crime
_____.

3. In 1727 Sir Isaac Newton became seriously ill, and on March 20 one of the greatest physicists of all time died. He was *accorded* a state funeral and interred in Westminster Abbey—a high and rare honor for a commoner.

—Adapted from Larry D. Kirkpatrick and Gregory E. Francis,
Physics: A World View, 5th ed.

Accorded means granted
_____.

4. At times, two sides cannot—or will not—agree. The speed and ease with which such an *impasse* is resolved depend in part on the nature of the contract issues.

—Adapted from Ricky W. Griffin and Ronald J. Ebert,
Business, 8th ed.

An *impasse* means a deadlocked situation
_____.

5. Social psychologist Robert Zajonc found that people like previously seen things better than unfamiliar ones; research shows that familiarity breeds not contempt but *affinity*.

—Adapted from Stephen M. Kosslyn and Robin S. Rosenberg, *Psychology: The Brain, the Person, the World*, 2nd ed.

Affinity means <u>attraction or liking</u>

_____.

exercise 2.4   **Context Clues in Short Passages**

Use context clues from each passage that follows to write the meaning of the italicized words.

Passage A
Blocked by her family and publicly *maligned*, Florence Nightingale struggled against *prevailing norms* to carve out her occupation. She was the daughter of a wealthy *gentry* family, and from her father she received a man's classical education. Women of her *milieu* were expected to be educated only in domestic arts.

—Adapted from Mark Kishlansky et al., *Civilization in the West*, 6th ed.

1. maligned <u>slandered or spoken ill of unjustly</u>

_____

2. prevailing <u>dominant</u>

_____

3. norms <u>standards</u>

_____

4. gentry <u>well-born, educated class of people</u>

_____

5. milieu <u>background</u>

_____

Passage B
The Clean Air Act, as *amended* in 1990, directed the U.S. Environmental Protection Agency (EPA) to issue regulations that require the gasoline used in pollution-*prone* areas to be "*reformulated*" in order to burn cleaner (that is, to reduce ozone-forming and toxic air pollutants) and not evaporate as easily. The Reformulated Gasoline Program was *implemented* in 1995. Reformulated gasoline is blended with chemicals commonly called "oxygenates," which raise the oxygen content of gasoline. Oxygen helps gasoline burn more completely, reducing harmful tailpipe emissions.

According to the EPA, reformulated gasoline produces 15 to 17 percent less pollution than *conventional* gasoline, and further improvements are expected as new formulas are developed.

—Frederick K. Lutgens and Edward J. Tarbuck,
The Atmosphere: An Introduction to Meteorology, 9th ed.

1. amended changed

2. prone predisposed; showing a tendency or likelihood

3. reformulated redesigned or changed

4. implemented put into effect

5. conventional usual or commonplace

exercise 2.5   **Context Clues in a Short Essay**

Use the context clues in the sentences to write the meaning of each word or phrase listed after the selection.

E. B.'S VIEW FROM THE COW PASTURE: HE'S BEEN SLEEPING IN MY BED

The Carolina Cattle Connection, *June 2003.*

E.B. Harris, a well-known North Carolina auctioneer of farm equipment, raises cattle and goats on his farm.

The other day I ran into a friend of mine who dates all the way back to my childhood. Her name is Brenda Davis Smith. Brenda's family and my family go back a long way. Brenda's daddy was sheriff of Warren County for many years.

Brenda had two brothers, Ashley and John Hugh. Ashley was the same age as me, and John Hugh was two years younger. Every Sunday afternoon after church they were at my house or I was at theirs, or we were in the woods playing. As a matter of fact, Ashley, John Hugh, and I are blood brothers. When we were about ten years old we did that cowboy and Indian trick. We got a little blood from each other by cutting with a dull knife from each one and rolling it in the cut of the next one. Back in those days, no one had heard of all the blood diseases that are going on now.

This incident I am going to tell you about with Brenda dates back to about 1969. At that time I was doing some custom disking about a mile from the Davis home in the community of Marmaduke for a man named Clifford Robertson. It was early to midspring and Clifford was fixing to put in some milo and had hired me to disk the land. That day I went on up there and finished his job. I was then planning to go to Warrenton to do some work for Hal Connell on the Bar C farm. Mr. Connell was a Charolais breeder and was going to put in some summer grazing.

After I finished the work at Clifford's I really did not feel that well. By the time I reached the Davis home, it was probably about 10:30 to 11:00 A.M. and I was really feeling bad. It was getting so warm, I pulled the tractor into the Davis yard and cut it off.

Rachel, their mom, wasn't there, but I made myself at home because Rachel had always called me one of her boys. The house was unlocked so I went in, lay down in the hallway where it was cool, and went to sleep. Rachel came in about 1:30 to 2:00 P.M. and woke me up. She asked if I was all right, and I told her that I really did not feel that well. She wanted to know if she could get me anything, and I told her no thank you. She then told me to lie in Brenda's bed until I felt better.

I got up out of the hall and lay down in Brenda's bed. Brenda was away at college. By around 3:00 P.M. I was feeling even worse. Rachel called my mama, and Mama and Daddy came and got me and carried me to the doctor's office.

I was running a high fever and they immediately put me in the hospital. About three days later and after a bunch of tests, I thought I was feeling better. I had started to turn yellow and they found out I had hepatitis. Mama came over and told me that I was going to be put in quarantine with no visitors for a week.

They immediately started calling all the folks that I had had close contact with to come and get vaccinated against hepatitis. Brenda had come home the next day after I had been at her house, so she was one of the ones who came to get a shot. Brenda told the nurse she had been in close contact with me. The nurse filling out the paperwork asked what kind of contact she had had with me.

Now Brenda is one of those people who say exactly what is on their mind. Brenda told her that I had been sleeping in her bed. You can imagine how that sounded. The rumor got started that Brenda and I had something going, which was the furthest thing from the truth. Brenda had to come back and clarify her statement.

I guess you have to be careful about what you say and who you say it to because the right thing can be taken the wrong way.

—By E. B. Harris
From *The Carolina Cattle Connection*, June 2003

1. go back a long way <u>have known each other a long time</u>

2. blood brothers <u>not actually related but mixed blood to pretend a relation</u>

3. blood diseases <u>HIV/AIDS</u>

4. custom disking <u>plowing a field for crops</u>

5. fixing to put in <u>preparing to plant</u>

6. early to midspring <u>April or May in North Carolina</u>

7. milo <u>crop</u>

8. Charolais breeder <u>cow farmer (note source for clue)</u>

9. hepatitis <u>highly contagious disease</u>

10. in quarantine <u>restricted from any visitors because contagious</u>

Multiple Meanings of a Word

Even when word meaning seems clear, many words—particularly short ones—can be confusing because they have more than one meaning. The word *bank*, for example, can be used as a noun to refer to a financial institution, the ground rising from a river, or a mass of clouds. As a verb, *bank* can mean to laterally incline an airplane, to accumulate, or to drive a billiard ball into a cushion. Thus, the meaning of the word depends on the sentence and paragraph in which the word is used. Be alert to context clues that indicate an unfamiliar use of a seemingly familiar word.

exercise 2.6   **Multiple Meanings**

The boldface words in the following sentences have multiple meanings. Write the definition of each boldface word as it is used in the sentence.

1. Despite a broken leg, the toddler was still amazingly **mobile.** <u>able to move</u>

2. Learning of its exclusive membership policy, she decided not to become a member of the **association.** <u>organization</u>

_____

3. The overcooked cauliflower emitted a **foul,** lingering odor. <u>offensive</u>

_____

4. With April 15 looming, the woman began to **comb** the den for her missing W2 forms. <u>search carefully</u>

_____

5. What she enjoyed most about early morning was that the world seemed so **still.** <u>calm; quiet</u>

_____

6. Having misplaced the overdue text, the library patron now owed a **fine** nearly equal to the cost of the book. <u>money paid as a penalty</u>

_____

Understanding the Structure of Words

What is the longest word in the English language and what does it mean? Maxwell Nurnberg and Morris Rosenblum, in *How to Build a Better Vocabulary* (Prentice-Hall, 1989), say that at one time the longest word in *Webster's New International Dictionary* was

pneumonoultramicroscopicsilicovolcanokoniosis

Look at the word again, and notice the smaller and more familiar word parts. Do you know enough of the smaller parts to figure out the meaning of the word? Nurnberg and Rosenblum unlock the meaning as follows:

pneumono: pertaining to the lungs, as in *pneumon*ia

ultra: beyond, as in *ultra*violet rays

micro: small, as in *micro*scope

scopic: from the root of Greek verb *skopein*, to view or look at

silico: from the element *silicon*, found in quartz, flint, and sand

volcano: the meaning of this is obvious

koni: the principal root, from a Greek word for dust

osis: a suffix indicating illness, such as trichinosis

Now putting the parts together again, we deduce that *pneumonoultramicro-scopicsilicovolcanokoniosis* is a disease of the lungs caused by extremely small particles of volcanic ash and dust.

This dramatic example demonstrates how an extremely long and technical word can become more manageable by breaking it into smaller parts. The same is true for many of the smaller words that we use every day. A knowledge of word parts will help you unlock the meaning of literally thousands of words. One vocabulary expert identified a list of thirty prefixes, roots, and suffixes and claims that knowing these 30 word parts will help unlock the meaning of 14,000 words.

Like people, words have families and, in some cases, an abundance of close relations. Clusters, or what might be called *word families*, are composed of words with the same base or **root**. For example, *bio* is a root meaning life. If you know that *biology* means the study of life, it becomes easy to figure out the definition of a word like *biochemistry*. Word parts form new words as follows:

prefix + base word or root   base word or root + suffix
prefix + base word or root + suffix

Prefixes and suffixes are added to root words to change the meaning. A **prefix** is added to the beginning of a word and a **suffix** is added to the end. For example, the prefix *il* means not. When added to the word *legal*, the resulting word, *illegal*, becomes the opposite of the original. Suffixes can change the meaning or change the way the word can be used in a sentence. The suffix *cide* means to kill. When added to *frater*, which means brother, the resulting word, *fratricide*, means to kill one's brother. Adding *ity* or *ize* to *frater* changes both the meaning and the way the word can be used grammatically in a sentence.

EXAMPLE To demonstrate how prefixes, roots, and suffixes overlap and make families, start with the root *gamy*, meaning marriage, and ask some questions.

1. What is the state of having only one wife called? _____
   (*mono* means one)

2. What is a man who has two wives called? _____
   (*bi-* means two and *ist* means one who)

3. What is a man who has many wives called? _____
   (*poly-* means many)

4. What is a woman who has many husbands called? _____
   (*andro-* means man)

5. What is someone who hates marriage called? _____
   (*miso-* means hater of)

EXPLANATION The answers are (1) monogamy, (2) bigamist, (3) polygamist, (4) polyandrist, and (5) misogamist. Notice that in several of the *gamy* examples, the letters change slightly to accommodate language sounds. Such variations of a letter or two are typical when you work with word parts. Often you have to drop or add letters to maintain the rhythm of the language, but the meaning of the word part remains the same regardless of the change in spelling. For example, the prefix *con* means with or together, as in *conduct*. This same prefix is used with variations in many other words:

cooperate	*collection*	*correlate*	*communicate*	*connect*

Thus, *con-, co-, col-, cor-*, and *com-* are all forms of the prefix that means with or together.

exercise 2.7   **Word Families**

Create your own word families from the word parts that are supplied. For each of the following definitions, supply a prefix, root, or suffix to make the appropriate word.

The prefix *bi-* means "two."

1. able to speak two languages: bi lingual
2. having two feet, like humans: bi ped
3. representing two political parties: bi partisan
4. occurring at two-year intervals: bi ennial
5. having two lenses on one glass: bi focals
6. cut into two parts: bi sect
7. mathematics expression with two terms: bi nomial
8. instrument with two eyes: bi noculars
9. tooth with two points: bi cuspid
10. coming twice a year: bi annual

The root *vert* means "to turn."

1. to change one's beliefs: _____ con vert
2. to go back to old ways again: _____ re vert
3. a car with a removable top: _____ con vert ible _____
4. to change the direction of a stream: _____ di vert
5. activities intended to undermine or destroy: _____ sub vers ive _____
6. an outgoing, gregarious person: _____ extro vert
7. a quiet, introspective, shy person _____ intro vert
8. conditions that are turned against you; misfortune

   _____ ad vers ity _____

9. one who deviates from normal behavior, especially sexual: _____ per vert

10. one who is sometimes introspective and sometimes gregarious: _____ ambi vert

The suffix *-ism* means "doctrine, condition, **or** characteristic."

1. addiction to alcoholic drink: _____ alcohol ism

2. a brave and courageous manner of acting: _____ hero ism

3. prejudice against a particular gender or sex: _____ sex ism

4. doctrine concerned only with fact and reality: _____ real ism

5. system using terror to intimidate: _____ terror ism

6. writing someone else's words as your own: _____ plagiar ism

7. driving out an evil spirit: _____ exorc ism

8. purification to join the church: _____ bapt ism

9. informal style of speech using slang: _____ colloquial ism

10. being obsessive or fanatical about something: _____ fanatic ism

exercise 2.8   **Prefixes, Roots, and Suffixes**

Using the prefix, root, or suffix provided, write the words that best fit the following definitions:

1. *con-* means "with"
   infectious or catching: con tagious _____

2. *sub-* means "under"
   under the conscious level of the mind: sub conscious _____

3. *post-* means "after"
   to delay or set back: post pone _____

4. *vita* means "life"
   a pill to provide essential nutrients: vita min _____

5. *pel* means "drive or push"
   to push out of school: _____ ex pel

6. *thermo* means "heat"
   device for regulating furnace heat: thermo stat _____

7. *ven* means "come"
   a meeting for people to come together: _____ con ven tion _____

8. *rupt* means "break or burst"
   a volcanic explosion: _____ <u>e rupt ion</u>

9. *meter* means "measure"
   instrument to measure heat: _____ <u>thermo</u> meter

10. *naut* means "voyager"
    voyager in space: _____ <u>astro</u> naut

Using a Dictionary

Do you have an excellent collegiate dictionary, such as *Merriam-Webster's Collegiate Dictionary?* Every college student needs two dictionaries: a small one for class and a large one to keep at home. In class, you may use a small paperback dictionary for quick spelling or word-meaning checks. The paperback is easy to carry but does not provide the depth of information needed for college study that is found in the larger collegiate editions.

Several online dictionaries offer easy and free access for limited use but require a yearly subscription fee for premium services. At http://www.Merriam-Webster.com/, for example, you can type your word into the Search window and receive the definition, word origin, pronunciation, and links to Top 10 Search Results (the word in use) for free. The site also provides an encyclopedia link, "Word of the Day" services, word games, an online thesaurus, a dictionary for kids, and an online store for purchases. Another easy-to-use free site, http://www.dictionary.com, includes definitions, foreign dictionaries, translations into foreign languages, a thesaurus, games, a word of the day, and a bookstore. Try these sites and see how they compare with your collegiate dictionary. In evaluating the sites, consider that good dictionaries not only contain the definitions of words but also provide the following additional information for each word.

Guide Words. The two words at the top of each dictionary page are the first and last entries on the page. They help guide your search for a particular entry by indicating what is covered on that page.

In the sample that follows, *flagrante delicto* is the first entry on the page of the dictionary on which *flamingo* appears, and *flappy* is the last entry. Note that the pronunciation of the word *flamingo* is followed by part of speech *(n)*, plural spellings, and the origin of the word.

flagrante delicto • flappy

fla·min·go \flə-ˈmiŋ-(ˌ)gō\ *n, pl* **-gos** *also* **-goes** [obs. Sp *flamengo* (now *flamenco*), lit., Fleming, German (conventionally thought of as ruddy-complexioned)] (1565) : any of several large aquatic birds (family Phoenicopteridae) with long legs and neck, webbed feet, a broad lamellate bill resembling that of a duck but abruptly bent downward, and usu. rosy-white plumage with scarlet wing coverts and black wing quills

\ə\ **abut** \ˀ\ **kitten,** F **table** \ər\ **further** \a\ **ash** \ā\ **ace** \ä\ **mop, mar**
\aù\ **out** \ch\ **chin** \e\ **bet** \ē\ **easy** \g\ **go** \i\ **hit** \ī\ **ice** \j\ **job**
\ŋ\ **sing** \ō\ **go** \ȯ\ **law** \ȯi\ **boy** \th\ **thin** \th̲\ **the** \ü\ **loot** \ù\ **foot**
\y\ **yet** \zh\ **vision** \k̲, ⁿ, œ, ue ˀ\ *see* **Guide to Pronunciation**

Pronunciation. The boldface main entry divides the word into sounds, using a dot between each syllable. After the entry, letters and symbols show the pronunciation. A diacritical mark (') at the end of a syllable indicates stress on that syllable. A heavy mark means major stress; a lighter one indicates minor stress.

As shown in the illustration on page 77, a key explaining the symbols and letters appears at the bottom of the dictionary page. For example, a word like *ragweed* (rag′-wēd) would be pronounced with a short *a* as in *ash* and a long *e* as in *easy*.

The *a* in *flamingo* sounds like the *a* in *abut*, and the final *o* has a long sound as in *go*. The stress is on the first syllable.

Part of Speech. The part of speech is indicated in an abbreviation for each meaning of a word. A single word, for example, may be a noun with one definition and a verb with another. The noun *flamingo* can be used as only one part of speech, but *sideline* can be both a noun and a verb (see the following entry).

> ¹**side·line** \-ˌlīn\ *n* (ca. 1862) **1** : a line at right angles to a goal line or end line and marking a side of a court or field of play for athletic games **2 a** : a line of goods sold in addition to one's principal line **b** : a business or activity pursued in addition to one's regular occupation **3 a** : the space immediately outside the lines along either side of an athletic field or court **b** : a sphere of little or no participation or activity — usu. used in pl.
> ²**sideline** *vt* (1943) : to put out of action : put on the sidelines

> By permission. From *Merriam-Webster's Collegiate® Dictionary*, Eleventh Edition;
> © 2006 by Merriam-Webster, Incorporated. (http://www.merriam-webster.com)

Spellings. Spellings are given for the plural of the word and for special forms. This is particularly useful in determining whether letters are added or dropped to form the new words. The plural of *flamingo* can be spelled correctly in two different ways. Both *flamingos* and *flamingoes* are acceptable.

Origin. For many entries, the foreign word and language from which the word was derived will appear after the pronunciation. For example, *L* stands for a Latin origin and *G* for Greek. A key for the many dictionary abbreviations usually appears at the beginning of the book.

The word *flamingo* has a rich history. It comes from the Spanish *(Sp)* word *flamenco*, which derived from the older, now obsolete *(obs. Sp)* word *flamengo*. It relates to the ruddy complexion once thought typical of German or Fleming (that is, Flemish, from a part of Belgium) people. That's a lot of information packed into an entry on a single pink bird!

Multiple Meanings. A single word can have many shades of meaning or several completely different meanings. The various meanings are numbered.

The word *flamingo* on page 77 has only one meaning. The word *sideline*, however, has several, as shown in the previous entry.

A sideline can be a business, a product, or a designated area. In addition, it can mean to move something out of the action. To select the appropriate meaning, consider the context or the way the word is used in the sentence. For example, consider the intended meaning in "As a sideline to being a full-time student, I also play in a band on the weekends."

exercise 2.9   **Using the Dictionary**

Answer the following questions, using the page from *Merriam-Webster's Collegiate Dictionary* reproduced on page 80. Write *T* (true) or *F* (false).

_____ F _____ 1. *Ammonia* is a white compound that is water soluble.

_____ T _____ 2. If something is *amiss*, it is out of place.

_____ T _____ 3. An *amoral* act could still be legal.

_____ F _____ 4. Couples in love are not *amorous*.

_____ T _____ 5. *Amnesia* and *amnesty* originate from the same Greek word.

_____ F _____ 6. *Ammo* is an abbreviation for *ammonia*.

_____ T _____ 7. *Ammonite* can refer to an ancient shell or to an ancient people.

_____ F _____ 8. The term *amoeba* is derived from older words meaning "to become."

_____ T _____ 9. *Among* and *amongst* are synonyms.

_____ F _____ 10. Geometric shapes are also *amorphous*.

Word Origins

The study of word origins is called **etymology.** Not only is it fascinating to trace a word back to its earliest recorded appearance, but your knowledge of the word's origin can strengthen your memory for the word. For example, the word *narcissistic* means egotistically in love with yourself. Its origin is a Greek myth in which a beautiful youth named Narcissus falls in love with his own reflection; he is punished for his vanity by being turned into a flower. Thus, the myth creates an intriguing image that can enhance your memory link for the word.

The amount of information on word origins varies with the type of dictionary. Because of its size, a small paperback dictionary such as the *American Heritage Dictionary* usually contains very little information on word origins, whereas a textbook-size edition of *Merriam-Webster's Collegiate Dictionary* offers more. For the most information on word origins, visit the reference room in your college library, and use an unabridged dictionary such as *Webster's Third New International Dictionary*, the *Random House Dictionary of the English Language*, or the *American Heritage Dictionary of the English Language*.

exercise 2.10   **Word Origins**

Read the following dictionary entries and answer the questions about the words and their origins.

*Amen fl*1693 Swiss Mennonite bishop] (1844) **:** of or relating to a strict sect of Mennonites who were followers of Amman and settled in America chiefly in the 18th century — **Amish** *n*

1**amiss** \ə-ˈmis\ *adv* (13c) **1 a :** in a mistaken way **:** WRONGLY ⟨if you think he is guilty, you judge ~⟩ **b :** ASTRAY ⟨something had gone ~⟩ **2 :** in a faulty way **:** IMPERFECTLY

2**amiss** *adj* (14c) **1 :** not being in accordance with right order **2 :** FAULTY, IMPERFECT **3 :** out of place in given circumstances — usu. used with a negative ⟨a few remarks may not be ~ here⟩

ami·to·sis \ˌā-mī-ˈtō-səs\ *n* [NL, fr. 2*a-* + *mitosis*] (1894) **:** cell division by simple cleavage of the nucleus and division of the cytoplasm without spindle formation or appearance of chromosomes — **ami·tot·ic** \-ˈtä-tik\ *adj* — **ami·tot·i·cal·ly** \-ti-k(ə-)lē\ *adv*

am·i·trip·ty·line \ˌa-mə-ˈtrip-tə-ˌlēn\ *n* [*amino* + *tryptophan* + *-yl* + 2*-ine*] (1961) **:** a tricyclic antidepressant drug $C_{20}H_{23}N$ used in the form of its hydrochloride salt

am·i·trole \ˈa-mə-ˌtrōl\ *n* [*amino* + *triazole*] (ca. 1960) **:** a systemic herbicide $C_2H_4N_4$ used in areas other than food croplands

am·i·ty \ˈa-mə-tē\ *n, pl* **-ties** [ME *amite,* fr. AF *amyté,* fr. ML *amicitas,* fr. L *amicus* friend — more at AMIABLE] (15c) **:** FRIENDSHIP; *esp* **:** friendly relations between nations

am·me·ter \ˈa-ˌmē-tər\ *n* [*ampere* + *-meter*] (1882) **:** an instrument for measuring electric current esp. in amperes

am·mine \ˈa-ˌmēn, a-ˈmēn\ *n* [ISV *ammonia* + 2*-ine*] (1897) **1 :** a molecule of ammonia as it exists in a coordination complex ⟨hex*ammine*-cobalt chloride $Co(NH_3)_6Cl_3$⟩ **2 :** a compound that contains an ammine

am·mo \ˈa-(ˌ)mō\ *n* [by shortening & alter.] (1911) **:** AMMUNITION

am·mo·nia \ə-ˈmō-nyə\ *n* [NL, fr. L *sal ammoniacus* sal ammoniac, lit., salt of Ammon, fr. Gk *ammōniakos* of Ammon, fr. *Ammōn* Ammon, Amun, an Egyptian god near whose temple at the Siwa oasis it was extracted] (1789) **1 :** a pungent colorless gaseous alkaline compound of nitrogen and hydrogen NH_3 that is very soluble in water and can easily be condensed to a liquid by cold and pressure **2 :** AMMONIA WATER

am·mo·ni·ac \ə-ˈmō-nē-ˌak\ *n* [ME & L; ME, fr. L *ammoniacum,* fr. Gk *ammōniakon,* fr. neut. of *ammōniakos* of Ammon] (15c) **:** the aromatic gum resin of a southwest Asian herb (*Dorema ammoniacum*) of the carrot family used as an expectorant and stimulant and in plasters

am·mo·ni·a·cal \ˌa-mə-ˈnī-ə-kəl\ *also* **am·mo·ni·ac** \ə-ˈmō-nē-ˌak\ *adj* (1646) **:** of, relating to, containing, or resembling ammonia

am·mo·ni·ate \ə-ˈmō-nē-ˌāt\ *vt* **-at·ed; -at·ing** (ca. 1928) **1 :** to combine or impregnate with ammonia or an ammonium compound **2 :** to subject to ammonification — **am·mo·ni·a·tion** \-ˌmō-nē-ˈā-shən\ *n*

ammonia water *n* (1852) **:** a water solution of ammonia

am·mo·ni·fi·ca·tion \ə-ˌmä-nə-fə-ˈkā-shən, -ˌmō-nə-\ *n* (1886) **1 :** the act or process of ammoniating **2 :** decomposition with production of ammonia or ammonium compounds esp. by the action of bacteria on nitrogenous organic matter — **am·mo·ni·fy** \-ˌfī\ *vb*

am·mo·nite \ˈa-mə-ˌnīt\ *n* [NL *ammonites,* fr. L *cornu Ammonis,* lit., horn of Ammon] (1758) **:** any of a subclass (Ammonoidea) of extinct cephalopods esp. abundant in the Mesozoic age that had flat spiral shells with the interior divided by septa into chambers — **am·mo·nit·ic** \ˌa-mə-ˈni-tik\ *adj*

Am·mon·ite \ˈa-mə-ˌnīt\ *n* [LL *Ammonites,* fr. Heb *ʽAmmōn* Ammon (son of Lot), descendant of Ammon] (1530) **:** a member of a Semitic people who in Old Testament times lived east of the Jordan between the Jabbok and the Arnon — **Ammonite** *adj*

am·mo·ni·um \ə-ˈmō-nē-əm\ *n* [NL, fr. *ammonia*] (1808) **:** an ion NH_4^+ derived from ammonia by combination with a hydrogen ion and known in compounds (as salts) that resemble in properties the compounds of the alkali metals

ammonium carbonate *n* (ca. 1829) **:** a carbonate of ammonium; *specif* **:** the commercial mixture of the bicarbonate and carbamate used esp. in smelling salts

ammonium chloride *n* (1869) **:** a white crystalline volatile salt NH_4Cl that is used in dry cells and as an expectorant — called also *sal ammoniac*

ammonium cyanate *n* (ca. 1881) **:** an inorganic white crystalline salt NH_4CNO that can be converted into organic urea

ammonium hydroxide *n* (1899) **:** a weakly basic compound NH_4OH that is formed when ammonia dissolves in water and that exists only in solution

ammonium nitrate *n* (1869) **:** a colorless crystalline salt NH_4NO_3 used in explosives and fertilizers and in veterinary medicine

ammonium phosphate *n* (1880) **:** a phosphate of ammonium; *esp* **:** DIAMMONIUM PHOSPHATE

ammonium sulfate *n* (1869) **:** a colorless crystalline salt $(NH_4)_2SO_4$ used chiefly as a fertilizer

am·mo·noid \ˈa-mə-ˌnȯid\ *n* (1884) **:** AMMONITE ⟨Mesozoic ~*s*⟩

am·mu·ni·tion \ˌam-yə-ˈni-shən\ *n* [obs. F *amunition,* fr. MF, alter. of *munition*] (1607) **1 a :** the projectiles with their fuses, propelling charges, or primers fired from guns **b :** CARTRIDGES **c :** explosive military items (as grenades or bombs) **2 :** material for use in attacking or defending a position ⟨~ for the defense lawyers⟩

Amn *abbr* airman

am·ne·sia \am-ˈnē-zhə\ *n* [NL, fr. Gk *amnēsia* forgetfulness, alter. of *amnēstia*] (1618) **1 :** loss of memory due usu. to brain injury, shock, fatigue, repression, or illness **2 :** a gap in one's memory **3 :** the selective overlooking or ignoring of events or acts that are not favorable or useful to one's purpose or position — **am·ne·si·ac** \-zhē-ˌak, -zē-\ *or* **am·ne·sic** \-zik, -sik\ *adj or n*

am·nes·ty \ˈam-nə-stē\ *n, pl* **-ties** [Gk *amnēstia* forgetfulness, fr. *amnēstos* forgotten, fr. *a-* + *mnasthai* to remember — more at MIND] (1580) **:** the act of an authority (as a government) by which pardon is granted to a large group of individuals — **amnesty** *vt*

am·nio \ˈam-nē-ō\ *n, pl* **am·ni·os** (1983) **:** AMNIOCENTESIS

am·nio·cen·te·sis \ˌam-nē-ō-(ˌ)sen-ˈtē-səs\ *n, pl* **-te·ses** \-ˌsēz\ [NL, fr. *amnion* + *centesis* puncture, fr. Gk *kentēsis,* fr. *kentein* to prick — more at CENTER] (1957) **:** the surgical insertion of a hollow needle through the abdominal wall and into the uterus to obtain amniotic fluid esp. for the determination of fetal sex or chromosomal abnormality

am·ni·on \ˈam-nē-ˌän, -ən\ *n, pl* **amnions** *or* **am·nia** \-nē-ə\ [NL, fr. Gk, caul, fr. *amnos* lamb — more at YEAN] (1667) **1 :** a thin membrane forming a closed sac about the embryos or fetuses of reptiles, birds, and mammals and containing the amniotic fluid **2 :** a membrane analogous to the amnion and occurring in various invertebrates — **am·ni·ot·ic** \ˌam-nē-ˈä-tik\ *adj*

am·ni·ote \ˈam-nē-ˌōt\ *n* [NL *Amniota,* fr. *amnion*] (1887) **:** any of a group (Amniota) of vertebrates that undergo embryonic or fetal development within an amnion and include the birds, reptiles, and mammals — **amniote** *adj*

amniotic fluid *n* (ca. 1855) **:** the serous fluid in which the embryo or fetus is suspended within the amnion

amniotic sac *n* (ca. 1881) **:** AMNION

amn't \ˈänt, ˈant, ˈa-mənt\ (1618) *chiefly Scot & Irish* **:** am not

amo·bar·bi·tal \ˌa-mō-ˈbär-bə-ˌtȯl\ *n* [*amyl* + *-o-* + *barbital*] (1949) **:** a barbiturate $C_{11}H_{18}N_2O_3$ used as a hypnotic and sedative; *also* **:** its sodium salt

amoe·ba *also* **ame·ba** \ə-ˈmē-bə\ *n, pl* **-bas** *or* **-bae** \-(ˌ)bē\ [NL, genus name, fr. Gk *amoibē* change, fr. *ameibein* to change — more at MIGRATE] (1855) **:** any of a large genus (*Amoeba*) of naked rhizopod protozoans with lobed and never anastomosing pseudopodia, without permanent organelles or supporting structures, and of wide distribution in fresh and salt water and moist terrestrial environments; *broadly* **:** a naked rhizopod or other amoeboid protozoan — **amoe·bic** \-bik\ *adj*

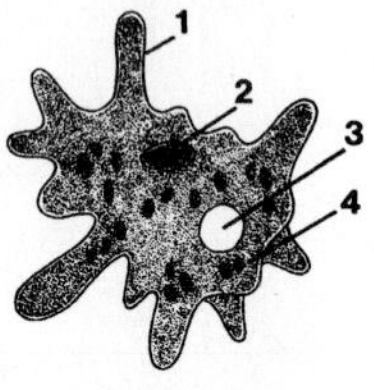

amoeba: *1* pseudopodium, *2* nucleus, *3* contractile vacuole, *4* food vacuole

amoebiasis *var of* AMEBIASIS

amoe·bo·cyte *also* **ame·bo·cyte** \ə-ˈmē-bə-ˌsīt\ *n* (1892) **:** a cell (as a phagocyte) having amoeboid form or movements

amoe·boid *also* **ame·boid** \ə-ˈmē-ˌbȯid\ *adj* (1856) **:** resembling an amoeba specif. in moving or changing in shape by means of protoplasmic flow

1**amok** \ə-ˈmək, -ˈmäk\ *or* **amuck** \ə-ˈmək\ *n* [Malay *amok*] (1665) **:** a murderous frenzy that has traditionally been regarded as occurring esp. in Malaysian culture

2**amok** *or* **amuck** *adv* (1672) **1 :** in a murderously frenzied state **2 a :** in a violently raging manner ⟨a virus that had run ~⟩ **b :** in an undisciplined, uncontrolled, or faulty manner ⟨films . . . about computers run ~ —*People*⟩

3**amok** *or* **amuck** *adj* (1944) **:** possessed with or motivated by a murderous or violently uncontrollable frenzy

amo·le \ə-ˈmō-lē\ *n* [AmerSp, fr. Nahuatl *ahmōlli* soap] (1831) **:** a plant part (as a root) possessing detergent properties and serving as a substitute for soap; *also* **:** a plant (as a yucca or agave) so used

among \ə-ˈməŋ\ *also* **amongst** \-ˈməŋ(k)st\ *prep* [*among* fr. ME, fr. OE *on gemonge,* fr. *on* + *gemonge,* dat. of *gemong* crowd, fr. *ge-* (associative prefix) + *-mong* (akin to OE *mengan* to mix); *amongst* fr. ME *amonges,* fr. *among* + *-es -s* — more at CO-, MINGLE] (bef. 12c) **1 :** in or through the midst of **:** surrounded by ⟨hidden ~ the trees⟩ **2 :** in company or association with ⟨living ~ artists⟩ **3 :** by or through the aggregate of ⟨discontent ~ the poor⟩ **4 :** in the number or class of ⟨wittiest ~ poets⟩ ⟨~ other things she was president of her college class⟩ **5 :** in shares to each of ⟨divided ~ the heirs⟩ **6 a :** through the reciprocal acts of ⟨quarrel ~ themselves⟩ **b :** through the joint action of ⟨made a fortune ~ themselves⟩ ***usage*** see BETWEEN

amon·til·la·do \ə-ˌmän-tə-ˈlä-(ˌ)dō, -ti(l)-ˈyä-(ˌ)t͟hō\ *n, pl* **-dos** [Sp, lit., done in the manner of *Montilla,* town in Andalusia] (1825) **:** a medium dry sherry

amor·al \(ˌ)ā-ˈmȯr-əl, (ˌ)a-, -ˈmär-\ *adj* (1779) **1 a :** being neither moral nor immoral; *specif* **:** lying outside the sphere to which moral judgments apply ⟨science as such is completely ~ —W. S. Thompson⟩ **b :** lacking moral sensibility ⟨infants are ~⟩ **2 :** being outside or beyond the moral order or a particular code of morals ⟨~ customs⟩ — **amor·al·ism** \-ə-ˌli-zəm\ *n* — **amo·ral·i·ty** \ˌā-mə-ˈra-lə-tē, ˌa-, -(ˌ)mȯ-\ *n* — **amor·al·ly** \ˌā-ˈmȯr-ə-lē, (ˌ)a-, -ˈmär-\ *adv*

amo·ret·to \ˌa-mə-ˈre-(ˌ)tō, ˌä-\ *n, pl* **-ti** \-(ˌ)tē\ *or* **-tos** [It, dim. of *amore* love, cupid, fr. L *amor*] (1622) **:** CUPID, CHERUB 2

am·or·ist \ˈa-mə-rist\ *n* (1581) **1 :** a devotee of love and esp. sexual love **:** GALLANT **2 :** one who writes about romantic love — **am·or·is·tic** \ˌa-mə-ˈris-tik\ *adj*

Am·o·rite \ˈa-mə-ˌrīt\ *n* [Heb *Ĕmōrī*] (1535) **:** a member of one of various Semitic peoples living in Mesopotamia, Syria, and Palestine during the third and second millennia B.C. — **Amorite** *adj*

am·o·rous \ˈa-mə-rəs, ˈam-rəs\ *adj* [ME, fr. AF, fr. ML *amorosus,* fr. L *amor* love, fr. *amare* to love] (14c) **1 :** strongly moved by love and esp. sexual love ⟨~ couples⟩ **2 :** being in love **:** ENAMORED — usu. used with *of* ⟨~ of the girl⟩ **3 a :** indicative of love ⟨received ~ glances from her partner⟩ **b :** of or relating to love ⟨an ~ novel⟩ — **am·o·rous·ly** *adv* — **am·o·rous·ness** *n*

amor·phous \ə-ˈmȯr-fəs\ *adj* [Gk *amorphos,* fr. *a-* + *morphē* form] (ca. 1731) **1 a :** having no definite form **:** SHAPELESS ⟨an ~ cloud mass⟩ **b :** being without definite character or nature **:** UNCLASSIFIABLE ⟨an ~ segment of society⟩ **c :** lacking organization or unity ⟨an ~ style of writing⟩ **2 :** having no real or apparent crystalline form ⟨an ~ mineral⟩ — **amor·phous·ly** *adv* — **amor·phous·ness** *n*

amort \ə-ˈmȯrt\ *adj* [short for *all-a-mort,* by folk etymology fr. MF *a la mort* to the death] (1546) *archaic* **:** being at the point of death

am·or·ti·za·tion \ˌa-mər-tə-ˈzā-shən *also* ə-ˌmȯr-\ *n* (1851) **1 :** the act or process of amortizing **2 :** the result of amortizing

am·or·tize \ˈa-mər-ˌtīz *also* ə-ˈmȯr-\ *vt* **-tized; -tiz·ing** [ME *amortisen* to kill, alienate in mortmain, fr. AF *amorteser,* alter. of *amortir,* fr. VL **admortire* to kill, fr. L *ad-* + *mort-, mors* death — more at MURDER] (1867) **1 :** to pay off (as a mortgage) gradually usu. by periodic payments of principal and interest or by payments to a sinking fund **2 :** to gradually reduce or write off the cost or value of (as an asset) ⟨~ goodwill⟩ ⟨~ machinery⟩ — **am·or·tiz·able** \-ˌtī-zə-bəl\ *adj*

\ə\ **abut** \ᵊ\ kitten, F table \ər\ **further** \a\ **ash** \ā\ **ace** \ä\ **mop, mar** \au̇\ **out** \ch\ **chin** \e\ **bet** \ē\ **easy** \g\ **go** \i\ **hit** \ī\ **ice** \j\ **job** \ŋ\ **sing** \ō\ **go** \ȯ\ **law** \ȯi\ **boy** \th\ **thin** \t͟h\ **the** \ü\ **loot** \u̇\ **foot** \y\ **yet** \zh\ **vision, beige** \k, ⁿ, œ, ue, ʸ\ *see* Guide to Pronunciation

¹bribe \'brīb\ *n* [ME, morsel given to a beggar, bribe, fr. AF, morsel] (15c)   **1** : money or favor given or promised in order to influence the judgment or conduct of a person in a position of trust   **2** : something that serves to induce or influence
²bribe *vb* **bribed; brib·ing** *vt* (1528) : to induce or influence by or as if by bribery ~ *vi* : to practice bribery — **brib·able** \'brī-bə-bəl\ *adj* —

By permission. From *Merriam-Webster's Collegiate® Dictionary*, Eleventh Edition; © 2006 by Merriam-Webster, Incorporated. (http://www.merriam-webster.com)

1. *Bribe* means <u>favor or money given for influence</u>

   _____ .

2. Explain the origin: <u>French, bread, given to a beggar</u>

   _____

   _____ .

¹scape·goat \'skāp-ˌgōt\ *n* [¹*scape;* intended as trans. of Heb '*azāzēl* (prob. name of a demon), as if '*ēz* '*ōzēl* goat that departs—Lev 16:8 (AV)] (1530)   **1** : a goat upon whose head are symbolically placed the sins of the people after which he is sent into the wilderness in the biblical ceremony for Yom Kippur   **2 a** : one that bears the blame for others   **b** : one that is the object of irrational hostility
²scapegoat *vt* (1943) : to make a scapegoat of — **scape·goat·ism** \-ˌgō-ˌti-zəm\ *n*

By permission. From *Merriam-Webster's Collegiate® Dictionary*, Eleventh Edition; © 2006 by Merriam-Webster, Incorporated. (http://www.merriam-webster.com)

3. *Scapegoat* means <u>one who is blamed for others' wrongdoing</u>

   _____ .

4. Explain the origin: <u>Hebrew, name of a demon or goat who bears the sins</u>

   <u>of people.</u> _____

   _____

mar·a·thon \'mer-ə-ˌthän, 'ma-rə-\ *n, often attrib* [*Marathon*, Greece, site of a victory of Greeks over Persians in 490 B.C., the news of which was carried to Athens by a long-distance runner] (1896)   **1** : a long-distance race: **a** : a footrace run on an open course usu. of 26 miles 385 yards (42.2 kilometers)   **b** : a race other than a footrace marked esp. by great length   **2 a** : an endurance contest   **b** : something (as an event, activity, or session) characterized by great length or concentrated effort

By permission. From *Merriam-Webster's Collegiate® Dictionary*, Eleventh Edition; © 2006 by Merriam-Webster, Incorporated. (http://www.merriam-webster.com)

5. *Marathon* means <u>26-mile run</u>

   _____ .

6. Explain the origin: <u>Greece, runner carried news of victory of Greeks over</u>

   <u>Persians at Marathon</u> _____

   _____

om·buds·man \'äm-ˌbu̇dz-mən, 'ȯm-, -bədz-, -ˌman; äm-'bu̇dz-, ȯm-\ *n*,
pl **-men** \-mən\ [Sw, lit., representative, fr. ON *umbothsmathr*, fr. *um-
both* commission + *mathr* man] (1959)   **1** : a government official (as in
Sweden or New Zealand) appointed to receive and investigate complaints made by individuals against abuses or capricious acts of public
officials   **2** : one that investigates reported complaints (as from students or consumers), reports findings, and helps to achieve equitable
settlements — **om·buds·man·ship** \-ˌship\ *n*

By permission. From *Merriam-Webster's Collegiate® Dictionary*, Eleventh Edition;
© 2006 by Merriam-Webster, Incorporated. (http://www.merriam-webster.com)

7. *Ombudsman* means <u>one who investigates reported complaints</u>

_____ .

8. Explain the origin: <u>a government representative in Sweden who</u>

<u>investigates complaints</u> _____

_____

_____

van·dal \'van-d²l\ *n* [L *Vandalii* (pl.), of Gmc origin] (1530)   **1** *cap* : a
member of a Germanic people who lived in the area south of the Baltic
Sea between the Vistula and the Oder rivers, overran Gaul, Spain, and
northern Africa in the fourth and fifth centuries A.D., and in 455
sacked Rome   **2** : one who willfully or ignorantly destroys, damages,
or defaces property belonging to another or to the public — **vandal**
adj, often cap

By permission. From *Merriam-Webster's Collegiate® Dictionary*, Eleventh Edition;
© 2006 by Merriam-Webster, Incorporated. (http://www.merriam-webster.com)

9. *Vandal* means <u>one who destroys property</u>

_____ .

10. Explain the origin: <u>Germanic people who sacked Rome</u>

_____

_____

_____

Using a Glossary

Each college subject seems to have a language, or jargon, of its own. For example, words like *sociocultural* or *socioeconomic* crop up in sociology. In truth,
these words are somewhat unique to the subject-matter area—they are *invented*
words. The best definitions of such words can usually be found in the textbook itself rather than in a dictionary. The definitions may be displayed in the *margins*
of a page, or more frequently, in a glossary of terms at the end of the book or each
chapter. The glossary defines the words as they are used in the textbook. At the
end of most textbooks is an index, which helps you find pages on which topics
are discussed. In some large texts, the glossary and index are combined.

Consider the following examples from the glossary of a psychology textbook. These terms are part of the jargon of psychology and would probably not be found in the dictionary.

latent learning   Hidden learning that is not demonstrated in performance until that performance is reinforced.

learning set   An acquired strategy for learning or problem solving; learning to learn.

exercise 2.11   **Using Your Glossary**

Turn to the glossary at the end of this book for help in defining the following terms. Write a definition for each in your own words. (Answers will vary.)

1. annotating: <u>a method of using symbols and notations to highlight textbook</u> <u>material for future study</u>

   _____

2. contrast: <u>a pattern of organization that presents items according to</u> <u>differences between or among them</u>

   _____

3. mnemonic: <u>a technique using images, numbers, rhymes, or letters to improve</u> <u>memory</u>

   _____

4. analogy: <u>a comparison showing connections with and similarities to previous</u> <u>experiences</u>

   _____

5. denotation: <u>the dictionary definition of a word</u>

   _____

   _____

Using a Thesaurus

A thesaurus is a writer's tool. It provides synonyms, that is, words similar in meaning, for the word you look up. It is not a dictionary, and it does not include all words. The first thesaurus was compiled in 1852 by Dr. Peter Mark Roget, an English physician, who collected lists of synonyms as a hobby. This book suggested synonyms for commonly used words, but it also included antonyms. A thesaurus entitled *Roget's Thesaurus* is organized according to Roget's format. There are other types of thesauruses available too.

Use a thesaurus to add variety to your writing and avoid repetitious wording. For example, if you find yourself repeating the word *guilt* in a research paper, consult a thesaurus for substitutes. *Roget's 21st Century Thesaurus* suggests synonyms such as *delinquency, fault, misconduct, shame,* and *transgression.*

guilt [*n*] *blame; bad conscience over responsibility*
answerability, blameworthiness, contrition, crime, criminality, culpability, delinquency, dereliction, disgrace, dishonor, error, failing, fault, indiscretion, infamy, iniquity, lapse, liability, malefaction, malfeasance, malpractice, misbehavior, misconduct, misstep, offense, onus, peccability, penitence, regret, remorse, responsibility, self-condemnation, self-reproach, shame, sin, sinfulness, slip, solecism, stigma, transgression, wickedness, wrong; SEE CONCEPTS *101,532, 645,690*

From *Roget's 21st Century Thesaurus*. Published by Dell Publishing, a Division of Random House. Copyright 1992, 1993, 1999 by the Philip Lief Group, Inc. Reprinted by permission.

At the end of the entry, the words SEE CONCEPTS (printed in capitals and followed by numbers) indicate that you can find additional synonyms under these numbers at the end of the book.

Most word-processing programs have an electronic thesaurus. Usually, it is found with the spelling checker or in the Tools pull-down menu. Use your cursor to highlight (select) the word for which you want alternatives, and then click on the thesaurus. Consider the context of your sentence as you choose from the array of words that appear. Be aware, though, that a thesaurus in book form will offer more choices.

exercise 2.12   **Using a Thesaurus**

Use the entries for *carry* in *The Oxford American Desk Dictionary and Thesaurus* to select an alternative word that fits the meaning of *carry* in the following sentences.

1. Pilates and yoga instructors encourage participants to *carry* themselves with good posture. _hold (as in a certain position)_

2. The infamous Typhoid Mary was able to *carry* her infectious disease to others through her employment as a cook. _transmit; spread_

3. When one of the wheels on my luggage broke, I was forced to carry my belongings in an expandable briefcase. _transport; haul_

4. Since he was running unopposed, the city councilor was able to easily *carry* the election. _win_

5. Positions of power also *carry* great responsibility. _involve; require_

car·ry /kárē/ • v. (**–ries**, **–ried**) **1** *tr.* support or hold up, esp. while moving. **2** *tr.* convey with one or have on one's person. **3** *tr.* conduct or transmit (*pipe carries water*). **4** *tr.* take (a process, etc.) to a specified point; continue (*carry into effect, carry a joke too far*). **5** *tr.* involve; imply; entail as a feature or consequence (*principles carry consequences*). **6** *tr.* (in reckoning) transfer (a figure) to a column of higher value. **7** *tr.* hold in a specified way (*carry oneself erect*). **8** *tr.* publish or broadcast esp. regularly. **9** *tr.* keep a regular stock of. **10** *intr.* be audible at a distance. **11** *tr.* **a** win victory or acceptance for (a proposal, etc.). **b** gain (a state or district) in an election. **c** *Golf* cause the ball to pass beyond (a bunker, etc.). **12** *tr.* endure the weight of; support. **13** *tr.* be pregnant with. • *n.* (*pl.* **–ries**) **1** act of carrying. **2** *Golf* distance a ball travels in the air. □ **carry away 1** remove. **2** inspire; affect emotionally or spiritually. **3** deprive of self-control (*got carried away*). **carry the day** be victorious or successful. **carry off 1** take away, esp. by force. **2** win (a prize). **3** (esp. of a disease) kill. **4** render acceptable or passable. **carry on 1** continue. **2** engage in (a conversation or a business). **3** *colloq.* behave strangely or excitedly. **4** advance (a process) by a stage. **carry out** put (ideas, instructions, etc.) into practice. **carry weight** be influential or important.

▪ *v.* **1, 2** transport, bear, deliver, bring, haul, lug, cart, ship, move, *colloq.* schlep, tote; drive, take; hold. **3** convey, take, transport, transfer, bear. **7** bear, deport, hold up, maintain, keep. **8** put out; air, screen; disseminate, communicate, present, announce, offer, give, release. **9** stock, keep, have in stock, sell, offer, trade in, deal in, have. **11 b** win, take, sweep, capture, pick up. **12** see SUPPORT *v.* 1, 2. □ **carry away 1** see REMOVE *v.* 2. **2** see INSPIRE 1, 2. **carry the day** see TRIUMPH *v.* 1. **carry off 1** abscond with, make away *or* off with, run off with, spirit off *or* away, whisk away *or* off, cart off, drag away, kidnap, abduct. **2** gain, capture, pick up, take, *colloq.* walk away *or* off with. **3** be *or* cause the death of, cause to die, *colloq.* finish off. **4** accomplish, achieve, perform, effect, effectuate, do, execute, succeed in *or* with, handle, manage, work, bring off, carry out *or* through, pull off. **carry on 1** go on, keep on; keep (on) going, last, remain; persist, persevere, push *or* press on. **2** be involved *or* busy, occupy oneself with; follow, pursue, prosecute; manage, conduct, operate, run, administer. **carry out** perform, continue, implement, administer, transact, see through, execute, discharge, prosecute, effect. complete. accomplish, conclude

From *The Oxford American Desk Dictionary and Thesaurus* (2003). By permission of Oxford University Press.

Using Analogies

Analogies are comparisons that call upon not only your word knowledge but also your ability to see relationships. They can be difficult, frustrating, and challenging. Use logical thinking and problem-solving skills to pinpoint the initial relationship, and then establish a similar relationship with two other words.

> **Reader's _Tip_** ——— Categories of Analogy Relationships
>
> - **Synonyms:** Similar in meaning
>   _Find_ is to _locate_ as _hope_ is to _wish_.
> - **Antonyms:** Opposite in meaning
>   _Accept_ is to _reject_ as _rude_ is to _polite_.
> - **Function, use, or purpose:** Identifies what something does; watch
>   for the object (noun) and then the action (verb)
>   _Pool_ is to _swim_ as _blanket_ is to _warm_.
> - **Classification:** Identifies the larger group association
>   _Sandal_ is to _shoe_ as _sourdough_ is to _bread_.
> - **Characteristics and descriptions:** Shows qualities or traits
>   _Nocturnal_ is to _raccoon_ as _humid_ is to _rainforest_.
> - **Degree:** Shows variations of intensity
>   _Fear_ is to _terror_ as _dislike_ is to _hate_.
> - **Part to whole:** Shows the larger group
>   _Page_ is to _book_ as _caboose_ is to _train_.
> - **Cause and effect:** Shows the reason (cause) and result (effect)
>   _Study_ is to _graduation_ as _caffeine_ is to _insomnia_.

exercise 2.13   **Identifying Types of Analogies**

Study the analogies that follow to establish the relationship of the first two words.
Record that relationship, using the categories outlined in the Reader's Tip. Then
choose the word that duplicates that relationship to finish the analogy.

1. _Trash_ is to _refuse_ as _soil_ is to ____b____ .

   Relationship ____synonyms____

   a. earthworms
   b. dirt
   c. minerals
   d. growing

2. _Burdened_ is to _overwhelmed_ as _tired_ is to ____b____ .

   Relationship ____synonyms _degree_____

   a. sleepy
   b. exhausted
   c. energetic
   d. rested

3. *Cappuccino* is to *coffee* as *jazz* is to _____d_____.

   Relationship _____classification_____

   a. singer
   b. opera
   c. rock
   d. music

4. *Excited* is to *dull* as *fancy* is to _____c_____.

   Relationship _____antonyms_____

   a. rich
   b. fortunate
   c. plain
   d. colorful

5. *Fork* is to *eat* as *television* is to _____c_____.

   Relationship _____function_____

   a. video
   b. actor
   c. entertain
   d. produce

6. *Sleeve* is *shirt* to as *lens* is to _____d_____.

   Relationship _____part to whole_____

   a. book
   b. motor
   c. movement
   d. camera

7. *Smart* is to *genius* as *rigid* is to _____a_____.

   Relationship _____characteristics_____

   a. steel
   b. comedy
   c. angle
   d. focus

8. *Recklessness* is to *accident* as *laziness* is to _____c_____.

   Relationship _____cause and effect_____

   a. work
   b. money
   c. failure
   d. ability

Easily Confused Words

Pairs or groups of words may cause confusion because they sound exactly alike, or almost alike, but are spelled and used differently. *Stationary* and *stationery* are examples of such words. You ride a stationary bike to work out and you write a business letter on your office stationery. For a memory link, associate the *e* in *letter* with the *e* in *stationery*. Students frequently confuse *your* and *you're*: *your* shows possession, and *you're* is a contraction for *you are*. To differentiate confusing words, create associations to aid memory. **Homonyms,** words with different meanings that are spelled and sound alike, are not as confusing. They tend to be simple words such as *bear* in "bear the burden" or "kill the bear."

exercise 2.14

Distinguishing Confusing Words

Study each set of easily confused words, and then circle the one that correctly fits in each sentence.

loose: unconfined; relaxed; not tight

lose: misplace

1. She enjoyed the comfort of long, **(loose, lose)** clothing during the warm summer months. _____loose_____

hole: opening

whole: entire object

2. His **(hole, whole)** check was insufficient to cover his monthly car payments. _____whole_____

there: a place

their: belonging to them

they're: they are

3. Over **(there, their, they're)** is the community shelter for the homeless. _____there_____

who's: who is

whose: belonging to whom

4. **(Whose, who's)** idea was it to attend that boring concert last weekend? _____Whose_____

heal: mend; cure

heel: part of foot; follow closely (dog)

5. A well-known saying about doctors is "*Physician,* **(*heal, heel*)** *thyself.*" _____heal_____

Recognizing Acronyms

An **acronym** is an abbreviation that is pronounced as a word. Acronyms can thus be considered invented words that are often thoughtfully contrived to simplify a lengthy name and gain quick recognition for an organization or agency. For example, *UNICEF* is the abbreviation for the United Nations International Children's Emergency Fund. The arrangement of consonants and vowels formed by the first letter of each word in the title creates an invented term that we can easily pronounce and quickly recognize. When names are created for new organizations, clever organizers thoughtfully consider the choice and sequence of words in order to engineer a catchy acronym. In some cases, acronyms have become so ingrained in our language that the abbreviations have become accepted as words with lowercase letters. An example of this is the word *radar*, which is a combination of the initial letters of the phrase *radio detecting and ranging*.

exercise 2.15   **Recognizing Acronyms**

The following letters are abbreviations made from the initial letters of words (and sometimes other letters as well). Write what each one stands for. Then place an A beside those that are pronounced as words and thus are considered acronyms.

_____ 1. ATV
        All Terrain Vehicle

___A___ 2. SCUBA
        Self Contained Underwater Breathing Apparatus

_____ 3. NPR
        National Public Radio

_____ 4. GPS
        Global Positioning System

___A___ 5. SONAR
        SOund Navigation And Ranging

_____ 6. DVR
        Digital Video Recorder

_____ 7. MRI
        Magnetic Resonance Imaging

___A___ 8. AMTRAK
        American Track

___A___ 9. NASCAR
        National Association for Stock Car Auto Racing

___A___ 10. CAT SCAN
        Computerized Axial Tomography Scan

Recognizing Transitional Words

Transitional words connect ideas and signal the direction of the writer's thought. These single words or short phrases lead the reader to anticipate a continuation or a change in thought. For example, the phrase *in addition* signals a continuation, whereas *but* or *however* signals a change.

Reader's *Tip* — Types of Transitional Words

- **To signal addition:** in addition, furthermore, moreover
- **To signal an example:** for example, for instance, to illustrate, such as
- **To signal time sequence:** first, second, finally, last, afterward
- **To signal comparison:** similarly, likewise, in the same manner
- **To signal contrast:** however, but, nevertheless, whereas, on the contrary, conversely, in contrast
- **To signal cause and effect:** thus, consequently, therefore, as a result, furthermore, similarly, consequently, however, for example

---

exercise 2.16   **Anticipating Transitions**

Read each sentence. Then choose a transitional word or phrase from the boxed list to complete each sentence.

in addition	first	likewise	whereas	therefore

1. Rather than immediately train to run in a marathon, you might _____first_____ consider entering a 5K or 10K race.

2. Couples do not always share personality traits; Tom is introverted _____whereas_____ his wife could be considered outgoing.

3. Since you already drank two cups of coffee __in addition__ to a glass of iced tea, it might be wise to switch to decaffeinated beverages for the rest of the night.

4. Cell phones must be turned off and put away before class; ___likewise___, your instructor expects you do to the same with all other electronic devices, except for laptops.

5. Rain seems to develop at the most inopportune moments; ___therefore___, it is wise to keep an umbrella handy.

Summary *Points*

➤ **How do you remember new words?**
To remember new words, use mnemonic devices to associate words in phrases, in families, and in images. Use concept cards to record a new word's definition with a phrase and an image that suggest the meaning.

➤ **What are context clues?**
The context clues in a sentence or paragraph can help unlock the meaning of unknown words. These can be definitions or synonyms, details, examples, and comparisons, contrasts, or antonyms.

➤ **Why learn prefixes, word roots, and suffixes?**
A knowledge of prefixes, roots, and suffixes can reveal smaller, more familiar word parts in unknown words.

➤ **What will you find in a dictionary?**
A collegiate dictionary contains definitions, word origins, pronunciations, and spellings.

➤ **What is a glossary?**
A glossary defines words that are unique to a subject matter area.

➤ **What is a thesaurus?**
A thesaurus is a reference book that contains synonyms for frequently used words to add variety to writing.

➤ **What are analogies?**
Analogies are comparisons that fall into different categories of relationships.

➤ **What are acronyms?**
Acronyms are abbreviations that are pronounced as words.

➤ **How are transitional words used?**
Transitional words connect ideas and signal the writer's train of thought.

 *Search* the Net

Use a search engine such as Google, AltaVista, Excite, Infoseek, Dogpile, Yahoo, or Lycos to find exercises on analogies. Select, print, and bring to class five sample analogies that your classmates would enjoy solving. For suggested Web sites and other research activities, go to http://www.ablongman.com/smith/.

Over, Under, Around, and Through

This is the first of ten end-of-chapter vocabulary lessons in this textbook designed to expand your vocabulary. Each lesson links words through shared prefixes, roots, and suffixes. The words are organized into different clusters or families to enhance memory, to organize your learning, and to emphasize that most new words are made up of familiar old parts. Strengthen your vocabulary by identifying your old friends in the new words. Then apply your knowledge of word parts to unlock and remember the meanings of the new words. You will learn more than 200 words through this easy word family approach.

Your instructor may choose to use these as weekly lessons by introducing the words at the beginning of the week, assigning review items for practice, and quizzing your knowledge of the words at the end of the week. All lessons follow the same format, except for slight variations in the lesson on doctors and the one on foreign terms. Following is the first one.

Study the following prefixes, words, and sentences.

| **Prefixes and Their Meanings** | *sur-:* over, above, more | *sub-:* under, beneath |
| | *amb-, ambi-:* around, about, both | *dia-:* through |

Words with *sur-:* "over, above, or more"

The fugitive *surrendered* himself to the police when he could no longer avoid capture.

- *surcharge:* an additional charge, tax, or cost

  The *surcharge* on an item such as cigarettes or alcohol is sometimes called a "sin tax" because these items are considered by some to be vices rather than necessities.

- *surface:* uppermost or outermost area; top layer

  When the deep-sea diver reached the *surface,* he saw that he had drifted far from his boat.

- *surfeit:* overindulgence in eating or drinking, an excessive amount

  Thanksgiving dinner usually means a *surfeit* of foods far beyond the usual amount served for an everyday meal.

- *surmise:* to guess, to infer without certain evidence

  At the point that Cindy and Gary were thirty minutes late to the ball game, I *surmised* that they probably were not coming.

- *surveillance:* a watch kept over someone or something

  The United States flies *surveillance* missions all over the world to collect information vital to our security.

- *surplus:* an amount greater than needed

  The government had collected more taxes than needed, so the *surplus* was returned to the taxpayers.

Words with *sub-:* "under, beneath"

Jorge's *subconscious* belief that he wasn't a good athlete probably contributed to his poor performance during basketball tryouts.

- *subsequent:* occurring later, following

  Ill health usually occurs *subsequent* to long periods of ignoring good nutrition and getting little sleep.

- *subservient:* excessively submissive

  Victorian husbands expected their wives to be *subservient*.

- *subsidiary:* subordinate or secondary

  The food products corporation decided to sell its *subsidiary* clothing company and to remain focused on foods.

- *substantiate:* to establish by proof

  A witness was able to *substantiate* Linda's story that the auto accident was not her fault.

- *subvert:* to overthrow something, such as a government; to cause the ruin of

  Castro's regime in Cuba came to power by *subverting* Batista's presidency.

- *subsistence:* a means of supporting life

  Her small *subsistence* check from the government was all the octogenarian had for living expenses after her husband died.

Words with *ambi-:* "around, about, both"

The horse's gait was kept to an *amble* as the jockey slowly walked him into the winner's circle.

- *ambiance* or *ambience:* the mood or atmosphere of a place or situation

  The day spa's low lighting, comfortable furnishings, and quiet music produced an *ambience* of soothing relaxation.

- *ambidextrous:* able to use both hands equally well; unusually skillful

  Being *ambidextrous* allows Keisha to write for long periods of time by switching hands when one gets tired.

- *ambiguous:* having two or more possible meanings

  Rosa was *ambiguous* when she said she fell on the skiing trip. We expected to see a cast on her leg, not a new boyfriend on her arm.

- *ambivalent:* fluctuating between two choices; having opposing feelings

  Jealousy and tremendous familial pride were the two *ambivalent* feelings Juan was experiencing over his brother's acceptance at a prestigious school.

- *ambulatory:* capable of walking

  Doctors didn't think Nora would be *ambulatory* again after the accident damaged her spinal cord.

- *ambition:* strong desire for fame or power

  His *ambition* to climb the corporate ladder drove Jim to work long hours to accomplish his goal.

Words with *dia-:* "through"

If you know the *diameter* of a circle, it is easy to find the circumference.

- *diagnosis:* a determination of the cause of medical symptoms; analysis of the cause of a situation

  The doctor's *diagnosis* of strep throat was proved correct by the lab report.

- *dialogue:* conversation between two or more persons

  The three actors practiced the scenes in which they had a humorous *dialogue* together.

- *diametrical:* pertaining to a diameter; at opposite extremes

  Susan was pro-life and *diametrically* opposed to any pro-choice legislation in Congress.

- *diatribe:* a bitter, abusive criticism

  After listening to a *diatribe* from her possessive boyfriend because she spent time with her girlfriends, Angelina decided to end the unhealthy relationship.

- *dialect:* a distinct variety of a language that differs from the standard

  Parts of rural England have *dialects* that differ from the English spoken in London.

- *diagonal:* an oblique or slanting line connecting opposite corners or angles

  Rather than being laid square, the floor tiles were laid on the *diagonal* for an additional decorative effect.

REVIEW QUESTIONS

Part I

Choose the best word from the box to complete each sentence.

surcharge	surveillance	subsidiary	subsistence	ambiance
ambivalent	ambulatory	diagnosis	surrender	subconscious

1. The mechanic was unable to make a thorough ___diagnosis___ of the engine trouble, as his computer system was temporarily out of order.

2. ___Ambivalent___ feelings of not knowing which choices to make can delay a decision.

3. During the Depression years, many unemployed Americans were surviving at barely a ___subsistence___ level.

4. ___Surveillance___ cameras were used in a traffic study of the intersection to determine the need for a stoplight.

5. Frequently, states gain revenue by imposing a hefty ___surcharge___ on luxury items such as alcohol and cigarettes.

6. ___Subsidiary___ businesses are generally formed as offshoots of the parent company.

7. ___Ambulatory___ patients are less likely to develop complications from surgery, such as blood clots and pneumonia, because they are mobile.

8. Shoppers tend to spend more in stores equipped with a pleasant ___ambience;___ relaxing music, attractive displays, peaceful lighting, and tables with sample items encourage the customer to buy.

9. Freud believed that the ___subconscious___ mind had a powerful influence on behavior.

10. After a week of very little rest, she was finally forced to ___surrender___ to her need for a good night's sleep.

Part II

Choose the best synonym from the boxed list for each word.

diametrical	dialogue	ambition	ambiguous	subvert
substantiate	subsequent	amble	surfeit	diagonal

11. opposite ___diametrical___

12. overthrow ___subvert___

13. following ___subsequent___

14. discussion ___dialogue___

15. unclear ___ambiguous___

16. excess ___surfeit___

17. walk ___amble___

18. prove ___substantiate___

19. desire ___ambition___

20. slanted ___diagonal___

Your instructor may choose to give you a multiple-choice review.

3 Strategic Reading and Study

- What is strategic reading?
- What is a study strategy?
- What are the three stages of reading?
- What are the strategies for previewing?
- Why should you activate your schemata?
- What is metacognition?
- What are the strategies for integrating knowledge during reading?
- Why recall or self-test what you have read?

Jacob Lawrence (1917–2000), *The Library*, 1960. Tempera on fiberboard, 24 × 29⅞ inches (60.9 × 75.8 cm). Courtesy of Artist Rights Society, New York.

What Is Strategic Reading?

In college you can expect a demanding course load and, most likely, a greater volume of difficult material than you have been assigned in the past. How can you meet the challenge and become a more effective reader? The answer is to have an arsenal of techniques, or strategies, to help you navigate through the required reading in your courses. For example, mastering the decoding, or sounding out, of words is one strategy. It is an initial and essential one, but college readers must go far beyond this level into the realm of associating and remembering.

Reading strategically means using specific techniques for understanding, studying, and learning. Research studies find that students who systematically learn such techniques score higher on reading comprehension tests. These strategies—previewing, questioning, connecting, recalling, determining the main idea, recognizing significant supporting details, drawing inferences, and others—will be presented throughout the various chapters in this text. Keep in mind, though, that for greatest success, you must do more than understand the strategies. You must also know when, why, and how to use them.

Four Types of Readers

Just as not all types of reading are the same, not all readers are the same. To understand how readers differ, read the following description of the four levels of reading and learning:[1]

- **Tacit learners/readers.** These readers lack awareness of how they think when reading.
- **Aware learners/readers.** These readers realize when meaning has broken down or confusion has set in but may not have sufficient strategies for fixing the problem.
- **Strategic learners/readers.** These readers use the thinking and comprehension strategies described in this text to enhance understanding and acquire knowledge. They are able to monitor and repair meaning when it is disrupted.
- **Reflective learners/readers.** These readers are strategic about their thinking and apply strategies flexibly depending on their goals or purposes for reading. In addition, they "reflect on their thinking and ponder and revise their future use of strategies."[2]

Which type describes your reading now? With this textbook, you are on your way to becoming a strategic and reflective learner and reader! The dynamic process of reading and learning can be broken into manageable pieces. Master the parts and see how they contribute to the whole. We begin by breaking reading into three stages and explaining strategies to use for each.

---

[1]S. Harvey and A. Goudvis, *Strategies That Work* (Portland, ME: Stenhouse Publishers, 2000), p. 17.

[2]D. Perkins, *Smart Schools: Better Thinking and Learning for Every Child* (New York: Free Press, 1992).

The Stages of Reading

In 1946, after years of working with college students at Ohio State University, Francis P. Robinson developed a textbook study system designed to help students efficiently read and learn from textbooks and effectively recall information for exams. The system was called SQ3R, with the letters standing for the following five steps: Survey, Question, Read, Recite, and Review.

Numerous variations have been developed since SQ3R was introduced. One researcher, Norman Stahl, analyzed sixty-five textbook reading/learning systems and concluded that they have more similarities than differences.[3] The common elements in the systems include a previewing stage, a reading stage, and a final self-testing stage.

In the *previewing* stage, which occurs before reading, students make predictions, ask questions, activate schemata (past knowledge), and establish a purpose for reading. In the *knowledge integration* stage, which occurs during reading, students make predictions, picture images, answer questions, continually relate and integrate old and new knowledge, monitor understanding to clarify confusing points, and use correction strategies. The *recall* stage, which occurs after reading, involves reviewing to self-test and improve recall, making connections to blend new information with existing knowledge networks, and reacting and reflecting to evaluate and accept or reject ideas.

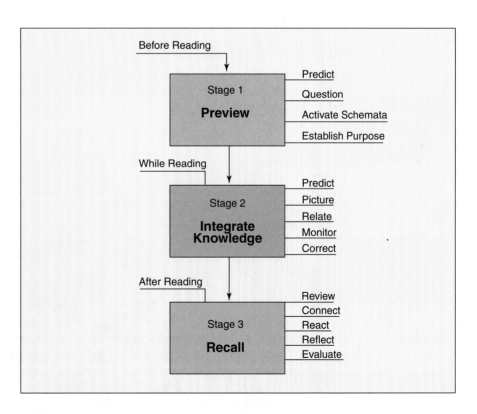

---

[3]N. A. Stahl, "Historical Analysis of Textbook Study Systems" (Ph.D. dissertation, University of Pittsburgh, 1983).

Stage 1: Strategies for Previewing

Previewing is a method of personally connecting with the material before you start to read. When you preview, you look over the material, predict what the material is probably about, ask yourself what you already know about the topic, decide what you will probably know after you read, and make a plan for reading. See the Reader's Tip for useful questions to ask before reading.

To preview, look over the material, think, and ask questions. The focus is "What do I already know, what do I need to know, and how do I go about finding it out?"

Signposts for Previewing

Like public speakers, textbook authors follow the rule "Tell them what you are going to tell them, tell them, and then tell them what you told them." Typically, a chapter begins with a brief overview of the topic, an outline, or questions. The ideas are then developed in clearly marked sections. Concluding statements at the end summarize the important points. Although this pattern does not apply in every case, use it when available as a guide in determining what to read when previewing textbook material.

Because of differences in writing styles, no one set of rules for previewing will work for all materials. Consider the following signposts when previewing.

Title. A title attracts attention, suggests content, and is the first and most obvious clue. Think about the title and turn it into a question. For an article entitled "Acupuncture," ask "What is acupuncture?" For other questions, use the "five-*W* technique" of journalists to find out *who, what, when, where,* and *why*.

Reader's *Tip*   Asking Questions Before Reading

- **What is the topic of the material?** What does the title suggest? What do the subheadings, italics, and summaries suggest?
- **What do I already know?** What do I already know about this topic or a related topic? Is this new topic a small part of a larger idea or issue that I have thought about before?
- **What is my purpose for reading?** What will I need to know when I finish?
- **How is the material organized?** What is the general outline or framework of the material? Is the author listing reasons, explaining a process, or comparing a trend?
- **What will be my plan of attack?** What parts of the textbook seem most important? Do I need to read everything with equal care? Can I skim some parts? Can I skip some sections completely?

Introductory Material. To get an overview of an entire book, refer to the table of contents and preface. Sophisticated students use the table of contents as a study guide, turning the chapter headings into possible exam items. Many textbook chapters open with an outline, preview questions, or an interesting anecdote that sets the stage for learning. Italicized inserts, decorative symbols, and colored type are also used to highlight key concepts. The first paragraph frequently sets expectations.

Subheadings. Subheadings are titles for sections within chapters. The subheadings, usually appearing in **boldface print** or *italics*, outline the main points of the author's message and thus give the reader an overview of the organization and the content. Turn these subheadings into questions to answer as you read.

Italics, Boldface Print, and Numbers. Italics and boldface print highlight words that merit special attention. These are usually new words or key words that you should be prepared to define and remember. For example, an explanation of sterilization in a biology text might emphasize the words *vasectomy* and *tubal ligation* in italics or boldface print. Numbers can also be used to signal a list of important details. The biology book might emphasize the two forms of sterilization with enumeration: (1) vasectomy and (2) tubal ligation.

Visual Aids. Photographs with their captions, charts, graphs, and maps emphasize important points and sometimes condense text. Reviewing visuals provides clues to what information will be significant.

Concluding Summary. Many textbooks include a summary at the end of each chapter to highlight the important points. The summary can serve not only as a review to follow reading but also as an overview of the chapter prior to reading.

exercise 3.1   **Previewing This Textbook for the Big Picture**

To get an overview of the scope of this textbook and its sequence of topics, look over the table of contents and preface. Think about how the chapter topics fit the goals of college reading. Glance at the chapters to get a sense of the organization, and then answer the following questions.

1. Who is the author? Was the author a professor? Brenda Smith; she was a
   professor at Georgia State University.
   _____

2. What seems to be the purpose of the Reader's Tip boxes throughout the text?
   To summarize the best reading approaches.
   _____

3. Does the book have specific exercises to help build vocabulary? Where are they located? <u>Yes; they are located at the end of most chapters, in addition</u> <u>to Chapter 2.</u>

4. Which chapter provides information about increasing reading rate? _____
<u>Chapter 11, Rate Flexibility</u>

5. Where might a student record scores received on the reading selections found throughout the text, in order to keep track of progress? <u>Inside</u> <u>the back cover</u>

6. Is there test-taking assistance provided within the book? <u>Yes: Chapter 12,</u> <u>Test Taking, provides tips and strategies for students.</u>

7. What seems to be the intent of the Search the Net activities following the longer textbook reading selections? <u>To give students experience with Internet</u> <u>searches on issues related to the particular selection.</u>

---

exercise 3.2   **Previewing This Chapter**

To get an overview of this chapter, first look at the table of contents at the beginning of the book, and then read the list of questions at the beginning of the chapter. Flip to the chapter summary points and read them. Use your previewing to answer the following questions.

1. What is strategic reading? <u>An organized approach to studying that includes</u> <u>previewing, reading, and self-testing</u>

2. What is a schema? <u>Your knowledge on a particular subject</u>

3. What is metacognition? <u>Knowing about knowing</u>

4. What is the purpose of a recall diagram? <u>To improve memory by self-testing</u>

5. Which reading selection do you think will be most interesting? _____
    Answers will vary.
    _____

6. What are the five thinking strategies used by good readers? Predict, picture,
    relate, monitor, and correct
    _____

Use your answers to these questions to help establish a purpose or a learning strategy goal for reading the chapter. Why is this chapter important, and what do you hope to gain from reading it?

Preview to Activate Schemata

What do you bring to the printed page? As a reader, you are thinking and interacting before, during, and after reading. Your previewing of material first helps you predict the topic. Then, as a further part of the prereading stage, you need to activate your schema for what you perceive the topic to be.

A **schema** (plural, *schemata*) is like a computer file in your brain that holds all you know on a subject. Each time you learn something new, you pull out the computer file on that subject, add the new information, and return the file to storage. The depth of the schema or the amount of information contained in the file varies according to previous experience. For example, a scientist would have a larger, more detailed file for DNA than would most freshman biology students.

The richness of your background determines the amount you can activate. In general, the more schemata you are able to activate, the more meaningful your reading will be. In fact, most experts agree that the single best predictor of your reading comprehension is what you already know. In other words, the rich get richer. Why is that good for you?

Once you have struggled with and learned about a subject, the next time you meet the subject, reading and learning will be easier. You will have greatly expanded your schema for the subject. Does this help explain why some say that the freshman year is the hardest? Some students who barely make C's in introductory courses end up making A's and B's in their junior and senior years. They profited from previous hard work to establish the frameworks of knowledge in building schemata. Comfort yourself during the early struggles by saying, "The smart get smarter, and I'm getting smart!"

Stage 2: Strategies for Integrating Knowledge While Reading

What are you thinking about when you read? Do you visualize? Do you make comparisons? If you don't understand, do you *notice* that you don't understand?

EXAMPLE   Read the following passage to answer the question "What are echinoderms?" Are your thoughts similar to the inserted thoughts of the reader?

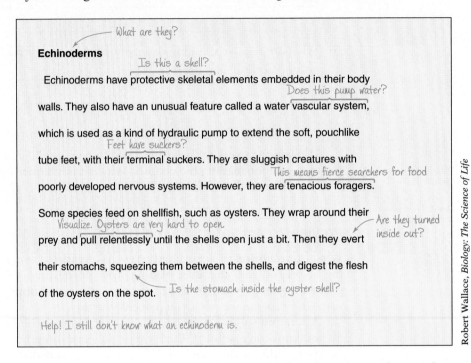

Were you able to follow the reader's inserted thoughts? Do you know what an echinoderm is? Can you guess? If you had known before reading that starfish are echinoderms, the passage would have been more entertaining and less challenging. If you have opened an oyster, you know the tenacity needed to open its shell. Reread the passage with this knowledge, and visualize the gruesome drama. Later in this chapter, be ready to pull out your now enlarged schema on echinoderms and network knowledge on a new passage.

Integrating Ideas: How Do Good Readers Think?

Understanding and remembering complex material requires as much thinking as reading. As illustrated in the previous passage, the good reader is always predicting, visualizing, and drawing comparisons to assimilate new knowledge. Beth Davey, a reading researcher, broke these thoughts down into five manageable and teachable strategies. The Reader's Tip lists the five thinking strategies of good readers.[4] Study them and visualize how you use each.

The first three thinking strategies used by good readers are perhaps the easiest to understand and the quickest to develop. From short stories as a young reader, you quickly learned to predict actions and outcomes. You would see the characters and scenes in your head. Such visualizing increased your level of involvement and enjoyment. You compared the character's reactions and adventures to your own.

---

[4]B. Davey, "Think Aloud—Modeling for Cognitive Processes of Reading Comprehension," *Journal of Reading* 27 (October 1983): 44–47.

Reader's *Tip* — Using Thinking Strategies While Reading

- **Make predictions.** Develop hypotheses.
  "From the title, I predict that this section will give another example of a critical time for rats to learn a behavior."
  "In this next part, I think we'll find out why the ancient Greeks used mnemonic devices."
  "I think this is a description of an acupuncture treatment."
- **Describe the picture you're forming in your head from the information.** Develop images during reading.
  "I have a picture of this scene in my mind. My pet is lying on the table with acupuncture needles sticking out of its fur."
- **Share an analogy.** Link prior knowledge with new information in text. We call this the *"like-a" step*.
  "This is like my remembering, 'In 1492 Columbus sailed the ocean blue.'"
- **Monitor your ongoing comprehension.** Clarify confusing points.
  "This is confusing."
  "This just doesn't make sense. How can redwoods and cypress trees both be part of the same family?"
  "This is different from what I had expected."
- **Correct gaps in comprehension.** Use fix-up correction strategies.
  "I'd better reread."
  "Maybe I'll read ahead to see if it gets clearer."
  "I'd better change my picture of the story."
  "This is a new word to me. I'd better check the context to figure it out."

When ideas get more complicated and reading becomes more difficult, however, the last two thinking strategies become essential elements in the pursuit of meaning. College textbooks are tough, requiring constant use of the monitoring strategy and frequent use of the correction strategy.

The final strategies involve a higher level of thinking than just picturing an oyster or a starfish. They reflect a deeper understanding of the process of getting meaning, and they require a reader who both understands the thinking process and controls that process. This ability to know and control is called *metacognition* (knowing about knowing).[5]

Metacognition

When you look at the following words, what is your reaction?

feeet	thankz	supplyyied

---

[5]A. L. Brown, "The Development of Memory: Knowing, Knowing About Knowing, and Knowing How to Know," in H. W. Reese, ed., *Advances in Child Development and Behavior*, vol. 10 (New York: Academic Press, 1975), pp. 104–46.

Your reaction is probably, "The words don't look right. They are misspelled." The reason you realize the errors so quickly is that you have a global understanding of the manner in which letters can and cannot occur in the English language. You instantly recognize the errors through an immediate scan of your knowledge of words and the rules of ordering letters. Through your efficient recognition and correction, you have used information that goes beyond knowing about each of the three individual words. You have demonstrated a metacognitive awareness and understanding of spelling in the English language.[6]

The term **metacognition** is a coined word. *Cognition* refers to knowledge or skills that you possess. The Greek prefix *meta-* suggests an abstract level of understanding, as if viewed from the outside. Thus, *metacognition* not only means having the knowledge but also refers to your own awareness and understanding of the thinking processes involved and your ability to regulate and direct these processes. If you know how to read, you are operating on a cognitive level. To operate on a metacognitive level, you must know the processes involved in reading—predicting, visualizing, relating new knowledge to old, clarifying points to monitor comprehension, and using correction strategies and be able to regulate them.

The Strategies of Metacognition

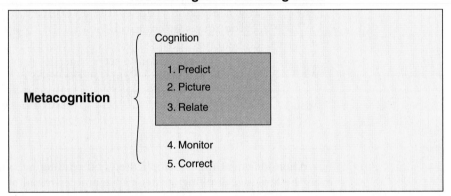

Let's take a real-life example. If you are reading a biology assignment and failing to understand it, you must first recognize that you are not comprehending. Next you must identify what and why you don't understand. Maybe you don't have enough background knowledge, your focus is overshadowed by details, you are relying on misconceptions that are not valid, or your attention is waning. Once you figure out the reason for your confusion, you can attempt a correction strategy. If your strategy does not work, try another and remain confident that you will succeed. The point of metacognition is to understand how to get meaning, to know when you don't have it, and to know what to do about straightening things out.

---

[6]The author is grateful to Professor Jane Thielemann, University of Houston (Downtown), for inspiring this paragraph.

Here is another example: Do you know when you are really studying? In other words, what is the difference between really studying and simply going through the motions of studying? Sometimes you can study intensely for an hour and accomplish a phenomenal amount. At other times, you can put in twice the time with books and notes but learn practically nothing. Do you know the difference, and do you know what to do about it?

Keep Your Eye on the Ball. Some students know the difference, whereas others do not. If you occasionally find yourself in the "going through the motions" frame of mind, think of your attention lapse not as lack of ability but as a wake-up call to reanalyze the task in front of you. Ask yourself, "What is my goal today? What can I do to focus more successfully on what needs to be done?" Picture yourself as an athlete who must keep an eye on the ball to win the game. Be your own coach by telling yourself that you can correct your problems and be more productive.

The Reader's Tip describes how you can improve your reading using metacognition.

Reader's *Tip* —— Developing Metacognition for Reading

With instruction and practice, you can improve your reading performance.

- **Know about reading.** Are you aware of the many strategies you use to comprehend? These include knowledge about words, main ideas, supporting details, and implied ideas. Also, think about the organization of the text and where meaning can be found.
- **Know how to monitor.** Monitor as an ongoing process throughout your reading. Use predicting and questioning to corroborate or discard ideas. Continually clarify and self-test to reinforce learning and pinpoint gaps in comprehension.
- **Know how to correct confusion.** Reread to reprocess a complex idea. Unravel a confusing writing style on a sentence level. Read ahead for ideas that unfold slowly. Consult a dictionary or other sources to fill in background knowledge you lack.

Gain Insight Through Think-Alouds. Experts say that the best way for instructors to teach comprehension strategies is not by just telling students what to do, but by showing them what to do.[7] Students seem to get the message best *when in-*

---

[7]S. Harvey and A. Goudvis, *Strategies That Work* (Portland, ME: Stenhouse Publishers, 2000), p. 13.

structors demonstrate how they themselves actually think while reading. How can that be done? Some instructors read a short passage aloud and verbalize internal thinking, similar to the thoughts inserted in the previous passage on echinoderms. Such modeling activities are called think-alouds. They will be inserted throughout this book to heighten your awareness of how good readers think.

EXAMPLE Apply both your cognitive and metacognitive knowledge to answer the following test item. Interact with the material, monitor, and predict the ending phrase before reading the options. The inserted handwriting simulates a think-aloud by modeling the thinking of a good reader.

Picture the comparison   *pollutes and kills*

What is euphemistically called an "oil spill" can very well become an oil

disaster for marine life. This is particularly true when refined or
                    wants to make more money
semirefined products are being transported. As the tankers get bigger, so

do the accidents, yet we continue to
                    key word

a. fight for clean water   c. use profits for cleanup
                                            shows a parallel idea
b. search for more oil   d. build larger vessels

Robert Wallace, *Biology: The Science of Life*

EXPLANATION Because you were an engaged thinker, you probably predicted the correct answer *d,* even before reading the four options.

In this test item as well as in the passage at the top of page 109, the inserted comments may be confusing to read because involvement differs and many thoughts occur on the subconscious level rather than on the conscious level. Stopping to consciously analyze these reactions may seem artificial and disruptive. It is important, however, to be aware of how you are incorporating the five thinking strategies into your reading.

The passage at the top of the next page illustrates the use of these thinking strategies with longer textbook material. Modeled thoughts of the reader are again inserted for a simulated think-aloud. Again, keep in mind that each reader reacts differently to material, depending on background and individual differences.

Exercise 3.3 will heighten your awareness of the process of interacting analytically with a piece of writing.

— What do I already know about this?

E-Commerce: Retail Sites

What is it?

The world of **electronic commerce**, or, more commonly, **e-commerce**, buying and

selling over the Internet, represents nothing less than a new economic order. Even the

Is this a new word? word *retail* is evolving to *etail*, for electronic retail. With a few clicks of your mouse,

you can buy a suit in Thailand, an out-of-print biography, a particular used car, or a

bargain airline ticket.

Think of what you have purchased on Internet.

— What is content?

Retail web sites have begun adding content to attract visitors and boost sales. That

is, rather than just the usual lists and views of products and prices, the site includes

something of more general interest to attract visitors. Lands' End, for example, a

Is this value added? retail clothier specializing in sportswear, has added true-life adventure tales, with text

and photos, to its site.

Interestingly, content-rich sites that were not originally retail sites are adding

Are they seizing the opportunity to sell? products and pitching sales. Thus the difference between content and commerce sites

is becoming more narrow.

Can critical readers spot the difference?

H. L. Capron, *Computers*

exercise 3.3   Integrating Knowledge While Reading

For the following passage, demonstrate with written notes the way you use the five thinking strategies as you read. The passage is double-spaced so you can insert your thoughts and reactions between the lines. Begin by looking at the title and pulling out your recently enhanced computer file. Make a conscious effort to implement all the following strategies as you read:

1. Predict (develop hypotheses).

2. Picture (develop images during reading).

3. Relate (link prior knowledge with new ideas).

4. Monitor your ongoing comprehension (clarify confusing points).

5. Correct gaps in comprehension (use correction strategies).

SEA STARS

Let's take a look at one class of echinoderms—the sea stars. Sea stars (starfish) are well known for their voracious appetite when it comes to gourmet foods, such as oysters and clams. Obviously, they are the sworn enemy of oystermen. But these same oystermen may have inadvertently helped the spread of the sea stars. At one time, when they caught a starfish, they chopped it apart and vengefully kicked the pieces overboard. But they were unfamiliar with the regenerative powers of the starfish. The central disk merely grows new arms, and a single arm can form a new animal.

Stars are slow-moving predators, so their prey, obviously, are even slower-moving or immobile. Their ability to open an oyster shell is a testimony to their persistence. When a sea star finds an oyster or clam, the prey clamps its shell together tightly, a tactic that discourages most would-be predators, but not the starfish. It bends its body over the oyster and attaches its tube feet to the shell, and then begins to pull. Tiring is no problem since it uses tube feet in relays. Finally, the oyster can no longer hold itself shut, and it opens gradually—only a tiny bit, but it is enough. The star then protrudes its stomach out through its mouth. The soft stomach slips into the slightly opened shell, surrounds the oyster, and digests it in its own shell.

—Robert Wallace,
Biology: The Science of Life

At first glance, you recognized the echinoderm as an old friend and activated your newly acquired schema. The description of the starfish lends itself to a vivid visualization. Were some of your predictions corroborated as you read the passage? Did you find yourself monitoring to reconcile new facts with old ideas? Did you need to use a correction strategy? Did you guess about the regenerative powers? Has your computer file been expanded?

Stage 3: Strategies for Recalling

To recall, you tell yourself what you have learned, relate it to what you already know, react, and evaluate. Actually, you do all this before and during reading, but a deliberate recall is necessary when you finish reading to assimilate knowledge and improve learning. Call it a short conversation with yourself to debrief and digest. You need to be sure you know the content, make connections, and update your schemata, or computer files.

Recalling Through Writing

Answering multiple-choice questions after reading requires one type of mental processing, but writing about the reading requires another type of processing. Experts define writing as a "mode of learning," which means that writing is a process that helps students blend, reconcile, and gain personal ownership of new knowledge. When you write about a subject, you not only discover how much you know and don't know, but you begin to unfold meaningful personal connections.

A humorous adage about the power of writing says, "How do I know what I think until I see what I say?" Writing can be hard work, but it helps you clarify and crystallize what you have learned. You discover your own thinking as you write. Use the power of this valuable tool to take your recall to a higher level. For the longer chapter reading selections in this text, both multiple-choice and writing questions are offered to help you learn.

The Three Steps of Recalling

Recall can be broken down into three manageable steps: self-test, make connections, and react and reflect.

Self-Test. First, test yourself to be sure you understand the content. To have confidence in your opinions, make sure that you clearly understand the facts. You can do this simply by taking a few minutes after reading to recap what you have learned. Do it either in your head or on paper. For practice, use a recall diagram as a learning tool to visualize the main points. On a straight line across the top of a piece of paper, briefly state the topic, or what the passage seems to be mainly about. Indent underneath the topic and state the most significant supporting details.

Make Connections. In the next step of recall, create bridges between what is new to you and what you already know. Ask yourself, "What do I already know that relates to this information?" Your answer will be unique because you are connecting the material to your own knowledge networks. Returning to the recall diagram you started in the previous step, draw a dotted line—your thought line—and write down a related idea, issue, or concern. Connect the text with your personal life experiences, with other things you have read, and with larger global issues. Researchers Harvey and Goudvis categorize these connections in the following way:[8]

---

[8]S. Harvey and A. Goudvis, *Strategies That Work* (Portland, ME: Stenhouse Publishers, 2000), p. 21.

- **Text-to-self.** Readers connect with their own personal experiences and background knowledge.
- **Text-to-text.** Readers connect new text with other written material.
- **Text-to-world.** Readers connect to bigger issues, events, or societal concerns.

How can you translate this theory into practice? Certainly, you can easily relate new reading to yourself. Relating to other written material may seem difficult initially but will be less challenging if you make everyday reading a part of your life. To help you with these connections, the longer reading selections in this text are preceded by a Contemporary Focus feature. These excerpts from recent publications introduce the selection, and later you are asked to answer a question that connects the two. Finally, your ability to make societal or global connections depends on your own interests and knowledge. Your awareness of these kinds of connections will encourage you to dig deeper to relate meaning.

React and Reflect. The final step in recalling is to react to the material. Formulate an opinion about the author and evaluate the message. Returning to your recall diagram, do you agree or disagree with the facts, opinions, and conclusions? How do you feel about the topic? Is this information significant to you? Did the author do a good job? Is this quality work? Your answers will be unique, and there are no right or wrong responses. You are thinking, and you are in control. In all three steps in recalling, you are strengthening your ties to new material. You must link it to own it.

Reader's *Tip*   Recalling After Reading

- **Pinpoint the topic.** Get focused on the subject. Use the title and the subheadings to help you recognize and narrow down the topic.
- **Select the most important points.** Poor readers want to remember everything, thinking all facts have equal importance. Good readers pull out the important issues and identify significant supporting information.
- **Relate the information.** Facts are difficult to learn in isolation. In history, events should not be seen as isolated happenings but rather as results of previous occurrences. Network your new knowledge to enhance memory. Relate new knowledge to yourself, to other written material, and to global issues.
- **React.** Form opinions and evaluate the material and the author. Decide what you wish to accept and what you will reject. Blend old and new knowledge, and write about what you have read.

EXAMPLE   **AUTOPSIES**

Today, many dead people receive some form of autopsy or postmortem examination. At least two main reasons for this are (1) the desire of the family to know the exact cause of death, and (2) the fact that increased medical knowledge results. Because of the important moral and legal restrictions on human experimentation, much of our knowledge of pathology comes from autopsies. This fact prompts many people to donate their bodies to medical schools and/or donate certain organs for possible transplantation.

—John Cunningham,
Human Biology, 2nd ed.

EXPLANATION   Remember that the recall diagram is a temporary and artificial format. The diagram below graphically demonstrates a process that you will learn to do in your head. Using the diagram will help you learn to organize and visualize your reading.

(Topic)	Why autopsies are done
(Significant details— examples, facts, or phrases)	To know exact cause of death
	To increase medical knowledge
	— thus donations
(Relate)	Do I want medical students studying my body?
(React)	I would donate my organs but not my body to medical school.

exercise 3.4   **Using Recall Diagrams**

After reading each of the following passages, stop to recall what the passage contained. Use recall diagrams to record what the passage seems to be mainly about. List significant supporting details; identify a related idea, issue, or concern to which you feel the information is connected; and react.

PASSAGE A: ELEPHANTS IN ANCIENT WARFARE

Elephants were the most spectacular, extravagant, and unpredictable element in ancient warfare. Since the time of Alexander the Great, Hellenistic kings and commanders had tried to use the great strength, size, and relative invulnerability of the animals to throw opposing infantry into confusion and flight. Elephants' unusual smell and loud trumpeting also panicked horses not accustomed to the strange beasts, wreaking havoc with cavalry units. Mahouts, or drivers, who were usually Indians, controlled and directed the animal from a seat on the elephant's neck. Normally each elephant carried a small, towerlike structure from which archers could shoot down on the massed infantry. However, as with modern tanks, the primary importance of the beasts was the enormous shock effect created by a charge of massed war elephants.

—Mark Kishlansky et al.,
Civilization in the West, 6th ed.

(Topic)	Reasons elephants were used in ancient battles
(Significant details)	Confused opposing infantry
	Panicked horses
	Archers able to shoot from atop elephant
	Provided shock effect
(Relate)	Answers will vary.
(React)	Answers will vary.

PASSAGE B: UNDERSTANDING DROUGHT

Drought is different from other natural hazards in several ways. First, it occurs in a gradual, "creeping" way, making its onset and end difficult to determine. The effects of drought accumulate slowly over an extended time span and sometimes linger for years after the drought has ended. Second, there is not a precise and universally accepted definition of drought. This adds to the confusion about whether or not a drought is actually occurring and, if it is, its severity. Third, drought seldom produces structural damages, so its social and economic effects are less obvious than damages from other natural disasters.

—Frederick K. Lutgens and Edward J. Tarbuck,
The Atmosphere: An Introduction to Meteorology, 9th ed.

(Topic)	Drought as a Different Natural Hazard
(Significant details)	Difficult to determine onset and end
	No universal definition
	Less obvious effects
(Relate)	Answers will vary.
(React)	Answers will vary.

Summary *Points*

➤ **What is strategic reading?**
Strategic reading is knowing and using techniques for understanding, studying, and learning.

➤ **What is a study strategy?**
All study systems include a previewing stage to ask questions and establish a purpose for reading, a reading stage to answer questions and integrate knowledge, and a final stage of self-testing and reviewing to improve recall.

➤ **What are the three stages of reading?**
Reading is an active rather than a passive process. Good readers preview before reading, integrate knowledge while reading, and recall after reading.

➤ **What are strategies for previewing?**
Previewing is a way to assess your needs before you start to read by deciding what the material is about, what needs to be done, and how to go about doing it.

➤ **Why should you activate your schema?**
If you brainstorm to make a connection with your reading topic before you begin to read, the information will be more meaningful and memorable.

➤ **What is metacognition?**
Good readers control and direct their thinking strategies as they read. They know about knowing.

➤ **What are the strategies for integrating knowledge during reading?**
Students make predictions, picture images, answer questions, continually relate and integrate old and new knowledge, monitor understanding to clarify confusing points, and use correction strategies.

➤ **Why recall or self-test what you have read?**
Recalling what you have read immediately after reading forces you to select the most important points, to relate the supporting details, to integrate new information into existing networks of knowledge, and to react.

1 selection

selection 1   History

Contemporary *Focus*

Madame C. J. Walker not only created wealth for herself, but she offered opportunities for success to others. In the late 1800s, the hair care needs of African American women were not being addressed. How are those needs being met today? Do new opportunities still exist in the hair care and beauty industry?

Entrepreneur Draws Inspiration from Cosmetics Industry Pioneer

By Maureen Milford
The News Journal (Wilmington, Delaware), October 7, 2005

Crystal Baynard-Norman, 49, of Wilmington, knows the juggling act performed by entrepreneurs who build businesses in their homes while holding down outside jobs.

"I would be sitting at work and thinking, 'Ooh, my gosh, I have to go home and make 20 hair ointments. I have to make 30 body lotions.' Then I'm staying up to 2 or 3 o'clock in the morning. But I love it," she said. Baynard-Norman founded her own hair and body products company, All God's Children Natural Hair & Body Care Products, in 2001.

But Baynard-Norman, who recruits family and friends to her manufacturing operation in her spacious, light-filled kitchen, has an inspiration: Madame C. J. Walker.

"I figured, if she could do it back then with no computers and no information, I could do it with all the information available," Baynard-Norman said.

Manufacturers' sales of ethnic hair-care products totaled $294 million in 2004, according to market research by Kline & Co. in Little Falls, New Jersey. The overall market for makeup and skin care products reached $13.5 billion last year, according Anna Wang, a consultant with Kline.

Last month, Baynard-Norman, a mother of three sons, introduced a line of cosmetics for children called Kidz Only. In addition, she makes more than a half-dozen products for adults, including hair ointment, body wash, body polish, scrubs, and massage oils. Products range in price from $2 to $20 for a gift set. Custom baskets run $40 and up.

COLLABORATE   Collaborate on responses to the following questions:

➤ How much do you spend per month on your hair?

➤ Why do people choose expensive hair care and beauty items over cheaper drug store brands?

➤ How much does a busy hair stylist make in a year?

Skill Development: Preview

Preview the next selection to predict its purpose and organization and to formulate your learning plan.

Activate Schema

What business opportunities were available for women in the late 1800s?
Why is hard work an important key to success? What else does it take?

Establish a Purpose for Reading

As a widowed mother with a child, she was working as a washerwoman and seemed destined to poverty. Read to find out how Madame C. J. Walker overcame obstacles, achieved success, and offered opportunities to others.

Increase Word Knowledge

What do you know about these words?

acumen	stimulate	lavish	philanthropic	patent
concoctions	implementing	burgeoning	consolidated	prosperous

Your instructor may give a true-false vocabulary review before reading.

Integrate Knowledge While Reading

Questions have been inserted in the margins to stimulate your thinking while reading. Remember to

Predict	Picture	Relate	Monitor	Correct

MADAME C. J. WALKER

"I am a woman who came from the cotton fields of the South. I was promoted from there to the washtub. Then I was promoted to the cook kitchen, and from there I promoted myself into the business of manufacturing hair goods and preparations."

What were her chances of success? →

With these words, Madame C. J. Walker introduced herself to the National Negro
5 Business League's 1912 convention and summed up her life to that time. Five years later, through her hard work and business acumen, this daughter of former slaves owned and ran the largest black-owned company in the United States.

The Madame C. J. Walker Manufacturing Company produced and distributed a line of hair and beauty preparations for black women, including conditioners to ease
10 styling, stimulate hair growth, and cure common scalp ailments, as well as an improved metal comb for straightening curly hair. So successful was she at marketing her products that Madame Walker became the first female African American millionaire. Her

self-made fortune allowed for a lavish personal lifestyle and extensive public philanthropic commitments, particularly to black educational institutions.

15   Walker was born Sarah Breedlove in 1867. Her parents, Owen and Minerva Breedlove, were former slaves who had chosen to remain as sharecroppers on the Burney family plantation near Delta, Louisiana. The family was poor, and both parents died by the time Sarah was seven. She was taken in by her old sister, Louvenia, and a few years later they moved to Vicksburg, Mississippi.

20   Sarah's education was extremely limited, and she was subjected to the cruelty of Louvenia's husband. To get away, she married a man named McWilliams when she was 14. In 1885 her daughter, Lelia, was born; two years later, McWilliams was killed, and the young widow moved to St. Louis, Missouri, where she worked as a washerwoman and domestic. Through hard work, she managed to see Lelia graduate from the St.

25 Louis public schools and attend Knoxville College, a black private college in Tennessee.

Shortly after her arrival in St. Louis, Sarah began losing her hair. Like many black women of her era, she would often divide her hair into sections, tightly wrap string around these sections, and twist them in order to make her hair straighter when it was combed out. Unfortunately, this hair-care ritual created such a strain

30 that it caused many women to lose their hair.

To keep her hair, Sarah tried every product she could find, but none worked. Desperate, she prayed to God to save her hair. "He answered my prayer," she later told a reporter for the *Kansas City Star* in a story recounted in *Ms.* magazine. "One night I had a dream, and in that dream a big black man appeared to me and told me what to mix

35 up for my hair. Some of the remedy was grown in Africa, but I sent for it, mixed it, put it on my scalp, and in a few weeks my hair was coming in faster than it had ever fallen out. I tried it on my friends; it helped them. I made up my mind to begin to sell it."

Would this approach work today? →

Walker experimented with patent medicines and hair products already on the market, developing different formulas and products in her wash tubs for testing on

40 herself, her family members, and friends. Realizing the commercial possibilities in the underserved market for black beauty products, she began selling her concoctions door-to-door in the local black community.

Madame C. J. walker sits proudly in the driver's seat of her own electric car.

A'Lelia Bundles/Walker Family Collection

Was she also an inventor?

After perfecting her "Wonderful Hair Grower" in 1905, she moved to Denver, Colorado, to join her recently widowed sister-in-law and nieces. Other products fol-
45 lowed, including "Glossine" hair oil, "Temple Grower," and a "Tetter Salve" for psoriasis of the scalp. These products, used along with her redesigned steel hot comb with teeth spaced far apart for thick hair, allowed black women to straighten, press, and style their hair more easily.

Soon she had enough customers to quit working as a laundress and devote all
50 her energy to her growing business. In 1906 she married Charles Joseph Walker, a Denver newspaperman. His journalistic background proved helpful in implementing advertising and promotional schemes for her products in various black publications, as well as through mail-order procedures. Though the marriage only lasted a few years, it provided a new professional name for herself and her company—the
55 Madame C. J. Walker Manufacturing Company.

Leaving Lelia in charge of her burgeoning mail-order operations in Denver, Walker traveled throughout the South and East, selling her products and teaching her hair care method. In 1908 she established a branch office and a school called Lelia College in Pittsburgh to train black hair stylists and beauticians in the Walker
60 System of hair care and beauty culture. While Lelia managed the school and office, Walker logged thousands of miles on the road, introducing her preparations to black women everywhere she went.

Does her success remind you of other women's achievements?

Stopping in Indianapolis in 1910, she was so impressed by the city's central location and transportation facilities that she decided to make it her headquarters.
65 That year she consolidated her operations by moving the Denver and Pittsburgh offices there and building a new factory to manufacture her hair solutions, facial creams, and related cosmetics. She also established a training center for her sales force, research and production laboratories, and another beauty school to train her "hair culturists."

70 On one of her many trips Walker met a train porter, Freeman B. Ransom, who was a Columbia University law student working during his summer vacation. After he graduated, she hired him to run her Indianapolis operations, freeing Lelia to move to New York in 1913 to expand activities on the East Coast and open another Lelia College. Walker herself continued to travel and promote her beauty program.

75 By 1917 the Madame C. J. Walker Manufacturing Company was the largest black-owned business in the country with annual revenues of approximately $500,000. Much of its success was built around the sales force—thousands of black women known as Walker agents. Dressed in white blouses and long black skirts, they became familiar sights in black communities throughout the United States and
80 the Caribbean. Walking door-to-door to demonstrate and sell Walker products, they easily outpaced their competitors in the newfound black beauty field.

Being a Walker agent or hair culturist was a rare career opportunity for black women in the rigidly segregated pre–World War I era. It enabled many to become financially independent, buy their own homes, and support their childrens' educa-
85 tions. Walker herself considered it one of her greatest accomplishments, telling delegates to the National Negro Business League, as recounted in *American History Illustrated:* "I have made it possible for many colored women to abandon the washtub for a more pleasant and profitable occupation…. The girls and women of our race must not be afraid to take hold of business enterprise."

90 Once her agents were making money, Walker encouraged them to donate to charitable causes in their own communities. Walker set a good example to her saleswomen by becoming the leading black philanthropist of her day.

Even with her generosity, Walker was able to lead a lavish lifestyle. Shrewd real estate investments complemented her self-made business fortune. A striking woman
95 nearly six feet tall, big boned, with brown skin and a broad face, she made heads turn by her presence whenever she entered a room. And her extravagant tastes only enhanced her public image. She dressed in the latest fashions, wore expensive jewelry, rode around in an electric car, was seen in the finer restaurants, owned townhouses in New York and Indianapolis and, befitting the first black female millionaire in the
100 country, built a $250,000, 20-room, elegant Georgian mansion, Villa Lewaro—complete with gold piano and $60,000 pipe organ—in Irvington-on-Hudson.

By 1918 Walker's nonstop pace and lifetime of hard work had begun to take their toll. Despite orders from doctors to slow down to ease her high blood pressure, she continued to travel. During a business trip to St. Louis she collapsed and
105 was transported back to her villa in a private railroad car. She died quietly of kidney failure resulting from hypertension in May of 1919 at the age of 52, leaving behind a prosperous company, extensive property, and a personal fortune in excess of $1 million. Summing up her life, the author of an editorial in *Crisis* said that Madame Walker "revolutionized the personal habits and appearance of millions of
110 human beings."

In her will, Walker bequeathed two-thirds of her estate to charitable and educational institutions, many of which she had supported during her lifetime. The remaining third was left to her daughter, now called A'Lelia, who succeeded her as company president. True to her beliefs, a provision in the will directed that the Madame C. J.
115 Walker Manufacturing Company always have a woman president. In 1927 the Walker Building, planned by Madame Walker, was completed in Indianapolis to serve as company headquarters.

Were hypertension drugs available in 1919?

(1,471 words)

From *Contemporary Black Biography* by Gale Research,
© 1994, Gale Research. Reprinted by permission of The Gale Group.

Recall

Stop to self-test, relate, and react.

Your instructor may choose to give you a true-false comprehension review.

Write About the Selection

What aspects of Walker's business show that she was a clever business strategist as well as an energetic and ambitious entrepreneur?

Response Suggestion: List the unique features of Walker's business plan, and explain how they contributed to her success.

Contemporary *Link*

Why and how does the salon business present such a lucrative opportunity for women? In what new areas might Madame C. J. Walker expand her business today?

Check Your Comprehension

After reading the selection, answer the following questions with *a, b, c,* or *d.* To help you analyze your strengths and weaknesses, the question types are indicated.

Main Idea ____a____ 1. Which is the best statement of the main idea of this selection?

a. Despite a discouraging early life, Walker became a very successful businesswoman.
b. Despite living a life of luxury, Walker gave a lot of money to charities.
c. The manufacturing of hair goods and preparations experienced a business boom in the early 1900s.
d. Walker carefully saved her money in order to become a successful millionaire.

Inference ____d____ 2. The quotation that opens the selection is most likely intended by the author to emphasize

a. the kinds of jobs women typically had in the early twentieth century.
b. the importance of receiving job promotions.
c. the importance of gaining experience in different lines of work.
d. Walker's decision to take charge of her own life.

Detail ____c____ 3. Each of the following is mentioned in the selection as one of the products manufactured and distributed by Walker *except*

a. hair conditioners.
b. facial creams.
c. hair coloring products.
d. a special hair comb.

Inference ____c____ 4. The selection suggests that Walker's development of various hair products was very much due to

a. reading insightful books on science and technology.
b. the guidance of a stranger who worked with her.
c. do-it-yourself trial and error.
d. assistance she received from her parents.

Detail ____c____ 5. Many African American women living in the early twentieth century lost their hair because they

a. had poor nutrition and thus lacked necessary vitamins.
b. used poor-quality hair shampoos.
c. used a harmful hair-straightening technique.
d. developed psoriasis of the scalp.

Detail ____a____ 6. Walker decided to establish her headquarters in Indianapolis because of the city's

a. location.
b. history.
c. laboratories.
d. factories.

Detail ____a____ 7. Lelia College was established to

    a. train women to be Walker System specialists.
    b. teach ladies to be sales agents.
    c. provide a business education for men and women.
    d. provide a liberal arts education to African American women.

Inference ____b____ 8. The reader can conclude that Walker spent most of her time

    a. decorating her mansion.
    b. taking business trips.
    c. teaching in her college.
    d. managing her head office on-site.

Inference ____d____ 9. The sales agents for Walker's company were easily identified because they

    a. were the only female sales agents in the field.
    b. were the only sales agents in the Caribbean market.
    c. gave away free samples.
    d. wore the same uniform.

Inference ____b____ 10. The author suggests that one of the most important benefits of being a Walker agent was

    a. the travel opportunities.
    b. the income.
    c. the free beauty products.
    d. the chance to meet people.

Answer the following with *T* (true) or *F* (false).

Detail ____F____ 11. Walker was at one time married to Freeman B. Ransom.

Inference ____F____ 12. Walker's products sold mostly through mail order.

Inference ____F____ 13. Walker's daughter, Lelia, worked in Denver and was not entrusted with major operational responsibilities in the Madame C. J. Walker Manufacturing Company.

Detail ____F____ 14. Walker gave generously to charities and schools but did not leave money in her will to her family.

Detail ____T____ 15. The director of the Madame C. J. Walker Manufacturing Company has always been a woman because of a stipulation in Walker's will.

Build Your Vocabulary

According to the way the italicized word was used in the selection, select *a, b, c,* or *d* for the word or phrase that gives the best definition. The number in parentheses indicates the line of the passage in which the word is located.

_____b_____ 1. "business *acumen*" (6)
   a. negotiations
   b. wisdom
   c. appeal
   d. training

_____a_____ 6. "selling her *concoctions*" (41)
   a. mixtures
   b. concepts
   c. ideas
   d. favorites

_____c_____ 2. "*stimulate* hair growth" (10)
   a. slow
   b. cure
   c. increase
   d. manage

_____d_____ 7. "*implementing* advertising" (51)
   a. imagining
   b. selling
   c. searching out
   d. accomplishing

_____b_____ 3. "*lavish* personal lifestyle" (13)
   a. interesting
   b. luxurious
   c. entertaining
   d. busy

_____a_____ 8. "*burgeoning* mail-order operations" (56)
   a. growing
   b. convenient
   c. new
   d. simple

_____d_____ 4. "*philanthropic* commitments" (13)
   a. institutional
   b. religious
   c. governmental
   d. charitable

_____a_____ 9. "*consolidated* her operations" (65)
   a. combined
   b. separated
   c. localized
   d. improved

_____a_____ 5. "*patent* medicines" (38)
   a. brands
   b. well known
   c. unreliable
   d. chemical

_____c_____ 10. "*prosperous* company" (107)
   a. large
   b. diverse
   c. wealthy
   d. cosmetic

Search the Net

Use a search engine such as Google, Yahoo, Ask.com, Excite, Dogpile, or Lycos to find information on other self-made American business women. Find the history of two other women and share their stories with your class.

Concept Prep for History

What events led up to World War II?

After Germany was defeated in World War I, supposedly the "war to end all wars," the **Allies** (United States, Britain, France, and Russia) expected Germany to pay for the war they helped start. The Allies also changed the world map by taking away much of the German empire. The German people were stunned at their defeat, angry over the demands of the victors, and eventually unable to meet their debt payments. **Adolf Hitler,** a skillful and charismatic leader, seized this opportunity and tapped into the country's anger. He promised to restore national pride, and consequently many Germans were drawn to him. He became the leader of the **Nazi** party, adopted the **swastika** as its symbol, and eventually became dictator of Germany.

Hitler strengthened the military, forged an alliance with Japan and Italy, and attacked and conquered much of continental Europe. When Britain, under the leadership of Prime Minister **Winston Churchill,** refused to bargain with Germany, Hitler ordered the **Luftwaffe,** the German air force, to destroy Britain from the air. The air raids, known as the **blitz,** failed in their purpose when the Royal Air Force (RAF) won the Battle of Britain. Hitler then attacked Russia.

Prime Minister Winston Churchill, President Franklin Roosevelt, and Soviet leader Joseph Stalin pose for pictures at the Yalta Conference in 1945.

Keystone/Hulton l Archive/Getty Images

What was the U.S. role in the war?

The United States, under **Franklin D. Roosevelt,** remained neutral. **Isolationists** opposed foreign involvement. That changed, however, on December 7, 1941, at 7:02 A.M., when the Japanese bombed **Pearl Harbor,** an American naval base in Hawaii. America declared war on that day. **General Douglas MacArthur** and **Admiral Chester Nimitz** were put in charge of forces in the Pacific, and **General Dwight D. Eisenhower** led the Allied soldiers in Europe.

What was D-Day?

Allied forces planned the liberation of Europe, and on June 6, 1944—on what came to be known as **D-Day**—thousands of brave soldiers secretly left England and stormed the beaches of Normandy, France. After two weeks of desperate fighting, the troops moved inland and liberated Paris by August. The Allied armies drove toward **Berlin,** the capital of Germany, and on April 30, Hitler committed suicide to avoid capture. The Germans surrendered one week later, and the European part of the war was over. Hitler, with his anti-Semitic hatred, had killed more than 6 million innocent Jews. Many were taken by trains to concentration camps for extermination in gas chambers. This horrible carnage was called the **Holocaust.**

How did the war with Japan end?

The American forces in the Pacific were moving from island to island against fierce Japanese resistance. Victories were won with great loss of life. Harry Truman had become president and was told of the **Manhattan Project,** a top-secret plan to develop an atomic bomb. On August 6, 1945, the **Enola Gay** flew over **Hiroshima, Japan,** and dropped an atomic bomb that obliterated the city. Three days later, a second bomb was dropped over **Nagasaki.** Within a few days, the Japanese asked for peace, and a month later they officially surrendered to General MacArthur aboard the battleship **U.S.S. *Missouri*** in Tokyo Bay. World War II had come to an end.

After studying the material, answer the following questions:

1. How did the end of World War I affect the beginning of World War II? _____
   Germany lost territory and had a national debt that it could not pay.
   _____

2. Why were the Germans drawn to Hitler's message? He promised to restore
   national pride.
   _____

3. Who were Germany's allies in World War II? Japan and Italy
   _____

4. Why did the Luftwaffe strike England? Because Churchill refused to
   bargain with Hitler
   _____

5. Who were the isolationists? Americans who opposed foreign involvement
   _____
   _____

6. What prompted the United States to enter the war? The bombing of
   Pearl Harbor
   _____

7. What was the Holocaust? The killing of six million Jews
   _____
   _____

8. What was D-Day? The Allied forces attack on the beaches of Normandy on
   June 6, 1944
   _____

9. What ended the war in Europe? Hitler committed suicide as Russian troops
   moved to take Berlin; Germany surrendered.
   _____

10. What ended the war in Japan? The United States dropped atomic bombs
    on Hiroshima and Nagasaki.
    _____

Your instructor may choose to give a true-false review of these history concepts.

selection 2 Sociology

Contemporary *Focus*

Experts say that oral communication is 7 percent actual spoken words, 35 percent tone of voice, and 55 percent body language. In a growing global economy, conducting business across cultures can be tricky. Extra care must be taken to avoid unintentionally offending other people.

Culture Clash: Closing Gaps between Different Worlds Is Crucial to Building Team Trust

By Mary Brandel

Computerworld, February 16, 2006. Reprinted with permission. Copyright © 2006 by Computerworld, Inc., Framington, MA 01701. All rights reserved.

An Indian firm recently sent a greeting card to coworkers worldwide with the image of a swastika, an ancient and sacred symbol in that country. "Many people went ballistic," says Gopal Kapur, founder of the Center for Project Management in San Ramon, California. In fact, it took five managers hours of telephone conversations and many e-mails to calm the waters. The work of 14 international team members came to a halt for more than 11 days, delaying the project and costing thousands of dollars.

With so much room for misinterpretation, it's important to play it straight with both speech and body language. Keep your vocabulary basic, and avoid jokes, Rosen cautions, as they never translate. Don't use a lot of hand gestures—a thumb's up and the OK sign are obscene in places like Brazil, Australia, Spain and the Middle East.

"Since gestures have different meanings in different parts of the world, they can cause confusion," says Terri Morrison, president of Getting Through Customs, which provides books and seminars for international travelers. This is particularly true in "high context" cultures such as Japan, France and many Arab countries.

"While Americans have no problem jumping into a business discussion as soon as a meeting begins, it's considered insulting in places like the Far East to begin negotiations before socializing and forming a relationship, even if that takes days," says Norbert Kubilus of Sunterra Corporation, a resort company in Las Vegas.

COLLABORATE Collaborate on responses to the following questions:

➤ When business is conducted in the United States, how is silence regarded?

➤ How would you react if a same-gender Russian businessperson kissed you on the mouth?

➤ Among Americans, what do words such as *issues* and *challenge* really mean in business conversations?

Skill Development: Preview

Preview the next selection to predict its purpose and organization and to formulate your learning plan.

Activate Schema

Is it wrong for primitive tribal people to wear no clothes?
Does social status exist in primitive cultures?
Would you eat insects if doing so meant survival?

Establish a Purpose for Reading

The phrase "unity in diversity" is a paradox. What does the author mean by this, and what do you expect to learn from this selection?

As you read, notice the author's use of examples to help you fully absorb the concepts of cultural universals, adaptation, relativity, ethnocentrism, norms, and values. Read with the intention of discovering that there are behavior patterns and institutions essential to all known societies, despite wide cultural variations in their expression.

Increase Word Knowledge

What do you know about these words?

curb	naïveté	adornments	articulate	bizarre
smirk	abstained	postpartum	agile	consign

Your instructor may give a true-false vocabulary review before or after reading.

Integrate Knowledge While Reading

Questions have been inserted in the margins to stimulate your thinking while reading. Remember to

Predict	Picture	Relate	Monitor	Correct

UNITY IN DIVERSITY

Does this title make sense, or are these words opposites?

What is more basic, more "natural" than love between a man and woman? Eskimo men offer their wives to guests and friends as a gesture of hospitality; both husband and wife feel extremely offended if the guest declines. The Banaro of New Guinea believe it would be disastrous for a woman to conceive her first child by her hus-
5 band and not by one of her father's close friends, as is their custom.

The real father is a close friend of the bride's father. . . . Nevertheless the first-born child inherits the name and possessions of the husband. An American would deem such a custom immoral, but the Banaro tribesmen would be equally shocked to discover that the first-born child of an Amer-
10 ican couple is the offspring of the husband.

selection 2

What would your parents do if you slapped either of them in the face?

The Yanomamö of Northern Brazil, whom anthropologist Napoleon A. Chagnon named "the fierce people," encourage what we would consider extreme disrespect. Small boys are applauded for striking their mothers and fathers in the face. Yanomamö parents would laugh at our efforts to curb aggression in children, much as they laughed at Chagnon's naïveté when he first came to live with them.

15
The variations among cultures are startling, yet all peoples have customs and beliefs about marriage, the bearing and raising of children, sex, and hospitality—to name just a few of the universals anthropologists have discovered in their cross-cultural explorations. But the *details* of cultures do indeed vary; in this country, not

20 so many years ago, when a girl was serious about a boy and he about her, she wore his fraternity pin over her heart; in the Fiji Islands, girls put hibiscus flowers behind their ears when they are in love. The specific gestures are different but the impulse to symbolize feelings, to dress courtship in ceremonies, is the same. How do we explain this unity in diversity?

CULTURAL UNIVERSALS

Why would incest have to be a taboo for a surviving culture?

25 *Cultural universals* are all of the behavior patterns and institutions that have been found in all known cultures. Anthropologist George Peter Murdock identified over sixty cultural universals, including a system of social status, marriage, body adornments, dancing, myths and legends, cooking, incest taboos, inheritance rules, puberty customs, and religious rituals.

30
The universals of culture may derive from the fact that all societies must perform the same essential functions if they are to survive—including organization, motivation, communication, protection, the socialization of new members, and the replacement of those who die. In meeting these prerequisites for group life, people inevitably design similar—though not identical—patterns for living. As Clyde Kluckhohn wrote,

35 "All cultures constitute somewhat distinct answers to essentially the same questions posed by human biology and by the generalities of the human situation."

The way in which a people articulates cultural universals depends in large part on their physical and social environment—that is, on the climate in which they live, the materials they have at hand, and the peoples with whom they establish contact.

In a traditional Indian wedding ceremony, the bride and groom pray at the altar.

Omni Photo Communications Inc./Index Stock Imagery, Inc.

40 For example, the wheel has long been considered one of humankind's greatest inventions, and anthropologists were baffled for a long time by the fact that the great civilizations of South America never discovered it. Then researchers uncovered a number of toys with wheels. Apparently the Aztecs and their neighbors did know about wheels; they simply didn't find them useful in their mountainous environment.

What is your mental picture?

ADAPTATION, RELATIVITY, AND ETHNOCENTRISM

45 Taken out of context, almost any custom will seem bizarre, perhaps cruel, or just plain ridiculous. To understand why the Yanomamö encourage aggressive behavior in their sons, for example, you have to try to see things through their eyes. The Yanomamö live in a state of chronic warfare; they spend much of their time planning for and defending against raids with neighboring tribes. If Yanomamö parents did not 50 encourage aggression in a boy, he would be ill-equipped for life in their society. Socializing boys to be aggressive is adaptive for the Yanomamö because it enhances their capacity for survival. "In general, culture is . . . adaptive because it often provides people with a means of adjusting to the physiological needs of their own bodies, to their physical-geographical environment and to their social environments as well."

55 In many tropical societies, there are strong taboos against a mother having sexual intercourse with a man until her child is at least two years old. As a Hausa woman explains,

> A mother should not go to her husband while she has a child who is sucking . . . if she only sleeps with her husband and does not become pregnant, 60 it will not hurt her child, it will not spoil her milk. But if another child enters in, her milk will make the first one ill.

Undoubtedly, people would smirk at a woman who nursed a two-year-old child in our society and abstained from having sex with her husband. Why do Hausa women behave in a way that seems so overprotective and overindulgent to us? In 65 tropical climates protein is scarce. If a mother were to nurse more than one child at a time, or if she were to wean a child before it reached the age of two, the youngster would be prone to *kwashiorkor*, an often fatal disease resulting from protein deficiency. Thus, long postpartum sex taboos are adaptive. In a tropical environment a postpartum sex taboo and a long period of breast-feeding solve a serious problem.

70 No custom is good or bad, right or wrong in itself; each one must be examined in light of the culture as a whole and evaluated in terms of how it works in the context of the entire culture. Anthropologists and sociologists call this *cultural relativity*. Although this way of thinking about culture may seem self-evident today, it is a *Why did missionaries* lesson that anthropologists and the missionaries who often preceded them to re-*want to clothe* 75 mote areas learned the hard way, by observing the effects their best intentions had *islanders?* on peoples whose way of life was quite different from their own. In an article on the pitfalls of trying to "uplift" peoples whose ways seem backward and inefficient, Don Adams quotes an old Oriental story:

> Once upon a time there was a great flood, and involved in this flood were 80 two creatures, a monkey and a fish. The monkey, being agile and experienced, was lucky enough to scramble up a tree and escape the raging waters. As he looked down from his safe perch, he saw the poor fish struggling against the swift current. With the very best intentions, he reached down and lifted the fish from the water. The result was inevitable.

What is the difference between adaptation and relativity?

85   *Ethnocentrism* is the tendency to see one's own way of life, including behaviors, beliefs, values, and norms as the only right way of living. Robin Fox points out that "any human group is ever ready to consign another recognizably different human group to the other side of the boundary. It is not enough to possess culture to be fully human, you have to possess *our* culture."

VALUES AND NORMS

90   The Tangu, who live in a remote part of New Guinea, play a game called *taketak*, which in many ways resembles bowling. The game is played with a top that has been fashioned from a dried fruit and with two groups of coconut stakes that are driven into the ground (more or less like bowling pins). The players divide into two teams. Members of the first team take turns throwing the top into the batch of
95   stakes; every stake the top hits is removed. Then the second team steps to the line and tosses the top into their batch of stakes. The object of the game, surprisingly, is not to knock over as many stakes as possible. Rather, the game continues until both teams have removed the *same* number of stakes. Winning is completely irrelevant.

    In a sense games are practice for "real life"; they reflect the values of the cul-
100   ture in which they are played. *Values* are the criteria people use in assessing their daily lives, arranging their priorities, measuring their pleasures and pains, choosing between alternative courses of action. The Tangu value equivalence: the idea of one individual or group winning and another losing bothers them, for they believe winning generates ill-will. In fact, when Europeans brought soccer to the Tangu,
105   they altered the rules so that the object of the game was for two teams to score the same number of goals. Sometimes their soccer games went on for days! American games, in contrast, are highly competitive; there are *always* winners and losers. Many rule books include provisions for overtime and "sudden death" to prevent ties, which leave Americans dissatisfied. World Series, Superbowls, cham-
110   pionships in basketball and hockey, Olympic Gold Medals are front-page news in this country. In the words of the late football coach Vince Lombardi, "Winning isn't everything, it's the only thing."

    Norms, the rules that guide behavior in everyday situations, are derived from values, but norms and values can conflict. You may recall a news item that appeared
115   in American newspapers in December 1972, describing the discovery of survivors of a plane crash 12,000 feet in the Andes. The crash had occurred on October 13; sixteen of the passengers (a rugby team and their supporters) managed to survive for sixty-nine days in near-zero temperatures. The story made headlines because, to stay alive, the survivors had eaten parts of their dead companions. Officials, speak-
120   ing for the group, stressed how valiantly the survivors had tried to save the lives of the injured people and how they had held religious services regularly. The survivors' explanations are quite interesting, for they reveal how important it is to people to justify their actions, to resolve conflicts in norms and values (here, the positive value of survival vs. the taboo against cannibalism). Some of the survivors compared their
125   action to a heart transplant, using parts of a dead person's body to save another person's life. Others equated their act with the sacrament of communion. In the words of one religious survivor, "If we would have died, it would have been suicide, which is condemned by the Roman Catholic faith."

(1,679 words)

—By Donald Light, Jr., and Suzanne Keller, *Sociology*, 5th ed.
Copyright © 1989 by The McGraw-Hill Companies, Inc.
Reproduced with permission of The McGraw-Hill Companies.

(margin annotations)
What will be covered in this next part?

How do you know appropriate dress for a place of worship? Are rules written on the door?

Recall

Stop to self-test, relate, and react. Use the subheadings in the recall diagram shown here to guide your thinking. For each subheading, jot down a key idea that you feel is important to remember.

(Topic)	Unity in Diversity
(Significant details)	Universals—behaviors and institutions found in all cultures
	Adaptation—a culture's specific expression of a universal
	Relativity—custom is neither good nor bad in itself
	Ethnocentrism—seeing one's own way of life as the only right way
	Values—criteria used to judge and assess actions
	Norms—rules that guide behavior in everyday situations
(Relate)	Answers will vary.
(React)	Answers will vary.

Your instructor may choose to give you a true-false comprehension review.

Write About the Selection

Define the following terms and describe two examples for each that are not mentioned in the selection:

cultural	universals	adaptation	relativity
ethnocentrism	norms	values	

Response Suggestion: Define the cultural concepts in your own words and relate examples from contemporary society.

Contemporary *Link*

Why might business meals be considered "minefields of opportunity" for embarrassment in foreign cultures? From a cultural relativity perspective, discuss how certain gestures can be acceptable in one culture but unacceptable in another.

Check Your Comprehension

After reading the selection, answer the following questions with *a, b, c,* or *d.* To help you analyze your strengths and weaknesses, the question types are indicated.

Main Idea _____d_____ 1. Which is the best statement of the main idea of this selection?

    a. Practices and customs in society show few threads of cultural unity.

    b. The unusual variations in societies gain acceptability because of the cultural universals in all known societies.

    c. A variety of cultural universals provides adaptive choices for specific societies.

    d. Cultural universals are found in all known societies, even though the details of the cultures may vary widely.

Inference _____c_____ 2. The author believes that the primary cultural universal addressed in the Eskimo custom of offering wives to guests is

    a. bearing and raising of children.

    b. social status.

    c. hospitality.

    d. incest taboos.

Detail _____a_____ 3. The custom of striking practiced by the Yanomamö serves the adaptive function of

    a. developing fierce warriors.

    b. binding parent and child closer together.

    c. developing physical respect for parents.

    d. encouraging early independence from parental care.

Detail _____b_____ 4. *Cultural universals* might be defined as

    a. each culture in the universe.

    b. similar basic living patterns.

    c. the ability for cultures to live together in harmony.

    d. the differences among cultures.

Inference _____d_____ 5. The author implies that cultural universals exist because of

    a. a social desire to be more alike.

    b. the differences in cultural behavior patterns.

    c. the competition among societies.

    d. survival needs in group life.

Inference _____a_____ 6. The author suggests that the wheel was not a part of the ancient Aztec civilization because the Aztecs

    a. did not find wheels useful in their mountainous environment.

    b. were not intelligent enough to invent wheels.

    c. were baffled by inventions.

    d. did not have the materials to develop them.

Inference _____b_____ 7. The underlying reason for the postpartum sexual taboo of the Hausa is

   a. sexual.
   b. nutritional.
   c. moral.
   d. religious.

Inference _____c_____ 8. The term *cultural relativity* explains why a custom can be considered

   a. right or wrong regardless of culture.
   b. right or wrong according to the number of people practicing it.
   c. right in one culture and wrong in another.
   d. wrong if in conflict with cultural universals.

Inference _____b_____ 9. The author relates Don Adams's Asian story to show that missionaries working in other cultures

   a. should be sent back home.
   b. can do more harm than good.
   c. purposely harm the culture to seek selfish ends.
   d. usually do not have a genuine concern for the people.

Inference _____b_____ 10. The tendency of ethnocentrism would lead most Americans to view the Eskimo practice of wife sharing as

   a. right.
   b. wrong.
   c. right for Eskimos but wrong for most Americans.
   d. a custom about which an outsider should have no opinion.

Answer the following questions with *T* (true) or *F* (false):

Inference _____T_____ 11. An American's acceptance of the Banaro tribal custom of fathering the firstborn is an example of an understanding by cultural relativity.

Inference _____T_____ 12. The author feels that the need to symbolize feelings in courtship is a cultural universal.

Inference _____F_____ 13. The author feels that culture is not affected by climate.

Detail _____T_____ 14. The author states that all societies must have a form of organization if they are to survive.

Inference _____F_____ 15. The author implies that the rugby team that crashed in the Andes could have survived without eating human flesh.

Build Your Vocabulary

According to the way the italicized word is used in the selection, select *a, b, c,* or *d* for the word or phrase that gives the best definition. The number in parentheses indicates the line of the passage in which the word is located.

_____d_____ 1. "efforts to *curb* aggression" (14)
a. stabilize
b. release
c. promote
d. restrain

_____a_____ 2. "To *symbolize* feelings" (23)
a. represent
b. hide
c. ignore
d. simplify

_____d_____ 3. "body *adornments*" (27)
a. ailments
b. treatments
c. scars
d. decorations

_____c_____ 4. "*articulates* cultural universals" (37)
a. remembers
b. designs
c. expresses clearly
d. substitutes

_____c_____ 5. "will seem *bizarre*" (45)
a. phony
b. unjust
c. very strange
d. unnecessary

_____b_____ 6. "*smirk* at a woman" (62)
a. refuse to tolerate
b. smile conceitedly
c. lash out
d. acknowledge approvingly

_____c_____ 7. "*abstained* from having sex" (63)
a. matured
b. regained
c. refrained
d. reluctantly returned

_____a_____ 8. "long *postpartum* sex taboos" (68)
a. after childbirth
b. awaited
c. subcultural
d. complicated

_____b_____ 9. "being *agile* and experienced" (80)
a. eager
b. nimble
c. young
d. knowledgeable

_____b_____ 10. "ready to *consign*" (87)
a. assign
b. transfer
c. reorganize
d. overlook

Search the Net

Use a search engine such as Google, AltaVista, Excite, Infoseek, Dogpile, Yahoo, or Lycos to find information on Latin American business and cultural etiquette, and highlight the differences. Pretend your company wishes to expand into Latin America, and write a memo to the company president summarizing your research. For suggested Web sites and other research activities, go to http://www.ablongman.com/smith/.

Concept Prep for Anthropology

Although the "Unity in Diversity" selection is from a sociology textbook, the passage deals with concepts in anthropology. Thus, this section will also explore anthropology.

What is anthropology?

Anthropology is the study of humankind. It focuses on the origins and development of humans and their diverse cultures. By seeking to understand, respect, and applaud human diversity, anthropology might be considered the first multicultural course on college campuses. Special areas that you can study in anthropology include the following:

- **Physical anthropology:** How did humans evolve? What does genetic and fossil evidence reveal about our place in the animal kingdom?
- **Cultural anthropology:** What was the purpose of primitive customs and behaviors, and what do they reveal about contemporary social problems?
- **Archaeology:** What can we reconstruct about extinct societies and their cultures from artifacts such as ancient bones, pieces of pottery, and excavated ruins?

Who are famous anthropologists?

- In search of our human origins, **Louis and Mary Leakey** sifted through the dirt of **Olduvai Gorge** in Tanzania, East Africa, for more than 25 years. Finally, in 1959 they unearthed a humanlike upper jaw with teeth and a skull. This discovery of a hominid 1.75 million years old revealed that the first humans originated in Africa.
- Cultural anthropology was popularized by **Margaret Mead** with the publication of her book *Coming of Age in Samoa*, published in 1928. Mead observed children moving into adolescence and described the transition as happy. She argued that the stress of adolescence is cultural, but others later disagreed. Mead also studied male and female roles in

Husband and wife Louis and Mary Leakey study fossilized skull fragments that might belong to the "missing link" between ape and man.

different societies and argued that gender roles are cultural rather than inborn.

Who were our early ancestors?

- **Lucy,** one of the greatest archaeological treasures, is the nickname for the most complete human skeleton of early ancestors ever found. Lucy is more than 3 million years old and was unearthed in Ethiopia.
- The **Cro-Magnons** were the earliest form of modern humans, who lived about 35,000 years ago. Their cave paintings in Europe are the first known human art.
- The earliest societies were **hunting and gathering societies.** People roamed widely to hunt wild animals and fish and to gather fruits and nuts. Usually, this **nomadic** wandering was seasonal and calculated to create the best opportunities for finding available food. Not until 10,000 years ago did humans begin to domesticate plants and animals and thus remain in one area.

After studying the material, answer the following questions:

1. Digging in New Mexico for prehistoric artifacts suggests what area of anthropology? archaeology

2. Living with tribal people in the Amazon to study their ways suggests what area of anthropology? cultural

3. Analyzing DNA to link Asian and African people suggests what area of anthropology? physical

4. What did Mary and Louis Leakey discover? A human skill, jaw bone, and teeth of a 1.75-million-year-old hominid

5. Why was the Leakey discovery especially significant? It showed that the first humans originated in Africa.

6. What did Margaret Mead investigate in Samoa? The transition from childhood to adolescence

7. Why was Mead's work especially significant? It popularized cultural anthropology, and it also suggested that gender roles are cultural rather than innate.

8. Why is Lucy significant? She is the most complete skeleton of a very early ancestor.

9. What was the artistic contribution of Cro-Magnons? Cave paintings

10. What phenomenon usually ends hunting and gathering societies? Domesticating plants and animals

Your instructor may choose to give a true-false review of these anthropology concepts.

selection 3 Business

Contemporary *Focus*

Restaurants depend on many low-wage employees to do grueling tasks and keep costs down. These service sector workers are usually entry-level employees, working at their first job to pay living expenses. The work has little status yet allows Americans to enjoy an inexpensive hamburger, fries, or salad for a quick lunch. How do you treat these service sector workers, and what does that say about you?

Watch How People Treat Staff

By Del Jones
USA Today, April 14, 2006. Reprinted with permission.

Office Depot CEO Steve Odland remembers like it was yesterday working in an upscale French restaurant in Denver.

The purple sorbet in cut glass he was serving tumbled onto the expensive white gown of an obviously rich and important woman. "I watched in slow motion ruining her dress for the evening," Odland says. "I thought I would be shot on sight."

Thirty years have passed, but Odland can't get the stain out of his mind, nor the woman's kind reaction. She was startled, regained composure and, in a reassuring voice, told the teenage Odland, "It's OK. It wasn't your fault." When she left the restaurant, she also left the future Fortune 500 CEO with a life lesson: You can tell a lot about a person by the way he or she treats the waiter.

Odland isn't the only CEO to have made this discovery. Rather, it seems to be one of those rare laws of the land that every CEO learns on his way up. It's hard to get a dozen CEOs to agree about anything, but all interviewed agree with the Waiter Rule.

Beware of anyone who pulls out the power card to say something like, "I could buy this place and fire you," or "I know the owner, and I could have you fired." Those who say such things have revealed more about their character than about their wealth and power.

Odland says he saw all types of people 30 years ago as a busboy. "People treated me wonderfully, and others treated me like dirt. There were a lot of ugly people. I didn't have the money or the CEO title at the time, but I had the same intelligence and raw ability as I have today."

COLLABORATE Collaborate on responses to the following questions:

➤ Have you ever worked in a service sector job? How was it?

➤ Why are so many young people and recent immigrants in service sector jobs?

➤ What would be the best and worst part of being a server?

Skill Development: Preview

Preview the next selection to predict its purpose and organization and to formulate your learning plan.

Activate Schema

How much do fast food jobs pay?
What advancement is available in fast food jobs?
Why are customers rude to service sector workers?

Establish a Purpose for Reading

In service sector jobs, the work is demanding, and the rewards are few. Read the selection to understand the difficulties of working in the service sector. As you read, learn what factors cause stress.

Increase Word Knowledge

What do you know about these words?

widespread	repetitive	endure	displacement	belittling
skimp	allocating	frequency	instability	rabid

Your instructor may give a true-false vocabulary review before or after reading.

Integrate Knowledge While Reading

Questions have been inserted in the margins to stimulate your thinking while reading. Remember to

Predict	Picture	Relate	Monitor	Correct

ON THE FRONT LINES OF THE SERVICE SECTOR

Why is fast food and grocery work considered high risk?

Work in fast food, grocery, and other low-end service jobs is, or can be, difficult, demanding, and unrewarding. Fast food and grocery work is high-stress, low-status, and low-wage work. It is work that, on the one hand, is subject to routinization, close surveillance, and management control. But, on the other hand, it calls for high
5 levels of self-motivation and investment from workers. It can also be physically dangerous. Grocery and restaurant workers throughout North America face some of the highest risks of all occupational groups of being injured, attacked, or even killed on the job.

STRESS

"I would say the stress is the worst thing about it," a young Fry House cashier
says of her fast food job. "Sometimes I get so stressed out, 'cause some days
you're in a bad mood yourself, you know, having to deal with people, you just
don't want to, you'd rather be somewhere else, anywhere except work." High
stress levels are the most widespread complaint young workers in Box Hill and
Glenwood have about their grocery and fast food employment. Stress can be
caused by many aspects of grocery and fast food work: difficult relations with
customers and managers; repetitive work tasks; low occupational status and
small paychecks; continual workplace surveillance; and hot, greasy, and often
dangerous work environments.

TIME FACTORS

But the number one factor young workers point to as the cause of workplace stress
is the lack of time to do the work they are expected to do. Either there are not
enough workers on shift to cover customer rushes and necessary preparation and
cleaning work, or workers are not given long enough shifts to get their work stations
ready for lunch and evening rushes and clean up after such rushes are through.

Lack of time lies behind almost all other causes of workplace stress. Young
workers regularly endure abuse from their customers. Workers are yelled at,
sworn at, and insulted by customers. They are frowned at, glared at, and sneered
at. They are ignored, treated as social inferiors, and assumed to be servants whose
role in life is to cater to and anticipate a customer's every whim and fancy. There
are different reasons for such abusiveness. Young grocery and fast food workers
make easy targets for the displacement of hostility. "Often people come into Fry
House," a cashier in Glenwood says, "because they've been yelled at by their
bosses. They don't have anybody they can yell at, so they yell at us 'cause they
think they can." "Customers go off on some grocery employee," says a stocker in
Box Hill, " 'cause it makes 'em feel powerful."

How does the atmosphere contribute to stress?

Do older workers get more respect?

Working at fast food restaurants and other service sector jobs can be very
stressful.

David Levenson/Alamy

selection 3

CUSTOMER INTEREST CONFLICTS

35 Grocery and fast food workers also incite abuse when their job responsibilities put them in conflict with customer interests. Checkers in Box Hill, for example, become the target of customers' anger when they are put in the position of having to police company rules on accepting checks or enforcing government laws for using food stamps or selling alcohol. In one supermarket, I witnessed a checker politely decline
40 to sell alcohol to a young couple who were clearly intoxicated—as she was required to do by law, under penalty of losing her job. The couple stalked out of the store, and on their way out turned to yell obscenities at the checker.

Beyond these various motivations, however, many young workers feel that grocery and fast food customers are abusive primarily because they fail to appreciate
45 the time pressure under which workers labor:

"That's the worst aspect of it for me, having to explain to people (customers) that, well, this is how it works, because they don't know . . . I've said, you're welcome to come back here, take a tour, sit here for an hour, watch us when it's busy, please. Actually, a lady who worked here for about a month, and then she got another job . . .
50 she said, "You know, I used to get really mad when I had to wait for stuff, but I have a total new respect for people that work in fast food. I know what you have to do. I know what it's like. I feel so bad for any time I ever blew up at anybody." She says, "I don't know how you guys do it, how you can handle it. I really, really, really admire you guys for that, for keeping your cool the way you do, 'cause it's hard to do."

55 "They think we're dumb and slow," a Fry House cashier complains of his customers, "but they don't understand. If they came in here and tried to do what we're doing, they'll be about three times as slow as we are." Young workers are often caught in difficult situations in their relations with customers. On the one hand, they are not given enough time or staff support by their employers to perform at the
60 speed and quality levels their customers would prefer; on the other hand, they lack the status to be able to persuade customers to respect them for the work that they do manage to do under what are often difficult and stressful working conditions.

How do time issues create conflict?

MANAGER CONFLICTS

Managers are another primary source of workplace stress. Like customers, some managers yell and swear at their young employees, talk down to them, and call
65 them "stupid," "incompetent," and "lazy." Many workers believe that the younger the worker, the more latitude managers feel they have in verbally attacking and belittling that worker. Managers in fast food and grocery, young workers say, often "go on power trips," order workers around, and "tell you every little thing you do wrong"—all the while failing to provide encouragement or acknowledgment of jobs
70 well done. Managers criticize workers behind their backs; worse, they dress employees down to their faces, in front of coworkers and customers. Young workers in both Box Hill and Glenwood complain widely of the stress caused by managerial favoritism. Managers pick on workers they dislike and confer favors on workers they prefer. Many feel that managers will abuse their power by trying to get rid of em-
75 ployees they don't want working in their stores. "When a manager doesn't want you to work there," explains a cook in Glenwood, "they look for things, they kinda set you up so they can give you something bad."

As it does with customer-caused stress, time pressure often stands behind manager-caused workplace stress. Workers, for example, sometimes encounter what
80 they refer to as "office managers"—managers who hide in their offices (claiming to

Is this also true for non-service sector jobs?

be doing needed paperwork) and avoid helping with rushes. Because stores' labor budgets generally assume that managers will work on the floor when needed, "office managers" put increased stress on already overloaded workers. Workers have to deal with "cheap" managers—managers who (in efforts to keep costs low and earn year-
85 end bonuses) skimp on allocating labor hours. Workers have to deal with managerial error—with managers who regularly screw up when submitting hours to company payroll, so that workers' checks are late or incorrect, or with managers who screw up scheduling, ordering, or inventory tasks. "I notice our managers forget a lot," one Fry House worker complained, "so we have to explain to our customers, 'We have
90 no fried chicken tonight.' 'How can you have no fried chicken when it's Fry House?' 'Well, our manager forgot to order chicken.' It's crazy!"

What impact do these conditions have on employees? → Managers in the grocery and (especially) fast food industries come and go with great frequency. Over time, management instability can be as stressful and wearing as bad or abusive management. "Every time a new manager comes in, they change
95 everything," complains a Fry House cashier. "It's just like being hired. They have to retrain you on everything. It's pretty hard, because once you get into something, you just keep with it. Then somebody else comes in, and they're like, 'No, no! You're doing it wrong; you have to do it this way.' "

LOW STATUS

The low status of grocery and fast food work feeds into general workplace stress.
100 Young grocery and fast food workers lack a "status shield" to protect them from customer and manager abuse. The low status of grocery and fast food work also feeds into low industry wages. Rabid employer determination to keep labor costs at a minimum, of course, further reinforces downward pressures on wages.

(1,388 words)

—Stuart Tannock
From *Youth at Work: The Unionized Fast-Food and Grocery Workplace*
Used by permission of Temple University Press. Copyright © 2001 by
Temple University. All Rights Reserved.

Recall

Stop to self-test, relate, and react.

Your instructor may choose to give you a true-false comprehension review.

Write About the Selection

What are the major factors that create stress and low morale in the fast food business? As a manager, what rule would you create to help employees deal with these major stressors?

Response Suggestion: List and explain four factors, and suggest a rule for dealing with each that would reduce employee stress.

Contemporary *Link*

If you were in a restaurant for an important business lunch and meeting afterward, what would you do if a server spilled a staining liquid on your light-colored jacket? Explain how you think the situation should be properly handled.

Check Your Comprehension

After reading the selection, answer the following questions with *a, b, c,* or *d*. To help you analyze your strengths and weaknesses, the question types are indicated.

Main Idea _____d_____ 1. Which is the best statement of the main idea of this selection?
  a. Service sector work can be physically dangerous.
  b. Service sector jobs are boring and repetitive.
  c. Service sector workers are often under surveillance.
  d. Service sector workers have very demanding and stressful jobs.

Inference _____c_____ 2. The reader can conclude that, for workers, the main cause of stress in service sector jobs is
  a. the risk of personal injury.
  b. working for critical managers.
  c. lack of time to do their jobs well.
  d. being yelled at by their customers.

Detail _____a_____ 3. The service sector workers quoted in the passage think that the customers who abuse them do so mainly because they
  a. fail to recognize the difficulty of the job.
  b. seem to have unusual personal problems.
  c. expect to be treated better than they are treated.
  d. enjoy going off on "power trips" on workers.

Inference _____b_____ 4. The author tells the story about the checkers in Box Hill primarily to point out that service sector workers must sometimes
  a. accept checks and ask for customer identification.
  b. enforce laws that anger customers.
  c. follow questionable company policies.
  d. disagree with a customer's opinion.

Inference _____b_____ 5. The author includes a long comment on line 46 (beginning with "That's the worst . . .") by an anonymous service sector worker mainly to
  a. reveal the complaints of an unhappy service sector worker.
  b. give an example of how a typical service sector worker feels.
  c. show how demanding employers can be in the service sector.
  d. suggest that fast food workers are treated with respect by most customers.

Detail _____d_____ 6. The author indicates that service sector jobs can be especially difficult for younger workers because customers
  a. want to be served by people nearer their own age.
  b. feel younger workers do not anticipate their needs.
  c. sense that younger workers do not work hard.
  d. fail to treat younger workers with much respect.

Inference _____c_____ 7. The reader can conclude that most problems service sector workers have with their managers come from

    a. lack of encouragement.
    b. frequent retraining for the job.
    c. the abuse of power.
    d. deliberate managerial mistakes.

Inference _____a_____ 8. The reader can conclude from the discussion of service sector managers that too many managers fail to

    a. give employees support and praise.
    b. offer employees raises.
    c. discipline bad employees.
    d. train employees.

Inference _____c_____ 9. The reader can infer that one difference between an "office manager" and a "cheap manager" is that a "cheap manager" is more likely to

    a. allocate hours fairly.
    b. allow ample time for setting up preparations.
    c. help work on the floor.
    d. engage in endless paperwork.

Inference _____c_____ 10. The reader can conclude that a "status shield" might be considered of all the following *except*

    a. a title of vice president.
    b. a high salary plus bonus options.
    c. workplace stress.
    d. respect for a significant worker.

Answer the following with *T* (true) or *F* (false).

Inference _____F_____ 11. A major source of stress for service sector workers is cooperating with coworkers who cannot perform their jobs adequately.

Detail _____T_____ 12. Many service sector workers think customers do not understand the demanding nature of their jobs.

Inference _____F_____ 13. Managers in fast food businesses are often unwilling to train their employees.

Inference _____T_____ 14. The author implies that service workers would probably get less abuse from customers if they had more job status.

Inference _____T_____ 15. The author's view of fast food managers is primarily negative.

selection 3

Build Your Vocabulary

According to the way the italicized word is used in the selection, select *a, b, c,* or *d* for the word or phrase that gives the best definition. The number in parentheses indicates the line of the passage in which the word is located.

_____d_____ 1. *"widespread* complaint" (13)
a. limited
b. distant
c. computer-generated
d. prevalent

_____b_____ 2. *"repetitive* work" (16)
a. rare
b. repeating
c. difficult
d. easy

_____a_____ 3. *"endure* abuse" (25)
a. tolerate
b. insight
c. encourage
d. depend on

_____d_____ 4. *"displacement* of hostility" (30)
a. sharpening
b. lack
c. target
d. shifting

_____c_____ 5. *"belittling* that worker" (66)
a. overlooking
b. training
c. degrading
d. promoting

_____b_____ 6. *"skimp* on" (85)
a. plentiful
b. hold back
c. skip out
d. cheat

_____d_____ 7. *"allocating* labor hours" (85)
a. charging
b. increasing
c. decreasing
d. assigning

_____a_____ 8. "with great *frequency"* (93)
a. regularity
b. politeness
c. hardships
d. happiness

_____b_____ 9. *"instability* can be stressful" (93)
a. firmness
b. unsteadiness
c. watchfulness
d. screaming

_____d_____ 10. *"rabid* employer determination" (102)
a. moderate
b. unfortunate
c. faulty
d. extreme

Search the Net

Use a search engine such as Google, Yahoo, Ask.com, AltaVista, Excite, or Dogpile to find information about stress levels at different types of jobs. What jobs are considered to have the highest stress levels? For suggested Web sites and other research activities, go to http://www.ablongman.com/smith/.

The Good, the Bad, and the Ugly

Prefixes	*bene-:* "well, good"	*eu-:* "good"
	mal-: "bad, evil"	*kakos- (caco-):* "harsh, bad, ugly"

Words with *bene-:* "well, good"

During the *benediction*, the minister blessed the infant and called for all family members to be positive influences on the child's life.

- **benefaction:** a charitable donation

  The anonymous *benefaction* came just in time to prevent the foreclosure on the school for the deaf.

- **beneficial:** producing a benefit; helpful

  The week away from work proved *beneficial* to Miguel, and he returned refreshed and cheerful.

- **beneficiary:** a person or group who receives advantages; one named to receive funds or property in a will

  The lawyer's call telling Rosa she was named as a *beneficiary* in a will came as a complete surprise to her.

- **benefit:** something that causes improvement or an advantage; a public event to raise money for a charitable cause

  As a prospective new father, Charles was relieved when he became eligible for medical *benefits* at work.

- **benevolent:** expressing goodwill or kindness; charitable; set up to do charitable works

  The *Benevolent* Women's Society set a priority of addressing the needs of the elderly in the community.

- **benefactor:** person who gives a benefit

  The wealthy *benefactor* achieved great satisfaction from donating money to the charity.

Words with *eu-:* "good"

The *eulogy* delivered at the funeral was full of praise, befitting the benevolent character of the deceased.

- *euphony:* a pleasant-sounding combination of words

  The poem had a lilting rhythm and a harmonious *euphony* that fell like music on the ears.

- *euphoria:* a feeling of well-being, confidence, or happiness

  After winning the State Salsa Championship, Jose and his dancing partner experienced a *euphoria* that lasted for days.

- *euphemism:* a substitution of a milder word or expression for a more blunt or offensive one

  Barry expressed his condolences to the widow at the funeral by using the *euphemism* "passed away" rather than expressing sorrow that her loved one had committed suicide.

- *euthanasia:* putting to death painlessly or allowing to die; mercy killing

  Dr. Jack Kevorkian is well known as an advocate of *euthanasia* for patients who are terminally ill and request his services.

- *eureka:* an exclamation of triumph at a discovery, meaning, "I have found it!"

  Archimedes exclaimed, "*Eureka!*" when he discovered a test for the purity of gold.

Words with *mal-:* "bad, evil"

After being confronted, Marie realized the pain she had caused Janice by continuing to *malign* her in public about a previous boyfriend.

- *maladroit:* lacking resourcefulness; awkward; not skillful in using the hands or body

  Because of his *maladroit* sawing and hammering, Jules wasn't going to sign up for the furniture-making class.

- *malady:* a sickness or disorder of the body; an unhealthy condition

  Some of the volunteers working in the impoverished country had come down with an unidentified *malady*.

- *malaise:* general weakness or discomfort usually before the onset of a disease

  Emily canceled her long-anticipated trip due to her general feelings of *malaise* for the past several days.

- *malapropism:* an amusing misuse of words that produces an inappropriate meaning

  After asking the waiter to bring the soap du jour, John was embarrassed to have made such a *malapropism*.

- *malcontent:* someone unsatisfied with current conditions

  Numerous *malcontents* were protesting outside the school about the hiring of the famous professor.

- *malevolent:* wishing evil or harm to others; injurious

  Georgia had *malevolent* feelings toward the girls on the newly selected cheer-leading squad and wished one of them would break a leg.

- *malfeasance:* misconduct or wrongdoing, especially by a public official

  Some voters feel that Bill Clinton committed the greatest *malfeasance* in office of any elected official—lying to the American people; others feel he committed a crime—lying under oath.

- *malfunction:* fail to function properly

  Although it worked well at the store, the computer *malfunctioned* when we got it home and set it up.

Words with *kakos- (caco-):* "harsh, bad, ugly"

- *cacophony:* a harsh, jarring sound; a discordant and meaningless mixture of sound

  The toddler's attempt to play an improvised drum set of pots, pans, and spoons created such a *cacophony* that her father required earplugs.

- *cacography:* bad handwriting; poor spelling

  His sister's beautiful calligraphy was in stark contrast to Mark's messy *cacography.*

REVIEW

Part I

Indicate whether the italicized word in each of the following sentences is used correctly (C) or incorrectly (I).

_____(C)_____ 1. *Malevolent* thoughts can occasionally lead to equally harmful actions.

_____(C)_____ 2. Some smokers consider a proposed law banning all smoking in public places to be pressure from nonsmoking *malcontents.*

_____(I)_____ 3. Upper class women of past centuries were often referred to as *malady* by members of lower social classes.

_____(C)_____ 4. Runners frequently claim to experience a state of *euphoria* in what is known as a "runner's high."

_____(I)_____ 5. Repeated *benevolent* acts may need to be corrected by counseling or behavior modification.

_____(C)_____ 6. Donations to the shelter were given at the *benefit* for feeding the homeless.

_____(C)_____ 7. Belonging to a campus organization can be *beneficial* for students who would like to expand their circle of friends.

_____(C)_____ 8. Tom blamed the poorly cooked meal on a *malfunctioning* oven.

_____(I)_____ 9. The noisy *cacography* of crows flying overhead caused people in the street to look up in amazement.

_____(I)_____ 10. An inspirational and touching *benefaction* was offered at the start of the wedding ceremony.

Part II

Choose the best synonym from the boxed list for the words below.

eulogy	maladroit	malaise	cacophony	malfeasance
malign	euthanasia	eureka	euphemism	malevolent

11. evil _____malevolent_____   16. awkward _____maladroit_____

12. harsh sound _____cacophony_____   17. death out of mercy _____euthanasia_____

13. substitute expression _____euphemism_____   18. weakness _____malaise_____

14. wrongdoing _____malfeasance_____   19. tribute _____eulogy_____

15. exclamation of discovery _____eureka_____   20. slander _____malign_____

4 Main Idea

- What is the difference between a topic and a main idea?
- What are the strategies for finding stated and unstated main ideas?
- What are the functions of major and minor supporting details?
- What is a summary?

Ford Smith, *Warm Embrace*, 2006. An original painting in acrylics on canvas, 30 × 30 inches.

What Is a Topic?

In this chapter we will discuss and practice what many experts believe is the most important reading skill and the key to comprehension: recognizing the main idea of a paragraph, passage, or selection. As you read—and regardless of what you are reading, whether it is a chapter from your history text or an article in the Sunday paper—it is important to answer the question "What's the point?" However, before attempting to discover the central point of a piece of writing, you must have a good sense of its topic.

A **topic** is like the title of a book or song. It is a word, name, or phrase that labels the subject but does not reveal the specific contents of the passage. Take a moment and flip back to the Table of Contents of this text. As you can see, the title of each chapter reflects its general topic. What's more, boldface heads within a chapter reflect subordinate topics, or subtopics. Similarly, individual passages beneath those heads have their own topics.

Think of the topic of a passage as a big umbrella under which specific ideas or details can be grouped. For example, consider the words *carrots, lettuce, onions,* and *potatoes.* What general term would pull together and unify these items?

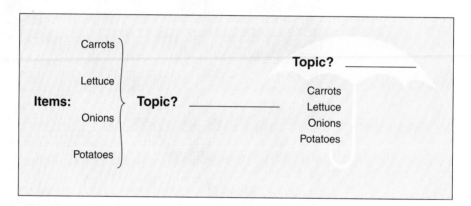

Topic: Vegetables

---

exercise 4.1 **Identifying Topics**

Each of the following lists includes three specific items or ideas that could relate to a single topic. At the top of each list, write a general topic under which the specific ideas can be grouped.

1. Potatoes
   french fried
   au gratin
   scalloped

2. Flowers
   tulip
   rose
   daisy

3. Dogs
   Poodle
   Schnauzer
   terrier

4. Precipitation
   snow
   rain
   sleet

5. Races
   triathlon
   5K
   marathon

What Is a Main Idea?

Using the topic as an initial indicator, the **main idea** of a passage becomes more focused and is the central message that the author is trying to convey about the material. It is a sentence that condenses thoughts and details into a general, all-inclusive statement of the author's point.

Reading specialists use various terms when referring to the main idea. In classroom discussions, a variety of words are used to help students understand its meaning. How many of these have you heard?

Main point

Central focus

Gist

Controlling idea

Central thought

Thesis

The last word on the list, *thesis*, is a familiar word in English composition classes. You have probably had practice in stating a thesis sentence for English essays, but you may not have had as much practice in stating the main idea of a reading selection. Can you see the similarity between a thesis and a main idea statement?

How important is it to be able to find and comprehend the main idea? Experts say that it is *crucial to your comprehension of any text*. In fact, if all reading comprehension techniques were combined and reduced to one essential question, that question might be "What is the main idea the author is trying to get across to the reader?" Whether you read a single paragraph, a chapter, or an entire book, your most important single task is to understand the main idea of what you read.

What Are Supporting Details?

Details are statements that support, develop, and explain a main idea. Specific details can include reasons, incidents, facts, examples, steps, and definitions.

There are important differences between *major details*, which are critical to the support of the main idea and your understanding of a passage, and *minor details*, which amplify the major details. One way to distinguish the two is to pay attention to signal words, which link thoughts and help you anticipate the kind of detail that is coming next. Key signal words for major supporting details are *one, first, another, furthermore, also,* and *finally*. Key signal words for minor details are *for example, to be specific, that is,* and *this means*. We will deepen our discussion of major and minor details later in this chapter.

Distinguishing Topics, Main Ideas, and Details: A Closer Look

We have seen that a topic is a general category, and that a main idea is the author's central message about the topic. Let's explore the difference between them—and the importance of supporting details—a little more closely.

Caffeine is a general term or topic that unifies the items *coffee, tea, cola,* and *chocolate*. If those items were used as details in a paragraph, the main idea could not be expressed by simply saying "caffeine." The word *caffeine* would answer the question, "What is the passage about?" However, only your evaluation of the supporting details in the paragraph would answer the question, "What is the author's main idea?"

Think of some of the very different paragraphs about caffeine that a writer could devise using the same four details as support. If you were that writer, what would be the main idea or thesis—using the four items as details—of your paragraph?

Topic: Caffeine

Main idea or thesis: _____

_____

EXAMPLE Read the following examples of different main ideas that could be developed in a paragraph about the topic of caffeine. Explanations appear in italicized type.

1. Consumption of caffeine is not good for your health. (*Details would enumerate health hazards associated with each item.*)
2. Americans annually consume astonishing amounts of caffeine. (*Details would describe amounts of each consumed annually.*)
3. Caffeine makes money as the Starbucks star rises. (*Details would show the profits and expansion of the coffee giant.*)
4. Reduce caffeine consumption with the decaffeinated version of popular caffeine-containing beverages. (*Details would promote the decaffeinated version of each item.*)

EXAMPLE Following are examples of a topic, main idea, and supporting detail.

Topic **EARLY COGNITIVE DEVELOPMENT**

Main Idea ⌐Cognitive psychologists sometimes study young children to observe the very beginnings of cognitive activity. For example, when children first begin to utter words and

Detail ⌐sentences, they overgeneralize what they know and make language more consistent than it actually is.

—Christopher Peterson,
Introduction to Psychology

EXPLANATION The topic pulls your attention to a general area, and the main idea provides the focus. The detail offers elaboration and support.

exercise 4.2 **Differentiating Topic, Main Idea, and Supporting Details**

This exercise is designed to check your ability to differentiate statements of the main idea from the topic and supporting details. Compare the items within each group, and indicate whether each one is a statement of the main idea *(MI)*, a topic *(T)*, or a specific supporting detail *(SD)*.

Group 1

_MI_ a. For poor farm families, life on the plains meant a sod house or a dugout carved out of the hillside for protection from the winds.

_SD_ b. One door and usually no more than a single window provided light and air.

_T_ c. Sod Houses on the Plains

—James W. Davidson et al.,
Nation of Nations

Group 2

_SD_ a. She was the daughter of English poet Lord Byron and of a mother who was a gifted mathematician.

_T_ b. Babbage and the Programming Countess

_MI_ c. Ada, the Countess of Lovelace, helped develop the instructions for doing computer programming computations on Babbage's analytical engine.

_SD_ d. In addition, she published a series of notes that eventually led others to accomplish what Babbage himself had been unable to do.

—Adapted from H. L. Capron,
Computers: Tools for an Information Age, 6th ed.

Group 3

_SD_ a. Fabiola Garcia worked at a 7-Eleven evenings and swing shifts, learning all aspects of the business as part of the screening and training process for prospective 7-Eleven franchise owners.

_T_ b. Evaluating a Franchising Opportunity

_MI_ c. One of the best ways to evaluate a prospective franchisor is to spend a few months working for someone who already owns a franchise you're interested in.

_SD_ d. Fabiola also worked at headquarters to learn the franchisor's paperwork procedures.

—Adapted from Michael Mescon et al.,
Business Today, 10th ed.

Group 4

_T_ a. Mexican American Political Gains

_SD_ b. During the 1960s, four Mexican Americans—Senator Joseph Montoya of New Mexico and Representatives Eligio de la Garza and Henry B. Gonzales of Texas and Edward R. Roybal of California—were elected to Congress.

_____ SD _____   c. In 1974, two Chicanos were elected governors—Jerry Apodaca in New Mexico and Raul Castro in Arizona—becoming the first Mexican American governors since early in this century.

_____ MI _____   d. Since 1960, Mexican Americans have made important political gains.

—James Kirby Martin et al.,
America and Its Peoples, vol. 2, 4th ed.

Group 5

_____ MI _____   a. Increased contact does reduce prejudice, particularly under certain conditions such as when working toward a shared goal.

_____ SD _____   b. For example, politically influential members of Israeli and Palestinian groups met informally for intense problem solving.

_____ T _____   c. Reducing Prejudice Through Contact

_____ SD _____   d. The meetings, although not designed to reduce prejudice, nonetheless fulfilled one of the steps in that direction.

—Adapted from Stephen Kosslyn and Robin Rosenberg,
Psychology, 2nd ed.

Prior Knowledge and Constructing the Main Idea

How exactly do you figure out the main idea of a paragraph or passage? Researchers have investigated the processes readers use to construct main ideas. One researcher, Peter Afflerbach, asked graduate students and university professors to "think aloud" as they read passages on both familiar and unfamiliar topics.[1] These expert readers spoke their thoughts to the researcher before, during, and after reading. From these investigations, Afflerbach concluded that expert readers use different strategies for familiar and unfamiliar materials.

Here is the important finding: This research showed that *already knowing something about the topic is the key* to easy reading. When readers are familiar with the subject, constructing the main idea is effortless and, in many cases, automatic. These readers quickly assimilate the unfolding text into already well developed knowledge networks. They seem to organize text into chunks for comprehension and later retrieval. These "informed" readers do not have to struggle with information overload. Again, this shows that the rich get richer, and the initial struggle to build knowledge has many benefits.

By contrast, expert readers with little prior knowledge of the subject are absorbed in trying to make meaning out of unfamiliar words and confusing sentences. Because they are struggling to recognize ideas, few mental resources remain

-----

[1] P. Afflerbach, "How Are Main Idea Statements Constructed? Watch the Experts!," *Journal of Reading* 30 (1987): 512–18; and "The Influence of Prior Knowledge on Expert Readers' Main Idea Construction Strategies," *Reading Research Quarterly* 25 (1990): 31–46.

for constructing a main idea. These "uninformed" experts are reluctant to guess at a main idea and to predict a topic. Instead, they prefer to read all the information before trying to make sense of it. Constructing the main idea is a difficult and deliberate task for these expert but uninformed readers. Even a proven expert reader in history, for example, might struggle to read chemistry books until enough knowledge is built for main idea construction to be automatic.

Strategies for Finding the Main Idea

The following strategies for getting the main idea were reported by Afflerbach's expert readers. Can you see the differences in the thinking processes of the informed and uninformed experts?

"Informed" Expert Readers

Strategy 1. The informed expert readers skimmed the passage before reading and took a guess at the main idea. Then they read for corroboration.

Strategy 2. The informed experts automatically paused while reading to summarize or condense information. They stopped at natural breaks in the material to let ideas fall into place.

"Uninformed" Expert Readers

Strategy 1. Expert readers who did not know about the subject were unwilling to take a guess at the main idea. Instead, they read the material, determined the topic, and then looked back to pull together a main idea statement.

Strategy 2. The uninformed experts read the material and reviewed it to find key terms and concepts. They tried to bring the key terms and concepts together into a main idea statement.

Strategy 3. The uninformed experts read the material and then proposed a main idea statement. They double-checked the passage to clarify or revise the main idea statement.

What differences do you see between these approaches? Since introductory college textbooks address many topics that are new and unfamiliar, freshmen readers will frequently need to use the strategies of uninformed expert readers to comprehend the main ideas of their college texts. Until you build up your reserves of prior knowledge through the college courses you take, constructing main ideas for course textbooks is likely to be a *conscious effort* rather than an automatic phenomenon.

Main Ideas in Sentences

Before identifying main ideas in paragraphs, practice with a simple list of sentences. Read the sentences in the following group. They are related to a single topic, with one sentence expressing a main idea and two other sentences expressing detailed support. Circle the number of the sentence that best expresses the main idea, and write the general topic for the group.

EXAMPLE
1. The 1960 debate between John Kennedy and Richard Nixon boosted Kennedy's campaign and elevated the role of television in national politics.
2. Televised presidential debates are a major feature of presidential elections.
3. Ronald Reagan's performance in 1980 and 1984 debates confirmed the public view of him as decent, warm, and dignified.

Topic: *importance of televised presidential debates*

—Adapted from James MacGregor Burns et al.,
Government by the People, 20th ed.

EXPLANATION The second sentence best expresses the main idea, declaring the importance of televised presidential debates. The other two sentences are details offering specific facts in support of the topic, which is the importance of televised presidential debates.

exercise 4.3 **Discovering Topics and Main Ideas in Sentence Groups**

Circle the number of the sentence that best expresses the general main idea, and write the general topic.

Group 1

1. Dentists are trying virtual reality headsets for their patients to help reduce anxiety about dental care.

2. Gradual exposure to takeoff and landing in a virtual environment allows would-be travelers to face their phobias and prepare to take the next step, a real flight.

(3.) Overcoming fear is a fast-growing application of virtual reality.

4. Topic: *Virtual Reality in Conquering Fear*

—Alan Evans et al.,
Technology in Action, 2nd ed.

Group 2

1. Men hunted, fished, and cleared land, but women controlled the cultivation, harvest, and distribution of crops, supplying probably three-quarters of their family's nutritional needs.

(2.) The role of women in the tribal economy reinforced the sharing of power between male and female.

3. When the men were away hunting, the women directed village life.

4. Topic: *Power Sharing in Tribal Economies*

—Gary B. Nash et al.,
The American People: Creating a Nation and a Society, 6th ed., vol. 1: To 1877

Group 3

(1.) At present, the meaning of correlations between brain size and intelligence is not clear.

2. For example, females have about the same average intelligence as males, but generally have smaller brains.

3. The Neanderthals had larger brains than we do, but there is no evidence that they were smarter.

4. Topic: Relationship between Brain Size and Intelligence

—Adapted from Stephen M. Kosslyn and Robin S. Rosenberg,
Psychology: The Brain, the Person, the World, 2nd ed.

Group 4

(1.) Relying on his extensive industry experience, JetBlue founder and CEO David Neeleman focused most of his energy on a few key factors that he felt would make or break his company.

2. JetBlue fills planes to capacity, gets more flying hours out of each aircraft, and saves on maintenance costs because its fleet is brand new.

3. By hiring younger, more productive workers and giving them stock options in lieu of high wages, JetBlue keeps labor expenses down to 25 percent of revenues (compared to Southwest's 33 percent and Delta's 44 percent).

4. Topic: Factors in JetBlue's Success

—Adapted from Ricky W. Griffin and Ronald J. Ebert,
Business, 8th ed.

Group 5

1. Despite its rapid growth, the company has no public relations department, no human resources department, and no recruiting apparatus.

(2.) The founders of Outback Steakhouse have proved that unconventional methods can lead to profitable results.

3. Methods include opening solely for dinner, sacrificing dining-room seats for back-of-the-house efficiency, limiting servers to three tables each, and handing 10 percent of the cash flow to the restaurants' general managers.

4. Topic: Outback's Unconventional Approach to Success

—Adapted from John R. Walker,
Introduction to Hospitality, 4th ed.

Questioning for the Main Idea

To determine the main idea of a paragraph, article, or book, follow the three basic steps shown in the box below, and ask the questions posed in the Reader's Tip on page 159. The order of the steps may vary depending on your prior knowledge of the material. If you are familiar with the material, you might find that constructing the main idea is automatic and you can select significant supporting details afterward. If you are unfamiliar with the material, as may often be the case in textbook reading, you would need to identify the details through key terms and concepts first, and from them you would form a topic and a main idea statement.

Routes to the Main Idea

For Familiar Material

Determine topic ▶ ▶ ▶ Identify key terms ▶ ▶ ▶ Find main idea

For Unfamiliar Material

Identify key terms ▶ ▶ ▶ Determine topic ▶ ▶ ▶ Find main idea

---

Stated Main Ideas

Like paragraphs, visual images also suggest main ideas. Photographers and artists compose and select images to communicate a message. Look at the picture shown below and then answer the questions that follow.

National Fluid Milk Processor Promotion Board

What is the general topic of the photograph? _____

_____

What details seem important? _____

_____

What is the main idea the photographer is trying to convey about the topic? _____

_____

_____

_____

    The topic of the picture is drinking milk. The details show football player Donovan McNabb holding a glass of it. From the white moustache on his upper lip, the viewer assumes that he has just had a sip of the beverage. Though the details are sparse, the viewer can spot references to McNabb's profession in the words on the poster, not to mention the padding he is wearing. The viewer can reason that McNabb is likely to drink milk to stay healthy, thus leading to peak performance in his sport. The main idea, "Drink milk to perform your best," is indirectly stated in the words under the photograph. The message is persuasive: We should imitate this noted athlete and take some time to drink a glass of milk.

Reader's *Tip*   Using Questions to Find the Main Idea

1. **Determine the topic.** *Who or what is this reading about?*
   Find a general word or phrase that names the subject. The topic should be broad enough to include all the ideas, yet restrictive enough to focus on the direction of the details. For example, the topic of an article might be correctly identified as Politics, Federal Politics, or Corruption in Federal Politics, but the last might be the most descriptive of the actual contents.
2. **Identify details.** *What are the major supporting details?*
   Look at the details and key terms that seem to be significant to see if they point in a particular direction. What aspect of the topic do they address? What seems to be the common message? Details such as kickbacks to senators, overspending on congressional junkets, and lying to the voters could support the idea of corruption in federal politics.
3. **Find the main idea.** *What is the message the author is trying to convey about the topic?*
   The statement of the main idea should be
   A complete sentence
   Broad enough to include the important details
   Focused enough to describe the author's slant
   The author's main idea about corruption in federal politics might be that voters need to ask for an investigation of seemingly corrupt practices by federal politicians.

The Topic Sentence

As in the photo, an author's main point can be directly stated in the material. When the main idea is stated in a sentence, the statement is called a **topic sentence** or **thesis statement**. Such a general statement is helpful to the reader because it provides an overview of the material.

Read the following examples and answer the questions for determining the main idea using the three-question technique.

EXAMPLE

Managers can regain control over their time in several ways. One is by meeting whenever possible in someone else's office, so that they can leave as soon as their business is finished. Another is to start meetings on time without waiting for late-comers. The idea is to let late-comers adjust their schedules rather than everyone else adjusting theirs. A third is to set aside a block of time to work on an important project without interruption. This may require ignoring the telephone, being protected by an aggressive secretary, or hiding out. Whatever it takes is worth it.

—Joseph Reitz and Linda Jewell,
Managing

1. Who or what is this passage about? _____

   _____

2. What are the major details? _____

   _____

   _____

3. What is the main idea the authors are trying to convey about the topic? _____

   _____

   _____

   _____

EXPLANATION   The passage is about managers controlling their time. The major details are *meet in another office, start meetings on time,* and *block out time to work.* The main idea, stated in the beginning as a topic sentence, is that managers can do things to control their time.

EXAMPLE

New high-speed machines also brought danger to the workplace. If a worker succumbed to boredom, fatigue, or simple miscalculation, disaster could strike. Each year of the late nineteenth century some 35,000 wage earners were killed by industrial accidents. In Pittsburgh iron and steel mills alone, in one year 195 men died from hot metal explosions, asphyxiation, and falls, some into pits of molten metal. Men and women working in textile mills were poisoned by the thick dust and fibers in the air; similar toxic atmospheres injured those working in anything from twine-making plants to embroidery factories. Railways, with their heavy equipment and unaccustomed speed, were especially dangerous. In Philadelphia over half the railroad workers who died between 1886 and 1890 were killed by accidents. For injury or death, workers and their families could expect no payment from employers, since the idea of worker's compensation was unknown.

—James W. Davidson et al.,
Nation of Nations

1. Who or what is this passage about? _____

_____

2. What are the major details? _____

_____

_____

3. What is the main idea the author is trying to convey about the topic? _____

_____

_____

_____

EXPLANATION The passage is about injuries from machines. The major details are *35,000 killed, 195 died from explosions and other accidents in iron and steel mills, poisoned dust killed workers in textile mills, and half of the rail workers who died were killed in accidents.* The main idea is that new high-speed machines brought danger to the workplace.

How Common Are Stated Main Ideas?

Research shows that students find passages easier to comprehend when the main idea is directly stated within the passage. How often do stated main ideas appear in college textbooks? Should the reader expect to find that most paragraphs have stated main ideas?

For psychology texts, the answer seems to be about half and half. One research study found that stated main ideas appeared in *only 58 percent* of the sampled paragraphs in introductory psychology textbooks.[2] In one of the books, the main idea was directly stated in 81 percent of the sampled paragraphs, and the researchers noted that the text was particularly easy to read.

Given these findings, we should recognize the importance of being skilled in locating and, especially, in constructing main ideas. In pulling ideas together to construct a main idea, you will be looking at the big picture and not left searching for a single suggestive sentence.

Where Are Stated Main Ideas Located?

Should college readers wish for all passages in all textbooks to begin with stated main ideas? Indeed, research indicates that when the main idea is stated at the beginning of the passage, the text tends to be comprehended more easily. In their

---

[2]B. Smith and N. Chase, "The Frequency and Placement of Main Idea Topic Sentences in College Psychology Textbooks," *Journal of College Reading and Learning* 24 (1991): 46–54.

research, however, Smith and Chase found only 33 percent of the stated main ideas to be positioned as the first sentence of the paragraph.

Main idea statements can be positioned at the beginning, in the middle, or at the end of a paragraph. Both the beginning and concluding sentences of a passage can be combined to form a main idea statement.

exercise 4.4 **Locating Stated Main Ideas**

The following diagrams and examples demonstrate the different possible positions for stated main ideas within paragraphs. Make notations as you read the examples, and then insert the main ideas and supporting details into the blank spaces provided beside the geometric diagrams.

1. **An introductory statement of the main idea is given at the beginning of the paragraph.**

EXAMPLE

Under hypnosis, people may recall things that they are unable to remember spontaneously. Some police departments employ hypnotists to probe for information that crime victims do not realize they have. In 1976, twenty-six young children were kidnapped from a school bus near Chowchilla, California. The driver of the bus caught a quick glimpse of the license plate of the van in which he and the children were driven away. However, he remembered only the first two digits. Under hypnosis, he recalled the other numbers and the van was traced to its owners.

—David Dempsey and Philip Zimbardo,
Psychology and You

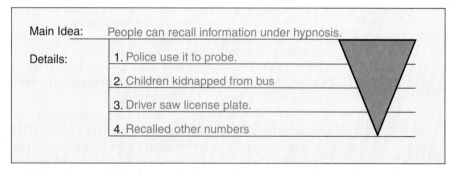

Main Idea: People can recall information under hypnosis.

Details:
1. Police use it to probe.
2. Children kidnapped from bus
3. Driver saw license plate.
4. Recalled other numbers

2. **A concluding statement of the main idea appears at the end of the paragraph.**

EXAMPLE

Research is not a once-and-for-all-times job. Even sophisticated companies often waste the value of their research. One of the most common errors is not providing a basis for comparisons. A company may research its market, find a need for a new advertising campaign, conduct the campaign, and then neglect to research the results. Another may simply feel the need for a new campaign, conduct it, and research the results. Neither is getting the full benefit of the research. When you fail to research either the results or your position *prior* to the campaign, you cannot know the effects of the campaign. For good evaluation you must have both before and after data.

—Edward Fox and Edward Wheatley,
Modern Marketing

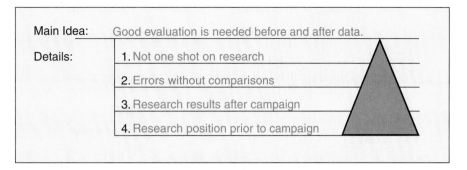

3. Details are placed at the beginning to arouse interest, followed by a statement of the main idea in the middle of the paragraph.

EXAMPLE

After losing $1 billion in Euro-Disney's first year of operation, the company realized that Paris was not Anaheim or Orlando. French employees were insulted by the Disney dress code, and European customers were not accustomed to standing in line for rides or eating fast food standing up. Disney had to adjust and customize its market mix after learning that international customers are not all alike. The company ditched its controversial dress code, authorized wine with meals, lowered admission prices, hired a French investor relations firm, and changed the name to Disneyland Paris to lure the French tourist.

—Adapted from Michael Mescon et al.,
Business Today, 8th ed.

4. Both the introductory and concluding sentences state the main idea.

EXAMPLE

You cannot avoid conflict but you can learn to face it with a four-step conflict resolution plan. Before you bring up the issue that's upsetting you, know what you want to achieve. Have a positive outcome in mind. Then listen to what the other side says, but go beyond that to try to understand as well. Express empathy for their position. It may not be easy, but try to see the big picture. Place the conflict in context. Finally, if at all possible, end your discussion on a positive note. Set the stage for further discussion by keeping those lines of communication open. Use these four strategies for handling tensions constructively and enjoy stronger social bonds.

—Adapted from Rebecca Donatelle,
Access to Health, 8th ed.

Main Idea:	Use conflict resolution strategies
Details:	1. Envision outcome
	2. Listen to other side
	3. Place in context
	4. Leave lines open for talk
Main Idea:	Use these four strategies

5. Details combine to make a point, but the main idea is not directly stated.

EXAMPLE

This creature's career could produce but one result, and it speedily followed. Boy after boy managed to get on the river. The minister's son became an engineer. The doctor's sons became "mud clerks"; the wholesale liquor dealer's son became a bar-keeper on a boat; four sons of the chief merchant, and two sons of the county judge, became pilots. Pilot was the grandest position of all. The pilot, even in those days of trivial wages, had a princely salary—from a hundred and fifty to two hundred and fifty dollars a month, and no board to pay. Two months of his wages would pay a preacher's salary for a year. Now some of us were left disconsolate. We could not get on the river—at least our parents would not let us.

—Mark Twain,
Life on the Mississippi

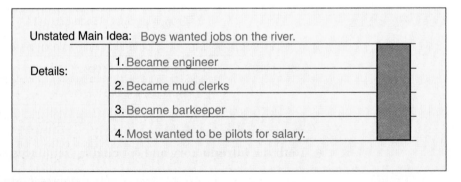

Unstated Main Idea:	Boys wanted jobs on the river.
Details:	1. Became engineer
	2. Became mud clerks
	3. Became barkeeper
	4. Most wanted to be pilots for salary.

EXPLANATION   Although not directly stated, the main idea is that young boys in the area have a strong desire to leave home and get a prestigious job on the Mississippi River.

exercise 4.5   **Using Questions to Find Stated Main Ideas**

Read the following passages, and use the three-question system to determine the author's main idea. For each passage in this exercise, the answer to the third question will be stated somewhere within the paragraph.

Passage A

The concept and practice of group harmony or *wa* is what most dramatically differentiates Japanese baseball from the American game. Contract holdouts for additional money, for example, are rare in Japan. A player usually takes what the club decides to give him, and that's that. Demanding more money is evidence that a player is putting his own interests before those of the team. Temper tantrums—along with practical joking, bickering, complaining, and other norms of American clubhouse life—are viewed in Japan as unwelcome intrusions into the team's collective peace of mind.

—Robert Whiting,
You Gotta Have Wa

1. Who or what is this about? Baseball in Japan vs. baseball in the U.S.A.

_____

_____

2. What are the major details? Holdouts are rare in Japan; players put team

interests before their own; actions that take away from team peace

are unwelcome.

_____

3. What is the main idea the author is trying to convey about the topic? _____

The practice of group harmony makes Japanese baseball quite different

from American baseball.

_____

4. Underline the main idea.

Passage B

Child labor is in great demand for several reasons. Children are more docile than adults, easier to discipline, and more often too frightened to complain. Their small frames and nimble fingers are considered an asset for certain kinds of work. Although only 7 to 10 years old, they are forced to work 12 to 14 hours a day. Most important, child labor is quite cheap; children are generally paid less than one-third of the adult wage. Not surprisingly, when children are given jobs, their parents may lose theirs.

—Adapted from Alex Thio,
Sociology: A Brief Introduction, 6th ed.

1. Who or what is this about? Reasons for child labor demand

_____

_____

2. What are the major details? <u>Children more docile than adults; easier to</u> <u>discipline, too frightened to complain; small bodies and quick fingers</u> <u>preferred for some work; 7- to 10-year-olds forced to work 12–14 hours daily;</u> <u>wages one-third of adult pay</u>

3. What is the main idea the author is trying to convey about the topic? _____ <u>Child labor is in great demand for several reasons.</u>

_____

_____

4. Underline the main idea.

Passage C

The participants were male college students. Each student, placed in a room by himself with an intercom, was led to believe that he was communicating with one or more students in an adjacent room. During the course of a discussion about personal problems, he heard what sounded like one of the other students having an epileptic seizure and gasping for help. During the "seizure," it was impossible for the participant to talk to the other students or to find out what, if anything, they were doing about the emergency. The dependent variable was the speed with which the participant reported the emergency to the experimenter. <u>The likelihood of intervention depended on the number of bystanders the participant thought were present.</u> The more people he thought were present, the slower he was in reporting the seizure, if he did so at all. Everyone in a two-person situation intervened within 160 seconds, but nearly 40 percent of those who believed they were part of a larger group never bothered to inform the experimenter that another student was seriously ill.

—Richard Gerrig and Philip Zimbardo,
Psychology and Life, 17th ed.

1. Who or what is this about? <u>Factors influencing whether or not people help</u> <u>others</u>

_____

2. What are the major details? <u>Experiment with college males; student in other</u> <u>room faked seizure; speed with which participant reported emergency</u> <u>measured; two-person groups quickest to intervene</u>

_____

3. What is the main idea the authors are trying to convey about the topic? _____ <u>The likelihood of intervention depended on the number of bystanders the</u> <u>participant thought were present.</u>

_____

4. Underline the main idea.

Passage D

Research has shown that girls and boys learn to use language differently in their sex-separate peer groups. Typically, a girl has a best friend with whom she sits and talks, frequently telling secrets. It's the telling of secrets, the fact and the way that they talk to each other, that makes them best friends. For boys, activities are central: their best friends are the ones they do things with. Boys also tend to play in larger groups that are hierarchical. High-status boys give orders and push low-status boys around. So boys are expected to use language to seize center stage: by exhibiting their skill, displaying their knowledge, and challenging and resisting challenges.

—Adapted from Deborah Tannen,
"How Male and Female Students Use Language Differently,"
The Chronicle of Higher Education, June 19, 1991.

1. Who or what is this about? Language use of boys and girls

2. What are the major details? Talking is central to female friendship; activities are central to male friendship; boys play in larger, hierarchical groups; boys use language to achieve center stage and establish rank.

3. What is the main idea the author is trying to convey about the topic? Girls and boys use language differently in their sex-separate peer groups.

4. Underline the main idea.

Passage E

The gulf separating people in Europe and North America was shaped not only by their cultures but also by the way they viewed the environment. Regarding the earth as filled with resources for man to use and exploit for human benefit, Europeans gained confidence that they could comprehend the natural world—and therefore eventually control it. For Native Americans, however, every aspect of the natural world was sacred. If one overfished or destroyed game beyond one's needs, the spirit forces in fish or animals would take revenge, because humans had broken the mutual trust that governed relations between all beings—human or nonhuman.

—Gary B. Nash et al.,
The American People: Creating a Nation and a Society,
6th ed., vol. 1: To 1877

1. Who or what is this about? How colonial Europeans and Native Americans viewed the environment

2. What are the major details? Europeans looked at nature as something to be controlled; Native Americans looked at nature as sacred

3. What is the main idea the author is trying to convey about the topic? The different ways in which the Europeans and Native Americans regarded their environment separated them.

4. Underline the main idea.

Passage F

The conquistadores were brave and imaginative men. It must not, however, be forgotten that they wrenched their empire from innocent hands. The settlement of the New World ranks among the most flagrant examples of unprovoked aggression in human history. When Columbus landed on San Salvador he planted a cross, "as a sign," he explained to Ferdinand and Isabella, "that your Highnesses held this land as your own." Of the Lucayans, the native inhabitants of San Salvador, Columbus wrote: "The people of this island . . . are artless and generous with what they have, to such a degree as no one would believe . . . If it be asked for, they never say no, but rather invite the person to accept it, and show as much lovingness as though they would give their hearts."

—Mark C. Carnes and John A. Garraty,
The American Nation: A History of the United States to 1877, 12th ed.

1. Who or what is this about? European aggression in settling the New World

2. What are the major details? New land taken from innocent victims; cross placed on San Salvador to claim it for Spain; generous nature of the native people

3. What is the main idea the authors are trying to convey? The settlement of the New World involved unprovoked aggression.

4. Underline the main idea.

What Are Major and Minor Details?

Textbooks are packed full of details, but fortunately all details are not of equal importance. Major details tend to support, explain, and describe main ideas—they are essential. Minor details, by contrast, tend to support, explain, and describe the major details. Ask the following questions to determine which details are major in importance and which are not:

1. Which details logically develop the main idea?
2. Which details help you understand the main idea?
3. Which details make you think the main idea you have chosen is correct?

Key signal words, like those listed in the Reader's Tip, form transitional links among ideas and can sometimes help you distinguish between major and minor details.

Reader's 𝒯ip   Signals for Significance

- Key words for major details:
  one   first   another   furthermore   also   finally

- Key words for minor details:
  for example   to be specific   that is   this means

EXAMPLE

Selena was the undisputed queen of Tejano, the music of the Texas-Mexico border. Her music epitomized the complexity of the border culture. Tejano music originated in the nineteenth century, when European immigrants introduced the accordion to the Texas-Mexico border. A fast-paced blend of Latin pop, German polka, and country rhythms, Tejano music combined the oompah music of Europeans with Mexican ballads known as *cumbias* and *rancheras*. Unlike many earlier Latina personalities, like Rita Hayworth and Raquel Welch, who gained their fame only after changing their names and projecting an exotic and sexy image, Selena never abandoned her Mexican American identity. Selena, who was 23 years old when she was slain, nevertheless achieved extraordinary popularity.

—Adapted from James Kirby Martin et al.,
America and Its Peoples, vol. 2, 5th ed.

1. The topic of the passage is
   a. Selena was slain.
   b. Tejano Music.
   c. Queen of Tejano Music.
   d. Mexican Ballads.

2. Indicate whether each of the following details is major or minor in support of the author's topic:

   a. Selena was true to her Mexican American identity.
   b. Raquel Welch changed her name.
   c. Selena was popular when she was slain at 23.

3. Underline the sentence that best states the main idea of this passage.

EXPLANATION For the first response, the topic of the passage is *c*. Both *b* and *d* are too broad and *a* is an unfortunate detail. For the second item, *a* is a major detail because her music is Tejano, *b* is a minor detail not directly related to Selena, and *c* is a major detail because she is no longer living. The first sentence states the main idea.

exercise 4.6   **Identifying Topics, Stated Main Ideas, and Details in Passages**

Read the following passages and apply the three-question system. Select the letter of the author's topic, identify major and minor details, and underline the main idea. For each passage in this exercise, the answer to the third question will be stated somewhere within the paragraph.

Passage A

Experts agree that the crux of Brazil's disastrous prison situation is rooted in overcrowding. Many prisons have two to five times the number of inmates they were designed to hold. A Human Rights Watch/Americas inspection team discovered that single-person cells contained eight to ten prisoners, with some inmates tied to windows to reduce demand for floor space. While some slept in hammocks suspended from the ceiling, others were forced to lie on top of hole-in-the floor toilets.

—Adapted from Steven Barkan and George Bryjak,
Fundamentals of Criminal Justice

_____b_____ 1. The topic of the passage is

   a. Human Rights Watch in Brazil
   b. Brazil's Prisons Overcrowded
   c. More Inspections Needed in Brazil
   d. Sleeping in Hammocks in Brazil

2. Indicate whether each of the following details is major or minor in support of the author's topic:

   Major a. Many prisons operate at two to five times capacity.

   Minor b. A Human Rights Watch team inspected prisons in Brazil.

   Major c. Single-person cells contained eight to ten prisoners.

3. Underline the sentence that best states the main idea of this passage.

Passage B

The term *vegetarian* means different things to different people. Strict vegetarians, or *vegans*, avoid all foods of animal origins, including dairy products and eggs. Far more common are *lacto-vegetarians,* who eat dairy products but avoid flesh foods. Their diets can be low in cholesterol, but only if they consume skim milk and other low- or nonfat products. **Ovo-vegetarians** add eggs to their diet, while *lacto-ovo-vegetarians* eat both dairy products and eggs. *Pesco-vegetarians* eat fish, dairy products, and eggs. Some people in the semivegetarian category prefer to call themselves "non–red meat eaters."

—Rebecca J. Donatelle,
Health: The Basics, 4th ed.

_____c_____ 1. The topic of the passage is

      a. Vegetarians Without Dairy Products.
      b. Becoming a Vegetarian.
      c. Different Vegetarian Categories.
      d. Health Issues for Vegetarians.

2. Indicate whether each of the following details is major or minor in support of the author's topic:

   Major a. Pesco-vegetarians eat fish.

   Minor b. Lacto-vegetarians have low-cholesterol diets if they consume skim milk.

   Major c. Ovo-vegetarians add eggs to their diet.

3. Underline the sentence that best states the main idea of this passage.

Passage C

Building and equipping the pyramids focused and transformed Egypt's material and human resources. Artisans had to be trained, engineering and transportation problems solved, quarrying and stone-working techniques perfected, and laborers recruited. In the Old Kingdom, whose population has been estimated at perhaps 1.5 million, more than 70,000 workers at a time were employed in building the great temple-tombs. No smaller work force could have built such a massive structure as the Great Pyramid of Khufu.

—Mark Kishlansky et al.,
Civilization in the West, 4th ed.

_____b_____ 1. The topic of the passage is

      a. Training Laborers for the Pyramids.
      b. Resources Needed for Building Pyramids.
      c. Pyramid Building Problems.
      d. The Pyramids.

2. Indicate whether each of the following details is major or minor in support of the author's topic:

    <u>Minor</u> a. The Old Kingdom had an estimated population of 1.5 million.

    <u>Major</u> b. More than 70,000 workers at a time were employed in building the great temple-tombs.

    <u>Major</u> c. Artisans had to be trained.

3. Underline the sentence that best states the main idea of this passage.

Passage D

If you're upset or tired, you're at risk for an emotion-charged confrontation. If you ambush someone with an angry attack, don't expect her or him to be in a productive frame of mind. Instead, give yourself time to cool off before you try to resolve a conflict. In the case of the group project, you could call a meeting for later in the week. By that time, you could gain control of your feelings and think things through. Of course, sometimes issues need to be discussed on the spot; you may not have the luxury to wait. But whenever it's practical, make sure your conflict partner is ready to receive you and your message. <u>Select a mutually acceptable time and place to discuss a conflict.</u>

—Adapted from Steven A. Beebe, Susan J. Beebe, and Diana K. Ivy, *Communication*

<u>a</u> 1. The topic of the passage is

    a. Planning for Conflict Resolution.
    b. Confrontation.
    c. Being Productive.
    d. Solving Problems.

2. Indicate whether each of the following details is major or minor in support of the author's topic:

    <u>Major</u> a. Give yourself time to cool off before you try to resolve a conflict.

    <u>Major</u> b. If you are upset, you are at risk for a confrontation.

    <u>Minor</u> c. Call a meeting a week later for a group project.

3. Underline the sentence that best states the main idea of this passage.

Passage E

In a Utah case, the defendant fell asleep in his car on the shoulder of the highway. Police stopped, smelled alcohol on his breath, and arrested him for driving while intoxicated. His conviction was reversed by the Utah Supreme Court because the defendant was not in physical control of the vehicle at the time, as required by the law. In freeing the defendant, the Supreme Court judged that the legal definition of sufficiency was not established in this case because the act observed by the police was not sufficient to confirm the existence of a guilty mind. In other words, the case against him failed because he was not violating the law at the time of the arrest and because it was also possible that he could have driven while sober, then pulled over, drank, and fell asleep.

—Adapted from Jay S. Albanese,
Criminal Justice, Brief Edition

_____d_____ 1. The topic of the passage is

      a. Driving Drunk.
      b. The Utah Supreme Court.
      c. Sleeping Behind the Wheel.
      d. Establishing Sufficiency for Drunken Driving.

2. Indicate whether each of the following details is major or minor in support of the author's topic:

   Major a. Police arrested the defendant for driving while intoxicated.

   Major b. The defendant was not violating a law at the time of the arrest.

   Minor c. The case was tried in Utah.

3. Underline the sentence that best states the main idea of this passage.

Unstated Main Ideas

Unfortunately, even if details are obvious, you cannot always depend on the author to provide a direct statement of a main idea. To add drama and suspense to a description or narrative, the main idea may be hinted at or implied rather than directly stated. Main ideas are often unstated in other media as well, such as movies and photographs.

Look at the details in the photo on page 174 to decide what message the photographer is trying to communicate. Determine the topic of the picture, propose a main idea using your prior knowledge, and then list some of the significant details that support this point.

AP Photo

What is the topic? _____

_____

_____

What are the significant supporting details? _____

_____

_____

What is the point the photograph is trying to convey about the topic? _____

_____

_____

The topic of the photo is an emergency rescue. The scene is dominated by a helicopter hovering over people stranded by flood waters that have nearly reached the roof of the home. The viewer can assume that these people were the occupants of the house. Some of their belongings are visible on the roof. Different areas of the roof appear to have had shingles ripped away, possibly from a storm and/or from the victims trying to crawl to the top of the building to save themselves. The main idea the photographer is trying to convey is that the family on the roof has been through a disastrous hurricane and could easily lose their lives without the rescue attempt. This main idea is suggested by the details but is not directly stated in the picture.

Unstated Main Ideas in Sentences

Before identifying unstated main ideas in paragraphs, practice with a simple list of sentences. First, read the related sentences in the following group. Next, create a sentence that states a general main idea for the three related thoughts.

EXAMPLE

1. A landmark 1990 study found that 30 percent of Americans under 35 had read a newspaper the day before—a much lower percentage than their parents.

2. Attempts to win a younger audience have included *USA Today*'s color and glitz, originally aimed at younger readers.

3. By 2000, daily newspaper circulation was down to 52.8 million from a 62.8 million high in 1988.

—John Vivian,
The Media of Mass Communication

Main idea: _____

_____

EXPLANATION The first sentence states that young readership is low. The second states an attempt to lure young readers, and the third states that circulation has declined by 10 million. The general main idea that reflects these sentences is that daily newspapers are not winning young readers and circulation is down.

exercise 4.7   **Determining Unstated Main Ideas**

Read the following related sentences and state the main idea:

Group 1

1. For over 200 years, *Encyclopedia Britannica* was considered the ultimate reference source.
2. *Britannica* looked the other way as competitors took advantage of new technologies and produced cheaper encyclopedias on CD-ROM.
3. *Britannica*'s sales slumped as consumers snapped up *Encarta* for $50 to $70 or enjoyed the free version installed on new computers.

—Michael Mescon et al.,
Business Today, 10th ed.

Main idea: *Britannica* failed to respond to technology and lost sales to *Encarta*.

_____

Group 2

1. The middle class seldom uses the double negative ("I can't get no satisfaction"), whereas the working class often does.
2. The middle class rarely drops the letter "g" in present participles ("doin'" for "doing," "singin'" for "singing"), perhaps because they are conscious of being correct.
3. The middle class also tends to say "lay" instead of "lie," as in "Let's lay on the beach," without suggesting a desire for sex.

—Alex Thio,
Sociology, 5th ed.

Main idea: Speech patterns differ between the middle and working classes.

Group 3

1. The AIDS virus (HIV), which seemed to arise abruptly in the early 1980s, and the new varieties of flu virus that frequently appear, are not the only examples of newly dangerous viruses.
2. A deadly virus called the Ebola virus menaces central African nations periodically, and many biologists fear its emergence as a global threat.
3. In 2003, a deadly new disease called SARS (severe acute respiratory syndrome) appeared in China and soon spread throughout the world.

—Neil Campbell et al.,
Essential Biology

Main idea: Dangerous, newly emerging viruses present a global threat.

Group 4

1. President George Washington converted the paper thoughts outlined in the Constitution into an enduring, practical governing process, setting precedents that balance self-government and leadership.
2. Thomas Jefferson, a skilled organizer and a resourceful party leader and chief executive, adapted the presidency to the new realities of his day with territorial expansions and sponsorship of the Lewis and Clark expedition westward.
3. President Lincoln is remembered for saving the Union and is revered as the nation's foremost symbol of democracy and tenacious leadership in the nation's ultimate crisis.

—James MacGregor Burns,
Government by the People, 20th ed.

Main idea: Early presidents made major contributions that strengthened the presidency and the country.

Group 5

1. Sales prospects are much more inclined to buy from people who make them feel good and with whom they have developed a personal bond, so begin by building a rapport.
2. Ask questions to find out the prospect's real needs, and describe the product or service accordingly to focus on the buyer's benefits.
3. Go for the final close and remember to ask for the order and stop talking so the customer can make the purchase.

—Michael Mescon et al.,
Business Today, 8th ed.

Main idea: Use these three steps in making an effective sales presentation.

Unstated Main Ideas in Paragraphs

Determining the main idea of a paragraph will be easier if you use the three-step questioning stategy on pages 158–159. The questions used to find an unstated main idea have a subtle difference, though. As you approach a passage with an implied or unstated main idea, begin by asking, "What is this about?" Reading carefully to identify key terms and major supporting details, draw a conclusion about the topic. Once you have determined the general topic of the paragraph, then ask yourself, "What do all or most of the key terms or major details suggest?" It is now up to you to figure out the author's point. Think as you read. Create an umbrella statement that brings these concepts together into a main idea statement.

EXAMPLE

Michael Harner proposes an ecological interpretation of Aztec sacrifice and cannibalism. He holds that human sacrifice was a response to certain diet deficiencies in the population. In the Aztec environment, wild game was getting scarce, and the population was growing. Although the maize-beans combination of food that was the basis of the diet was usually adequate, these crops were subject to seasonal failure. Famine was frequent in the absence of edible domesticated animals. To meet essential protein requirements, cannibalism was the only solution. Although only the upper classes were allowed to consume human flesh, a commoner who distinguished himself in a war could also have the privilege of giving a cannibalistic feast. Thus, although it was the upper strata who benefited most from ritual cannibalism, members of the commoner class could also benefit. Furthermore, as Harner explains, the social mobility and cannibalistic privileges available to the commoners through warfare provided a strong motivation for the "aggressive war machine" that was such a prominent feature of the Aztec state.

—Serena Nanda,
Cultural Anthropology, 4th ed.

1. Who or what is this about? _____

_____

_____

2. What are the major details? _____

_____

_____

3. What is the main idea the author is trying to convey about the topic?

_____

_____

EXPLANATION   The passage is about Aztec sacrifice and cannibalism. The major details are: diet deficiencies occurred, animals were not available, and members of the upper class and commoners who were war heroes could eat human flesh. The main idea is that Aztec sacrifice and cannibalism met protein needs of the diet and motivated warriors to achieve.

exercise 4.8   **Identifying Unstated Main Ideas**

Read the following passages and apply the three-question system. Select the letter of the author's topic, identify major and minor details, and choose the letter of the sentence that best states the main idea.

Passage A

Until recently, the U.S. census, which is taken every ten years, offered only the following categories: Caucasian, Negro, Indian, and Oriental. After years of complaints from the public the list was expanded. In the year of the 2000 census, everyone had to declare that they were or were not "Spanish/Hispanic/Latino." They had to mark "one or more races" that they "considered themselves to be." Finally, if these didn't do it, you could check a box called "Some Other Race" and then write whatever you wanted. For example, Tiger Woods, one of the top golfers of all time, calls himself Cablinasian. Woods invented this term as a boy to try to explain to himself just who he was—a combination of Caucasian, Black, Indian, and Asian. Woods wants to embrace both sides of his family.

—Adapted from James M. Henslin,
Sociology, 5th ed.

_____d_____ 1. The topic of the passage is

a. Tiger Woods Speaks Out.
b. The U.S. Census.
c. Identify Your Race.
d. The Emerging Multiracial Identity.

2. Indicate whether each of the following details is major or minor in support of the author's topic:

Minor a. Tiger Woods is one of the top golfers of all time.

Minor b. Tiger Woods wants to embrace both sides of his family.

Major c. Until recently, the U.S. census offered only four racial categories.

_____b_____ 3. The sentence that best states the main idea of this passage is

    a. Citizens complained about the four categories of the previous census.

    b. The 2000 census took a new approach and allowed citizens to identify themselves as being of more than one race.

    c. Tiger Woods considers himself a combination of Caucasian, Black, Indian, and Asian.

    d. Information from the 2000 census will be more useful than data gathered from the previous census.

Passage B

The rate of incarceration of women in prison increased from 27 per 100,000 women in 1985 to 57 per 100,000 in 1998. Men still outnumber women in the inmate population by a factor of about 14 to 1, but the gap is narrowing—from 17 to 1 a decade ago. Women constituted only 4 percent of the total prison and jail population in the United States in 1980 but more than 6 percent in 1998.

—Adapted from Jay S. Albanese,
Criminal Justice, Brief Edition

_____c_____ 1. The topic of the passage is

    a. Men Versus Women in Jail.

    b. Incarceration in America.

    c. The Increasing Number of Women in Jail.

    d. Overcrowded Prisons.

2. Indicate whether each of the following details is major or minor in support of the author's topic:

    Major a. The rate of incarceration of women in prison in 1985 was 27 per 100,000.

    Major b. The rate of incarceration of women in prison in 1998 was 57 per 100,000.

    Minor c. A decade ago men outnumbered women 17 to 1.

_____c_____ 3. Which sentence best states the main idea of this passage?

    a. Men continue to outnumber women in the prison and jail population.

    b. The rate of incarceration is increasing for both men and women.

    c. In the last decade, the rate of women incarcerated has doubled.

    d. The role of women in society has changed in the last decade.

Passage C

Each year in the United States approximately 50,000 miscarriages are attributed to smoking during pregnancy. On average, babies born to mothers who smoke weigh less than those born to nonsmokers, and low birth weight is correlated with many developmental problems. Pregnant women who stop smoking in the first three or four months of their pregnancies give birth to higher-birth-weight babies than do women who smoke throughout their pregnancies. Infant mortality rates are also higher among babies born to smokers.

—Rebecca J. Donatelle,
Health: The Basics, 4th ed.

_____c_____ 1. The topic of the passage is

    a. Infant Mortality.
    b. Smoking.
    c. Smoking and Pregnancy.
    d. Smoking and Miscarriages.

  2. Indicate whether each of the following details is major or minor in support of the author's topic:

    Minor a. Low birth weight is correlated with many developmental problems.

    Major b. Infant mortality rates are also higher among babies born to smokers.

    Major c. Babies born to mothers who smoke weigh less than those born to nonsmokers.

_____a_____ 3. Which sentence best states the main idea of this passage?

    a. Smoking during pregnancy increases the chance of miscarriages, low-weight babies, and infant mortality.
    b. Smoking during pregnancy causes many miscarriages.
    c. Ceasing smoking during pregnancy can increase infant birth weight.
    d. Smoking is a major contributor to infant mortality.

Passage D

The young reporter with the slow Missouri drawl stamped the cold of the high Nevada desert out of his feet as he entered the offices of the Virginia City *Territorial Enterprise*. It was early in 1863. The newspaper's editor, Joseph T. Goodman, looked puzzled at seeing his Carson City correspondent in the home office, but Samuel Clemens came right to the point: "Joe, I want to sign my articles. I want to be identified to a wider audience." The editor, already impressed with his colleague of six months, readily agreed. Then came the question of a pen name, since few aspiring writers of the time used their legal names. Clemens had something in mind: "I want to sign them 'Mark Twain,'" he declared. "It is an old river term, a leadsman's call, signifying two fathoms—twelve feet. It has a richness about it; it was always a pleasant sound for a pilot to hear on a dark night; it meant safe water."

—Roderick Nash and Gregory Graves,
From These Beginnings, vol. 2, 6th ed.

_____b_____ 1. The topic of the passage is

    a. Becoming a Reporter.
    b. How Mark Twain Got His Name.
    c. Safe Water on the River.
    d. Working for the Virginia City *Territorial Enterprise*.

2. Indicate whether each of the following details is major or minor in support of the author's topic:

Minor a. Clemens had worked for the newspaper for six months.

Minor b. The newspaper's editor was Joseph T. Goodman.

Major c. Clemens wanted to sign his articles to be known to a wider audience.

_d_ 3. Which sentence best states the main idea of this passage?

    a. Samuel Clemens worked as a young reporter for the Virginia City *Territorial Enterprise.*
    b. The newspaper's editor, Joseph T. Goodman, was impressed with the young reporter, Samuel Clemens.
    c. "Mark Twain" is a river term that means two fathoms—twelve feet.
    d. The young reporter, Samuel Clemens, decided to take the pen name "Mark Twain."

Passage E

Credit card companies entice students to apply for cards and take on debt with free T-shirts, music CDs, and promises of an easy way to pay for spring break vacations. Many students, however, can't even keep up with the minimum payment. In fact, it is estimated that in one year 150,000 people younger than 25 will declare personal bankruptcy. That means for 150,000 young people, their first significant financial event as an adult will be to declare themselves a failure. And for each one who goes into bankruptcy, there are dozens just behind them, struggling with credit card bills. In one 4-month period, for instance, a Texas A&M freshman piled up $2,500 of charges on two Visa cards and four retail credit cards. The student couldn't afford to pay the $25 minimum a month on all the cards, so she accumulated $150 in late fees and over-credit-limit fees.

—Adapted from Michael Mescon et al.,
Business Today, 8th ed.

_d_ 1. The topic of the passage is

    a. The Credit Card Industry.
    b. Paying Off Debt.
    c. Bankruptcy Options.
    d. Danger of Credit Cards for College Students.

2. Indicate whether each of the following details is major or minor in support of the author's topic:

Minor a. Credit card companies give away music CDs.

Major b. Young people are declaring bankruptcy over credit cards.

Minor c. A Texas A&M freshman cannot pay her minimum payments.

_____c_____ 3. Which sentence best states the main idea of this passage?

    a. Credit card companies engage in illegal activities to hook students on debt.

    b. It should be illegal for credit card companies to enroll college students who have no means of payment.

    c. Credit-card companies entice college students into debt that can be financially disastrous.

    d. Bankruptcy is an easy option for college students with over-whelming credit card debt.

exercise 4.9 Writing Unstated Main Ideas

Read the following passages and use the three-question system to determine the author's main idea. Pull the ideas together to state the main ideas in your own words.

Passage A

According to the U.S. Department of the Census, the demographic shift in the population will be "profound" in the next 50 years. By 2050, Hispanics will make up 24.5 percent of the population, up from 10.2 percent in 1996. The annual growth rate of the Hispanic population is expected to be 2 percent through the year 2030. To put this growth in perspective, consider the fact that even at the height of the baby boom explosion in the late 1940s and early 1950s, the country's annual population increase never reached 2 percent. Demographers, it seems, are alerting us to the enormous importance of such change. Says Gregory Spencer, Director of the Census Bureau's Population Projections Branch, "The world is not going to be the same in thirty years as it is now."

—Ronald Ebert and Ricky Griffin,
Business Essentials, 2nd ed.

1. Who or what is this about? Hispanic population growth

2. What are the major details? Hispanics 24.5 percent of population by 2050; annual growth rate of 2 percent until 2030; change of enormous importance

3. What is the main idea the author is trying to convey about the topic? _____
Demographers feel the rapid growth in the Hispanic population in the 2000s is of enormous importance.

Passage B

Prior to the time of Jan Baptiste van Helmont, a Belgian physician of the 17th century, it was commonly accepted that plants derived their matter from materials in the soil. (Probably, many people who haven't studied photosynthesis would go along with this today.) We aren't sure why, but van Helmont decided to test the idea. He carefully stripped a young willow sapling of all surrounding soil, weighed it, and planted it in a tub of soil that had also been carefully weighed. After five years of diligent watering (with rain water), van Helmont removed the greatly enlarged willow and again stripped away the soil and weighed it. The young tree had gained 164 pounds. Upon weighing the soil, van Helmont was amazed to learn that it had lost only 2 ounces.

—Robert Wallace et al.,
Biology: The Science of Life, 3rd ed.

1. Who or what is this about? _Van Helmont's plant experiment_

2. What are the major details? _Van Helmont tested a willow; weighed soil and planted; watered 5 yrs and weighed; tree gained 164 lbs; soil lost 2 oz._

3. What is the main idea the author is trying to convey about the topic? _____ _Van Helmont conducted an experiment that proved that trees do not derive their matter from materials in the soil._

Passage C

The Aswan High Dam, built in Egypt with Russian support, was supposed to provide hydroelectric power and to increase Egypt's food supply by controlling the unpredictable Nile River. The project meant that great art treasures were flooded as submerged land was drained for cultivation. However, only one-tenth of an acre of land was made available for each person added to Egypt's population during the period of construction. One result of the dam was that the Nile no longer flooded the delta farmlands annually. These annual floods served to restore the farmland fertility with deposited silt. This no longer the case, the quality of the farmland decreased. The dam also cut off the nutrients that had been washed to the Mediterranean Sea as a result of the annual floodings. Because of this, or the change in the salinity of the sea that the dam produced, the sardine catch dropped from 18,000 tons per year to 500 tons per year. The stable lake created by the dam allowed aquatic snails to flourish. The snails serve as an intermediate host to a blood fluke that bores into humans causing the dreaded disease, schistosomiasis. The construction of the dam had important political implications at the time.

—Robert Wallace,
Biology: The World of Life

1. Who or what is this about? <u>The Aswan High Dam</u>

   _____

   _____

2. What are the major details? <u>For power and increased food supply; no annual</u>
   <u>flood; farmland quality decreased without silt; nutrients washed in Med.;</u>
   <u>sardine drop; snail and fluke increase</u>

   _____

3. What is the main idea the author is trying to convey about the topic? _____
   <u>The Aswan Dam controlled the flooding of the Nile but caused other</u>
   <u>environmental problems never initially envisioned.</u>

   _____

Passage D

If using sunscreen, apply it at least 30–45 minutes before exposure, then reapply it periodically, especially after you swim or sweat. It is especially important to protect children. One or more severe sunburns with blisters in childhood or adolescence can double the risk of the skin cancer melanoma later in life. Additional protection can be provided by a wide-brimmed hat to protect your head and face, and opaque clothing to cover those body areas you wish to protect. Any fabric or material you can see through, including some beach umbrellas, does not give full protection. You should stay out of the sun between 10 A.M. and 2 P.M. when the rays are strongest.

—Curtis O. Byer and Louis W. Shainberg,
Living Well: Health in Your Hands, 2nd ed.

1. Who or what is this about? <u>Protection from the sun</u>

   _____

   _____

2. What are the major details? <u>Use sunscreen and reapply; sunburns lead to</u>
   <u>later skin cancer; use hat and opaque clothing, see-through fabrics do not</u>
   <u>protect; avoid midday sun.</u>

   _____

3. What is the main idea the author is trying to convey about the topic? _____
   <u>There are several ways to protect yourself from the sun and from developing</u>
   <u>skin cancer later.</u>

   _____

Passage E

In 1979 when University of Minnesota psychologist Thomas Bouchard read a newspaper account of the reuniting of 39-year-old twins who had been separated from infancy, he seized the opportunity and flew them to Minneapolis for extensive tests. Bouchard was looking for differences. What "the Jim twins," Jim Lewis and Jim Springer, presented were amazing similarities. Both had married women named Linda, divorced, and married women named Betty. One had a son James Alan, the other a son James Allan. Both had dogs named Toy, chain-smoked Salems, served as sheriff's deputies, drove Chevrolets, chewed their fingernails to the nub, enjoyed stock car racing, had basement workshops, and had built circular white benches around trees in their yards. They also had similar medical histories: Both gained 10 pounds at about the same time and then lost it; both suffered what they mistakenly believed were heart attacks, and both began having late-afternoon headaches at age 18.

Identical twins Oskar Stohr and Jack Yufe presented equally striking similarities. One was raised by his grandmother in Germany as a Catholic and a Nazi, while the other was raised by his father in the Caribbean as a Jew. Nevertheless, they share traits and habits galore. They like spicy foods and sweet liqueurs, have a habit of falling asleep in front of the television, flush the toilet before using it, store rubber bands on their wrists, and dip buttered toast in their coffee. Stohr is domineering toward women and yells at his wife, as did Yufe before he was separated.

—David G. Myers,
Psychology

1. Who or what is this about? <u>Similarities between twins</u>

   _____

   _____

2. What are the major details? <u>"Jim twins" married, divorced, remarried</u>

   <u>women of same name; both had same habits, cars, hobbies, and medical</u>

   <u>histories; Stohr and Yufe had same traits and habits.</u>

   _____

3. What is the main idea the author is trying to convey about the topic?

   <u>Studies show that identical twins, even those separated at birth, have amazing</u>

   <u>similarities.</u>

   _____

Interpreting the Main Idea of Longer Selections

Understanding the main idea of longer selections requires a little more thinking than does finding the main idea of a single paragraph. Since longer selections, such as articles or chapters, contain more material, tying the ideas together can be a challenge. Each paragraph of a longer selection usually represents a new aspect of a supporting detail. In addition, several major ideas may contribute to developing the overall main idea. Your job is to group the many pieces under one central theme.

For longer selections, add an extra step between the two questions "What is the topic?" and "What is the main idea the author is trying to convey?" The step involves organizing the material into manageable subunits and then relating those to the whole. Ask the following two additional questions: "Under what subsections can these ideas be grouped?" and "How do these subsections contribute to the whole?"

Use the suggestions in the Reader's Tip to determine the main idea of longer selections. The techniques are similar to those used in previewing and skimming, two skills that also focus on the overall central theme.

Reader's *Tip* — Getting the Main Idea of Longer Selections

- **Think about the title.** What does the title suggest about the topic?
- **Read the first paragraph or two to find a statement of the topic or thesis.** What does the selection seem to be about?
- **Read the subheadings** and, if necessary, glance at the first sentences of some of the paragraphs. Based on these clues, what does the article seem to be about?
- **Look for clues that indicate how the material is organized.** Is the purpose to define a term, to prove an opinion or explain a concept, to describe a situation, or to persuade the reader toward a particular point of view? Is the material organized into a list of examples, a time order or sequence, a comparison or contrast, or a cause-and-effect relationship?
- **As you read, organize the paragraphs into subsections.** Give each subsection a title. Think of it as a significant supporting detail.
- **Determine how the overall organization and subsections relate to the whole.** What is the main idea the author is trying to convey in this selection?

---

exercise 4.10   **Getting the Main Idea of Longer Selections**

Read each passage, and use the strategies in the Reader's Tip to determine the author's main idea.

Passage A: The Benefits of a Good Night's Sleep

College students are well known for "all nighters," during which they stay up through the night to study for an exam or to finish—or even to start—a paper due in the morning. Lack of sleep is nothing to brag or laugh about. Sleep is vital to your life and can help you function at optimal levels both physically and mentally.

On the physical side, sleep helps regulate your metabolism and your body's state of equilibrium. On the mental side, it helps restore your ability to be optimistic and to have a high level of energy and self-confidence. To keep your body in balance, more sleep is needed when you are under stress, experiencing emotional fatigue, or undertaking an intense intellectual activity such as learning.

During sleep, most people experience periods of what is called rapid eye movement (REM). These movements can be observed beneath closed eyelids. In REM sleep, the body is quiet but the mind is active, even hyperactive. Some researchers believe that REM sleep helps you form permanent memories; others believe that this period of active brain waves serves to rid your brain of overstimulation and useless information acquired during the day. REM sleep is the time not only for dreams but also for acceleration of the heart rate and blood flow to the brain.

During non-REM sleep, in contrast, the body may be active—some people sleepwalk during this period—but the mind is not. In spite of this activity, non-REM sleep is the time when the body does its repair and maintenance work, including cell regeneration.

Although much still needs to be learned about sleep and its functions, few would disagree that sleep plays a role in the maintenance of good mental health.

—B. E. Pruitt and Jane J. Stein,
Decisions for Healthy Living

1. What does the title suggest about the topic? It is about the benefits of sleep.

   _____

   _____

2. What sentence in the first paragraph suggests the main idea? The last
   sentence

   _____

3. What subtitles would you give the second, third, and fourth paragraphs? _____
   Answers may vary; Physical and Mental Benefits, REM Sleep, Non-REM Sleep

   _____

4. What is the main idea of the selection? Sleep is vital for physical and mental
   health.

   _____

Passage B: Clothing as Communication

Besides protecting us from the elements, clothing is a means of nonverbal communication, providing a relatively straightforward (if sometimes expensive) method of impression management. Clothing can be used to convey economic status, educational level, social status, moral standards, athletic ability and/or interests, belief system (political, philosophical, religious), and level of sophistication.

Research shows that we do make assumptions about people based on their clothing. Communicators who wear special clothing often gain persuasiveness. For example, experimenters dressed in uniforms resembling police officers were more successful than those dressed in civilian clothing in requesting pedestrians to pick up litter and in persuading them to lend a dime to an overparked motorist. Likewise, solicitors wearing sheriff's and nurse's uniforms increased the level of contributions to law enforcement and healthcare campaigns.

Uniforms aren't the only kind of clothing that carries influence. In one study, a male and female were stationed in a hallway so that anyone who wished to go by had to avoid them or pass between them. In one condition, the conversationalists wore "formal daytime dress"; in the other, they wore "casual attire." Passersby behaved differently toward the couple depending on the style of clothing: They responded positively with the well-dressed couple and negatively when the same people were casually dressed.

Similar results in other situations show the influence of clothing. We are more likely to obey people dressed in a high-status manner. Pedestrians were more likely to return lost coins to well-dressed people than to those dressed in low-status clothing. We are also more likely to follow the lead of high-status dressers even when it comes to violating social rules. Eighty-three percent of the pedestrians in one study followed a well-dressed jaywalker who violated a "wait" crossing signal, whereas only 48 percent followed a person dressed in lower-status clothing. Women who are wearing a jacket are rated as being more powerful than those wearing only a dress or skirt and blouse.

As we get to know others better, the importance of clothing shrinks. This fact suggests that clothing is especially important in the early stages of a relationship, when making a positive first impression is necessary in order to encourage others to get to know us better. This advice is equally important in personal situations and in employment interviews. In both cases, your style of dress (and personal grooming) can make all the difference between the chance to progress further and outright rejection.

—Ronald B. Adler and George Rodman,
Understanding Human Communication, 8th ed.

1. What does the title suggest about the topic? It implies that clothing is more than simply a way to keep warm; it is a means of expression.

2. What sentence in the first paragraph suggests the main idea? The first sentence

3. What subtitles would you give the second, third, fourth, and fifth paragraphs? (Answers may vary) 2nd—Special Clothing and Persuasiveness, 3rd—Clothing and First Impressions, 4th—Clothing and Power, 5th—Clothing and Relationships

4. What is the main idea of the selection? Clothing is a means of communication that creates impressions of and assumptions about the wearer.

Passage C: Immigration in the 1800s

What had been a trickle in the 1820s—some 128,502 foreigners came to U.S. shores during that decade—became a torrent in the 1850s, with more than 2.8 million migrants to the United States. Although families and single women emigrated, the majority of the newcomers were young European men of working age.

This vast movement of people, which began in the 1840s and continued throughout the nineteenth century, resulted from Europe's population explosion and the new farming and industrial practices that undermined or ended traditional means of livelihood. Poverty and the lack of opportunity heightened the appeal of leaving home. As one Scottish woman wrote to an American friend in 1847, "We cannot make it better here. All that we can do is if you can give us any encouragement is to immigrate to your country."

Famine uprooted the largest group of immigrants: the Irish. In 1845, a terrible blight attacked and destroyed the potato crop, the staple of the Irish diet. Years of devastating hunger followed. One million Irish starved to death between 1841 and 1851; another million and a half emigrated. Although not all came to the United States, those who did arrived almost penniless in eastern port cities without the skills needed for good jobs. With only their raw labor to sell, employers, as one observer noted, "will engage Paddy as they would a dray horse." Yet, limited as their opportunities were, immigrants saved money to send home to help their families or to pay for their passage to the United States.

German immigrants, the second largest group of newcomers during this period (1,361,506 arrived between 1840 and 1859), were not facing such drastic conditions. But as Henry Brokmeyer observed, "Hunger brought me . . . here, and hunger is the cause of European immigration to this country."

—Gary B. Nash et al.,
The American People, 6th ed., vol. 1

1. What does the title suggest about the topic? It is about immigration in the 1800s.

2. What subtitles could you give paragraphs one through four? Answers may vary; 1—Immigration Increase, 2—Immigration Causes, 3—Irish Famine, 4—German Hunger

3. Is there one sentence that sums up the main idea in the passage? No, not completely

4. What is the main idea of the selection? A number of factors contributed to the large increase in European immigrants in the mid-1800s.

Summary Writing: A Main Idea Skill

A **summary** is a series of brief, concise statements, in your own words, of the main idea and the significant supporting details. The first sentence should state the main idea or thesis; subsequent sentences should incorporate the significant details. Minor details and material irrelevant to the learner's purpose should be omitted. The summary should be written in paragraph form and should always be shorter than the material being summarized.

Why Summarize?

Summaries can be used for textbook study and are particularly useful in anticipating answers for essay exam questions. For writing research papers, summarizing is an essential skill. Using your own words to put the essence of an article into concise sentences requires a thorough understanding of the material. As one researcher noted, "Since so much summarizing is necessary for writing papers, students should have the skill before starting work on research papers. How much plagiarism is the result of inadequate summarizing skills?"[3]

Writing a research paper may mean that you will have to read as many as 30 articles and four books over a period of a month or two. After each reading, you want to take enough notes so you can write your paper without returning to the library for another look at the original reference. Since you will be using so many different references, do your note taking carefully. The complete sentences of a summary are more explicit than underscored text or the highlighted topic-phrase format of an outline. Your summary should demonstrate a synthesis of the information. The Reader's Tip outlines how to write an effective summary.

Reader's *Tip*   How to Summarize

- **Keep in mind the purpose of your summary.** Your task or assignment will determine which details are important and how many should be included.
- **Decide on the main idea the author is trying to convey.** Make this main idea the first sentence in your summary.
- **Decide on the major ideas and details that support the author's point.** Mark the key terms and phrases. Include in your summary the major ideas and as many of the significant supporting details as your purpose demands.
- **Do not include irrelevant or repeated information.** A summary stays very focused and concise.
- **Use appropriate transitional words and phrases.** They'll show the relationship between ideas.
- **Use paragraph form.** Don't use a list or write in incomplete sentences.
- **Do not add your personal opinion.** Stick to the content of the material you are summarizing.

---

[3]K. Taylor, "Can College Students Summarize?" *Journal of Reading* 26 (March 1983): 540–44.

Read the following excerpt on political authority as if you were doing research for a term paper and writing a summary on a note card. Mark key terms that you would include. Before reading the example provided, anticipate what you would include in your own summary.

Types of Authority

Where is the source of the state's authority? Weber described three possible sources of the right to command, which produced what he called traditional authority, charismatic authority, and legal authority.

Traditional Authority

In many societies, people have obeyed those in power because, in essence, "that is the way it has always been." Thus, kings, queens, feudal lords, and tribal chiefs did not need written rules in order to govern. Their authority was based on tradition, on long-standing customs, and it was handed down from parent to child, maintaining traditional authority from one generation to the next. Often, traditional authority has been justified by religious tradition. For example, medieval European kings were said to rule by divine right, and Japanese emperors were considered the embodiment of heaven.

Charismatic Authority

People may also submit to authority, not because of tradition, but because of the extraordinary attraction of an individual. Napoleon, Gandhi, Mao Tse-tung, and Ayatollah Khomeini all illustrate authority that derives its legitimacy from *charisma*—an exceptional personal quality popularly attributed to certain individuals. Their followers perceive charismatic leaders as persons of destiny endowed with remarkable vision, the power of a savior, or God's grace. Charismatic authority is inherently unstable. It cannot be transferred to another person.

Legal Authority

The political systems of industrial states are based largely on a third type of authority: legal authority, which Weber also called *rational authority*. These systems derive legitimacy from a set of explicit rules and procedures that spell out the ruler's rights and duties. Typically, the rules and procedures are put in writing. The people grant their obedience to "the law." It specifies procedures by which certain individuals hold offices of power, such as governor or president or prime minister. But the authority is vested in those offices, not in the individuals who temporarily hold the offices. Thus, a political system based on legal authority is often called a "government of laws, not of men." Individuals come and go, as American presidents have come and gone, but the office, "the presidency," remains. If individual officeholders overstep their authority, they may be forced out of office and replaced.

—Alex Thio,
Sociology, 3rd ed.

1. To begin your summary, what is the main point? _____

_____

_____

_____

2. What are the major areas of support? _____

_____

_____

3. Should you include an example for each area? _____

_____

_____

Begin your summary with the main point, which is that Weber describes the three sources of authority as traditional, charismatic, and legal. Then define each of the three sources, but do not include examples.

Read the following summary and notice how closely it fits your own ideas.

Political Authority

Weber describes the three command sources as traditional, charismatic, and legal authority. Traditional authority is not written but based on long-standing custom such as the power of queens or tribal chiefs. Charismatic authority is based on the charm and vision of a leader such as Gandhi. Legal authority, such as that of American presidents, comes from written laws and is vested in the office rather than the person.

---

exercise 4.11 **Summarizing Passages**

Read the following passages, and mark the key terms and phrases. Begin your summary with a statement of the main point, and add the appropriate supporting details. Use your markings to help you write the summary. Be brief, but include the essential elements.

Passage A: Prosecutors

The task of prosecutors is to represent the community in bringing charges against an accused person. The job of the prosecutor is constrained by political factors, caseloads, and relationships with other actors in the adjudication process.

First, most prosecutors are elected (although some are appointed by the governor), so it is in their interests to make make "popular" prosecution decisions—and in some cases these may run counter to the ideals of justice. For example, prosecution "to the full extent of the law" of a college student caught possessing a small amount of marijuana may be unwarranted, but failure to prosecute may be used by political opponents as evidence that the prosecutor is "soft on crime."

A second constraint is caseload pressures, which often force prosecutors to make decisions based on expediency rather than justice. A prosecutor in a jurisdiction where many serious crimes occur may have to choose which to prosecute to the full extent of the law and which ones to plea-bargain.

Third, prosecutors must maintain good relationships with the other participants in the adjudication process: police, judges, juries, defense attorneys, victims, and witnesses. Cases typically are brought to prosecutors by the police, and police officers usually serve as witnesses.

—Jay S. Albanese,
Criminal Justice

Use your marked text to write a summary.

Passage B: Suicide Among College Students

Compared to nonstudents of the same age, the suicide rate among college students is somewhat higher. Why is this so? For one thing, among the younger college students who commit suicide (ages 18–22), a common thread is the inability to separate themselves from their family and to solve problems on their own. College presents many of these younger students with the challenge of having to be independent in many ways while remaining dependent on family in other ways, such as financially and emotionally.

Several other characteristics of the college experience may relate to suicide. A great emphasis is put on attaining high grades, and the significance of grades may be blown out of proportion. A student may come to perceive grades as a measurement of his or her total worth as a person, rather than just one of many ways a person can be evaluated. If a student is unable to achieve expected grades, there may be a total loss of self-esteem and loss of hope for any success in life.

In the college setting, where self-esteem can be tenuous, the end of a relationship can also be devastating. A student who has recently lost a close friend or lover can become so deeply depressed that suicide becomes an attractive alternative. The problem can be compounded when depression interferes with coursework and grades slip.

—Curtis O. Byer and Louis W. Shainberg,
Living Well: Health in Your Hands, 2nd ed.

Use your marked text to write a summary.

Passage C: Alcohol Advertising and College Students

The alcohol industry knows a receptive market when it sees it. Each year, college students spend a reported $5.5 billion ($446 per student) on alcohol, consuming some 4 billion cans' worth of alcohol and accounting for 10 percent of total beer sales. For brewers, student beer drinking spells not just current sales, but future profits as well, because most people develop loyalty to a specific beer between the ages of 18 and 24. To secure this lucrative market, brewers and other alcohol producers spend millions of dollars each year promoting their products to college students. One conservative estimate places annual expenditures for college marketing between $15 million and $20 million. According to one survey, alcohol advertising of local specials in many college newspapers has increased by more than half over the past decade, stymying college and community efforts to reduce binge drinking.

—Rebecca J. Donatelle,
Health: The Basics, 4th ed.

Use your marked text to write a summary.

Passage D: Using Tree Rings to Study Past Climates

If you examine the top of a tree stump or the end of a log, you will see that it is composed of a series of concentric rings. Each of these tree rings becomes larger in diameter outward from the center. Every year in temperate regions trees add a layer of new wood under the bark. Characteristics of each tree ring, such as size and density, reflect the environmental conditions (especially climate) that prevailed during the year the ring formed. Favorable growth conditions produce a wide ring; unfavorable ones produce a narrow ring. Trees growing at the same time in the same region show similar tree-ring patterns.

Because a single growth ring is usually added each year, the age of the tree when it was cut can be determined by counting the rings. If the year of cutting is known, the age of the tree and the year in which each ring formed can be determined by counting back from the outside ring. This procedure can be used to determine the dates of recent environmental events such as the maximum number of years since a new land surface was created by a landslide or a flood. The dating and study of annual rings in trees is called dendrochronology.

—Frederick K. Lutgens and Edward J. Tarbuck,
The Atmosphere, 9th ed.

Use your marked text to write a summary.

Passage E: Advantages of Community Colleges

Community colleges provide a number of specific benefits. First, their low tuition cost places college courses and degrees within the reach of millions of families that could not otherwise afford them. Today, it is at community colleges that we find many students who are the first generation of their families to pursue a postsecondary degree. Compared to students who attend four-year colleges, a larger share of community college students are also paying their own way. The low cost of community colleges is especially important during periods of economic recession. Typically, when the economy slumps (and people lose their jobs), college enrollments—especially at community colleges—soar.

Second, community colleges have special importance to minorities. Currently, one-half of all African American and Hispanic undergraduates in the United States attend community colleges.

Third, although it is true that community colleges serve local populations, many two-year colleges also attract students from around the world. Many community colleges recruit students from abroad, and more than one-third of all foreign students enrolled on a U.S. campus are studying at community colleges.

Finally, while the highest priority of faculty who work at large universities typically is research, the most important job for community college faculty is teaching. Thus, although teaching loads are high (typically four or five classes each semester), community colleges appeal to faculty who find their greatest pleasure in the classroom. Community college students often get more attention from faculty than their counterparts at large universities.

—John J. Macionis,
Sociology, 10th ed.

Use your marked text to write a summary.

Summary *Points*

➤ **What is the difference between a topic and a main idea?**
The topic of a passage is the general term that forms an umbrella for the specific ideas presented, whereas the main idea is the message the author is trying to convey about the topic.

➤ **What are the strategies for finding stated and unstated main ideas?**
In some passages the main idea is stated in a sentence, and in others it is unstated. For both, ask, "Who or what is this about?" to establish the topic. Then look for the key supporting details that seem to suggest a common message. Finally, focus on the message of the topic by asking, "What is the main idea the author is trying to convey about the topic?"

➤ **What are the functions of major and minor supporting details?**
Major details support, develop, and explain the main idea, whereas minor details develop the major details.

➤ **What is a summary?**
Summaries condense material and include the main ideas and major details.

1 selection

selection 1   Psychology

Contemporary *Focus*

What is the bond between a mother and infant, and why is it important? What is the long-term strength of that bond? Researchers have sought to define this special relationship and to test its lasting significance to the infant's development.

Mother's Love Works Like Opiate

By Benedict Carey
From "Addicted to Mother's Love: It's Biology, Stupid," *New York Times*, June 29, 2004.
Copyright © 2004 by The New York Times Co. Reprinted with permission.

A mother's love is like a drug, psychologists say, a potent substance that cements the parent-infant bond and has a profound impact on later development.

Warm, attentive parenting can, in fact, help baby animals overcome some genetic differences. In a series of experiments, scientists at McGill University in Montreal have shown that baby rats repeatedly groomed, cuddled and licked by their mothers grow up to be less anxious than those who received less coddling. In a study appearing in *Nature Neuroscience*, they report that this physical mothering early in life prompts long-lasting changes in the rats' genes that help the animals manage stress throughout their lives.

Researchers at the U.S. National Institutes of Health have demonstrated a similar effect in monkeys: Having parents that are warm and attentive protects young animals from a specific genetic variation that would—in the absence of such comfort and support—put them at high risk for aggressive, disruptive behavior. These well-nurtured monkeys tend to become attentive parents themselves. Their attachment to their mothers provides a model for the relationships they will form much later with their own children.

"The important part of all this is that we're showing that an attentive caregiver can actually alter the baby's genes, for the better," says Dr. Allan Schore, who studies attachment at the School of Medicine at the University of California, Los Angeles.

COLLABORATE   Collaborate on responses to the following questions:

➤ How could early nurturing promote a lasting defense against stress?

➤ How is mothering learned by the next generation?

➤ Why do people think that being a good parent is an instinctive behavior?

Preview

Preview the next selection to predict its purpose and organization and to formulate your learning plan.

Activate Schema

Do parents who were not nurtured as children later abuse their own children?
As a child, what brought you the most emotional comfort?

Establish a Purpose for Reading

What does monkey love have to do with human behavior? In this selection, discover how scientists explain the importance of contact comfort and trust in an infant-mother relationship. Notice how the Harlows came to understand the psychological needs of an infant monkey and the effects that deprivation of those needs can have on the whole pattern of psychological development. As you read, predict what the implications of the Harlows' animal research might be for our understanding of human development.

Increase Word Knowledge

What do you know about these words?

surrogate	functional	anatomy	tentatively	novel
desensitized	ingenious	deprived	persisted	deficient

Your instructor may give a true-false vocabulary review before or after reading.

Integrate Knowledge While Reading

Questions have been inserted in the margins to stimulate your thinking while reading. Remember to

Predict	Picture	Relate	Monitor	Correct

MONKEY LOVE

The scientist who has conducted the best long-term laboratory experiments on love is surely Harry Harlow, a psychologist at the University of Wisconsin. Professor Harlow did not set out to study love—it happened by accident. Like many other psychologists, he was at first primarily interested in how organisms learn. Rather
5 than working with rats, Harlow chose to work with monkeys.

Since he needed a place to house and raise the monkeys, he built the Primate Laboratory at the University of Wisconsin. Then he began to study the effects of brain lesions on monkey learning. But he soon found that young animals reacted somewhat differently to brain damage than did older monkeys, so he and his wife
10 Margaret devised a breeding program and tried various ways of raising monkeys in the laboratory. They rapidly discovered that monkey infants raised by their mothers often caught diseases from their parents, so the Harlows began taking the infants away from their mothers at birth and tried raising them by hand. The

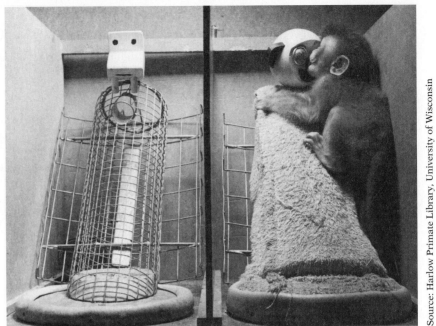

Source: Harlow Primate Library, University of Wisconsin

Although the monkey receives milk from Harlow's wire mother, it spends most of its time with the terry cloth version and clings to the terry-cloth mother when frightened.

baby monkeys had been given cheesecloth diapers to serve as baby blankets.
15 Almost from the start, it became obvious to the Harlows that their little animals
developed such strong attachments to the blankets that, in the Harlows' own
terms, it was often hard to tell where the diaper ended and the baby began. Not
only this, but if the Harlows removed the "security" blanket in order to clean it,
the infant monkey often became greatly disturbed—just as if its own mother had
20 deserted it.

Did you have a "security blanket" as a child?

THE SURROGATE MOTHER

What the baby monkeys obviously needed was an artificial or *surrogate* mother—
something they could cling to as tightly as they typically clung to their own
mother's chest. The Harlows sketched out many different designs, but none really
appealed to them. Then, in 1957, while enjoying a champagne flight high over the
25 city of Detroit, Harry Harlow glanced out of the airplane window and "saw" an
image of an artificial monkey mother. It was a hollow wire cylinder, wrapped with a
terry-cloth bath towel, with a silly wooden head at the top. The tiny monkey could
cling to this "model mother" as closely as to its real mother's body hair. This surrogate
mother could be provided with a functional breast simply by placing a milk bottle so
30 that the nipple stuck through the cloth at an appropriate place on the surrogate's
anatomy. The cloth mother could be heated or cooled; it could be rocked mechani-
cally or made to stand still; and, most important, it could be removed at will.

While still sipping his champagne, Harlow mentally outlined much of the research that kept him, his wife, and their associates occupied for many years to
35 come. And without realizing it, Harlow had shifted from studying monkey learning
to monkey love.

INFANT-MOTHER LOVE

The chimpanzee or monkey infant is much more developed at birth than the human infant, and apes develop or mature much faster than we do. Almost from the moment it is born, the monkey infant can move around and hold tightly to its
40 mother. During the first few days of its life the infant will approach and cling to almost any large, warm, and soft object in its environment, particularly if that object also gives it milk. After a week or so, however, the monkey infant begins to avoid newcomers and focuses its attentions on "mother"—real or surrogate.

During the first two weeks of its life warmth is perhaps the most important
45 psychological thing that a monkey mother has to give to its baby. The Harlows discovered this fact by offering infant monkeys a choice of two types of mother-substitutes—one wrapped in terry cloth and one that was made of bare wire. If the two artificial mothers were both the same temperature, the little monkeys always preferred the cloth mother. However, if the wire model was heated, while the cloth
50 model was cool, for the first two weeks after birth the baby primates picked the warm wire mother-substitutes as their favorites. Thereafter they switched and spent most of their time on the more comfortable cloth mother.

Why is cloth preferable to bare wire? Something that the Harlows called *contact comfort* seems to be the answer, and a most powerful influence it is. Infant
55 monkeys (and chimps too) spend much of their time rubbing against their mothers' skins, putting themselves in as close contact with the parent as they can. Whenever the young animal is frightened, disturbed, or annoyed, it typically rushes to its mother and rubs itself against her body. Wire doesn't "rub" as well as does soft cloth. Prolonged "contact comfort" with a surrogate cloth mother appears to instill confi-
60 dence in baby monkeys and is much more rewarding to them than is either warmth or milk. Infant monkeys also prefer a "rocking" surrogate to one that is stationary.

According to the Harlows, the basic quality of an infant's love for its mother is *trust*. If the infant is put into an unfamiliar playroom without its mother, the infant ignores the toys no matter how interesting they might be. It *screeches* in terror and
65 curls up into a furry little ball. If its cloth mother is now introduced into the playroom, the infant rushes to the surrogate and clings to it for dear life. After a few minutes of contact comfort, it apparently begins to feel more secure. It then climbs down from the mother-substitute and begins tentatively to explore the toys, but often rushes back for a deep embrace as if to reassure itself that its mother is still
70 there and that all is well. Bit by bit its fears of the novel environment are "desensitized," and it spends more and more time playing with the toys and less and less time clinging to its "mother."

GOOD MOTHERS AND BAD

The Harlows found that, once a baby monkey has come to accept its mother (real or surrogate), the mother can do almost no wrong. In one of their studies, the
75 Harlows tried to create "monster mothers" whose behavior would be so abnormal that the infants would desert the mothers. Their purpose was to determine whether maternal rejection might cause abnormal behavior patterns in the infant monkeys similar to those responses found in human babies whose mothers ignore or punish their children severely. The problem was—how can you get a terry-cloth mother to
80 reject or punish its baby? Their solutions were ingenious—but most of them failed in their main purpose. Four types of "monster mothers" were tried, but none of them was apparently "evil" enough to impart fear or loathing to the infant monkeys.

One such "monster" occasionally blasted its babies with compressed air; a second shook so violently that the baby often fell off; a third contained a catapult that fre-
85 quently flung the infant away from it. The most evil-appearing of all had a set of metal spikes buried beneath the terry cloth; from time to time the spikes would poke through the cloth making it impossible for the infant to cling to the surrogate.

The baby monkeys brought up on the "monster mothers" did show a brief pe-riod of emotional disturbance when the "wicked" temperament of the surrogates
90 first showed up. The infants would cry for a time when displaced from their moth-ers, but as soon as the surrogates returned to normal, the infant would return to the surrogate and continue clinging, as if all were forgiven. As the Harlows tell the story, the only prolonged distress created by the experiment seemed to be that felt by the experimenters!

95 There was, however, one type of surrogate that uniformly "turned off" the in-fant monkeys. S. J. Suomi, working with the Harlows, built a terry-cloth mother with ice water in its veins. Newborn monkeys would attach themselves to this "cool momma" for a brief period of time, but then retreated to a corner of the cage and rejected her forever.

100 From their many brilliant studies, the Harlows conclude that the love of an in-fant for its mother is *primarily a response to certain stimuli the mother offers*. Warmth is the most important stimulus for the first two weeks of the monkey's life, then contact comfort becomes paramount. Contact comfort is determined by the soft-ness and "rub-ability" of the surface of the mother's body—terry cloth is better than
105 are satin and silk, but all such materials are more effective in creating love and trust than bare metal is. Food and mild "shaking" or "rocking" are important too, but less so than warmth and contact comfort. These needs—and the rather primitive re-sponses the infant makes in order to obtain their satisfaction—are programmed into the monkey's genetic blueprint. The growing infant's requirement for social and in-
110 tellectual stimulation becomes critical only later in a monkey's life. And yet, if the baby primate is deprived of contact with other young of its own species, its whole pattern of development can be profoundly disturbed.

MOTHER-INFANT LOVE

The Harlows were eventually able to find ways of getting female isolates pregnant, usually by confining them in a small cage for long periods of time with a patient and
115 highly experienced normal male. At times, however, the Harlows were forced to help matters along by strapping the female to a piece of apparatus. When these iso-lated females gave birth to their first monkey baby, they turned out to be the "mon-ster mothers" the Harlows had tried to create with mechanical surrogates. Having had no contact with other animals as they grew up, they simply did not know what
120 to do with the furry little strangers that suddenly appeared on the scene. These motherless mothers at first totally ignored their children, although if the infant per-sisted, the mothers occasionally gave in and provided the baby with some of the contact and comfort it demanded.

Surprisingly enough, once these mothers learned how to handle a baby, they
125 did reasonably well. Then, when they were again impregnated and gave birth to a second infant, they took care of this next baby fairly adequately.

Maternal affection was totally lacking in a few of the motherless monkeys, however. To them the newborn monkey was little more than an object to be abused the way a human child might abuse a doll or a toy train. These motherless mothers

Do abused children return to cruel mothers?

Is mothering an instinctive or learned behavior?

130 stepped on their babies, crushed the infant's face into the floor of the cage, and once or twice chewed off their baby's feet and fingers before they could be stopped. The most terrible mother of all popped her infant's head into her mouth and crunched it like a potato chip.

We tend to think of most mothers—no matter what their species—as having
135 some kind of almost divine "maternal instinct" that makes them love their children and take care of them no matter what the cost or circumstance. While it is true that most females have built into their genetic blueprint the tendency to be interested in (and to care for) their offspring, this inborn tendency is always expressed in a given environment. The "maternal instinct" is strongly influenced by the mother's past
140 experiences. Humans seem to have weaker instincts of all kinds than do other animals— since our behavior patterns are more affected by learning than by our genes, we have greater flexibility in what we do and become. But we pay a sometimes severe price for this freedom from genetic control.

Normal monkey and chimpanzee mothers seldom appear to inflict real phys-
145 ical harm on their children; human mothers and fathers often do. Serapio R. Zalba, writing in a journal called *Trans-action*, estimated in 1971 that in the United States alone, perhaps 250,000 children suffer physical abuse by their parents each year. Of these "battered babies," almost 40,000 may be very badly injured. The number of young boys and girls killed by their parents annually is not
150 known, but Zalba suggests that the figure may run into the thousands. Parents have locked their children in tiny cages, raised them in dark closets, burned them, boiled them, slashed them with knives, shot them, and broken almost every bone in their bodies. How can we reconcile these facts with the much-discussed maternal and paternal "instincts"?

155 The research by the Harlows on the "motherless mothers" perhaps gives us a clue. Mother monkeys who were themselves socially deprived or isolated when young seemed singularly lacking in affection for their infants. Zalba states that most of the abusive human parents that were studied turned out to have been abused and neglected *themselves* as children. Like the isolated monkeys who seemed unable
160 to control their aggressive impulses when put in contact with normal animals, the abusive parents seem to be greatly deficient in what psychologists call "impulse control." Most of these parents also were described as being socially isolated, as having troubles adjusting to marriage, often deeply in debt, and as being unable to build up warm and loving relationships with other people—including their own children.
165 Since they did not learn how to love from their own parents, these mothers and fathers simply did not acquire the social skills necessary for bringing up their own infants in a healthy fashion.

How can the cycle of abuse be broken?

(2,192 words)

—From James V. McConnell,
Understanding Human Behavior. Copyright © 1974.
Reprinted with permission of Wadsworth, a division of Thomson Learning.

Recall

Stop to self-test, relate, and react.

Your instructor may choose to give you a true-false comprehension review.

Write About the Selection

Explain and give examples of findings from the Harlows' experiments that you believe are applicable to human infants.

Response Suggestion: Describe the experimental finding and use examples to relate it to the psychological needs of human infants.

Contemporary *Link*

Research shows that the nurturing hand of a mother can release endorphins in the body to give feelings of relief and comfort, as well as positive messenger chemicals in the brain, such as dopamine. Accepting this, why are some people drawn into abuse? Why is this a generational cycle that is so difficult to break? What suggestions would you have for breaking the cycle for both the victims and the abuser?

Summarize

Using this selection as a source, summarize on index cards the information that you might want to include in a research paper entitled "Animal Rights: Do Scientists Go Too Far?"

Skill Development: Find the Main Idea

Answer the following with *T* (true) or *F* (false):

____T____ 1. The main point of the first four paragraphs is that the Harlows' shift to studying monkey love occurred by accident.

____T____ 2. In the second section titled "Infant-Mother Love," the main point is that an infant monkey needs the "contact comfort" of the mother to give it a feeling of security while interacting with the environment.

____F____ 3. In the beginning of the section titled "Good Mothers and Bad," the main point is that baby monkeys will reject monster mothers.

____F____ 4. In the beginning of the section titled "Mother-Infant Love," the main point is that the maternal instinct is not influenced by the mother's past experiences.

Check Your Comprehension

After reading the selection, write the topic and main idea to answer item 1. Answer items 2–10 with *a, b, c,* or *d.* To help you analyze your strengths and weaknesses, the question types are marked.

Main Idea

1. Who or what is the topic? Infant-mother relationship
_____

_____

What is the main idea the author is trying to convey about the topic?

An infant develops a love or comfort relationship with its mother and

initiates the same relationship with its own child.

Inference _____c_____ 2. When Harry Harlow originally started his experiments with monkeys, his purpose was to study

a. love.
b. breeding.
c. learning.
d. disease.

Inference _____d_____ 3. The reason that the author mentions Harry Harlow's revelations on the airplane is to show

a. that he had extrasensory perception.
b. that he liked to travel.
c. that he was always thinking of his work.
d. in what an unexpected way brilliant work often starts.

Detail _____b_____ 4. In their experiments, the Harlows used all the following in designing his surrogate mothers *except*

a. a terry-cloth bath towel.
b. real body hair.
c. a rocking movement.
d. temperature controls.

Detail _____a_____ 5. The Harlows manipulated their experiments to show the early significance of warmth by

a. heating wire.
b. changing from satin to terry cloth.
c. equalizing temperature.
d. creating "monster mothers."

Inference _____c_____ 6. The Harlows found that for contact comfort, the cloth mother was preferable to the wire mother for all the following reasons *except*

a. the cloth mother instilled confidence.
b. the wire mother didn't "rub" as well.
c. the wire mother was stationary.
d. with the cloth mother, the infant felt a greater sense of security when upset.

Detail _____c_____ 7. The Harlows' studies show that when abused by its mother, the infant will

    a. leave the mother.
    b. seek a new mother.
    c. return to the mother.
    d. fight with the mother.

Detail _____b_____ 8. The Harlows' studies show that for an infant to love its mother, in the first two weeks the most important element is

    a. milk.
    b. warmth.
    c. contact comfort.
    d. love expressed by the mother.

Inference _____b_____ 9. The Harlows' studies with motherless monkeys show that the techniques of mothering are

    a. instinctive.
    b. learned.
    c. inborn.
    d. natural.

Inference _____d_____ 10. The Harlows feel that child abuse is caused by all the following problems *except*

    a. parents who were abused as children.
    b. socially isolated parents.
    c. parents who cannot control their impulses.
    d. parents who are instinctively evil.

Answer the following with *T* (true) or *F* (false):

Inference _____T_____ 11. The author feels that love in infant monkeys has a great deal of similarity to love in human children.

Inference _____T_____ 12. The author implies that isolated monkeys have difficulty engaging in normal peer relationships.

Detail _____T_____ 13. After learning how to handle the first baby, many motherless mothers became better parents with the second infant.

Inference _____T_____ 14. Zalba's studies support many of the findings of the Harlow studies.

Detail _____F_____ 15. Harlow had initially planned to perform drug experiments on the monkeys.

Build Your Vocabulary

According to the way the italicized word was used in the selection, indicate *a, b, c,* or *d* for the word or phrase that gives the best definition. The number in parentheses indicates the line number of the passage in which the word is located.

____d____ 1. "*surrogate* mother"(21)
   a. mean
   b. thoughtless
   c. loving
   d. substitute

____b____ 2. "a *functional* breast"(30)
   a. mechanical
   b. operational
   c. wholesome
   d. imitation

____a____ 3. "on the surrogate's *anatomy*" (32)
   a. body
   b. head
   c. offspring
   d. personality

____b____ 4. "begins *tentatively* to explore" (68)
   a. rapidly
   b. hesitantly
   c. aggressively
   d. readily

____d____ 5. "fears of the *novel* environment" (70)
   a. hostile
   b. literary
   c. dangerous
   d. new

____a____ 6. "fears . . . are '*desensitized*'" (70)
   a. made less sensitive
   b. made more sensitive
   c. electrified
   d. communicated

____c____ 7. "solutions were *ingenious*" (80)
   a. incorrect
   b. noble
   c. clever
   d. honest

____b____ 8. "*deprived* of contact"(111)
   a. encouraged
   b. denied
   c. assured
   d. ordered into

____b____ 9. "if the infant *persisted*" (121)
   a. stopped
   b. continued
   c. fought
   d. relaxed

____a____ 10. "to be greatly *deficient*" (161)
   a. lacking
   b. supplied
   c. overwhelmed
   d. secretive

Search the Net

Use a search engine such as Google, Yahoo, AltaVista, Ask.com, Excite, Dogpile, or Lycos to find information on the signs of child abuse. List five indicators that a child may be suffering from abuse or neglect. For suggested Web sites and other research activities, go to http://www.ablongman.com/smith/.

What is classical conditioning?

Classical conditioning is the learning that takes place when a subject is taught, or conditioned, to make a new response to a neutral stimulus. This is illustrated by the research of **Ivan Pavlov,** a Russian scientist in the late nineteenth century. Pavlov was studying the basic processes of digestion, focusing on salivation in dogs. Because salivation is a **reflex,** it is an unlearned, automatic response in dogs. When presented with food, dogs will automatically salivate. As his research progressed, Pavlov noticed that the dogs would salivate at the sight of the assistant who delivered the food. At this point, Pavlov decided to investigate learning.

Pavlov reasoned that no learning was involved in the dog's automatic salivation (the **unconditioned response**) when presented with food (the **unconditioned stimulus**). He wondered, however, if he could teach the dogs to salivate at the sound of a bell. To investigate this, Pavlov decided to pair the sound of a bell with the presentation of the food—sound first, food second. The bell alone was a **neutral stimulus** that had never before caused salivation. After a number of **trials** (presenting sound and food together), the dogs became conditioned to associate the sound of the bell with the food. The dogs soon would salivate at the sound, even when the food was withheld. Learning had taken place; Pavlov had taught the dogs to react to a neutral stimulus. Once learning or conditioning had taken place, the sound became a **conditioned stimulus** and the salivation became a **conditioned response.** To take this experiment a step further, if the sound is consistently presented without food, the salivation response will gradually weaken until the dogs completely stop salivating at the sound of the bell (**extinction**). Pavlov's work on animals and learning laid the groundwork for the American behaviorists of the twentieth century.

What is behaviorism?

At the beginning of the twentieth century, many American psychologists disagreed with Freud's

Two pigeons seek food in a box developed by psychologist B.F. Skinner as part of his operant conditoing research.

psychoanalytical approach (see page 46). They wanted to measure behavior in the laboratory and explain personality in terms of learning theories and observable behaviors. **B. F. Skinner** was a leader in this new movement. He borrowed from Pavlov's work and conducted research on operant conditioning.

Skinner posed questions such as, What are your beliefs about rewards and punishments? Do consequences affect your behaviors? Are you a reflection of your positive and negative experiences? Skinner believed that consequences shape behavior and that your personality is merely a reflection of your many learned behaviors.

Skinner demonstrated **operant conditioning** (behaviors used to operate something) by putting a rat inside a small box that came to be known as a **"Skinner box."** The rat explored the box until eventually it found that it could make food appear by pressing a lever. The rat enjoyed the food and dramatically increased the lever pressings. The food was a **positive reinforcer** for the lever pressing. In other words, the food reinforced the behavior and increased it. To stop the lever-pressing behavior (**extinction**), the rat was given a shock each time the lever was touched. The shock was a **negative reinforcer.** Rewards are positive reinforcers, and punishments are negative reinforcers.

Behavior modification, a type of **behavior therapy,** uses the principles of classical and operant conditioning to increase desired behaviors and decrease problem behaviors. You can use these principles to train a pet, stop a smoking habit, or overcome a fear of flying. Does the desire to make a good grade (reward) affect your studying behavior? Skinner would say yes.

Review Questions

After studying the material, answer the following questions:

1. Who was Ivan Pavlov? Russian scientist who studied classical conditioning

2. What is a reflex? An unlearned, automatic response

3. What is a neutral stimulus? Something that draws no response, like a bell that draws no response from a dog

4. Why is the response to the food called unconditioned? The response is a reflex that is automatic.

5. What is a conditioned stimulus? A previously neutral stimulus that now draws a response

6. What is extinction? The loss of the conditioned response

7. How did B. F. Skinner differ from Freud? He explained personality in terms of learning theories and observable behaviors.

8. How does operant conditioning differ from classical conditioning? The subject has to operate or manipulate something.

9. What is the role of a positive reinforcer? It satisfies you and makes you want to repeat a behavior.

10. In behavior modification, what makes you want to change behaviors? Rewards and punishments

Your instructor may choose to give a true-false review of these psychology concepts.

selection 2 Short Story

2 selection

Contemporary *Focus*

What motivates urban youth to join violent street gangs? Do they think they are bullet proof and invincible? Can members ever break free, or are they forever brothers, warriors, and criminals?

A Chance for a Clean Start

By David Cho

The Washington Post, February 20, 2005, p. T03. © 2005, The Washington Post, reprinted with permission.

Dr. Colin Berry's office in Yorktown, Virginia offers more than a tattoo removal service. It is where former gang members who are willing to endure a little pain can find redemption.

Fairfax County has offered free tattoo removals since 1999. Clients must be younger than 22 and willing to participate in at least 40 hours of community service.

The procedure is painful because the carbon particles explode and sometimes burn the flesh. It often takes repeated sessions for a tattoo to be fully removed, and even then there can be scarring.

One patient, a 19-year-old from Richmond who had been in a violent gang known as the Bloods for five years, came so he could have "THUG LIFE" removed from just below his knuckles. He said he saw the shallowness of the group while in prison.

The gang's leaders had pressured him into robbing a store, he said. He was arrested and sentenced to two years in prison. No one visited him during those lonely days behind bars. He couldn't even get anyone to pick him up after he finished his term, so he called his mother.

Prison "felt like you are dead for two years," he said. "I realized the only people who love me is my family."

The young man spoke on the condition that his name not be used because he was afraid of retribution from former gang friends. He said he planned to join the army, which would not accept him unless he removed his tattoos.

COLLABORATE Collaborate on responses to the following questions:

➤ Why is removing a tattoo a key to a clean start?

➤ Why is forty hours of community service an important part of the tattoo removal program?

➤ What do you know about gang activity in your area of the country?

Preview

Preview the next selection to predict its purpose and organization and to formulate your learning plan.

Activate Schema

What is the proper ethical response to encountering a seriously injured person?
Why do teens join street gangs?
What kind of violence is prevalent among urban street gangs?

Establish a Purpose for Reading

Why is someone on the sidewalk, bleeding? In this story, read about the fatal consequences of an act of gang violence with the intention of discovering the author's unstated message about gang culture in our society. As you read, be aware of the author's use of symbolism, and note the way the rainy setting and the reactions of other characters contribute to the story's mood and the main character's realizations.

Increase Word Knowledge

What do you know about these words?

excruciating	clutching	rumble	neon	lurched
soothing	relentless	foraging	loathing	hysterically

Your instructor may give a true-false vocabulary review before or after reading.

Integrate Knowledge While Reading

Questions have been inserted in the margins to stimulate your thinking while reading. Remember to

Predict	Picture	Relate	Monitor	Correct

ON THE SIDEWALK, BLEEDING

The boy lay on the sidewalk bleeding in the rain. He was sixteen years old, and he wore a bright purple silk jacket, and the lettering across the back of the jacket read THE ROYALS. The boy's name was Andy, and the name was delicately scripted in black thread on the front of the jacket, just over the heart. ANDY.

5   He had been stabbed ten minutes ago. The knife entered just below his rib cage and had been drawn across his body violently, tearing a wide gap in his flesh. He lay on the sidewalk with the March rain drilling his jacket and drilling his body and washing away the blood that poured from his open wound. He had known excruciating pain when the knife had torn across his body, and then sudden comparative

10   relief when the blade was pulled away. He had heard the voice saying, "That's for you, Royal!" and then the sound of footsteps hurrying into the rain, and then he had fallen to the sidewalk, clutching his stomach, trying to stop the flow of blood.

Why would the author choose the name Royal?

why are these words in italics?

He tried to yell for help, but he had no voice. He did not know why his voice had deserted him, or why the rain had become so steadily fierce, or why there was an open hole in his body from which his life ran redly, steadily. It was 11:13 P.M., but he did not know the time.

There was another thing he did not know.

He did not know he was dying. He lay on the sidewalk, bleeding, and he thought only: *That was a fierce rumble. They got me good that time*, but he did not know he was dying. He would have been frightened had he known. In his ignorance he lay bleeding and wishing he could cry out for help, but there was no voice in his throat. There was only the bubbling of blood from between his lips whenever he opened his mouth to speak. He lay in his pain, waiting, waiting for someone to find him.

He could hear the sound of automobile tires hushed on the rain-swept streets, far away at the other end of the long alley. He lay with his face pressed to the sidewalk, and he could see the splash of neon far away at the other end of the alley, tinting the pavement red and green, slickly brilliant in the rain.

He wondered if Laura would be angry.

He had left the jump to get a package of cigarettes. He had told her he would be back in a few minutes, and then he had gone downstairs and found the candy store closed. He knew that Alfredo's on the next block would be open until at least two, and he had started through the alley, and that was when he had been ambushed.

The two tattooed men are members of the Los Angeles-based 18th Street Gang. The man on the left flashes a gang-related hand sign.

Eros Hoagland/Redux

He could hear the faint sound of music now, coming from a long, long way off. He wondered if Laura was dancing, wondered if she had missed him yet. Maybe she
35 thought he wasn't coming back. Maybe she thought he'd cut out for good. Maybe she had already left the jump and gone home. He thought of her face, the brown eyes and the jet-black hair, and thinking of her he forgot his pain a little, forgot that blood was rushing from his body.

Someday he would marry Laura. Someday he would marry her, and they would
40 have a lot of kids, and then they would get out of the neighborhood. They would move to a clean project in the Bronx, or maybe they would move to Staten Island. When they were married, when they had kids . . .

He heard footsteps at the other end of the alley, and he lifted his cheek from the sidewalk and looked into the darkness and tried to cry out, but again there was
45 only a soft hissing bubble of blood on his mouth.

The man came down the alley. He had not seen Andy yet. He walked, and then stopped to lean against the brick of the building, and then walked again. He saw Andy then and came toward him, and he stood over him for a long time, the minutes ticking, ticking, watching him and not speaking.

50 Then he said, "What's a matter, buddy?"

Andy could not speak, and he could barely move. He lifted his face slightly and looked up at the man, and in the rain-swept alley he smelled the sickening odor of alcohol and realized the man was drunk. He did not know he was dying, and so he felt only mild disappointment that the man who found him was drunk.

55 The man was smiling.

"Did you fall down, buddy?" he asked. "You mus' be as drunk as I am." He grinned, seemed to remember why he had entered the alley in the first place, and said, "Don' go way. I'll be ri' back."

The man lurched away. Andy heard his footsteps, and then the sound of the man
60 colliding with a garbage can, and some mild swearing, and then the sound of the man urinating, lost in the steady wash of the rain. He waited for the man to come back.

It was 11:39.

When the man returned, he squatted alongside Andy. He studied him with drunken dignity.

65 "You gonna catch cold there," he said. "What's the matter? You like layin' in the wet?"

Andy could not answer. The man tried to focus his eyes on Andy's face. The rain spattered around them.

"You like a drink?"

70 Andy shook his head.

"I gotta bottle. Here," the man said. He pulled a pint bottle from his inside jacket pocket. He uncapped it and extended it to Andy. Andy tried to move, but pain wrenched him back flat against the sidewalk.

"Take it," the man said. He kept watching Andy. "Take it." When Andy did not
75 move, he said, "Nev' mind, I'll have one m'self." He tilted the bottle to his lips, and then wiped the back of his hand across his mouth. "You too young to be drinkin' anyway. Should be 'shamed of yourself, drunk and layin' in a alley, all wet. Shame on you. I gotta good mind to call a cop."

Andy nodded. Yes, he tried to say. Yes, call a cop. Please. Call one.

80 "Oh, you don' like that, huh?" the drunk said. "You don' wanna cop to fin' you all drunk an' wet in an alley, huh: Okay, buddy. This time you get off easy." He got

How was the drunk compassionate?

to his feet. "This time you lucky," he said again. He waved broadly at Andy, and then almost lost his footing. "S'long, buddy," he said.

Wait, Andy thought. *Wait, please, I'm bleeding.*

85 "S'long," the drunk said again, "I see you aroun'," and then he staggered off up the alley.

Andy lay and thought: *Laura, Laura. Are you dancing?*

The couple came into the alley suddenly. They ran into the alley together, running from the rain, the boy holding the girl's elbow, the girl spreading a newspaper over her

90 head to protect her hair. Andy lay crumpled on the pavement and he watched them run into the alley laughing, and then duck into the doorway not ten feet from him.

"Man, what rain!" the boy said. "You could drown out there."

"I have to get home," the girl said. "It's late, Freddie. I have to get home."

"We got time," Freddie said. "Your people won't raise a fuss if you're a little late.

95 Not with this kind of weather."

"It's dark," the girl said, and she giggled.

"Yeah," the boy answered, his voice very low.

"Freddie? . . ."

"Um?"

100 "You're . . . standing very close to me."

"Um."

There was a long silence. Then the girl said, "Oh," only that single word, and Andy knew she had been kissed, and he suddenly hungered for Laura's mouth. It was then that he wondered if he would ever kiss Laura again. It was then that he

105 wondered if he was dying.

No, he thought, *I can't be dying, not from a little street rumble, not from just being cut. Guys get cut all the time in rumbles. I can't be dying. No, that's stupid. That don't make any sense at all.*

"You shouldn't," the girl said.

110 "Why not?"

"I don't know."

"Do you like it?"

"Yes."

"So?"

115 "I don't know."

"I love you, Angela," the boy said.

"I love you, too, Freddie," the girl said, and Andy listened and thought: *I love you, Laura. Laura, I think maybe I'm dying. Laura, this is stupid but I think maybe I'm dying. Laura, I think I'm dying.*

120 He tried to speak. He tried to move. He tried to crawl toward the doorway where he could see two figures embrace. He tried to make a noise, a sound, and a grunt came from his lips, and then he tried again, and another grunt came, a low animal grunt of pain.

"What was that?" the girl said, suddenly alarmed, breaking away from the boy.

125 "I don't know," he answered.

"Go look, Freddie."

"No. Wait."

Andy moved his lips again. Again the sound came from him.

"Freddie!"

130 "What?"

"I'm scared."

"I'll go see," the boy said.

He stepped into the alley. He walked over to where Andy lay on the ground. He stood over him, watching him.

135 "You all right?" he asked.

"What is it?" Angela said from the doorway.

"Somebody's hurt," Freddie said.

"Let's get out of here," Angela said.

"No. Wait a minute." He knelt down beside Andy. "You cut?" he asked.

140 Andy nodded. The boy kept looking at him. He saw the lettering on the jacket then. THE ROYALS. He turned to Angela.

"He's a Royal," he said.

"Let's . . . what . . . what . . . do you want to do, Freddie?"

"I don't know. I don't know. I don't want to get mixed up in this. He's a Royal.

145 We help him, and the Guardians'll be down on our necks. I don't want to get mixed up in this, Angela."

"Is he . . . is he hurt bad?"

"Yeah, it looks that way."

"What shall we do?"

150 "I don't know."

"We can't leave him here in the rain," Angela hesitated. "Can we?"

"If we get a cop, the Guardians'll find out who," Freddie said. "I don't know, Angela. I don't know."

Angela hesitated a long time before answering. Then she said, "I want to go

155 home, Freddie. My people will begin to worry."

"Yeah," Freddie said. He looked at Andy again. "You all right?" he asked. Andy lifted his face from the sidewalk, and his eyes said: *Please, please help me*, and maybe Freddie read what his eyes were saying, and maybe he didn't.

Behind him, Angela said, "Freddie, let's get out of here! Please!" There was ur-

160 gency in her voice, urgency bordering on the edge of panic. Freddie stood up. He looked at Andy again, and then mumbled, "I'm sorry." He took Angela's arm and together they ran towards the neon splash at the other end of the alley.

What would you have done at this point? What is ethical?

Why, they're afraid of the Guardians, Andy thought in amazement. *But why should they be? I wasn't afraid of the Guardians. I never turkeyed out of a rumble with*

165 *the Guardians. I got heart. But I'm bleeding.*

The rain was soothing somehow. It was a cold rain, but his body was hot all over, and the rain helped cool him. He had always liked rain. He could remember sitting in Laura's house one time, the rain running down the windows, and just looking out over the street, watching the people running from the rain. That was

170 when he'd first joined the Royals.

He could remember how happy he was when the Royals had taken him. The Royals and the Guardians, two of the biggest. He was a Royal. There had been meaning to the title.

Now, in the alley, with the cold rain washing his hot body, he wondered about

175 the meaning. If he died, he was Andy. He was not a Royal. He was simply Andy, and he was dead. And he wondered suddenly if the Guardians who had ambushed him and knifed him had ever once realized he was Andy. Had they known that he was Andy or had they simply known that he was a Royal wearing a purple silk jacket? Had they stabbed *him*, Andy, or had they only stabbed the jacket and the title and

180 what good was the title if you were dying?

I'm Andy, he screamed wordlessly, *For Christ's sake, I'm Andy*.

An old lady stopped at the other end of the alley. The garbage cans were stacked there, beating noisily in the rain. The old lady carried an umbrella with broken ribs, carried it with all the dignity of a queen. She stepped into the mouth of
185 the alley, shopping bag over one arm. She lifted the lids of the garbage cans delicately, and she did not hear Andy grunt because she was a little deaf and because the rain was beating a steady relentless tattoo on the cans. She had been searching and foraging for the better part of the night. She collected her string and her newspapers, and an old hat with a feather on it from one of the garbage cans, and a bro-
190 ken footstool from another of the cans. And then delicately she replaced the lids and lifted her umbrella high and walked out of the alley mouth with a queenly dignity. She had worked quickly and soundlessly, and now she was gone.

The alley looked very long now. He could see people passing at the other end of it, and he wondered who the people were, and he wondered if he would ever get
195 to know them, wondered who it was of the Guardians who had stabbed him, who had plunged the knife into his body.

"That's for you, Royal!" the voice had said, and then the footsteps, his arms being released by the others, the fall to the pavement. "That's for you, Royal!" Even in his pain, even as he collapsed, there had been some sort of pride in knowing he was
200 a Royal. Now there was no pride at all. With the rain beginning to chill him, with the blood pouring steadily between his fingers, he knew only a sort of dizziness. He could only think: *I want to be Andy.*

It was not very much to ask of the world.

He watched the world passing at the other end of the alley. The world didn't
205 know he was Andy. The world didn't know he was alive. He wanted to say, "Hey, I'm alive! Hey, look at me! I'm alive! Don't you know I'm alive? Don't you know I exist?"

He felt weak and very tired. He felt alone, and wet and feverish and chilled, and he knew he was going to die now, and the knowledge made him suddenly sad. He was not frightened. For some reason, he was not frightened. He was filled with
210 an overwhelming sadness that his life would be over at sixteen. He felt all at once as if he had never done anything, never seen anything, never been anywhere. There were so many things to do, and he wondered why he'd never thought of them before, wondered why the rumbles and the jumps and the purple jackets had always seemed so important to him before, and now they seemed like such small things in
Does Andy deserve to die? How is his life wasted? 215 a world he was missing, a world that was rushing past at the other end of the alley.

I don't want to die, he thought. *I haven't lived yet.*

It seemed very important to him that he take off the purple jacket. He was very close to dying, and when they found him, he did not want them to say, "Oh, it's a Royal." With great effort, he rolled over onto his back. He felt the pain tearing at his
220 stomach when he moved, a pain he did not think was possible. But he wanted to take off the jacket. If he never did another thing, he wanted to take off the jacket. The jacket had only one meaning now, and that was a very simple meaning.

What is the author's view of gang culture? If he had not been wearing the jacket, he wouldn't have been stabbed. The knife had not been plunged in hatred of Andy. The knife hated only the purple jacket. The
225 jacket was a stupid meaningless thing that was robbing him of his life. He wanted the jacket off his back. With an enormous loathing, he wanted the jacket off his back.

He lay struggling with the shiny wet material. His arms were heavy; pain ripped fire across his body whenever he moved. But he squirmed and fought and twisted until one arm was free and then the other, and then he rolled away from the
230 jacket and lay quite still, breathing heavily, listening to the sound of his breathing and the sounds of the rain and thinking: *Rain is sweet, I'm Andy.*

She found him in the doorway a minute past midnight. She left the dance to look for him, and when she found him, she knelt beside him and said, "Andy, it's me, Laura."

He did not answer her. She backed away from him, tears springing into her eyes, and 235 then she ran from the alley hysterically and did not stop running until she found a cop.

And now, standing with the cop, she looked down at him, and the cop rose and said, "He's dead," and all the crying was out of her now. She stood in the rain and said nothing, dead boy on the pavement, looking at the purple jacket that rested a foot away from his body.

240 The cop picked up the jacket and turned it over in his hands.

"A Royal, huh?" he said.

The rain seemed to beat more steadily now, more fiercely.

She looked at the cop and, very quietly, she said, "His name is Andy."

What happens next? → The cop slung the jacket over his arm. He took out his black pad, and he 245 flipped it open to a blank page.

"A Royal," he said.

Then he began writing.

(3,040 words)

—By Evan Hunter
Happy New Year, Herbie and Other Stories

Recall

Stop to self-test, relate, and react.

Your instructor may choose to give you a true-false comprehension review.

Write About the Selection

How do Andy's thoughts of his own life evolve from the beginning to the end of the story?

Response Suggestion. Use the italicized thoughts to trace Andy's emotional journey.

Contemporary *Link*

If you had survived being a member of a street gang, what would you do to persuade your children never to join such a gang?

Skill Development: Find the Main Idea

Answer the following with *T* (true) or *F* (false):

_____T_____ 1. One of the central themes of this story is that Andy initially thought the jacket gave him identity, but he learned instead that it robbed him of his identity.

_____F_____ 2. The main point of the story is that Andy could have lived if others had helped him.

_____F_____ 3. The fact that the murder happened in March is a major detail.

Check Your Comprehension

After reading the selection, answer the first item in your own words and answer the subsequent questions with *a, b, c,* or *d.* To help you analyze your strengths and weaknesses, the question types are indicated.

1. Who or what is the topic? <u>Andy's dying</u>

Main Idea   What is the main idea the author is trying to convey about the topic?

<u>Andy wants to die as Andy, but he is dying as a Royal.</u>

Detail   __d__   2. All of the following are true about Andy's jacket *except*

a. it was purple.
b. *The Royals* was written on the back.
c. *Andy* was written on the left side of the front.
d. it was torn in the back from the stab wounds.

Inference   __b__   3. The reader can assume that the primary reason Andy was stabbed was because

a. he was threatening a member of the Guardian gang.
b. he was wearing a jacket that said *The Royals.*
c. he witnessed Guardians engaged in illegal activity in the alley.
d. he was dating a girlfriend of the Guardians.

Inference   __a__   4. The reader can conclude that the drunk

a. thought he was helping Andy.
b. was afraid and did not want to help Andy.
c. understood that Andy was dying.
d. saw the blood and left.

Inference   __c__   5. The reader can conclude that Angela and Freddie

a. would not have called the police if Andy did not have the jacket.
b. recognized Andy from the dance.
c. feared retribution from the Guardians.
d. contacted Laura so that she could find Andy.

Inference   __d__   6. The reader can conclude all the following about the old lady *except*

a. she never heard Andy.
b. she was salvaging items from trash, as if poor or homeless.
c. the author felt she carried herself with dignity despite her actions.
d. she saw trouble and wanted no involvement.

Inference   __c__   7. The author suggests that the person who could most accurately be called a coward in the story is

a. the drunk.
b. the old lady.
c. Freddie.
d. Laura.

Inference _____c_____ 8. The author suggests that Andy took off the jacket because

    a. he did not want Laura to find him wearing the jacket.
    b. he wanted other members of the Royals to be proud of him.
    c. he wanted to reclaim his personal identity.
    d. as a sign of honor, he wanted to avoid implicating gang members in his death.

Inference _____a_____ 9. The author suggests all the following about the cop *except*

    a. he recognized Andy as a person.
    b. he recorded the death as a meaningless gang killing.
    c. he was familiar with the activities of the gangs.
    d. he recognized Laura from a previous incident.

Inference _____c_____ 10. The author suggests that Andy's anger at his death was directed primarily toward

    a. the Guardians.
    b. the Royals.
    c. himself.
    d. Angela and Freddie.

Answer the following with *T* (true) or *F* (false):

Inference _____T_____ 11. The jacket was first a symbol of inclusion for Andy and then it became a symbol of meaningless death.

Inference _____F_____ 12. According to the story, the time that elapsed from the stabbing until Andy was found by Laura was 58 minutes.

Detail _____F_____ 13. Andy cut through the alley because it was the shortest way to the candy store, which was open until 2:00.

Inference _____T_____ 14. The author suggests that there are other gangs in the area besides the Guardians and the Royals.

Inference _____T_____ 15. As Andy got closer to death, he thought more about his wasted life and less about Laura.

Build Your Vocabulary

According to the way the italicized word was used in the selection, select *a*, *b*, *c*, or *d* for the word or phrase that gives the best definition. The number in parentheses indicates the line of the passage in which the word is located.

_____d_____ 1. "*scripted* in black thread" (3)
    a. painted
    b. carved
    c. blocked
    d. handwritten

_____c_____ 2. "known *excruciating* pain" (8)
    a. immediate
    b. humiliating
    c. agonizing
    d. tantalizing

_____a_____ 3. *"clutching* his stomach"
(12)
a. tightly holding
b. scratching
c. tearing
d. skinning

_____c_____ 4. "fierce *rumble*" (19)
a. knife
b. gang member
c. gang fight
d. gang order

_____b_____ 5. "man *lurched* away" (59)
a. sneaked
b. staggered
c. ran
d. excused himself

_____c_____ 6. "rain was *soothing*"
(166)
a. cold
b. endless
c. calming
d. irritating

_____d_____ 7. "steady *relentless* tattoo"
(187)
a. noisy
b. ugly
c. rhythmical
d. persistent

_____b_____ 8. *"foraging* for the better
part" (188)
a. singing
b. searching for food
c. speaking aloud
d. hiding

_____a_____ 9. "enormous *loathing*" (226)
a. hatred
b. eagerness
c. strain
d. energy

_____d_____ 10. "ran from the alley
hysterically" (235)
a. quickly
b. fearfully
c. sadly
d. frantically

$\mathcal{S}earch$ the Net

Use a search engine such as Google, AltaVista, Excite, Yahoo, Ask.com, Dogpile, or Lycos to find information on urban street gangs. Choose a major U.S. city and describe its gang problems. For suggested Web sites and other research activities, go to http://www.ablongman.com/smith/.

Concept Prep for Literature

What is literature?

Literature, the art form of language, is invented from the author's imagination. The purpose is to entertain an audience, to explore the human condition, and to reveal universal truths through shared experiences. As a reader, you are allowed inside the minds of characters, and you feel what they feel. You learn about life as the characters live it or as the poet entices you to feel it. After reading, you are enriched, not just entertained. Literature includes four categories, or **genres:** essays, fiction, poetry, and drama. Although the four genres differ in intent, they share many of the same elements.

Awarded the Nobel Prize for Literature in 1993, author Toni Morrison also won a Pulitzer Prize for her bestselling novel Beloved, *which was later made into a movie.*

What are literary elements?

Plot. The **plot** describes the action in a story, play, or epic poem. It is a sequence of incidents or events linked in a manner that suggests their causes.

Incidents in the story build progressively to reveal conflict to the reader. The **conflict** is a struggle or a clash of ideas, desires, or actions. Conflicts can exist between the main character and another character, a group, external forces, or within the character.

As the plot moves forward, the **suspense** builds. You are concerned about the character's well-being. The conflict intensifies to a peak, or **climax,** which comes near the end of the story and is the turning point, for better or worse. The **denouement** is the outcome of conflicts. Then the action falls and leads to a **resolution,** which answers any remaining questions and explains the outcome.

Characters. In literature you are told what characters think and feel. Thus you are better able to understand the complexities of human nature. By the shared experience of "living through" significant events with the character, you learn compassion for others.

Characters should be consistent in behavior, and they should grow and change according to their experiences in the story. You learn what kind of person the character is by what the character does and says, and by what others say about the character.

Point of View. The **point of view** in literature is not defined as bias or opinion as it is in Chapter 8. Rather, it describes who tells the story. It can be in *first person*, as the *I* in a diary; *second person*, using the word *you*; or most commonly, *third person*, in which the author is the omniscient or all-knowing observer revealing what all characters think and do.

Tone. The **tone** is the writer's attitude toward the subject or the audience. When people speak, we recognize their tone of voice. In stories, however, we must rely on the author's choice of words to convey attitudes. Word clues may suggest that the author is being humorous. Cutting remarks, on the other hand, may suggest *sarcasm*, which is an expression of disapproval designed to cause pain. The author's emotional and intellectual attitude toward the subject also describes the **mood,** or overall feeling of the work.

Setting. All stories exist in a time and place. Details must be consistent with the setting or else they distract your attention. The **setting** is the backdrop for the story and the playground for the characters.

Figures of Speech and Symbolism. Literary writing appeals to the five senses and, unlike scientific or academic writing, uses images to convey a figurative or symbolic meaning rather than an exact literal meaning. Consider the noun *hunger*. Other than simply wanting a hamburger, a student may hunger for the reassuring touch of a friend's hand. *Metaphors* and *similes* are the most common, and they both suggest a comparison of unlike things. For more on figurative language, see Chapter 7.

The imagery or **symbolism** in a story can be an object, action, person, place, or idea that carries a condensed and recognizable meaning. For example, an opened window might represent an opportunity for a new life.

Theme. The **theme** is the main idea or the heart and soul of the work. The theme is a central insight into life or universal truth. This message is never preached but is revealed to your emotions, senses, and imagination through powerful, shared experiences. Too often readers want to oversimplify and reduce the theme to a one-sentence moral such as "Honesty is the best policy" or "Crime does not pay." To deduce the theme, ask yourself, "What has the main character learned during the story?" or "What insight into life does the story reveal?"

Review *Questions*

After studying the material, answer the following questions:

1. What is literature? Literature is the art form of language, which includes essays, fiction, poetry, and drama.

2. What is plot? Plot is the action in a story, the sequence of incidents or events linked to suggest cause.

3. What is the climax of "On the Sidewalk, Bleeding"? The climax, the peak, or turning point in the conflict is when Andy dies.

4. What is the resolution? The resolution is at the end when the action falls and remaining questions are answered.

5. How do you learn about the characters in "On the Sidewalk, Bleeding"? You learn about characters from what they do and say, what others say about them, and what the author says about them. In this story, we learn from Andy's thoughts.

6. What is the most common point of view in a story? Third person is the most common point of view.

7. How does the definition of *point of view* differ in literature and in the question, "What is your point of view on cloning?" Your point of view on cloning is your opinion or bias, whereas the point of view in a story is first, second, or third person.

8. What do you feel is the author's attitude toward the subject in "On the Sidewalk, Bleeding"? _The writer's attitude or tone is one of sympathy or regret for the young man who has lost his life for nothing. Answers will vary._

9. What is the overriding symbol in "On the Sidewalk, Bleeding"? _The overriding symbol is the jacket with the label on it that has robbed Andy of his identity as an individual._

10. What is the theme of a story? _The theme of a story is the main idea, central insight into life, or universal truth._

Your instructor may choose to give a true-false review of these literary concepts.

selection 3 | Criminal Justice

Contemporary *Focus*

Would you prefer that your 911 call be answered by a male or a female police officer? Studies show that female police officers are making progress toward equality, but biases do exist with public perception and within police departments. How do women actually perform on the job, and what changes are offering new opportunities?

Arresting Development

By Anna Morrell
Western Mail, February 25, 2006

Chief Superintendent Michele Williams of North Wales Police says, "With almost 30 years as an operational police officer I have personally witnessed a sea of change in attitudes towards women officers by both colleagues and members of the public and am encouraged by the opportunities now available to women in the service.

"I started my career in 1976 and was posted to Caernarfon where I was invariably detailed to station duty on a Friday and Saturday night, effectively preventing me from gaining experience in dealing with public order. These were the days when the specialist departments tended to have one token female who dealt, in the main, with issues surrounding women and children, and if you found yourself pregnant, then resignation was your only option (unless you could afford a full-time nanny). Your uniform was comprised of a pencil skirt, fitted tunic, and air hostess style hat with a complimentary handbag in which you placed your 8-inch wooden baton for protection when you were let out on your own! Opportunities were limited, and there were male and female supervisors who were distinctly suspicious and unnerved by any woman who challenged the status quo."

"On reflection, I did that a number of times, not always in the most tactful of ways, but experience is a great teacher, and I look back with some pride at the changes that I have brought about personally and with the support of my male and female colleagues. Over the next ten to fifteen years I believe that women can be equally represented across all specialists and ranks. This may have to be achieved through government-imposed targets but will be possible. It is encouraging that there is a will at the highest level for this to be achieved."

COLLABORATE Collaborate on responses to the following questions:

➤ How are you biased against policewomen?

➤ What roles do you view as best for policewomen?

➤ What do you think about government-imposed targets to achieve equity for women in police ranks?

Preview

Preview the next selection to predict its purpose and organization and to formulate your learning plan.

Activate Schema

Think about the female police officers within your community. How effective are they in conducting police business? Are there some aspects of the job in which they might excel because of their gender?

Establish a Purpose for Learning

Police work is a job that attracts and needs both men and women. What are the realities of the job for women? In the following selection, learn the challenges faced by policewomen. As you read, ask yourself about the biases, the performance realities, and the progress being made.

Increase Word Knowledge

What do you know about these words?

criteria	eliminated	restricted	conviction	debunked
peers	aggressive	dominated	perceptions	affront

Your instructor may give a true-false vocabulary review before or after reading.

Integrate Knowledge While Reading

Questions have been inserted in the margins to stimulate your thinking while reading. Remember to

Predict	Picture	Relate	Monitor	Correct

FEMALE POLICE OFFICERS

In 1910 Alice Stebbins Wells became the first woman to hold the title of police officer (in Los Angeles) and to have arrest powers. For more than half a century, female officers endured separate criteria for selection. They were given menial tasks, and were denied the opportunity for advancement. Some relief was gained with the
5 passage of the Civil Rights Act of 1964 and its amendments. Courts have supported the addition of women to police forces by striking down entrance requirements that eliminated almost all female candidates but could not be proven to predict job performance (such as height and upper body strength). Women do not do as well as men on strength tests and are much more likely to fail the entrance physical than

10 male recruits. Critics contend that many of these tests do not reflect the actual tasks that police do on the job. Nonetheless, the role of women in police work is still restricted by barriers that have been difficult to remove. Today, about 6 percent of all sworn officers are women.

Women continue to be underrepresented in the senior administrative ranks.
15 Many believe they are assigned duties that underutilize their skills and training. If they aspire to rise in the police force, policewomen become frustrated when they begin to recognize that few women get promoted to command positions. Female recruits often lack successful female role models on which to shape their career plans. It may not be surprising, then, that female officers report higher levels of job-
20 related stress than male officers.

Is the same true at the upper levels of other professions?

WORK PERFORMANCE

Gender bias is not supported by existing research, which indicates that women are highly successful police officers. In an important study of recruits in Washington, D.C., policewomen were found to display extremely satisfactory work performances. Compared with male officers, women were found to respond to similar
25 types of calls. The arrests they made were as likely to result in conviction. Women were more likely than their male colleagues to receive support from the community and were less likely to be charged with improper conduct. Policewomen seem to be more understanding and sympathetic to crime victims than male officers and are more likely to offer them treatment.

Are criminals less likely to become violent with female officers?

30 Research has also debunked another myth about female officers. Because they are less capable of subduing a suspect physically, they will be more likely to use their firearms. Actually, the opposite is true. Policewomen are less likely to use their firearms in violent confrontations than their male partners. Policewomen are more emotionally stable and are less likely to seriously injure a citizen. They are no more
35 likely to suffer injuries than their male partners. These generally positive results are similar to findings in other studies conducted in major U.S. cities.

Jeff Greenberg/Alamy

The female police officer photographed here works the crowd as a member of the City of Miami Police Department.

selection 3

GENDER CONFLICTS

Despite the overwhelming evidence supporting their performance, policewomen have not always been fully accepted by their male peers or the general public. Male officers complain that female officers lack the emotional and physical strength to
40 perform well in situations involving violence. Some officers' wives resent their husbands' having a female partner because they consider the policewoman not only a sexual threat but poor support in a violent encounter.

Studies of policewomen indicate that they are still struggling for acceptance. They believe that they do not receive equal credit for their job performance. They
45 report that it is common for them to be sexually harassed by their co-workers. Female officers may also be targeted for more disciplinary actions by administrators. If cited, they are more likely to receive harsher punishment than male officers.

Surveys of male officers show that only one-third actually accept a woman on patrol. More than one-half do not think that women can handle the physical re-
50 quirements of the job as well as men.

DEFINING THE FEMALE POLICE ROLE

Those female officers who fail to catch on to the unwritten police subculture are often written off as "bad police material." Women who prove themselves tough enough to gain respect as police officers are then labeled as "lesbians" or "bitches" to neutralize their threat to male dominance, a process referred to as **defeminization.**
55 Male officers also generally assume that female offices who adopt an aggressive style of policing will be quicker to use deadly force than their male counterparts. Women working in this male-dominated culture may experience stress and anxiety. It is not surprising, then, that significantly more female than male officers report being the victim of discrimination on the job. Male officers who claim to have experienced
60 gender-based discrimination suggest that it comes at the hands of female officers who use their "sexuality" for job-related benefits.

Is strength essential? What about older and/or out-of-shape male officers?

These perceptions of female officers are often based on gender stereotypes and are incorrect. Nonetheless, policewomen are frequently caught in the classic "catch 22" dilemma. If they are physically weak, male partners view them as a risk in street
65 confrontations. If they are actually more powerful and aggressive than their male partners, they are regarded as an affront to the policeman's manhood.

(821 words)

—From Joseph J. Senna and Larry J. Siegel,
Introduction to Criminal Justice, 9th ed. Copyright © 2002.
Reprinted with permission of Wadsworth, a division of Thomson Learning.

Skill Development: Recall

Stop to self-test, relate, and react.

Your instructor may choose to give you a true-false comprehension review.

Write About the Selection

What are the challenges and drawbacks of being a policewoman? Consider both public perception and the police subculture in answering the question.

Response Suggestion: List challenges that are real and those that are not based on fact but exist in the minds of the public and male police coworkers.

Contemporary *Link*

Women are meeting with increasing success in police work. Even on television, women are given starring roles in crime investigations. What special skills do women add to police work? Beyond their individual skills, how can women add strength to the mix?

Skill Development: Find the Main Idea

Answer the following with *T* (true) or *F* (false):

F _____ 1. The main idea of the third paragraph (Work Performance heading) is that research studies show that the work performance of female police officers is only slightly below that of male officers.

T _____ 2. A major detail in the passage is that male officers complain that female officers lack qualities to perform well in violent situations.

F _____ 3. A minor detail in the passage is that women continue to be under-represented in senior administrative offices.

Check Your Comprehension

After reading the selection, answer the following questions with *a, b, c,* or *d*. To help you analyze your strengths and weaknesses, the question types are indicated.

Main Idea   __a__   1. Which of the following best states the main idea of the selection?

     a. Female police officers are subject to unjustified gender bias.
     b. Female police officers are better than male police officers.
     c. Women should not become police officers.
     d. The gender discrimination experienced by those in the police force is worse than that of other occupations.

Detail   __c__   2. When women first became police officers,

     a. they did not have the power to arrest people.
     b. they did not have to take any physical tests.
     c. they were given unimportant tasks to do.
     d. they were given many opportunities to advance.

Detail   __c__   3. Physical tests required by applicants to the police force have been criticized

     a. for being too easy.
     b. for being too hard.
     c. for not being relevant to actual police work.
     d. for not taking height and weight into consideration.

Detail   __b__   4. Few women hold senior administrative and command positions in the police force because few women

     a. apply for such positions.
     b. get promoted to such positions.
     c. have the skills and training required for such positions.
     d. want the stress related to such positions.

Detail   __d__   5. Compared to male police officers, female police officers

     a. respond to calls more often.
     b. receive more satisfactory work performance reports.
     c. are more likely to be accused of improper conduct.
     d. are more likely to offer help to crime victims.

Detail   __b__   6. Because female officers, as compared to male officers, are less capable of subduing a suspect, it is wrongly believed that

     a. they will be seriously injured more often.
     b. they will be more likely to use firearms.
     c. they will make fewer arrests.
     d. they will not respond to the more dangerous calls.

selection **3**

Detail _____a_____ 7. Both male police officers and their wives voice concerns about the behavior of female police officers

    a. when in violent situations.
    b. when off the job.
    c. when they hold supervisory positions.
    d. when they use firearms.

Inference _____a_____ 8. The author implies that one of the unwritten rules of the subculture is that

    a. men make better police officers than women do.
    b. suspects should be treated as if they are always guilty.
    c. there is no such thing as discrimination.
    d. the chain of command must always be followed.

Inference _____d_____ 9. In the police subculture, the process of "defeminization" as described in the passage implies that

    a. women who use their sexuality for job-related advancements are not "real" women.
    b. women are most threatened by not being considered feminine.
    c. women express aggression more directly than men do.
    d. women are most threatening to men when they are both feminine and successful.

Inference _____b_____ 10. By using the term "catch 22," the author suggests that female police officers are often

    a. in a "no need for action" situation.
    b. in a "no win" situation.
    c. in a position to win praise.
    d. in a position to use power over men.

Answer the following with *T* (true) or *F* (false):

Detail _____F_____ 11. Women have been police officers for over two hundred years in the United States.

Detail _____F_____ 12. Arrests made by female police officers are less likely to result in conviction.

Inference _____F_____ 13. The reader can conclude that a citizen fearing injury at the hands of police officers should be more concerned about female police officers than male police officers.

Detail _____T_____ 14. Most male police officers would rather partner with another male police officer.

Inference _____F_____ 15. The reader can conclude that most female police officers are lesbians.

Build Your Vocabulary

According to the way the italicized word was used in the selection, select *a, b, c,* or *d* for the word or phrase that gives the best definition. The number in the parentheses indicates the line of the passage in which the word is located.

b 1. "separate *criteria*" (3)
    a. heights
    b. standards
    c. powers
    d. opportunities

c 6. "male *peers*" (38)
    a. strangers
    b. opponents
    c. equals
    d. relatives

c 2. "*eliminated* almost all" (7)
    a. added
    b. heightened
    c. removed
    d. required

c 7. "*aggressive* style" (56)
    a. happy
    b. masculine
    c. combative
    d. deadly

d 3. "still *restricted*" (11)
    a. released
    b. required
    c. underrepresented
    d. limited

a 8. "male-*dominated* culture" (57)
    a. ruled
    b. subordinate
    c. insignificant
    d. referred

b 4. "result in *conviction*" (25)
    a. proof of innocence
    b. proof of guilt
    c. proof of support
    d. proof of sympathy

c 9. "These *perceptions*" (63)
    a. prejudices
    b. lies
    c. viewpoints
    d. gossiping

c 5. "also *debunked*" (30)
    a. proved
    b. theorized
    c. discredited
    d. liked

b 10. "an *affront*" (67)
    a. endorsement
    b. insult
    c. offer
    d. recognition

Search the Net

Use a search engine such as Google, Yahoo, Ask.com, Excite, Dogpile, or Lycos to find information about female police officers in other countries. Do they experience discrimination, and is it different or similar to the bias encountered by female officers in the United States? For suggested Web sites and other research activities, go to http://www. ablongman.com/smith/.

Who's Who in Medicine?

Suffixes	-ist, -ician: "one who"	-ologist: "one who studies"

- **dermatologist:** skin doctor (*derma:* skin)

  Dermatologists remove skin cancers.

- **internist:** medical doctor for internal organs (*internus:* inside)

  The *internist* will administer a series of tests to determine the cause of Ben's mysterious pain.

- **intern:** a medical school graduate serving an apprenticeship at a hospital

  The *interns* work under the close supervision of doctors on the staff.

- **gynecologist:** doctor for reproductive systems of women (*gyne:* women)

  The *gynecologist* recommended a Pap smear to check for cervical cancer.

- **obstetrician:** doctor who delivers babies (*obstetrix:* midwife)

  Many *obstetricians* are also gynecologists.

- **pediatrician:** doctor for children (*paidos:* children)

  Pediatricians use antibiotics to treat infections.

- **ophthalmologist** or **oculist:** doctor who performs eye surgery

  The *ophthalmologist* performed cataract surgery on the woman.

- **optometrist:** specialist for measuring vision

  An *optometrist* tests eyesight and fits glasses and contact lenses.

- **optician:** specialist who makes visual correction lenses for eyeglasses and contact lenses

  Opticians usually work behind the scene, often at an optometrist's office.

- **orthopedist:** doctor who corrects abnormalities in bones and joints (*orthos:* straight or correct)

  The *orthopedist* set up his practice near a ski area.

- **orthodontist:** dentist for straightening teeth

  Her braces had to be adjusted every six weeks by the *orthodontist*.

- **cardiologist:** heart doctor (*cardio:* heart)

  Cardiologists treat patients who have had heart attacks.

- **psychiatrist:** doctor for treating mental disorders (*psycho:* mind)

  The *psychiatrist* prescribed drugs for the treatment of depression.

- **psychologist:** counselor for treating mental disorders

  The *psychologist* administered tests to determine the cause of the child's behavior.

- **neurologist:** doctor for disorders of the brain, spinal cord, and nervous system (*neuron:* nerve)

  Neurologists are searching for new treatments for patients who have suffered spinal cord injuries.

- **oncologist:** doctor for treating cancer and tumors (*onkos:* mass)

  The *oncologist* recommended various methods for dealing with the cancerous tumor.

- **urologist:** doctor specializing in the urinary tract (*ouro:* urine)

  The urologist was treating several patients for impotence.

- **podiatrist:** specialist in the care and treatment of the foot (*pod:* foot)

  The *podiatrist* knew the best way to deal with blisters, corns, and bunions.

- **anesthesiologist:** doctor who administers anesthesia to patients undergoing surgery (*anesthesia:* insensibility)

  Usually a patient will meet the *anesthesiologist* just before surgery.

- **hematologist:** doctor who studies the blood and blood-forming organs (*hemat:* blood)

  A hematoma is treated by a *hematologist*.

- **radiologist:** doctor using radiant energy for diagnostic and therapeutic purposes (*radio:* radiant waves)

  After the removal of a cancerous tumor, further treatment by a *radiologist* is usually recommended.

REVIEW

Part I

Indicate whether the following sentences are true (*T*) or false (*F*):

_____T_____ 1. *Radiologists* are physicians who evaluate x-rays.

_____T_____ 2. A *psychologist* is unable to prescribe medications for patients.

_____T_____ 3. If a mental illness is suspected, a patient may be referred to a *psychiatrist*.

_____F_____ 4. An *internist* is a medical school graduate serving an apprenticeship at a hospital.

_____T_____ 5. *Dermatologists* recommend the daily use of sunscreen.

_____F_____ 6. A *neurologist* specializes in the treatment of heart attacks.

_____F_____ 7. Medical school is required in order to become an *optician*.

_____T_____ 8. *Pediatricians* examine babies.

_____F_____ 9. *Oncologists* specialize in eye treatment.

_____T_____ 10. A *hematologist* might help a patient whose blood fails to clot properly.

Part II

Choose the doctor from the boxed list that best fits the job description.

anesthesiologist	podiatrist	urologist	cardiologist	orthodontist
orthopedist	optometrist	obstetrician	intern	ophthalmologist

11. Performs eye surgery ___ophthalmologist___

12. Treats diseases of the foot ___podiatrist___

13. Delivers babies ___obstetrician___

14. Works with bones and joints ___orthopedist___

15. Treats disorders of the urinary tract ___urologist___

16. Administers anesthesia ___anesthesiologist___

17. Dispenses contact lenses ___optometrist___

18. Treats heart problems ___cardiologist___

19. Corrects problems with teeth ___orthodontist___

20. Apprentice to physician or surgeon ___intern___

Your instructor may choose to give a multiple-choice review.

5 Patterns of Organization

- How do transitional words signal organizational patterns?
- What organizational patterns are used in textbooks?
- Why are several organizational patterns sometimes combined to develop a main idea?

Jane Wooster Scott (b.1939/American), *Heroes on Wheels*, 1985. Oil on canvas.

Textbook Organization: The Big Picture

The **pattern of organization** in a textbook is the presentation plan, format, or structure for the message. Why is it important to identify organizational patterns in textbooks and other pieces of writing? Basically, such patterns serve as the book's blueprint, showing the reader how the book was built. They signal how facts and ideas are presented. The number of details in a textbook can be overwhelming. Identifying the pattern of organization of a section or chapter can help you master the complexities of the material. If you know the pattern of organization, you can predict the format of upcoming information.

Although key transitional words can signal a particular pattern, the most important clue to the pattern is the main idea itself because it usually dictates the organizational pattern. Your aim as a reader is to identify the main idea, be alert to the signal words, anticipate the overall pattern of organization, and place the major supporting details into the outline or pattern used by the author.

What Do Transitional Words Do?

Small words can carry a big load. A single word can signal the level of importance, a connection, or a direction of thought. For example, if a friend begins a sentence by saying "I owe you $100," would you prefer that the next word be *and* or that it be *but*? The word *and* signals addition and would give you high hopes for the return of your money. However, the word *but* signals a change of thought which, in this case, would be in a negative direction. If the next word were *first*, you would anticipate a sequence of events before repayment. If it were *consequently*, you would hope the positive result would be your $100.

Such words are **transitional words**—sometimes called *signal words*—that connect parts of sentences or whole sentences and lead you to anticipate either a continuation of or a change in thought. Transitions show the relationships of ideas within sentences, between sentences, and between paragraphs. Writers use transitions to keep their readers' comprehension on track and to guide them through the logic of the message. To avoid repetition, authors choose from a variety of signal words to indicate the transition of thought. These signal words or transitions can be categorized as shown in the following examples and in the Reader's Tip on page 236.

Words That Signal Addition

in addition	moreover	furthermore	and	also	another

EXAMPLE José was given a raise after six months at his job. *In addition*, he became eligible for health insurance benefits.

After causing a disturbance in the movie theater, Brian and his friends were asked to leave. *Furthermore*, they were barred from attending that theater ever again.

Words That Signal Examples or Illustrations

for example	for instance	to illustrate	such as	including

EXAMPLE

Traffic seems to be getting heavier. *For instance*, last year it took only twenty minutes to get to school, and now it takes thirty.

Some experts believe that a fetus in the womb can be affected by sounds *such as* classical music or the mother's voice.

Words That Signal Time or Sequence

first	second	finally	last	afterward	after	during
while	before	then	previously	until	now	next

EXAMPLE

Apply sunscreen while walking on the beach and *before* swimming in the surf. *Afterward*, reapply the sunscreen even if it is waterproof.

To build a good financial foundation, *first* pay yourself in the form of savings, and *then* pay your bills.

Words That Signal Comparison

similarly	likewise	in the same manner	like	as	just as	as well

EXAMPLE

If you treat someone with kindness, he or she will probably treat you in kind. *Likewise*, if you treat someone with disrespect, you will probably be disrespected.

Portland is a port city in Oregon; *similarly*, it is a seaport in Maine.

Words That Signal Contrast

however	but	nevertheless	whereas
on the contrary	conversely	yet	in contrast
even though	on the other hand	although	instead

EXAMPLE

Using a knife to cut a bagel can be dangerous to the fingers. *On the other hand*, using a bagel holder keeps fingers safe from the falling blade.

Today many families eat dinner separately and on the run, *whereas* in the past the family dinner hour was a time for bonding and an opportunity to instill values or share dreams.

Words That Signal Cause and Effect

thus	consequently	therefore	as a result	because
accordingly	since	so	because of	

EXAMPLE *Because of* his work to end apartheid in South Africa, Nelson Mandela spent twenty-seven years in prison. Upon his release, Mandela treated his oppressors with respect and worked to unite the country. *Consequently*, he shared a Nobel Peace Prize with then-president de Klerk.

There has been a severe shortage of rainfall this year. *Therefore*, we have instituted a ban on outdoor watering.

Reader's *Tip* ─────── Signal Words for Transition ────────────────

➤ **Addition:** in addition • furthermore • moreover
➤ **Examples:** for example • for instance • to illustrate • such as
➤ **Time:** first • second • finally • last • afterward
➤ **Comparison:** similarly • likewise • in the same manner
➤ **Contrast:** however • but • nevertheless • whereas • on the contrary • conversely • in contrast
➤ **Cause and Effect:** thus • consequently • therefore • as a result

---

exercise 5.1 **Signal Words**

Choose a signal word from the boxed lists to complete the sentences that follow.

however	for example	in addition	consequently	in the meantime

1. Forget the boring tourist narrative and turn walking around a city into a hip audio tour experience with Soundwalk CDs. In New York, ___for example___, you can pop in a fifty-minute audio CD to explore Chinatown, the meat-packing district, or Wall Street.

2. The United States has an ever-increasing demand for oil. ___Consequently___, we are researching alternative sources of energy, such as solar energy, to reduce our dependence on oil.

3. ___In addition___ to alternative energy research, we may begin drilling for oil on a small portion of our public lands to lessen our dependence on foreign sources of oil.

4. Drilling on public lands, _____however_____, is not popular with environmentalists who believe the drilling cannot be done without spoiling the land.

5. ___In the meantime___, we can strive to be more fuel efficient to help reduce our demand for energy.

| therefore | on the contrary | for instance |
| in the same manner | furthermore | |

6. One way to conserve energy is to drive a fuel-efficient car. ___For instance___, some hybrid cars that run on both gas and electricity are currently available. ___Furthermore___, these cars get up to sixty-eight miles per gallon.

7. The ancient Chinese practice of acupuncture is based on a belief that chi, a life force, flows along meridians throughout the body. ___In the same manner___, Feng Shui practitioners believe that the same chi flows throughout the earth, and that by harnessing the chi of our surroundings, we can improve the flow of energy in our bodies.

8. Coretta Scott King felt strongly that her husband's legacy should be celebrated nationally. ___Therefore___, she worked successfully with others to have Martin Luther King Jr.'s birthday recognized as a federal holiday beginning in 1983.

9. The U.S. Postal Service works to raise social awareness of important issues. ___For instance___, the USPS has issued commemorative stamps for causes that include diabetes awareness, breast cancer awareness, and hospice care.

10. The popular Harry Potter books are not only for children. ___On the contrary___, many adults enjoy reading about Harry's magical adventures at Hogwarts.

| furthermore | for example | nevertheless | finally | in contrast |

11. African American music in twentieth-century America evolved from ragtime, to jazz, to rhythm and blues, to soul, and ___finally___, to rap.

12. The concert tickets were outrageously priced. ___Nevertheless___, this was a once-in-a-lifetime opportunity, and other luxuries would have to be sacrificed to compensate for the expense.

13. Mardi Gras as celebrated in New Orleans is similar to Carnaval as celebrated throughout Latin America. Carnaval lasts for five days; ___in contrast___, Mardi Gras lasts only one day.

14. Internet car sales, rather than hurting auto dealerships, have actually helped them. ___For example___, most customers conduct research on the Net but still visit a dealer to actually buy automobiles. A well-informed consumer who is ready to purchase makes the salesperson's job easier.

15. Since Melissa failed to notify her parents that she had backed into another vehicle in the college parking lot, they were outraged to learn of the accident through a third party. ___Furthermore___, due to her lack of honesty, Melissa's parents decided that she would no longer be covered under their auto insurance policy.

---

moreover	but	simultaneously	as a result	similarly

---

16. Nutritionists note that a diet for good health includes five or more servings of fruits and vegetables daily. ___Moreover___, nutritional studies indicate that an increase in the consumption of these healthful foods can reduce rates of heart disease and cancer.

17. Is chocolate a food or a drug? Chocolate contains antioxidants and minerals like many foods, ___but___ it also contains a neurotransmitter naturally found in the brain that, like many drugs, makes us feel good.

18. The 2000 U.S. Census shows a dramatic increase in the Hispanic population in the South. This influx was due to a recession in California occurring ___simultaneously___ with a robust economy in the South during the 1990s.

19. Musicians protested the swapping of their songs on the Napster Web site without royalties being paid. ___Similarly___, journalists have protested their past works being electronically reproduced without royalty payments.

20. Gamblers with an illusion of control delude themselves into thinking that they can control outcomes in games of chance. ___As a result___, they lose substantial sums at casinos, racetracks, lotteries, and Internet gaming sites.

Patterns of Organization in Textbooks

As transitional words signal connections and relationships of ideas within and among sentences, they also help signal the overall organizational pattern of the message. When you write, you choose a pattern for organizing your thoughts. That organizational pattern is probably dictated by the main idea of your message. Before beginning to write, you must ask, "If this is what I want to say, what is the best logical pattern to organize my message?"

The next exercise contains examples of the patterns of organization you will encounter in textbooks. Some are used much more frequently than others, and some are typical of particular disciplines. For example, history textbooks often use the patterns of time order and cause and effect. Management textbooks frequently use the simple listing pattern, whereas psychology textbooks make heavy use of the definition-and-example pattern. *The Reader's Tip* following the exercise (see page 247) lists each type of pattern of organization along with some related signal words.

exercise 5.2

Patterns of Organization

Notice the outline that accompanies each pattern of organization described in the following paragraphs. After reading each example, enter the key points into the blank outline display to show that you understand the pattern.

Simple Listing

With **simple listing,** items are randomly listed in a series of supporting facts or details. These supporting elements are of equal value, and the order in which they are presented is of no importance. Changing the order of the items does not change the meaning of the paragraph.

Signal words, often used as transitional words to link ideas in a paragraph with a pattern of simple listing, include *in addition, also, another, several, for example, a number of.*

EXAMPLE   WORK-RELATED STRESS

Work-related stress has increased significantly in the last few years. People are spending more hours at work and bringing more work home with them. Job security has decreased in almost every industry. Pay, for many, has failed to keep up with the cost of living. Women are subject to exceptionally high stress levels as they try to live up to all the expectations placed on them. Finally, many people feel that they are trapped in jobs they hate but can't escape.

—Curtis O. Byer and
Louis W. Shainberg,
Living Well: Health in Your Hands,
2nd ed.

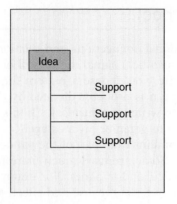

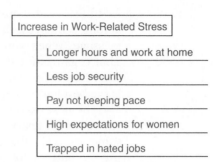

Definition

Frequently in a textbook, an entire paragraph is devoted to defining a complex term or idea. With **definition,** the concept is defined initially and then expanded with examples and restatements. In a textbook, a defined term is usually signaled by *italic* or **bold** type.

EXAMPLE   ULTRASOUND

Ultrasound is a technique that uses sound waves to produce an image that enables a physician to detect structural abnormalities. Useful pictures can be obtained as early as five or six weeks into pregnancy. Ultrasound is frequently used in conjunction with other techniques such as amniocentesis and fetoscopy.

—John Dacey and John Travers,
Human Development, 2nd ed.

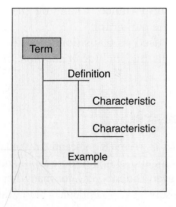

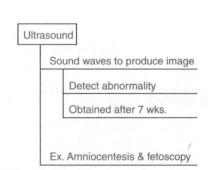

Description

Description is like listing; the characteristics that make up a description are no more than a definition or a simple list of details.

EXAMPLE   CARIBBEAN

Caribbean America today is a land crowded with so many people that, as a region (encompassing the Greater and Lesser Antilles), it is the most densely populated part of the Americas. It is also a place of grinding poverty and, in all too many localities, unrelenting misery with little chance for escape.

—H. J. De Blij and Peter O. Muller,
Geography: Realms, Regions, and Concepts, 7th ed.

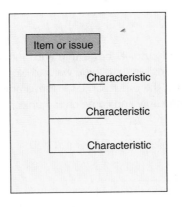

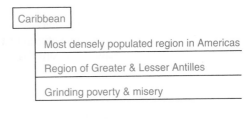

Time Order, Sequence, or Narration

Items are listed in the order in which they occurred or in a specifically planned order in which they must develop. In this case, the **time order** is important, and changing it would change the meaning. Narrative writing, which tells a story, is an example of writing in which time order is important.

Signal words that are often used for time order, sequence, or narration include *first, second, third, after, before, when, until, at last, next, later.* Actual time periods, such as days or years, also signal sequence and time.

EXAMPLE   **THE MORMON MOVEMENT**

The idea of the Mormon Church began when a young Joseph Smith, Jr., went into the New York woods in 1820 and was told by God that the true church of God would be reestablished. In 1823, another revelation led him to find buried golden plates and translate the *Book of Mormon*. Smith attracted thousands of followers and in the 1830s moved from Ohio to Missouri to Illinois to seek religious freedom for his group. In 1844 Smith was shot by an angry mob. After his death, a new leader, Brigham Young, led the Mormons to the Great Salt Lake.

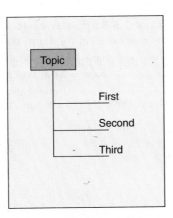

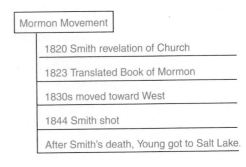

Contrast

With **contrast,** items are presented according to differences between or among them. Signal words that are often used for contrast include *different, in contrast, on the other hand, but, however, bigger than.*

EXAMPLE ORANGES

An orange grown in Florida usually has a thin and tightly fitting skin, and it is also heavy with juice. Californians say that if you want to eat a Florida orange you have to get into a bathtub first. On the other hand, California oranges are light in weight and have thick skins that break easily and come off in hunks.

—John McPhee,
Oranges

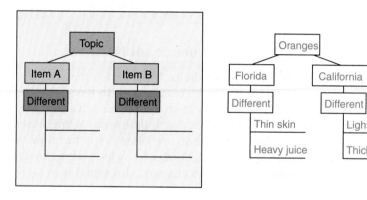

Comparison

With **comparison,** items are presented according to similarities between or among them. Signal words that are often used for comparison include *similar, in the same way, likewise, just like.*

EXAMPLE JAZZ GREATS

Jazz greats Louis Armstrong and Billie Holiday overcame similar obstacles in their struggling early years. Both were raised in the slums by working mothers, and both learned the discipline needed for success through hard work. As a teen, Armstrong hauled coal from 7 A.M. to 5 P.M. for 75 cents a day and then practiced on his trumpet after work. Similarly, after school, Holiday scrubbed the white stone steps of neighbors' houses to earn an average of 90 cents a day, and then she came home to practice her singing.

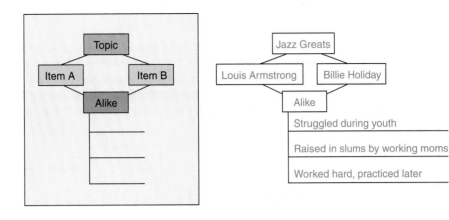

Comparison-Contrast

Some passages combine comparison and contrast into a single paragraph. This combination is called a **comparison-contrast** pattern and is demonstrated in the following examples.

HISPANIC AMERICANS

The primary groups in the rising new minority are Mexican Americans and Cuban Americans. Mexican Americans are heavily concentrated in the Southwest, whereas Cuban Americans are concentrated in Florida, particularly in the Miami area. Together the groups are called Hispanic Americans or Latinos. Although their histories are different, they share several similarities. They both speak the Spanish language and most of them, at least 85 percent, are Roman Catholic.

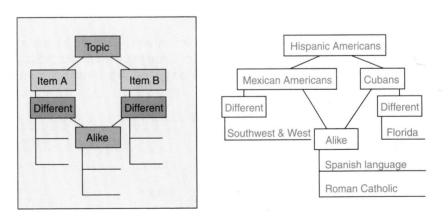

Cause and Effect

With **cause and effect,** an element is shown as producing another element. One is the *cause* or the "happening" that stimulated the particular result or *effect*. A paragraph may describe one cause or many causes, as well as one or many results. Signal words that are often used for cause and effect include *for this reason, consequently, on that account, hence, because.*

EXAMPLE   **WINTER CAMP AT VALLEY FORGE**

General George Washington's Continental army set up camp on the frozen grounds of Valley Forge in December 1777 and experienced dire consequences. The winter was particularly cold that year, and the soldiers lacked straw and blankets. Many froze in their beds. Food was scarce, and soldiers died of malnutrition. Because of the misery and disease in the camp, many soldiers deserted the army and went home.

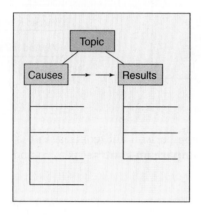
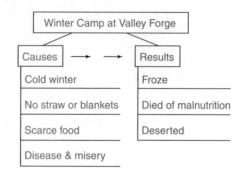

Classification

To simplify a complex topic, authors frequently begin introductory paragraphs by stating that the information that follows is divided into a certain number of groups or categories. The divisions are then named and the parts are explained. Signal words often used for **classification** include *two divisions, three groups, four elements, five classes, six levels, seven categories,* and so on.

EXAMPLE   **PREDATION**

Predation, the interaction in which one species kills and eats another, involves two groups. The predator, or consumer, must be alert and skillful to locate and capture the prey. The consumable group, or prey, constantly must adapt its behavior to defend against being eaten.

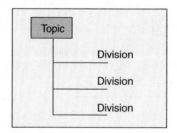
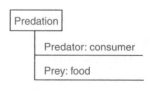

Addition

The addition pattern is used to provide more information related to something that has already been explained. Signal words are *furthermore, again, also, further, moreover, besides, likewise.*

EXAMPLE **ENTREPRENEUR QUINCY JONES**

Not only is Quincy Jones the talented producer who helped drive Michael Jackson's "Beat It" to a number one hit and "Thriller" to the best-selling album of all time, he is also the founder of *VIBE* magazine and the co-owner of *SPIN* magazine. Furthermore, Jones, who has been awarded twenty-six Grammys and a Grammy Legend, is chairman and CEO of the Quincy Jones Media Group.

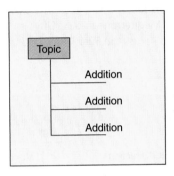

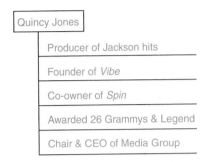

Summary

A **summary,** which usually comes at the end of an article or chapter, condenses the main idea or thesis into a short and simple concluding statement with a few major supporting details. Signal words are *in conclusion, briefly, to sum up, in short, in a nutshell.*

EXAMPLE **WWII TOTAL WAR**

In conclusion, World War II was more of a total war than any previous war in history. Some 70 nations took part in the war, and fighting took place on the continents of Europe, Asia, and Africa. Entire societies participated, either as soldiers, war workers, or victims of occupation and mass murder.

—Adapted from James Kirby Martin et al.,
America and Its People

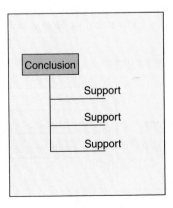

Location or Spatial Order

Location or **spatial order** identifies the whereabouts of a place or object. Signal words are *north, east, south, west, next to, near, below, above, close by, within, without, adjacent to, beside, around, to the right or left side, opposite.*

EXAMPLE   EGYPT

The Republic of Egypt is located in the northeastern corner of Africa. The northern border of Egypt is the Mediterranean Sea. Libya is the country to the west, and the Sudan lies to the south. Across the Suez Canal and to the east lies Israel.

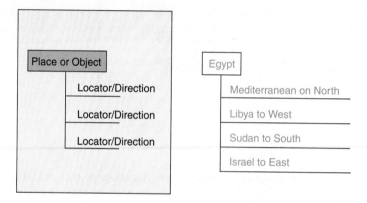

Generalization and Example

In the **generalization-and-example** pattern, a general statement or conclusion is supported with specific examples. Signal words include *to restate that, that is, for example, to illustrate, for instance.*

EXAMPLE   SMOKING

To restate it in simple terms, smoking kills. The American Cancer Society estimates that tobacco smoking is the cause of 30 percent of all deaths from cancer. Lung cancer is the leading cause of death from cancer in the United States, with 85 percent to 90 percent of these cases linked to smoking. Save your life by not smoking.

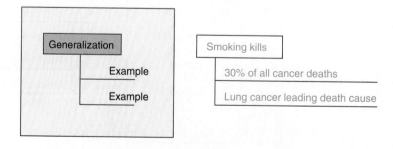

Reader's *Tip* — Patterns of Organization and Signal Words

➤ **Addition:** furthermore • again • also • further • moreover • besides • likewise
(provides more information)
➤ **Cause and Effect:** because • for this reason • consequently • hence • as a result • thus • due to • therefore
(shows one element as producing or causing a result or effect)
➤ **Classification:** groups • categories • elements • classes • parts
(divides items into groups or categories)
➤ **Comparison:** in a similar way • similar • parallel to • likewise • in a like manner
(lists similarities among items)
➤ **Contrast:** on the other hand • bigger than • but • however • conversely • on the contrary • although • nevertheless
(lists differences among items)
➤ **Definition:** can be defined • means • for example • like
(initially defines a concept and expands with examples and restatements)
➤ **Description:** is • as • is made up of • could be described as
(lists characteristics or details)
➤ **Generalization and Example:** to restate • that is • for example • to illustrate • for instance
(explains with examples to illustrate)
➤ **Location or Spatial Order:** next to • near • below • above • close by • within • without • adjacent to • beside • around • to the right or left side • opposite
(identifies the whereabouts of objects)
➤ **Simple Listing:** also • another • several • for example
(randomly lists items in a series)
➤ **Summary:** in conclusion • briefly • to sum up • in short • in a nutshell
(condenses major points)
➤ **Time Order, Sequence, or Narration:** first • second • finally • after • before • next • later • now • at last • until • thereupon • while • during
(lists events in order of occurrence)

exercise 5.3 **Identifying Paragraph Patterns**

Each of the following items presents the first two sentences of a paragraph stating the main idea and a major supporting detail. Select the letter that indicates the pattern of organization that you would predict for each.

_____c_____ 1. Jim Vicary coined the term *subliminal advertising,* claiming that inserting messages like "Eat popcorn" and "Drink Coca-Cola" into movies would increase consumption. According to Vicary, the messages, flashed too fast for the human eye to recognize but registered in the brain, would prompt a rush to the snack bar.

   a. summary
   b. classification
   c. definition
   d. comparison-contrast

_____b_____ 2. Now an integral part of the recruiting strategy, companies of all sizes are finding that e-cruiting, job recruiting over the Internet, has many benefits. To begin, the Internet is a fast, convenient, and inexpensive way to find prospective job candidates.

   a. description
   b. simple listing
   c. time order
   d. classification

_____a_____ 3. Most prisons are designed to have three levels of custody: maximum, medium, and minimum. Maximum security prisons usually have a 25-foot wall surrounding the entire facility to prevent the escape of dangerous felons.

   a. classification
   b. cause and effect
   c. definition
   d. comparison

_____c_____ 4. As a result of the Great Depression, Hollywood flourished. Cheap tickets, free time, and the lure of fantasy brought 60 million to 80 million Americans to the movies each week.

   a. comparison-contrast
   b. simple listing
   c. cause and effect
   d. description

_____d_____ 5. Queens ruled England in the second half of the sixteenth century. In 1553, Mary I took the throne. She was followed in 1558 by Elizabeth I, who ruled for the next 45 years.

   a. summary
   b. contrast
   c. classification
   d. time order

_____a_____ 6. The great white shark is a 6- to 7-meter predator. This most dangerous of all sharks gets extra power and speed from its warm muscles.

  a. description
  b. addition
  c. location or spatial order
  d. generalization and example

_____b_____ 7. Although both artists lived in Spain, Pablo Picasso and Salvador
Dali had styles that differed dramatically. Picasso depicted his subjects in abstract terms, whereas Dali painted the stark reality of the
image.

  a. description
  b. comparison-contrast
  c. time order
  d. simple listing

_____c_____ 8. Michelangelo depicted the creation of Eve on a panel that is almost
in the center of the Sistine Chapel ceiling. The Creation of Adam, a
larger and more famous panel, is located adjacent to it and toward
the back of the chapel.

  a. simple listing
  b. time order
  c. location or spatial order
  d. definition

_____b_____ 9. In short, the Internet can be a source of dangerous misinformation.
Anyone can develop a Web site and fill it with distortions of the
truth and inflammatory accusations.

  a. classification
  b. summary
  c. definition
  d. time order

_____d_____ 10. In case of a sprained ankle, you should first apply ice to constrict
the blood vessels and stop internal bleeding. Next, elevate your foot
above the level of your heart to further control bleeding by making
the blood flow away from the injured area.

  a. summary
  b. classification
  c. generalization and example
  d. sequence

exercise 5.4   **Patterns of Organization and Main Idea**

Read the following passages, and use the three-question system you learned in Chapter 4 to determine the author's main idea. In addition, indicate the dominant pattern of organization used by the author. Select from the following list:

classification	definition	description
example	cause and effect	comparison-contrast

Passage A

Also called ice pellets, sleet is formed when raindrops or melted snowflakes freeze as they pass through a subfreezing layer of air near Earth's surface. Sleet does not stick to trees and wires, and it usually bounces when it hits the ground. An accumulation of sleet sometimes has the consistency of dry sand.

—Frederick K. Lutgens and Edward J. Tarbuck,
The Atmosphere, 9th ed.

1. Who or what is this about? <u>Sleet</u>

2. What are the major details? <u>Sleet is also called ice pellets; sleet is formed</u>
   <u>when raindrops or melted snow pass through cold air; sleet does not stick to</u>
   <u>trees and wires; sleet bounces on impact; accumulated sleet is like dry sand.</u>

3. What is the overall pattern of organization? <u>Definition</u>

4. What is the main idea the authors are trying to convey about the topic? <u>Sleet</u>
   <u>is formed when liquid precipitation freezes near the Earth's surface.</u>

Passage B

A man bought his first new Lexus—a $45,000 piece of machinery. He took delivery of his new honey and started to drive it home. The lights, the windshield washer, the gizmo cup holder that popped out of the center console, the seat heater that warmed him on a cold winter morning—he tried them all. On a whim, he turned on the radio. His favorite classical music station came on in splendid quadrophonic sound. He pushed the second button. It was his favorite news station. The third button brought his favorite talk station that kept him awake on long trips. The fourth button was set to his daughter's favorite rock station. The customer was delighted.

—Adapted from Denny Hatch, "Delight Your Customers,"
Target Marketing, April 1, 2002

1. Who or what is this about? <u>A man's new Lexus</u>

2. What are the major details? The car's luxuries and the radio

_____

_____

_____

3. What is the overall pattern of organization? Description

4. What is the main idea the author is trying to convey about the topic? The new Lexus owner was delighted with his car.

_____

_____

Passage C

There are so many types of water available to drink in the United States, how can we group them and distinguish among them? If we prefer to drink water with bubbles—carbonation—we can choose carbonated water. This type of water contains carbon dioxide gas that either occurs naturally or is added to the water. Mineral water is another beverage option. Mineral waters contain 250 to 500 parts per million of minerals. While many people prefer the unique taste of mineral water, a number of brands contain high amounts of sodium so they should be avoided by people who are trying to reduce their sodium intake. Distilled water is processed in such a way that all dissolved minerals are removed. This type of water is often used in steam irons, as it will not clog the iron with mineral buildup. Purified water has been treated so that all dissolved minerals and contaminants are removed, making this type of water useful in research and medical procedures. Of course, we can also drink the tap water found in our homes and in public places.

—Adapted from Janice Thompson and Melinda Manore,
Nutrition: An Applied Approach

1. Who or what is this about? Types of drinking water

_____

2. What are the major details? Carbonated, mineral, distilled, purified, and tap

_____

_____

_____

3. What is the overall pattern of organization? Classification

4. What is the main idea the authors are trying to convey about the topic?
There are several distinct categories of drinking water.

_____

_____

Passage D

The law of demand states that the quantity demanded will increase as the price is lowered as long as other factors that affect demand do not change. The makers of M&M candy conducted an experiment in the law of demand, holding the necessary demand-affecting conditions constant. Over a 12-month test period, the price of M&Ms was held constant in 150 stores while the content weight of the candy was increased. By holding the price constant and increasing the weight, the price (per ounce) was lowered. In the stores where the price was dropped, sales rose by 20 to 30 percent almost overnight. As a result of the law of demand, a reduction in prices caused the quantity demanded to rise.

—Adapted from Paul R. Gregory,
Essentials of Economics, 6th ed.

1. Who or what is this about? <u>M&Ms and the law of demand</u>

2. What are the major details? <u>Quantity demanded increases with lowered per-</u>
   <u>ounce price; the M&M study supported the law of demand.</u>

3. What is the overall pattern of organization? <u>Cause and effect</u>

4. What is the main idea the author is trying to convey about the topic? <u>The</u>
   <u>M&M experiment supports the law of demand—the quantity demanded will</u>
   <u>increase as the price is lowered, with all other factors remaining constant.</u>

Passage E

One overlooked part of many presidents' emotional makeup has been their extraordinarily close relationship with their mothers. These mothers were strong, religious women who dominated the raising of their favorite sons. To illustrate the closeness of a few, Harry Truman had a portrait of his mom hung in the White House, and Calvin Coolidge died carrying a picture of his. In Richard Nixon's Watergate farewell address, he called his mother a "saint." Lyndon Johnson declared his mother "the strongest person I ever knew." Sara Roosevelt rented an apartment in Cambridge to be near Franklin at college. Years later when some New York political bosses asked him to run for office, he responded, "I'd like to talk with my mother about it first."

—Gary Wasserman,
The Basics of American Politics, 12th ed.

1. Who or what is this about? <u>Presidents' relationships with their mothers</u>

2. What are the major details? How Harry Truman, Calvin Coolidge, Richard Nixon, Lyndon Johnson, and Franklin Roosevelt each felt about his mother

_____

_____

3. What is the overall pattern of organization? Example _____

4. What is the main idea the author is trying to convey about the topic? Several presidents had very close relationships with their strong, dominating mothers.

_____

Passage F

I immediately noted differences in the early [basketball] practices. Girls' attention to directions was far superior to the boys', most of whom found it physically impossible not to be distracted by any movement anywhere in the gym. Whereas the boys generally either went deadpan or shot me the evil "how dare you" death stare when I corrected their play, the girls often sincerely apologized for any mistake. My stereotypically gawky center, when told not to leave her feet on defense, said, "I know. I'm sorry. I'm terrible." Strangest of all, they actually wanted to talk to me and the other coach, something teenage boys found equivalent to having their nose hairs individually plucked out in front of an audience.

—Brendan O'Shaughnessy,
"It's a Whole New Ballgame for Veteran Coach"

1. Who or what is this about? Basketball practice differences between boys and girls

_____

_____

2. What are the major details? Girls had better attention to directions; girls often apologized for mistakes; girls enjoyed talking with the coaches.

_____

_____

3. What is the overall pattern of organization? Comparison and contrast ____

4. What is the main idea the author is trying to convey about the topic? _____ Coaching girls is a different experience than coaching boys.

_____

_____

Mixed Organizational Patterns

Suppose you were writing an orientation article describing support services available at your own college. You could present the resources in a **simple listing** pattern, or you could discuss them in the **sequence** or **time order** in which a freshman is likely to need them or in terms of the most convenient geographic **locations** to students. Within your article, you might use a **description** or **definition** pattern to identify a relatively unknown service on campus, with **examples** of how it has helped others. You could demonstrate **cause and effect** with facts and statistics on how using services has helped students. You might also choose to **compare and contrast** a special service with that at another college.

You could supply **additional** information by presenting the qualifications of professional staff providing the services. To wrap things up, you could create an overall **summary** about the support services. Thus, one long article might have an overall **simple listing** pattern of organization yet contain individual paragraphs that follow other patterns.

---

exercise 5.5 | **Identifying Combined Organizational Patterns**

Read the following textbook excerpts and answer the questions that follow. Note how combined organizational patterns may help you understand the main idea of a longer piece of writing. Signal words are set in bold type to help you identify a particular pattern.

Does the title suggest a pattern?

Passage 1
What Are Dust Devils?
A common phenomenon in arid regions of the world is the whirling vortex called the dust devil. Although they resemble tornadoes, dust devils are generally much smaller and less intense than their destructive cousins. Most dust devils are only a few meters in diameter and reach heights no greater than about 100 meters (300 feet). **By definition,** these whirlwinds are usually short-lived microscale phenomena. Most form and die out within minutes. In rare instances dust devils have lasted for hours.

Unlike tornadoes, which are associated with convective clouds, dust devils form on days when clear skies dominate. **In contrast,** these whirlwinds form from the ground upward, exactly opposite of tornadoes. Because surface heating is critical to their formation, dust devils occur most frequently in the afternoon when surface temperatures are highest.

Which pattern is suggested by the boldface words?

When the air near the surface is considerably warmer than the air a few dozen meters overhead, the layer of air near Earth's surface becomes unstable. In this situation warm surface air begins to rise, **causing** air near the ground to be drawn into the developing whirlwind. **As a result,** the rotating winds that are associated with dust devils are produced by the same phenomenon that causes ice skaters to spin faster as they pull their arms closer to their bodies. As the inwardly spiraling air rises, it carries sand, dust, and other loose debris dozens of meters into the air. It is this material that makes a dust devil visible. Occasionally, dust devils form above vegetated surfaces. Under these conditions, the vortices may go undetected unless they interact with objects at the surface.

—Adapted from Frederick K. Lutgens and Edward J. Tarbuck,
The Atmosphere, 9th ed.

1. Who or what is this about? Dust devils

_____

2. What overall pattern is suggested by the title? Definition

_____

3. What is the pattern of organization in the first paragraph? Definition

_____

4. What is the pattern of organization in the second paragraph? Contrast

_____

5. What is the pattern of organization in the third paragraph? Cause and effect

_____

6. What is the main idea the authors are trying to convey about the topic?

While dust devils may be considered relatives of tornadoes, several

differences distinguish the two phenomena.

_____

Passage 2
The Success of eBay

eBay is one of the most successful e-commerce businesses. **Unlike** Amazon.com, it does not need expensive warehouses and storage facilities. eBay earns its revenues by charging a small fee to sellers who list their products on eBay for sale. **While other** dot-com companies have suffered losses in recent years, eBay, **on the other hand,** has been consistently profitable, earning almost $150 million in annual profits.

eBay exists in all major countries (eBay Germany, eBay Austria, eBay Canada, and so on). It operates a worldwide virtual auction market in which registered sellers can list products and registered buyers can enter bids for them. Participants in this virtual market can follow the progress of bids online as each auction progresses. (Usually an ending time of each auction is listed.)

Products auctioned on eBay range from the ordinary to the unique or exotic. On a given day, wooden crates of rough jade ($15.95), a Tibetan bronze Buddha ($88), a 1913 Catholic dictionary ($204), a 1725 bible ($348), and an 1895 U.S. Navy steam launch engine ($2,025) can be found on auction.

eBay deals with problems of dishonesty. **That is,** eBay maintains bulletin boards of comments submitted by eBay subscribers, organized by the identification number of eBay buyers and sellers. These ratings provide information on records of past honesty and reliability. A "cheating" buyer or seller would not be able to buy or sell on eBay after disclosure of negative comments.

eBay **offers several** enormous **advantages** to buyers and sellers. **First,** the seller can gain access to a large number of potential buyers of unusual products by paying a small fee to eBay. **Second,** buyers have the opportunity to bid on thousands of products and services without leaving the comfort of their homes. Historically, exotic products such as Rembrandt paintings and Kennedy presidential memorabilia were auctioned by prestigious auction houses such as Sotheby's, which typically collected fees of 15 percent or more. It appears to be only a matter of time until rare and expensive items will be auctioned on eBay.

—Adapted from Paul R. Gregory,
Essentials of Economics, 6th ed.

1. Who or what is this about? How eBay has become successful

2. What overall pattern is suggested by the title? Cause and effect

3. What is the pattern of organization in the first paragraph? Contrast

4. What is the pattern of organization in the second paragraph? Definition

5. What is the pattern of organization in the third paragraph? Simple listing

6. What is the pattern of organization in the fourth paragraph? Generalization and example

7. What is the pattern of organization in the final paragraph? Simple listing

Summary *Points*

➤ **What are transitional words?**
Transitional or signal words connect parts of sentences and lead you to anticipate a continuation or a change in thoughts. They guide you through the logic of the message by showing the relationships of ideas within sentences, between sentences, and between paragraphs.

➤ **What is an organizational pattern, and how many types of patterns can be used in textbooks?**
An organizational pattern is the presentation plan, format, or structure of a message. It is a way to present ideas with logic. There are at least thirteen possible configurations or patterns for logically presenting details.

➤ **Why are several organizational patterns sometimes combined to develop a main idea?**
To fully present and explore the message, one long article may have a general overall pattern of organization yet contain individual paragraphs that follow other patterns.

selection 1   Narrative

Contemporary *Focus*

How is marriage changing in America? What do the statistics reveal? Young adults are establishing themselves in careers and marrying later. How does this affect behavior, expectations, and the eventual marriage relationship?

So Many Men, So Few Women

By Sam Roberts
New York Times, February 12, 2006. Copyright © 2006 by The New York Times Co. Reprinted with permission.

People are attracted to one another for lots of reasons, of course, but numbers count, too. And while sex ratios vary by place, nationwide the Census Bureau calculates that among single non-Hispanic whites in their 20's, there are 120 men for every 100 women. The comparable figures are 153 Hispanic men, 132 Asian men and 92 black men for every 100 single women in their 20's of the same race or ethnicity.

Overall, there are 120 men in their 20's who have never been married, widowed, or divorced for every 100 women in the same category.

The median age for first marriages was 25.8 for women and 27.4 for men in 2004, the highest on record. Among whites, Hispanics and Asians, most women marry by their late 20's and men by their early 30's.

These statistics, however, don't tell the whole story. "People's behavior about marriage changed more in the past 30 years than in the last 3,000," said Professor Stephanie Coontz, a sociology professor at Evergreen State College in Washington and author of *Marriage: A History.*

"Women," she added, "are tending with the new equality to be more cautious about an institution that comes with a lot of expectations about women doing the comfort-generating work."

COLLABORATE   Collaborate on responses to the following questions:

➤ Why has the median age for first marriages increased?

➤ How does this increased median age change the dynamics of a marriage?

➤ How does this increased median age change social interaction for young adults?

Skill Development: Preview

Preview the next selection to predict its purpose and organization and to formulate your learning plan.

Activate Schema

What is a curandera?
How much would you pay to have your fortune told?
Are fortune tellers accurate?

Establish a Purpose for Reading

Read the short story to be entertained and to understand the cultural differences between the author and her family.

Increase Word Knowledge

What do you know about these words?

wilt	overwrought	epiphany	equate	inhabited
banishing	vixen	ingrates	imploring	contradiction

Your instructor may give a true-false vocabulary review before or after reading.

Integrate Knowledge While Reading

Questions have been inserted in the margin to stimulate your thinking while reading. Remember to

Predict	Picture	Relate	Monitor	Correct

WHAT I DID FOR LOVE

How does the author express this cultural conflict?

I know what I will be serving at my wedding. My mother's neighbor Doña Ester García will make carne guisada, beef stew, for the main course. My uncle has volunteered one of his steers. I am wondering whether it should be a huge affair, a la Mexicana, with a guest list including the mailman and distant relatives of my sec-
5   ond cousin's inlaws. Or a simple, more Americanized ceremony, with only those by my side who have been part of my most recent life. I have some time to work out the details since I still don't have the groom.

I'm a 25-year-old Mexican American whose relationships wilt faster than orchids in the Texas sun. And that, according to my aunts and cousins, makes me an old maid.
10   Never mind that I've spent the last seven years living and working in major cities throughout the United States where women tend to get married in their late 20s and early 30s. Whenever I come back home to La Joya, Texas, my family is quick to remind me that time is running out. My love life, or lack of it, is especially troubling to my aunts, most of whom have children who are at least seven years
15   younger than I and already married.

I know about the chisme that the aunts swap as they huddle over the kitchen table making tamales.

"She studies way too much. All that work can't be good for her head," says one as she spreads masa on a cornhusk and tops it with a spoonful of beef.
20   "Maybe she doesn't like men. You know, in San Francisco where she used to live, there are a lot of gay people," another tía adds.

I suspect they also talk about me while they watch their favorite Spanish-language soap operas, overwrought stories that always involve a poor girl crying crocodile tears as she calls out, "Carlos José! No me dejes. Yo te amo." (Carlos José! Don't leave me. I love you.)

It was probably during one of those pain-filled telenovelas that one of my tias had an epiphany. Something, she realized, must have happened to me during my childhood, some awful trauma that has made it impossible for me to keep a man.

I'll admit I can scare men off. But I think if has more to do with growing up with four older brothers who rarely spoke to me unless they wanted a shirt ironed or dinner cooked. At an early age, I began to equate marriage with slavery. I couldn't see myself spending the rest of my life washing someone else's underwear.

My relatives view my attitude on the subject as a disease that seems to be getting worse.

It's no secret that my mother has been praying for years for a "good man who can take care of you." And if all the prayer hasn't helped, my Tía Nelly concluded, I must be cursed.

She knew the perfect person to help me: a curandera, a healer who can cure a person of lovelessness just as easily as colic.

"I don't believe in it," my cousin said to me, "but maybe you should go."

I thought about it for a week. If I went, I'd be admitting that I have a problem. If I didn't, I might miss out on a cure.

why did she decide to go?

I picked a Friday afternoon. I decked myself out in a short black dress and red lipstick so the curandera couldn't blame my anemic love life on the way I dressed. Tía Nelly and I drove 35 minutes to Rio Grande City and the curandera's storefront office.

I hid my truck in an alley so nobody I knew would see it. The store looked like an herb shop one might find on South Street in Philadelphia, except this one inhabited

Some women feel pressured by family and friends to get married by a certain age.

Imape 100/Alamy

an old grocery. Inside were long aisles of neatly displayed candles, religious statuettes, soaps and good luck charms. One wall offered packages of herbs and spices.

50   In Latino neighborhoods curanderas are considered not only healers, but also spiritual advisers. They are like doctors, psychiatrists and priests rolled into one.

I am told my father's grandfather, Emeterio Chasco, was a curandero. He didn't charge his clients money; in exchange for banishing a fright, bad luck or a rash, he'd receive chickens, boxes of fruit and personal favors.

55   The only curandero I'd ever met was El Papi, one of my mother's younger cousins. A dark-skinned man who never married and lived with his parents in Mexico, El Papi had big crooked teeth that you saw even when he wasn't smiling. My mother doubted his spiritual powers, but people from nearby towns and ranches consulted with him in his bedroom, which was also the family living room. Nonetheless, I ex-
60   pected my curandera to be an older woman, with hands as worn and soft as my grandmother's. Her touch, I imagined, would be magical enough to cure anything.

Did the curandera's appearance affect the author's belief in her capabilities?

But this curandera greeted me wearing a tight purple shirt and black pants that hugged a killer figure—curves that the bottle-blond healer told me were the prod-uct of hours at the gym. She was a middle-aged vixen, not a grandmotherly adviser.
65   A thoroughly modern healer who drives a white convertible and recently divorced her husband of more than 20 years.

She performed her consults in the area once designated "for employees only." For $20 she gave me a card reading that she said would give us both a better handle on mi problema. She asked me to shuffle the tarot cards and then split the deck into
70   three stacks. She instructed me to use my left hand to place the different piles back into one. I kept my left hand on the pile. She covered it with her left hand and prayed. Then she began to deal the cards. Her long, pearl-colored acrylic nails made clicking noises every time she placed one down, face up. She spread the cards out on her desk. "Your problem," she said, "is a sentimental one."

75   No one could hear our conversation, so I decided to be honest. "My aunt said maybe you could help me because I can't seem to find the right guy or even keep the bad ones I date."

"This is not logical. You are very pretty," she said, looking me straight in the eye. "Men are desgraciados [ingrates]. You can give everything except your heart, be-
80   cause they will hurt you."

After a few more minutes of reading my life in the cards, she looked at me as if to say: "This is more serious than I thought."

"There was a woman about five years ago, and her name starts with the letter M," she said. "There was money paid to keep men away from you, and it was proba-
85   bly done in Mexico because they will do anything over there."

But that was all she could tell me. I would, she said, have to come back the next morning so she could start doing some work on me. She asked for $48 to buy 40 candles that she'd burn while she prayed that night in hopes that everything we needed to know about the mysterious M would reveal itself. I would also need to
90   pay $20 for a barrida, a cleansing ritual.

The next day the curandera was 10 minutes late—she had just finished a two-hour workout. She said she had news for me. Her overnight mediation had revealed two more letters of the mystery woman's name: A and R.

"Do you know anyone whose name starts with M-A-R?" she asked. Half of the
95   Latinas I know have names that start with M-A-R: Maria, Martina, Marisa, Marisela, Marielena, Marina, Marta, Margarita.

Well, she said, the women in question now dyes her hair guerro, blond. That only disqualified half.

"Last night," she said, "I saw a small black-and-white photo, probably from a yearbook."

Then the curandera explained what was wrong. The evil MAR woman, she said, had loved someone I was dating and had paid a dark man from Mexico to curse me, to keep men from sticking around.

Does the author still have faith in the curandera?

The curse, she said, could be removed for $275, and even if I opted to go somewhere else, she advised me to get help as soon as possible. I couldn't remember dating anyone within the last five years who was so special that another woman would pay to have him. But I told her she could give me a barrida.

That, she promised, would definitely make me feel better, but I still needed to have the curse removed.

For the barrida, she had me stand just outside her office, facing south, in the middle of a circle that looked as if it had been burned into the floor. She instructed me to stretch my arms over my head as if I were singing or praising the Lord at church.

She doused her hands with lavender-scented alcohol and touched my neck, arms, hands and legs. She then began making the sign of the cross with a brown-shelled egg that she said had been laid by a black hen. The egg was cold. I couldn't help but wonder whether it had lost its magic while sitting in the refrigerator.

The curandera prayed, fast and in Spanish, imploring the bad spirits to leave. She then lighted a candle and walked around me, asking some invisible power to illuminate me. She put the candle down and crumbled some dried leaves around the circle and poured alcohol on them. She grabbed the candle and set the circle on fire.

Her praying was so fervent and so rapid that I could understand only a few phrases: "Give her a pure love," "send her a good man." Essentially, the same thing my mom had been asking for.

It was getting hot. The flames were inching closer to my toes and there was smoke. Just when I thought I might melt I heard her say: "Jump over the flame." I did.

For the next three days, she said, before I ate anything else I was to drink half a cup of water mixed with sugar followed by a single banana cut into slices and covered with honey. She sold me two $10 candles that I was supposed to light and pray to.

Then she calmly reminded me that I still had to come back to get the curse removed.

But I'd had enough. I had no intention of drinking sugar water, eating honey-coated slices of banana or lighting candles. Maybe I was afraid to rely on some vague magic I didn't understand.

Or maybe I believed in it too much and couldn't bear the thought that it might not work.

When you live squeezed between two cultures, two languages, you are often a walking contradiction. Sometimes there is little you can do to keep both worlds at peace.

For days after the barrida I thought about everything the curandera told me. I held on to the things I wanted to believe—that I was too pretty not to attract men, that I would eventually end up with a successful, good man. And weighed those I didn't—that unless I reversed the curse there was no hope.

I wondered why a modern woman like me should listen to a curandera, even a with-it one clad in spandex. And then I remembered the words of another curandero: El Papi.

I was in the fourth grade and we were visiting his family in Nuevo Leon.

He and I were standing in the middle of the woods and I was watching him break an egg over a pile of sticks he was about to set on fire.

"Can you make someone fall in love with someone else?" I asked.

150   He looked up.

"Yes. I can," he said. "But that wouldn't be true love. You can't force love. You just have to wait for it to happen."

(1,980 words)

—Macarena del Rocío Hernández;
from *The Philadelphia Inquirer*

How does El Papi's advice contradict that of the curandera?

Recall

Stop to self-test, relate, and react.

Your instructor may choose to give you a true-false comprehension review.

Write About the Selection

Why does the author describe herself as a "walking contradiction"? What does she mean by this phrase? Why does she tell her story with humor?

Response Suggestion: Define "walking contradiction" and list examples from the story that show contradictions in her personality.

Contemporary *Link*

College provides many opportunities to meet people of the opposite sex. The workplace, however, is different, and social interaction may require more thought or planning. What suggestions for meeting potential mates would you make to unmarried college graduates in their late twenties? List at least five options, and explain the advantages and disadvantages of each.

Skill Development: Identify Organizational Patterns

Answer the following questions with *T* (true) or *F* (false).

_____T_____ 1. The organizational pattern is narrative or time order.

_____T_____ 2. The author flashes back in time to tell the story.

Check Your Comprehension

After reading the selection, answer the following questions with *a*, *b*, *c*, or *d*. To help you analyze your strengths and weaknesses, the question types are indicated.

Main Idea   __d__ 1. Which of the following best states the main idea of this selection?

    a. A young woman's family accepts her failure to find a husband.

    b. A young woman returns home to learn about her future from a curandera.

    c. A young woman challenges the culture that expects an early marriage.

    d. A young woman reflects on her adventures in reaction to her family's eagerness for her to marry.

Inference   __b__ 2. The reader can conclude from the narrator's tone or attitude that she

    a. is not respectful of her family.

    b. does not take herself too seriously.

    c. is excessively concerned about how her wedding ceremony will be conducted.

    d. is not an independent thinker.

Inference   __c__ 3. The narrator's description of her aunts' comments shows that she feels her aunts are

    a. being mean.

    b. not concerned with her welfare.

    c. tied to tradition.

    d. against education.

Inference   __c__ 4. When the narrator says that her "relationships wilt faster than orchids in the Texas sun," she means that

    a. she doesn't really want a romantic relationship.

    b. she doesn't know how to get along with men.

    c. none of her relationships last very long.

    d. her relationships in La Joya never work out.

Detail   __a__ 5. When the narrator meets the curandera in Rio Grande City, she is surprised because the curandera

    a. does not fit her preconception.

    b. is located in a converted herb shop.

    c. wants money right away.

    d. is painfully direct with her.

Detail   __c__ 6. The total amount of money the narrator paid the *curandera* seems to be closest to

    a. $20.

    b. $48.

    c. $108.

    d. $275.

Inference   ___b___   7. When the narrator wonders if the brown-shelled egg "had lost its magic while sitting in the refrigerator," she is most probably revealing her

    a. concern for her love life.
    b. doubts about the curandera.
    c. interest in the barrida.
    d. worry about the barrida's cost.

Inference   ___b___   8. The reader can conclude that the purpose of the barrida the narrator experiences is to

    a. teach a prayer.
    b. cleanse the spirit.
    c. bring love.
    d. test the will.

Inference   ___c___   9. The reader can conclude that the narrator is willing to go along with Tía Nelly and actually see a curandera partly because she

    a. resents the advice of her aunts.
    b. knows that her uncle has helped other people.
    c. feels a mixed attraction to the culture in which she was raised.
    d. believes in the power of a barrida.

Inference   ___d___   10. When the narrator describes herself as "a walking contradiction," she means that she

    a. contradicts people on cultural issues.
    b. means different things to different people.
    c. wishes that she were not an educated woman.
    d. feels torn between two ways of life.

Answer the following with *T* (true) or *F* (false).

Inference   ___F___   11. The narrator implies that her friends in the big city where she lives and works think of her as an old maid.

Detail   ___T___   12. The narrator's family views the narrator's unmarried state as a very serious problem that needs to be solved.

Detail   ___F___   13. The narrator admits being in love once but losing the man to another.

Detail   ___T___   14. The narrator credits her brothers with making her equate marriage with slavery.

Detail   ___F___   15. The narrator feels that her aunts gain valuable insights by watching their telenovelas.

Build Your Vocabulary

According to the way the italicized word was used in the selection, indicate *a, b, c,* or *d* for the word or phrase that gives the best definition. The number in parentheses indicates the line of the passage in which the word is located.

_____b_____ 1. "relationships *wilt*" (8)
    a. increase
    b. dry up
    c. grow
    d. hide

_____d_____ 2. "*overwrought* stories" (23)
    a. calm
    b. silly
    c. unbelievable
    d. emotional

_____b_____ 3. "had an *epiphany*" (27)
    a. epileptic fit
    b. sudden insight
    c. dream
    d. flashback

_____c_____ 4. "*equate* marriage" (31)
    a. dislike
    b. believe
    c. associate
    d. downgrade

_____c_____ 5. "*inhabited* an old grocery" (47)
    a. abandoned
    b. was next to
    c. occupied
    d. shared with

_____b_____ 6. "*banishing* a fright" (53)
    a. curing
    b. sending away
    c. causing
    d. making up

_____b_____ 7. "middle-aged *vixen*" (64)
    a. ghost
    b. attractive woman
    c. victim
    d. gym instructor

_____d_____ 8. "Men are desgraciados [*ingrates*]" (79)
    a. incapable of relationships
    b. very strong
    c. extremely needy
    d. ungrateful people

_____b_____ 9. "*imploring* the bad spirits" (117)
    a. hoping
    b. begging
    c. searching
    d. cursing

_____b_____ 10. "a walking *contradiction*" (137)
    a. agreement
    b. conflict
    c. athlete
    d. healer

Search the Net

Use a search engine such as Google, Yahoo, Ask.com, Excite, Dogpile, or Lycos to find information on the average age of marriage for men and women in the United States. Compare the average age now to the average age 20 years ago and 100 years ago. Explain reasons for the differences. For suggested Web sites and other research activities, go to http://www.ablongman.com/smith/.

Contemporary *Focus*

Dr. Condoleezza Rice is the first African American woman to be secretary of state. She has brains, bravado, and a commanding presence. She loves foreign policy, fashion, and football. While growing up, Rice recalls that parental expectations were always high. In an interview she said, "My parents had me absolutely convinced that, well, you may not be able to have a hamburger at Woolworth's, but you can be president of the United States."

What Makes Condi Run

By Ann Reilly Dowd
AARP Magazine, September–October, 2005

Born in 1954 in Birmingham, Alabama, during the heart of racial darkness when little black girls couldn't eat at Woolworth's, Condoleezza—named after the Italian musical term *con dolcezza*, to perform "with sweetness"—has spent a half century breaking molds and busting stereotypes: child-prodigy pianist; competitive ice skater; top Soviet advisor at age 34 to President George H. W. Bush; Stanford University's youngest, first female, and first non-white provost; and George W's premier national-security and foreign policy advisor.

Condi's parents indulged their only child, who inherited her taste for fancy clothes from her mother, who loved to shop. She joined the Girl Scouts, took private language lessons (French and Spanish), and read stacks of books. And there was her music; even while Birmingham was plunged into racial torment, she was taking advanced classical piano at the Birmingham Conservatory—a first for a black youngster—and practicing hours a day. Even back then her discipline was extraordinary. At St. Mary's Academy in Denver, the first integrated school Condi attended, she was a straight-A student and a competitive ice skater. Her typical day: up at 4:30 A.M., hit the rink at 5,

practice until 7, then school, piano, back to the rink for an hour, then more piano.

But at 17, she found a new love: geopolitics and, in particular, all things Soviet—the language, the culture, the weaponry, the diplomacy (she even named her car Boris). Her inspiration was a political science professor at the University of Denver, where she was able to enroll at the age of 15, having skipped both first grade and seventh grade. He was former secretary of state Madeleine Albright's father, Czech diplomat and political refugee Josef Korbel. By then Condi had decided she was not a "phenomenal talent" as a pianist.

She still gets up early (5 A.M.) to lift weights or hit the treadmill, her headphones often blaring heavy metal legend Led Zeppelin. She also plays tennis and is taking golf lessons (really). And while she's had some awesome musical moments—playing a Brahms duet with cellist Yo-Yo Ma at Constitution Hall and now being wooed to play with the National Symphony Orchestra Pops by conductor and composer Marvin Hamlisch—she still finds time to play chamber music with a group of friends. And yes, she watches TV. Her favorite shows: *Law & Order* and *Cold Case Files*.

 Collaborate on responses to the following questions:

➤ What is the job of the secretary of state?

➤ Who is Madeleine Albright?

➤ What other president did Condoleezza Rice work for, and what was her job?

Skill Development: Preview

Preview the next selection to predict its purpose and organization and to formulate your learning plan.

Activate Schema

Who was Sojourner Truth?

Why did the Civil War throw women into many leadership roles?

Establish a Purpose for Reading

Although history books tend to be mostly about the accomplishments of men, over time, women also have made contributions and pursued political and other professions. Who were some of the early women leaders? After recalling what you already know about women in history, read the selection to explain the contributions of individuals and groups toward changing the image of women.

Increase Word Knowledge

What do you know about these words?

restrictive	detriment	defiant	communal	hecklers
pursue	hygiene	incessant	convalescent	naive

Your instructor may give a true-false vocabulary review before or after reading.

Integrate Knowledge While Reading

Questions have been inserted in the margin to stimulate your thinking while reading. Remember to

Predict	Picture	Relate	Monitor	Correct

WOMEN IN HISTORY

THREE RADICAL WOMEN

Amelia Bloomer (1818–1894) published the first newspaper issued expressly for women. She called it *The Lily*. Her fame, however, rests chiefly in dress reform. For six or eight years she wore an outfit composed of a knee-length skirt over full pants

gathered at the ankle, which were soon known everywhere as "bloomers." Wherever
5   she went, this style created great excitement and brought her enormous audiences—
including hecklers. She was trying to make the serious point that women's fashions,
often designed by men to suit their own tastes, were too restrictive, often to the
detriment of the health of those who wore them. Still, some of her contemporaries
thought she did the feminist movement as much harm as good.

Why would Bloomer have hurt the movement?

10   Very few feminists hoped to destroy marriage as such. Most of them had husbands and lived conventional, if hectic, lives. And many of the husbands supported
their cause. Yet the feminists did challenge certain marital customs. When Lucy
Stone married Henry Blackwell, she insisted on being called "Mrs. Stone," a defiant
gesture that brought her a lifetime of ridicule. Both she and her husband signed a
15   marriage contract, vowing "to recognize the wife as an independent, rational being."
They agreed to break any law which brought the husband "an injurious and unnatural superiority." But few of the radical feminists indulged in "free love" or joined
communal marriage experiments. The movement was intended mainly to help
women gain control over their own property and earnings and gain better legal
20   guardianship over their children. Voting also interested them, but women's suffrage
did not become a central issue until later in the century.

Why was voting a later issue?

Many black women were part of the movement, including the legendary
Sojourner Truth (1797–1883). Born a slave in New York and forced to marry a man

Former slave Isabella Van Wagener became the abolitionist
Sojourner Truth.

MPI/Hulton Archive/Getty Images

approved by her owner, Sojourner Truth was freed when the state abolished slavery.
25 After participating in religious revivals, she became an active abolitionist and feminist. In 1851 she saved the day at a women's rights convention in Ohio, silencing
hecklers and replying to a man who had belittled the weakness of women:

> The man over there says women need to be helped into carriages and lifted
> over ditches, and to have the best place everywhere. Nobody ever helps me
> 30 into carriages or over puddles, or gives me the best place—and ain't I a
> woman? . . . Look at my arm! I have ploughed and planted and gathered
> into barns, and no man could head me—and ain't I a woman? I could work
> as much and eat as much as a man—when I could get it—and bear the lash
> as well! And ain't I a woman? I have borne thirteen children, and seen
> 35 most of 'em sold into slavery, and when I cried out my mother's grief, none
> but Jesus heard me—and ain't I a woman?

What makes this speech powerful? Read it aloud.

CHANGING THE IMAGE AND THE REALITY

The accomplishments of a few women who dared pursue professional careers had
somewhat altered the image of the submissive and brainless child-woman. Maria
Mitchell of Nantucket, whose father was an astronomer, discovered a comet at the
40 age of twenty-eight. She became the first woman professor of astronomy in the U.S.
(at Vassar in 1865). Mitchell was also the first woman elected to the American
Academy of Arts and Sciences and a founder of the Association for the
Advancement of Women. Elizabeth Blackwell applied to twenty-nine medical
schools before she was accepted. She attended all classes, even anatomy class, de-
45 spite the sneers of some male students. As a physician, she went on to make important contributions in sanitation and hygiene.

Why would there be sneers in anatomy?

By about 1860 women had effected notable improvements in their status.
Organized feminists had eliminated some of the worst legal disadvantages in fifteen
states. The Civil War altered the role—and the image—of women even more drasti-
50 cally than the feminist movement did. As men went off to fight, women flocked
into government clerical jobs. And they were accepted in teaching jobs as never before. Tens of thousands of women ran farms and businesses while the men were
gone. Anna Howard Shaw, whose mother ran a pioneer farm, recalled:

How did the Civil War force an image change?

> It was an incessant struggle to keep our land, to pay our taxes, and to live.
> 55 Calico was selling at fifty cents a yard. Coffee was one dollar a pound.
> There were no men left to grind our corn, to get in our crops, or to care for
> our livestock; and all around us we saw our struggle reflected in the lives of
> our neighbors.

Women took part in crucial relief efforts. The Sanitary Commission, the Union's
60 volunteer nursing program and a forerunner of the Red Cross, owed much of its
success to women. They raised millions of dollars for medicine, bandages, food, hospitals, relief camps, and convalescent homes.

North and South, black and white, many women served as nurses, some as
spies and even as soldiers. Dorothea Dix, already famous as a reformer of prisons
65 and insane asylums, became head of the Union army nurse corps. Clara Barton
and "Mother" Bickerdyke saved thousands of lives by working close behind the

front lines at Antietam, Chancellorsville, and Fredericksburg. Harriet Tubman led a party up the Combahee River to rescue 756 slaves. Late in life she was recog-
70 nized for her heroic act by being granted a government pension of twenty dollars per month.

Southern white women suffered more from the disruptions of the Civil War than did their northern sisters. The proportion of men who went to war or were killed in battle was greater in the South. This made many women self-sufficient during the war. Still, there was hardly a whisper of feminism in the South.
75 The Civil War also brought women into the political limelight. Anna Dickson skyrocketed to fame as a Republican speaker, climaxing her career with an address to the House of Representatives on abolition. Stanton and Anthony formed the National Woman's Loyal League to press for a constitutional amendment banning slavery. With Anthony's genius for organization, the League in one year collected
80 400,000 signatures in favor of the Thirteenth Amendment.

Once abolition was finally assured in 1865, most feminists felt certain that suf-
frage would follow quickly. They believed that women had earned the vote by their patriotic wartime efforts. Besides, it appeared certain that black men would soon be allowed to vote. And once black men had the ballot in hand, how could anyone jus-
85 tify keeping it from white women—or black women? Any feminist who had pre-
dicted in 1865 that women would have to wait another fifty-five years for suffrage would have been called politically naive.

Why was suffrage slow to come?

(1,102 words)

—From Leonard Pitt,
We Americans

Recall

Stop to self-test, relate, and react.

Your instructor may choose to give you a true-false comprehension review.

Write About the Selection

Have we been taught to believe that dynamic women are the exception rather than the rule in history? Is this idea confirmed when we see stories of women only in box inserts and footnotes in history textbooks? How did the actions of many early women "somewhat alter the image of the submissive and brainless child-woman"? Is that image still being altered?

Response Suggestion: List some dynamic women, and discuss how each has changed stereotypical thinking.

Contemporary *Link*

How does Condoleezza Rice continue to change the image of and the prospects for women? What characteristics do you admire about her? How would you compare her to the three radical women in the selection?

Skill Development: Identify Organizational Patterns

Fill in the organizational diagram to reflect the simple-listing pattern of the first part of the selection.

Women & Accomplishments
Bloomer: fashion statement
Stone: legal gains
Truth: freed slaves & proclaimed strength of women
Mitchell: professor of astronomy
Blackwell: physician

Check Your Comprehension

After reading the selection, answer the following questions with *a, b, c,* or *d.* To help you analyze your strengths and weaknesses, the question types are indicated.

Main Idea   ___b___   1. What is the best statement of the main point of this selection?

    a. Women made impressive gains because of their work during the Civil War.

    b. Many women made early contributions to changing the stereotypical image of the female role.

    c. Bloomer, Stone, and Truth changed a radical image into a reality.

    d. Women were slow to get the right to vote despite their efforts.

Detail   ___b___   2. In originating "bloomers," Amelia Bloomer's greatest concern was

    a. fashion.

    b. principle.

    c. expense.

    d. good taste.

Inference   ___c___   3. The major purpose of Sojourner Truth's quoted speech was to

    a. prove that women are stronger than men.

    b. reprimand men for social courtesy.

    c. dramatize the strengths of women.

    d. praise childbearing as a womanly virtue.

Detail   ___d___   4. Lucy Stone's major motive in retaining the name "Mrs. Stone" after marriage was to

    a. condone "free love" without marriage.

    b. de-emphasize the responsibilities of marriage.

    c. purchase property in her own name.

    d. be recognized as an independent person equal to her husband.

Detail   ___d___   5. The article explicitly states that women worked during the Civil War in all the following *except*

    a. farms and businesses.

    b. the military.

    c. government clerical jobs.

    d. the Red Cross.

Inference   ___d___   6. The author implies that the eventual assumption of responsible roles by large numbers of women was primarily due to

    a. the feminist movement.

    b. the determination and accomplishments of female professionals.

    c. a desire to give women a chance.

    d. economic necessity.

Inference _____a_____ 7. The author believes that the Civil War showed southern women to be

    a. as capable as but less vocal than northern women.
    b. more capable than their northern sisters.
    c. capable workers and eager feminists.
    d. less able to assume responsible roles than northern women.

Inference _____b_____ 8. The author's main purpose in mentioning the accomplishments of Maria Mitchell is to point out that

    a. she discovered a comet.
    b. her professional achievements in astronomy were exceptional and thus somewhat improved the image of women.
    c. she was the first woman professor of astronomy in the United States.
    d. she was a founder of the Association for the Advancement of Women.

Detail _____a_____ 9. The article states or implies that all the following women worked to abolish slavery *except*

    a. Anna Howard Shaw.
    b. Harriet Tubman.
    c. Anna Dickson.
    d. Stanton and Anthony.

Inference _____b_____ 10. In the author's opinion, the long wait by women after the Civil War for suffrage

    a. was predictable in 1865.
    b. would not have been expected in 1865.
    c. was due to the vote of black men.
    d. was justified.

Answer the following with *T* (true) or *F* (false).

Detail _____T_____ 11. Women were granted the right to vote in 1920.

Detail _____F_____ 12. Sojourner Truth had been a southern slave.

Inference _____F_____ 13. The author implies that feminist leaders were more concerned with their own right to vote than with the abolition of slavery.

Detail _____F_____ 14. From the very beginning, the right to vote was the focal point of the women's movement.

Detail _____T_____ 15. Sojourner Truth had thirteen children.

Build Your Vocabulary

According to the way the italicized word was used in the selection, indicate *a, b, c,* or *d* for the word or phrase that gives the best definition. The number in parentheses indicates the line of the passage in which the word is located.

____d____ 1. "were too *restrictive*" (7)
   a. showy
   b. expensive
   c. complicated
   d. confining

____a____ 2. "to the *detriment* of" (8)
   a. harm
   b. anger
   c. apology
   d. objection

____b____ 3. "a *defiant* gesture" (13)
   a. unlucky
   b. resistant
   c. admirable
   d. ignorant

____b____ 4. "*communal* marriage experiments" (18)
   a. permanent
   b. living together in groups
   c. illegal
   d. uncommon

____d____ 5. "silencing *hecklers*" (27)
   a. soldiers
   b. rioters
   c. disciples
   d. verbal harassers

____a____ 6. "*pursue* professional careers" (37)
   a. strive for
   b. abandon
   c. acknowledge
   d. indicate

____c____ 7. "sanitation and *hygiene*" (46)
   a. garbage disposal
   b. biology
   c. preservation of health
   d. mental disorders

____d____ 8. "an *incessant* struggle" (54)
   a. earlier
   b. final
   c. novel
   d. unceasing

____d____ 9. "*convalescent* homes" (62)
   a. sanitary
   b. government
   c. reclaimed
   d. recuperating

____a____ 10. "called politically *naive*" (87)
   a. unsophisticated
   b. well informed
   c. dishonest
   d. unfortunate

Search the Net

Use a search engine such as Google, Yahoo, Ask.com, AltaVista, Excite, Dogpile, Yahoo, or Lycos to find information on Rosa Parks. Explain her pivotal role in the civil rights movement. For suggested Web sites and other research activities, go to http://www.ablongman.com/smith/.

Concept Prep for Art History

Why study art history?

Just as written history is a verbal record of the events and people of the past, fine art is a visual interpretation of reality and a reflection of past taste and values. Art tells us about people and their culture, as illustrated in the earliest primitive cave drawings depicting animals and hunters or in the elaborate tombs in the Egyptian pyramids, built for the pharaohs. Through art, we can glimpse a likeness of Elizabeth I, feel the power of a ship battle at sea, or view the majesty of the American frontier. Artists link us to the past through beauty, creativity, and emotion.

When we say "the arts," what do we mean?

The **arts** and the **fine arts** refer to creative works in painting, sculpture, literature, architecture, drama, music, opera, dance, and film. A work that is exceptionally well crafted is said to aspire to the level of fine art.

Museums, a word derived from Greek to mean places presided over by the Muses, display fine arts in paintings and sculpture. Some of the greatest museums in the world are the **Louvre** in Paris, the **Prado** in Madrid, and the **Metropolitan Museum of Art** in New York City.

Who are some of the great artists?

- One of the most extraordinary artists was **Leonardo da Vinci** (1452–1519). He was considered a **Renaissance man** because of his genius, insatiable curiosity, and wide interests in art, engineering, anatomy, and aeronautics. He painted the *Mona Lisa,* the world's most famous painting. This woman with the mysterious smile whose eyes seem to follow you is displayed in the Louvre behind several layers of bulletproof glass.
- **Michelangelo** (1475–1564) was a sculptor, painter, architect, and poet. Before he was 30 years old, he created the famous marble statue of *David,* which portrays the biblical king in his youth. Michelangelo was commissioned by the pope to paint the ceiling of the **Sistine**

Ram's Head, White Hollyhock-Hills (Ram's Head and White Hollyhock, New Mexico) by Georgia O'Keeffe, 1935. Oil on canvas, 20 × 36" (76.2 × 91.44 cm). Brooklyn Museum of Art. Bequest of Edith and Milton Lowenthal, 1992.11.28. © 2006 The Georgia O'Keeffe Foundation/Artist Rights Society (ARS), New York

Chapel in the Vatican in Rome. For four years, the artist worked on his back in the chapel to complete *The Creation of Adam,* which contains more than 400 individual figures.

- The founder and leading artist of the **impressionists** was **Claude Monet** (1840–1926). Critics said the feathery brushstrokes and play of light in his works conveyed the "impression" of a particular moment. Monet advocated getting out of the studio and painting outdoors, facing the subject. He painted many scenes of the gardens and water lily ponds surrounding his home in **Giverny** near Paris.
- **Vincent van Gogh** (1853–1890) borrowed from the impressionists but achieved another dimension in the swirling brushstrokes of his work to convey his unique vision. His sunflower paintings and *Starry Night* are among his most famous works, now popularized in mass reproductions, but in his lifetime van Gogh sold only one painting. He suffered from depression and spent his last years in a mental institution. In an argument with another artist,

he cut off his own ear, which he later sent to a prostitute.

- **Pablo Picasso** (1881–1973) is one of the most influential of all modern artists. Because traditional skills in painting were so easy for him, he looked for new modes of expression. He was the originator of cubism, an abstract style of painting that displays several perspectives of an object simultaneously. One of his most acclaimed paintings is *Guernica,* a haunting visual protest against the savagery of war.
- By the twentieth century, female artists were becoming more prominent. **Mary Cassatt** (1861–1914), an impressionist, holds a unique place in American art. She was one of the first women artists to succeed professionally. Cassatt began her work in Pennsylvania but later settled in Paris. Domestic scenes became her theme, and she portrayed women and children in intimate relationships.

- **Frida Kahlo** (1907–1954), a Mexican artist, is sometimes called the "portrait genie." She dramatized her life story in self-portraits, interweaving them with symbolism, myth, and surrealistic elements. Kahlo was studying to be a physician when a serious car accident hospitalized her. She took up painting and did not return to medicine. Her colorful creations reflect the endurance of life and the traditions of Mexico.
- **Georgia O'Keeffe** (1887–1986) was one of the first American artists to experiment with abstract form. She interpreted nature in beautiful geometric shapes. O'Keeffe combined the appearance of sculpture and photography in her paintings of flowers, sunbleached animal bones, clouds, and surreal desert scenes. Her clear, bright colors reflect her love of the Southwest and her American independence.

Review *Questions*

After studying the material, answer the following questions:

1. What do works included in "the arts" have in common? They are creative and well crafted.

2. Where is the Louvre? Paris

3. What is a Renaissance man? An accomplished person with a wide range of interests

4. What is unusually engaging about Mona Lisa's face? Her smile is mysterious, and her eyes follow you.

5. What story is painted on the ceiling of the Sistine Chapel? The biblical story of the creation of Adam

6. How did the impressionists get their name? _From a critic who said they_ _painted the impression of the moment_

7. What scenes did Monet paint at Giverny? _The gardens and water lily ponds_ _surrounding his home_

8. Which painter advocated painting outdoors? _Monet_

9. How did Van Gogh disfigure himself? _He cut off his ear._

10. Why did Picasso turn to cubism? _He was seeking a new mode of expression._

Your instructor may choose to give a true-false review of these art history concepts.

selection 3   Business

Contemporary *Focus*

Did you know that 17 percent of all restaurants in our nation are pizza restaurants? Approximately 3 billion pizzas were sold in the United States in 2005. Pizza is a $30 billion per year business. Imagine the many other businesses that benefit from the pizza boom. For example, the pizza business affects the cheese, pepperoni, and tomato businesses. Is there still money to be made in inventing products that support the pizza industry?

Inventors Hope for Slice of Pizza Box Business

By Dave Hall

National Post's Financial Post & FP Investing, Canada, March 23, 2006

Tired of searching for plates or ripping strips of cardboard off pizza box lids, owners of a Windsor company have designed a revolutionary new environmentally friendly perforated lid that breaks up into slice-shaped pieces that replace plates.

The company hopes to corner a fraction of North America's multi-million-unit-per-month pizza box business.

"We're changing the way the world eats pizza," said Rob Tulk, one of the owners of the company. "It's a box with the plates on top."

Mr. Tulk said the idea originated with Chris Holden, his business partner, who was hosting an outdoor pizza party and ended up ripping the box apart to use as plates.

"We talked, and I sort of took the idea from there, worked with it, and came up with the idea we're now trying to market," said Mr. Tulk, who

said the new box has been patented and trademarked.

By reducing the need for paper, plastic, or foam plates, Mr. Holden believes the new box lids are environmentally friendly and will reduce waste.

The box, which has undergone a number of design changes in the past few years, costs no more to make than a regular box, and, despite the perforations, is strong enough to withstand a number of pizzas being piled on top without collapsing.

Ron Martinello, owner of Windsor's Pizza King, said, "The idea has merit, and the theory is good, especially for groups such as schools and workplaces, where you're always scrambling around for plates.

"At home, you might prefer to use a real plate, while guys sitting around eating pizza and drinking beer usually don't need napkins, much less plates," said Mr. Martinello, laughing.

COLLABORATE   Collaborate on responses to the following questions:

➤ What kind of toppings do you order on your pizza?

➤ How do you select a pizza when many options are available?

➤ Why do you think the new pizza boxes could be successful?

➤ What new products would you suggest for the competitive pizza business?

Skill Development: Preview

Preview the next selection to predict its purpose and organization and to formulate your learning plan.

Activate Schema

Do you prefer pizzas from Domino's, Pizza Hut, or Papa John's?
If your dream could become a reality, what small business would you start?

Establish a Purpose for Reading

Downsizing, outsourcing, women's increasing presence in the workforce, and Internet technology are now shaping the American entrepreneurial spirit. The advantages and rewards of small business ownership are great, but so are the risks. What do you expect to learn from this selection about Papa John's and small businesses? After recalling what you already know about start-up businesses, read the selection to learn what defines a small business, why people open them, and why Papa John's is successful.

Increase Word Knowledge

What do you know about these words?

| void | successive | droves | dominant | titans |
| novice | debut | vaulted | stagnant | heritage |

Your instructor may give a true-false vocabulary review before or after reading.

Integrate Knowledge While Reading

Questions have been inserted in the margin to stimulate your thinking while reading. Remember to

| Predict | Picture | Relate | Monitor | Correct |

WHY IS PAPA JOHN'S ROLLING IN THE DOUGH?

As a high school student working at a local pizza pub, John Schnatter liked everything about the pizza business. "I liked making the dough; I liked kneading the dough; I liked putting the sauce on; I liked putting the toppings on; I liked running the oven," recalls Schnatter. Obsessed with perfect pizza topping and bubble-free melted cheese, Schnatter knew that something was missing from national pizza chains: superior-quality traditional pizza delivered to the customer's door. And his dream was to one day open a pizza restaurant that would fill that void.

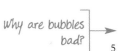
Why are bubbles bad?

Schnatter worked his way through college making pizzas, honing the techniques and tastes that would someday become Papa John's trademark. Shortly after graduating from Ball State University with a business degree, he faced his first business challenge. His father's tavern was $64,000 in debt and failing. So Schnatter sold his car, used the money to purchase $1,600 of used restaurant equipment, knocked out a broom closet in the back of his father's tavern, and began selling pizzas to the tavern's customers. Soon the pizza became the tavern's main attraction and helped turn the failing business around. In 1985 Schnatter officially opened the first Papa John's restaurant. Then he set about opening as many stores as the market would bear.

But Schnatter needed a recipe for success. With Little Caesar's promoting deep discounts and Domino's emphasizing fast delivery, Papa John's needed a fresh approach to compete successfully with the big chains. If you were John Schnatter, how would you grow a small pizza operation into one that could compete with national players? Would you franchise your concept? Would you remain a private enterprise or go public? Would you expand overseas? Where would you focus your efforts?

UNDERSTANDING THE WORLD OF SMALL BUSINESS

Many small businesses start out like Papa John's: with an entrepreneur, an idea, and a drive to succeed. In fact, the United States was originally founded by people involved in small business—the family farmer, the shopkeeper, the craftsperson. Successive waves of immigrants carried on the tradition, launching restaurants and laundries, providing repair and delivery services, and opening newsstands and bakeries.

What companies succeeded?

The 1990s were a golden decade of entrepreneurship in the United States. Entrepreneurs launched small companies in droves to fill new consumer needs. Many took advantage of Internet technologies to gain a competitive edge. Some succeeded; others failed. But the resurgence of small businesses helped turn the U.S. economy into the growth engine for the world.

Today, over 5.8 million small companies exist in the United States. But defining what constitutes a small business is surprisingly tricky, because *small* is a relative term.

One reliable source of information for small businesses is the Small Business Administration (SBA). This government agency serves as a resource and advocate for small firms, providing them with financial assistance, training, and a variety of helpful programs. The SBA defines a **small business** as a firm that (a) is independently owned and operated, (b) is not dominant in its field, (c) is relatively small in terms of annual sales, and (d) has fewer than 500 employees. The SBA reports that 80 percent of all U.S. companies have annual sales of less than $1 million and that about 60 percent of the nation's employers have fewer than five workers.

FACTORS CONTRIBUTING TO THE INCREASE IN THE NUMBER OF SMALL BUSINESSES

Three factors are contributing to the increase in the number of small businesses today: technological advances, an increase in the number of women and minority business owners, and corporate downsizing and outsourcing.

TECHNOLOGY AND THE INTERNET

Do Internet companies have low start-up costs?

The Internet, together with e-commerce, has spawned thousands of new business ventures. ShippingSupply.com is one such firm. Karen Young, a collector of knick-knacks, founded this small business when she was looking for affordable packing and shipping materials for her mail-order items. On a whim, Young decided to market

50 bubble wrap, plastic foam, and shipping tubes she purchased directly from manufacturers to eBay sellers. Today, ShippingSupply.com has eight full-time employees, occupies 7,000 feet of warehouse space, and has over 35,500 customers in its database.

RISE IN NUMBER OF WOMEN AND MINORITY SMALL-BUSINESS OWNERS

The number of women-owned small businesses has also increased sharply over the past three decades—from 5 percent to over 39 percent of all small businesses. These
55 businesses now employ more than 18.5 million people and ring up more than $3.1 trillion in annual sales. Women are starting small businesses for a number of reasons. Some choose to run their own companies so they can enjoy a more flexible work arrangement; others start their own businesses because of barriers to corporate advancement, known as the glass ceiling. Josie Natori is a perfect example of such a
60 scenario. By her late twenties, Natori was earning six figures as the first female vice president of investment banking at Merrill Lynch. But Natori knew that her chances of further advancement were slim in the male-dominated financial world. So she started her own lingerie line. Today, Natori is the owner of a multi-million-dollar fashion empire that sells elegant lingerie and evening wear.

DOWNSIZING AND OUTSOURCING

65 Contrary to popular wisdom, business start-ups soar when the economy sours. During hard times, many companies downsize or lay off talented employees, who then have little to lose by pursuing self-employment. In fact, several well-known companies were started during recessions. Tech titans William Hewlitt and David Packard joined forces in Silicon Valley in 1938 during the Great Depression. Bill
70 Gates started Microsoft during the 1975 recession. And the founders of Sun Microsystems, Compaq Computer, Adobe Systems, Silicon Graphics, and Lotus Development started their companies in 1982—in the midst of a recession and high unemployment.

John Schnatter, founder and president of the Papa John's Pizza chain, makes a surprise check at one of his outlets.

Taro Yamasaki/Time Life Pictures/Getty Images

selection 3

75

*Is this a cause and
effect relationship?*

To make up for layoffs of permanent staff, some companies **outsource** or sub-contract special projects and secondary business functions to experts outside the organization. Others turn to outsourcing as a way to permanently eliminate entire company departments. Regardless of the reason, the increased use of outsourcing provides opportunities for smaller businesses to serve the needs of larger enterprises.

BEHIND THE SCENES: PAPA JOHN'S PIPING HOT PERFORMANCE

80

John Schnatter did a remarkable job of expanding from a single pizza store he started in his father's tavern. Three years after Schnatter opened his first Papa John's, he expanded outside of the Louisville, Kentucky, area. He was no novice. He knew the grass roots of the pizza business, he had an intuitive grasp on what customers wanted, and he knew how to make pizzas taste a little bit better than the competition. Moreover, he had the qualities of an entrepreneur: driven, intense,

85

willing to make things happen, visionary, and very competitive.

John Schnatter used franchising to grow the business. Today about 75 percent of Papa John's are franchised; the rest are company owned. He was encouraged by Kentucky Fried Chicken, Long John Silver's, Chi Chi's, and other Kentucky-born restaurants that had successfully taken their franchised restaurants national. Schnatter

90

thought, "What the heck, maybe I could do it too." But to keep growth under control, Papa John's didn't just move into an area and open up 200 stores. Schnatter grew the stores one at a time—spending up to six months to a year assessing an area's potential.

It wasn't long before Papa John's began grabbing business from such giants as Pizza Hut, Little Caesar's, and delivery king Domino's. Then in 1999 Papa John's made its

95

European debut by acquiring Perfect Pizza Holdings, a 205-unit delivery and carryout pizza chain in the United Kingdom. The acquisition gave Papa John's instant access to proven sites that would have been difficult to obtain. Besides the real estate, Perfect Pizza had a good management team that Schnatter could fold into his organization.

Today, Papa John's has vaulted past Little Caesar's to become the nation's

100

third-largest pizza chain. The company now boasts over 2,700 stores in 47 states and 9 international markets. Annual sales have mushroomed to about $1.7 billion. In spite of its tremendous growth, Schnatter insists on maintaining the highest quality standards. He does so by keeping things simple. About 95 percent of the restau-

*Does lack of
diversity lower costs?*

rants are takeout only. The menu is simple—just two types of pizza, thin crust or

105

regular—no exotic toppings, no salads, no sandwiches, and no buffalo wings. Owners are trained to remake pies that rate less than 8 on the company's 10-point scale. If the cheese shows a single air bubble or the crust is not golden brown, out the offender goes. Schnatter's attention to product quality has earned the company awards. Papa John's was twice voted number one in customer satisfaction among all

110

fast-food restaurants in the American Consumer Satisfaction Index.

To keep things in order, Schnatter visits four to five stores a week, often unannounced. He also trains managers how to forecast product demand. Stores project demand one to two weeks in advance. They factor in anything from forthcoming promotions to community events to the next big high school football game. If a big game is on

115

TV, Schnatter wants to make sure the store owners are ready for the surge in deliveries.

Still, like many companies today, Papa John's faces new challenges. It's becoming increasingly difficult to grow the company's share of the pie. Although Americans consume pizza at a rate of 350 slices a second, the pizza industry is stagnant and highly competitive. Growth usually comes at the expense of a competitor's

120

existing business. Moreover, to keep profitability in line, Schnatter has scaled back company expansion plans and even closed some unprofitable outlets. But Schnatter

is determined to succeed. And if one strength rises above the others in Schnatter's path to success, it's his ability to recruit and retain the right people. "There's nothing special about John Schnatter except the people around me," Schnatter says. "They
125 make me look better" and they make Papa John's what it is—committed to its heritage of making superior-quality, traditional pizza.

(1,640 words)

—Courtland Bovee, John Thill, Barbara Schatzman,
Business in Action

Recall

Stop to self-test, relate, and react.

Your instructor may choose to give you a true-false comprehension review.

Write About the Selection

What factors contribute to the opening of small businesses? Why did John Schnatter open his pizza business?

Response Suggestion: Discuss and explain the cause and effect relationship of at least five factors that prompt people to take risks and start something new.

Contemporary *Link*

Entrepreneurs could seek profits in the fast food pizza business through innovations that support the current industry or through expanding product offerings. Can you think of clever innovations, such as plate-boxes, or perhaps a new product? To counter the stiff competition in the pizza business, perhaps new items should be considered. For example, McDonald's did not always have breakfast and the Egg McMuffin. What menu items or services would you add to expand pizza restaurant sales, and why? What trend would you set, or what needs would you seek to meet?

Skill Development: Identify Organizational Patterns

Answer the following with *T* (true) or *F* (false).

_____T_____ 1. The first and last sections are examples with anecdotal information about a real business.

_____T_____ 2. The section "Understanding the World of Small Business" defines a small business.

_____T_____ 3. The organizational pattern of the section "Factors Contributing to the Increase in the Number of Small Businesses" is simple listing.

_____F_____ 4. The organizational pattern of the section "Downsizing and Outsourcing" is comparison-contrast.

Check Your Comprehension

After reading the selection, answer the following questions with *a, b, c,* or *d.* To help you analyze your strengths and weaknesses, the question types are indicated.

Main Idea ____c____ 1. Which is the best statement of the main idea of this selection?

     a. Through hard work, Papa John's has expanded globally and become the third-largest pizza company in the world.

     b. The golden decade for entrepreneurship has peaked but is not over, as proved by Papa John's Pizza.

     c. Current factors are contributing to a rise in the number of small businesses, and Papa John's Pizza is a glowing example of one such entrepreneurial success.

     d. The highly competitive pizza business requires more than good tomato sauce to turn dough into dollars.

Detail ____d____ 2. When John Schnatter started his pizza business, he had all the following *except*

     a. years of experience making pizza dough.

     b. a college degree in business.

     c. training in running the pizza ovens.

     d. restaurant equipment from his father's business.

Inference ____a____ 3. The author implies that John Schnatter

     a. pulled his father's business out of a $64,000 debt.

     b. closed his father's tavern to open his pizza parlor.

     c. was financed in the pizza business by his father.

     d. continued to use the formula of liquor sales with pizza.

Detail ____c____ 4. As defined by the Small Business Administration, a small business is all of the following *except*

     a. it has fewer than 500 employees.

     b. it is independently operated.

     c. it is owned by stock holders.

     d. it is not dominant in its field.

Inference ____d____ 5. The author suggests that Karen Young's ShippingSupply.com business is

     a. primarily a retail store that customers enter to buy supplies.

     b. a prime candidate for franchising.

     c. a mail-order knickknack venture.

     d. a firm that conducts business over the Internet, with supplies shipped from a warehouse.

Inference ____a____ 6. The author implies that a glass ceiling is

     a. a barrier to high-level corporate advancement.

     b. a more flexible work arrangement.

     c. an entry into investment banking.

     d. a barrier to male-dominated entry-level positions.

Detail _____b_____ 7. Downsizing in a company means to

    a. fire incompetent workers.
    b. lay off valued employees.
    c. freeze hiring until profits improve.
    d. subcontract for special projects.

Inference _____c_____ 8. An example of outsourcing done by an American company would be

    a. selling products in India.
    b. hiring experienced European workers for an American company.
    c. contracting for payroll accounting to be done by a company in Ireland.
    d. buying coffee beans from Latin America and processing them in the United States.

Inference _____b_____ 9. The author suggests that Schnatter's success can be attributed to all the following *except*

    a. hiring good people.
    b. adding a variety of items to the menu.
    c. insisting on high-quality standards for pizzas.
    d. personally visiting stores to keep things in order.

Inference _____c_____ 10. The reader can conclude that of the company's 2,700 stores,

    a. most are owned by Schnatter.
    b. all but 340 stores are now franchised.
    c. the company owns about 675 of them.
    d. Perfect Pizza Holdings franchised 2,400 stores.

Answer the following with *T* (true), *F* (false), or *CT* (can't tell).

Detail _____F_____ 11. During a recession and times of high unemployment, few new businesses are started.

Detail _____T_____ 12. According to the Small Business Administration, over half of the small American businesses hire fewer than five workers.

Inference _____F_____ 13. Schnatter bought Perfect Pizza in the United Kingdom because it was poorly managed.

Inference _____F_____ 14. The author suggests that Papa John's plans to expand into salads and sandwiches.

Inference _____CT_____ 15. The author suggests that the pizza industry is rapidly increasing its customer base and adding new patrons who have never tried pizza.

Build Your Vocabulary

According to the way the italicized word was used in the selection, select *a, b, c,* or *d* for the word or phrase that gives the best definition. The number in parentheses indicates the line of the passage in which the word is located.

_____b_____ 1. "would fill that *void*" (7)
  a. goal
  b. empty space
  c. union
  d. demand

_____a_____ 2. "*Successive* waves of immigrants" (26)
  a. one after another
  b. eager
  c. unsteady
  d. overwhelming

_____d_____ 3. "launched small companies in *droves*" (29)
  a. efforts
  b. desperation
  c. reactions
  d. large numbers

_____b_____ 4. "not *dominant* in its field" (39)
  a. growing
  b. foremost
  c. secure
  d. competitive

_____c_____ 5. "Tech *titans*" (68)
  a. enthusiasts
  b. explorers
  c. giants
  d. hobbiests

_____a_____ 6. "was no *novice*" (81)
  a. beginner
  b. pushover
  c. coward
  d. follower

_____c_____ 7. "its European *debut*" (95)
  a. achievement
  b. marketing ploy
  c. market entry
  d. diversity

_____c_____ 8. "has *vaulted* past Little Caesar's" (99)
  a. sneaked
  b. crawled
  c. leaped
  d. slowly moved

_____d_____ 9. "pizza industry is *stagnant*" (118)
  a. nervous
  b. cutthroat
  c. small
  d. not growing

_____d_____ 10. "committed to its *heritage*" (125)
  a. logo
  b. brand
  c. management
  d. tradition

Search the Net

Use a search engine such as Google, AltaVista, Excite, Infoseek, Dogpile, Yahoo, or Lycos to find information on the nutritional value of your favorite slice of pizza, as well as two other frequently consumed fast-food items. List the calories, carbohydrates, fats, and proteins for each. For suggested Web sites and other research activities, go to http://www.ablongman.com/smith/.

Concept Prep for Business

What is a CD?

When you put money into a **CD (certificate of deposit)** through a bank, you are essentially lending the bank money for a fixed interest rate and for a designated period, called the **maturity.** The CD matures for one month or up to five years, and the interest rate is higher for the longer maturities. Banks then lend out the money at a higher rate for people to buy cars or houses. With a CD, the return of your **principal** (original money) is guaranteed. You do not have to worry about losing your money.

What is a bond?

A **bond** is a loan to a government or a corporation. For example, many cities sell **municipal bonds** to finance infrastructure improvements or schools. When you buy bonds, you are lending the city money, and the taxpayers will pay you interest. The interest rate on bonds is usually higher than that on CDs, but the risk is greater. You have a promise that you will be paid back at **maturity** (a specified period), and you hope the city will be able to fulfill this promise. If you buy a **U.S. Treasury Bill** or a **savings bond,** you are lending money to the federal government, which uses the money to pay down the national debt. Because U.S. Treasury bills are backed by the federal government, they are safer investments than are municipal bonds.

What is a mutual fund?

A **mutual fund** is a company that pools the investment money of many individuals and purchases a **portfolio** (array of holdings) of stocks, bonds, and other securities. Each investor then shares accordingly in the profits or losses. Investors also pay a fee for professionals to manage the portfolio, which includes bookkeeping, researching, buying, and selling. All fees for management come out of profits before they are shared.

An advantage of mutual funds is that they offer instant **diversification.** With a $1,000 purchase, you can have a part ownership in many different stocks

John H. Johnson, the late former publisher of *Ebony* magazine, and his daughter, Linda Johnson Rice, company president, ran the fifty-year-old publishing business.

or bonds. Also, if you do not have the expertise to research individual stocks, you can rely on the judgment of the professional money managers. Different mutual funds specialize in different areas such as large companies, small companies, or even IPOs, which are initial public offerings of stock. You would want to find one that matches your investment interests and also has a positive track record of growth.

What is a capital gain?

A capital gain is a profit on the sale of a property or a security. A **short-term capital gain** is a profit made on stocks or bonds owned for less than one year. This profit is taxed as ordinary income and may be as high as 40 percent for people in upper tax brackets. A **long-term capital gain,** on the other hand, is a profit on a property or security owned for over a year. On this, investors are taxed at a maximum of 15 percent.

After studying the material, answer the following questions:

1. Are CD rates better for a month or a year? <u>A year</u>

2. What does the bank do with your CD money? <u>Lends it out to others at a higher rate</u>

3. What is your principal? <u>Your original money that was invested</u>

4. What is a municipal bond? <u>Money you are lending to a city</u>

5. What are the advantages of a mutual fund? <u>You can own a variety of securities and have a professional manager.</u>

6. Is tax greater on a short- or long-term capital gain? <u>Short-term</u>

7. How long must you hold a property before selling to achieve a long-term capital gain? <u>One year</u>

8. What is a portfolio? <u>A collection of different types of investments, including stocks, bonds, money market funds, and so on</u>

9. For the safest choice, should you pick bonds, CDs, or a mutual fund? <u>CDs</u>

10. What does diversification mean? <u>You own a variety of investments.</u>

Your instructor may choose to give a true-false review of these business concepts.

What's In, What's Out? What's Hot, What's Not?

Prefixes	Root
en-, em-: "in"	*e-, ec-, ef-, ex-:* "out"
non-: "not"	*calor:* "heat"

Words with *en-, em-:* "in"

Jackson was able to *employ* several of his friends as tech reps for his Internet software company.

- *encapsulate:* to place in a capsule; to condense or summarize

    Drug manufacturers *encapsulate* some medications so that they are easier to swallow.

- *enclave:* any small, distinct area or group within a larger one

    Before the Berlin Wall came down, West Berlin was a democratic *enclave* surrounded by communist East Germany.

- *enmesh:* to catch in a net; entangle

    Animal rights groups are against the use of nets in tuna fishing because dolphins become *enmeshed* in the nets and die.

- *ensemble:* all parts of a thing considered only as the whole, not separately, such as an entire costume or a group of musicians, singers, dancers, or actors.

    The cast of ABC's drama *Grey's Anatomy* is an *ensemble* of nine actors.

- *embed:* to fix or place firmly in a surrounding mass; to insert, as a clause in a sentence

    The senator knew that to get her controversial proposal passed by Congress, she had to *embed* it in a more popular bill.

- *embroiled:* to be involved in conflict or confusion

    The twins were *embroiled* in a wrestling match when their father finally had to separate them.

- *embellish:* to beautify with ornamental or elaborate details

    The speechwriter's goal was to enhance but not overly *embellish* the governor's speeches.

- *enroll:* to register or become a member of a group

    Jenny needed to *enroll* in the Psychology 101 class before it became filled.

Words with *e-, ec-, ef-, ex-:* "out"

Renew your driver's license before it *expires*, so you can avoid taking the driving test again.

- *eclipse:* any obscuring of light (darkening) especially of planets; to surpass by comparison

    To protect your eyes during a solar *eclipse*, wear sunglasses and look at the sun only through a pinhole in a piece of paper.

- *emaciated:* abnormally thin, as if wasting away

    Tanica had lost so much weight on a fad diet that she looked *emaciated*.

- *eccentric:* peculiar or odd; not having the same center

    The neighbor on the corner is an *eccentric* man who wears pajamas to the grocery store.

- *effervescent:* bubbling; lively or enthusiastic

    The *effervescent* spring water foamed and sparkled as Juan poured it.

- *exalt:* raise or elevate in rank or character; praise highly

    In his opening remarks, the club president *exalted* the literary talent and accomplishments of the guest speaker.

- *exaggerate:* to stretch the limits of the truth or overstate

    John always *exaggerates* the size of the fish he claims he almost caught.

Words with *non-:* "not"

Military personnel such as surgeons or chaplains who are not fighters are considered *noncombatants*.

- *nonchalant:* coolly indifferent, unconcerned, unexcited

    Tonia's *nonchalant* way of accepting dates makes it seem that she just has nothing better to do.

- *nondescript:* undistinguished or dull, a person or thing of no specific type or kind; not easy to describe

    Students decorated the *nondescript* dorm rooms to reflect their own tastes and personalities.

- *nonpartisan:* objective; not controlled by an established political party

    It is necessary to forge *nonpartisan* politics when the government is split evenly between two parties.

- *nonplussed:* completely puzzled, totally perplexed so as to become unable to continue

The stand-up comedian was inexperienced and became totally *nonplussed* by the hecklers in the audience.

- **nonconformist:** someone who refuses to act in accordance with established customs

A *nonformist* would not be a good candidate for a private school where uniforms are worn.

Words with *calor-:* "heat"

When capitalized, the word *Calorie* refers to a kilocalorie (1,000 small calories) and is used to measure the amount of energy produced by food when oxidized in the body.

- **calorie:** a specific unit of heat (cal.) in physics; a unit expressing the energy value of food (Cal.) in nutrition

Judy tries to eat low-*calorie* meals, including salads, fish, lots of vegetables, and few desserts, to maintain a healthy weight.

- **caloric:** of or pertaining to calories or heat; high in calories

People who eat highly *caloric* meals must exercise more to maintain a healthy weight.

- **scald:** to burn with hot liquid or steam; to bring to a temperature just short of the boiling point

Some recipes require the cook to *scald* milk before adding it to the other ingredients.

- **caldera:** a basinlike depression or collapsed area caused by the explosion of the center of a volcano

The scientists were injured by hot lava when they got too close to the edge of the *caldera* of a still-active volcano.

- **cauldron:** a large kettle for boiling

Shakespeare's *Macbeth* includes a scene with witches stirring a boiling mixture in a *cauldron*.

REVIEW QUESTIONS

Part I

Indicate whether the following sentences are true (*T*) or false (*F*).

___T___ 1. A person known to *embellish* is not a plain speaker.

___F___ 2. We tend to *exalt* those whom we hold in low regard.

___F___ 3. A *nonchalant* attitude could also be described as deeply caring.

___F___ 4. A chef can *scald* milk without cooking it.

_____T_____ 5. The brass instruments are a part of the band's *ensemble*.

_____T_____ 6. An *eccentric* relative likely has some unusual behaviors.

_____F_____ 7. Someone who dresses in a *nondescript* manner would stand out in a crowd.

_____F_____ 8. *Nonconformists* are likely to care a good deal about what others think of them.

_____T_____ 9. A dormitory room could be considered an *enclave* within the dorm itself.

_____T_____ 10. Jewelers have a talent for *embedding* precious stones in gorgeous settings.

Part II

Choose the best antonym from the boxed list for the words below.

criticize	compliant	chill	dislodge	fatten	interested
	minimized	undecorated	untangled	usual	

11. eccentric _____usual_____

12. embellished _____undecorated_____

13. exalt _____criticize_____

14. exaggerated _____minimized_____

15. emaciate _____fatten_____

16. enmeshed _____untangled_____

17. embed _____dislodge_____

18. nonchalant _____interested_____

19. scald _____chill_____

20. nonconformist _____compliant_____

Your instructor may choose to give a multiple-choice review.

6 Organizing Textbook Information

- What is study reading?
- What is annotating?
- What is the Cornell Method of note taking?
- What is outlining?
- What is mapping?

Guy Billout, *Maze*, 1995. Watercolor and airbrush. 4 11/16 × 5 1/16 inches.

The Demands of College Study

If you are like most students, you have already confronted new challenges in college. Your courses may cover a great deal of information more rapidly than you are used to, and the study techniques you used in high school may not be as effective in college. In a sense, college textbook assignments are like the Olympics of reading. Can you train like an athlete to meet the challenge?

exercise 6.1 ### Discovering Your Fitness as a Reader

Take the following inventory to see how you already measure up. Check *yes* or *no* for your response.

What Kind of Reader Are You?

1. Do you mark your text while reading?   Yes—— No——

2. Do you make marginal notes while reading?   Yes—— No——

3. Do you take notes on paper while reading?   Yes—— No——

4. Do you differentiate between details and main ideas?   Yes—— No——

5. Do you stop to summarize while reading?   Yes—— No——

6. Do you have a purpose behind note taking?   Yes—— No——

7. Do you review your textbook notes?   Yes—— No——

8. Do you review class lecture notes within 24 hours?   Yes—— No——

9. Do you link old and new information to remember it?   Yes—— No——

10. Do you use maps or charts to condense notes for study? Yes—— No——

If all your answers were yes, you are well on your way to becoming an Olympic champ in the college arena! If some of your answers were no, you will want to start training now.

Your first assignment in most college courses will be to read Chapter 1 of the assigned textbook. At that time, you will immediately discover that a textbook chapter contains an amazing amount of information. Your instructor will continue to assign the remaining chapters in rapid succession. Don't panic! Your task is to select the information that you need to remember, learn it, and organize it for future study for a midterm or final exam that is weeks or months away.

In a study of the demands on students in introductory college history courses during a ten-week period,[1] three professors analyzed the actual reading demands of classes they observed and found that students were asked to read an average of 825 pages over the course of each class. The average length of weekly assignments was more than 80 pages, but the amount varied both with

---

[1]J. G. Carson, N. D. Chase, S. U. Gibson, and M. F. Hargrove, "Literacy Demands of the Undergraduate Curriculum," *Reading, Research, and Instruction* 31 (1992): 25–30.

the professor and the topic. In one class, students had to read 287 pages in only ten days.

Students were expected to grasp relationships between parts and wholes, place people and events in historical context, and retain facts. Professors spent 85 percent of class time lecturing and 6 percent of the time giving tests, which often amounted to 100 percent of the final grade. In short, the demands were high and students were expected to work independently to organize textbook material efficiently and effectively to prepare for that crucial 6 percent of test-taking time.

The task is difficult, but you have seen many others succeed—and even earn A's. Train for the challenge by using the skills of a successful learner. Consciously build knowledge networks—your foundation for thought interaction—and organize your materials for learning.

Building Knowledge Networks

The old notion of studying and learning is that studying is an information-gathering activity. Knowledge is the "product" you can acquire by transferring information from the text to your memory. According to this view, good learners locate important information, review it, and then transfer the information to long-term memory. The problem with this model is that review does not always guarantee recall, and rehearsal is not always enough to ensure that information is encoded into long-term memory.

Experts now know that studying and learning involve more than review, rehearsal, and memorization; they require making meaningful connections. Cognitive psychologists focus on schemata, or prior knowledge, and the learner's own goals. To understand and remember, you must link new information to already existing schemata, creating networks of knowledge. As your personal knowledge expands, you create new networks. As the learner, you—not your professor—decide how much effort you need to expend, and you adjust your studying according to your answers to questions such as "How much do I need to know?" "Will the test be multiple-choice or essay?" and "Do I want to remember this forever?" In this way, you make judgments and select the material to remember and integrate into knowledge networks.

Organizing Textbook Information

In this chapter, we discuss four methods of organizing textbook information for future study: (1) annotating, (2) note taking, (3) outlining, and (4) mapping. Why four? In a review of more than five hundred research studies on organizing textbook information, two college developmental reading professors concluded that "no one study strategy is appropriate for all students in all study situations."[2] On the basis of these findings, they established guidelines encouraging students to develop a repertoire of skills in study reading. They felt that students need to know, for example, that underlining takes less time than note taking but that note taking or outlining can result in better test scores.

---

[2]D. Caverly and V. Orlando, *Textbook Strategies in Teaching Reading and Study Strategies at the College Level* (Newark, NJ: International Reading Association, 1991), pp. 86–165.

Your selection of a study-reading strategy for organizing textbook material will vary based on the announced testing demands, the nature of the material, the amount of time you have to devote to study, and your preference for a particular strategy. Being familiar with all four strategies affords a repertoire of choices.

The following comments on organizing textbook and lecture materials come from college freshmen taking an introductory course in American history. These students were enrolled in a Learning Strategies for History course that focused on how to be a successful student. Their comments probably address some of your experiences in trying to rapidly organize large amounts of textbook material.

From a student who earned an A:

Organization of my class notes is very important. The notes can be very easy to refer to if they are organized. This enables me to go back and fill in information, and it also helps me to understand the cycle of events that is taking place. I generally try to outline my notes by creating sections. Sections help me to understand the main idea or add a description of a singular activity. I usually go back and number the sections to make them easy for reference.

Taking notes can be very difficult sometimes. In class, if my mind strays just a few times, I can easily lose track of where my notes were going. Then again, when I am reading my textbook, I may read without even realizing what I just read. The difference in class and the textbook is that I can go back and reread the text.

It is very easy to overdo the notes that I take from the text. Originally, I tended to take too much information from the book, but now, as I read more, I can better grasp the main idea. Underlining also makes a big difference. When I underline, I can go back and reread the book.

From another student who earned an A:

I think that the best way to do it is to completely read the assignment and then go back over it to clear up any confusion. I would also recommend going over your lecture notes before starting your reading assignment, which is something I didn't do this past week. I also try to key in on words like "two significant changes" or "major factors." Sometimes you may go three or four pages without seeing anything like that. My question is, "What do you do then?" I think that you should write down the point or points that were repeated the most or stressed the most.

From a student who earned a B:

Taking notes is no longer something that you can just do and expect to have good and complete notes. I have learned that taking notes is a process of learning within itself.

From a student who earned a C:

In starting college, I have made a few changes in how I take notes. For instance, I am leaving a lot more space in taking notes. I find that they are easier to read when they are spread out. I have also been using a highlighter and marking topics and definitions and people's names. I make checks near notes that will definitely be on a test so I can go over them.

When I am reading, I have begun to do a lot of underlining in the book, which I would never do before because my school would not take back books if they were marked. I have also started to note important parts with a little star and confusing parts with a question mark.

All these students were successful in the history class, although the final grades varied. Each student's reflection offers sincere and sound advice. Regardless of the way you organize material—by annotating, note taking, outlining, or mapping—your goal should be to make meaning by making connections.

Annotating

Which of the following would seem to indicate the most effective use of the textbook as a learning tool?

1. A text without a single mark—not even the owner's name has spoiled the sacred pages
2. A text ablaze with color—almost every line is adorned with a red, blue, yellow, or green colored marker
3. A text with a scattered variety of markings—highlighting, underlines, numbers, and stars are interspersed with circles, arrows, and short, written notes

Naturally, option three is the best. The rationale for the first is probably for a better book resale value, but usually used books resell for the same price whether they are marked or unmarked. The reason for the second is probably procrastination in decision making. Students who highlight everything—the "yellow book disease"—rely on coming back later to figure out what is *really* important. Although selective highlighting in a light color such as yellow is a helpful strategy, highlighting everything is inefficient. The variety of markings in the third strategy enables you to pinpoint ideas for later study.

Why Annotate?

The textbook is a learning tool and should be used as such; it should not be preserved as a treasure. A college professor requires a particular text because it contains information vital to your understanding of the course material. The text places a vast body of knowledge in your hands, much more material than the professor could possibly give in class. It is your job to cull through this information, make some sense out of it, and select the important points that need to be remembered.

Annotating is a method of highlighting main ideas, major supporting details, and key terms. The word *annotate* means "to add marks." By using a system of symbols and notations rather than just colored stripes, you mark the text after the first reading so that a complete rereading will not be necessary. The markings indicate pertinent points to review for an exam. If your time is short, however, highlighting with a colored marker is better than not making any marks at all. The Reader's Tip on page 298 offers an example of annotation.

Marking in the textbook itself is frequently faster than summarizing, outlining, or note taking. In addition, since your choices and reactions are all in one place, you can view them at a glance for later study rather than referring to separate notebooks. Your textbook becomes a workbook.

Students who annotate, however, will probably want to make a list of key terms and ideas on their own paper to have a reduced form of the information for review and self-testing.

Reader's *Tip* ──── How to Annotate
───

Develop a system of notations. Use circles, stars, numbers, and whatever else helps you put the material visually into perspective. *Anything that makes sense to you is a correct notation.* Here is an example of one student's marking system:

Main idea	( )
Supporting material	───────
Major trend or possible essay exam question	*
Important smaller point to know for multiple-choice item	✓
Word that you must be able to define	⬭
Section of material to reread for review	{ }
Numbering of important details under a major issue	(1), (2), (3)
Didn't understand and must seek advice	?
Notes in the margin	Ex., Def., Topic
Questions in the margin	Why signif.?
Indicating relationships	〜
Related issue or idea	← R

When to Annotate

Plan to annotate after a unit of thought has been presented and you can view the information as a whole. This may mean marking after a single paragraph or after three pages; your marking will vary with the material.

When you are first reading, every sentence seems of major importance as each new idea unfolds, and you may be tempted to annotate too much. Resist this tendency, as overmarking wastes both reading time and review time. Instead, be patient and read through a passage or section until the end, at which point the author's complete thought will have been fully developed; and the major points will emerge from a background of lesser details. With all the facts at your fingertips and in your consciousness, you can decide what you want to remember. At the end of the course, your textbook should have that worn but well-organized look.

EXAMPLE   The following passage is taken from a biology textbook. Notice how the annotations have been used to highlight main ideas and significant supporting details. This same passage will be used throughout this chapter to demonstrate each of the four methods of organizing textbook material.

Circulatory Systems

When we examine the systems by which blood reaches all the cells of an animal, we find two general types, known as open and closed circulatory systems.

Def. I

Open Circulatory Systems

The essential feature of the **open circulatory system** is that the blood moves through a body cavity—such as the abdominal cavity—and bathes the cells directly. The open circulatory system is particularly characteristic of insects and other arthropods, although it is also found in some other organisms. *Ex.*

In most insects the blood does not take a major part in oxygen transport. Oxygen enters the animal's body through a separate network of branching tubes that open to the atmosphere on the outside of the animal. (This type of respiratory system will be discussed in more detail in the next chapter.) Blood in an open circulatory system moves somewhat more slowly than in the average closed system. The slower system is adequate for insects because it does not have to supply the cells with oxygen.

Def. II

Closed Circulatory Systems

In a **closed circulatory system**, the blood flows through a well-defined system of vessels with many branches. In the majority of closed systems the blood is responsible for oxygen transport. To supply all the body cells with sufficient oxygen, the blood must move quickly through the blood vessels. A closed circulatory system must therefore have an efficient pumping mechanism, or heart, to set the blood in motion and keep it moving briskly through the body.

Ex. 4

All vertebrates possess closed circulatory systems. Simple closed systems are also found in some invertebrates, including annelid worms. A good example of such a simple closed circulatory system can be seen in the earthworm.

Ex. R ——→ regeneration?

exercise 6.2 **Annotating**

Using a variety of markings, annotate the following selection as if you were preparing for a quiz on the material. Remember, do not underscore as you read, but wait until you finish a paragraph or a section, and then mark the important points.

WORK SCHEDULES

Several work-scheduling trends are evident in the new millennium: flextime, job sharing, job splitting, permanent part-time workers, telecommuting, and employee leasing. Companies are increasing their use of these flexible approaches to work. For example, Merck has reported increased use of flextime, telecommuting, and job sharing. The composition of Merck's workforce is also illustrative of trends for the future, as women make up 52 percent of its U.S. employees while minorities account for 24 percent. More significantly, in its U.S. operations 32 percent of the company's managerial positions are held by women while minorities account for 16 percent. All of these trends present unique challenges and opportunities for supervisors.

Flextime allows people to vary their starting and ending times. A company may specify a core time, requiring all employees to be on the job from 10:00 A.M. until 1:00 P.M., but some may start as early as 6:00 A.M. or as late as 10:00 A.M. Some may go home as early as 1:00 P.M. Flexible scheduling appeals to working parents with school-age children and to a growing number of self-managing information workers. But such work schedules make it difficult for one supervisor to manage people who work over a span of 10 or more hours. **Compressed work weeks** of four 10-hour days also help organizations meet the needs of employees.

The Bechtel Group, a construction and engineering firm, has 27,800 employees worldwide. It offers a flexible schedule to its employees in Houston, Texas. Under the plan, employees work nine-hour days, Monday through Thursday each week. Each Friday, about half the employees work eight hours, and the other half have the day off. All employees work 80 hours in nine days. Management initially feared that longer work days would mean lower productivity, but productivity has improved. Employees seemed to be scheduling more of their personal business for their off time.

Job sharing allows two or more people to work at one full-time job. A growing number of people want to work part time, and a growing number of businesses want more part-time employees. The employer benefits in several ways. It gets double the creativity for each shared job. It may also cut benefit costs, which often add 30 to 40 percent to an employee's salary. People come to work refreshed and eager to perform and experience less fatigue and stress. Boring jobs can be more attractive when performed for fewer than 40 hours each week.

Permanent part-time workers usually work for small companies that do not have enough work for a full-timer to perform. Part-time work may be for any number of hours and days per week, up to 35 hours. Older individuals, such as those who may have retired from other jobs, provide a source of reliable employees who may be interested in permanent part-time work.

Temporary workers or contingent workers fill millions of jobs in the United States each year. The U.S. Bureau of Labor has estimated, using a broad definition of "contingent workers," that 4.4 percent of the employed population consists of contingent workers. A somewhat lower estimate is provided by the CEO of Manpower Inc., who has estimated that 2.5 percent of the U.S. workforce is made up of temporary workers. Temporary work agencies provide people to work part time for clients who need temporary help. Most come well trained for their jobs and work in skilled areas such as computer services, secretarial services, manufacturing, and accounting. Another view of the broad presence of temporary workers in the workforce is provided by the president of a temporary help firm that provides temporary employees to such employers as Sun Microsystems and Silicon Graphics: "There's not a single major company in the United States that doesn't have a substantial percentage of the work force as contingent workers."

Telecommuting allows a full- or part-time employee to work at home while remaining connected to the employer by telecommunications devices such as computers, e-mail, the Internet, and fax machines. Estimates of the number of telecommuters in the United States vary widely, with numbers ranging from 9 million to 24 million. More than half of the Fortune 500 companies reported that 1 to 5 percent of their employees are involved in telecommuting, and some companies have large numbers of telecommuters. For example, Merrill Lynch has 3,500 telecommuters. Nortel, one of the pioneers in this area, had 3,600 telecommuters at one point. In addition, AT&T has announced a telecommuting day, encouraging and making arrangements for any worker who can to telecommute. Telecommuters can increase their quality of life by living in geographic areas that are long distances from their offices and combining work at home with child care arrangements. In addition, major disasters quickly isolate people from their jobs and places of employment. The terrorist attack on the World Trade Center on September 11, 2001, earthquakes, floods, and hurricanes have highlighted the value of telecommuting—within hours, companies whose physical plants were in ruins were making alternative arrangements to meet their customers' needs, thanks to cellular communications.

—Charles R. Greer and W. Richard Plunkett,
Supervision: Diversity and Teams in the Workplace, 10th ed.

Review your annotations. Have you sufficiently highlighted the main idea and the significant supporting details?

Note Taking

Many students prefer **note taking,** or jotting down on their own paper brief sentence summaries of important textbook information. With this method, margin space to the left of the summaries can be used to identify topics. Thus, important topics and their explanations are side by side on notepaper for later study. To reduce notes for review and trigger thoughts for self-testing, highlight key terms with a yellow marker. The Reader's Tip on page 302 summarizes one note-taking method.

Why Take Textbook Notes?

Students who prefer note taking say that working with a pencil and paper while reading keeps them involved with the material and thus improves concentration. This method takes longer than annotating, but after annotating the text, you may at times feel an additional need—based on later testing demands, time, and the complexity of the material—to organize the information further into notes.

Reader's $\mathcal{T}ip$ ────── How to Take Notes: The Cornell Method

One of the most popular systems of note taking is called the Cornell Method. The steps are as follows:

1. Draw a line down your paper two and one-half inches from the left side to create a two-and-one-half-inch margin for noting key words and a six-inch area on the right for sentence summaries.

2. After you have finished reading a section, tell yourself what you have read, and jot down sentence summaries in the six-inch area on the right side of your paper. Use your own words, and make sure you have included the main ideas and significant supporting details. Be brief, but use complete sentences.

3. Review your summary sentences and underline key words. Write these key words in the column on the left side of your paper. These words can be used to stimulate your memory of the material for later study.

You can use the Cornell Method to take notes on classroom lectures. The chart shown below, developed by Norman Stahl and James King, explains the procedure and gives a visual display of the results.

The example on pages 302–303 applies the Cornell Method of note taking to the biology passage on the circulatory system that you have already read (see page 299). Although the creators of this method recommend the writing of sentence summaries, you may find that short phrases can sometimes be as or more efficient and still adequately communicate the message for later study.

Taking Class Notes: The Cornell Method

← 2½ INCHES →	← 6 INCHES →
REDUCE IDEAS TO CONCISE JOTTINGS AND SUMMARIES AS CUES FOR RECITING.	*RECORD THE LECTURE AS FULLY AND AS MEANINGFULLY AS POSSIBLE.*
Cornell Method	This sheet demonstrates the Cornell Method of taking classroom notes. It is recommended by experts from the Learning Center at Cornell University.
Line drawn down paper	You should draw a line down your notepage about 2½ inches from the left side. On the right side of the line simply record your classroom notes as you usually do. Be sure that you write legibly.

After the lecture	After the lecture you should read the notes, fill in materials that you missed, make your writing legible, and underline any important materials. Ask another classmate for help if you missed something during the lecture.
Use the recall column for key phrases	The recall column on the left will help you when you study for your tests. Jot down any important words or key phrases in the recall column. This activity forces you to rethink and summarize your notes. The key words should stick in your mind.
Five Rs	The Five Rs will help you take better notes based on the Cornell Method.
Record	1. Record any information given during the lecture which you believe will be important.
Reduce	2. When you reduce your information you are summarizing and listing key words/phrases in the recall column.
Recite	3. Cover the notes you took for your class. Test yourself on the words in the recall section. This is what we mean by recite.
Reflect	4. You should reflect on the information you received during the lecture. Determine how your ideas fit in with the information.
Review	5. If you review your notes you will remember a great deal more when you take your midterm.
Binder & paper	Remember it is a good idea to keep your notes in a standard-sized binder. Also you should use only full-sized binder paper. You will be able to add photocopied materials easily to your binder.
Hints	Abbreviations and symbols should be used when possible. Abbrev. & sym. give you time when used automatically.

Circulatory System

Two types Open and closed	There are two types, the open and the closed, by which blood reaches the cells of an animal.
Open	In the open system, found mostly in insects and other arthropods, blood moves through the body and bathes the cells directly. The blood moves slower
Bathes cells	than in the closed system, and oxygen
Oxygen from outside	is supplied from the outside air through tubes.

(continued)

Closed Blood vessels Blood carries oxygen Heart pumps	In the _closed system_, blood flows through a _system of vessels_, _oxygen_ is _carried_ by the blood so it must move _quickly_, and the _heart_ serves as a _pumping_ mechanism. All vertebrates, as well as earthworms, have closed systems.

exercise 6.3   **Note Taking**

Using a variety of markings, annotate the following selection as if you were preparing for a quiz on the material. Remember, do not underscore as you read, but wait until you finish a paragraph or a section, and then mark the important points.

WHY THE FOOD PYRAMID HAS BEEN REVISED

The limitations of the USDA Food Guide Pyramid have resulted in serious criticisms about the effectiveness of the Pyramid as a tool and led nutrition experts to question its usefulness in designing a healthful diet. One major criticism is that it is overly simple and does not help consumers make appropriate food selections within each food group. For example, all the grains and cereals are grouped into one category with no distinction made between whole and refined grains or carbohydrates. A serving of Fruit Loops "counts" the same as a serving of oatmeal.

Yet nutritionists know that whole-grain foods contain important nutrients, such as fiber, vitamins, and minerals—nutrients that are typically lost when grains are refined. To help make up for this loss, some of these nutrients, but not all, are added back through a process called enrichment (or fortification). Whole grains are also high in fiber, increase the feeling of fullness, and are typically digested more slowly than refined grains, gradually releasing glucose into the blood. In contrast, refined-grain foods are low in fiber and typically high in simple sugars, causing a spike in blood glucose and contributing to increased hunger shortly after their consumption.

A second criticism is that the Pyramid makes a poor distinction between healthful and unhealthful fats. All the fats are lumped together at the tip of the Pyramid, and consumers are told to use them "sparingly." Not all fats have the same effect on health so they cannot be easily grouped together. We want to limit our intake of saturated and trans fats, while making sure our diets are adequate in the monounsaturated and polyunsaturated fats that are essential for good health and may protect against disease.

A third criticism is that the serving sizes suggested in the Food Guide Pyramid are unrealistic or do not coincide with typical serving sizes of foods listed on food labels. For instance, one serving of a muffin as defined in the Food Guide Pyramid is 1.5 ounces, but most muffins available to consumers range from 2 ounces to 8 ounces! The way that foods are packaged is also confusing to consumers. Unless people read food labels carefully, it is easy to consume an entire package of a food that contains multiple servings and assume that the entire package is equal to one serving. For example, it is common to find soft drinks sold in 20 fluid ounce bottles. Although the serving size listed on the label is 8 fluid ounces, and total servings per bottle is listed as 2.5, most people just drink the entire bottle in one sitting and assume they had one soft drink.

—Janice Thompson and Melinda Manore,
Nutrition: An Applied Approach

Review your annotations. Have you sufficiently highlighted the main idea and the significant supporting details?

exercise 6.4   **Note Taking**

In college courses, you will usually take notes on lengthy chapters or entire books. For practice with note taking here, use the passage "Work Schedules," which you have already annotated (see pages 300–301). Prepare a two-column sheet, and take notes using the Cornell Method.

exercise 6.5   **Note Taking**

For more practice with note taking, use the passage "Why the Food Pyramid Has Been Revised," which you have already annotated (see pages 304–305). Prepare a two-column sheet, and take notes using the Cornell Method.

Outlining

Outlining enables you to organize and highlight major points and subordinates items of lesser importance. In a glance, the indentations, Roman numerals, numbers, and letters quickly show how one idea relates to another and how all aspects relate to the whole. The layout of the outline is simply a graphic display of main ideas and significant supporting details.

The following example is a picture-perfect version of the basic outline form. In practice your "working outline" would probably not be as detailed or as regular as this. Use the tools of the outline format, *especially the indentations and numbers*, to devise your own system for organizing information.

I. First main idea
  A. Supporting idea
    1. Detail
    2. Detail

      3. Detail

         a. Minor detail

         b. Minor detail

   B. Supporting idea

      1. Detail

      2. Detail

   C. Supporting idea

II. Second main idea

   A. Supporting idea

   B. Supporting idea

Why Outline?

Students who outline usually drop the precision of picture-perfect outlines but still make good use of the numbers, letters, indentations, and mixture of topics and phrases to show levels of importance. A quick look to the far left of an outline indicates the topic, with subordinate ideas indented underneath. The letters, numbers, and indentations form a visual display of the parts that make up the whole. Good outliners use plenty of paper so the levels of importance are evident at a glance.

Another use of the outline is to organize notes from class lectures. During class, most professors try to add to the material in the textbook and put it into perspective for students. Since the notes taken in class represent a large percentage of the material you need to know to pass the course, they are extremely important.

How to Outline

While listening to a class lecture, you must almost instantly receive, synthesize, and select material and, at the same time, record something on paper for future reference. The difficulty of the task demands order and decision making. Do not be so eager to copy down every detail that you miss the big picture. One of the most efficient methods of taking lecture notes is to use a modified outline form—a version that adds stars, circles, and underlines to emphasize further the levels of importance.

Professors say that they can walk around a classroom and look at the notes students have taken from the text or from a lecture and tell how well each student has understood the lesson. The errors most frequently observed fall into the following categories. The Reader's Tip provides more details about how to outline.

1. Poor organization
2. Failure to show importance
3. Writing too much
4. Writing too little

Reader's *Tip* — Guidelines for Successful Outlining

The most important thing to remember when outlining is to ask yourself, *"What is my purpose?"* You don't need to include everything, and you don't need a picture-perfect version for study notes. Include only what you believe you will need to remember later, and use a numbering system and indentations to show how one item relates to another. There are several other important guidelines to remember:

- **Get a general overview before you start.**
  How many main topics do there seem to be?
- **Use phrases rather than sentences.**
  Can you state it in a few short words?
- **Put it in your own words.**
  If you cannot paraphrase it, do you really understand it?
- **Be selective.**
  Are you highlighting or completely rewriting?
- **After outlining, indicate key terms with a yellow marker.**
  Highlighting makes them highly visible for later review and self-testing.

EXAMPLE   Notice how numbers, letters, and indentations are used in the following outline to show levels of importance.

Circulatory System

I. Open circulatory system
   A. Blood moves through the body and bathes cells directly
   B. Examples—insects and other arthropods
   C. Oxygen supplied from outside air through tubes
   D. Slower blood movement since not supplying cells with oxygen
II. Closed circulatory system
   A. Blood flows through system of vessels
   B. Oxygen carried by blood so it must move quickly
   C. Heart serves as pumping mechanism
   D. Example—all vertebrates
   E. Example—earthworms

exercise 6.6 **Outlining**

Outline the key ideas in the following selection as if you were planning to use your notes to study for a quiz. You may want to annotate before you outline.

REACTING TO STRESS WITH DEFENSE MECHANISMS

Stress may occasionally promote positive outcomes. Motivated to overcome stress and the situations that produce it, we may learn new and adaptive responses. It is also clear, however, that stress involves a very unpleasant emotional component. **Anxiety** is a general feeling of tension or apprehension that often accompanies a perceived threat to one's well-being. It is this unpleasant emotional component that often prompts us to learn new responses to rid ourselves of stress.

There are a number of techniques, essentially self-deception, that we may employ to keep from feeling the unpleasantness associated with stress. These techniques, or tricks we play on ourselves, are not adaptive in the sense of helping us to get rid of anxiety by getting rid of the source of stress. Rather, they are mechanisms that we can and do use to defend ourselves against the *feelings* of stress. They are called **defense mechanisms.** Freud believed defense mechanisms to be the work of the unconscious mind. He claimed that they are ploys that our unconscious mind uses to protect us (our *self* or *ego*) from stress and anxiety. Many psychologists take issue with Freud's interpretation of defense mechanisms and consider defense mechanisms in more general terms than did Freud, but few will deny that defense mechanisms exist. It *is* true that they are generally ineffective if consciously or purposively employed. The list of defense mechanisms is a long one. Here, we'll review some of the more common defense mechanisms, providing an example of each, to give you an idea of how they might serve as a reaction to stress.

Repression. The notion of **repression** is the most basic of all the defense mechanisms. It is sometimes referred to as *motivated forgetting,* which gives us a good idea of what is involved. Repression is a matter of conveniently forgetting about some stressful, anxiety-producing event, conflict, or frustration. Paul had a teacher in high school he did not get along with at all. After spending an entire semester trying his best to do whatever was asked, Paul failed the course. The following summer, while walking with his girlfriend, Paul encountered this teacher. When he tried to introduce his girlfriend, Paul could not remember his teacher's name. He had repressed it. As a long-term reaction to stress, repressing the names of people we don't like or that we associate with unpleasant, stressful experiences is certainly not a very adaptive reaction. But at least it can protect us from dwelling on such unpleasantness.

Denial. **Denial** is a very basic mechanism of defense against stress. In denial, a person simply refuses to acknowledge the realities of a stressful situation. When a physician first tells a patient that he or she has a terminal illness, a common reaction is denial; the patient refuses to believe that there is anything seriously wrong.

Other less stressful events than serious illness sometimes evoke denial. Many smokers are intelligent individuals who are well aware of the data and the statistics that can readily convince them that they are slowly (or rapidly) killing themselves by continuing to smoke. But they deny the evidence. Somehow they are able to convince themselves that they aren't going to die from smoking; that's something that happens to other people, and besides, they *could* stop whenever they wanted.

Rationalization. **Rationalization** amounts to making excuses for our behaviors when facing the real reasons for our behaviors would be stressful. The real reason Kevin failed his psychology midterm is that he didn't study for it and has missed a number of classes. Kevin hates to admit, even to himself, that he could have been so stupid as to flunk that exam because of his own actions. As a result, he rationalizes: "It wasn't really *my* fault. I had a lousy instructor. We used a rotten text. The tests were grossly unfair. I've been fighting the darn flu all semester. And Marjorie had that big party the night before the exam." Now Susan, on the other hand, really did want to go to Marjorie's party, but she decided that she wouldn't go unless somebody asked her. As it happens, no one did. In short order, Susan rationalized that she "didn't want to go to that dumb party anyway"; she needed to "stay home and study."

Compensation. We might best think of **compensation** in the context of personal frustration. This defense mechanism is a matter of overemphasizing some positive trait or ability to counterbalance a shortcoming in some other trait or ability. If some particular goal-directed behavior becomes blocked, a person may compensate by putting extra effort and attention into some other aspect of behavior. For example, Karen, a seventh grader, wants to be popular. She's a reasonably bright and pleasant teenager, but isn't—in the judgment of her classmates—very pretty. Karen *may* compensate for her lack of good looks by studying very hard to be a good student, or by memorizing jokes and funny stories, or by becoming a good musician. Compensation is not just an attempt to be a well-rounded individual. It is a matter of expending *extra* energy and resources in one direction to offset shortcomings in other directions.

Fantasy. **Fantasy** is one of the more common defense mechanisms used by college students. It is often quite useful. Particularly after a hard day when stress levels are high, isn't it pleasant to sit in a comfortable chair, kick off your shoes, lie back, close your eyes, and daydream, perhaps about graduation day, picturing yourself walking across the stage to pick up your diploma—with honors?

When things are not going well for us, we may retreat into a world of fantasy where everything always goes well. Remember that to engage from time to time in fantasizing is a normal and acceptable response to stress. You should not get worried if you fantasize occasionally. On the other hand, you should realize that there are some potential dangers here. You need to be able to keep separate those activities that are real and those that occur in your fantasies. And you should realize that fantasy in itself will not solve whatever problem is causing you stress. Fantasizing about academic successes may help you feel better for a while, but it is not likely to make you a better student.

Projection. **Projection** is a matter of seeing in others those very traits and motives that cause us stress when we see them in ourselves. Under pressure to do well on an exam, Mark may want to cheat, but his conscience won't let him. Because of projection, he may think he sees cheating going on all around him.

Projection is a mechanism that is often used in conjunction with hostility and aggression. When people begin to feel uncomfortable about their own levels of hostility, they often project their aggressiveness onto others, coming to believe that others are "out to do me harm," and "I'm only defending myself."

Regression. To employ **regression** is to return to earlier, even childish, levels of behavior that were once productive or reinforced. Curiously enough, we often find regression in children. Imagine a four-year-old who until very recently was an only child. Now Mommy has returned from the hospital with a new baby sister. The four-year-old is no longer "the center of the universe," as her new little sister now gets parental attention. The four-year-old reverts to earlier behaviors and starts wetting the bed, screaming for a bottle of her own, and crawling on all fours in an attempt to get attention. She is regressing.

Many defense mechanisms can be seen on the golf course, including regression. After Doug knocks three golf balls into the lake, he throws a temper tantrum, stamps his feet, and tosses his three-iron in the lake. His childish regressive behavior won't help his score, but it may act as a release from the tension of his stress at the moment.

Displacement. The defense mechanism of **displacement** is usually discussed in the context of aggression. Your goal-directed behavior becomes blocked or thwarted. You are frustrated, under stress, and somewhat aggressive. You cannot vent your aggression directly at the source of the frustration, so you displace it to a safer outlet. Dorothy expects to get promoted at work, but someone else gets the new job she wanted. Her goal-directed behavior has been frustrated. She's upset and angry at her boss, but feels (perhaps correctly) that blowing her top at her boss will do more harm than good. She's still frustrated, so she displaces her hostility toward her husband, children, and/or the family cat.

Displacement doesn't have to involve hostility and aggression. A young couple discovers that having children is not going to be as easy as they thought. They want children badly, but there's an infertility problem that is causing considerable stress. Their motivation for love, sharing, and caring may be displaced toward a pet, nephews and nieces, or some neighborhood children—at least until their own goals can be realized with children of their own.

The list of defense mechanisms provided above is not an exhaustive one. These are among the most common, and this list gives you an idea of what defense mechanisms are like.

—Josh Gerow,
Psychology: An Introduction, 2nd ed.

exercise 6.7 **Outlining**

For additional practice, outline the selection on "Work Schedules" beginning on page 300. Use your annotations and notes to help.

exercise 6.8 **Outlining**

For further practice, outline the selection "Why the Food Pyramid Has Been Revised" beginning on pages 304–305. Use your annotations and notes to help.

Mapping

Mapping is a visual system of condensing material to show relationships and levels of importance. A map is a diagram of the major points, with their significant subpoints, that support a topic. The purpose of mapping as an organizing strategy is to improve memory by grouping material in a highly visual way.

Why Map?

Proponents of popular learning style theories (see the discussion of multiple intelligences in Chapter 1) would say that mapping offers a visual organization that appeals to learners with a preference for spatial representation, as opposed to the linear mode offered by outlining and note taking. A map provides a quick reference to overviewing an article or a chapter and can be used to reduce notes for later study. The Reader's Tip shows the steps in mapping.

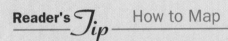

Reader's *Tip* ———— How to Map

Use the following steps for mapping:

- **Draw a circle or a box** in the middle of a page, and in it write the subject or topic of the material.
- **Determine the main ideas** that support the subject, and write them on lines radiating from the central circle or box.
- **Determine the significant details,** and write them on lines attached to each main idea. The number of details you include will depend on the material and your purpose.

Maps are not restricted to any one pattern but can be formed in a variety of creative shapes, as the diagrams illustrate below.

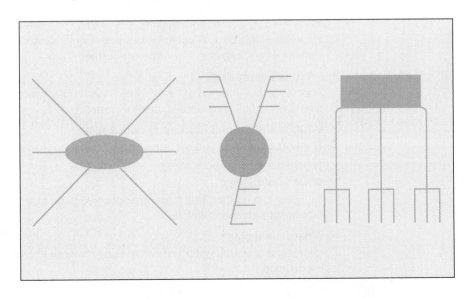

The following map highlights the biology passage on the circulatory system (see page 299). Notice how the visual display emphasizes the groups of ideas supporting the topic.

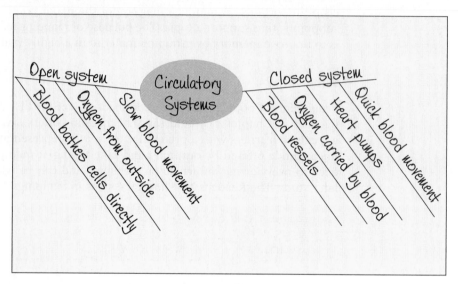

exercise 6.9 **Mapping**

Return to Exercise 6.6 and design a map for the selection entitled "Reacting to Stress with Defense Mechanisms," which you previously outlined. Use your outline to help you design the map. Experiment with several different shapes for your map patterns on notebook or unlined paper. For additional practice, design maps for the selections in Exercises 6.2 and 6.3.

Summary *Points*

➤ **What is study reading?**
Study reading is textbook reading. It is reading to learn and involves establishing knowledge networks. Students must select which textbook information to remember and organize it to facilitate further study.

➤ **What is annotating?**
Annotating is a method of using symbols and notations to highlight main ideas, significant supporting details, and key terms.

➤ **What is the Cornell Method of note taking?**
The Cornell Method is a system of note taking that includes writing summary sentences and marginal notes.

➤ **What is outlining?**
Outlining is a method that follows a specified sequence of main ideas and significant supporting details.

➤ **What is mapping?**
Mapping is a visual system of condensing material to show relationships and importance.

selection 1 — Communications

Contemporary *Focus*

Will the Internet change the magazine market? In considering the present influence of magazines, what do the sales numbers say about subscriptions and individual purchases? Magazine are highly visible in grocery check-out lines, particularly glossy publications with celebrities on the cover, but are average sales up or down? What are your favorite magazines? What prompts you to purchase a magazine?

Snuffing Out Magazines

By Jeff Sturgeon
The Roanoke Times, Virginia, September 3, 2006

Americans still read magazines. There were 18,267 magazines published in this country last year, 2,000 more than 10 years earlier, according to the latest data from Magazine Publishers of America, a trade group. The top three subject categories were entertainment/celebrity, wearing apparel and accessories, and home furnishings and management. New-magazine launches in 2005 totaled 350. Advertising revenue has doubled since mid-1997 to more than $23 billion.

But the Internet and pricing trends that make subscribing the best value have reduced the need for magazine stands to sell them one at a time, according to David Sumner, a magazine industry guru and magazine writing instructor at Ball State University who wrote a newly re-

leased book, *Magazines: A Complete Guide to the Industry.*

According to Sumner, single-copy magazine sales have dropped from between 40 percent and 50 percent of all magazine sales during the 1960s to 13 percent last year. Last year, the average price of a single magazine was $4.40, up from $2.93 in 1995, while subscriptions have fallen to $26.78 from $29.42 over the same period, the publishing group said.

The magazine category that's taken perhaps the biggest hit from the Web is pornography, he said. Adult magazines have endured "a tremendous decline," he said, noting the drop in *Playboy*'s circulation to perhaps half of what it was 30 years ago.

COLLABORATE **Collaborate on responses to the following questions:**

➤ What magazines do you read regularly?

➤ Why does celebrity gossip sell magazines?

➤ Why are magazines placed at the grocery checkout?

Skill Development: Preview

Preview the next selection to predict its purpose and organization and to formulate your learning plan.

Activate Schema

Which print or electronic magazines do you read regularly?

Why do you think people participate in blogging and Web sites like My Space and Facebook?

Establish a Purpose for Reading

What impact have magazines had on our culture? What do you expect to learn from this selection? After recalling what you already know about the history and evolution of magazines, read the selection to find out how we are influenced by magazines. What early innovations made magazines such a popular medium?

Increase Word Knowledge

What do you know about these words?

means	vie	aficionados	haunting	indelible
universal	diminutive	scoffers	novel	disdained

Your instructor may give a true-false vocabulary review before or after reading.

Integrate Knowledge While Reading

Questions have been inserted in the margin to stimulate your thinking while reading. Remember to

Predict	Picture	Relate	Monitor	Correct

Skill Development: Note Taking

Annotate this selection and then make a study outline for the key ideas as if you were planning to use your notes to study for a quiz.

INFLUENCE OF MAGAZINES

The first successful magazines in the United States, in the 1820s, were much less expensive than books. People of ordinary means could afford them. Unlike newspapers, which were oriented to their cities of publication, early magazines created national audiences. This contributed to a sense of nationhood at a time when an
5 American culture, distinctive from its European heritage, had not yet emerged. The American people had their magazines in common. The *Saturday Evening Post*, founded in 1821, carried fiction by Edgar Allan Poe, Nathaniel Hawthorne and Harriet Beecher Stowe to readers who could not afford books. Their short stories

What is a national identity? →

and serialized novels flowed from the American experience and helped Americans
10 establish a national identity.

With the Postal Act of 1879, Congress recognized the role of magazines in creating a national culture and promoting literacy—in effect, binding the nation. The law allowed a discount on mailing rates for magazines, a penny a pound. Magazines were being subsidized, which reduced distribution costs and sparked dramatic cir-
15 culation growth. New magazines cropped up as a result.

NATIONAL ADVERTISING MEDIUM

Advertisers used magazines through the 1800s to build national markets for their products, which was an important factor in transforming the United States from an agricultural and cottage industry economy into a modern economy. This too contributed to a sense of nationhood.

MASSIVE MAGAZINE AUDIENCE

20 The American people have a tremendous appetite for magazines. According to magazine industry studies, almost 90 percent of U.S. adults read an average 10

How many do I read? →

issues a month. Although magazines are affordable for most people, the household income of the typical reader is 5 percent more than the national average. In general, the more education and higher income a person has, the greater the person's maga-
25 zine consumption.

The massiveness of the audience makes the magazine an exceptionally competitive medium. About 12,000 magazines vie for readers in the United States, ranging from general interest publications such as *Reader's Digest* to such specialized publications as *Chili Pepper*, for people interested in hot foods, and *Spur*, for racehorse
30 aficionados. In recent years 500 to 600 new magazines have been launched annually, although only one in five survives into its third year. Even among major magazines, a huge following at the moment is no guarantee of survival. Of the 23 U.S. magazines with a circulation of more than 1 million in 1946, 10 no longer exist. Magazine publishing is a risky business.

MAGAZINES AS MEDIA INNOVATORS

35 Magazines have led other media with significant innovations in journalism, photojournalism, circulation, and niche marketing

MARGARET BOURKE-WHITE'S PHOTOJOURNALISM

The oversized *Life* magazine created by Henry Luce was the perfect forum for the work of Margaret Bourke-White. The giant pages, $13\frac{1}{2}$ inches high and opening to 21-inch spreads, gave such impact to photos that they seemed to jump off the page
40 at readers. Bourke-White was there at the beginning, shooting the immense Fort Peck Dam in Montana for *Life*'s first cover in 1936. Over her career, Bourke-White shot 284 assignments for *Life*, many of them enduring images from World War II. These included Holocaust victims in a Nazi concentration camp, great military movements, and the leaders of the time in both triumph and defeat. She was among
45 the first great photojournalists.

Bourke-White's photojournalism went beyond the news and emotions of any given day to penetrate the core of great social problems. In collaboration with writer Erskine Caldwell, to whom she was later married, Bourke-White created a

photo documentary on the tragic lives of sharecroppers in the American South.
50 Later, in South Africa, she went underground to photograph gold miners who were
known only by numbers. Her haunting photos from the Midwest drought of the
1930s created indelible images in the minds of a generation. These were socially significant projects that moved people and changed public policy.

Did her stories change their lives?

DEWITT AND LILA WALLACE'S MASS CIRCULATION

Reader's Digest is usually considered to have the largest circulation of any U.S. mag-
55 azine. Dewitt and Lila Wallace had an idea but hardly any money. The idea was a
pocket-sized magazine that condensed informational, inspiring and entertaining
nonfiction from other publications—a digest. With borrowed money the Wallaces
brought out their first issue of *Reader's Digest* in 1922.

The rest, as they say, is history. In 1947 the *Digest* became the first magazine to
60 exceed a circulation of 9 million. Except for the Sunday newspaper supplement
Parade, *Reader's Digest* has been the nation's largest-circulation magazine most of

Oscar Graubner/Time Life/Getty Images

American photographer and journalist Margaret Bourke-White focuses a camera
on New York City from a perch on an eagle head at the top of the Chrysler
Building in 1935.

the time since then. In 1999 *Reader's Digest* circulation was 12.6 million—not counting an additional 12.2 million overseas in 18 languages.

Why has it been so popular?

65 The magazine has remained true to the Wallaces' successful formula. DeWitt and Lila Wallace, children of poor Presbyterian clergy, wanted "constructive articles," each with universal appeal. The thrust was upbeat but not Pollyanna. Digested as they were, the articles could be quickly read. America loved it.

For its first 33 years, *Reader's Digest* was wholly reader supported. It carried no advertising. Rising postal rates forced a change in 1955. There was scoffing about
70 whether advertisers would go for "postage-stamp-sized ads" in *Reader's Digest* with its diminutive pages, but the scoffers were wrong. Today, advertisers—except for cigarette manufacturers—pay more than $100,000 a page for a color advertisement. Consistent with the Wallaces' standards, cigarette advertisements are not accepted and never have been.

HALE'S WOMEN'S MAGAZINE

75 The first U.S. magazine edited to interest only a portion of the mass audience, but otherwise to be of general interest, was *Ladies' Magazine*, which later became *Godey's Lady's Book*. Sara Josepha Hale helped start the magazine in 1828 to uplift and glorify womanhood. Its advice on fashion, morals, taste, sewing and cooking developed a following, which peaked with a circulation of 150,000 in 1860.

80 During her tenure Hale defined women's issues and in indirect ways contributed importantly to women's liberation. She campaigned vigorously for educational opportunities for women. When Matthew Vassar was setting up a women's college, she persuaded him to include women on the faculty—a novel idea for the time. Unlike other magazine editors of the time, she disdained reprinting articles
85 from other publications. Hence, *Ladies' Magazine* created opportunities for new writers, particularly women, and enriched the nation's literary output.

The tradition is maintained today in seven competing magazines known as the Seven Sisters because of their female following: *Better Homes & Gardens, Family Circle, Good Housekeeping, Ladies' Home Journal, McCall's, Redbook* and *Woman's Day.*

JOHNSON'S *EBONY*

90 One entrepreneur who decided to do something to serve the media needs of African Americans in the mid-1900s was John H. Johnson, then a young African American whose hometown high school in Arkansas City, Arkansas, was "whites only." As a result, John's family moved to Chicago, where Johnson got his formal high school education. His mother funded his business undertaking by pawning her
95 household furniture and giving her son $500 to start *Ebony* magazine. *Ebony* became one of the leading magazines targeting the interests of African Americans, with a circulation of more than 1.5 million. Johnson became one of the leading cross-media owners in the United States, with a book publishing company, a nationally syndicated television program, and two radio stations.

What other magazines target African American readers?

(1,178 words)

—From John Vivian,
The Media of Mass Communication, 6th ed.
Published by Allyn and Bacon, Boston, MA. Copyright © 2002 by
Pearson Education. Reprinted by permission of the publisher.

Recall

Stop to self-test, relate, and react. Review your study outline.

Your instructor may choose to give you a true-false comprehension review.

Write About the Selection

How did magazines help create a national identity for a young United States, and how did the later innovations continue to strengthen that common bond?

Response Suggestion: List ways in which magazines subtly drew a large national audience toward common concerns and pleasures. Explain how later innovations continued to build unity by targeting causes and audiences.

Contemporary *Link*

Given the influence of magazines in forging a national identity and uplifting the spirits, what positive and negative effects on society do you see emerging from contemporary print, broadcast, and electronic media? What trends do you see? Are the media changing the way we think?

Check Your Comprehension

After reading the selection, answer the following questions with *a, b, c,* or *d*. To help you analyze your strengths and weaknesses, the question types are indicated.

Main Idea ___d___ 1. Which is the best statement of the main idea of this selection?

    a. Magazines increased in American popularity because they were much less expensive than books.

    b. Magazines created a medium for mass advertising before the advent of television.

    c. Magazines enriched the nation's literary output by providing a vehicle for gifted American fiction writers to reach the public.

    d. Magazines created national audiences, a sense of nationhood, and innovations in mass communication.

Detail ___b___ 2. The success of magazines in the 1800s can be attributed to all of the following *except*

    a. they were affordable.

    b. they were oriented toward their cities of publication.

    c. they included quality fiction from books readers could not afford to buy.

    d. they created a national audience with a common bond.

Inference ___a___ 3. The Postal Act of 1879 subsidized magazine mailings, which means that

    a. the postal rate for magazines was less than its true cost and thus was supported by tax money.

    b. the laws for magazines and newspapers were the same.

    c. cheaper mailing rates were available if the contents of the magazine were approved by the government.

    d. both letters and magazines could be delivered for a penny a pound.

Inference ___b___ 4. The phrase "an agricultural and cottage industry economy" refers to

    a. farms with tenant farmers working the land while living in cottages on the property.

    b. family farms and small, locally owned businesses.

    c. a barter economy in which goods were traded rather than sold.

    d. farmers supplying the goods for urban economies.

Detail ___b___ 5. According to magazine industry studies, the typical adult magazine reader

    a. reads fewer than 10 issues a month.

    b. has a household income 5 percent more than the national average.

    c. shows no change in magazine consumption in accordance with education.

    d. reads fewer magazines as income increases.

Detail _____d_____ 6. According to the passage, if 500 new magazines were launched this year, the predicted number to survive into the third year would be

    a. 10.
    b. 23.
    c. 50.
    d. 100.

Inference _____d_____ 7. The author suggests that Bourke-White's photojournalism was socially significant and changed public policy because

    a. her pictures opened to 21-inch spreads.
    b. she showed the immenseness of the Fort Peck Dam for *Life's* first cover.
    c. she shot the news and emotions of World War II and Nazi concentration camps.
    d. she showed the suffering at the core of the social problems of southern sharecroppers, South African gold miners, and victims of the Midwestern drought.

Inference _____c_____ 8. With the *Reader's Digest*, DeWitt and Lila Wallace wanted all the following *except*

    a. previously published nonfiction.
    b. inspiring articles.
    c. quality fiction.
    d. condensed nonfiction.

Inference _____d_____ 9. The author suggests that Sara Josepha Hale

    a. created a magazine to voice ideas of social reform for women.
    b. was the first woman to work on a national magazine.
    c. initially tried to appeal to the household interests of both men and women.
    d. indirectly promoted woman's liberation while focusing primarily on fashion, morals, taste, sewing, and cooking.

Inference _____c_____ 10. The author suggests all the following about John H. Johnson *except*

    a. he was born in a time of overt racial prejudice.
    b. his family wanted him to get a good education.
    c. his mother was against his starting a risky magazine venture.
    d. his family hoped for greater opportunities in Chicago.

Answer the following with *T* (true), *F* (false), or *CT* (can't tell):

Inference _____T_____ 11. The reader can conclude that Congress appreciated the national propaganda value of magazines.

Inference _____T_____ 12. The serialized novels in early magazines were broken into small, readable segments for the monthly publication.

Inference _____T_____ 13. The reader can conclude that *Reader's Digest* would probably not accept liquor advertisements.

Inference ____F____ 14. The phrase "but not Pollyanna," in referring to *Reader's Digest* articles, means not too feminine to attract male readers.

Inference ____T____ 15. The reader can conclude that niche marketing refers to appealing to a specific population or interest group.

Build Your Vocabulary

According to the way the italicized word was used in the selection, select *a*, *b*, *c*, or *d* for the word or phrase that gives the best definition. The number in parentheses indicates the line of the passage in which the word is located.

____d____ 1. "People of ordinary *means*" (2)
a. ability
b. intelligence
c. talent
d. income

____c____ 6. "*universal* appeal" (66)
a. limited
b. sophisticated
c. widespread
d. cultured

____b____ 2. "*vie* for readers" (27)
a. line up
b. compete
c. publish
d. circulate

____a____ 7. "*diminutive* pages" (71)
a. very small
b. divided
c. congested
d. overpriced

____b____ 3. "racehorse *aficionados*" (30)
a. owners
b. devotees
c. jockeys
d. gamblers

____b____ 8. "*scoffers* were wrong" (71)
a. staff members
b. mocking disbelievers
c. subscribers
d. mail carriers

____a____ 4. "*haunting* photos" (51)
a. unforgettable
b. unrealistic
c. elegant
d. happy

____a____ 9. "*novel* idea" (83)
a. new
b. unpopular
c. controversial
d. thoughtful

____d____ 5. "created *indelible* images" (52)
a. delicate
b. large
c. artistic
d. permanent

____b____ 10. "*disdained* reprinting" (84)
a. prohibited
b. looked down on
c. promoted
d. incorporated

1 selection

Search the Net

Use a search engine such as Google, Yahoo, Ask.com, AltaVista, Excite, Dogpile, or Lycos to find the classic cover photographs for *Life* magazine. Notice Margaret Bourke-White's Fort Peck Dam cover. Select, print, and share your three favorite covers with classmates. For suggested Web sites and other research activities, go to http://www.ablongman.com/smith/.

Concept Prep for Communications and Language

What is communications?

Little wonder, given the importance of mass communication in our daily lives, that **communications** is one of the fastest growing departments in many colleges. The courses that focus on technologically based means of communicating examine the role of mass media in educating the public and influencing cultural, social, and economic change. Popular courses include mass media, journalism, film, and video. Other communications courses, the ones you are more likely to take as introductory courses, focus on interpersonal and intrapersonal communications. The courses are usually interactive and stress group and team performance by learning leadership and responsible group membership skills.

American civil rights activist Dr. Martin Luther King Jr. addresses a large crowd gathered at the Lincoln Memorial for the March on Washington.

Hulton Archive/Getty Images

What are the important elements of communications?

- Public speakers and others in leadership roles usually have **charisma,** a magnetically charming personality and an extraordinary power to inspire loyalty and enthusiasm in others. Leaders such as John F. Kennedy and Martin Luther King Jr. are described as charismatic.
- **Ethics** is another significant aspect of sound leadership, team performance, and business. Ethical decision making and behavior are aimed at distinguishing between right and wrong and acting in a manner that is morally correct and virtuous.
- When speaking formally, use fresh and concise language. Avoid using **clichés** such as "Don't let the cat out of the bag" and "Let's get down to brass tacks." These hackneyed, overused expressions were probably humorous when first used but are now considered tiresome. If interpreted **literally,** exactly word for word, the phrases do not make sense. The words are intentionally designed to take on a new descriptive or **figurative** meaning. In the previous phrases, the "cat in the bag" is a secret, and the "brass tacks" are the real issues. Such phrases are also called **idioms,** and they are especially confusing to people who speak English as a second language.
- Use appropriate **diction** for your audience. Diction refers to your choice of words. It can also refer to the quality of your pronunciation. Use clear and effective words, and enunciate them correctly.
- If you don't want snickers in the audience, avoid **double entendres**—expressions that have a double meaning. The second meaning is usually a mischievous and sexual interpretation of an innocent expression, such as "The athletes were hanging out in the locker room."
- More snickers may come if you make a **malapropism,** a humorous confusion of two words that sound alike. Saying "a blue tarpon was spread over the building under repair" will have your audience envisioning a huge blue fish covering the structure rather than a large plastic tarp.
- Give credit when you use the words or ideas of another person. To steal the thoughts of others

and use them as your own is **plagiarism.** Acknowledging credit to others does not detract from your work but enhances your status as a researcher.

- If you are duplicating published materials for distribution to a group, obtain **copyright** permission so that you are not acting illegally. A copyright is a legal protection granted to an author or publishing company to prevent others from pirating a body of work. To obtain reprint permission, you will probably need to pay a fee.

- When receiving constructive criticism, don't be a **prima donna.** The word is derived from Latin and refers to the "first lady" in an opera.

The connotation, however, is that the person is overly sensitive and difficult to work with. If you become a prima donna, you may suddenly discover that you are a ***persona non grata,*** a person who is no longer acceptable or in favor.

- Strive for excellence, and perhaps you will graduate with honors or **cum laude.** Colleges differ on the grade point averages required for different designations of distinction and high honor. At some institutions, a cumulative grade point average of 3.500–3.699 is required for **cum laude,** a 3.700–3.899 for **magna cum laude,** and a 3.900–4.000 for **summa cum laude.** Some students, however, are satisfied to graduate with a "Thank the Lordy."

Review Questions

After studying the material, answer the following questions:

1. What areas are usually included in a communications department? Speech, journalism, film, and video

2. What is ethical behavior? Distinguishing between right and wrong and acting correctly

3. What is a cliché? An overused expression

4. What is good diction? An appropriate choice of words and clear enunciation

5. What is a double entendre? A word or expression having a double meaning, often with sexual overtones

6. What is a malapropism? Misusing a word that sounds like another one

7. What is plagiarism? _Using someone's ideas and words as your own_

8. What is a prima donna? _A temperamental person who is hard to work with_

9. What is a _persona non grata_? _An unacceptable person_

10. What is summa cum laude? _An award recognizing graduation with the highest distinction_

Your instructor may choose to give a true-false review of these communications and language concepts.

selection

2

selection 2 | Health

Contemporary *Focus*

The demands of college can certainly be stressful. With assignments, exams, work schedules, room-mates, and personal responsibilities, life can become hectic, and your body and mind may be absorbing the trauma. What do you do to take care of your body and keep energized for studying?

Drink and Be Wary?

By Valerie Phillips
Deseret Morning News, April 26, 2006

Increasingly, people are looking for it in a can with revved-up names like AMP, Full Throttle, Adrenaline Rush, Socko! and Wired. "Energy drinks" are supposed to fuel a hectic lifestyle with quick bursts of energy.

But, while these gulp-and-go cocktails deliver nearly the same caffeine buzz as a cup of coffee, they're a poor substitute for proper rest and nutrition, according to Stacie Wing-Gaia, a University of Utah professor and sports dietitian, and Leslie Bonci, Director of the University of Pittsburgh Medical Center's Sports-Nutrition Department.

In an article for the Gatorade Sports Science Institute, Bonci concluded, "Being optimally 'energized' requires a suitable level of physical activity,

adequate sleep, effective fueling and hydration strategies, and probably other unknown factors that affect neurochemicals in the brain. An energy drink alone will never make up for all of these elements."

Energy drinks are banned in France due to food safety concerns. But, in the rest of the world, the energy drink category has grown by 55 percent.

Wing-Gaia said energy drinks are a poor choice before or during strenuous exercise because their high carbohydrate content slows fluid absorption and delays hydration of the body. Sports drinks such as Gatorade or Powerade are only six to eight percent carbohydrate, with electrolytes added to enhance hydration.

COLLABORATE Collaborate on responses to the following questions:

➤ What is your experience with energy or caffeine drinks?

➤ What is your typical sleep schedule? Does it create or reduce stress?

➤ Do cluttered surroundings make you feel unsettled and add to stress?

Skill Development: Preview

Preview the next selection to predict its purpose and organization and to formulate your learning plan.

Activate Schema

What causes stress for you, and what is your response to it?
What do you think of the low-carbohydrate diet craze that has swept the nation?

Establish a Purpose for Reading

Do you have bad habits that sabotage your energy? What can you do to attain a higher level of performance? After recalling what you already know about keeping your body healthy, read this selection to explain the scientific impact of nutrition, exercise, and stress on the body.

Increase Word Knowledge

What do you know about these words?

attribute	crankiness	optimal	judiciously	mimic
aroused	prone	precursor	salient	euphoria

Your instructor may give a true-false vocabulary review before or after reading.

Integrate Knowledge While Reading

Questions have been inserted in the margin to stimulate your thinking while reading. Remember to

Predict	Picture	Relate	Monitor	Correct

Skill Development: Note Taking

Use an informal outline to take notes for later study.

NUTRITION, HEALTH, AND STRESS

NUTRITION AND STRESS: RUNNING ON EMPTY

Good nutrition and eating habits contribute significantly to good health and stress resistance. They are especially important during high-stress times, but these may be the times when we are least likely to eat well! The cupboard is bare, we have no time to plan a shopping list and no money to go shopping, so we skip meals or grab
5 whatever fast food is closest at hand. Sometimes we depend on a dining hall whose schedule doesn't match our own, or whose ideas of good nutrition and fine cuisine are limited to meat, potatoes, and overcooked vegetables with lots of butter. Dessert is usually the high point of every meal.

What should I eat?

2 selection

The Image Bank/Getty Images

Exercising several times a week along with eating healthy food promotes emotional and physical well-being.

FOOD AND ENERGY: THE ROLE OF BLOOD SUGAR

Everyone has experienced the fatigue and irritability that can result from being
10 hungry. While many of the body's systems can make energy from fat, the central nervous system, including the brain, relies primarily on blood sugar, or glucose, for fuel. When blood sugar falls, these symptoms of fatigue result. Parents and people who work with children have observed the hungry-cranky connection on many occasions. As adults, we tend to attribute our moods to external events and ignore our
15 internal physiology, but hunger can cause crankiness in us just the same.

After you consume a meal, your blood glucose level rises as sugar enters the bloodstream from the digestive tract. A rising blood sugar level signals the pancreas to release **insulin.** Insulin is a hormone that allows sugar to enter the cells and be used for energy. As the glucose gradually leaves the bloodstream, blood glucose lev-
20 els begin to decrease.

Some people have more trouble regulating blood sugar than others and are prone to **hypoglycemia,** or low blood sugar, especially if they forget to eat or when they participate in physical activity. Symptoms of hypoglycemia include hunger, shakiness, nervousness, dizziness, nausea, and disorientation.

Do I have hypoglycemia?

25 The following are recommendations for keeping your blood sugar at a healthful level without peaks and dips.

Eat Regularly

Your body likes a regular schedule. Skipping meals means guaranteed hypoglycemia in people prone to this condition. Set up times for meals and snacks that are convenient for your schedule and stick to this routine as much as possible. This may mean
30 planning ahead and carrying snacks with you if you are at work or out running errands. Many people, including those with hypoglycemia, find that eating five or six small meals or snacks each day helps them feel more energetic than three large meals.

Include Protein Foods at Every Meal

Carbohydrate foods eaten without foods containing much protein are digested and enter the bloodstream quickly and are thus likely to challenge blood sugar regulatory processes in people prone to hypoglycemia. Protein slows digestion and allows blood sugar to rise more gradually. Protein servings may be small: a slice or two of meat or cheese; a half-cup of cottage cheese, yogurt, or tuna salad; small servings of fish or shellfish; a dish made with lentils or other legumes; or soy products like tofu.

Avoid Sugar Overload

Do sweets work as snacks?

When you eat a large amount of carbohydrates, blood sugar rises quickly. A high blood sugar level calls forth a high insulin response, which in some people causes a sort of rebound effect: glucose enters the cells, and the blood sugar level drops quickly, causing hypoglycemia. While you may feel energized for a short period of time after too much sugar, you may eventually begin to feel tired, irritable, and hungry.

Drink Plenty of Fluids

Many people fail to maintain optimal levels of hydration. The next time you feel tired, try drinking a glass of water. Dehydration causes fatigue and irritability. Thirst is not an adequate indicator of dehydration; you become dehydrated before you get thirsty. Nutritionists advise drinking at least eight cups of fluid each day, more with physical activity or hot weather. Caffeinated and alcoholic beverages don't count. Not only do they increase your stress, but they also dehydrate you and thus increase your fluid needs. Your urine will be pale if you are adequately hydrated; dark-colored urine is a sign of dehydration.

Limit Caffeine

Caffeine is a **sympathomimetic** substance, which means its effects mimic those of the sympathetic nervous system and thus cause the fight-or-flight response. If you add caffeine to an already aroused sympathetic nervous system, the results can be stressful and produce high levels of anxiety, irritability, headache, and stress-related illness. Most caffeine drinks, including coffee, tea, and cola soft drinks, can also cause stomachaches and nausea, which often get worse under stress.

Why do people consume too much caffeine?

One or two caffeinated beverages consumed judiciously at appropriate times during the day appear to do no harm for most people. Indeed, a little caffeine can increase alertness. The problem with caffeine is that people are likely to overindulge in it when they are stressed. When summoning the energy necessary to get through the day feels like trying to squeeze water from a rock, they reach for a shot of caffeine. Caffeine cannot substitute for a good night's sleep, however. When you are truly fatigued, caffeine does not help you concentrate; it simply leaves you wired, too jittery to sleep, and too tired to do anything productive.

EATING IN RESPONSE TO STRESS: FEEDING THE HUNGRY HEART

Why do we celebrate with food?

Few people look on eating and food only in terms of hunger and nutrition. Every culture in the world has evolved rituals around food and eating. Feasting and fasting carry layers of religious, cultural, and emotional overtones. As children, we learn to associate food with security, comfort, love, reward, punishment, anger, restraint. It's no wonder that we eat for many reasons other than hunger: because we're lonely, angry, sad, happy, nervous, or depressed. Unlike alcohol, which we can give up if we are prone to a drinking problem, we must learn to live with food. If eating is the

only way we take the time to nurture ourselves, we eat more than we are really hungry for. In extreme cases, an inability to control eating can develop into an eat-
75 ing disorder, known as **compulsive overeating,** that often gets worse under stress.

FOOD AND MOOD: THE ROLE OF NEUROTRANSMITTERS

Most people feel relaxed and lazy after a big feast. For this reason many cultures have incorporated a siesta after the large midday meal, and professors who teach a class right after lunch or dinner rarely turn out the lights for a slide show. Why do we feel tired? Certainly our blood sugar should be adequate after eating all that
80 food. Changes in brain biochemistry may be the reason. The food we eat supplies the precursor molecules for manufacturing neurotransmitters that influence our emotions and mood. Some researchers believe that by selecting the right kinds of food we can encourage states of relaxation or alertness.

Big meals, especially those with a lot of fat, take a long time to digest, and with
85 a full stomach we feel like relaxing rather than working. On the other hand, smaller meals low in fat take less time and energy to digest and leave us feeling more ener-getic and alert.

Meals that are composed primarily of carbohydrates encourage production of the neurotransmitter *serotonin*, which makes us feel drowsy and relaxed. High-
90 carbohydrate meals are a prescription for relaxation and may be the reason some people overeat: it makes them feel good. A small, high-carbohydrate snack before bedtime can encourage sleep. Many people find that eating carbohydrates helps them feel less stressed and more relaxed. Some people find that a meal or snack with carbohydrate but little protein, especially in the middle of the day, leaves
95 them feeling tired.

What would be a great lunch for me? →

Meals that include a small serving of protein foods, with or without carbohy-drates, encourage alertness by favoring production of neurotransmitters such as *dopamine* and *norepinephrine*. A small lunch that includes protein foods is best for students who need to stay alert for a 1:00 class.

PHYSICAL ACTIVITY AND STRESS RESISTANCE

100 Participation in regular physical activity is one of the most effective ways to in-crease your stress resistance. Countless studies comparing people with high and low levels of stress resistance have found exercise to be one of the most salient discrim-inators between these two groups. An important note is that the amount and inten-sity of exercise required to produce stress management benefits need not be over-
105 whelming. While many athletes enjoy extended periods of intense activity, other people find stress relief with a brisk walk, an hour of gardening, or a game of volley-ball on the beach.

Exercise High: Endorphins, Hormones, and Neurotransmitters

In addition to canceling the negative effects of stress, exercise may induce some positive biochemical changes. Many exercisers report feelings of euphoria and states
110 of consciousness similar to those described by people using drugs such as heroin. Such accounts have led to use of the term *runner's high*, since these descriptions first came primarily from long-distance runners. These reports have intrigued both exercise scientists and the lay public and have suggested the possibility that certain types of exercise, particularly vigorous exercise of long duration, may cause bio-
115 chemical changes that mimic drug-induced euphoria.

As scientists have come to understand something of brain biochemistry, some interesting hypotheses have emerged. The most publicized of these has focused on a group of chemical messengers found in the central nervous system (brain and spinal cord) called opioids, since they are similar in structure and function to 120 the drugs that come from the poppy flower: opium, morphine, and heroin. **Beta-endorphins** belong to this group. They not only inhibit pain but also seem to have other roles in the brain as well, such as aiding in memory and learning and registering emotions. It is difficult for scientists to measure opioid concentrations in the central nervous system of humans, but animal research has suggested that en- 125 dogenous (produced by the body) opioid concentrations increase with level of exercise: more exercise, more opioids.

Rhythmic Exercise: Relaxed Brain Waves

What will be my exercise regimen?

Rhythmic exercises such as walking, running, rowing, and swimming increase **alpha-wave** activity in the brain. The electrical activity of the brain can be monitored in the laboratory using an instrument called an **electroencephalograph** 130 **(EEG).** Alpha waves are associated with a calm mental state, such as that produced by meditation or chanting. The rhythmic breathing that occurs during some forms of exercise also contributes to an increase in alpha-wave activity. Rhythmic activity performed to music may be stress relieving in other ways as well.

(1,727 words)

—From Barbara Brehm,
Stress Management

Finding Your Life Stress Score

To assess your life in terms of life changes, check all the events listed that have happened to you in the past year. Add up the points to derive your life stress score.

Rank	Life Event	Life Change Unit Value	Your Points
1.	Death of spouse	100	_____
2.	Divorce	73	_____
3.	Separation from living partner	65	_____
4.	Jail term or probation	63	_____
5.	Death of close family member	63	_____
6.	Serious personal injury or illness	53	_____
7.	Marriage or establishing life partnership	50	_____
8.	Getting fired at work	47	_____
9.	Marital or relationship reconciliation	45	_____
10.	Retirement	45	_____
11.	Change in health of immediate family member	44	_____
12.	Pregnancy or causing pregnancy	40	_____
13.	Sex difficulties	39	_____

(continued)

Rank	Life Event	Life Change Unit Value	Your Points
14.	Gain of new family member	39	_____
15.	Business or work role change	39	_____
16.	Change in financial state	38	_____
17.	Death of a close friend (not a family member)	37	_____
18.	Change to different line of work	36	_____
19.	Change in number of arguments with spouse or life partner	35	_____
20.	Taking a mortgage or loan for a major purpose	31	_____
21.	Foreclosure of mortgage or loan	30	_____
22.	Change in responsibilities at work	29	_____
23.	Son or daughter leaving home	29	_____
24.	Trouble with in-laws or with children	29	_____
25.	Outstanding personal achievement	28	_____
26.	Spouse begins or stops work	26	_____
27.	Begin or end school	26	_____
28.	Change in living conditions (visitors, roommates, remodeling)	25	_____
29.	Change in personal habits (diet, exercise, smoking)	24	_____
30.	Trouble with boss	23	_____
31.	Change in work hours or conditions	20	_____
32.	Moving to new residence	20	_____
33.	Change in schools	20	_____
34.	Change in recreation	19	_____
35.	Change in religious activities	19	_____
36.	Change in social activities (more or less than before)	18	_____
37.	Taking out a loan for a lesser purchase (car or TV)	17	_____
38.	Change in sleeping habits	16	_____
39.	Change in frequency of family get-togethers	15	_____
40.	Change in eating habits	15	_____
41.	Vacation	13	_____
42.	Presently in winter holiday season	12	_____
43.	Minor violation of the law	11	_____
		LIFE STRESS SCORE:	_____

Adapted from the "Social Readjustment Rating Scale," by Thomas Holmes and Richard Rahe. The scale was first published in the *Journal of Psychosomatic Research*, vol. II, p. 214, Copyright 1967. Reprinted by permission of Elsevier, Inc., Philadelphia, PA.

Researchers Holmes and Rahe claim that there is a connection between the degree of life stress and major health problems. A person who scores 300 or more on the life stress test runs an 80 percent risk of suffering a major health problem within the next two years. Someone who scores 150 to 300 has a 50 percent chance of becoming ill.

Recall

Stop to self-test, relate, and react. Study your informal outline.

Your instructor may choose to give you a true-false comprehension review.

Write About the Selection

Explain how you can use the health and nutritional information in this selection to energize and stimulate your mental performance during exam week.

Response Suggestion: List your energizing ideas with a purpose and examples for each.

Contemporary *Link*

During stressful times, some people eat more and some eat less. The "Freshman 15" refers not to an athletic team but to the 15 pounds that students often gain during the first year of college. Other students who are concerned with body image obsess about their weight and follow overly restrictive diets. How do you plan to use this information about nutrition, exercise, and stress to identify your needs and avoid unhealthy behaviors leading to excessive weight gain or loss?

Check Your Comprehension

After reading the selection, answer the following questions with *a, b, c,* or *d.* To help you analyze your strengths and weaknesses, the question types are indicated.

Main Idea   __b__   1. Which is the best statement of the main idea of this selection?

       a. A balanced diet is the most effective way to decrease stress.
       b. Regular exercise and good eating habits contribute to stress reduction and both physical and emotional well-being.
       c. Stress negatively affects mental and physical performance.
       d. Avoiding sugar overload and including protein at every meal help regulate blood sugar.

Detail   __b__   2. The pancreas is signaled to release insulin when

       a. protein is consumed.
       b. blood glucose levels rise.
       c. physical activity increases.
       d. blood sugar levels decrease.

Inference   __c__   3. By using the term *fine cuisine,* the author suggests that

       a. "fine" meals include meat, potatoes, and vegetables.
       b. dessert is an important part of "fine dining."
       c. dining halls do not always serve good, nutritional meals.
       d. vegetables should be cooked without fats.

Detail   __a__   4. People who experience symptoms of hypoglycemia should do all the following *except*

       a. eat three large meals per day and vary the times.
       b. combine proteins with carbohydrates.
       c. limit sugar intake.
       d. eat several small meals or snacks throughout the day.

Inference   __c__   5. The implied similarity between drinking and eating problems is that

       a. many people who abuse alcohol are also prone to eating problems.
       b. compulsive eating is treated more easily than compulsive drinking.
       c. drinking alcohol and eating food sometimes are misguided responses to stress.
       d. the consumption of both food and alcohol releases endorphins, which reduce stress.

Detail   __a__   6. The production of norepinephrine is stimulated by eating

       a. proteins.
       b. fats.
       c. carbohydrates.
       d. caffeine.

Detail _____c_____ 7. The beta-endorphins believed to be released by exercise have all the following benefits *except*

    a. inducing feelings of euphoria.
    b. inhibiting pain.
    c. regulating blood sugar.
    d. aiding memory.

Inference _____b_____ 8. The activity most likely to increase alpha-wave activity in the brain would be

    a. playing a game of chess.
    b. jogging.
    c. lifting weights.
    d. playing baseball.

Inference _____a_____ 9. For a midnight snack before bed, the author would most likely recommend

    a. a bagel.
    b. cappuccino.
    c. peanuts.
    d. a chicken leg.

Detail _____b_____ 10. The author's attitude toward the use of caffeine by most people is that

    a. caffeine can be used to decrease fear because it arouses the fight-or-flight response.
    b. light amounts of caffeine appear harmless and can increase alertness.
    c. caffeine should be avoided because it causes stomachaches, nausea, headaches, and irritability.
    d. when a person is truly fatigued, caffeine can increase concentration.

Answer the following with *T* (true) or *F* (false).

Detail _____T_____ 11. Glucose provides the primary fuel for the brain.

Detail _____F_____ 12. Thirst is an adequate indicator of the body's optimal hydration level.

Inference _____T_____ 13. The term *hungry heart* implies a need that food cannot satisfy.

Detail _____F_____ 14. A glass of cola can be counted toward the number of cups of fluid the body needs each day.

Inference _____F_____ 15. The author suggests that serotonin is more important for effective studying than dopamine and norepinephrine.

Build Your Vocabulary

According to the way the italicized word was used in the selection, select *a, b, c,* or *d* for the word or phrase that gives the best definition. The number in parentheses indicates the line of the passage in which the word is located.

____b____ 1. "to *attribute* our moods"
(14)
a. dissociate
b. credit
c. explain
d. reject

____b____ 2. "can cause *crankiness*" (15)
a. rage
b. irritability
c. drowsiness
d. fatigue

____c____ 3. "*optimal* levels"
(44)
a. medium
b. low
c. most desirable
d. regulatory

____b____ 4. "its effects *mimic*"
(52)
a. distort
b. imitate
c. confuse
d. falsify

____a____ 5. "an already *aroused*"(54)
a. excited
b. not stimulated
c. settled
d. relaxed

____c____ 6. "beverages consumed
judiciously" (58)
a. recklessly
b. hastily
c. cautiously
d. carelessly

____b____ 7. "we are *prone*" (72)
a. damaged by
b. inclined
c. addicted
d. connected

____d____ 8. "the *precursor* molecules"
(81)
a. necessary
b. final
c. active
d. forerunner

____a____ 9. "*salient* discriminators"
(102)
a. noticeable
b. instructive
c. irrelevant
d. damaging

____c____ 10. "drug-induced *euphoria*"
(115)
a. insanity
b. disorientation
c. exhilaration
d. serenity

Search the Net

Use a search engine such as Google, Yahoo, Ask.com, AltaVista, Excite, Dogpile, or Lycos to search for foods that can serve as remedies for specific ailments. Search for foods that help the body fight acne, cold sores, high blood pressure, and insomnia. For suggested Web sites and other research activities, go to http://www.ablongman.com/smith/.

Concept Prep for Health

What is blood pressure?

Blood pressure is the measure of the pressure exerted by the blood as it flows through the arteries. Blood moves in waves and is thus measured in two phases. The **systolic pressure** is the pressure at the height of the blood wave when the left ventricle of the heart contracts to push the blood through the body. The **diastolic pressure** is the pressure when the ventricles are at rest and filling with blood. The figures are expressed as the systolic "over" the diastolic pressure. The average blood pressure of a healthy adult is **120 over 80.**

What can happen to arteries as we age?

Cholesterol—a white soapy substance that is found in the body and in foods such as animal fats—can accumulate on the inner walls of arteries—blood vessels that carry blood away from the heart—and narrow the channels through which blood flows. Nutritionists recommend eating **unsaturated fats** such as vegetable or olive oils as opposed to **saturated fats** (animal fats), which are solid at room temperature.

Another condition that lessens the flow of blood through the arteries is hardening of the arteries or **arteriosclerosis.** A surgical technique called an **angioplasty** is used to clear the arteries. A catheter with a small balloon is inserted into the arteries around the heart to compress fatty deposits and restore the flow of blood.

What are some frequently discussed medical procedures?

- A **CAT scan** (computerized axial tomography) is a painless, noninvasive procedure that uses radiation to show a three-dimensional image of the body. The diagnostic procedure is used to detect tumors and other conditions. It shows differences in the density of soft tissue,

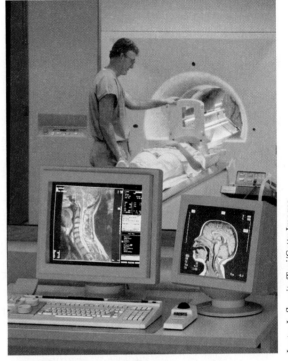

Radiologists are physicians who specialize in imaging technologies such as magnetic resonance imaging (MRI) for medical diagnosis.

Lester Lefkowitz/Taxi/Getty Images

with high-density substances appearing white and low-density substances appearing dark.
- An **MRI** (magnetic resonance imaging) uses magnetic fields and radio waves to detect hidden tumors and other conditions by mapping the vibration of atoms. An MRI is painless and does not use radiation.
- **Chemotherapy** is a treatment for cancer in which the patient receives chemicals that destroy cancer cells. Currently, more than 50 anticancer drugs are available for use. Temporary hair loss is a common side effect of chemotherapy.
- **Radiation** is another treatment for destroying malignant cancer cells. Unfortunately, it also destroys some healthy cells.

Copyright © 2008 by Pearson Education, Inc.

337

- A **mammogram** is an x-ray of the breast to detect tumors that are too small to be detected by other means.
- A **Pap test** is a procedure in which cells are taken from the cervical region and tested for cancer.
- **PSA** (prostate-specific antigen) levels in the blood are measured to detect prostate cancer in men. A **prostatic ultrasound** can also be used.

- A **sonogram** or **ultrasound** test uses high-frequency sound waves to detect abnormalities. It is a noninvasive procedure that can be used to view the size, position, and sex of a fetus.
- **Amniocentesis** is a procedure for detecting abnormalities in the fetus. Fluid is drawn from the liquid surrounding the fetus by a needle through the mother's stomach. The fluid contains cells of the fetus that can be analyzed.

Review Questions

After studying the material, answer the following questions:

1. What is the difference between systolic and diastolic pressure? Systolic pressure is the height of the pressure as the heart pumps, and diastolic pressure is when the heart is resting and filling with blood.

2. Which type of pressure should be higher? Systolic

3. How does cholesterol harm the body? It accumulates on the inner walls of arteries and slows the flow of blood.

4. How can you distinguish saturated fats? These animal fats are solid at room temperature.

5. What does an angioplasty do? It opens the arteries with a balloon.

6. What medical procedure uses drugs to cure cancer? Chemotherapy

7. What procedure uses magnetic fields and radio waves to detect tumors and other conditions without radiation? MRI

8. What test can indicate prostate cancer? PSA

9. What procedure extracts fetal cells for diagnosis? Amniocentesis

10. What type of x-ray is used to detect breast cancer? Mammogram

Your instructor may choose to give a true-false review of these health concepts.

selection 3 | Criminal Justice

Contemporary *Focus*

Legend has it that electronic monitoring bracelets were inspired by Spiderman. In 1984, a New Mexico judge persuaded the Honeywell Electronics Company to design a device to "tag" offenders for law enforcement just as Spiderman tagged villains in the comic strip. How effective are these bracelets, and what future roles will they play in law enforcement?

Can I Cut Off My Electronic Monitoring Bracelet?

Daniel Engber

Slate.com and WashingtonPost.Newsweek Interactive

How easy is it to cut off one of those bracelets?

All you need is a pair of scissors. Electronic monitoring bracelets aren't designed to stay on at all costs. A device that can't be removed without special tools would pose a serious health risk to its wearer. A bracelet might get caught in heavy machinery, for example, or paramedics might need to remove it to provide emergency medical care. Most of the monitoring bracelets on the market can be easily cut in two, or even ripped off if enough pressure is applied.

If you slice through your bracelet, you'll probably set off an alarm. A radio transmitter embedded in the bracelet is programmed to send a distress signal as soon as it's tampered with. Bracelet manufacturers won't discuss the specifics of tamper-proofing, but many pieces of monitoring jewelry use a wire that runs the length of the band. Cutting the wire breaks a circuit and sends an alert to the authorities. Some bracelets also use internal light sensors to catch anyone who manages to pry open the transmitter's housing.

Anyone can cut off a bracelet and go into hiding, but it's very difficult to take one off and put it back on later. Parole officers or other supervisors are supposed to examine the bracelets on a regular basis. If they see any signs of tampering "like cut marks or twisted plastic" the offender is considered to have violated the terms of the monitoring program. The fact that most bracelets are worn on the ankle makes them very difficult to remove intact. (Someone wearing a device on his wrist might be able to slide it over a greased-up hand.)

COLLABORATE Collaborate on responses to the following questions:

➤ What type of offender might most likely be tagged with an electronic monitoring bracelet?

➤ Why are electronic systems frequently mentioned as appropriate for pedophiles?

➤ If bracelets are easy to cut, why do they work?

Skill Development: Preview

Preview the next selection to predict its purpose and organization and to formulate your learning plan.

Activate Schema

Who is Martha Stewart, and why was she electronically monitored for a period of time?
How is electronic monitoring a form of "big brother"?

Establish a Purpose for Reading

Though intended to offer rehabilitation, prisons are often "graduate schools" for crime. Can technology address some of the problems associated with imprisonment? Read about the advantages and disadvantages of electronic monitoring and how the system works.

Increase Word Knowledge

What do you know about these words?

monitor	verifier	recidivism	sanction	drawbacks
rehabilitation	deterrent	libertarians	erode	virtue

Your instructor may give a true-false vocabulary review before or after reading.

Integrate Knowledge While Reading

Questions have been inserted in the margin to stimulate your thinking while reading. Remember to

Predict	Picture	Relate	Monitor	Correct

Skill Development: Annotating and Outlining

Annotate the selection, and make an informal study outline.

ELECTRONIC MONITORING

For house arrest to work, sentencing authorities must be assured that arrestees are actually at home during their assigned times. Random calls and visits are one way to check on house arrest orders. However, one of the more interesting developments in the criminal justice system has been the introduction of electronic monitoring
5 (EM) devices to manage offender obedience to home confinement orders.

Electronic monitoring programs have been around since 1964, when Ralph Schwitzgabel of Harvard University experimented with linking offenders with a central monitoring station. EM can be used with offenders at a number of points in the criminal justice system, ranging from pretrial release to parole. Today, about
10   14,000 probationers are being monitored electronically. However, in all, approximately 1,500 programs exist and 95,000 EM units are in use, including those being used by individuals on pretrial status, home detention, and parole, as well as in juvenile detention.

ACTIVE AND PASSIVE SYSTEMS

How obvious are these devices? →   The electronically monitored offender wears a device around the ankle, wrist, or
15   neck that sends signals back to a control office. Two basic types of systems are used: active and passive. Active systems constantly monitor the offender by continuously sending a signal back to the central office. If the offender leaves home at an unauthorized time, the signal is broken and the "failure" recorded. In some cases, the control officer is automatically notified electronically through a beeper. Passive sys-
20   tems usually involve random phone calls by a computer to which the offender must respond within a specified time (such as 30 seconds). Some passive systems require that the offender place the monitoring device into a verifier box that sends a signal

Shannon Stapleton/Reuters/Landov

Entertainment maven Martha Stewart models her electronic monitoring bracelet during a taping of her show.

back to the control computer. Another approach is to have the arrestee repeat words that are analyzed by a voice verifier and compared to tapes of the client's voice.

25 Other systems use radio transmitters that receive a signal from a device worn by the offender and relay it back to the computer monitoring system via telephone lines.

ADVANTAGES OF ELECTRONIC MONITORING

Supporters of EM point to its relatively low cost and high security, while helping offenders avoid overcrowded and dangerous jails. Electronic monitoring is capital-rather than labor-intensive. Since offenders are monitored by computers, an initial

30 investment in hardware rules out the need for hiring many more supervisory officers to handle large numbers of clients. It is not suprising, then, that the public supports EM as a cost-effective alternative to prison sentences.

There are some indications that EM can be an effective addition to the mix of alternative sanctions, providing judges with an enhanced supervision tool. Program

35 evaluations with pretrial, probation, and parole groups indicate that recidivism rates are no higher than in traditional programs, costs are lower, and system overcrowding is reduced. For example, one study of the cost savings potential of using house arrest with EM as an alternative to jail for drunk drivers in a Pennsylvania county found that the program was able to save money and avoid new construction costs

40 without widening the net of social control.

Research shows that although many EM clients are cited for program violations, recidivism rates are low. Clients find the program valuable, and many use the opportunity to obtain jobs and improve family relationships. If the program can service defendants who would otherwise have been jailed (for example, people con-

45 victed of drunk driving), it will prove to be an effective correctional option that works as well as, if not better than, a probation sentence.

Are those undergoing electronic monitoring required to notify employers?

DISADVANTAGES OF ELECTRONIC MONITORING

Electronic monitoring holds the promise of becoming a widely used intermediate sanction in the new millenium. Nevertheless, a few critics charge that the concept has drawbacks as a form of low-cost confinement.

50 First, current technology is limited. Existing systems can be affected by faulty telephone equipment; by radio beams from powerful transmitters, such as those located at airports or radio stations; by storms and weather disturbances; and even by large concentrations of iron and steel, which can block signals or cause electromagnetic interference. There have also been cases of EM's being "defeated" by people

55 using call-forwarding systems and prerecorded messages to fool monitors. Assessing what the proper response should be when tracking equipment reveals a breach of home confinement is difficult. Can we punish someone for what might be an equipment failure? New methods are now being developed to improve the efficiency of EM.

60 Second, it may be inaccurate to assume that electronic monitoring can provide secure confinement at a relatively low cost. In addition to the initial outlay for the equipment, other expenses involved with electronic monitoring include overtime pay for control officers who must be on duty nights or weekends, the cost of training personnel to use the sophisticated equipment, and the cost of educating judges

65 in the legality of home confinement. The cost of home confinement with electronic monitoring is estimated to be four times greater than that of traditional probation.

selection 3

What makes
probation more
rehabilitative than
EM?

Third, most electronic monitoring or house arrest programs do not provide for rehabilitation services. The focus is on guaranteeing the location of offenders, not their treatment. Thus, electronic monitoring may lack the deterrent power of
70 a prison sentence while offering little of the rehabilitative effect of traditional probation.

It is assumed that EM will be used as a cost-saving alternative to jail or prison. Unfortunately, alternative sanctions are often directed at offenders who might otherwise have received easier sentences. Electronic monitoring will not save money
75 unless it eliminates the need for new jail and prison construction. It is unlikely that staff in existing institutions will be let go because offenders are being monitored in their homes.

Finally, some civil libertarians are troubled by EM's potential to erode privacy and liberty. Do we really want U.S. citizens watched over by a computer? What are
80 the limits of electronic monitoring? Can it be used with mental patients? HIV carriers? Suicidal teenagers? Those considered high-risk future offenders? While promising to reduce the correctional population, EM actually has the potential to substantially increase it by turning homes into prisons.

EM seems to hold great promise, but neither its effectiveness nor its virtue
85 has been determined. It is not yet clear whether EM is a correctional savior or a temporary fad.

(1,030 words)

—From Joseph J. Senna and Larry J. Seigel,
Introduction to Criminal Justice, 9th ed. Copyright
© 2002. Reprinted with permission of Wadsworth,
a division of Thomson Learning.

Recall

Stop to self-test, relate, and react. Study your informal outline.

Your instructor may choose to give you a true-false comprehension review.

Write About the Selection

What are the advantages and disadvantages of using an electronic monitoring system? What types of offenders should be eligible for electronic monitoring?

Response Suggestion: Describe a scenario in which electronic monitoring would be particularly effective.

Contemporary *Link*

Since legend has it that electronic monitoring bracelets were inspired by Spiderman, what fictional or factual improvements in the system can you envision? Knowing some of the difficulties of electronic monitoring and recognizing the overcrowding in prisons, what innovations would you suggest to improve the situation?

Check Your Comprehension

After reading the selection, answer the following questions with *a, b, c,* or *d.* To help you analyze your strengths and weaknesses, the question types are indicated.

Main Idea _____b_____ 1. Which is the best statement of the main idea of this selection?

    a. EM appears likely to change the criminal justice system, thus reducing the need for lengthy jail terms.

    b. EM has its pluses and minuses, but it is too early to know how much it will change our criminal justice system.

    c. EM will lead to an increase in home confinement for convicted criminals who have been charged with drunk driving.

    d. EM has good and bad features, but experts in the criminal justice system have determined that it is a cost-saving alternative.

Inference _____d_____ 2. The reader can conclude that EM devices were developed mainly in order to

    a. cut back on existing staff at jails.

    b. change the attitude of convicted criminals.

    c. discourage repeat offenders.

    d. make house arrest more effective.

Detail _____c_____ 3. An important difference between active EM systems and passive EM systems is that active EM systems

    a. use telephone signals to function.

    b. utilize random calls by a computer.

    c. operate constantly, day and night.

    d. cannot be "defeated" by offenders.

Inference _____a_____ 4. The reader can conclude that supporters of EM are likely to emphasize that EM

    a. saves taxpayers' money.

    b. increases public safety.

    c. reduces crime rates.

    d. helps rehabilitate criminals.

Detail _____d_____ 5. One obvious benefit of using EM for pretrial, probation, and parole groups is that

    a. progress can be monitored more rapidly for offenders.

    b. recidivism rates are cut almost in half.

    c. few visitors are allowed.

    d. prisoners are probably safer than they would be in jail.

Detail   b   6. According to critics, a major shortcoming of EM devices is that they

        a. can be "defeated" by most criminals.
        b. rely on undependable technology.
        c. are made of concentrated iron and steel.
        d. allow criminals too much freedom.

Detail   a   7. The author states that electronic monitoring will save the criminal justice system money only if it

        a. does away with the need to build new jails.
        b. allows a reduction in prison staff.
        c. develops technology that is foolproof.
        d. rehabilitates offenders better than jail does.

Inference   c   8. The questions the author asks in the next-to-last paragraph are mainly concerned with

        a. the general economics of EM.
        b. additional safety benefits of EM.
        c. potential social and legal issues related to EM.
        d. public opinion about EM.

Inference   b   9. The ending of the selection reveals that the author's feelings about EM are

        a. enthusiastically supportive of expansion.
        b. somewhat guarded at present.
        c. negative.
        d. strongly influenced by costs.

Inference   a   10. It can reasonably be assumed that a major reason for inventing EM was that

        a. prisons were getting dangerously overcrowded.
        b. many criminals did not deserve to be in prison for a full term.
        c. prisons were not effectively rehabilitating offenders.
        d. politicians wanted to widen the net of social control.

Answer the following with *T* (true) or *F* (false).

Detail   T   11. Most passive EM devices involve using the telephone.

Inference   T   12. The reader can conclude that the focus of a capital-intensive system requires money.

Detail   F   13. The cost of traditional probation is roughly four times as much as electronic monitoring.

selection 3

Detail _____T_____ 14. The author indicates the use of EM allows for the possible improvement of family relationships whereas prison offers no such benefit.

Inference _____F_____ 15. The author supports using EM to lengthen sentences for offenders who might normally have been set free earlier.

Build Your Vocabulary

According to the way the italicized word was used in the selection, select *a, b, c,* or *d* for the word or phrase that gives the best definition. The number in parentheses indicates the line of the passage in which the word is located.

_____b_____ 1. "constantly *monitor*" (16)
a. shock
b. observe
c. selectively ignore
d. respond to

_____a_____ 2. "*verifier* box" (22)
a. confirmation
b. contradiction
c. closed
d. tracking

_____a_____ 3. "*recidivism* rates" (35/42)
a. return to criminal behavior
b. return to being a good citizen
c. return home
d. return court

_____c_____ 4. "intermediate *sanction*" (48)
a. prison
b. police
c. penalty
d. judge

_____b_____ 5. "has *drawbacks*" (49)
a. promise
b. flaws
c. advantages
d. electronics

_____c_____ 6. "*rehabilitation* services" (68)
a. management
b. direction
c. treatment
d. listening

_____d_____ 7. "*deterrent* power" (69)
a. money
b. monitoring
c. confinement
d. preventive

_____d_____ 8. "civil *libertarians*" (78)
a. people who believe in constant monitoring
b. people who believe in no privacy or free will
c. people who believe in authority
d. people who believe in free will

_____b_____ 9. "*erode* privacy" (78)
a. resist
b. break down
c. watch
d. increase

_____b_____ 10. "*virtue* has been determined" (84)
a. disadvantage
b. value
c. evilness
d. inefficiency

Search the Net

Use a search engine such as Google, Yahoo, Ask.com, AltaVista, Excite, Dogpile, or Lycos to find information about different programs used to manage offenders. Describe three alternatives to traditional jail or prison sentences and discuss the pros and cons of each program. For suggested Web sites and other research activities, go to http://www.ablongman.com/smith/.

Vocabulary Booster

The Sun, the Moon, and the Stars

Roots		
	sol, helio: "sun"	*luna:* "moon"
	aster, astro: "star"	

Words with *sol, helio:* "sun"

A sundial is a primitive example of a *solar* chronometer, a device indicating the time by means of the sun.

- *solar:* of or pertaining to the sun; proceeding from the sun; operating on energy from the sun

  Solar panels on rooftops to heat water for homes have become a popular way to conserve energy.

- *solarium:* a glass-enclosed room that is exposed to the sun's rays

  A *solarium* in a home usually becomes the favorite spot in winter because it is naturally warmed by the sun.

- *solstice:* either of two times a year when the sun is farthest from the equator

  The summer *solstice,* the longest day in the Northern Hemisphere, occurs around June 21 or 22 when the sun is farthest north of the equator.

- *heliotherapy:* treatment of disease by exposure to sunlight

  Heliotherapy is prescribed sunbathing for certain illnesses such as tuberculosis or rickets.

- *heliotropic:* turning or growing toward the light or sun

  Without frequent turning, some *heliotropic* houseplants would grow only in one direction—toward the sunlight.

- *helium:* an inert gaseous element present in the sun's atmosphere and in natural gas

  Because *helium* is a chemically inactive gas, it is used as a substitute for flammable gases in dirigibles (blimps).

Words with *luna:* "moon"

The small *demilune* table was just the right size for the narrow foyer because its half-moon shape did not extend far into the room.

- *lunar:* of or pertaining to the moon; round or crescent-shaped; measured by the moon's revolutions

A *lunar* month is equal to one revolution of the moon around the earth, approximately 29½ days.

- *lunatic:* an insane or recklessly foolish person

  The old gentleman was labeled a *lunatic* and unable to handle his legal affairs responsibly.

- *lunatic fringe:* members on the edges of a group, such as a political or religious group, who hold extreme views

  Members of the *lunatic fringe* of some environmentalist movements have destroyed property to protest further building in certain areas.

- *lunar eclipse:* an obscuring of the light of the moon when the earth is positioned between the moon and the sun

  During a *lunar eclipse,* the earth casts its shadow on the moon.

- *lunar year:* a division of time equal to twelve lunar months

  In a *lunar year* the moon orbits the earth twelve times.

Words with *aster, astro:* "star"

An *aster* is a daisylike flower with colored petals radiating around a yellow disk.

- *asterisk:* a small, starlike symbol (*) used in writing and printing to refer to footnotes or omissions

  An *asterisk* can be used to refer readers to an explanation of an item in the written material.

- *asteroid:* a small, solid body orbiting the sun between Mars and Jupiter

  Scientists believe that *asteroids* collided with Earth in the past and predict they will do so again.

- *astronomy:* the science that deals with the universe beyond the Earth's atmosphere

  Astronomy involves studying the motion, position, and size of celestial bodies.

- *astronomical:* pertaining to astronomy; extremely large or enormous

  Projected costs for the new hospital wing were so *astronomical* that the board decided to postpone the project.

- *astrology:* the study that attempts to foretell the future by interpreting the influence of the stars on human lives

  Most people don't believe in *astrology;* they believe they are responsible for what happens in their future.

- *astronauts:* a person trained for space flight

  The *astronauts* all went to bed early the night before their scheduled space shuttle mission.

REVIEW

Part I

Choose the word from the boxed list that best completes each of the sentences below.

lunatic	astronomical	astronomy	astrology
solarium	heliotropic	lunar eclipse	astronauts

1. A ___heliotropic___ plant might be compared to a person who is a sun worshipper.

2. The world's population appears to be growing at an alarmingly large, or ___astronomical___, rate.

3. Someone branded a ___lunatic___ would not be sought out for sound advice.

4. The competition is fierce for gaining admittance to the training program for ___astronauts___ in Houston.

5. Black holes, supernovas, and constellations are all studied in the science of ___astronomy.___

6. A warm ___solarium___ is the perfect place to keep plants alive during the winter months.

7. According to ___astrology___, personality traits are determined by the planetary alignments on a person's birthday.

8. In ancient times, the appearance of a ___lunar eclipse___ was mistakenly thought to be a sign that the end of the world was near.

Part II

Indicate whether the italicized words are used correctly (C) or incorrectly (I) in the following sentences:

___C___ 9. *Solar* panels are becoming more popular in home design as the costs of other forms of energy continue to rise.

___I___ 10. *Lunar* explorations involve spacecraft searching for proof of life on Mars.

___I___ 11. Years ago native people celebrated the winter *solstice*, which is the coldest day of the year.

___C___ 12. A sun worshipper would likely be happy with a prescription for *heliotherapy*.

___C___ 13. An *asterisk* is on one of the keys on most cell phones.

___I___ 14. *Asters* are small planets of varying sizes, often confused with meteors.

___C___ 15. A person labeled a *lunatic* is not known for giving wise advice.

Your instructor may choose to give you a multiple-choice review.

7 Inference

- What is an inference, and what does it mean to read between the lines?
- What is the connotation of a word?
- Why do authors use figurative language, and how can understanding it enhance comprehension?
- Why is prior knowledge needed for implied meaning?
- How does a reader draw conclusions?

Rafal Oblinski, *Graceful Dream of Poetic Glory*, 1995. Acrylic on canvas. 28 x 20 inches.

What Is an Inference?

At the first and most basic level of reading, the *literal level*—the level that presents the facts—you can actually point to the words on the page to answer a literal question. However, at the second and more sophisticated level of reading—the *inferential level*—you no longer can point to such an answer but instead must form it from clues and suggestions within the text.

EXAMPLE In the following passage from Michael Ondaatje's novel *The English Patient*, the author implies an activity, and the reader infers what is happening. Mark the point at which you understand the activity.

> She moves backwards a few feet and with a piece of white chalk draws more rectangles, so there is a pyramid of them, single then double then single, her left hand braced flat on the floor, her head down, serious. . . .
>
> She drops the chalk into the pocket of her dress. She stands and pulls up the looseness of her skirt and ties it around her dress. She pulls from another pocket a piece of metal and flings it out in front of her so it falls just beyond the farthest square.
>
> She leaps forward, her legs smashing down, her shadow behind her curling into the depth of the hall. She is very quick, her tennis shoes skidding on the numbers she has drawn into each rectangle, one foot landing, then two feet, then one again until she reaches the last square.[1]

EXPLANATION How many sentences did it take for you to infer that she is playing the game of hopscotch? You may have visualized the activity as early as the author's description of drawing "single then double then single"; or perhaps you caught on a bit later, when she jumps. In any case, you were able to make the inference when the clues from the text merged with your own prior knowledge.

Two different terms are used in discussing inferential thinking: the writer or speaker *implies* and the reader or listener *infers*. This merging of suggested thought is also figuratively called **reading between the lines.** Throughout this text, many of the thought questions, or think-alouds, appearing in the margins alongside the longer reading selections ask you to read between the lines.

At the inferential level, authors not only entertain readers but also subtly manipulate them. When you read, always consider what is left unsaid. This is true for the spoken word. For example, when asked, "How do you like your new boss?" you might answer, "She is always well dressed" rather than "I don't like her." By not volunteering information that directly answers the question, you convey your lack of approval or, certainly, your lack of enthusiasm. In some cases, this lack of information might send a damaging message. For example, when you graduate and look for that perfect position, you will need to ask professors and previous employers for job recommendations. Take care that the person you ask to recommend you is 100 percent on your team. The following exercise illustrates the power of what is left unsaid.

---

[1]As quoted in Stephanie Harvey and Anne Goudvis. *Strategies That Work* (Portland, ME: Stenhouse Publishers, 2000), p. 37.

exercise 7.1   **Reading Between the Lines**

Read the two recommendations and decide whom you would hire.

> **Carlos** has been working as an assistant for one year and has been a valuable member of our team. He aggressively tackles new accounts, making calls after hours to track down customers and ship needed products. He excels in sales and follows through with the details in keeping customers satisfied. We want to keep Carlos but have no openings for advanced positions. I highly recommend him for the position at your company.

> **Roger** has worked for our company for one year as an assistant. Our company sells chicken by-products, mostly thighs and legs that are not used in America, to Russia and third-world countries. Because of the international nature of our business, communication is extremely important. During his year with us, Roger has faithfully attended all meetings and has been friendly with our staff. We certainly wish him well.

Which one would you hire? Why? Carlos. He is aggressive, makes calls, excels in sales, and tends to details. His current employer wants to keep him and explicitly recommends him. Roger, on the other hand, is described only in terms of his personality and attendance. Nothing is said about his performance. Roger is not directly recommended.

_____

_____

_____

Any employer is wise enough to infer the meaning of a vaguely worded reference. Similarly, inferential skills are important in interpreting persuasive reports and arguments because facts that are detrimental to the supported position might be omitted to manipulate a reader's opinion. Such omissions send a "Reader Beware" signal. One of the most effective tools that selectively uses words and photos to send persuasive messages is advertising.

Cigarette advertisements, for example, entice the public through suggestion, not facts, to spend millions of dollars on a product that is known to be unhealthy. They use words and photos in a sophisticated way to lure consumers. Depending on the brand, smoking offers the refreshment of a mountain stream or the sophisticated elegance of the rich and famous. Never do the ads directly praise smoking or promise pleasure; instead, the ads _imply_ smoking's positive aspects. The cigarette advertisers avoid lawsuits for false advertising by never putting anything tangible into print. The emotionalism of a full-page advertisement is so overwhelming that the consumer hardly notices the cautionary note in small print at the bottom of the page: "Warning: The Surgeon General Has Determined That Cigarette Smoking Is Dangerous to Your Health."

exercise 7.2 **Implied Meaning in Advertisements**

Advertisers can directly state that a detergent cleans, but the task of advertising other products can be more complicated. Look through magazines and newspapers to locate three advertisements: one each for cigarettes, alcoholic beverages, and fragrances. Answer the following questions about each:

1. What is directly stated about the product?
2. What does the advertisement suggest about the product?
3. Who seems to be the suggested audience or customer for the product? Why?

Authors and advertisers have not invented a new comprehension skill; they are merely capitalizing on a highly developed skill of daily life. Think, for example, of the inferences you make every day by noticing what people say or don't say, by examining what they do or don't do, and by interpreting what others say or don't say about them. In fact, if you lacked these skills, you would miss out on a lot of the humor in jokes, cartoons, and sitcoms.

Implied Meaning in Humor

Jokes and cartoons require you to read between the lines and make connections. They are funny not so much because of what is said but because of what has been left unsaid. When you "catch on" to a joke, it simply means that you make the connection and recognize the **implied meaning.** To enjoy the joke, you link prior knowledge to what is being said. If you are telling a joke and your listener lacks the background knowledge to which the joke refers, your attempt will fall flat because the listener cannot understand the implied meaning. Listeners cannot connect with something they don't know, so be sure to choose the right joke for the right audience.

Biting humor has two levels of implied meaning. On the surface the joke makes us laugh. At a deeper level, however, the humor ridicules our beliefs, practices, or way of life.

"We built a snowperson!"

EXAMPLE   What inference makes this joke funny?

> At an airline ticket counter, a small boy with his mother told the agent he was two years old. The man looked at him suspiciously and asked, "Do you know what happens to little boys who lie?"
> "Yes. They get to fly at half-price."

—Marleene Freedman
in *Chevron USA: Laughter, the Best Medicine*

EXPLANATION   The inference is that the boy and his mother had lied about his age so he could fly for half the price. Children tend to speak the truth.

exercise 7.3   **Implied Humor in Jokes**

Explain the inferences that make the following jokes funny.

Joke 1

"Take a pencil and paper," the teacher said, "and write an essay with the title 'If I Were a Millionaire.'"

> Everyone but Philip, who leaned back with arms folded, began to write furiously. "What's the matter?" the teacher asked. "Why don't you begin?"
> "I'm waiting for my secretary," he replied.

—Bernadette Nagy,
Laughter, the Best Medicine

Inference: Philip has probably not thought of anything to write, but he has a clever reason for delay. He uses the stereotype that millionaires don't write; they hire secretaries for that.

_____

Joke 2

Mel's son rushed in the door. "Dad! Dad!" he announced. "I got a part in the school play!"

> "That's terrific," Mel said proudly. "What part is it?"
> "I play the part of the dad."
> Mel thought this over. "Go back tomorrow," he instructed, "and tell them you want a speaking role."

—Darleen Giannini,
Laughter, the Best Medicine

Inference: Fathers are portrayed in the media as not able to get a word into family conversations, so getting a part as a dad is not much of an acting debut.

_____

_____

Joke 3

A woman in Atlantic City was losing at the roulette wheel. When she was down to her last $10, she asked the fellow next to her for a good number. "Why don't you play your age?" he suggested.

The woman agreed, and then put her money on the table. The next thing the fellow with the advice knew, the woman had fainted and fallen to the floor. He rushed right over. "Did she win?" he asked.

"No," replied the attendant. "She put $10 on 29 and 41 came in."

—Christine L. Castner,
Laughter, the Best Medicine

Inference: She lied about her age, which is a vanity of human nature. She was really 41.

---

exercise 7.4 **Implied Meaning in Cartoons**

Explain the inferences that make the following cartoons funny.

"Oh no, we're being spammed!"

Inference: The inference relates to the persistence of unwanted spam in electronic communication. Even the stranded men in the cartoon can't escape the constant stream of useless messages. Rescuers, however, have been unable to locate the men, considering the beards.

THE FAR SIDE® By GARY LARSON

"I've got it too, Omar ... a strange feeling like we've just been going in circles."

Inference: They may be Viking leaders, but they have put all the strong rowers on one side of the boat and all the weak ones on the other. Thus, the boat will turn to the side of strength and go in a circle. The leaders need to turn around and observe the obvious.

In cartoons, subtle expressions in the drawings, along with the words, imply meaning. In speech or writing, carefully chosen words imply attitude and manipulate the emotions of the reader.

Connotations of Words

Notice the power of suggested meaning as you respond to the following questions:

1. If you read an author's description of classmates, which student would you assume is smartest?

   a. A student annotating items on a computer printout
   b. A student with earphones listening to a CD
   c. A student talking with classmates about *The Sopranos*

2. Which would you find discussed in a vintage small town of the 1940s?

   a. Movies
   b. Cinema
   c. Picture shows

3. Who probably earns the most money?

   a. A businessperson in a dark suit, white shirt, and tie
   b. A businessperson in slacks and a sport shirt
   c. A businessperson in a pale-blue uniform

Can you prove your answers? It's not the same as proving when the Declaration of Independence was signed, yet you still have a feeling for the way each question should be answered. Even though a right or wrong answer is difficult to explain in this type of question, certain answers can still be defended as most accurate; in the preceding questions, the answers are *a, c,* and *a.* The answers are based on feelings, attitudes, and knowledge commonly shared by members of society.

A seemingly innocent tool, word choice is the first key to implied meaning. For example, compare the following sentences:

   Esmeralda is skinny.

   Esmeralda is slender or slim.

If she is skinny, she is unattractive; but if she is slender or slim, she must be attractive. All three adjectives might refer to the same underweight person, but *skinny* communicates a negative feeling, whereas *slender* or *slim* communicates a positive one. This feeling or emotionalism surrounding a word is called **connotation. Denotation,** on the other hand, is the specific meaning of a word. The connotative meaning goes beyond the denotative meaning to reflect certain attitudes and prejudices of society. Even though it may not seem premeditated, writers select words, just as advertisers select symbols and models, to manipulate the reader's opinions.

exercise 7.5   **Recognizing Connotation in Familiar Words**

In each of the following word pairs, write the letter of the word with the more positive connotation:

  _a_   1. (a) issue   (b) problem

  _b_   2. (a) loneliness   (b) independence

  _a_   3. (a) tolerant   (b) pushover

  _b_   4. (a) difficult   (b) challenging

  _b_   5. (a) pale   (b) fair

  _a_   6. (a) direct   (b) rude

  _b_   7. (a) cop   (b) officer

  _a_   8. (a) take   (b) steal

  _b_   9. (a) lazy   (b) easygoing

  _a_ 10. (a) unanswered   (b) ignored

  _b_ 11. (a) smart   (b) brilliant

_____b_____ 12. (a) abandon   (b) leave

_____b_____ 13. (a) know-it-all   (b) wise

_____a_____ 14. (a) lead   (b) dominate

_____b_____ 15. (a) make   (b) create

_____b_____ 16. (a) mutt   (b) puppy

_____a_____ 17. (a) late   (b) delinquent

_____a_____ 18. (a) reasonable   (b) cheap

_____a_____ 19. (a) call   (b) yell

_____a_____ 20. (a) request   (b) beg

_____a_____ 21. (a) tell   (b) command

_____a_____ 22. (a) question   (b) interrogate

_____a_____ 23. (a) gift   (b) solicitation

_____a_____ 24. (a) discuss   (b) complain

_____a_____ 25. (a) clever   (b) underhanded

exercise 7.6   Choosing Connotative Words

For each word listed, write a word with a similar denotative meaning that has a positive (or neutral) connotation and one that has a negative connotation. Answers will vary.

	Positive	**Negative**
EXAMPLE eat	dine	devour
1. child	youngster	brat
2. ruler	leader	dictator
3. innocent	pure	clueless
4. supportive	helpful	overbearing
5. quiet	calm	dull

exercise 7.7   Connotation in Textbooks

For each of the underlined words in the following sentences, indicate the meaning of the word and reasons why the connotation is positive or negative.

EXAMPLE

While the unions fought mainly for better wages and hours, they also championed various social reforms.

—Leonard Pitt,
We Americans

Championed: Means "supported"; suggests heroes and thus a positive cause

1. The ad was part of the oil companies' program to sell their image rather than their product to the public. In the ad they <u>boasted</u> that they were reseeding all the disrupted areas with a newly developed grass that grows five times faster than the grass that normally occurs there.

   —Robert Wallace,
   Biology: The World of Life

   boasted: <u>Negative, sounds self-serving</u>

   _____

2. At noon, a group of prominent bankers met. To stop the <u>hemorrhaging</u> of stock prices, the bankers' pool agreed to buy stocks well above the market.

   —James Kirby Martin et al.,
   America and Its People

   hemorrhaging: <u>Negative, suggests life-threatening bleeding or dangerous</u>
   <u>loss of money</u>

3. Tinbergen, like Lorenz and von Frisch, entered retirement by continuing to work. Tinbergen was a hyperactive child who, at school, was allowed to periodically dance on his desk to let off steam. So in "<u>retirement</u>" he entered a new arena, stimulating the use of ethological methods in autism.

   —Robert Wallace,
   Biology: The World of Life

   "retirement": <u>Quotation marks suggest irony, that he is working hard</u>

   _____

4. The nation's capital is <u>crawling</u> with lawyers, lobbyists, registered foreign agents, public relations consultants, and others—more than 14,000 individuals representing nearly 12,000 organizations at last count—all seeking to influence Congress.

   —Robert Lineberry et al.,
   Government in America, Brief Version, 2nd ed.

   crawling: <u>Negative, suggesting lowly worms or snakes</u>

   _____

5. Not since Wilson had tried to <u>ram</u> the League of Nations through the Senate had any president put more on the line.

   —Leonard Pitt,
   We Americans

   ram: <u>Negative, suggesting pushing with force</u>

   _____

Euphemisms and Politically Correct Language

A **euphemism** is a substitution of a mild, indirect, or vague term for one that is considered harsh, blunt, or offensive. It is a polite way of saying something that is embarrassing or indelicate. In the funeral business, for example, euphemisms abound. In fact, one Web site lists 213 terms for *death* or *dying* such as *pass to the great beyond* or *big sleep*.

When used to hide unpleasant ideas in politics or social interaction, euphemisms are sometimes called doublespeak or **politically correct language.** For example, *collateral damage* refers to civilian casualties. Other examples are the janitor being called the *sanitation engineer,* a handicapped person being called *differently abled,* or someone with a missing tooth being called *dentally disadvantaged.*

EXAMPLE Euphemism: My stomach feels unsettled.

Politically correct: The troops were hit by friendly fire.

Figurative Language

What does it mean to say "She worked like a dog"?

To most readers it means that she worked hard, but since few dogs work, the comparison is not literally true or particularly logical. **Figurative language** is, in a sense, another language because it is a different way of using "regular" words so that they take on new meaning. For example, "It was raining buckets" and "raining cats and dogs" are lively, figurative ways of describing a heavy rain. New speakers of English, however, who comprehend on a literal level, might look up in the sky for the descending pails or animals. The two expressions create an exaggerated, humorous effect, but on a literal level, they do not make sense.

Consider an example from a Shakespearean play. When Hamlet prepares to confront his mother, he says, "I will speak daggers to her, but use none." With an economy of expression, he vividly suggests his feelings. Much more is implied than merely saying, "I will speak sternly to her." No one expects he will use a knife on his mother, but the connotation is that the words will be sharp, piercing, and wounding. Words can be hurtful or enriching; and an author uses figurative language, sometimes called **imagery,** to stimulate readers' minds to imagine beyond the printed page by adding color, attitude, or wit.

Idioms

When first used, the phrases "works like a dog" and "raining cats and dogs" were probably very clever. Now they have lost their freshness but still convey meaning for those who are "in the know." Such phrases are called **idioms,** or expressions that do not make literal sense but have taken on a new, generally accepted meaning over many years of use.

EXAMPLE She tried to keep a stiff upper lip during the ordeal.

His eyes were bigger than his stomach.

EXPLANATION The first means to maintain control and the second means to ask for more food than you are able to eat.

exercise 7.8   **Understanding Idioms**

What do the following idioms mean?

1. burning the candle at both ends <u>constantly busy, early and late</u>

2. to have the Midas touch <u>to have luck; to make money</u>

3. walking on air <u>extraordinarily happy; elated</u>

4. to beef up <u>to add substance or bulk</u>

5. costs an arm and a leg <u>is quite expensive</u>

Similes

A **simile** is a comparison of two unlike things, using the word *like* or *as*.

EXAMPLE

And every soul, it passed me by,
Like the whizz of my crossbow!

—Samuel Taylor Coleridge,
The Rime of the Ancient Mariner

Metaphors

A **metaphor** is a direct comparison of two unlike things (without using *like* or *as*).

EXAMPLE

The corporate accountant is a computer from nine to five.

Miss Rosie was a wet brown bag of a woman who used to be the best looking gal in Georgia.

—Lucille Clifton,
Good Times

Literary Analogies

A **literary analogy** is a comparison of two unlike things that can be a simile or a metaphor.

EXAMPLE   Workers are the clockwork in assembly line production. (metaphor)

Time is like a river. (simile)

Hyperbole

Hyperbole, sometimes called **overstatement,** is an exaggeration to describe some-thing as being more than it actually is. For example, *the lights of the village were brighter than a thousand stars.* An **understatement,** on the other hand, minimizes a point, such as saying, *"I covered expenses"* after winning $3 million in Las Vegas.

EXAMPLE   Hyperbole: I could sleep for twenty days and nights and still be tired.

Understatement: His clothes have seen better days.

Personification

Personification is the process of attributing human characteristics to nonhuman things.

EXAMPLE   The birds speak from the forest.

Time marches on.

Verbal Irony

Verbal irony is the use of words to express a meaning that is the opposite of what is literally said.[2] If the intent is to hurt, the irony is called **sarcasm.**

EXAMPLE   "What a great looking corporate outfit!" (Said to someone wearing torn jeans)

"There is nothing like a sunny day for a picnic." (Said during a thunder-storm)

exercise 7.9   **Discovering Figurative Language in Essays**

Read the following essay titled "The Barrio" and enjoy the figurative language. Indicate *a* or *b* for the type of figurative language used, and write a response to each question.

The train, its metal wheels squealing as they spin along the silvery tracks, rolls slower now. Through the gaps between the cars blinks a streetlamp and this pulsing light on a barrio streetlamp beats slower, like a weary heartbeat, until the train shudders to a halt, the light goes out, and the barrio is deep asleep.

---

[2]In situational irony, events occur contrary to what is expected, as if in a cruel twist of fate. For example, Juliet awakens and finds that Romeo has killed himself because he thought she was dead.

Members of the barrio describe the entire area as their home. It is a home, but it is more than this. The barrio is a refuge from the harshness and the coldness of the Anglo world. It is a forced refuge. There is no want to escape, for the feeling of the barrio is known only to its inhabitants, and the material needs of life can also be found here.

The *tortilleria* [tortilla factory] fires up its machinery three times a day, producing steaming, round, flat slices of barrio bread. In the winter, the warmth of the tortilla factory is a wool *sarape* [blanket] in the chilly morning hours, but in the summer, it unbearably toasts every noontime customer.

The *panaderia* [bakery] sends its sweet messenger aroma down the dimly lit street, announcing the arrival of fresh, hot sugary *pan dulce* [sweet rolls].

The pool hall is a junior level country club where *chucos* [young men], strangers in their own land, get together to shoot pool and rap, while veterans, unaware of the cracking, popping balls on the green felt, complacently play dominoes beneath rudely hung *Playboy* foldouts.

—Richard Ramirez,
in *Models for Writers*, 8th ed.,
by Alfred Rosa and Paul Escholz

_____a_____ 1. metal wheels squealing: a. personification   b. simile

_____a_____ 2. blinks a streetlamp: a. personification   b. simile

_____b_____ 3. like a weary heartbeat: a. metaphor   b. simile

_____a_____ 4. train shudders to a halt: a. personification   b. simile

_____a_____ 5. the barrio is deep asleep: a. personification   b. simile

_____a_____ 6. tortilla factory is a wool *sarape*: a. metaphor   b. simile

_____a_____ 7. toasts every noontime customer: a. personification   b. simile

_____a_____ 8. [the aroma] announcing the arrival: a. personification   b. simile

_____b_____ 9. pool hall is a junior level country club: a. personification
                b. metaphor

10. How does the figurative language add to the pleasure of the essay? _You can_
    see, feel, hear, smell and taste the barrio.
    _____

11. Why does the author use Spanish vocabulary words? _To add actual sounds_
    heard in a barrio.
    _____

12. What is the connotation of words like *home* and *refuge* in describing the barrio?
    The words are positive and add to the feeling of warmth.
    _____

Copyright © 2008 by Pearson Education, Inc.

exercise 7.10   **Figurative Language in Textbooks**

The figurative expressions in the following sentences are underlined. Identify the type, define each expression, and if possible, suggest the reason for its use.

EXAMPLE

> As a trained nurse working in the immigrant slums of New York, she knew that <u>table-top abortions</u> were common among poor women, and she had seen some of the tragic results.
>
> —Leonard Pitt,
> *We Americans*

EXPLANATION   table-top abortions: It is a metaphor, which may now be an idiom, and means "illegal." The connotation suggests the reality of where the operations probably occurred.

1. The Confederate States of America adopted a constitution and elected Jefferson Davis, a Mississippi senator and cotton planter, its provisional president. The <u>divided house</u> had fallen, as Lincoln had predicted.

   —Adapted from Gary B. Nash et al.,
   The American People: Creating a Nation and a Society, 6th ed., vol. 1: To 1877

   divided house: <u>Metaphor for the United States at the time of the Civil War</u>

   _____

2. Henry VIII <u>lived large</u>. He was <u>a bear of a man</u>, famed for his ability to hunt all day while wearing out a pack of trained horses, for his prowess in wrestling bouts, including one with King Francis I of France, and of course, for having six wives.

   —Mark Kishlansky et al.,
   Civilization in the West 6th ed.

   lived large: <u>Idiom for doing things in a grand manner or to an extreme</u>

   _____

   a bear of a man: <u>Idiom for large in stature; rough</u>

   _____

3. For some reason, I knew they were going to stop me. My heart clenched <u>like a fist</u>; the muscles in my back knotted up.

   —Chris Anderson and Lex Runciman,
   Open Questions: Readings for Critical Thinking and Writing

   like a fist: <u>Simile for feeling apprehension or fear</u>

   _____

4. The line moved rapidly toward its destination as the prisoners shuffled their feet in unison, without lifting them from the ground. Because this nonstop shuffle was "encouraged" by the use of the lash, any prisoner who fell out of lockstep risked a broken ankle or other serious injury from the steadily moving formation.

—Adapted from Harry E. Allen et al.,
Corrections in America: An Introduction, 10th ed.

"encouraged": Quotation marks suggest verbal irony, as the prisoners were forced, rather than encouraged, to keep in formation or risk being whipped or trampled

5. And the word *Environment*. Such a bloodless word. A flat-footed word with a shrunken heart. A word increasingly disengaged from its association with the natural world. Urban planners, industrialists, economists, and developers use it. It's their word now.

—Adapted from Chris Anderson and Lex Runciman,
Open Questions: Readings for Critical Thinking and Writing

bloodless, flat-footed, with a shrunken heart: Personification of the word *environment*, which the author feels has lost positive connotation—she indicates that the word's meaning has become bland—more of a catchword for big business than a reference to the wonder of nature

Figurative Language in Poetry

Poets use connotations and imagery to appeal to the senses and convey striking pictures to us with great economy of words. Because much of the meaning in poetry is implied, this literary form can seem challenging. The highly condensed language of poetry makes every word valuable.

Some poems consist of short rhymes or descriptions of love or emotion, whereas others have a plot and characters. To understand a poem, read it several times and at least once aloud. Know the meanings of words, and pay attention to sentence structure and line breaks. Visualize what you read, and use each part of the poem to help you understand the other parts.[3]

---

[3]William Heffernan, Mark Johnston, and Frank Hodgins, *Literature: Art and Artifact* (New York: Harcourt Brace Jovanovich, 1987), p. 555.

EXAMPLE The haiku poetic form, adapted from Japanese tradition, expresses an insight or impression in about 17 syllables and is usually arranged in three lines. What is the image and impression in the following by poet Raymond Roseliep?

> campfire extinguished
> the woman washing dishes
> in a pan of stars

EXPLANATION When all light is extinguished outside, the stars are so bright that they illuminate the pan for washing.

exercise 7.11 **Understanding Poetry**

Read the following poems, and answer the questions. The first poem builds on similes, and the second tells a story.

Poem 1

A DREAM DEFERRED

> What happens to a dream deferred?
> Does it dry up
> Like a raisin in the sun?
> Or fester like a sore—
> And then run?
> Does it stink like rotten meat?
> Or crust and sugar over—
> Like a syrupy sweet?
>
> Maybe it just sags
> Like a heavy load.
>
> Or *does it explode?*
>
> —By Langston Hughes

1. What is the meaning of *deferred*? Delayed or put off to another time _____

_____

2. List the five similes the author uses, and explain the meaning of each.

dry up "Like a raisin in the sun" means to lose value and die; "fester like

a sore" means to become diseased and infected; "stink like rotten meat"

means to spoil or decay; "crust and sugar over—Like a syrupy sweet" means

to harden and become unusable; "sags/Like heavy load" means to be a

burden or feel depressed

_____

3. How many metaphors does the author use? Explain. One, "explode," to suggest a bomb

_____

_____

4. If a dream deferred was compared to a luscious bunch of grapes rather than a raisin, how would the poem's meaning change? The grapes would be positive, which negates the meaning that nothing is done and it shrivels with age.

_____

5. Why does the poet save *explode* to the end? Because it is a major action that can have massive results

_____

_____

6. What is the meaning the poet is trying to convey? If your goals in life or deepest desires are postponed, it can lead to serious negative effects or destruction.

_____

Poem 2

MID-TERM BREAK

I sat all morning in the college sick bay
Counting bells knelling classes to a close.
At two o'clock our neighbors drove me home.
In the porch I met my father crying—
He had always taken funerals in his stride—
And Big Jim Evans saying it was a hard blow.
The baby cooed and laughed and rocked the pram
When I came in, and I was embarrassed
By old men standing up to shake my hand
And tell me they were "sorry for my trouble,"
Whispers informed strangers I was the eldest,
Away at school, as my mother held my hand
In hers and coughed out angry tearless sighs.
At ten o'clock the ambulance arrived
With the corpse, stanched and bandaged by the nurses.
Next morning I went up into the room. Snowdrops
And candles soothed the bedside; I saw him
For the first time in six weeks. Paler now,
Wearing a poppy bruise on his left temple,
He lay in the four foot box as in his cot.

No gaudy scars, the bumper knocked him clear.
A four foot box, a foot for every year.

—By Seamus Heaney

1. What figure of speech is *bells knelling classes to a close,* and how does it fit the rest of the poem? Metaphor suggesting funeral bells

    _____

2. What images of grief does the narrator encounter upon entering the house? Father crying, Big Jim saying it was a hard blow, old men standing, whispers

    _____

3. What form of figurative language is "sorry for my trouble"? What does it mean? Euphemism for sorry about the death of your brother

    _____

4. What happened to the brother? He was killed by a car.

    _____

5. How old was the brother? Four years old

    _____

6. How is this poem like a mystery? The story unfolds bit by bit and you do not know what happened until the end.

More Types of Inferences

Many types of text—not just advertising, humor, and poetry—demand that you read between the lines in order to understand the author's goals or meaning. You can make inferences based on facts, the voice of a narrator, descriptions, and actions.

Inferences from Facts

The way in which facts are juxtaposed can imply a certain message. For example, an author selected the following facts from issues of *Time* magazine and presented them consecutively to suggest an inference. No direct connection is stated, so the reader must thoughtfully reflect on the suggested message. This pause for thought adds power to the message.

EXAMPLE

28%   Proportion of public libraries in the United States that offered Internet access in 1996

95%   Proportion of libraries that offered Internet access in 2002

17%   Increase in library attendance between 1996 and 2002

Inference: _____

EXPLANATION   The inference is that library attendance has improved because many more libraries have Internet access. Before libraries buy more computers, however, specific data on daily use should be collected.

exercise 7.12   **Drawing Inferences from Facts**

400,000	Number of hot dogs ordered for the Winter Olympics
10	Number of days it took to go through the hot-dog supply

1. Inference: People at the Winter Olympics liked to eat hot dogs. Although consumption rates might vary by day, approximately 40,000 hot dogs were ordered each day.

1 billion	Number of birds killed by flying into glass windows in the United States each year.
121 million	Number of birds killed annually by U.S. hunters

2. Inference: Birds are significantly more endangered by glass windows than by guns in the United States.

408	Species that could be extinct by 2050 if global warming trends continue.
6.6 tons	Average amount of greenhouse gases emitted annually by each American, an increase of 3.4% since 1990.

3. Inference: Greenhouse gases are contributing to global warming, and Americans are creating more of it.

42%	Percentage of adults who say the toothbrush is the one invention they could not live without
6%	Percentage who say the personal computer is the one invention they could not live without.

4. Inference: The percentage of adults who could not live without their toothbrush is seven times that of those who could not live without their computer. We hope they are brushing!

1	Rank of Super Bowl Sunday, among all the days of the year, in pizza sales at the major U.S. pizza chains
20%	Increase in frozen-pizza sales on Super Bowl Sunday

5. Inference: Super Bowl Sunday is still the best day for chain pizza sales,

although more people are cooking frozen ones at home. Maybe the frozen

products are getting better!

© *Time* Magazine, March 4, 2002; March 1, 2004;
January 19, 2004; February 3, 2003; February 2, 2004.

Inferences About a Speaker or Narrator

Read the following excerpt about children and see if you can guess who is complaining.

> Children now love luxury. They have bad manners, contempt for authority. They show disrespect for elders. They contradict their parents, chatter before company, cross their legs and tyrannize their teachers.[4]

Did you assume that this is a contemporary description of modern youth? Although it may sound that way, actually the Greek philosopher Plato attributed the quotation to his student and fellow philosopher Socrates, who lived more than 2,300 years ago. Perhaps the only phrase in the excerpt that does not fit a modern speaker is the "cross their legs." The rest of the clues sound deceptively modern, leading readers to make an inappropriate assumption.

How can you tell whether an inference is valid or invalid? If an inference is appropriate or valid, it can be *supported by the clues within the passage*. The clues "add up," and the logic allows you to feel confidence in making certain assumptions. On the other hand, an inappropriate or invalid inference goes beyond the evidence and may be an "off the wall" stab at meaning that was never suggested or intended.

Readers and listeners alike are constantly making inferences; and as more information is revealed, self-corrections are sometimes necessary. For example, as we listen to strangers talk, we make assumptions about their backgrounds, motives, and actions. Thus, dialogue is an especially fertile ground for observing how the active mind looks for hidden meaning.

exercise 7.13 **Inferences from Dialogue**

Considering the facts presented in the passage, mark the inferences as *V* (valid) or *I* (invalid).

Passage 1

I'm eight years old. But I have the mind of a nineteen-year-old. Mom says it's making up for all the wrong Dad did. Today there's going to be a whole camera crew here. They're going to film different angles of me beating myself at chess. Then they want

---

[4]Suzy Platt, *Respectfully Quoted* (Washington, DC: Library of Congress, 1989), p. 42.

me to walk around the neighborhood in my Eagle Scout uniform. Dad doesn't want to talk to them. So I guess they'll do an exterior of the penitentiary.

—Matt Marinovich,
The Quarterly

___V___ 1. A film is being shot about the child because he is so smart for his age.

___V___ 2. The child is a boy.

___I___ 3. The father was abusive to the mother and child.

___V___ 4. The child has been raised by his mother.

___V___ 5. The father is in jail.

Passage 2

"Now how are we going to get across this monster?" Lisa asked.

"Easy," said John. "We take the rope over, get it around that big tree and use the winch to pull the Jeep across."

"But who swims the flood with the rope?"

"Well, I can't swim," he said, "but you're supposed to be so good at it."

—Anne Bernays and Pamela Painter,
What If?

___V___ 1. John wants Lisa to swim the rope across the water to attach it to the tree.

___V___ 2. Water has flooded the path of the Jeep.

___I___ 3. Lisa and John anticipated that they would be crossing water with the Jeep.

___I___ 4. Lisa and John are driving on a mountain trail after a storm.

___I___ 5. Lisa and John work together on a film crew.

Passage 3

So this ordinary patrolman drove me home. He kept his eye on the road, but his thoughts were all on me. He said that I would have to think about Mrs. Metzger, lying cold in the ground, for the rest of my life, and that if he were me, he would probably commit suicide. He said that he expected some relative of Mrs. Metzger would get me sooner or later, when I least expected it—maybe the very next day, or maybe when I was a man, full of hopes and good prospects, and with a family of my own. Whoever did it, he said, would probably want me to suffer some.

—Kurt Vonnegut Jr.,
Deadeye Dick

___I___ 1. The patrolman witnessed a murder.

___V___ 2. The patrolman thinks his passenger killed Mrs. Metzger.

_____I_____ 3. Mrs. Metzger's family is associated with violent organized crime.

_____V_____ 4. The patrolman is trying to scare his passenger.

_____I_____ 5. The patrolman knew the family of Mrs. Metzger.

Inferences Based on Action and Description

Reading would be rather dull if authors stated every idea, never giving you a chance to figure things out for yourself. For example, in a mystery novel, you carefully weigh each word, each action, each conversation, each description, and each fact in an effort to identify the villain and solve the crime before it is revealed at the end. Although textbook material may not have the Sherlock Holmes spirit of high adventure, authors use the same techniques to imply meaning.

Note the inferences in the following example.

EXAMPLE

JOHNSON IN ACTION

Lyndon Johnson suffered from the inevitable comparison with his young and stylish predecessor. LBJ was acutely aware of his own lack of polish; he sought to surround himself with Kennedy advisers and insiders, hoping that their learning and sophistication would rub off on him. Johnson's assets were very real—an intimate knowledge of Congress, an incredible energy and determination to succeed, and a fierce ego. When a young Marine officer tried to direct him to the proper helicopter, saying, "This one is yours," Johnson replied, "Son, they are all my helicopters."

LBJ's height and intensity gave him a powerful presence; he dominated any room he entered, and he delighted in using his physical power of persuasion. One Texas politician explained why he had given in to Johnson: "Lyndon got me by the lapels and put his face on top of mine and he talked and talked and talked. I figured it was either getting drowned or joining."

—Robert A. Divine et al.,
America Past and Present

Answer the following with *T* (true) or *F* (false).

_____ 1. Johnson was haunted by the style and sophistication of John F. Kennedy.

_____ 2. Johnson could be both egotistical and arrogant about his presidential power.

_____ 3. Even if he did not mentally persuade, Johnson could physically overwhelm people into agreement.

EXPLANATION The answer to question 1 is *True*. He "suffered from the inevitable comparison" and he went so far as to retain the Kennedy advisers. Question 2 is *True*. The anecdote about the helicopters proves that. Question 3 is *True*. His delight in "using his physical powers of persuasion" and the anecdote about the Texas politician support that.

In the following exercises, you can see how authors use suggestions. From the clues given, you can deduce the facts.

exercise 7.14 ## Inferences Based on Description of a Person

Looking back on the Revolutionary War, one cannot say enough about Washington's leadership. While his military skills proved less than brilliant and he and his generals lost many battles, George Washington was the single most important figure of the colonial war effort. His original appointment was partly political, for the rebellion that had started in Massachusetts needed a commander from the South to give geographic balance to the cause. The choice fell to Washington, a wealthy and respectable Virginia planter with military experience dating back to the French and Indian War. He had been denied a commission in the English army and had never forgiven the English for the insult. During the war he shared the physical suffering of his men, rarely wavered on important questions, and always used his officers to good advantage. His correspondence with Congress to ask for sorely needed supplies was tireless and forceful. He recruited several new armies in a row, as short-term enlistments gave out.

—Leonard Pitt,
We Americans

Answer the following with *T* (true) or *F* (false):

____F____ 1. The author regards George Washington as the most brilliant military genius in American history.

____F____ 2. A prime factor in Washington's becoming president of the United States was a need for geographic balance.

____T____ 3. Washington resented the British for a past injustice.

____T____ 4. The Revolutionary War started as a rebellion in the northeast.

____T____ 5. The author believes that Washington's leadership was courageous and persistent even though not infallible.

exercise 7.15 ## Inferences Based on Action

When he came to the surface he was conscious of little but the noisy water. Afterward he saw his companions in the sea. The oiler was ahead in the race. He was swimming strongly and rapidly. Off to the correspondent's left, the cook's great white and corked back bulged out of the water, and in the rear the captain was hanging with his one good hand to the keel of the overturned dinghy.

There is a certain immovable quality to a shore, and the correspondent wondered at it amid the confusion of the sea.

—Stephen Crane,
The Open Boat

Answer the following with *a*, *b*, *c*, or *d*. Draw a map indicating the shore and the positions of the four people in the water to help you visualize the scene.

_____c_____ 1. The reason that the people are in the water is because of

    a. a swimming race.
    b. an airplane crash.
    c. a capsized boat.
    d. a group decision.

_____b_____ 2. In relation to his companions, the correspondent is

    a. closest to the shore.
    b. the second or third closest to the shore.
    c. farthest from the shore.
    d. in a position that is impossible to determine.

_____d_____ 3. The member of the group that had probably suffered a previous injury is the

    a. oiler.
    b. correspondent.
    c. cook.
    d. captain.

_____c_____ 4. The member of the group that the author seems to stereotype negatively as least physically fit is the

    a. oiler.
    b. correspondent.
    c. cook.
    d. captain.

_____b_____ 5. The story is being told through the eyes of the

    a. oiler.
    b. correspondent.
    c. cook.
    d. captain.

exercise 7.16   **Inferences Based on Description of a Place**

Mexico, by many indicators, should be among the most prosperous nations on earth. It is a large country, occupying some 72 percent of the land of Middle America and containing 57 percent of the population of that area. It has benefited throughout its history from some of the richest mineral deposits on earth—first its silver in the colonial period and now its petroleum and natural gas. Mexico's proximity to the technologically advanced and wealthy United States is also a potential economic advantage of significance as are its varied agricultural landscapes, which range from irrigated deserts in the north to tropical rain forests in parts of the gulf coastal lowlands. To understand Mexico's limited economic achievement, we must evaluate the treatment of its people.

—David Clawson and Merrill Johnson,
World Regional Geography, 8th ed.

Answer the following with *T* (true) or *F* (false):

___T___ 1. The author implies that Mexico has fallen short of its economic potential.

___T___ 2. The author implies that Mexico's lag in economic achievement is due to the treatment of its people.

___F___ 3. The author implies that profits from Mexico's silver, oil, and gas were exploited or stolen by other countries.

___F___ 4. The author implies that Mexico does not have enough resources to compensate for its natural physical limitations.

___T___ 5. The author implies that economic trade advantages can be derived from bordering a wealthy country.

Using Prior Knowledge to Make Inferences

Just as a joke is funny only if you have the right background knowledge, college reading is easier if you have **prior knowledge** needed to grasp the details that are frequently implied rather than directly spelled out. For example, if a sentence began, "Previously wealthy investors were leaping from buildings in the financial district," you would know that the author was referring to the stock market crash of 1929 on Wall Street in New York City. The details fall into an already existing schema. Although the specifics are not directly stated, you have used prior knowledge and have "added up" the details to infer time and place.

exercise 7.17 | **Inferring Time and Place**

Read the following passages and indicate *a*, *b*, or *c* for the suggested time and place. Use your prior knowledge of "anchor dates" in history to logically think about the possible responses. Underline the clues that helped you arrive at your answers.

Passage A

For disgruntled or abused women, divorce was sometimes available. Wives with grievances could sue for divorce in some colonies. For instance, although Puritan colonists preferred to keep couples together and often fined troublesome spouses or ordered them to "live happily together," they believed that some marriages could not be saved. Because Puritans viewed marriage as a legal contract rather than a religious sacrament, if one party violated the terms of a marital contract the marriage could be dissolved.

—Glenda Riley,
Inventing the American Woman: An Inclusive History,
3rd ed., vol. 1: To 1877

___a___ 1. The time period that this passage refers to is probably

    a. the 1600s–1700s.
    b. the 1800s–1900s.
    c. the 1900s–2000s.

_____b_____ 2. The part of colonial America discussed here is likely

   a. uncolonized territory in the west.
   b. the northeast.
   c. the southern colonies.

3. Underline the clues to your answers.

Passage B

Families at dinner were startled by the sudden gleam of bayonets in the doorway and rose up to be driven with blows and oaths along the weary miles to the stockade. Men were seized in their fields or going along the road, women were taken from their wheels and children from their play. In many cases, on turning for one last look as they crossed the ridge, they saw their homes in flames, fired by the lawless rabble that followed on the heels of the soldiers to loot and pillage. So keen were these outlaws on the scent that in some instances they were driving off the cattle and other stock of the Indians almost before the soldiers had fairly started their owners in the other direction. Systematic hunts were made by the same men for Indian graves, to rob them of the silver pendants and other valuables deposited with the dead. A volunteer, afterward a colonel in the Confederate service, said: "I fought through the Civil War and have seen men shot to pieces and slaughtered by thousands, but the Cherokee removal was the cruelest work I ever knew."

—James Mooney,
Myths of the Cherokee, 19th Annual Report,
Bureau of American Ethnology

_____c_____ 4. The time period discussed is probably

   a. the 1600s.
   b. the 1700s.
   c. the 1800s.

_____b_____ 5. The place is most likely

   a. the Great Lakes region of the United States.
   b. the southeastern United States.
   c. the Texas-Mexican border.

6. Underline the clues to your answers.

Passage C

As unskilled workers, most found employment in the low-status, manual-labor jobs in the factories, mines, needle trades, and construction. At that time, workers had no voice in working conditions, for labor unions had not yet become effective. The 84-hour workweek (14 hours per day, 6 days per week) for low wages was common. Jobs offered no paid vacations, sick pay, or pension plans. Child labor was commonplace, and entire families often worked to provide a subsistence-level family income. Lighting, ventilation, and heating were poor. In the factories, moving parts of machinery were dangerously exposed, leading to numerous horrific accidents. There was no workers' compensation, although many laborers were injured on the job. A worker who objected was likely to be fired and blacklisted. Exploited by the captains of industry, the immigrants became deeply involved in the labor-union movement, so much so that to tell the story of one without the other is virtually impossible.

—Vincent N. Parrillo,
Strangers to These Shores: 8th ed. Published by
Allyn and Bacon, Boston, MA. Copyright © 2005 by Pearson
Education. Reprinted by permission of the publisher.

_____c_____ 7. The time period discussed is probably

    a. the late 1600s.
    b. the late 1700s.
    c. the late 1800s.

_____b_____ 8. The place is probably

    a. California.
    b. New York.
    c. Mississippi.

     9. Underline the clues to your answers.

Expanding Prior Knowledge

Your response on the previous passages depends on your previous knowledge of history and your general knowledge. If you did not understand many of the inferences, you might ask, "How can I expand my prior knowledge?" The answer is not an easy formula or a quick fix. The answer is part of the reason that you are in college; it is a combination of broadening your horizons, reading more widely, and being an active participant in your own life. Expanding prior knowledge is a slow and steady daily process.

Drawing Conclusions

To arrive at a conclusion, you must make a logical deduction from both stated ideas and from unstated assumptions. Using hints as well as facts, you rely on prior knowledge and experience to interpret motives, actions, and outcomes. You draw conclusions on the basis of perceived evidence, but because perceptions differ, conclusions can vary from reader to reader. Generally, however, authors attempt to direct readers to preconceived conclusions. Read the following example and look for a basis for the stated conclusion.

EXAMPLE   **UNDERGROUND CONDUCTOR**

Harriet Tubman was on a northbound train when she overheard her name spoken by a white passenger. He was reading aloud an ad which accused her of stealing $50,000 worth of property in slaves, and which offered a $5000 reward for her capture. She lowered her head so that the sunbonnet she was wearing hid her face. At the next station she slipped off the train and boarded another that was headed south, reasoning that no one would pay attention to a black woman traveling in that direction. She deserted the second train near her hometown in Maryland and bought two chickens as part of her disguise. With her back hunched over in imitation of an old woman, she drove the chickens down the dusty road, calling angrily and chasing them with her stick whenever she sensed danger. In this manner Harriet Tubman was passed by her former owner who did not even notice her. The reward continued to mount until it reached $40,000.

—Leonard Pitt,
We Americans

Conclusion: Harriet Tubman was a clever woman who became a severe irritant to white slave owners.

What is the basis for this conclusion?

_____

_____

EXPLANATION Her disguise and subsequent escape from the train station provide evidence of her intelligence and resourcefulness. The escalating amount of the reward, finally $40,000, proves the severity of the sentiment against her.

Reader's *Tip* ——— Making Inferences
_____

- Consider the attitude implied in the author's choice of words.
- Think about what might have been left out.
- Unravel actions.
- Interpret motives.
- Use suggested meaning and facts to make assumptions.
- Draw on prior knowledge to make connections.
- Base conclusions on stated ideas and unstated assumptions.

---

exercise 7.18   **Drawing Conclusions**

Read the following passages. For the first passage indicate evidence for the conclusion that has been drawn. For the latter passages, write your own conclusion as well as indicate evidence. Use the suggestions in the Reader's Tip.

Passage A
Albert Einstein did not begin to talk until he was three years old, and he wasn't entirely fluent even by the time he was nine. His language skills were so poor that his parents seriously worried that he might be mentally retarded! Nevertheless, he eventually learned to speak not only his native German, but also French and English. However, he mixed German with his French, and he had a strong accent. His English,

learned later in life, never became fluent—as countless satirists have noted, he made grammatical mistakes and had a heavy German accent.

—Stephen M. Kosslyn and Robin S. Rosenberg,
Psychology: The Brain, the Person, the World, 2nd ed.

Conclusion: Einstein's language skills were not an accurate reflection of his true intelligence.

What is the basis for this conclusion? Einstein's speech developed later than normal, causing his parents to question his intelligence. By prior knowledge, we know that Einstein was, in fact, a gifted thinker, especially in terms of physics. The last two sentences of the paragraph imply that Einstein's intelligence lay in the realm of reasoning and problem solving.

Passage B

In Massachusetts, Nicola Sacco and Bartolomeo Vanzetti—an immigrant shoe-factory worker and a poor fish peddler—were charged with and convicted of robbery and murder in 1920. The prosecutor insulted immigrant Italian defense witnesses and appealed to the prejudices of a bigoted judge and jury. Despite someone else's later confession and other potentially exonerating evidence, their seven-year appeals fight failed to win them retrial or acquittal. They were executed in 1927. At his sentencing in 1927, Vanzetti addressed presiding judge Webster Thayer. At one point in his moving speech, he said,

"I would not wish to a dog or a snake, to the most low and misfortunate creature of the earth—I would not wish to any of them what I have had to suffer for the things that I am not guilty of . . . I have suffered because I was an Italian, and indeed I am an Italian."

—Vincent N. Parrillo,
Strangers to These Shores: 8th ed. Published by
Allyn and Bacon, Boston, MA. Copyright © 2005 by
Pearson Education. Reprinted by permission of the publisher.

Conclusion: Sacco and Vanzetti were wrongly convicted of a crime because of ethnic prejudice.

What is the basis for this conclusion? The prosecutor insulted Italian defense witnesses. The judge and jury were referred to as "bigoted." Another person confessed, and evidence surfaced that may have proved Sacco and Vanzetti innocent. They were not allowed a retrial or acquital. Vanzetti's sentencing speech discussed suffering because of his Italian heritage.

Passage C

A scientist wrote a report attesting to Mozart's musical ability and age. The proof that he was indeed a boy and not a midget came at the end of a rigorous series of musical examinations:

> "While he was playing to me, a cat came in, upon which he immediately left his harpsichord, nor could we bring him back for a considerable time. He would also sometimes run about the room with a stick between his legs for a horse."

—Jeremy Yudkin,
Understanding Music, 4th ed.

Conclusion: Young Mozart was so gifted musically that a scientist was brought in to determine whether or not he was truly a child.

_____

What is the basis for this conclusion? A scientist tested him and judged him to be a boy on evidence of his childlike behavior—leaving his instrument to go to a cat and pretending to use a stick as a horse.

_____

_____

Passage D

A seventy-five-year-old man who loved to square dance suddenly had a sharp pain in his left knee. He went to his doctor to find out what the trouble was. The doctor noted his age, gave his knee a fairly superficial examination, and said, "I can't find anything obviously wrong with your knee. It must be due to your age." The man asked the doctor to explain. The doctor launched into a discussion of various theories of aging and how they might explain his knee problem, and concluded, "Now do you understand?" The old man replied, "No, I don't, because my right knee is just as old as my left knee, and it's not giving me a bit of trouble!"

—Erdman Palmore,
The Facts on Aging Quiz, 2nd ed.

Conclusion: When his doctor bases his diagnosis on age, not knee pain, as the cause of the older man's problem, the patient feels his physician is failing to make a thorough assessment of his condition because of ageism.

What is the basis for this conclusion? Seventy-five-year-old man; a fairly superficial examination; "It must be due to your age"; "my right knee is just as old as my left knee, and it's not giving me a bit of trouble!"

_____

_____

_____

Passage E

Many Irish were single women taking jobs as domestics or nannies for the native-born urban elite. In 1800, there was 1 domestic servant for every 20 families, but by 1840, the ratio had dropped to 1 servant for every 10 families. Unmarried Irish (and Scandinavian) young women often came first and worked in U.S. homes. Their daily typical workload was 16 hours of cooking, cleaning, tending to the children, and nursing the sick, six days a week. With little time to themselves, these women saved their earnings for passage money for other family members. Records from the Boston Society for the Prevention of Pauperism offer one illustration of the difficulties women had seeking jobs in a household compared to men finding work in labor gangs. Between 1845 and 1850, it received employment applications from 14,000 female foreigners in contrast to 5,034 male applications.

—Vincent N. Parrillo,
Strangers to These Shores:
Race and Ethnic Relations in the United States, 8th ed.

Conclusion: In the mid-1800s, competition for domestic employment among women increased significantly and was far greater than the competition men experienced when applying for jobs as laborers.

What is the basis for this conclusion? Statistics show that the ratio of domestic servants to families was halved from 1800 to 1840. Records also list nearly three times the number of female applicants for household work as men applying to labor gangs between 1845 and 1850.

exercise 7.19   **Building a Story Based on Inferences**

The following story unfolds as the reader uses the clues to predict and make inferences. To make sense out of the story, the reader is never told—but must figure out—who the main character is, what he is doing, and why he is doing it. Like a mystery, the story is fun to read because you are actively involved. Review the strategies for making inferences, and then use your inferential skills to figure it out.

CAGED

Emphatically, Mr. Purcell did not believe in ghosts. Nevertheless, the man who bought the two doves, and his strange act immediately thereafter, left him with a distinct sense of the eerie.

Purcell was a small, fussy man; red cheeks and a tight, melon stomach. He owned a pet shop. He sold cats and dogs and monkeys; he dealt in fish food and bird seed, and prescribed remedies for ailing canaries. He considered himself something of a professional man.

There was a bell over the door that jangled whenever a customer entered. This morning, however, for the first time Mr. Purcell could recall, it failed to ring. Simply he glanced up, and there was the stranger, standing just inside the door, as if he had materialized out of thin air.

The storekeeper slid off his stool. From the first instant he knew instinctively, unreasonably, that the man hated him; but out of habit he rubbed his hands briskly together, smiled and nodded.

"Good morning," he beamed. "What can I do for you?"

The man's shiny shoes squeaked forward. His suit was cheap, ill-fitting, but obviously new. A gray pallor deadened his pinched features. He had a shuttling glance and close-cropped hair. He stared closely at Purcell and said, "I want something in a cage."

"Something in a cage?" Mr. Purcell was a bit confused. "You mean—some kind of pet?"

"I mean what I said!" snapped the man. "Something alive that's in a cage."

"I see," hastened the storekeeper, not at all certain that he did. "Now let me think. A white rat, perhaps."

"No!" said the man. "Not rats. Something with wings. Something that flies."

"A bird!" exclaimed Mr. Purcell.

"A bird's all right." The customer pointed suddenly to a suspended cage which contained two snowy birds. "Doves? How much for those?"

"Five-fifty. And a very reasonable price."

"Five-fifty?" The sallow man was obviously crestfallen. He hesitantly produced a five-dollar bill. "I'd like to have those birds. But this is all I got. Just five dollars."

Mentally, Mr. Purcell made a quick calculation, which told him that at a fifty-cent reduction he could still reap a tidy profit. He smiled magnanimously. "My dear man, if you want them that badly, you can certainly have them for five dollars."

"I'll take them." He laid his five dollars on the counter. Mr. Purcell teetered on tiptoe, unhooked the cage, and handed it to his customer. The man cocked his head to one side, listening to the constant chittering, the rushing scurry of the shop. "That noise?" he blurted. "Doesn't it get you? I mean all this caged stuff. Drives you crazy, doesn't it?"

Purcell drew back. Either the man was insane, or drunk.

"Listen." The staring eyes came closer. "How long d'you think it took me to make that five dollars?"

The merchant wanted to order him out of the shop. But he heard himself dutifully asking, "Why—why, how long *did* it take you?"

The other laughed. "Ten years! At hard labor. Ten years to earn five dollars. Fifty cents a year."

It was best, Purcell decided, to humor him. "My, my! Ten years—"

"They give you five dollars," laughed the man, "and a cheap suit, and tell you not to get caught again."

Mr. Purcell mopped his sweating brow. "Now, about the care and feeding of—"

"Bah!" The sallow man swung around, and stalked abruptly from the store.

Purcell sighed with sudden relief. He waddled to the window and stared out. Just outside, his peculiar customer had halted. He was holding the cage shoulder-high, staring at his purchase. Then, opening the cage, he reached inside and drew out one of the doves. He tossed it into the air. He drew out the second and tossed it after the first. They rose like wind-blown balls of fluff and were lost in the smoky grey of the wintry city. For an instant the liberator's silent and lifted gaze watched after them. Then he dropped the cage. A futile, suddenly forlorn figure, he shoved both hands deep in his trouser pockets, hunched down his head and shuffled away. . . .

The merchant's brow was puckered with perplexity. "Now why," Mr. Purcell muttered, "did he do that?" He felt vaguely insulted.

—Lloyd Eric Reeve,
Household Magazine

1. Where had the man been? <u>Jail</u>

2. How do you know for sure? Underline the clues. <u>Ten years to earn five dollars;</u> <u>not to get caught again</u>

3. When did you figure it out? Circle the clincher. <u>Answers will vary.</u>

4. Why does he want to set the birds free? <u>He wants to give freedom to</u> <u>something else that has been imprisoned.</u>

5. Why should the shopkeeper feel insulted? <u>You can infer that the customer is</u> <u>accusing the shopkeeper of being a warden and running a jail.</u>

6. After freeing the birds, why is the stranger "a futile, suddenly forlorn figure," rather than happy and excited? <u>He has accomplished his goal or dream and</u> <u>now must think of his own life.</u>

Summary Points

➤ **What is an inference?**
The inferential level of reading deals with motives, feelings, and judgments. The reader must read between the lines and look for the implied meaning in words and actions. Understanding implied meaning can be the determining factor in a reader's comprehension of jokes, advertisements, poetry, and some prose.

➤ **What is the connotation of a word?**
The feeling or emotion surrounding a word is its connotation. The connotation reflects certain attitudes and prejudices that can be positive or negative. The author's choice of words can manipulate the reader.

➤ **What is figurative language?**
Figurative language creates images to suggest attitudes. It is a different way of using "regular" words so that the words take on new meaning. A simile is a comparison of two unlike things using the word *like* or *as,* whereas a metaphor is a directly stated comparison. A literary analogy includes both similes and metaphors. A euphemism is a more pleasant way of saying something that is embarrassing or indelicate. Hyperbole is a figurative exaggeration. Personification attributes human characteristics to nonhuman things. Verbal irony expresses a meaning the opposite of what is literally said.

➤ **Why is prior knowledge needed to grasp implied meaning?**
The reader must have background knowledge of a subject to understand the suggested or implied meaning.

➤ **How does a reader draw conclusions?**
The reader makes a logical deduction from hints, facts, and prior knowledge.

selection 1 Short Story

Contemporary *Focus*

An intriguing short story is a work of art. The format is ideally suited for a lunch break or a daily commute. Thirty years ago, short stories were printed in glossy magazines, but now they are harder to find. Is there a modern market for a clever short story?

Short in Length But Large in Stature

Western Morning News (Plymouth, UK), February 15, 2005. Copyright © 2005 Western Morning News. Reprinted with permission.

The demise of the short story is just about the saddest fact in modern publishing life. Yet many of us believe short story readers have never disappeared into thin air—like a ghost in a tale by Jean Stubbs or James Turner. You will find them in bookshops browsing and buying something else, usually a novel, because the choice is no longer there.

The truth is that the short story, at its best, is a satisfying art form for author and reader. The experienced writer knows all about the importance of sound construction and in view of the limited space, he or she keeps the time span fairly short.

The novelist can pack a lifetime into his volume, but the short story author cannot have such length and luxury. Taut is the word.

Maybe a renaissance is on the way. Will an enterprising publisher one day produce a book of the best short stories through the ages? A rich harvest is there for the picking.

COLLABORATE Collaborate on responses to the following questions:

➤ What short stories did you enjoy in high school?

➤ What is meant by the word *taut*?

➤ Why are people reading novels now?

Skill Development: Preview

Preview the next selection to predict its purpose and organization and to formulate your learning plan.

Activate Schema

What do you expect from a short story?
What kind of security do hotels usually have?

Establish a Purpose for Reading

Short stories entertain, so read to enjoy and predict the outcome.

Increase Word Knowledge

What do you know about these words?

genteel	indigo	retreated	diffused	purity
cascading	insinuating	sanatorium	scurrying	swag

Your instructor may give a true-false vocabulary review before or after reading.

Integrate Knowledge While Reading

Inference questions have been inserted in the margin to stimulate your thinking and help you read between the lines. Remember to

Predict	Picture	Relate	Monitor	Correct

A DIP IN THE POOLE

Why was the narrator watching Mr. Stuyvesant?

I was sitting in a heavy baroque chair in the Hotel Poole's genteel lobby, leafing through one of the plastic-encased magazines provided by the management, when the girl in the dark tweed suit picked Andrew J. Stuyvesant's pockets.

She worked it very nicely. Stuyvesant—a silver-haired old gentleman who car-
5 ried a malacca walking stick and had fifteen or twenty million dollars in Texas oil—
had just stepped out of one of the chrome-and-walnut elevators directly in front of me. The girl appeared from the direction of the curving marble staircase, walking rapidly and with elaborate preoccupation, and collided with him. She excused herself. Bowing in a gallant way, Stuyvesant allowed as how it was perfectly all right,
10 my dear. She got his wallet and the diamond stickpin from his tie, and he neither felt nor suspected a thing.

The girl apologized again and then hurried off across the padded indigo carpeting toward the main entrance at the lobby's opposite end, slipping the items into a tan suede bag she carried over one arm. Almost immediately, I was out of my chair
15 and moving after her. She managed to thread her way through the potted plants and the dark furnishings to within a few steps of the double-glass doors before I caught up with her.

I let my hand fall on her arm. "Excuse me just a moment," I said, smiling.

She stiffened. Then she turned and regarded me as if I had crawled out from
20 one of the potted plants. "I beg your pardon?" she said in frosty voice.

"You and I had best have a little chat."

"I am not in the habit of chatting with strange men."

"I think you'll make an exception in my case."

Her brown eyes flashed angrily as she said, "I suggest you let go of my arm. If
25 you don't, I shall call the manager."

I shrugged. "There's no need for that."

"I certainly hope not."

"Simply because he would only call me."

"What?"

30 "I'm chief of security at the Hotel Poole, you see," I told her. "What was once referred to as the house detective."

Conde Nast Archive/Corbis

She grew pale, and the light dimmed in her eyes. "Oh," she said.

I steered her toward the arched entrance to the hotel's lounge, a short distance on our left. She offered no resistance. Once inside, I sat her down in one of the
35 leather booths and then seated myself opposite. A blue-uniformed waiter approached, but I shook my head and he retreated.

I examined the girl across the polished surface of the table. The diffused orange glow from the small lantern in its center gave her classic features the impression of purity and innocence, and turned her seal-brown hair into a cascading black wave. I
40 judged her age at about twenty-five. I said, "Without a doubt, you're the most beautiful dip I've ever encountered."

"I . . . don't know what you're talking about."

"Don't you?"

"Certainly not."

45 "A dip is underworld slang for a pickpocket."

She tried to affect indignation. "Are you insinuating that *I* . . . ?"

"Oh come on," I said. "I saw you lift Mr. Stuyvesant's wallet and his diamond stickpin. I was sitting directly opposite the elevator, not fifteen feet away."

She didn't say anything. Her fingers toyed with the catch on the tan suede bag.
50 After a moment, her eyes lifted to mine, briefly, and then dropped again to the bag. She sighed in a tortured way. "You're right, of course. I stole those things."

Why did he memorize this information?

I reached out, took the bag from her and snapped it open. Stuyvesant's wallet, with the needle-point of the stickpin now imbedded in the leather, lay on top of the various feminine articles inside. I removed them, glanced at her identification long 55 enough to memorize her name and address, reclosed the bag and returned it to her.

She said softly, "I'm . . . not a thief, I want you to know that. Not really, I mean." She took her lower lip between her teeth. "I have this . . . *compulsion* to steal. I'm powerless to stop myself."

"Kleptomania?"

60 "Yes. I've been to three different psychiatrists during the past year, but they've been unable to cure me."

I shook my head sympathetically. "It must be terrible for you."

"Terrible," she agreed. "When . . . when my father learns of this episode, he'll have me put into a sanatorium." Her voice quavered. "He threatened to do just that 65 if I ever stole anything again, and he doesn't make idle threats."

I studied her. Presently, I said, "Your father doesn't have to know what happened here today."

"He . . . he doesn't?"

"No," I said slowly. "There was no real harm done, actually. Mr. Stuyvesant will 70 get his wallet and stickpin back. And I see no reason for causing the hotel undue embarrassment through the attendant publicity if I report the incident."

Her face brightened. "Then . . . you're going to let me go?"

I drew a long breath. "I suppose I'm too soft-hearted for the type of position that I have. Yes, I'm going to let you go. But you have to promise me that you'll 75 never set foot inside the Hotel Poole again."

What is the significance of the story's title?

"Oh, I promise!"

"If I see you here in the future, I'll have to report you to the police."

"You won't!" she assured me eagerly. "I . . . have an appointment with another psychiatrist tomorrow morning. I feel sure he can help me."

80 I nodded. "Very well, then." I turned to stare through the arched lounge entrance at the guests and uniformed bellboys scurrying back and forth in the lobby. When I turned back again, the street door to the lounge was just closing and the girl was gone.

I sat there for a short time, thinking about her. If she was a kleptomaniac, I re-85 flected, then I was Mary, Queen of Scots. What she was, of course, was an accomplished professional pickpocket—her technique was much too polished, her hands much too skilled—and an extremely adept liar.

I smiled to myself, and stood and went out into the lobby again. But instead of resuming my position in the baroque chair before the elevator bank, or approaching 90 the horseshoe-shaped desk, I veered left to walk casually through the entrance doors and out to Powell Street.

As I made my way through the thickening late-afternoon crowds—my right hand resting on the fat leather wallet and the diamond stickpin in my coat pocket—I found myself feeling a little sorry for the girl. But only just a little.

How is this ending ironic?

95 After all, Andrew J. Stuyvesant had been *my* mark from the moment I first noticed him entering the Hotel Poole that morning—and after a three-hour vigil I had been within fifteen seconds of dipping him myself when she appeared virtually out of nowhere.

Wouldn't you say I was entitled to the swag?

(1,155 words)

—By Bill Pronzini

Recall

Stop to self-test, relate, and react.

Your instructor may choose to give you a true-false comprehension review.

Write About the Selection

When did you figure out the ending? Was the ending predictable? How did the author manipulate and entertain you?

> *Response Suggestion:* Evaluate the craft of this short story. How is the author a master of the format? What structural factors contributed to your enjoyment?

Skill Development: Implied Meaning

According to the implied meaning in the selection, answer the following items with *T* (True) or *F* (false).

___T___ 1. The reader can logically conclude that *swag* is most likely loot acquired by unlawful means.

___F___ 2. When the man says, "Excuse me just a moment" to the female pickpocket, she looks at him with admiration.

___F___ 3. The woman admits her guilt to the thief because she wants help for her kleptomania.

___F___ 4. The man lets the woman pickpocket go because he is too soft-hearted.

___F___ 5. The man implies that Mary, Queen of Scots, was also a kleptomaniac.

Check Your Comprehension

Answer the following items with *a, b, c,* or *d.* To help you analyze your strengths and weaknesses, the question types are indicated.

Main Idea _____d_____ 1. Which is the best statement of the main idea of this selection?

    a. A life of crime has many risks.
    b. Lying can get you both into and out of jams.
    c. Criminals deceive by presenting themselves as law enforcement agents.
    d. A thief is cheated by another clever thief.

Inference _____c_____ 2. The reader can conclude that the man sitting in the hotel lobby chair thinks that the woman pickpocket is

    a. somewhat inexperienced.
    b. unattractive.
    c. extremely skilled.
    d. quite polite.

Inference _____b_____ 3. When the man catches up with the woman pickpocket at the hotel doors, he speaks to her in

    a. an evil way.
    b. an official manner.
    c. a joking voice.
    d. an icy fashion.

Inference _____a_____ 4. The narrator does not want the woman to ever return to the hotel because

    a. he wants the territory for himself.
    b. he wants to protect the hotel.
    c. he does not want her to get caught.
    d. she is a kleptomaniac and needs treatment.

Inference _____d_____ 5. The reader can conclude that the "light dimmed in her eyes" when the woman pickpocket realizes that

    a. the man wants the wallet she stole.
    b. the man is extremely angry with her.
    c. her father will be angry that she has stolen again.
    d. she has been caught in the act.

Inference _____b_____ 6. The narrator would describe the actual concern experienced by the woman's father as

    a. sympathetic.
    b. nonexistent.
    c. therapeutic.
    d. threatening.

Inference _____a_____ 7. The ending to this story indicates that when the man says earlier in the story, "It must be terrible for you," he was

    a. insincere.
    b. concerned.
    c. annoyed.
    d. troubled.

Inference _____c_____ 8. By saying she has "an appointment with another psychiatrist tomorrow morning," the reader can conclude that the woman is

    a. finally ready to get help.
    b. following her father's orders.
    c. making up a story.
    d. planning another crime.

Inference _____b_____ 9. The reader can infer from the phrase "the thickening late-afternoon crowds" that people are

    a. walking too slowly.
    b. just getting off work.
    c. out enjoying the weather.
    d. arriving at the hotel.

Inference _____a_____ 10. The narrator's description of his sitting in the hotel lobby reveals that he is very

    a. patient.
    b. brave.
    c. sincere.
    d. talkative.

Answer the following with *T* (true) or *F* (false).

Detail _____F_____ 11. The narrator suggests that he will use physical force if the woman pickpocket will not confess to her crime.

Inference _____F_____ 12. The woman finally realizes that the narrator is a thief.

Inference _____F_____ 13. When the woman pickpocket describes what will happen if her father learns of the episode, the narrator thinks her fear is reasonable.

Inference _____F_____ 14. The reader can conclude that the narrator memorized the woman's name and address so that he can later report her to the hotel.

Inference _____T_____ 15. The story title is a humorous play on words.

Build Your Vocabulary

According to the way the italicized word was used in the selection, select *a, b, c,* or *d* for the word or phrase that gives the best definition. The number in parentheses indicates the line of the passage in which the word is located.

___a___ 1. *"genteel* lobby" (1)
    a. formal
    b. run-down
    c. tacky
    d. gentle

___c___ 6. *"cascading* black wave" (39)
    a. increasing
    b. swimming
    c. falling
    d. wet

___b___ 2. *"indigo* carpeting" (12)
    a. thick
    b. blue
    c. antique
    d. new

___d___ 7. *"insinuating* that" (46)
    a. lying
    b. accusing
    c. hoping
    d. suggesting

___a___ 3. "he *retreated*" (36)
    a. withdrew
    b. hid
    c. sat in another booth
    d. returned to the kitchen

___b___ 8. "into a *sanatorium*" (64)
    a. health spa
    b. hospital
    c. condo
    d. convent

___d___ 4. *"diffused* orange glow" (37)
    a. pretty
    b. bright
    c. small
    d. scattered

___a___ 9. *"scurrying* back" (81)
    a. rushing
    b. walking
    c. skating
    d. looking

___c___ 5. "impression of *purity*" (39)
    a. harshness
    b. blandness
    c. innocence
    d. dimness

___b___ 10. "the *swag*" (99)
    a. a depression in the earth
    b. profits
    c. decoration
    d. sway

Search the Net

Use a search engine such as Google, Yahoo, Ask.com, Excite, Dogpile, or Lycos to find information about confidence schemes. Describe three schemes and how people can protect themselves from these crimes. For suggested Web sites and other research activities, go to http://www.ablongman.com/smith/.

Concept Prep for Philosophy and Literature

The ancient Greeks laid the foundations for Western traditions in science, philosophy, literature, and the arts. They set the standards for proportion and beauty in art and architecture, and we continue to ponder their questions about the good life, the duties of a citizen, and the nature of the universe.

Who were the most notable Greek philosophers?

- One of the most notable philosophers was **Socrates,** the teacher of Plato. Socrates sought an understanding of the world while other teachers of the time taught students how to get along in the world. Socrates proclaimed himself to be the wisest of all the thinkers because he knew how little he knew. He used a method of teaching that explored a subject from all sides with questions and answers, as opposed to the lecture method. Today this teaching technique is known as the **Socratic method.** Socrates took no pay for his teachings. As an old man, he was condemned to death by the citizens of Athens who claimed he denied the gods and corrupted the youth. More likely, however, Socrates was a natural target for enemies and was made the scapegoat for the city's military defeat. As ordered, Socrates drank the poison hemlock and died. He left behind no written works, but his pupil Plato later immortalized Socrates' lively discussions in his own works.
- **Plato** is often considered the most important figure in Western philosophy. Without him, the thoughts of Socrates and previous philosophers might not be recorded. Plato used a dialogue format to explore many subjects such as ethics and politics. He founded a school in Athens called the Academy and became the teacher of Aristotle.
- **Aristotle** was a disciple of Plato and then broke away to develop his own philosophy and school, called the Lyceum. He wrote on virtu-

In Raphael's painting *School of Athens*, Plato and Aristotle converse.

ally every subject and laid the foundation for analytical reasoning and logic. He was the tutor of Alexander the Great. In the political unrest following Alexander's death, Aristotle remembered the fate of Socrates and fled Athens to escape prosecution.

What are literary genres?

Over hundreds of years, certain stories, essays, and poems have remained timeless in their appeal and relevance to human life. These works are considered **literature,** the art form of language. As you read a piece of literature, you are allowed inside the minds of characters, and you feel what they feel. You learn about life as the characters live it or as the poet entices you to feel it. After reading, you are enriched, as well as entertained. As defined in most college courses, literature includes four categories, or **genres:** poetry, drama, fiction, and essays.

Poetry

Poetry has its roots in the pleasure of rhythm, repetition, and sound. Before the written word, rhythm and repetition were used to help people organize and recall episodes in history. Poetry was danced, chanted, and performed with the whole body in tribal cultures as a way of keeping cultural truths alive. In the *Odyssey,* an ancient Greek epic by **Homer** that recounts the adventures of Odysseus during his return from the war in Troy to his home on a Greek island, the rhyme format made the epic easier to remember. Thus the poem became a vehicle for preserving the lore of the sea, warfare, and Greek mythology.

Poetry appeals to the senses, offering strong visual images and suggestive symbolism to enhance pleasure. **Lyric** poems are brief and emotional, **narrative** poems tell a story with plot and characters, **dramatic** poems use dialogue to express emotional conflict, and **epic** poems tell a long narrative with a central hero of historical significance.

Drama

The origins of **drama** lie in religious ceremonies in ancient Greece, where masters of Greek drama competed for prizes. Without movies or television, the ancient Greeks created plays for religious instruction and for entertainment. These dramatic performances eventually evolved into the categories of comedy, tragedy, and romantic tragedy.

Plays are narratives and thus contain all the literary elements of short stories and novels. As in works of fiction, the main character in a play is sometimes called a **protagonist,** from the Greek word for "first actor." The character who is trying to move against or harm the main character is called the **antagonist** (from the prefix *anti-*).

Plays are written to be performed rather than read. The actors interpret the actions for the audience, and a single play can seem vastly different depending on which production company performs it. After hundreds of years, the plays of **William Shakespeare** are still relevant to the human condition; they entertained audiences in England in the late 1500s, on the American frontier in the mid-1800s, and both on stages and in movie theaters in the 2000s.

Fiction

Fiction creates an illusion of reality to share an experience and communicate universal truths about the human condition. Each work of fiction is subject to interpretation on many different levels. Short stories and novels are written to entertain by engaging you in the life of another human being.

- A **short story** is a brief work of fiction ranging from 500 to 15,000 words. It is a narrative with a beginning, middle, and end that tells about a sequence of events. The **plot** of the story involves **characters** in one or more **conflicts.** As the conflict intensifies, the **suspense** rises to a **climax,** or turning point, which is followed by the **denouement,** or unraveling. Then the action falls for a **resolution.** Because the short story is brief and carefully crafted, some literary experts recommend reading a short story three times: first to enjoy the plot, second to recognize the elements, and third to appreciate how the elements work together to support the theme. Setting, point of view, tone, and symbolism all contribute to this appreciation.
- The **novel** is an extended fictional work that has all the elements of a short story. Because of its length, a novel usually has more characters and more conflicts than a short story.

The Essay

An **essay** is a short work of nonfiction that discusses a specific topic. Much of your own college writing will follow an essay format. The **title** of an essay suggests the contents, the **thesis** is usually stated in the **introduction,** the **body** provides evidence to prove the thesis, and the **conclusion** summarizes in a manner to provoke further thought.

After studying the material, answer the following questions:

1. What is the Socratic method of teaching? Asking questions to explore a subject from all sides

2. For what underlying reason was Socrates forced to drink poison? The people of Athens wanted a scapegoat for their military defeat.

3. Why was Plato particularly important to the teachings of Socrates? Plato wrote down the teachings of Socrates.

4. What acronym might you devise to remind you of the chronological order of the lives of the three famous philosophers? SPA, for Socrates, Plato, and Aristotle (Answers may vary.)

5. What was a significant contribution of Aristotle? The development of the foundation for analytical reasoning and logic

6. What is a literary genre? A category of literature, such as essay, fiction, poetry, or drama

7. What was the original purpose of drama? For religious instruction and for entertainment

8. What was the purpose of the *Odyssey*? To keep cultural truths alive by recounting the adventures of Odysseus during his return from the Trojan War

9. Which genre is most frequently written by the majority of college students in the classroom setting? Essay

10. What is the typical relationship between the protagonist and the antagonist? The protagonist is the main character, whom the antagonist tries to harm.

Your instructor may choose to give a true-false review of these philosophy and literature concepts.

selection 2 Short Story

Contemporary *Focus*

You have probably read "The Gift of the Magi," the popular Christmas classic of unselfish love and sacrifice. Written by William Sydney Porter, who wrote under the pen name of O. Henry, it tells of a young wife who sells her beautiful hair to buy a watch chain for her husband, Jim. Meanwhile, Jim sells his watch to buy expensive combs for his wife's long hair. With such twists of irony, O. Henry surprises and delights his readers in 256 short stories.

Today in History: O. Henry

By Mark Watson
The Commercial Appeal (Memphis, Tennessee), April 10, 2006. p. A2. Copyright, The Commercial Appeal, Memphis, TN. Used with permission.

He was born William S. Porter in Greensboro, North Carolina in 1862. At 15, he started work in a drugstore.

He moved to Texas in 1882 and worked on a ranch and then at an Austin bank.

In 1894, he started a humorous weekly, *The Rolling Stone.* After it failed, he joined the *Houston Post* staff.

In 1896, he was indicted for embezzling bank funds. He fled to the Honduras. His wife's illness lured him back. After she died, he was convicted and spent 1898 to 1901 in an Ohio prison.

While in prison, he wrote popular stories of the Southwest and Central America. He emerged from prison as O. Henry. From 1903 to 1906, he wrote a story a week for the *New York World.* Another work by O. Henry, "The Four Million," explored New Yorker's adventures and romances.

Plagued by ill health, a bad marriage, alcoholism, and desperate finances, he died June 5, 1910, in New York.

COLLABORATE Collaborate on responses to the following questions:

➤ How were O. Henry's short stories published?
➤ Why might O. Henry be surprised by his success?

➤ How might being in jail enrich a person's writing skills and understanding of different characters?

Skill Development: Preview

Preview the next selection to predict its purpose and organization and to formulate your learning plan.

Activate Schema

When you see people repeatedly but do not know them, do you make up stories about their lives?
Should you secretly try to help someone or instead announce your good deed?

Establish a Purpose for Reading

When we wonder about the people we meet in everyday life, we sometimes make inappropriate assumptions about their lives. Read this short story to find out about the consequences of this misjudgment.

Increase Word Knowledge

| garret | draughty | cunning | meager | affront |
| edibles | emblem | deception | viciously | ferociously |

Your instructor may give a true-false vocabulary review before or after reading.

Integrate Knowledge While Reading

Inference questions have been inserted in the margin to stimulate your thinking and help you read between the lines. Remember to

| Predict | Picture | Relate | Monitor | Correct |

WITCHES' LOAVES

Miss Martha Meacham kept the little bakery on the corner (the one where you go up three steps, and the bell tinkles when you open the door).

Was she attractive?

Miss Martha was forty, her bank-book showed a credit of two thousand dollars, and she possessed two false teeth and a sympathetic heart. Many people have mar-
5 ried whose chances to do so were much inferior to Miss Martha's.

Two or three times a week a customer came in in whom she began to take an interest. He was a middle-aged man, wearing spectacles and a brown beard trimmed to a careful point.

He spoke English with a strong German accent. His clothes were worn and
10 darned in places, and wrinkled and baggy in others. But he looked neat, and had very good manners.

He always bought two loaves of stale bread. Fresh bread was five cents a loaf. Stale ones were two for five. Never did he call for anything but stale bread.

Once Miss Martha saw a red and brown stain on his fingers. She was sure then

Are these appropriate inferences?

15 that he was an artist and very poor. No doubt he lived in a garret, where he painted pictures and ate stale bread and thought of the good things to eat in Miss Martha's bakery.

Often when Miss Martha sat down to her chops and light rolls and jam and tea she would sigh, and wish that the gentle-mannered artist might share her tasty meal
20 instead of eating his dry crust in that draughty attic. Miss Martha's heart, as you have been told, was a sympathetic one.

In order to test her theory as to his occupation, she brought from her room one day a painting that she had bought at a sale, and set it against the shelves behind the bread counter.

25   It was a Venetian scene. A splendid marble *palazzio* (so it said on the picture) stood in the foreground—or rather forewater. For the rest there were gondolas (with the lady trailing her hand in the water), clouds, sky, and *chiaro-oscuro* in plenty. No artist could fail to notice it.

    Two days afterward the customer came in.

30   "Two loafs of stale bread, if you blease.

    "You haf here a fine bicture, madame," he said while she was wrapping up the bread.

    "Yes?" says Miss Martha, reveling in her own cunning. "I do so admire art and" (no, it would not do to say "artists" thus early) "and paintings," she substituted. "You
35 think it is a good picture?"

    "Der balace," said the customer, "is not in good drawing. Der bairspective of it is not true. Goot morning, madame."

    He took his bread, bowed, and hurried out.

why didn't she ask about his job? →   Yes, he must be an artist. Miss Martha took the picture back to her room.

40   How gently and kindly his eyes shone behind his spectacles! What a broad brow he had! To be able to judge perspective at a glance—and to live on stale bread! But genius often has a struggle before it is recognized.

What was she thinking? →   What a thing it would be for art and perspective if genius were backed by two thousand dollars in the bank, a bakery, and a sympathetic heart to—But these were
45 daydreams, Miss Martha.

    Often now when he came he would chat for a while across the showcase. He seemed to crave Miss Martha's cheerful words.

    He kept on buying stale bread. Never a cake, never a pie, never one of her delicious Sally Lunns.

50   She thought he began to look thinner and discouraged. Her heart ached to add something good to eat to his meager purchase, but her courage failed at the act. She did not dare affront him. She knew the pride of artists.

Why was she changing? →   Miss Martha took to wearing her blue-dotted silk waist behind the counter. In the back room she cooked a mysterious compound of quince seeds and borax. Ever
55 so many people use it for the complexion.

A bakery shop worker sells her goods in Boston, Massachusetts.

One day the customer came in as usual, laid his nickel on the showcase, and called for his stale loaves. While Miss Martha was reaching for them there was a great tooting and clanging, and a fire engine came lumbering past.

The customer hurried to the door to look, as any one will. Suddenly inspired, 60 Miss Martha seized the opportunity.

On the bottom shelf behind the counter was a pound of fresh butter that the dairyman had left ten minutes before. With a bread knife Miss Martha made a deep slash in each of the stale loaves, inserted a generous quantity of butter, and pressed the loaves tight again.

65 When the customer turned once more she was tying the paper around them.

When he had gone, after an unusually pleasant little chat, Miss Martha smiled to herself, but not without a slight fluttering of the heart.

Had she been too bold? Would he take offense? But surely not. There was no language of edibles. Butter was no emblem of unmaidenly forwardness.

70 For a long time that day her mind dwelt on the subject. She imagined the scene when he should discover her little deception.

He would lay down his brushes and palette. There would stand his easel with the picture he was painting in which the perspective was beyond criticism.

He would prepare for his luncheon of dry bread and water. He would slice into 75 a loaf—ah!

Miss Martha blushed. Would he think of the hand that placed it there as he ate? Would he—

The front door bell jangled viciously. Somebody was coming in, making a great deal of noise.

80 Miss Martha hurried to the front. Two men were there. One was a young man smoking a pipe—a man she had never seen before. The other was her artist.

His face was very red, his hat was on the back of his head, his hair was wildly rumpled. He clinched his two fists and shook them ferociously at Miss Martha. *At Miss Martha.*

85 *"Dummkopf!"* he shouted with extreme loudness; and then *"Tausendonfer!"* or something like it in German.

The young man tried to draw him away.

"I vill not go," he said angrily, "else I shall told her."

He made a bass drum of Miss Martha's counter.

90 "You haf shpoilt me," he cried, his blue eyes blazing behind his spectacles. "I vill tell you. You vas von *meddingsome old cat!"*

Miss Martha leaned weakly against the shelves and laid one hand on her blue-dotted silk waist. The younger man took the other by the collar.

"Come on," he said, "you've said enough." He dragged the angry one out at the 95 door to the sidewalk, and then came back.

"Guess you ought to be told, ma'am," he said, "what the row is about. That's Blumberger. He's an architectural draftsman. I work in the same office with him.

"He's been working hard for three months drawing a plan for a new city hall. It was a prize competition. He finished inking the lines yesterday. You know, a drafts-100 man always makes his drawing in pencil first. When it's done he rubs out the pencil lines with handfuls of stale bread crumbs. That's better than India rubber.

"Blumberger's been buying the bread here. Well, to-day—well, you know, ma'am, that butter isn't—well, Blumberger's plan isn't good for anything now except to cut up into railroad sandwiches."

105   Miss Martha went to the back room. She took off the blue-dotted silk waist and put on the old brown serge she used to wear. Then she poured the quince seed and borax mixture out of the window into the ash can.

(1,261 words)

—By O. Henry

Recall

Stop to self-test, relate, and react.

Your instructor may choose to give you a true-false comprehension review.

Write About the Selection

What clues lead Miss Martha to her incorrect assumptions? How did Miss Martha incorrectly stereotype the man?

Response Suggestion: List Miss Martha's assumptions and the possible clues that led her to make them.

Contemporary *Link*

How does O. Henry achieve, as one New York Times interviewer wrote, "sobs, sniffles and smiles, with sniffles predominating" in this story? How does he show the characters as individuals rather than simply blue-collar workers of the masses?

Skill Development: Implied Meaning

According to the implied meaning in the selection, answer the following with *T* (true) or *F* (false):

_____F_____ 1. By describing Miss Martha's bakery as the one where "the bell tinkles when you open the door," the author implies that the store was always full of customers.

_____T_____ 2. The Venetian scene in the painting depicted a palace with water and boats.

_____T_____ 3. Miss Martha's fear of adding the butter was that it would be too flirtatious.

_____F_____ 4. The compound of quince and borax was used to wash the pans from cooking.

_____T_____ 5. The author suggests that Miss Martha did not ask Blumberger about adding a treat to the stale bread because she feared hurting his pride.

Check Your Comprehension

Answer the following with *a, b, c,* or *d.* To help you analyze your strengths and weaknesses, the question types are indicated.

Main Idea ____b____ 1. Which is the best statement of the main idea of this selection?

    a. Miss Martha used her bread to further her own selfish interests and was not rewarded.

    b. Based on false assumptions and without communication, well-meaning Miss Martha took action that led to unexpected negative results.

    c. Miss Martha's actions showed that she was not worthy of being called Blumberger's friend

    d. Miss Martha's goals were unrealistic because she wanted more than she could possibly have.

Detail ____c____ 2. The author describes Miss Martha as all the following *except*

    a. 40 years old.

    b. having two thousand dollars.

    c. overweight because she baked delicious foods.

    d. capable of daydreaming.

Inference ____a____ 3. By saying that "Many people have married whose chances to do so were much inferior to Miss Martha's," the author implies

    a. Miss Martha was a more acceptable mate than many who were already married.

    b. Miss Martha was inferior to most women who were already married.

    c. Miss Martha's eligibility for marriage was greater than that of most young, single women.

    d. Miss Martha would have been among the last women a man would consider for marriage.

Detail ____b____ 4. Blumberger was described as all the following *except*

    a. middle-aged.

    b. well dressed.

    c. German.

    d. mannerly.

Detail ____a____ 5. All of Miss Martha's assumptions about Blumberger were incorrect *except* that

    a. he had paint on his fingers because he had been working.

    b. he was an artist.

    c. he was poor and without money to buy fresh bread.

    d. he ate the stale bread.

Detail ____d____ 6. In speaking with his German accent, Blumberger mispronounced words by saying all the following *except*

    a. b for p.
    b. t for d.
    c. v for w.
    d. d for v.

Inference ____b____ 7. The reader can assume that Blumberger commented on the palace in the Venetian painting because

    a. he was an artist.
    b. he drew buildings.
    c. he recognized the splendid marble palazzio.
    d. the perspective of the water in the foreground was confusing.

Inference ____b____ 8. The reader can assume that

    a. the bread did not erase the pencil marks.
    b. the butter smeared the ink in the drawing.
    c. Blumberger had an additional copy of his drawing.
    d. Blumberger would still be able to enter the competition.

Inference ____c____ 9. By calling Miss Martha a "meddingsome old cat," Blumberger indicated that he thought

    a. she put the butter in the bread by accident.
    b. she was trying to cause him to lose the competition.
    c. she added the butter because she thought he was poor.
    d. she considered him to be an artist.

Inference ____c____ 10. The irony of this story is that

    a. good deeds should be announced rather than done in secret.
    b. asking questions reveals truth.
    c. a sympathetic act unintentionally turned into a destructive one.
    d. poor communication causes unfortunate errors.

Answer the following with *T* (true) or *F* (false).

Detail ____T____ 11. Blumberger purchased stale bread for half the price of fresh bread.

Inference ____T____ 12. In her thoughts of Blumberger, Miss Martha imagined herself married and sharing her finances with Blumberger to further his artistic career.

Inference ____T____ 13. Miss Martha wore the blue-dotted shirt because she wanted to look more attractive to Blumberger.

Inference ____T____ 14. The reader can assume that prior to the butter incident, Blumberger had little interest in talking to Miss Martha.

Inference ____T____ 15. Without the interruption of the fire engine, Blumberger might have entered his drawing in the prize competition.

Build Your Vocabulary

According to the way the italicized word was used in the selection, select *a, b, c,* or *d* for the word or phrase that gives the best definition. The number in parentheses indicates the line of the passage in which the word is located.

_____c_____ 1. "lived in a *garret*" (15)
a. house
b. studio
c. attic loft
d. barn

_____b_____ 2. "*draughty* attic" (20)
a. ugly
b. poorly insulated
c. large
d. cluttered

_____d_____ 3. "her own *cunning*" (33)
a. joy
b. happiness
c. curiosity
d. craftiness

_____a_____ 4. "his *meager* purchase" (51)
a. skimpy
b. unappetizing
c. unhealthy
d. unfortunate

_____c_____ 5. "dare *affront* him" (52)
a. scold
b. scare
c. offend
d. fool

_____a_____ 6. "language of *edibles*" (69)
a. food
b. traditions
c. flirtations
d. courting

_____c_____ 7. "no *emblem* of" (69)
a. lie
b. fortune
c. symbol
d. misconception

_____c_____ 8. "her little *deception*" (71)
a. sorry
b. wish
c. trick
d. favor

_____d_____ 9. "bell jangled *viciously*" (78)
a. knowingly
b. suddenly
c. surprisingly
d. nastily

_____a_____ 10. "shook them *ferociously*" (83)
a. fiercely
b. hesitantly
c. continuingly
d. righteously

Search the Net

Use a search engine such as Google, Yahoo, Ask.com, Excite, Dogpile, or Lycos to find information about miscommunication. Look specifically for material on miscommunication between different cultures. How does miscommunication occur between cultures? How can miscommunication be avoided? For suggested Web sites and other research activities, go to http://www.ablongman.com/smith/.

selection 3 | Narrative Nonfiction

Contemporary *Focus*

What contributions did Malcolm X make to the civil rights movement? How did a hustler who spent years in prison rise to become a leader and spokesman for the cause?

Remembering A Civil Rights Hero

By Adil Ahmad

The Dartmouth via University Wire, Dartmouth College, April 12, 2004

Martin Luther King Jr. Day is celebrated every year. Unfortunately, a different hero of the Civil Rights Movement of the 1950s and '60s remains forgotten. That man is El-Hajj Malik El-Shabazz, or Malcolm X, as he is more commonly known.

Malcolm X was born Malcolm Little into a poor Baptist family in Omaha, Neb., on May 19, 1925. The son of a Baptist preacher and "outspoken promoter of social and economic independence for blacks" who was brutally murdered by white supremacists, Malcolm had political activism in his blood.

After his house was burned down by the Ku Klux Klan, Little and his siblings were forced into foster homes and reform schools. Little moved to Boston to live with his half-sister in 1941 after he dropped out of school at age 15, then fell into the underworld of Harlem, New York, at the age of 17. There, he turned to a life of crime and drug-addiction, committing armed robberies for a living.

At the age of 21, he was sentenced to 10 years in prison for a minor robbery. In prison, Little began to read with enthusiasm. He started to read about Elijah Muhammad and his mis-named Nation of Islam, a Black Nationalist organization whose followers were called Black Muslims. After his release from prison in 1952, Little went to Detroit to become a full member of the Nation of Islam.

He changed his name to Malcolm X, dropping the "slave name" of Little. With his dazzling oratorical and people skills, Malcolm X soon rose up the ladder of the Nation of Islam. He soon surpassed Elijah as the foremost spokesman of the Nation.

However, Malcolm X's high-profile, radical agenda, and popularity among black Muslims and whites alike put him in direct conflict with Elijah Muhammad, and Malcolm X was consequently disbarred from the Nation in 1964.

Soon after, he started a new organization to promote his own beliefs. In 1964, he made a pilgrimage to Mecca, Saudi Arabia, and visited several other African and Muslim nations in which he was treated as a hero. On this trip he realized that his theories of black supremacy were false, and that whites were not necessarily evil after all. He then converted to Sunni Islam and changed his name to El-Hajj Malik El-Shabazz. After his return to the United States, he created the Organization of Afro-American Unity (OAAU), a nationalist organization that sought to unite all black organizations fighting racism against blacks. He renounced his racism against whites and began to encourage blacks to vote, to participate in the political system, and to work with each other and with sympathetic whites and Hispanics for an end to all forms of racial discrimination.

Malik El-Shabazz was assassinated on February 21, 1965, by members of the Nation of Islam, who, under orders from Elijah Muhammad, felt that El-Shabazz was a danger to their organization.

 Collaborate on responses to the following questions:

➤ What factors caused Malcolm X to end up in jail?

➤ Why was Malcolm X assassinated?

➤ How did Malcolm X's philosophy change with each of his name changes?

Skill Development: Preview

Preview the next selection to predict its purpose and organization and to formulate your learning plan.

Activate Schema

Why do we hear more about Martin Luther King Jr. than Malcolm X?
Why was Malcolm X considered controversial?

Establish a Purpose for Reading

Malcolm X was a strong voice in the civil rights struggle of the 1960s. With his background, how did he become an educated spokesperson for a movement? Recall what you already know about Malcolm X, and read the following selection to find out how he learned to read.

Increase Word Knowledge

What do you know about these words?

articulate	functional	emulate	riffling	burrowing
wedge	devour	engrossing	intervals	feigned

Your instructor may give a true-false vocabulary review before or after reading.

Integrate Knowledge While Reading

Inference questions have been inserted in the margin to stimulate your thinking and help you read between the lines. Remember to

Predict	Picture	Relate	Monitor	Correct

Learning to Read: Malcolm X

It was because of my letters that I happened to stumble upon starting to acquire some kind of a homemade education.

I became increasingly frustrated at not being able to express what I wanted to convey in letters that I wrote, especially those to Mr. Elijah Muhammad. In the street, I had been the most articulate hustler out there—I had commanded attention when I said something. But now, trying to write simple English, I not only wasn't articulate, I wasn't even functional. How would I sound writing in slang, the way I would *say* it, something such as, "Look, daddy, let me pull your coat about a cat, Elijah Muhammad—"

How did he become so famous?

Many who today hear me somewhere in person, or on television, or those who read something I've said, will think I went to school far beyond the eighth grade. This impression is due entirely to my prison studies.

It had really begun back in Charlestown Prison, when Bimbi first made me feel envy of his stock of knowledge. Bimbi had always taken charge of any conversations he was in, and I had tried to emulate him. But every book I picked up had few sentences which didn't contain anywhere from one to nearly all of the words that might as well have been in Chinese. When I just skipped those words, of course, I really ended up with little idea of what the book said. So I had come to the Norfolk Prison Colony still going through only book-reading motions. Pretty soon, I would have quit even these motions, unless I had received the motivation that I did.

I saw that the best thing I could do was get hold of a dictionary—to study, to learn some words. I was lucky enough to reason also that I should try to improve my penmanship. It was sad. I couldn't even write in a straight line. It was both ideas together that moved me to request a dictionary along with some tablets and pencils from the Norfolk Prison Colony school.

I spent two days just riffling uncertainly through the dictionary's pages. I'd never realized so many words existed! I didn't know *which* words I needed to learn. Finally, just to start some kind of action, I began copying.

American civil rights leader Malcolm X speaks at an outdoor rally in 1963.

Bob Parent/Hulton | Archive/Getty Images

30   In my slow, painstaking, ragged handwriting, I copied into my tablet everything printed on that first page, down to the punctuation marks.

How did he read the defining words?

    I believe it took me a day. Then, aloud, I read back, to myself, everything I'd written on the tablet. Over and over, aloud, to myself, I read my own handwriting.

    I woke up the next morning, thinking about those words—immensely proud to
35 realize that not only had I written so much at one time, but I'd written words that I never knew were in the world. Moreover, with a little effort, I also could remember

How was he a strategic learner?

what many of these words meant. I reviewed the words whose meaning I didn't remember. Funny thing, from the dictionary's first page right now, that "aardvark" springs to my mind. The dictionary had a picture of it, a long-tailed, long-eared,
40 burrowing African mammal, which lives off termites caught by sticking out its tongue as an anteater for ants.

    I was so fascinated that I went on—I copied the dictionary's next page. And the same experience came when I studied that. With every succeeding page, I also learned of people and places and events from history. Actually the dictionary
45 is like a miniature encyclopedia. Finally the dictionary's A section had filled a whole tablet—and I went on into the B's. That was the way I started copying what eventually became the entire dictionary. It went a lot faster after so much practice helped me to pick up handwriting speed. Between what I wrote in my tablet, and writing letters, during the rest of my time in prison I would guess I
50 wrote a million words.

    I suppose it was inevitable that as my word-base broadened, I could for the first time pick up a book and read and now begin to understand what the book was saying. Anyone who has read a great deal can imagine the new world that opened. Let me tell you something: from then until I left that prison, in every free moment I
55 had, if I was not reading in the library, I was reading on my bunk. You couldn't have gotten me out of books with a wedge. Between Mr. Muhammad's teachings, my correspondence, my visitors, . . . and my reading of books, months passed without my even thinking about being imprisoned. In fact, up to then, I never had been so truly free in my life.

60   The Norfolk Prison Colony library was in the school building. A variety of classes was taught there by instructors who came from such places as Harvard

In what U.S. state was the prison?

and Boston universities. The weekly debates between inmate teams were also held in the school building. You would be astonished to know how worked up convict debaters and audiences would get over subjects like "Should Babies Be
65 Fed Milk?"

    Available on the prison library's shelves were books on just about every general subject. Much of the big private collection that Parkhurst had willed to the prison was still in crates and boxes in the back of the library—thousands of old books. Some of them looked ancient: covers faded, old-time parchment-looking binding.
70 Parkhurst . . . seemed to have been principally interested in history and religion. He had the money and the special interest to have a lot of books that you wouldn't have in a general circulation. Any college library would have been lucky to get that collection.

    As you can imagine, especially in a prison where there was heavy emphasis on
75 rehabilitation, an inmate was smiled upon if he demonstrated an unusually intense interest in books. There was a sizable number of well-read inmates, especially the popular debaters. Some were said by many to be practically walking encyclopedias.

How do values change in prison?

They were almost celebrities. No university would ask any student to devour literature as I did when this new world opened to me, of being able to read and *understand*.

80   I read more in my room than in the library itself. An inmate who was known to read a lot could check out more than the permitted maximum number of books. I preferred reading in the total isolation of my own room.

When I had progressed to really serious reading, every night at about ten P.M. I would be outraged with the "lights out." It always seemed to catch me right in the
85   middle of something engrossing.

Fortunately, right outside my door was a corridor light that cast a glow into my room. The glow was enough to read by, once my eyes adjusted to it. So when "lights out" came, I would sit on the floor where I could continue reading in that glow.

90   At one-hour intervals at night guards paced past every room. Each time I heard the approaching footsteps, I jumped into bed and feigned sleep. And as soon as the guard passed, I got back out of bed onto the floor area of that light-glow, where I would read for another fifty-eight minutes until the guard approached again. That went on until three or four every morning. Three or four
95   hours of sleep a night was enough for me. Often in the years in the streets I had slept less than that.

(1,245 words)

—From *The Autobiography of Malcolm X*
as told to Alex Haley

Recall

Stop to self-test, relate, and react.

Your instructor may choose to give you a true-false comprehension review.

Write About the Selection

If you did not know how to read at 21 years of age, what methods would you use to teach yourself? Would you copy the dictionary? How did Malcolm X use some of the learning tips in this textbook to remember the words on the dictionary pages? How did he seize an unfortunate circumstance and make it into an opportunity? How are his efforts at self-improvement inspirational?

Response Suggestion: Relate your own ideas to the path taken by Malcolm X.

Contemporary *Link*

Although Malcolm X changed, initially he opposed Martin Luther King Jr.'s movement to promote racial change through nonviolence. He wanted a black revolution rather than compromise. How do you think the background experiences of Malcolm X might have shaped his beliefs and pulled him more toward violence than peaceful change?

Response Suggestion: List the different events and influences on his life and learning. Suggest how each experience shaped his philosophy.

Skill Development: Implied Meaning

According to the implied meaning in the selection, answer the following with *T* (true) or *F* (false).

__F__ 1. The phrase "let me pull your coat about a cat" probably means that we need to put a coat around the cat to keep it warm.

__F__ 2. The phrase "let me pull your coat about a cat" is a simile.

__T__ 3. The phrase "gotten me out of books with a wedge" is an idiom.

__T__ 4. It is ironic that Malcolm X felt truly free in prison.

__T__ 5. The Norfolk Prison Colony was probably in the Northeast.

Check Your Comprehension

After reading the selection, answer the following questions with *a, b, c,* or *d.* To help you analyze your strengths and weaknesses, the question types are indicated.

Main Idea _____b_____ 1. Which is the best statement of the main idea of this selection?

    a. Malcolm X was motivated by educated prisoners to change his life.
    b. While in prison, Malcolm X learned to read by copying and studying the dictionary.
    c. Malcolm X spent his time in prison helping fellow prisoners.
    d. Although mistreated in prison, Malcolm X was able to go to the library to read.

Detail _____b_____ 2. Malcolm initially began his reading program because

    a. he wanted to read the Parkhurst books in the library.
    b. he wanted to write letters to Elijah Muhammad.
    c. he wanted to debate Bimbi.
    d. he wanted to entertain himself at night during the long hours of "lights out."

Inference _____b_____ 3. Malcolm X describes his learning as a "homemade education" because

    a. he started it at home.
    b. he made it up himself without professional help.
    c. it was designed by prison teachers.
    d. it was modeled after other efforts of prison education.

Detail _____c_____ 4. Malcolm X described his reading at Charlestown Prison as

    a. knowing most words in the sentences.
    b. knowing at least half the words in sentences.
    c. not knowing one to all words in most sentences.
    d. not knowing half the words in a few sentences.

Inference _____c_____ 5. Malcolm X would define book-reading motions as

    a. reading with understanding.
    b. reading aloud.
    c. reading without understanding.
    d. not bothering to try to read.

Detail _____c_____ 6. Malcolm X's decision to copy each page of the dictionary was motivated by all the following *except*

    a. a desire to learn words.
    b. a desire to improve his handwriting.
    c. a proven method.
    d. not knowing with which words to begin.

selection **3**

Inference ___a___ 7. Malcolm X mentions *aardvark* because

    a. it is a funny word that he still remembers from the first page of the dictionary.
    b. he has used the word many times.
    c. he thinks that *aardvark* is an important word for all to know.
    d. he is still not sure what the word means.

Inference ___a___ 8. Malcolm X mentions the debate topic "Should Babies Be Fed Milk?" to show that

    a. the inmate debaters would get excited over any topic, even if it was irrelevant to them.
    b. the debaters were qualified on a wide range of subjects.
    c. the convicts took a special interest in family issues.
    d. it was a favorite topic with the inmate debaters and the audience.

Inference ___a___ 9. Malcolm X implies that prison officials

    a. encouraged education.
    b. discouraged education.
    c. were not concerned with rehabilitation.
    d. gave favors for good behavior but not for educational efforts.

Inference ___d___ 10. The reader can appropriately assume all the following *except*

    a. after "lights out," no reading was allowed.
    b. the glow of the corridor light after "lights out" was not strong enough to allow Malcolm to lie in his bunk and read.
    c. the night guards would object to Malcolm X's reading after "lights out."
    d. other prisoners would complain to the guards if Malcolm X read after "lights out."

Answer the following with *T* (true) or *F* (false).

Detail ___T___ 11. Malcolm X dropped out of school in the eighth grade.

Detail ___T___ 12. Malcolm X began his attempts at reading at Charlestown Prison before he went to Norfolk Prison Colony.

Inference ___F___ 13. Bimbi suggested that Malcolm X use a dictionary to learn words.

Inference ___F___ 14. Prisoners at Norfolk Prison Colony looked down on fellow inmates who were well read.

Inference ___F___ 15. Malcolm X suggests that university reading demands are insufficient.

Build Your Vocabulary

According to the way the italicized word was used in the selection, select *a, b, c,* or *d* for the word or phrase that gives the best definition. The number in parentheses indicates the line of the passage in which the word is located.

____d____ 1. *"articulate* hustler" (5)
    a. dangerous
    b. crafty
    c. unclear
    d. well-spoken

____b____ 2. "wasn't even *functional"* (7)
    a. interested
    b. useful
    c. vocal
    d. determined

____b____ 3. "tried to *emulate* him" (15)
    a. convince
    b. copy
    c. argue with
    d. advise

____c____ 4. *"riffling* uncertainly through" (27)
    a. studying
    b. memorizing
    c. flipping
    d. reading

____a____ 5. *"burrowing* African mammal" (40)
    a. tunneling
    b. insect-eating
    c. slow moving
    d. shy

____b____ 6. "with a *wedge"* (56)
    a. bet
    b. tapered block
    c. hammer
    d. slap

____a____ 7. *"devour* literature" (78)
    a. consume
    b. be assigned
    c. require
    d. discuss

____a____ 8. "something *engrossing"* (85)
    a. absorbing
    b. confusing
    c. historical
    d. religious

____d____ 9. "one-hour *intervals"* (90)
    a. watches
    b. reports
    c. walks
    d. periods

____c____ 10. *"feigned* sleep" (91)
    a. begged for
    b. hoped for
    c. pretended
    d. accomplished

Search the Net

Use a search engine such as Google, Yahoo, Ask.com, Excite, Dogpile, or Lycos to find how Malcolm X's beliefs changed. Compare his initial beliefs with those he held when he died. For suggested Web sites and other research activities, go to http://www.ablongman.com/smith/.

"One of the difficult lessons we have learned," wrote Martin Luther King Jr., "is that you cannot depend on American institutions to function without pressure. Any real change in the status quo depends on continued creative action to sharpen the conscience of the nation." Although the equal protection clause in the Fourteenth Amendment has been a part of the Constitution since 1868, social reformers such as Malcolm X and Martin Luther King Jr. challenged and changed the interpretation of that amendment. Civil rights activists maintained that the Constitution was color-blind, and court decisions supported that policy.

What is the U.S. Constitution?

The **Constitution** is a document that defines the structure of our government and the roles, powers, and responsibilities of public officials. It was signed in Philadelphia in 1787. Before the Constitution, the **Declaration of Independence** in 1776 affirmed our independence from England. The **Articles of Confederation** were written to govern the resulting new union of states that joined to fight for freedom and forge a new democracy. The articles created a loose union and left most of the authority with the individual states. After the Revolution, as economic conflicts arose and more central control was needed, the Constitution was written to give more power to the federal government, replacing the Articles of Confederation. Our country is still governed by this same Constitution of 1787, which also guarantees our civil liberties and civil rights, including freedom of expression, due process, and equal protection.

Because no document is perfect, the writers of the Constitution allowed for amendments, and the Constitution has been amended 27 times.

What are the three branches of government?

The Constitution divides the federal government into the executive, legislative, and judicial branches.

- The **executive branch** consists of the president, whose powers include approving or vetoing (refusing to sign) laws passed by Congress, and the **president's cabinet,** an advisory group of 13 government department heads appointed by the president. For example, Madeleine Albright was a member of former president Bill Clinton's cabinet.
- The **legislative branch** of the government consists of the two houses of Congress: the Senate and the House of Representatives. The **Senate** with 100 members (two from each state) and the **House of Representatives** with 435 members (apportioned to each state according to population) pass federal laws and serve on committees that investigate problems and oversee the executive branch.
- The **judicial branch** consists of a system of federal courts, the highest of which is the **Supreme**

Voters using electronic voting machines cast ballots.

Bob Daemmrich/PhotoEdit Inc.

413

Court. It consists of a chief justice and eight associate justices who are appointed by sitting presidents. The Supreme Court ensures uniformity in the interpretation of national laws.

Each of the three branches has checks and balances over the other branches so that power is shared.

What are political parties?

- Our president, senators, and representatives are nominated for office by a political party, an organization formed to support and elect candidates who uphold the views and beliefs of the group. Over the years, political parties have changed and some have disappeared. Today the two major parties are Republican and Democrat.
- The **Republican Party,** also called the GOP, for "Grand Old Party," began in 1854. Its symbol is the elephant, and Abraham Lincoln was the first Republican president. The party tends to be against expanding the size and responsibilities of the federal government and to support private enterprise. The party image is **conservative,** an ideology or set of beliefs that prefers the existing order and opposes change.
- The **Democratic Party** was organized by Thomas Jefferson in the late eighteenth century, and its first elected president was Andrew Jackson. The party tends to support the expansion of federal programs and a tax system with a greater burden on the rich and corporations. Its symbol is the donkey. The party image is **liberal,**

an ideology that supports the strong role of government in economic and social issues.

Before elections, both parties pay organizations such as **Gallup** to conduct **polls,** questioning voters about the most important issues and sampling public opinion on voting preferences.

What are capitalism, communism, and socialism?

- **Capitalism** is an economic system based on a free market for goods and services. Production centers such as factories seek profits and are owned by individuals as well as corporations and their stockholders, not the government. The United States has a capitalist economy, although it is not purely capitalistic since government does impose regulations on business.
- **Communism** is almost the opposite of capitalism. It is an economic, political, and social system in which there is no individual ownership. The government controls businesses, and goods and property are owned in common by all citizens. Goods are available to all people as they are needed. The communist system was envisioned by Karl Marx and is associated with the former Soviet Union and China.
- **Socialism** is an economic system advocating government or collective ownership of goods, rather than private ownership. In Karl Marx's theory, it represents the transition between capitalism and communism in which people are paid according to work done. Communists are socialists, but not all socialists are communists.

Review *Questions*

After studying the material, answer the following questions:

1. Why were the Articles of Confederation replaced? The union of states needed a stronger central authority.

2. How does the Declaration of Independence differ from the Constitution? The first declared independence from England and resolved to fight for it; the second set up the structure of our current government.

3. Which branch of the government has the fewest appointed members? _____ judicial

4. In which branch of the government do members of the cabinet serve? ____ executive

5. Which branch of the government has the most elected members? legislative

6. In which house of Congress does each state have the same number of representatives? Senate

7. How do Republican and Democratic views on federal government expansion differ? Democrats want expanded government programs; Republicans do not.

8. Would a push to reduce corporate taxes most likely be a liberal or conservative cause? conservative

9. Would a dynamic business owner prefer capitalism or socialism? capitalism

10. In theory, under which system—capitalism or communism—does a worker share equally in goods regardless of the work he or she does? communism

Your instructor may choose to give a true-false review of these political science concepts.

Can I Get That in Writing?

Roots	*graph:* "write"	*scrib, scrip:* "write"

Words with *graph:* "write"

Tests that use computer-readable answer sheets require that a no. 2 *graphite* pencil be used for marking the answers.

- *graph:* something written; a diagram or chart; a network of lines connecting points

  The calculus homework required a written solution and a corresponding *graph* for each problem.

- *graphic:* described in realistic detail; vivid; pertaining to any of the graphic arts such as painting, drawing, and engraving

  The movie's *graphic* violence guaranteed that it would not get anything other than an R rating.

- *phonograph:* a machine for reproducing sound from records in the form of cylinders or spiral-grooved rotating disks

  The early *phonograph* had a tuba-like device that transmitted sound.

- *cinematography:* the art or technique of motion-picture photography

  The movie that won Best Picture at the Academy Awards also won the award for *cinematography.*

- *polygraph:* a lie detector

  A *polygraph* records changes in pulse rate or respiration to determine if a person is telling the truth.

- *geography:* the science dealing with differences between areas of the earth's surface, such as climate, population, elevation, vegetation, or land use

  Interactions between populations may be explained by *geography*—such as whether mountains or rivers separate them or whether they are in close proximity.

- *telegraph:* a system for sending distant messages or signals between two electronic devices connected by wire

  The telephone and e-mail have largely replaced the *telegraph* as a means of communicating.

Words with *scrib, scrip:* "write"

The bride and groom had an inscription engraved inside their wedding rings.

- *scribble:* to write hastily or carelessly; to cover with meaningless marks

  Before running to catch my bus, I quickly *scribbled* a note to my roommate that I would not be home for dinner.

- *transcribe:* to make a written or typed copy of spoken material; to translate into another language

  Saundra loved her job at the UN, where she *transcribed* multilingual meetings into English.

- *transcript:* a written, typewritten, or printed copy of something

  An official *transcript* of your college records is required when you transfer to another school.

- *ascribe:* to assign or attribute to a particular cause or source

  Stephen *ascribes* his good looks to his father's genes.

- *subscription:* a sum of money pledged as a contribution; the right to receive a magazine or other service for a sum; the act of appending one's signature to a document

  Public television relies on *subscriptions* pledged during its annual fund-raising drives.

- *prescription:* a written direction from a doctor for the preparation and use of a medicine

  Pharmacists read and fill *prescriptions* and usually warn about possible side effects of the prescribed drugs.

- *circumscribe:* to draw a circle around; to enclose within bounds or confine

  Since Emilio had just started to drive, he had a *circumscribed* area out of which he was not allowed to take the family car.

- *script:* handwriting; written text of a play, movie, or television program

  The *script* of the play was revised when the screenwriters started work on the movie version of the story.

- *postscript:* an addition to a concluded and signed letter; a supplement appended to a book

  I forgot to tell my mom about my promotion until after I had signed the letter, so I added a *postscript* telling her about my new position.

- *description:* a representation of something in words or pictures; a sort or variety of thing

  The witness to the robbery gave the police sketch artist a good *description* of the suspect.

REVIEW

Part I

Choose the best synonym from the boxed list for the words and phrases below.

graphic	scribble	transcript	subscription	prescription
script	postscript	transcribe	inscription	circumscribe

1. document showing dialogue __script__
2. addendum __postscript__
3. scrawl __scribble__
4. direction __prescription__
5. purchase __subscription__

6. a copy __transcript__
7. vivid __graphic__
8. translate __transcribe__
9. written or carved words __inscription__
10. limit __circumscribe__

Part II

From the boxed list, choose the word that best completes each sentence below.

transcript	telegraph	geography	polygraph	cinematography
phonograph	ascribe	graphic	graph	prescription

11. You must supply the most recent copy of your college __transcript__ when transferring to another university.

12. Cult members tend to __ascribe__ only the best qualities to their leader.

13. __Graphic__ violence in a film results in a restricted rating.

14. Findings obtained from __polygraph__ tests are not ordinarily admitted as legal evidence in court.

15. If you are a visual learner, you prefer gaining information through pictures or a __graph__ rather than a lecture.

16. In the 1960s, people used the __phonograph__ to listen to music, since CD players were not yet available.

17. Studies of the __geography__ of the Appalachian Mountains found them to be among the oldest land masses in the United States.

18. Prior to the invention of the __telephone__, the telegraph allowed traveling news reporters to transmit their breaking stories promptly back to city newspapers.

19. The older woman's __prescription__ for a long, healthy life included proper nutrition, adequate exercise and rest, and lots of laughter.

20. Exceptional __cinematography__ can make the viewer feel transported to another place.

8 Point of View

- Is a textbook influenced by the author's point of view?
- What is the author's point of view?
- What is the reader's point of view?
- What is the difference between a fact and an opinion?
- What is the author's purpose?
- What is the author's tone?

Eyvind Earl, *Horses by the Sea.* 1981, 40 x 30 inches.

Textbooks and the Author's Point of View

If you are like many people, you might assume that textbooks contain facts rather than opinions, that historical accounts are based on fact and do not vary from one author to another, and that textbooks are free from an author's bias. Nothing could be further from the truth. Textbooks are replete with interpretation, opinion, and slanted—rather than balanced—views. In short, they reflect the author's point of view and the "politically correct" winds of change.

For example, in your world civilization textbook, you will read about the wealthy and cosmopolitan Persian Empire, whose kings were righteous rulers believed to be elected by the gods. About 2,500 years ago, the Persian Empire was at its height, with spectacular public buildings and palaces at the capital, Persepolis, located in what is now Iran. Yes, *you* will read about the splendor of the empire, but twenty-first-century inhabitants of the region will not. Read what one textbook author has to say about the way historical facts about that region are treated:

> Islam denigrates the earlier cultures of its converts, just as it was noted that Christianity can. Everything before Islam was, in Arabic, *jahiliya*, "from the age of ignorance." This leaves little room in these peoples' historical consciousness for their pre-Islamic past, so they often lack interest in it. For example, despite Persia's brilliant antique history, for contemporary Iranians the glory began with the coming of Islam. Many people in Muslim countries view their own ancient cultural landscapes without interest. They may even discourage tourists from viewing pre-Islamic ruins.
>
> Edward Bergman and William Renwick,
> *Introduction to Geography*, 2nd ed.

In other violent changes of regime, such as the communist takeover of the Russian Empire, new leaders have also thrown out the old history books and written new ones to reflect the new political thinking. Even in American history books, you now see more about women and minorities—not because historical records have recently been unearthed, but in response to public demand. Thus, no purity rule applies to textbook writing.

The slant may start with, but is not limited to, what is included in the book; it continues with the author's interpretation. For example, the view of government in political science texts varies with liberal and conservative authors. Global warming, cloning, and stem cell replacement therapy can be opinion-laden topics in biology texts. And although the name of the first U.S. president does not vary from one American history book to another, the emphasis on the importance of Washington's administration might vary, depending on the author's point of view.

In short, *everything you read is affected by the author's point of view, purpose, tone, and presentation of facts and opinions.*

What Is the Author's Point of View?

An author's opinions and theories concerning factual material will influence the presentation of the subject matter. Although the author of a British textbook might describe American history during Revolutionary times as a colonial uprising on a

distant continent, an American author would praise the heroic struggle for personal freedom and survival. Each of the two authors would write from a different **point of view** and express particular opinions because they have different ways of looking at the subject.

Recognizing the author's point of view is part of understanding what you read. Sophisticated readers seek to identify the beliefs of the author to know "where he or she is coming from." When the point of view is not directly stated, the author's choice of words and information provide clues for the reader.

What Is Bias?

The terms *point of view* and *bias* are very similar and are sometimes used interchangeably. When facts are slanted, though not necessarily distorted, to reflect the author's personal beliefs, the written material is said to reflect the author's bias. Thus, a **bias** is simply an opinion or position on a subject. As commonly used, however, *bias* has a negative connotation suggesting narrow-mindedness and prejudice, whereas *point of view* suggests thoughtfulness and openness. Perhaps you would like to refer to your own opinion as a point of view and to those of others, particularly if they disagree with you, as biases!

EXAMPLE Read the following passage and use the choice of information and words to identify the author's point of view or bias.

> As president, Richard Nixon enjoyed the pomp and circumstance of office. He liked to listen to the presidential song, "Hail to the Chief," and to review at strict attention ranks of marching soldiers. Nixon's vaguely royal pretensions seemed harmless enough initially, but after Watergate many people began to feel that an all-too-royal president was endangering democratic practice.
>
> —Morris Fiorina and Paul Peterson,
> *The New American Democracy*, 3rd ed.

What is the author's point of view? Underline clues that support your answer.

_____

EXPLANATION   The author feels that former President Nixon began to think that he was king of the country rather than president of a democracy. This is suggested by the passage and by words such as *pomp and circumstance, royal pretensions, all-too-royal* and *endangering democratic practice.*

exercise 8.1   **Recognizing an Author's Point of View**

Read the following passages, and use the choice of information and words to identify the author's point of view or bias.

Passage 1
Commercial fishing vessels, which can catch massive amounts of fish using dragnets, have emptied coastal waters of fish, often with the help of government subsidies. No longer is the sea an inexhaustible source of food, as 60 percent of all fishing regions are now showing a decline in catch.

—Christian Goergen,
Politics in a Globalized World

What is the author's point of view? Underline clues that support your answer.
Commercial fishing, along with governmental support of it, has had an

unnatural and harmful ecological impact throughout the world.

_____

Passage 2
"I suppose that I need not tell you that as regards Hawaii I take your views absolutely, as indeed I do on foreign policy generally. If I had my way we would annex those islands tomorrow. If that is impossible I would establish a protectorate over them."

—David Goldfield et al.,
The American Journey: A History of the United States,
vol. II, 3rd ed.

What is the point of view of the person quoted? Underline clues that support your answer.   The person would like to gain control of the Hawaiian islands.

_____

_____

Passage 3
Unless you are willing to argue that single mothers are lazier than others, it will be hard to deny that circumstances and government policies matter for poverty. Single mothers are the largest group among the poor, because they are caught between a rock and a hard place. They need to take care of their children—often without support from a father—but without support from others, they also need to work to make money. Especially if they are young and do not have a good education, it will be very

hard to find a job that pays enough for childcare and a decent living. Thus, many women are forced to rely on the welfare system.

—Christian Goergen,
Politics in a Globalized World

What is the author's point of view? Underline clues that support your answer.

The author has empathy for the plight of single working mothers.

_____

_____

exercise 8.2   **Comparing Points of View of Different Authors**

Read the following two descriptions of Mary Stuart, queen of Scotland, from two different history books. Although both include positive and negative comments, the second author obviously finds the subject more engaging and has chosen to include more positive details.

Portrait of Mary Stuart, Queen of Scots, Anonymous, 16th Century.

Scala/Art Resource, NY

Passage A

Mary Stuart returned to Scotland in 1561 after her husband's death. She was a far more charming and romantic figure than her cousin Elizabeth, but she was no stateswoman. A convinced Catholic, she soon ran head-on into the granitelike opposition of Knox and the Kirk. In 1567 she was forced to abdicate, and in the following year she fled from Scotland and sought protection in England from Elizabeth. No visitor could have been more unwelcome.

—Joseph R. Strayer et al.,
The Mainstream of Civilization, 4th ed.

Passage B

Mary Stuart was an altogether remarkable young woman, about whom it is almost impossible to remain objectively impartial. Even when one discounts the flattery that crept into descriptions of her, one is inclined to accept the contemporary evidence that Mary was extraordinarily beautiful, though tall for a girl—perhaps over six feet. In addition to beauty, she had almost every other attractive attribute in high degree: courage, wit, resourcefulness, loyalty, and responsiveness, in short everything needful for worldly greatness save discretion in her relations with men and a willingness to compromise, if need be, on matters of religion. She was a thoroughgoing Roman Catholic, a good lover, and a magnificent hater.

—Shepard B. Clough et al.,
A History of the Western World

1. How are the two descriptions alike? <u>Both say Mary Stuart was charming and a</u>
   <u>very devout Catholic.</u>

2. How do the two descriptions differ? <u>The first is more critical; the second has</u>
   <u>more positive detail.</u>

3. Which do you like better, and why? <u>Answers will vary.</u>

4. Which clues signal that the author of the second description is more biased
   than the first? <u>He suggests that he is biased, and his choice of words and</u>
   <u>attitude show it.</u>

5. What is the suggested meaning in the following phrases:

   a. "no stateswoman" <u>not a politician</u>

   b. "A convinced Catholic" <u>narrow-minded on religion</u>

   c. "granitelike opposition" <u>strong opposition</u>

   d. "more unwelcome" <u>not wanted</u>

   e. "save discretion in her relations with men" <u>not secretive about her lovers</u>

   f. "thoroughgoing Roman Catholic" <u>religiously narrow-minded</u>

   g. "magnificent hater" <u>ironic use of positive adjective for negative emphasis</u>

What Is the Reader's Point of View?

Thus far we have considered only the author's point of view. However, to recognize a point of view, a reader must know enough about the subject to realize that there is another opinion beyond the one being expressed. Therefore, prior knowledge and a slightly suspicious nature will open the mind to countless other views and alternative arguments.

On the other hand, prior knowledge can lead to a closed mind and rigid thinking. Existing opinions affect the extent to which readers accept or reject what they read. If their beliefs are particularly strong, sometimes they refuse to hear what is said or they hear something that is not said. Research has shown that readers will actually "tune out" new material that expresses views drastically different from their own. For example, if you were reading that the AIDS virus should not be a concern for most middle-class Americans, would you be "tuned in" or "tuned out"?

EXAMPLE Read the following passage on smoking from the point of view of a non-smoker. Next, reread it from the point of view of a smoker. Finally, answer the questions.

> Smoke can permanently paralyze the tiny cilia that sweep the breathing passages clean and can cause the lining of the respiratory tract to thicken irregularly. The body's attempt to rid itself of the smoking toxins may produce a deep, hacking cough in the person next to you at the lunch counter. Console yourself with the knowledge that these hackers are only trying to rid their bodies of nicotines, "tars," formaldehyde, hydrogen sulfide, resins, and who knows what. Just enjoy your meal.
>
> —Robert Wallace,
> *Biology: The World of Life*

1. Is the author a smoker? Underline the clues suggesting your answer. _____

   _____

2. What is your view on smoking? _____

   _____

3. Reading this passage in the guise of a nonsmoker, what message is conveyed

   to you? _____

   _____

4. Assuming the role of a smoker, what message is conveyed to you? _____

   _____

5. What is the main point the author is trying to convey? _____

   _____

Answers will vary.

EXPLANATION Although it is possible that both the smoker and nonsmoker would get exactly the same message, it is more likely that the nonsmoker would be disgusted by the health risks, whereas the smoker would find the author guilty of exaggeration and discrimination. The main point is that smoking causes permanent physical damage. The attitude suggests that the author is probably not a smoker.

exercise 8.3   **Identifying Points of View**

Read the following passages and answer the questions about point of view.

Passage A: Columbus

On August 3, 1492, Columbus and some ninety mariners set sail from Palos, Spain, in the *Niña, Pinta,* and *Santa Maria.* Based on faulty calculations, the Admiral estimated Asia to be no more than 4500 miles to the west (the actual distance is closer to 12,000 miles). Some 3000 miles out, his crew became fearful and wanted to return home. But he convinced them to keep sailing west. Just two days later, on October 12, they landed on a small island in the Bahamas, which Columbus named San Salvador (holy savior).

A fearless explorer, Columbus turned out to be an ineffective administrator and a poor geographer. He ended up in debtor's prison, and to his dying day in 1506 he never admitted to locating a world unknown to Europeans. Geographers overlooked his contribution and named the Western continents after another mariner, Amerigo Vespucci, a merchant from Florence who participated in a Portuguese expedition to South America in 1501. In a widely reprinted letter, Vespucci claimed that a new world had been found, and it was his name that caught on.

—James Kirby Martin et al.,
America and Its Peoples

1. Which paragraph sounds more like the Columbus you learned about in elementary school? Both are critical, but the first gives the usual facts.

2. What is the author's position on Columbus? Underline clues for your answer.
He was a fearless explorer but no administrator or intellect.

3. What is your view of Columbus? What has influenced your view? Answers will vary.

4. What is the main point the author is trying to convey? Columbus made many mistakes and is a tarnished hero.

Passage B: Mexican Cession

The tragedy of the Mexican cession is that most Anglo-Americans have not accepted the fact that the United States committed an act of violence against the Mexican people when it took Mexico's northwestern territory. Violence was not limited to the taking of the land; Mexico's territory was invaded, her people murdered, her land raped, and her possessions plundered. Memory of this destruction generated a distrust and dislike that is still vivid in the minds of many Mexicans, for the violence of the United States left deep scars. And for Chicanos—Mexicans remaining within the boundaries of the new United States territories—aggression was even more insidious, for the outcome of the Texas and Mexican-American wars made them a conquered people. Anglo-Americans were the conquerors, and they evinced all the arrogance of military victors.

In material terms, in exchange for 12,000 lives and more than $100,000,000, the United States acquired a colony two and a half times as large as France, containing rich farm lands and natural resources such as gold, silver, zinc, copper, oil, and uranium which would make possible its unprecedented industrial boom. It acquired ports on the Pacific which generated further economic expansion across that ocean. Mexico was left with its shrunken resources to face the continued advances of the expanding capitalist force on its border.

—Rodolfo Acuña,
Occupied America: A History of Chicanos

1. What is the author's point of view? Underline clues. The United States violently conquered Mexican territory, took resources, and treated people with arrogance.

2. How does this author's view differ from what you would expect in most American history texts? History describes the glory of conquerors rather than the unfairness to the conquered.

3. What is your point of view on the subject? Answers will vary.

4. What is the main point the author is trying to convey? The United States violently conquered Mexican land and people and took resources.

Passage C: Surviving in Vietnam

Vietnam ranks after World War II as America's second most expensive war. Between 1950 and 1975, the United States spent $123 billion on combat in Southeast Asia. More importantly, Vietnam ranks—after our Civil War and World Wars I and II—as the nation's fourth deadliest war, with 57,661 Americans killed in action.

Yet, when the last U.S. helicopter left Saigon, Americans suffered what historian George Herring terms "collective amnesia." Everyone, even those who had fought in 'Nam, seemed to want to forget Southeast Asia. It took nearly ten years for the government to erect a national monument to honor those who died in Vietnam.

Few who served in Vietnam survived unscathed, whether psychologically or physically. One of the 303,600 Americans wounded during the long war was 101st Airborne platoon leader James Bombard, first shot and then blown up by a mortar round during the bitter Tet fighting at Hue in February 1968. He describes his traumatic experience as

> feeling the bullet rip into your flesh, the shrapnel tear the flesh from your bones and the blood run down your leg. . . . To put your hand on your chest and to come away with your hand red with your own blood, and to feel it running out of your eyes and out of your mouth, and seeing it spurt out of your guts, realizing you were dying. . . . I was ripped open from the top of my head to the tip of my toes. I had forty-five holes in me.

Somehow Bombard survived Vietnam.

Withdrawing U.S. forces from Vietnam ended only the combat. Returning veterans fought government disclaimers concerning the toxicity of the defoliant Agent Orange. VA hospitals across the nation still contain thousands of para- and quadriplegic Vietnam veterans, as well as the maimed from earlier wars. Throughout America the "walking wounded" find themselves still embroiled in the psychological aftermath of Vietnam.

—James Divine et al.,
America: Past and Present

1. What is the author's own view of the war? Underline clues for your answer.
   The war was costly in human life, suffering, and money.

2. What is your own position on the Vietnam War? Answers will vary.

3. What is the purpose of Bombard's quotation? To personalize the pain of war and get a negative reaction from the reader

4. How do you feel about war after reading this passage? Discuss student responses.

5. What is the main point the author is trying to convey? The Vietnam War created suffering and a tragic waste of human life.

What Are Fact and Opinion?

For both the reader and the writer, a point of view is a position or belief that logically evolves over time through gained knowledge and experience and is usually based on both facts and opinions. For example, what is your position on city curfews for youth, on helping the homeless, and on abortion? Are your views on these issues supported solely by facts? Do you recognize the difference between the facts and the opinions used in your thinking?

Both facts and opinions are used persuasively to support positions. You have to determine which is which and then judge the issue accordingly. A **fact** is a statement based on actual evidence or personal observation. It can be checked objectively with empirical data and proved to be true. By contrast, an **opinion** is a statement of personal feeling or judgment. It reflects a belief or an interpretation of evidence, rather than evidence itself; it cannot be proved true. Adding the quoted opinion of a well-known authority to a few bits of evidence does not improve the data, yet this is an effective persuasive technique. Even though you may believe an opinion is valid, it is still an opinion.

EXAMPLE

Fact: Freud developed a theory of personality.

Fact: Freud believed that the personality is divided into three parts.

Opinion: Freud constructed the most complete theory of personality development.

Opinion: The personality is divided into three parts: the id, the ego, and the superego.

Authors mix facts and opinions, sometimes in the same sentence, to win you over to a particular point of view. Persuasive tricks include quoting a source of facts who then voices an opinion or hedging a statement with "It is a fact that" and attaching a disguised opinion. Recognize that both facts and opinions are valuable, but be able to distinguish between the two. The questions listed in the Reader's Tip can help you.

Reader's *Tip* — Questions to Uncover Bias

- What is your opinion on the subject?
- What is the author's opinion on the subject?
- What are the author's credentials for writing on the subject?
- What does the author have to gain?
- Does the author use facts or opinions as support?
- Are the facts selected and slanted to reflect the author's bias?

---

exercise 8.4   **Differentiating Beween Facts and Opinions**

Read each statement, and indicate *F* for fact and *O* for opinion.

_____O_____ 1. Regarding the drugs that can cause death from overdose, the dangers have been blown wildly out of proportion.

—Jeffrey Reiman,
The Rich Get Richer and the Poor Get Prison:
Ideology, Class, and Criminal Justice, 7th ed.

_____O_____ 2. Jefferson was feared, honestly feared, by almost all Federalists.

—Morton Borden,
America's Eleven Greatest Presidents.

_____F_____ 3. A misdemeanor is a crime punishable by less than one year in prison.

—Adapted from John J. Macionis,
Social Problems, 2nd ed.

_____O_____ 4. The most controversial tax is a general sales tax, which is levied by all but a few states on the sale of most goods, sometimes exempting food and drugs.

—Adapted from David B. Magleby et al.,
Government by the People, Teaching and
Learning Classroom Edition, 6th ed.

_____F_____ 5. Phosphorus, found in detergents, causes an overgrowth of algae, which then consume all the available oxygen in the water, making it incapable of supporting any flora or fauna.

—Ricky W. Griffin and Ronald J. Ebert,
Business, 8th ed.

_____F_____ 6. Witnesses who identify culprits (from photos or police lineups) within 10 seconds are 90% accurate, whereas those who take longer than 12 seconds are only 50% accurate.

—Lester A. Lefton and Linda Brannon,
Psychology, 9th ed.

_____F_____ 7. When you feel anger, your heart rate increases and so does the temperature of your skin; and when you feel fear, your heart rate increases but your skin temperature actually decreases.

—Stephen M. Kosslyn and Robin S. Rosenberg,
Psychology: The Brain, the Person, the World, 2nd ed.

_____O_____ 8. Today colleges and universities increasingly tend to circumvent the courts and bury serious criminal cases in their own judicial systems.

—John Silber,
"Students Should Not Be Above the Law,"
New York Times, May 9, 1996.

_____O_____ 9. Convicted juveniles, like adult offenders, often gain early and undeserved release from jail.

—Judy Sheindlin,
*Don't Pee On My Leg and Tell Me It's Raining:
America's Toughest Family Court Judge Speaks Out*

_____F_____ 10. In all states, compulsory-attendance laws forbid students to drop out until they turn 16 and sometimes until they turn 18 or even older.

—Jackson Toby,
"Obsessive Compulsion: The Folly of Mandatory High School Attendance."

_____O_____ 11. Repairing the meetinghouse, building a school, aiding a widowed neighbor—such were the proper uses of wealth.

—Gary B. Nash et al.,
The American People, 6th ed., vol. 1

_____F_____ 12. If you are like most people in the United States, you eat only about 2 servings of fruits or vegetables each day, a figure below the 5 to 9 recommended servings.

—Janice Thompson and Melinda Manore,
Nutrition: An Applied Approach

_____O_____ 13. Although there are a large number of Web browsers, some developed by Internet giants such as Microsoft, the dominant Web browser is Google, which has gained dominance by offering the most efficient search engine on the Web.

—Paul R. Gregory,
Essentials of Economics, 6th ed.

_____O_____ 14. Americans are poorly informed about politics.

—Gary Wasserman,
The Basics of American Politics, 12th ed.

_____O_____ 15. Bach was by no means considered the greatest composer of his day, though he was recognized as the most well-known organist, harpsichordist, and improviser (one who creates music at the same time it is performed).

—Roger Kamien,
Music: An Appreciation, Brief 5th ed.

exercise 8.5

Discerning Fact and Opinion in Textbooks

The following passage from a history text describes Sigmund Freud. Notice the mixture of facts and opinions in developing a view of this scientist. Mark the items that follow with *F* for fact and *O* for opinion.

Passage A

Sigmund Freud was a disciplined man, precise and punctual in his habits. In many ways, his life was typical of the life of a Viennese bourgeois professional at the end of the nineteenth century. His day was like a railway timetable, scheduled to the minute—whether seeing patients, dining with his family, or taking his daily constitutional. He even calculated his pleasures, counting as his only indulgence the 20 cigars he smoked every day.

The order in Freud's life seemed curiously at odds with his dedication to the study of disorder. He was a man of science, a medical doctor specializing in *organic* diseases of the nervous system. Early in his career, he began to question *physiological* explanations for certain nervous disorders and to search for another reason for the disorders of the mind. His exploration took him to Paris in 1885 to study with the leading French neurologist, Jean Martin Charcot (1825–1893), whose work on hysteria had won him an international reputation.

Surrounded by hysterics in Charcot's clinic, Freud wondered whether organic physical illnesses could be traced to psychological problems. Freud explored the value of hypnosis as a technique for uncovering the secret workings of the mind. He learned that emotions alone could produce physical symptoms such as blindness and paralysis. By hypnotizing patients, Freud caught glimpses of the world of the unconscious as a vast and hidden terrain. He approached the new territory as an explorer.

Freud created a new science of the unconscious, psychoanalysis, when he rejected physiological causes for nervous disorders in favor of psychological ones. He intended psychoanalysis as a theory of personality and a method of treatment or therapy. That was a dramatic break with existing theories of madness and mental disorder. On his seventieth birthday, Freud looked back over his own career and described his achievement: "The poets and philosophers before me discovered the unconscious; what I discovered was the scientific method by which the unconscious can be studied."

—Mark Kishlansky et al.,
Civilization in the West, 6th ed.

___F___ 1. Freud smoked 20 cigars each day.

___O___ 2. He lived the life of a typical Viennese professional of his era.

___O___ 3. The order in Freud's life was at odds with his dedication to the study of disorder.

___F___ 4. Freud was a medical doctor specializing in organic disorders of the nervous system.

___F___ 5. Freud created the science of psychoanalysis.

The following passage from a business text discusses Winston Churchill's leadership capabilities. Notice the mixture of facts and opinions in developing a view of this former British leader. Mark the items that follow with *F* for fact and *O* for opinion.

Passage B

Successful leaders often have the experience of prevailing in the face of adversity and learning from earlier failures. Leaders' skills also must match the circumstances. Winston Churchill's career provides a classic example.

Churchill began his remarkable political career in 1901 when he became a member of the House of Commons at the age of 26. Prior to his entry into Parliament he had seen combat as a cavalry officer in India, Cuba, and the Sudan and was awarded several medals for valor. He rose quickly in politics and governmental service, becoming the First Lord of the Admiralty (civilian head of the British Navy) in 1911. One of Churchill's decisions about deployment of naval forces in 1915 during World War I resulted in failure and marked the end of his fast-track career. Churchill returned to combat, serving as an infantry officer in 1917. After World War I Churchill returned to public office but was essentially relegated to the sidelines of politics. His calls for rearmament, warnings about the intentions of the Nazis between 1933 and 1939, and criticisms of the government's attempts to appease the Nazis were ignored. When things looked the worst in May 1940, the country turned to the 65-year-old Churchill for leadership as Prime Minister. It is said that Churchill "stood out as the one man in whom the nation could place its trust."

In June 1940 Britain had been at war with Germany for a year. British soldiers had been driven out of France and narrowly escaped capture through an evacuation from Dunkirk. France surrendered on June 22, and the United States had not yet entered World War II. The Battle of Britain, which involved heavy bombing of Britain's major cities, was about to begin, and it appeared that Germany would invade Britain. The outcome looked bleak. Churchill's hats, cigars, and two-fingered "v" for victory signs were distinctive, as well as symbolic, and endeared him to his followers. There were other qualities about Churchill as well that made him well-suited for the challenges of leadership during these difficult times. Two specific examples of his personal risk-taking are described as follows:

> Churchill as Prime Minister frequently and deliberately ran terrible personal risks. But the people admired him for it, and loved his offhand disregard for danger. Once, when a German bomb landed near his car and nearly tipped it over, he joked, "Must have been my beef that kept the car down"—a reference to his pudginess.
>
> Windston Churchill was another who liked to leave his underground air-raid shelter in Whitehall for the streets the moment bombs began falling. Attempts were made to stop him, because the risk of getting one's head blown off or losing a limb from shrapnel was great. . . . "I'll have you know," thundered Churchill, "that as a child my nursemaid could never prevent me from taking a walk in the Green Park when I wanted to do so. And, as a man, Adolf Hitler certainly won't."

At the end of World War II in 1945, Churchill lost his bid for reelection because he was unresponsive to the needs for social change after the war. He returned to office again as Prime Minister from 1951 to 1955, but his performance was limited by age and health problems. In general, his service as a peace-time Prime Minister did not measure up to his service during war time.

—Charles R. Greer and W. Richard Plunkett,
Supervision: Diversity and Teams in the Workplace, 10th ed.

_____O_____ 1. The skills of leaders must also match their circumstances.

_____F_____ 2. Churchill began his political career at the age of 26 in the House of Commons.

_____O_____ 3. Things looked the worst for England in May of 1940.

_____F_____ 4. France surrendered to Germany on June 22, 1940, but the United States had not yet entered the war.

_____F_____ 5. Churchill wore hats, smoked cigars, and made the two-finger "v" for victory sign.

_____O_____ 6. Churchill was unresponsive to social issues after World War II.

_____O_____ 7. Churchill was a frequent and deliberate risk-taker.

_____O_____ 8. Churchill was a better leader during the war than during peacetime.

What Is the Author's Purpose?

A textbook author can shift from an objective and factual explanation of a topic to a subjective and opinionated treatment of the facts. Recognizing the author's purpose does not mean that you won't buy the product; it just means that you will be a more cautious, well-informed consumer.

An author always has a **purpose** in mind when putting words on paper. A textbook reader expects that the author's purpose is to inform or explain objectively—and, in general, this is true. At times, however, an author can slip from factual explanation to opinionated treatment of the facts, or persuasion. The sophisticated reader recognizes this shift in purpose and becomes more critical in evaluating the content. For example, a persuasive paragraph for or against more air quality control regulations should alert you to be more skeptical than you would be while reading a paragraph that only explains how air quality control works.

The author can have a single purpose or more than one of the following:

inform	argue	entertain
explain	persuade	narrate
describe	condemn	shock
enlighten	ridicule	investigate

Read the following passage to determine the author's purpose.

EXAMPLE

love, *n.* A temporary insanity curable by marriage or by removal of the patient from the influences under which he incurred the disorder. This disease, like caries and many other ailments, is prevalent only among civilized races living under artificial conditions; barbarous nations breathing pure air and eating simple food enjoy immunity from its ravages. It is sometimes fatal, but more frequently to the physician than to the patient.

—Ambrose Bierce,
The Devil's Dictionary

EXPLANATION   The author defines love in a humorous and exaggerated manner for the purpose of entertaining the reader.

exercise 8.6   **Determining the Author's Purpose**

Read the following passage and answer the questions about the author's purpose.

ISABELLA KATZ AND THE HOLOCAUST: A LIVING TESTIMONY

No statistics can adequately render the enormity of the Holocaust, and its human meaning can perhaps only be understood through the experience of a single human being who was cast into the nightmare of the Final Solution. Isabella Katz was the eldest of six children—Isabella, brother Philip, and sisters Rachel, Chicha, Cipi, and baby Potyo—from a family of Hungarian Jews. She lived in the ghetto of Kisvarda, a provincial town of 20,000 people, where hers was a typical Jewish family of the region—middle-class, attached to Orthodox traditions, and imbued with a love of learning.

In 1938 and 1939 Hitler pressured Hungary's regent, Miklós Horthy, into adopting anti-Jewish laws. By 1941 Hungary had become a German ally, and deportations and massacres were added to the restrictions. Isabella's father left for the United States, where he hoped to obtain entry papers for his family, but after Pearl Harbor, Hungary was at war with America and the family was trapped. In the spring of 1944, when Hitler occupied Hungary, the horror of the Final Solution struck Isabella. On March 19 Adolf Eichmann, as SS officer in charge of deportation, ordered the roundup of Jews in Hungary, who numbered some 650,000. On May 28, Isabella's nineteenth birthday, the Jews in Kisvarda were told to prepare for transportation to Auschwitz on the following morning. Isabella recalled:

> And now an SS man is here, spick-and-span, with a dog, a silver pistol, and a whip. And he is all of sixteen years old. On his list appears the name of every Jew in the ghetto. . . . "Teresa Katz," he calls—my mother. She steps forward. . . . Now the SS man moves toward my mother. He raises his whip and, for no apparent reason at all, lashes out at her.

En route to Auschwitz, crammed into hot, airless boxcars, Isabella's mother told her children to "stay alive":

> Out there, when it's all over, a world's waiting for you to give it all I gave you. Despite what you see here . . . believe me, there is humanity out there, there is dignity. . . . And when this is all over, you must add to it, because sometimes it is a little short, a little skimpy.

Isabella and her family were among more than 437,000 Jews sent to Auschwitz from Hungary.

When they arrived at Auschwitz, the SS and camp guards divided the prisoners into groups, often separating family members. Amid the screams and confusion, Isabella remembered:

> We had just spotted the back of my mother's head when Mengele, the notorious Dr. Josef Mengele, points to my sister and me and says, "Die Zwei" [those two]. This trim, very good-looking German, with a flick of his thumb and a whistle, is selecting who is to live and who is to die.

Isabella's mother and her baby sister perished within a few days.

> The day we arrived in Auschwitz, there were so many people to be burned that the four crematoriums couldn't handle the task. So the Germans built big

open fires to throw the children in. Alive? I do not know. I saw the flames. I heard the shrieks.

Isabella was to endure the hell of Auschwitz for nine months.

The inmates were stripped, the hair on their heads and bodies was shaved, and they were herded into crude, overcrowded barracks. As if starvation, forced labor, and disease were not enough, they were subjected to unspeakable torture, humiliation, and terror, a mass of living skeletons for whom the difference between life and death could be measured only in an occasional flicker of spirit that determined to resist against impossible odds. Isabella put it this way:

> Have you ever weighed 120 pounds and gone down to 40? Something like that—not quite alive, yet not quite dead. Can anyone, can even I, picture it? . . . Our eyes sank deeper. Our skin rotted. Our bones screamed out of our bodies. Indeed, there was barely a body to house the mind, yet the mind was still working, sending out the messages "Live! Live!"

In November, just as Isabella and her family were lined up outside a crematorium, they were suddenly moved to Birnbäumel, in eastern Germany—the Russians were getting nearer, and the Nazis were closing down their death camps and moving the human evidence of their barbarism out of reach of the enemy. In January, as the Russians and the frigid weather closed in, the prisoners were forced to march through the snows deeper into Germany, heading toward the camp at Bergen-Belsen. Those who could not endure the trial fell by the side, shot or frozen to death. On January 23, while stumbling through a blizzard with the sound of Russian guns in the distance, Isabella, Rachel, and Chicha made a successful dash from the death march and hid in an abandoned house. Two days later Russian soldiers found them. Philip had been sent to a labor camp, and Cipi made it to Bergen-Belsen, where she died.

Isabella later married and had two children of her own, making a new life in America. Yet the images of the Holocaust remain forever in her memory. "Now I am older," she says, "and I don't remember all the pain. . . . That is not happiness, only relief, and relief is blessed. . . . And children someday will plant flowers in Auschwitz, where the sun couldn't crack through the smoke of burning flesh."

—Richard L. Greaves et al.,
Civilizations of the World, 3rd ed.

1. What is the author's purpose for including this story in a history textbook?
   To feel the terror rather than only learn the facts (emotional appeal)

2. What does the author mean by "its human meaning can perhaps only be understood through the experience of a single human being"? One person's suffering is stronger than facts on thousands. The story creates a personal image.

3. Why does the author include Isabella's quotations? For us to become eye witnesses. Her language is simple and innocent.

4. Why does the author include Isabella's quotation about the SS man? _____
   To visualize the cruelty of a 16-year-old versus innocent people

   _____

5. What is Isabella's purpose in relating her story? For us to remember, so that
   such crimes do not happen again

   _____

6. Is the passage predominantly developed through facts or opinions? Give an
   example of each. Fact: dates, places, numbers, and factual description;
   Opinion: Mother's quotation on human dignity

   _____

7. How does the passage influence your thinking about the Holocaust? _____
   Answers will vary. Discuss responses.

   _____

   _____

What Is the Author's Tone?

The author's purpose directly affects the **tone.** If the purpose is to criticize, the tone will probably be condemning and somewhat mean-spirited. If the purpose is to entertain, the tone may be humorous and playful. To put it in simple terms, the tone of an author's writing is similar to the tone of a speaker's voice. For listeners, telling the difference between an angry tone and a romantic tone is easy; you simply notice the speaker's voice. Distinguishing among humor, sarcasm, and irony, however, may be more difficult. **Humorous** remarks are designed to be comical and amusing, whereas **sarcastic** remarks are designed to cut or inflict pain. As discussed in Chapter 7, **ironic** remarks express the opposite of the literal meaning and show the incongruity between the actual and the expected. Making such precise distinctions requires a careful evaluation of what is said. Because the sound of the voice is not heard in reading, clues to the tone must come from the writer's presentation of the message. Your job is to look for clues to answer the question "What is the author's attitude toward the topic?" The list in the Reader's Tip on pages 438–439 shows the many ways a writer can express tone.

Try being an author yourself. Imagine that you have been waiting a half-hour for one of your friends to show up for a meeting, and you can wait no longer. You decide to leave a note. On your own paper, write your friend three different notes—one in a sympathetic tone, one in an angry tone, and one in a sarcastic tone. Notice in doing this how your tone reflects your purpose. Which note would you really leave and to which friend?

Reader's *Tip* ———— Recognizing an Author's Tone

The following words with explanations can describe an author's tone or attitude:

- **Absurd, farcical, ridiculous:** laughable or a joke
- **Apathetic, detached:** not caring
- **Ambivalent:** having contradictory attitudes or feelings
- **Angry, bitter, hateful:** feeling bad and upset about the topic
- **Arrogant, condescending:** acting conceited or above others
- **Awestruck, wondering:** filled with wonder
- **Cheerful, joyous, happy:** feeling good about the topic
- **Compassionate, sympathetic:** feeling sorrow at the distress of others
- **Complex:** intricate, complicated, and possibly confusing
- **Congratulatory, celebratory:** honoring an achievement or festive occasion
- **Cruel, malicious:** mean-spirited
- **Cynical:** expecting the worst from people
- **Depressed, melancholy:** sad, dejected, or having low spirits
- **Disapproving:** judging unfavorably
- **Distressed:** suffering strain, misery, or agony
- **Evasive, abstruse:** avoiding or confusing the issue
- **Formal:** using an official style; of a high social class, genteel
- **Frustrated:** blocked from a goal
- **Gentle:** thoughtful, not pushy, kind
- **Ghoulish, grim:** robbing graves or feeding on corpses; stern and forbidding
- **Hard:** unfeeling, strict, and unrelenting
- **Humorous, jovial, comic, playful, amused:** being funny
- **Incredulous:** unbelieving
- **Indignant:** outraged
- **Intense, impassioned:** extremely involved, zealous, or agitated
- **Ironic:** stating the opposite of what is expected; having a twist at the end
- **Irreverent:** lacking respect for authority
- **Mocking, scornful, caustic, condemning:** ridiculing the topic
- **Objective, factual, straightforward, critical:** using facts without emotions
- **Obsequious:** fawning for attention
- **Optimistic:** looking on the bright side
- **Outspoken:** speaking one's mind on issues

(continued)

- **Pathetic:** moving one to compassion or pity
- **Pessimistic:** looking on the negative side
- **Prayerful:** religiously thankful
- **Reticent:** shy and not speaking out
- **Reverent:** showing respect
- **Righteous:** morally correct
- **Romantic, intimate, loving:** expressing love or affection
- **Sarcastic:** saying one thing and meaning another
- **Satiric:** using irony, wit, and sarcasm to discredit or ridicule
- **Sensational:** overdramatized or overhyped
- **Sentimental, nostalgic:** remembering the good old days
- **Serious, sincere, earnest, solemn:** being honest and concerned
- **Straightforward:** forthright, direct
- **Subjective, opinionated:** expressing opinions and feelings
- **Tragic:** regrettable or deplorable
- **Uneasy:** restless or uncertain
- **Vindictive:** seeking revenge

EXAMPLE   Identify the tone of the following passage.

> As a father of two pre-teen boys, I have in the last year or so become a huge fan of the word "duh." This is a word much maligned by educators, linguistic Brahmins and purists, but they are all quite wrong.
>
> Duh has elegance. Duh has shades of meaning, even sophistication. Duh and its perfectly paired linguistic partner, "yeah, right," are the ideal terms to usher in the millennium and the information age, and to highlight the differences from the stolid old 20th century.
>
> —From Kirk Johnson.
> "Today's Kids Are, Like, Killing the English Language,"
> *New York Times,* August 9, 1998. Copyright © 1998
> by The New York Times Co. With permission.

The author's tone is _____

a. nostalgic.
b. humorous.
c. angry.

EXPLANATION   The author's tone is humorous (*b*). By juxtaposing the attributes of the word, or nonword, *duh* with complex terms such as *linguistic Brahmins* and *linguistic partner,* the author pokes fun at the way teens communicate or fail to communicate. For an additional clue to the author's tone and intent, read the title of the selection from which this excerpt is taken.

exercise 8.7   **Identifying Tone**

Mark the letter that identifies the tone for each of the following examples.

_____c_____ 1. Must I recycle everything? I don't want any more gifts of brown, "earth friendly" stationery. I want to exercise my right to burn my newspapers and throw my soda can in the trash.

  a. objective
  b. nostalgic
  c. angry

_____b_____ 2. Health experts and environmentalists now look to birth control to save us from a growing world population that already exceeds 5.5 billion. Yet, as recently as 1914, the distribution of birth control information was illegal. In that year, Margaret Higgins Sanger, founder of the magazine *The Woman Rebel,* was arrested and indicted for sending birth control information through the mail.

  a. optimistic
  b. ironic
  c. sentimental

_____b_____ 3. The Golden Age or heyday of Hollywood was in the 1930s. Americans, economically crippled by the Great Depression, went to movies for fantasy escapes into worlds created by entertainers such as Clark Gable, Greta Garbo, and the Marx Brothers.

  a. objective
  b. nostalgic
  c. bitter

_____c_____ 4. Doublespeak hides the truth, evades the issues, and misleads. No one gets fired these days. They disappear due to downsizing, workforce adjustments, and head-count reductions. After eliminating 8,000 jobs, an automobile company called it "a volume-related production schedule adjustment." Perhaps the families of the workers called it an "involuntary lifestyle reduction."

  a. sensational
  b. impassioned
  c. bitter

_____a_____ 5. In his early thirties, Beethoven's gradual hearing loss became total. This prevented him from playing the piano properly but not from continuing to write music. His three most complex and acclaimed symphonies were written when he was stone deaf. He never heard them played.

  a. ironic
  b. sarcastic
  c. opinionated

exercise 8.8   **Identifying the Author's Tone in Paragraphs**

Read the following passages to determine the author's tone and attitude toward the subject.

Passage A: The Fence

My fingers wanted to reach through the wire fence, not to touch it, not to feel it, but to break it down, with what I did not understand. The burning was not there to be understood. Something was burning, the side of me that knew I was treated different, would always be treated different because I was born on a particular side of a fence, a fence that separated me from others, that separated me from the past, that separated me from the country of my genesis and glued me to the country I did not love because it demanded something of me I could not give. Something was burning now, and if I could have grasped the source of that rage and held it in my fist, I would have melted that fence.

—Benjamin Alire Saénz,
"Exile, El Paso, Texas"

1. What is the author's tone? (Answers may vary.) Angry, distressed, intense, indignant, outspoken

2. Underline the words and phrases that suggest this tone.

3. What is the author's point of view? He sees the border fence as a symbol of separation—one that is keeping him from belonging to any country.

4. What is your own point of view on the subject? Answers will vary.

5. What is the main point the author is trying to convey? The author feels caught between two worlds and not a part of either, due to circumstances beyond his control.

Passage B: Make the Parents Pay

Too many people treat the juvenile system as a joke. That would change overnight if we required parents to pay for their children's defense attorneys according to their means, even if it is a percentage of their welfare benefits. Furthermore, in too many states, welfare keeps flowing while the kids are in jail, or middle-class parents continue to claim children as tax deductions even as the state pays for their upkeep in detention facilities. We must demand that parents reimburse the state for housing their failures.

—Adapted from Judy Sheindlin,
Don't Pee On My Leg and Tell Me It's Raining:
America's Toughest Family Court Judge Speaks Out

1. What is the author's tone? (Answers may vary.) Angry

2. Underline the words and phrases that suggest this tone.
3. What is the author's point of view? Parents treat the juvenile justice system as a joke.

4. What is your point of view on the subject? Answers will vary.

5. What is the main point the author is trying to convey? Parents need to face financial consequences for children involved in the juvenile justice system.

Passage C: A Whole New Ballgame

The first day of freshman basketball tryouts, I learned that coaching girls is different. I was demonstrating the correct way to set a cross screen. I positioned my legs shoulder-width apart and crossed my hands—fists clenched—over my groin to protect myself from the injury that all men fear. I paused, confused, understanding from the girls' bewildered looks that something was wrong. The other coach, a 15-year veteran of coaching girls, recognized my rookie mistake and bailed me out. He raised his arms and covered his chest, and I knew that I had entered alien territory.

—Brendan O'Shaughnessy,
"It's a Whole New Ballgame for Veteran Coach,"
Chicago Tribune, December 1, 2002.

1. What is the author's tone? Humorous

2. Underline the words and phrases that suggest this tone.
3. What is the author's point of view? Coaching girls is different than coaching boys.

4. What is your own point of view on the subject? Answers will vary.

5. What is the main point the author is trying to convey? As a rookie girls' basketball coach, the author made some mistakes by trying to coach girls the way he had coached boys.

Passage D: Why Women Smile

After smiling brilliantly for nearly four decades, I now find myself <u>trying to quit</u>. Or, at the very least, seeking <u>to lower the wattage a bit</u>.

Smiles are not the small and innocuous things they appear to be: Too many of us smile in lieu of showing what's really on our minds. Despite all the work we American women have done to get and <u>maintain full legal control of our bodies, not to mention our destinies</u>, we still don't seem to be <u>fully in charge of a couple of small muscle groups in our faces</u>.

Our smiles have their roots in the greetings of monkeys, who pull their lips up and back to show their fear of attack, as well as their reluctance to vie for a position of dominance. And <u>like the opossum</u> caught in the light by a clattering garbage can, we, too, <u>flash toothy grimaces</u> when we make major mistakes. By <u>declaring ourselves nonthreatening</u>, our smiles provide an extremely versatile means of protection.

—Amy Cunningham,
"Why Women Smile"

1. What is the author's tone? <u>Angry, sad, disillusioned</u>

2. Underline the words and phrases that suggest this tone.

3. What is the author's point of view? <u>Women should not feel forced to smile.</u>

4. What is your own point of view on the subject? <u>Answers will vary.</u>

5. What is the main point the author is trying to convey? <u>Women feel forced to smile even when they don't feel like it.</u>

Passage E: The Comma

The commas are the most useful and usable of all the stops. It is highly important to put them in place as you go along. If you try to come back after doing a paragraph and stick them in the various <u>spots that tempt you</u> will discover that they tend <u>to swarm like minnows into all sorts of crevices</u> whose existence you hadn't realized and before you know it the whole long sentence <u>becomes immobilized and lashed up squirming in commas</u>. Better to use them sparingly, and with affection, precisely when the need for each one arises, nicely, by itself.

—Lewis Thomas,
The Medusa and the Snail

1. What is the author's tone? <u>Humorous</u>

2. Underline the words and phrases that suggest this tone.

3. What is the author's point of view? <u>He likes correctly used commas.</u>

4. What is your own point of view on the subject? <u>Answers will vary.</u>

5. What is the main point the author is trying to convey? <u>Commas should be used sparingly and only when needed.</u>

Points of View in Editorial Cartoons

Editorial cartoons vividly illustrate how an author or an artist can effectively communicate point of view without making a direct verbal statement. Through their drawings, cartoonists have great freedom to be extremely harsh and judgmental. For example, they take positions on local and national news events and frequently depict politicians as crooks, thieves, or even murderers. Because the accusations are implied rather than directly stated, the cartoonist communicates a point of view but is still safe from libel charges.

EXAMPLE Study the cartoon on the next page to determine what the cartoonist believes and is saying about the subject. Use the following steps to analyze the implied meaning and point of view.

1. Glance at the cartoon for an overview.

2. Answer the question "What is this about?" to determine the general topic.

3. Study the details for symbolism. Who or what is represented by the images shown?

4. With all the information in mind, explain the main point that the cartoonist is trying to get across. _____

_____

_____

5. What is the tone of the cartoon? _____

_____

_____

6. What is the cartoonist's purpose? _____

_____

_____

7. What is the cartoonist's point of view or position on the subject? What is your point of view? _____

_____

_____

_____

Mike Lane/Cagle Cartoons, Inc.

EXPLANATION   Global warming is the topic of the cartoon, as suggested by the question on the back of the newspaper. The carefree polar bear sunbathes as the polar ice shelf cracks beneath the lounge chair. As the sun beams and the ice melts, the bear acclimates with sun shades, suntan oil, and an iced drink from the "Kool-R." The main point of the cartoon is that we, like the polar bear, are ignoring the reality of global warming, and we will suffer the disastrous consequences. The question "What global warming?" suggests that we are in as much denial as the polar bear. The tone is sarcastic and pleading. The cartoonist's purpose is to spur us into action before it is too late.

exercise 8.9   **Interpreting an Editorial Cartoon**

Use the same steps to analyze the message and answer the questions about the cartoon shown on page 447.

1. What is the general topic of this cartoon? College application procedures

2. What is represented by the objects such as the circular slide, the hoop, and the tires? These items liken the college application process to getting through a series of obstacles successfully. As in the course depicted, college applicants must prove themselves successful. In the case of college, this is done by things such as providing evidence of class rank rather than jumping through a hoop, but the cartoonist is drawing a parallel between the two.

3. What is the main point the cartoonist is trying to convey? Completing college applications is a series of challenges, with an element of chance mixed in (note the roulette wheel), most of which are rather rough on the student.

4. What is the cartoonist's purpose? To compare the college application process to completing an obstacle course

5. What is the tone of the cartoon? (Answers may vary.) Sarcastic, sympathetic to college students, mocking, satiric

6. What is the cartoonist's point of view? He views the college application procedure as overly difficult and likely to harm rather than help a student.

7. What is your point of view on the subject? Answers will vary.

_____

_____

_____

Cartoons are fun but challenging because they require prior knowledge for interpretation. To understand current news cartoons, you have to be familiar with the latest happenings. Look on the editorial page of your newspaper to enjoy world events from a cartoonist's point of view. If you prefer viewing them online, the home pages of some Internet service providers include links to the day's best cartoons; or you can do a Google search for cartoon sites.

As stated in the beginning of the chapter, even in college textbooks, authors' attitudes and biases slip through. Your responsibility as a reader is to be alert for signs of manipulation and to be ready—by noticing not only what is said but also what is not said—to question interpretations and conclusions. Sophisticated readers draw their own conclusions based on their own interpretation of the facts.

Summary *Points*

➤ **Does a textbook reflect the author's point of view?**
Authors have opinions, theories, and prejudices that influence their presentation of material. When facts are slanted, though not necessarily distorted, the material is biased in favor of the author's beliefs.

➤ **What is the author's point of view?**
A bias is a prejudice, a preference, or an inclination. The bias, in a sense, creates the point of view—the particular angle from which the author views the material.

➤ **What is the reader's point of view?**
The reader's point of view is the prejudice or bias the reader has concerning the subject. Readers should not let their viewpoint impede their understanding of the author's opinions and ideas.

➤ **What is the difference between a fact and an opinion?**
A fact is a statement that can be proved true; an opinion is a statement of feeling or a judgment. Both facts and opinions are used persuasively to support positions.

➤ **What is the author's purpose?**
The author's purpose may be to inform, to persuade, to entertain, or to achieve some other goal. An author always has a purpose in mind, and to be a well-informed consumer, a sophisticated reader should recognize that purpose.

➤ **What is the author's tone?**
The tone of an author's writing is similar to the tone of a speaker's voice. The reader's job is to look for clues to determine the author's attitude about the subject.

selection 1 Essay

Contemporary *Focus*

Is life as a twenty-something filled with questions and uncertainty? After college, is the path predictable? What are the crucial questions confronting college graduates and young working adults?

Growing Up Is Taking Longer Than It Used To

By Jordan Capobianco
The Oracle, University of South Florida, May 15, 2006

Where's my $100,000 Mercedes S-Class?

As spoiled as that question may sound, it's a tune that more and more young adults are humming. The 18-to-35 crowd wants everything from true love to a high-paying, enjoyable job.

And they want it plenty.

The problem is that most emerging adults aren't exactly sure how to get it. Graduating from college and being employed by a company for the entirety of one's working life is less possible now than it was when the parents of this generation were emerging into adulthood. Choosing one career path and sticking to it is also less desirable today and borders on boring. With all of the options that are available, doing so is like going to a large Chinese buffet and just eating the fried rice.

However, there is a problem: When young adults find themselves in such a position of not knowing what to do or how to get what they want, they flounder. It's referred to as a "quarter-life crisis," and it's a phenomenon occurring in many places. It is not a disease, nor is it indicative of a lack of values. It is merely a change in the way life is led, and every new generation experiences such changes to some degree.

 Collaborate on responses to the following questions:

➤ How is attending school a goal setting, structured experience?

➤ How do you find a job that is more than a paycheck?

➤ How often can you change jobs and still have a respectable employment record?

Skill Development: Preview

Preview the next selection to predict its purpose and organization and to formulate your learning plan.

Activate Schema

What do you predict will be your first job as a college graduate?
How long will you stay in your first job?
How do you plan to meet friends after college?

Establish a Purpose for Reading

Much attention has been given to the midlife crisis. What is a quarterlife crisis? Read to learn the challenges facing young adults as they seek to establish their careers and social networks.

Increase Word Knowledge

What do you know about these words?

inevitable	scorned	ponder	relevant	devastating
chaotic	stagnancy	desperation	trepidation	barrage

Your instructor may give a true-false vocabulary review before or after Readings.

Integrate Knowledge While Reading

Questions have been inserted in the margin to stimulate your thinking and help you read between the lines. Remember to

Predict	Picture	Relate	Monitor	Correct

WHAT IS THE QUARTERLIFE CRISIS?

Jim, the neighbor who lives in the three-story colonial down the block, has recently turned 50. You know this because Jim's wife threw him a surprise party about a month ago. You also know this because, since then, Jim has dyed his hair blond, purchased a leather bomber jacket, traded in his Chevy Suburban for a sleek Miata, and
5 ditched the wife for a girlfriend half her size and age.

Yet, aside from the local ladies' group's sympathetic clucks for the scorned wife, few neighbors are surprised at Jim's instant lifestyle change. Instead, they nod their heads understandingly. "Oh, Jim," they say. "He's just going through a midlife crisis. Everyone goes through it." Friends, colleagues, and family members excuse his
10 weird behavior as an inevitable effect of reaching this particular stage of life. Like millions of other middle-aged people, Jim has reached a period during which he

Do women also have midlife crises?

believes he must ponder the direction of his life—and then alter it. Jim's midlife crisis is relevant to you because it is currently the only age-related crisis that is widely
recognized as a common, inevitable part of life. The midlife crisis, however, is not
15 the only age-related crisis that we experience.

This other crisis can be just as, if not more, devastating than the midlife crisis. It
can throw someone's life into chaotic disarray or paralyze it completely. It may be
the single most concentrated period during which individuals relentlessly question
their future and how it will follow the events of their past. It covers the transition
20 from the academic world to the "real" world—an age group that can range from late
adolescence to the mid-thirties but is usually most intense in twentysomethings. It
is what we call the quarterlife crisis, and it is a real phenomenon.

The quarterlife crisis and the midlife crisis stem from the same basic problem,
but the resulting panic couldn't be more opposite. At their cores, both the quarter-
25 life and the midlife crisis are about a major life change. Often, for people experiencing a midlife crisis, a sense of stagnancy sparks the need for change. During this period, a middle-aged person tends to reflect on his past, in part to see if his life to
date measures up to the life he had envisioned as a child (or as a twentysomething).
The midlife crisis also impels a middle-aged person to look forward, sometimes
30 with an increasing sense of desperation, at the time he feels he has left.

What causes the quarterlife crisis? →

In contrast, the quarterlife crisis occurs precisely because there is none of that
predictable stability that drives middle-aged people to do unpredictable things.
After about twenty years in a sheltered school setting many graduates undergo
some sort of culture shock. In the academic environment, goals were clear-cut and
35 the ways to achieve them were mapped out distinctly. To get into a good college or
graduate school, it helped if you graduated with honors. To graduate with honors,
you needed to get good grades. To get good grades, you had to study hard. If your
goals were athletic, you worked your way up from junior varsity or walk-on to varsity
by practicing skills, working out in the weight room, and gelling with teammates
40 and coaches. The better you were, the more playing time you got, the more impressive your statistics could become.

Twenty-somethings may become disillusioned with their life's path.

But after graduation, the pathways blur. In the "real world," there is no defini-
tive way to get from point A to point B, regardless of whether the points are related
to a career, financial situation, home, or social life. The extreme uncertainty that
45 twenty-somethings experience after graduation occurs because what was once a
solid line that they could follow throughout their series of educational institutions
has now disintegrated into millions of different options. The sheer number of possibilities can certainly inspire hope. That is why people say that twenty-somethings
have their whole lives ahead of them. But the endless array of decisions can also
50 make a recent graduate feel utterly lost.

Would there be a crisis if fewer choices existed?

WHY WORRY ABOUT A QUARTERLIFE CRISIS?

The whirlwind of new responsibilities, new liberties, and new choices can be entirely overwhelming for someone who has just emerged from the shelter of twenty
years of schooling. We don't mean to make graduates sound as if they have been
hibernating since they emerged from the womb; certainly it is not as if they have
55 been slumbering throughout adolescence (though some probably tried). They have
in a sense, however, been encased in a bit of a cocoon, where someone or something—parents or school, for example—has protected them from a lot of the scari-
ness of their surroundings. As a result, when graduates are let loose into the world,
their dreams and desires can be tinged with trepidation. They are hopeful, but at
60 the same time they are also, to put it simply, scared silly.

Why are people at midlife and twentysomethings the most likely groups to experience a crisis?

The revelation that life simply isn't easy is one of the most distressing aspects of the quarterlife crisis, particularly for individuals who do not have large
support networks or who doubt themselves often. It is in these situations that
the quarterlife crisis can become hazardous. Depression is one common result of
65 the quarterlife crisis. That is why it is so important to acknowledge this transition
period.

Another way the quarterlife crisis can show up is in a feeling of disappointment, of "This is all there is?" Maybe the job turns out to be not so glamorous
after all, or maybe it just doesn't seem to lead anywhere interesting. Perhaps the
70 year of travel in Europe was more of a wallet buster than previously imagined. Or
maybe the move to a hip, new city just didn't turn out to be as fabulous a reloca-
tion as expected.

What are some strategies twentysomethings might use to combat the crisis?

Twenty-somethings are particularly vulnerable to doubts. They doubt their decisions, their abilities, their readiness, their past, present, and future. But most of
75 all, they doubt themselves. The twenties are a period of intense questioning. The
questions can range from seemingly trivial choices—"Should I really have spent
$100 to join that fantasy baseball league?"—to much larger decisions—"When is
the right time for me to start a family?"

But if the questioning becomes constant and the barrage of doubts never seems
80 to cease, twenty-somethings can feel as if it is hard to catch their breath, as if they
are spiraling downward. Many times the doubts increase because twenty-somethings
think it is abnormal to have them in the first place. No one talks about having
doubts at this age, so when twentysomethings do find that they are continuously
questioning themselves, they think something is wrong with them.

(1,092 Words)

—Alexandra Robbins and Abby Wilner,
from *Quarterlife Crisis*

Recall

Stop to self-test, relate, and react.

Your instructor may choose to give you a true-false comprehension review.

Write About the Selection

Is there a legitimate quarter life crisis? What factors merge for twentysomethings to cause this uncertainty?

   Response Suggestion: List and explain the causes of the crisis.

Armed with information about a looming quarterlife crisis, what can you do to lessen the impact? What questions would you ask the authors of this selection?

Skill Development: Explore Point of View

Form a collaborative group to discuss the following questions:

- What is the author's point of view on the quarterlife crisis?
- What is your point of view on the quarterlife crisis?
- Why should people feel disappointed to be out of school?
- How do expectations for school and expectations for work differ?
- After graduating from college, how do you become your own boss?

Check Your Comprehension

After reading the selection, answer the following questions with *a, b, c,* or *d.* To help you analyze your strengths and weaknesses, the question types are indicated.

Main Idea   __d__   1. What is the best statement of the main idea of this selection?

     a. People who have a quarterlife crisis will most likely not have a midlife crisis.
     b. Graduating from college does not prevent a quarterlife crisis.
     c. The quarterlife crisis is an extension of the predictable academic plan for the future.
     d. The quarterlife crisis is a time of uncertainty as twenty-somethings chart paths for the future.

Inference   __d__   2. The authors suggest that each of the following is true *except*

     a. many people are familiar with the term "midlife crisis."
     b. many people tend to change their values in a midlife crisis.
     c. the midlife crisis involves reflection and change.
     d. the midlife crisis is experienced only by men.

Detail   __a__   3. The quarterlife crisis

     a. marks the transition from the academic world to the "real" world.
     b. occurs in late adolescence as college draws near.
     c. lasts longer than a midlife crisis.
     d. is seldom an intense experience.

Inference   __b__   4. An important difference between the midlife crisis and the quarterlife crisis is that

     a. the midlife crisis is stressful.
     b. the midlife crisis is triggered by the long established and predictable routine of one's life.
     c. the quarterlife crisis involves looking forward.
     d. the quarterlife crisis is age-related.

Inference   __c__   5. The authors discuss the connections between schools, grades, and studying most likely in order to

     a. indicate that the stress of the quarterlife crisis is due to school, grades, and studying.
     b. suggest that academic success can reduce the severity of a quarterlife crisis.
     c. illustrate that in the academic world, the rules and goals are clear.
     d. indicate that there are few connections between academic success and career success.

Detail _____b_____ 6. According to the selection, a significant source of stress for people experiencing a quarterlife crisis is that

    a. parental expectations conflict with the expectations of twenty-somethings.
    b. there are no clear directions to follow.
    c. good grades are required to get into graduate school.
    d. the unemployment rate is increasing, and job security is decreasing.

Inference _____a_____ 7. The authors suggest that the sheer number of possibilities facing people after graduation

    a. can both inspire and overwhelm.
    b. is an indication of our improving standard of living.
    c. is not a factor in the quarterlife crisis.
    d. should make young people feel confident of success.

Inference _____a_____ 8. The authors suggest that college contributes to the quarterlife crisis because it

    a. protects students from much of the "real" world.
    b. fails to provide skills that can be used in the "real" world.
    c. costs so much that graduates have no financial resources left to start a career.
    d. leads students to believe that few employment activities will be structured.

Inference _____c_____ 9. By saying, "People have to invent their own road map," the authors mean that presently young people must

    a. study hard and get a good job.
    b. seek security in a job and satisfaction will follow.
    c. think creatively in choosing from the many options for success.
    d. follow a predictable path without the guarantee of financial success.

Inference _____a_____ 10. The authors suggest that

    a. the twenties are not necessarily the best years of one's life.
    b. decisions made in one's twenties are usually not realistic.
    c. most people in their twenties suffer from job-related depression.
    d. twentysomethings should travel in Europe before getting a job.

Answer the following with *T* (true) or *F* (false).

Detail _____F_____ 11. The authors suggest that the "cocoon" in which twentysomethings have previously been encased is a web of addiction, anxiety, and depression.

Inference _____T_____ 12. The tone of the statement "It is not as if they have been slumbering throughout adolescence (though some probably tried)" is humorous and a little sarcastic.

Inference   __T__   13. Doubt can be a major problem for people experiencing a quarterlife crisis.

Inference   __F__   14. The authors suggest that figuring out the meaning of life before you're fifty will alleviate the stress of a midlife crisis.

Inference   __T__   15. People in a quarterlife crisis often think they are the only ones who feel the way they do.

Build Your Vocabulary

According to the way the italicized word was used in the selection, select *a, b, c,* or *d* for the word or phrase that gives the best definition. The number in parentheses indicates the line of the passage in which the word is located.

__c__ 1. "the *scorned* wife" (6)
   a. endangered
   b. intelligent
   c. disrespected
   d. liberated

__b__ 2. "*inevitable effect*" (10)
   a. uncertain
   b. unavoidable
   c. silly
   d. normal

__c__ 3. "*ponder* the direction" (12)
   a. discard
   b. overlook
   c. think about
   d. reject

__a__ 4. "crisis is *relevant*" (13)
   a. significant
   b. commonplace
   c. entertaining
   d. refreshing

__b__ 5. "can be just as, if not more, *devastating*" (16)
   a. thought provoking
   b. distressing
   c. meaningful
   d. lonely

__b__ 6. "*chaotic* disarray" (17)
   a. harmful
   b. disorderly
   c. faster
   d. needed

__a__ 7. "sense of *stagnancy*" (26)
   a. standing still
   b. moving rapidly
   c. uncertainty
   d. dissatisfaction

__a__ 8. "sense of *desperation*" (30)
   a. despair
   b. unknowing
   c. isolation
   d. guilt

__d__ 9. "tinged with *trepidation*" (59)
   a. hopefulness
   b. delight
   c. eagerness
   d. uneasiness

__a__ 10. "*barrage* of doubts" (79)
   a. rapid outpouring
   b. feeling
   c. conversation
   d. argument

Search the Net

Use a search engine such as Google, Yahoo, Ask.com, Excite, Dogpile, or Lycos to find information about major life changes that cause the most stress. List the events such as a death in the family and changing jobs and explain why some changes cause more stress than others. For suggested Web sites and other research activities, go to http://www.ablongman.com/smith/.

selection 1

Selection 2 Communications

Contemporary *Focus*

Why do men and women use computers differently? Does it reflect essential gender differences in communication, and is it a reason for concern?

Study Reveals Gender Divide in Use of News Media

By Owen Gibson

From "More Likely to Have a Mobile, Use the Net, Listen to Radio and Read Papers: It's the Girl," *The Guardian* (London), May 3, 2006. Copyright Guardian Newspapers Limited 2006.

They mature more quickly, are said to be more responsible and do better at school. Now media-savvy girls are putting another one over the boys by leading the digital communications revolution.

After one of the most comprehensive studies of the effect on children of the explosion in media choices of the past 15 years, Ofcom, an agency designed to boost media literacy, said girls aged 12 to 15 are more likely than boys to have a mobile phone, use the Internet, listen to the radio and read newspapers or magazines. Only when it comes to playing computer and console games do boys overtake girls.

Given the historic domination of the home telephone by teenage girls, perhaps it is not surprising they are using the Internet to communicate with friends for hours on end. Almost all children between 12 and 15 with the Internet at home said they were "confident" surfing the Web and did so on average for eight hours a week. But girls are more likely than boys to use the Web as a communication tool.

The [British] culture secretary, Tessa Jowell, has frequently referred to the challenge of equipping people to handle an ever-wider array of media sources as one of the most pressing facing society. "I do not exaggerate when I say that media literacy in its widest sense is as important to our development as was universal literacy in the 19th century," said Jowell. "Then, the written word was the only passport to knowledge. Now, there are many more. And the most insidious digital divide is between those equipped to understand that and those who aren't."

 **COLLABORATE**   Collaborate on responses to the following questions:

➤ How many e-mails do you receive, on average, each day?

➤ Do you e-mail jokes to friends?

➤ What computer games do you play?

Skill Development: Preview

Preview the next selection to predict its purpose and organization and to formulate your learning plan.

Activate Schema

Are you happy or bothered to get e-mails?
How long are you engaged in using e-mail each day?
How much time do you spend at the computer each day?

Establish a Purpose for Reading

Are there gender differences in the use of computers? Read to discover what the author proposes. As you read, decide if you agree or disagree.

Increase Word Knowledge

novice	maven	obliquencess	reveal	captivated
defiance	vituperative	deluge	bombarded	waned

Integrate Knowledge While Reading

Questions have been inserted in the margin to stimulate your thinking and help you read between the lines. Remember to

Predict	Picture	Relate	Monitor	Correct

GENDER GAP IN CYBERSPACE

I was a computer pioneer, but I'm still something of a novice. That paradox is telling.

I was the second person on my block to get a computer. The first was my colleague Ralph. It was 1980. Ralph got a Radio Shack TRS-80; I got a used Apple II+.
5 He helped me get started and went on to become a maven, reading computer magazines, hungering for the new technology he read about, and buying and mastering it as quickly as he could afford. I hung on to old equipment far too long because I dislike giving up what I'm used to, fear making the wrong decision about what to buy, and resent the time it takes to install and learn a new system.

10   My first Apple came with videogames; I gave them away. Playing games on the computer didn't interest me. If I had free time I'd spend it talking on the telephone to friends.

Why do females prefer e-mail to games? →   Ralph got hooked. His wife was often annoyed by the hours he spent at his computer and the money he spent upgrading it. My marriage had no such strains—
15 until I discovered e-mail. Then I got hooked. E-mail draws me the same way the phone does: it's a souped-up conversation.

E-mail deepened my friendship with Ralph. Though his office was next to mine, we rarely had extended conversations because he is shy. Face to face he mumbled so, I could barely tell he was speaking. But when we both got on e-mail, I
20 started receiving long, self-revealing messages; we poured our hearts out to each

Women enjoy using the computer as a communication tool.

other. A friend discovered that e-mail opened up that kind of communication with her father. He would never talk much on the phone (as her mother would), but they have become close since they both got online.

Why, I wondered, would some men find it easier to open up on e-mail? It's a combination of the technology (which they enjoy) and the obliqueness of the written word, just as many men will reveal feelings in dribs and drabs while riding in the car or doing something, which they'd never talk about sitting face to face. It's too intense, too bearing-down on them, and once you start you have to keep going. With a computer in between, it's safer.

How do males try to dominate the computer?

It was on e-mail, in fact, that I described to Ralph how boys in groups often struggle to get the upper hand whereas girls tend to maintain an appearance of cooperation. And he pointed out that this explained why boys are more likely to be captivated by computers than girls are. Boys are typically motivated by a social structure that says if you don't dominate you will be dominated. Computers, by their nature, balk; you type a perfectly appropriate command and it refuses to do what it should. Many boys and men are incited by this defiance: "I'm going to whip this into line and teach it who's boss! I'll get it to do what I say!" (and if they work hard enough, they always can). Girls and women are more likely to respond, "This thing won't cooperate. Get it away from me!"

Although no one wants to think of herself as "typical"—how much nicer to be *sui generis*—my relationship to my computer is—gulp—fairly typical for a woman. Most women (with plenty of exceptions) aren't excited by tinkering with the technology, grappling with the challenge of eliminating bugs or getting the biggest and best computer. These dynamics appeal to many men's interest in making sure they're on the top side of the inevitable who's-up-who's-down struggle that life is for them. E-mail appeals to my view of life as a contest for connections to others. When I see that I have fifteen messages. I feel loved.

What makes it easier to communicate via e-mail?

I once posted a technical question on a computer network for linguists and was flooded with long dispositions, some pages long. I was staggered by the generosity

50 and the expertise, but wondered where these guys found the time—and why all the answers I got were from men.

Like coed classrooms and meetings, discussions on e-mail networks tend to be dominated by male voices, unless they're specifically women-only, like single-sex schools. Online, women don't have to worry about getting the floor (you just send a
55 message when you feel like it), but, according to linguists Susan Herring and Laurel Sutton, who have studied this, they have the usual problems of having their messages ignored or attacked. The anonymity of public networks frees a small number of men to send long, vituperative, sarcastic messages that many other men either can tolerate or actually enjoy, but that turn most women off.

60 The anonymity of networks leads to another sad part of the e-mail story: there are men who deluge women with questions about their appearance and invitations to sex. On college campuses, as soon as women students log on, they are bombarded by references to sex, like going to work and finding pornographic posters adorning the walls.

How do men and women differ in their purposes for computer use?

65 Most women want one thing from a computer—to work. This is significant counterevidence to the claim that men want to focus on information while women are interested in rapport. That claim I found was often true in casual conversation, in which there is no particular information to be conveyed. But with computers, it is often women who are more focused on information, because they don't respond
70 to the challenge of getting the equipment to submit.

Once I had learned the basics, my interest in computers waned. I use it to write books (though I never mastered having it do bibliographies or tables of contents) and write checks (but not balance my check book). Much as I'd like to use it to do more, I begrudge the time it would take to learn.

75 Ralph's computer expertise costs him a lot of time. Chivalry requires that he rescue novices in need, and he is called upon by damsel novices far more often than knaves. More men would rather study the instruction booklet than ask directions, as it were, from another person. "When I do help men," Ralph wrote (on e-mail, of course), "they want to be more involved. I once installed a hard drive
80 for a guy, and he wanted to be there with me, wielding the screwdriver and giving his own advice where he could." Women, he finds, usually are not interested in what he's doing; they just want him to get the computer to the point where they can do what they want.

Which pretty must explains how I managed to be a pioneer without becoming
85 an expert.

(1,101 Words)

—Deborah Tannen
Newsweek, May 16, 1994

Recall

Stop to self-test, relate, and react.

Your instructor may choose to give you a true-false comprehension review.

Write About the Selection

How does the author's use of e-mail compare with a teenage girl's use of the telephone?

Response Suggestion: List the author's uses, and make comparisons.

Contemporary *Link*

How do the Ofcom findings for 12- and 15-year-olds reflect gender differences in communication? How would Tannen interpret the findings?

Skill Development: Explore Point of View

Form a collaborative group to discuss the following questions:

- What is the author's point of view about how men and women differ in using computers?
- What is your point of view about how men and women differ in using computers?
- How does Tannen stereotype gender behavior?
- Why is Ralph more expressive with e-mail than with face-to-face communication? Which way of communicating allows you to be more expressive?
- How would you react to a lengthy e-mail question from a stranger?

Check Your Comprehension

After reading the selection, answer the following questions with *a*, *b*, *c*, or *d*. To help you analyze your strengths and weaknesses, the question types are indicated.

Main Idea _____b_____ 1. Which is the best statement of the main idea of this selection?

    a. Men like to know how to fix computers, but women want someone else to make repairs.
    b. Men use computers for a variety of personal reasons, but women see computers mainly as tools.
    c. Men tend to embrace new technology, but women usually try to avoid new technology.
    d. Men and women buy computers for different reasons, but they use computers in much the same way.

Detail _____d_____ 2. The narrator's comparison of her initial interest in computers and Ralph's shows that Ralph's interest was

    a. less emotional in nature.
    b. less time consuming.
    c. more to do with work.
    d. more of an obsession.

Inference _____a_____ 3. In the beginning of the narrator's discussion of men using e-mail, the narrator is curious about why

    a. men prefer e-mail to face-to-face communication.
    b. women get hooked on e-mail as most men do.
    c. e-mail encourages men to be more polite than they are in conversation.
    d. women enjoy writing lengthy e-mails.

Inference _____c_____ 4. When the narrator says that communication by e-mail is "safer" for men, she means that it is

    a. less likely to involve untruths.
    b. easier to avoid answering messages.
    c. emotionally less threatening.
    d. personally less satisfying.

Inference _____d_____ 5. From the narrator's discussion of computers, the reader can conclude that men tend to see a computer malfunction as a

    a. negative reflection of their own inability.
    b. reason to stop and cool off.
    c. failure in social life.
    d. kind of personal challenge to be conquered.

selection 2

Inference   _b_   6. When the narrator says that "most women . . . aren't excited by tinkering with the technology" of a computer, she is stating a

    a. claim based on proof provided later in the selection.
    b. personal opinion based on her own experiences.
    c. stereotype that was disproved later in the selection.
    d. negative comment made by men who feel overlooked.

Inference   _b_   7. The reader can conclude that the most important and satisfying function of e-mail for the narrator is that it helps her

    a. perform better in her job.
    b. social interaction.
    c. learn from linguists.
    d. correspond without being dominated by men.

Detail   _a_   8. In comparing boys and girls, the author asserts that girls are more

    a. seemingly cooperative.
    b. dominating.
    c. captivating.
    d. aggressive.

Inference   _d_   9. The comments made by the narrator's friend Ralph in the next-to-last paragraph are intended to

    a. show that men and women are both interested in computer repair.
    b. reveal how much computers changed Ralph's life.
    c. explain why men are more self-sufficient than women.
    d. suggest that men like to learn things on their own.

Inference   _c_   10. The reader can conclude that the writing in this selection is meant to be

    a. detailed and serious.
    b. dramatic and impersonal.
    c. casual and personal.
    d. one-sided and factual.

Answer the following with *T* (true) or *F* (false).

Detail   _F_   11. The narrator claims that women are primarily interested in computers as a way to strengthen relationships.

Inference   _T_   12. The narrator is not really interested in how computers work.

Detail   _F_   13. The author lives next door to Ralph's house.

Detail   _T_   14. According to the passage, more women than men are turned off by long, sarcastic messages.

Inference   _F_   15. From the responses to her technical questions to linguists, the author concludes that the men wanted to be sarcastic and criticize her work.

Build Your Vocabulary

According to the way the italicized word was used in the selection, select *a, b, c,* or *d* for the word or phrase that gives the best definition. The number in parentheses indicates the line of the passage in which the word is located.

_____c_____ 1. "something of a *novice*"
(1)
a. thinker
b. professional
c. beginner
d. complainer

_____b_____ 2. "become a *maven*"
(5)
a. consumer
b. expert
c. bookworm
d. intellectual

_____d_____ 3. "*obliqueness* of the written
word" (25)
a. directness
b. safety
c. clarity
d. indirectness

_____c_____ 4. "*reveal* feelings" (26)
a. organize
b. hide
c. show
d. condense

_____a_____ 5. "*captivated* by computers"
(33)
a. fascinated
b. mystified
c. puzzled
d. bored

_____d_____ 6. "incited by this *defiance*"
(36)
a. failure
b. level of detail
c. opportunity
d. rebelliousness

_____b_____ 7. "*vituperative*, sarcastic
messages" (58)
a. controlling
b. verbally abusing
c. complimentary
d. irrelevant

_____c_____ 8. "*deluge* women" (61)
a. interrupt
b. flatter
c. overwhelm
d. correct

_____d_____ 9. "*bombarded* by
references" (62)
a. offended
b. confused
c. monitored
d. constantly contacted

_____a_____ 10. "interest in computers
waned" (71)
a. lessened
b. grew
c. continued
d. multiplied

Search **the Net**

Use a search engine such as Google, Yahoo, Ask.com, Excite, Dogpile, or Lycos to find information about how men and women vary in the way they communicate. Discuss what women and men are trying to accomplish while communicating and if there are differences. For suggested Web sites and other research activities, go to http://www.ablongman.com/smith/.

Selection 3 Sociology

Contemporary *Focus*

According to research, 70 percent of lottery winners lose their wealth within a few years. About one-third of them eventually declare bankruptcy. How difficult is it to play it safe and be a winner for life?

Obtain Professional Advice If You Win Big

By Fiona Anderson
The Vancouver Sun, British Columbia, May 5, 2006

Tonight, some very lucky person could be $35 million richer, the estimated size of today's Lotto Super 7 jackpot.

"For that person, the first thing to do is scream," said Robert Pasion, a financial planner with Coast Capital Savings in White Rock.

But once you've got that out of your system, it's time to get serious.

"The knee-jerk reaction is to quit your job and spend a big chunk of the money on traveling or buying a fancy car or house," Pasion said. But just going out and spending the money is not really the best thing to do.

Pasion recommends putting the money immediately into a savings account.

"Just leave it there until you can get your head on straight," Pasion said. "Don't make any rash decisions, [because] rash decisions aren't the best decisions to make."

Once you've gotten over the initial shock, that's when you can start thinking about what to do. Quitting your job may be an option for the $35-million winner, but not when a smaller jackpot is the prize.

Coast Capital also recommends writing a will.

"Since the chances of dying within 15 minutes of buying your lotto ticket are roughly the same as winning, consider estate planning."

COLLABORATE **Collaborate on responses to the following questions:**

➤ Why do people have trouble holding on to lottery winnings?

➤ Why do people lose friends after lottery wins?

➤ As a lotto winner, would you continue to go to college?

Skill Development: Preview

Preview the next selection to predict its purpose and organization and to formulate your learning plan.

Activate Schema

How often have you bought lottery tickets?
Who tends to buy lottery tickets?

Establish a Purpose for Reading

Can you be convinced that winning a jackpot has a negative side? Read to find out how lottery winners can have difficulties.

Increase Word Knowledge

What do you know about these words?

glimmering	systematic	apparent	consequence	topsy-turvy
moorings	anomie	daze	anchors	poses

Your instructor may give a true-false vocabulary review before or after reading.

Integrate Knowledge While Reading

Questions have been inserted in the margin to stimulate your thinking and help you read between the lines. Remember to

Predict	Picture	Relate	Monitor	Correct

THE BIG WIN: LIFE AFTER THE LOTTERY

"If I just win the lottery, life will be good. These problems I've got, they'll be gone. I can just see myself now."

So goes the dream. And many Americans shell out megabucks every week, with the glimmering hope that "Maybe this week, I'll hit it big."

5   Most are lucky to hit for $10, or maybe just win another scratch-off ticket.

But there are the big hits. What happens to these winners? Are their lives all roses and chocolate afterwards?

Unfortunately, we don't yet have any systematic studies of the big winners, so I can't tell you what life is like for the average winner. But several themes are appar-
10 ent from reporters' interviews.

The most common consequence of hitting it big is that life becomes topsy-turvy. All of us are rooted somewhere. We have connections with others that provide the basis for our orientations to life and how we feel about the world. Sudden wealth can rip these moorings apart, and the resulting *status inconsistency* can lead
15 to a condition sociologists call *anomie*.

why this reaction? →   First comes the shock. As Mary Sanderson, a telephone operator in Dover, New Hampshire, who won $66 million, said, "I was afraid to believe it was real, and

Reuters/Landov

The lives of lottery winners do not always change for the better.

afraid to believe it wasn't." Mary says she never slept worse than her first night as a multimillionaire. "I spent the whole time crying—and throwing up"

20   Reporters and TV cameras appear on your doorstep. "What are you going to do with all that money?" they demand. You haven't the slightest idea, but in a daze you mumble something.

How could someone win and avoid the accompanying publicity?

Then come the calls. Some are welcome. Your mom and dad call to congratulate you. But long-forgotten friends and distant relatives suddenly remember how 25 close they really are to you—and strangely enough, they all have emergencies that your money can solve. You even get calls from strangers who have sick mothers, sick kids, sick dogs . . .

You have to unplug the phone and get an unlisted number.

Some lottery winners are flooded with marriage proposals. These individuals 30 certainly didn't become more attractive or sexy overnight—or did they? Maybe money makes people sexy.

What other groups of people might experience similar reactions?

You can no longer trust people. You don't know what their real motives are. Before, no one could be after your money because you didn't have any. You may even fear kidnappers. Before, this wasn't a problem—unless some kidnapper wanted 35 the ransom of a seven-year-old car.

The normal becomes abnormal. Even picking out a wedding gift is a problem. If you give the usual toaster, everyone will think you're stingy. But should you write a check for $25,000? If you do, you'll be invited to every wedding in town—and everyone will expect the same.

40   Here is what happened to some lottery winners:

How common are these sorts of situations?

As a tip, a customer gave a lottery ticket to Tonda Dickerson, a waitress at the Waffle House in Grand Bay, Alabama. She won $10 million. (Yes, just like the Nicholas Cage movie, *It Could Happen to You.*) Her coworkers sued her, saying they had always agreed to split such winnings.

45   Then there is Michael Klingebiel of Rahway, New Jersey. When he won $2 million, his mother, Phyllis, said they had pooled $20 a month for years to play the

lottery. He said that was true, but his winning ticket wasn't from their pool. He bought this one on his own. Phyllis sued her son.

Frank Capaci, a retired electrician in Streamwood, Illinois, who won $195 mil-
50 lion, is no longer welcome at his neighborhood bar, where he had hung out for years. Two bartenders had collected $5 from customers and driven an hour to Wisconsin to buy tickets. When Frank won, he gave $10,000 to each of them. They said he promised them more. Also, his former friends say that Capaci started to act "like a big shot," buying rounds of drinks but saying, "Except him," while pointing to
55 someone he didn't like.

Those who avoid *anomie* seem to be people who don't make sudden changes in their lifestyle or their behavior. They hold on to their old friends, routines, and other moorings in life that give them identity. Some even keep their old jobs—not for the money, of course, but because it anchors them to an identity with which they are
60 familiar and comfortable.

Sudden wealth, in other words, poses a threat that has to be guarded against. And I can just hear you say, "I'll take the risk!"

(741 Words)

—James M. Henslin,
Sociology: A Down-to-Earth Approach, 7th ed. Published by
Allyn and Bacon, Boston, MA. Copyright © 2005 by Pearson
Education. Reprinted by permission of the publisher.

Recall

Stop to self-test, relate, and react.

Your instructor may choose to give you a true-false comprehension review.

Write About the Selection

What are the difficulties faced by winners of a $35 million jackpot?
Response Suggestion: List and explain the potential problems.

Contemporary *Link*

If you won a $35 million jackpot, what would you do? List how you would spend some of the money and the steps you would take to preserve the rest.

Explore Point of View

Form a collaborative group to discuss the following questions:

- What is your point of view about playing the lottery?
- What is the author's point of view about winning the lottery?
- What is your point of view about winning the lottery?
- What is your point of view about lottery winners who later go bankrupt?

Check Your Comprehension

Answer the following with *a, b, c,* or *d.* To help you analyze your strengths and weaknesses, the question types are indicated.

Main Idea   __d__   1. Which is the best statement of the main idea of this selection?

       a. Sudden wealth leads to problems with a person's value system.
       b. Winning a lot of money enables people to enjoy life more fully.
       c. Sudden wealth creates many more problems than it solves.
       d. Winning a lot of money can change a person's life in unexpected ways.

Inference   __a__   2. The way the author says "So goes the dream" suggests that he feels that winning the lottery

       a. is not at all what people imagine it will be.
       b. should not be a dream for most people.
       c. is not something worth thinking about.
       d. is a false goal for too many people.

Inference   __c__   3. The reader can conclude that the information presented in this selection comes mainly from

       a. formal studies done by the author.
       b. the author's interviews with winners.
       c. media articles.
       d. research in foreign countries.

Inference   __b__   4. The author's mention of *anomie* and *status inconsistency* are related to his feeling that winning the lottery can

       a. change how the winner behaves in public.
       b. disconnect winners from their usual lives.
       c. cause winners to be more materialistic.
       d. make winners give away more money than they should.

Inference   __d__   5. The author's tone when he writes that "long-forgotten friends and distant relatives suddenly remember how close they really are to you" is best described as

       a. thoughtful.
       b. sympathetic.
       c. pleased.
       d. sarcastic.

Inference   __c__   6. The reader can conclude that one of the main reasons the lives of lottery winners change so much is that

       a. they must be concerned about kidnappers and theft.
       b. their old problems are solved by money.
       c. people want to take advantage of their winnings.
       d. they use the money to help others.

selection 3

Inference _____b_____ 7. The story about the waitress who received the lottery ticket as a tip is meant to illustrate that people

    a. want what they cannot have.
    b. are greedy.
    c. feel entitled to a good life.
    d. are lucky and generous.

Inference _____c_____ 8. The story about Frank Capaci is told to make the point that some lottery winners

    a. win by joining together in a group.
    b. give money to the people who buy their tickets.
    c. are changed for the worse by money.
    d. experience little status inconsistency or anomie.

Inference _____b_____ 9. The reader can conclude that the author's first advice to suddenly wealthy lottery winners would be to

    a. give some of their winnings to charitable causes.
    b. avoid dramatic changes in the way they live.
    c. keep some distance from current and former friends.
    d. get informed about how to invest the money.

Inference _____a_____ 10. The reader can conclude from the ending of the selection that the author understands the desire of many to win a lottery but hopes that those who do win

    a. exercise caution.
    b. show generosity.
    c. learn to trust others again.
    d. enjoy comfortable but not extravagant lifestyles.

Answer the following with *T* (true) or *F* (false).

Detail _____F_____ 11. The author feels that having a lot of money does not solve any problems.

Inference _____T_____ 12. *Status inconsistency* refers to feeling important one day but unimportant a week later or vice versa.

Inference _____T_____ 13. The author suggests that anomie can be avoided if lottery winners do not lose touch with the things that previously gave their lives meaning.

Inference _____T_____ 14. The author feels that most people would be happy to win the lottery even though their lives would change dramatically because of sudden wealth.

Inference _____F_____ 15. Most of the author's comments are based on years of research studies compiled on the lives of actual lottery winners.

Build Your Vocabulary

According to the way the italicized word was used in the selection, select *a*, *b*, *c*, or *d* for the word or phrase that gives the best definition. The number in parentheses indicates the line of the passage in which the word is located.

_____a_____ 1. "*glimmering* hope" (4)
   a. faint
   b. glaring
   c. inspiring
   d. greatest

_____c_____ 2. "*systematic* studies" (8)
   a. difficult
   b. college
   c. thoroughgoing
   d. unclear

_____a_____ 3. "themes are *apparent*" (9)
   a. obvious
   b. hidden
   c. located
   d. inconsistent

_____b_____ 4. "common *consequence*" (11)
   a. theme
   b. outcome
   c. relations
   d. demand

_____c_____ 5. "becomes *topsy-turvy*" (11)
   a. organized
   b. rich
   c. confused
   d. neat

_____b_____ 6. "rip these *moorings*" (14)
   a. employment opportunities
   b. connections
   c. ties
   d. ideas

_____d_____ 7. "call *anomie*" (15)
   a. condition characterized by uncontrollable spending
   b. condition characterized by extreme happiness
   c. condition characterized by great generosity
   d. condition characterized by disorientation, anxiety, and isolation

_____c_____ 8. "in a *daze*" (21)
   a. dilemma
   b. fight
   c. trance
   d. tragedy

_____a_____ 9. "*anchors* them" (59)
   a. secures
   b. releases
   c. drags
   d. changes

_____b_____ 10. "*poses* a threat" (61)
   a. models
   b. sets forth
   c. encounters
   d. ends

$\mathcal{S}earch$ the Net

Use a search engine such as Google, Yahoo, Ask.com, Excite, Dogpile, or Lycos to find information about the pros and cons of lotteries and stories of lottery winners. Explain the reasons why many people do not support the idea of lotteries. Explore what the money made from lotteries is intended to support and if that is happening. Also explore what group of people is most likely to spend their money on lotteries, problems with gambling, and whether lotteries create legal problems. For suggested Web sites and other research activities, go to http://www.ablongman .com/smith/.

Vocabulary *Booster*

Say, What?

Roots	*dic, dict:* "say"	*locu, loqui:* "speak"
	lingu: "tongue"	

Words with *dic, dict:* "say"

Each morning Rose used a word processor to transcribe *dictation* from a recording machine on which her boss had recorded letters and memos the previous day.

- *dictate:* to say or read aloud for transcription; to command with authority

  Sarena's parents *dictated* the nonnegotiable conditions of her upcoming slumber party: no boys, no alcohol.

- *dictator:* a ruler using absolute power without hereditary right or consent of the people

  Fidel Castro, who staged a coup to oust former president Batista of Cuba, is a *dictator* who has remained in power for many years.

- *diction:* that aspect of speaking or writing dependent on the correct choice of words; the voice quality of a speaker or singer

  Listening to public speakers with fine *diction* is much easier than trying to decipher the words of those whose speech is not clear and distinct.

- *contradict:* to state the opposite of or deny; to imply denial with actions

  Mark's wild lifestyle seems to *contradict* his claim of being the quiet, studious type.

- *indict:* to charge with a crime; to seriously criticize or blame

  The grand jury *indicted* the alleged computer hacker for breaking into banking system computers to illegally move funds electronically.

- *predict:* to declare in advance or foretell the future

  Meteorologists *predict* the weather based on facts, experience, and use of complex meteorological instruments.

- *dictionary:* a reference book of alphabetically arranged words and their meanings

  Word-processing computer programs usually contain a *dictionary* and can run a spelling check on documents.

Words with *locu, loqui:* "speak"

The defendant's attorney was skilled in fluent, forceful, and persuasive speech, so it came as no surprise that his closing statement was *eloquent* enough to convince the jury of his client's innocence.

- *elocution:* the study and practice of public speaking; a style of speaking or reading aloud

  Julianne was taking speech classes for all her electives, hoping that the *elocution* practice would help in the frequent presentations required in her chosen career of public relations.

- *locution:* a word or phrase as used by a particular person or group

  In the late 1960s and early 1970s, hippies used *locutions* such as "groovy" or "way out, man."

- *colloquial:* characteristic of informal speech or writing; conversational

  Choosing the word "nope" instead of "no" is an example of using a *colloquial* expression.

- *soliloquy:* the act of speaking to oneself; a speech in a drama in which a character reveals innermost thoughts

  Aspiring actors often use *soliloquies* from Shakespeare's plays as audition monologues.

- *loquacious:* tending to talk too much or too freely; garrulous

  When meeting new people, Nadia often becomes nervous and *loquacious,* and tends to chatter on and on about unimportant things.

- *circumlocution:* a roundabout or indirect way of speaking; using more words than necessary

  After all the *circumlocution* in Sydney's story, such as what she was wearing, what she had to eat, and what time they left, we finally got to hear whether or not she liked her blind date.

Words with *lingu:* "tongue"

When you visit the doctor it is customary for the nurse to take your *sublingual* temperature and your blood pressure.

- *linguistics:* the study of language

  Phonetics is the branch of *linguistics* involving the study of the production of speech sounds and the written symbols representing them.

- *multilingual:* able to speak several languages with some ease

  Some public schools in the United States are experiencing a need for *multilingual* teachers due to the influx of immigrants who do not yet speak English.

REVIEW

Part I

Choose the best antonym from the boxed list for each of the words below.

| acquit or discharge | confirm | dialogue | directness | elected ruler |
| formal speech | obey | recall | silent | unconvincing |

1. contradict _____confirm_____
2. circumlocution _____directness_____
3. dictate _____obey_____
4. predict _____recall_____
5. loquacious _____silent_____

6. dictator _____elected ruler_____
7. indict _____quit or discharge_____
8. eloquent _____unconvincing_____
9. soliloquy _____dialogue_____
10. colloquial _____formal speech_____

Part II

From the boxed list, choose the word that best completes each of the sentences below.

| locution | dictionary | indict | dictate | linguistics |
| diction | elocution | sublingual | dictation | contradict |

11. His outstanding performance in the classroom seemed to _____contradict_____ his rather ordinary test scores.

12. Studies indicate that multiples such as twins and triplets often communicate with their own unique words and phrases, or forms of _____locution_____.

13. To help with the study of technical vocabulary, a specialized _____dictionary_____ would be a useful purchase.

14. With infants, health care professionals often opt for another means of assessing fever in lieu of a _____sublingual_____ temperature reading.

15. Several colleges offer a camera for _____elocution_____ practice in speech labs.

16. The number of white collar criminals that courts are choosing to _____indict_____ has increased.

17. As a result of downsizing, middle managers often type their own documents instead of relying on the _____dictation_____ of notes to a secretary or administrative assistant.

18. A speaker with clear, distinct _____diction_____ is more easily understood than one with a regional accent.

19. Her friends are wondering how much longer she will remain in a relationship with a domineering person who seems to ___dictate___ rather than communicate.

20. Some researchers in the field of ___linguistics___ specialize in the study of the development of regional dialects.

9 Critical Thinking

- What is thinking?
- What is critical thinking?
- What are the characteristics of critical thinkers?
- What are the barriers to critical thinking?
- How do critical thinkers analyze an argument?
- What is the difference between inductive and deductive reasoning?
- What does creative thinking add to critical thinking?

Guy Billout, *Diving Board*, 1986. Watercolor and airbrush. 6 × 7½ inches.

What Is Thinking?

Thinking is an organized and controlled mental activity that helps you solve problems, make decisions, and understand ideas. To think is not simply to ponder; it is demanding, challenging, and rewarding work requiring skill and confidence.

All thinkers experience confusion, mental blocks, and failure at times. When faced with such adversity, poor thinkers get frustrated. They initially have trouble knowing where to begin and tend to jump haphazardly from one part of the problem to another. Lacking confidence, they eventually give up. Good thinkers, on the other hand, are strategic. They form a plan and systematically try different solutions. They work with confidence, persistently stick with the task, and find solutions.

exercise 9.1 | **Problem Solving**

Experience the thinking processes of good thinkers by solving the following problem. Warm up your thinking skills, formulate a plan, believe that you can do it (I did it, so can you!), be persistent, and solve this problem. Have fun with it!

Record your solution patterns as you "pour water" into empty glasses. If one approach fails, try another. This is not a trick but a problem that can be systematically solved—without throwing water away or estimating amounts. Use the illustration shown below to stimulate your thinking.

> Rowena has three unmarked glasses of different sizes: 3 ounces, 5 ounces, and 8 ounces. The largest glass is full, and the other two glasses are empty. What can Rowena do to get 4 ounces of liquid into each of the two larger glasses?

—Adapted from Vincent Ryan Ruggiero,
The Art of Thinking 7th ed.

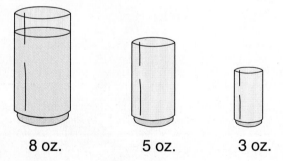

8 oz.   5 oz.   3 oz.

There are several ways to solve this problem.

1. Fill the 3-oz. glass and empty it into the 5-oz. glass. Fill it a second time, and empty as much as will fit into the 5-oz. glass. Now, the 3-oz. glass contains 1 oz., the 5-oz glass has 5 ozs., and the 8-oz. glass has 2 ozs.

2. Empty 5 ozs. into the 8-oz. glass. Then empty 3 ozs. into the 5-oz. glass. Now the 3-oz. glass is empty, the 5-oz. glass contains 1 oz., and the 8-oz. glass contains 7 ozs.

3. Fill the 3-oz. glass from the 8-oz. Empty 3-ozs. into the 5-oz. glass. Now the 3-oz. glass will be empty, and the 5- and 8-oz. glasses each contain 4 ozs.

If you worked on the exercise at length, you have now experienced the rigors of earnest thinking. Did you work strategically? What was your plan? What were the frustrations? Were you persistent? Did you believe in your ability to find a solution? Did you enjoy using thinking for problem solving?

Problems in real life are usually expressed as questions that need an action plan. For example, how would you respond if company executives decided that your job required you to solve the following problems?

- How can workers be enticed to car pool?
- How can awards be distributed to employees to mark each five years of service?
- How can a dead elephant be removed from the parking lot after an unfortunate media event?

You would, of course, work systematically to find solutions to the stated problems.

What does all of this have to do with critical thinking? Assuming it was your managers who identified the bigger issues regarding the need for car pooling, five-year awards, and elephant removal, they were the ones who did the critical thinking, and you were the one who got to do the problem solving.

What Is Critical Thinking?

While problem solving is important in any job, **critical thinking**—deliberating in a purposeful, organized manner to assess the value of old and new information—precedes it and defines the problems to be solved. Critical thinkers search, compare, analyze, clarify, evaluate, and conclude. They build on previous knowledge, recognize both sides of an issue, and evaluate the reasons and evidence in support of each. And they often deal with issues that can be controversial and can be seen from several different viewpoints. The words "How can" usually begin a problem-solving question, whereas "Should" begins a critical thinking question.

For example, imagine the critical thinking needed to answer the controversial question "Should state legislators vote to take away the driver's licenses of students ages 16 through 18 who drop out of school?" Supporters would say that such a law would improve the educational system by reducing the number of high

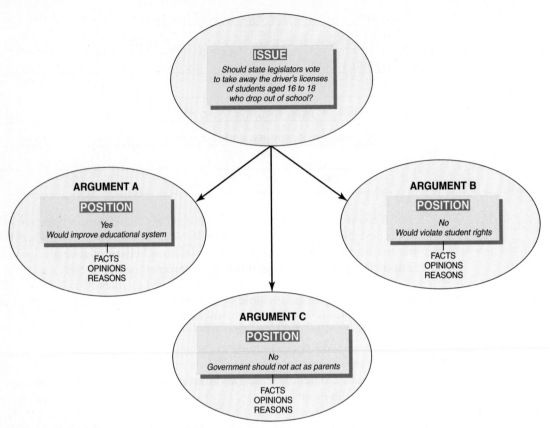

Depending on your position, many different arguments can be constructed for a single issue.

school dropouts; detractors would contend it would violate the rights of students; and others would dismiss the idea on the basis that government should not be in the parenting business. After forming a position, each side would line up evidence to build a persuasive argument to use in lobbying legislators. Both the developers of the arguments and the legislators would be critical thinkers. For the 16- to 18-year-old dropouts, the stakes would be high. The diagram illustrates the parts and possibilities.

Some professors speak of critical thinking as if it were a special discipline rather than an application of many known skills. However, critical thinking actually uses the many skills covered in the preceding chapters of this textbook. Keep reading to discover how "old friends" like *topic, main idea, details,* and *point of view* can connect with new terminology to become powerful vehicles of persuasion. In this chapter, we discuss a few new techniques for identifying and evaluating the support in an argument.

Critical Thinking Skills and College Goals

Many colleges cite the ability to think critically as one of the essential academic outcomes of a college education. An educated person is expected to think systematically, to evaluate, and to draw conclusions based on logic. At your college, an emphasis on critical thinking probably crosses the curriculum and thus becomes a part of every college course. When an instructor returns a paper to you with notes like "Good logic" or "Not enough support" written on it, the comments are referring to critical thinking. The same is true if you make a class presentation and are told either that your thesis is very convincing or that you are missing vital support. See the Reader's Tip for four habits of effective critical thinkers.

Reader's *Tip* — Four Habits of Effective Critical Thinkers

- **Be willing to plan.** Think first and write later. Don't be impulsive. Develop a habit of planning.
- **Be flexible.** Be open to new ideas. Consider new solutions for old problems.
- **Be persistent.** Continue to work even when you are tired and discouraged. Good thinking is hard work.
- **Be willing to self-correct.** Don't be defensive about errors. Figure out what went wrong, and learn from your mistakes.

Critical thinking instruction has its own specialized vocabulary, often using seemingly complex terms for simple ideas. As you work through this chapter, you will become familiar with the critical thinking application of the following terminology:

analogy	argument	assertion	believability	conclusion	consistency
deduction	fallacy	induction	premise	relevance	reliability

Barriers to Critical Thinking

Some people are mired in their own belief systems and do not want to rethink, change, or be challenged. They may be gullible and thus easily persuaded by a slick presentation or an illogical argument. For many people, the following barriers interfere with critical thinking:[1]

1. **Frame of reference.** Each of us has an existing belief system that influences the way we deal with incoming information. We interpret new experiences according to what we already believe. We are culturally conditioned to resist change and feel that our own way is best. We refuse to look at the merits of something our belief system rejects, such as the advantages of legalizing drugs, for example.

---

[1]J. Rudinow and V. E. Barry, *Invitation to Critical Thinking* (New York: Harcourt Brace, 1994), pp. 11–19.

2. **Wishful thinking.** We talk ourselves into believing things that we know are not true because we want them to be true. We irrationally deceive ourselves and engage in self-denial. For example, we might refuse to believe well-founded claims of moral corruption leveled at our favorite relative or a politician we voted for.

3. **Hasty moral judgments.** We tend to evaluate someone or something as good or bad, right or wrong, and remain fixed in this thinking. Such judgments are often prejudiced, intolerant, emotional, and self-righteous. An example of this type of barrier to thinking critically would be the statement "Abortion should never be legal."

4. **Reliance on authority.** An authority such as a clergy member, a doctor, or a teacher is an expert source of information. We give authorities and institutions such as churches or governments the power to think for us and thus block our own abilities to question and reason.

5. **Labels.** Labels ignore individual differences and lump people and things into categories. Labels oversimplify, distort the truth, and usually incite anger and rejection. For example, to say, "People who love America and people who do not" forces others to take sides as a knee-jerk reaction.

exercise 9.2 **Identifying Types of Barriers**

Read the numbered statements below and identify with *a, b, c,* or *d* the type of barrier the statement best represents:

a. Wishful thinking
b. Frame of reference or hasty moral judgment
c. Reliance on authority
d. Labels

EXAMPLE The new drug will not be helpful because the FDA has not yet approved it.

EXPLANATION The answer is c, reliance on authority, which in this case is a government agency. A critical thinker might argue that the FDA is slow to test and respond to new drugs, and that many drugs are used safely and successfully in other countries before the FDA grants approval for Americans.

___a___ 1. Since attendance is not taken for each class session, unlimited absences are acceptable for the course.

___c___ 2. According to the director of writing assistance, students are more likely to feel comfortable with peer tutors than with college instructors.

___d___ 3. City dwellers are an impatient lot; they are rude and in a hurry.

___b___ 4. Offering financial assistance to people who have fallen on hard times keeps them from learning to stand on their own two feet.

Recognizing an Argument

Just as we may have barriers to critical thinking, we also need to recognize that not every statement is an argument. **Assertions** such as "I like soy milk" or "We had a huge overnight snowfall, and my car is covered" are nonargumentative statements that are intended to inform or explain. An **argument,** on the other hand, is an assertion that supports a conclusion and is intended to persuade. The difference is intent and purpose. For example, the statement "The grass is wet because it rained last night" is an explanation, not an argument. To say, however, "You should water the grass tonight because rain is not predicted for several days" constitutes an argument. In the latter case, the conclusion of watering the grass is based on a "fact," the forecast, and the intent is to persuade by appealing to reason. To identify arguments, use inferential skills and recognize the underlying purpose or intent of the author.

exercise 9.3 | **Identifying Arguments**

Practice recognizing arguments by identifying each of the following statements with *A* (argument) or *N* (nonargumentative statement of information).

EXAMPLE   The foods in salad bars sometimes contain preservatives to keep them looking fresh and appealing.

>   **EXPLANATION**   This is not an argument. It is not intended to move you to action. It is a statement of fact similar to "It sometimes snows at night."

_____N_____ 1. Brown eyes and brown hair are dominant over blue eyes and blond hair.

_____A_____ 2. Since summer enrollment is low, the college should initiate a parking fee to offset lost income.

_____A_____ 3. Student employment should first be offered to those who have demonstrated the most significant financial need.

_____N_____ 4. Americans own more radios than they do television sets.

_____A_____ 5. College students should date people their own age.

Steps in Analyzing an Argument

Analyzing an argument through critical thinking and evaluation combines the use of most of the skills that have been taught in this text. The amount of analysis depends on the complexity of the argument. Some arguments are simple; others are lengthy and complicated. The following is a four-step procedure that you can use to guide your critical thinking:

1. Identify the position on the issue.
2. Identify the support in the argument.
3. Evaluate the support.
4. Evaluate the argument.

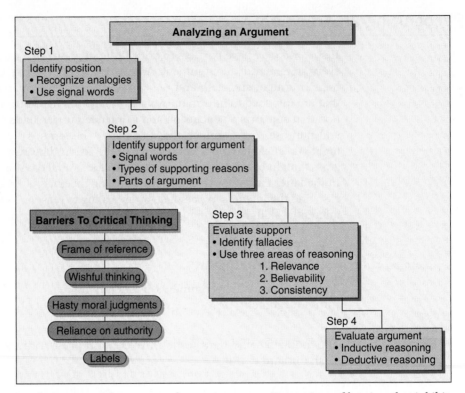

Use four sequential steps to analyze an argument. Be cautious of barriers that inhibit critical thinking.

Step 1: Identify the Position on the Issue

To identify the position on an issue or the conclusion in persuasive writing, use your main-idea reading skills. First, determine the topic that is the issue by asking yourself, "What is the passage primarily about?" Then ask, "What is the author trying to convey about the issue?" Your answer will be a statement of the position that is being argued—in other words, the main point, thesis, or conclusion. For example, on the topic or issue of searching school lockers for weapons, one position or main point might be that it can prevent violence and a contrasting position or main point might be that it is an invasion of privacy.

In a college course on critical thinking or logic, the parts of an argument that you would be asked to identify would probably be called the **conclusion** and the **premises.** The conclusion is the position on the issue or the main point, and the premises are the supporting points. For example, an argument now exists on the death of Alexander the Great more than 2,300 years ago. The conclusion that some epidemiologists have reached is that he died of West Nile virus rather than typhoid or malaria. One premise states that he became paralyzed before he died, and paralysis is a symptom of the brain infection that marks West Nile virus. Another premise holds that Alexander saw ravens pecking one another, and some fell dead in front of him, and ravens are among the types of birds that are particularly susceptible to West Nile virus.

When reading an argument, be aware of the author's bias and your own biases. Do not allow your own beliefs to cloud your thinking. Guard against falling for the barriers to critical thinking that include limited frame of reference, wishful thinking, hasty moral judgments, reliance on authority, and labeling. Be sensitive to emotional language and the connotation of words. Cut through the rhetoric, and get to the heart of the matter.

EXAMPLE Read the following passage, and identify the position on the issue that is being argued.

> The technology for television has far exceeded the programming. Viewers are recipients of crystal clear junk. Network programming appeals to the masses for ratings and advertising money and thus offers little creative or stimulating entertainment.

EXPLANATION Several debatable issues about television are suggested by this passage. They include the abundance of technological advancement, the power of ratings, and the importance of advertising money. The topic or issue, however, concerns the quality of network programming. Although it is not directly stated, the argument or central issue is "Network television programming offers little creative or stimulating entertainment."

Signal Words We have said that the position on the issue may be stated as the thesis or main point. However, it does not necessarily appear at the beginning of an argument. Instead, it might be embedded within the passage or stated at the end as a conclusion. Look for the following key words that may be used to signal the central issue:

as a result	finally	in summary	therefore
consequently	for these reasons	it follows that	thus, should

EXAMPLE What is the position on the issue that is being argued in the following passage?

> Although a year in a U.S. prison costs more than a year at Harvard, almost no one leaves prison rehabilitated. Prisoners meet and share information with other hardened criminals to refine their "skills." It seems reasonable, therefore, to conclude that prisons in the United States are societal failures.

EXPLANATION The position on the issue of prison rehabilitation in this argument is directly stated in the last sentence. Note the inclusion of the signal word *therefore.*

exercise 9.4

Identifying the Position on the Issue

Read the following sentence groups, and indicate the number of the sentence that states the position on the issue.

1. (1)Ten is the new twenty. (2)In modern America, the stage of late childhood has all but disappeared. (3)Parents allow their under-thirteens to play video games rated for mature audiences and to view movies intended for teens or adults.

    Position on issue: ____2____

2. (1)There should be a special parking area devoted to students who achieve grade-point averages of 3.0 or above. (2)These students are less likely to be involved in collisions. (3)They also deserve to be rewarded for their efforts in school.

   Position on issue: _____1_____

3. (1)Online courses are often a time-saver for students who live far from campus. (2)The majority of institutions offering these classes are accredited and have experienced faculty. (3)Consider taking courses online because of the many advantages that come with this option for learning.

   Position on issue: _____3_____

4. (1)The amount of time a doctor spends with a patient has declined over the past few decades. (2)Managed care has led to quantity over quality, when it comes to patient appointments. (3)Doctors see a prescribed number of patients within an allotted time period, regardless of the medical issues involved.

   Position on issue: _____2_____

5. (1)The age group born after the Generation Xers is looking out for number one. (2)Sociologists refer to post–Generation X as Generation Me.

   Position on issue: _____1_____

6. (1)We are fast becoming a nation of perfectionists. (2)We trim our body fat, color our hair, and pump our muscles. (3)Our teeth are whitened, our bodies dieted and exercised, and, in some cases, "perfection" is even attempted via surgery.

   Position on issue: _____1_____

7. (1)Some parts of the country encourage this support by providing curbside collection of recyclables at no cost to the consumer. (2)Other places charge the same amount to collect recycled products as they do for general refuse. (3)If policies that entice consumers to recycle were implemented nationwide, our country's rate of recycling would certainly increase greatly.

   Position on issue: _____3_____

8. (1)Our legislators ought to consider enforcing mandatory arbitration to discourage frivolous lawsuits. (2)The rising cost of malpractice insurance for physicians is a case in point. (3)While many lawsuits against physicians are valid, studies indicate that approximately 40 percent are baseless.

   Position on issue: _____1_____

Step 2: Identify the Support in the Argument

In a college logic course, after identifying the position on the issue of an argument, you would be asked to identify and number the premises, or support statements.

For example, in an argument about searching school lockers, a proponent's first premise or support statement might be that *guns and knives are always found in searches*. Other premises, such as *the school owns the lockers* and *metal detectors at the school's entrance miss harmful, illegal drugs*, would have added further supporting evidence. In short, to identify the premises, simply identify significant supporting details for the main point.

Signal Words   Supporting reasons may be directly stated or may be signaled. The key words that signal support for an argument are in some cases the same as those that signal significant supporting details. They include the following:

because	if	assuming that
since	first, second, finally	given that

EXAMPLE   What happens when the passage about U.S. prisons (see page 487) is rewritten so that signal words introduce supporting details? Read the following:

> One can conclude that prisons in the United States are societal failures. First, almost no one leaves prison rehabilitated. Second, prisoners meet and share information with other hardened criminals to refine their "skills." Taxpayers should also consider that a year in prison costs more than a year at Harvard.

EXPLANATION   The argument is the same with or without the signal words. In a longer passage, the signal words usually make it easier to identify the significant supporting details or reasons.

exercise 9.5   **Identifying Support for the Argument**

Read the following sentence groups. Record the number of the sentence that states the position on the issue that is being argued and the numbers of the support statements.

1. [1]Some college sports involve more bodily contact than others. [2]With a surface injury, the chance of bleeding could be high. [3]Thus, college athletes on teams with high levels of bodily contact, such as wrestlers, should have mandatory testing for AIDS.

   Position on issue: ___3___ Support: ___1, 2___

2. [1]Radar detectors on cars warn drivers of police surveillance. [2]At the beep, drivers slow down to avoid tickets. [3]Such devices should be banned because they promote driving beyond the legal speed limit.

   Position on issue: ___3___ Support: ___1, 2___

3. [1]Because of certain characteristics, shad and salmon are the best choices for sea ranching. [2]These fish use their own energy to swim upstream. [3]They grow in open waters and then swim back to be harvested.

   Position on issue: ___1___ Support: ___2,3___

4. (1)Major game reserves in Africa such as the Ngorongoro Crater are in protected areas, but many lie adjacent to large tracts of land with no conservation status. (2)Animals that migrate off the reserves compete with humans for food and are endangered. (3)Thus, clear boundaries between areas for animals and people would minimize friction.

Position on issue: ___3___ Support ___1, 2___

5. (1)Some state laws prohibit the sale of obscene material to minors. (2)Consequently, in these states musicians who sell CDs with obscene lyrics should be prosecuted. (3)Such lyrics brutalize women and are audio pornographic.

Position on issue: ___2___ Support ___1, 3___

6. (1)Doctors should try to make a patient's visit to the office less humiliating. (2)First, you see a receptionist who tells you to fill out forms and wait your turn. (3)Next, the nurse takes your blood pressure and extracts blood while you look at the diplomas on the wall. (4)Finally, you are led into a cold room to strip down and wait still longer for the doctor to appear for a few expensive minutes of consultation.

Position on issue: ___1___ Support ___2, 3, 4___

7. (1)In most companies, college graduates get higher-paying jobs than those who do not attend college. (2)As the years go by in a company, promotions and their accompanying raises tend to go primarily to the college graduates. (3)Thus, it can be concluded that a college degree is worth money.

Position on issue: ___3___ Support ___1, 2___

8. (1)Some parents overreact at Little League games. (2)They scream for home runs. (3)Defeat is upsetting. (4)As a result, parents put intense pressure on their children to compete and win, which can be harmful.

Position on issue: ___4___ Support ___1, 2, 3___

Types of Supporting Reasons Readers would probably prefer support for an argument to be in the simple form of a smoking gun with fingerprints on it, but such conclusive evidence is usually hard to find. Evidence comes in many different forms and may be tainted with opinion. The Reader's Tip on page 491 contains some categories of "evidence" typically used as supporting reasons in an argument. Each type, however, has its pitfalls and should be immediately tested with an evaluative question.

Step 3: Evaluate the Support

As a reader, you will decide to accept or reject the author's conclusion based on the strength and acceptability of the reasons and evidence. Keep in mind that although strong arguments are logically supported by valid reasons and evidence, weak, invalid arguments also may be supported by the crafty use of reason and evidence. Your job is to assess the validity of the support.

Reader's *Tip* ————— Types of Support for Arguments

- **Facts:** objective truths
  Ask: How were the facts gathered? Are they true?
- **Examples:** anecdotes to demonstrate the truth
  Ask: Are the examples true and relevant?
- **Analogies:** comparisons to similar cases
  Ask: Are the analogies accurate and relevant?
- **Authority:** words from a recognized expert
  Ask: What are the credentials and biases of the expert?
- **Causal relationship:** saying that one thing caused another
  Ask: Is it an actual cause or merely an association?
- **Common knowledge claim:** assertion of wide acceptance
  Ask: Is it relevant? Does everyone really believe it?
- **Statistics:** numerical data
  Ask: Do the numbers accurately describe the phenomenon?
- **Personal experiences:** personal anecdotes
  Ask: Is the experience applicable to other situations?

Teachers of logic warn students to beware of fallacies when they evaluate the support for an argument. A **fallacy** is an inference that appears to be reasonable at first glance, but closer inspection proves it to be unrelated, unreliable, or illogical. For example, to say that something is right because everybody is doing it is not a convincing reason for accepting an idea. Such "reasoning," however, can be compelling and is used so frequently that it is labeled a *bandwagon fallacy*.

Logicians have categorized, labeled, and defined more than two hundred types of fallacies or tricks of persuasion. For critical thinkers, however, the emphasis should be less on memorizing a long list of fallacy types and more on understanding how such irrelevant reasoning techniques can manipulate logical thinking. Fallacies are tools employed in constructing a weak argument that critical thinkers should spot. In a court of law, the opposing attorney would shout "Irrelevant, Your Honor!" to alert the jury to the introduction of fallacious evidence.

Evaluate the support for an argument according to three areas of reasoning: (1) relevance, (2) believability, and (3) consistency. The following list of fallacies common to each area can sensitize you to the "tools" of constructing a weak argument.

1. **Relevance fallacies: Is the support related to the conclusion?**
   - ***Ad hominem.*** An attack on the person rather than the issue is used in the hope that the idea will be opposed if the person is opposed.
     Example: Do not listen to Mr. Hite's views on education because he is a banker.
   - **Bandwagon.** Everybody is doing it, and you will be left out if you do not quickly join the crowd.
     Example: Everybody around the world is drinking Coke, so you should too.

- **Misleading analogy.** Two things are compared, suggesting that they are similar when they are in fact distinctly different.
  Example: College students are just like elementary school students; they need to be taught self-discipline.
- **Straw person.** A distorted or exaggerated form of the opponent's argument is introduced and knocked down as if to represent a totally weak opposition.
  Example: When a teenage daughter is told she cannot go out on the week-night before a test, she replies, "It's unreasonable to say that I can never go out on a weeknight."
- **Testimonials.** Respected celebrities make strong, convincing claims, though they are not actually experts.
  Example: A famous actor endorses a headache pill.
- **Transfer.** An association with a positively or negatively regarded person or thing lends the same association to the argument (also called guilt or virtue by association).
  Example: A local politician quotes President Lincoln in a speech as if to imply that Lincoln would have agreed with and voted for the candidate.

2. **Believability fallacies: Is the support believable or highly suspicious?**
   - **Incomplete facts** or **card stacking.** Factual details are omitted to misrepresent reality.
     Example: Buy stock in this particular restaurant chain because it is under new management and people eat out a lot.
   - **Misinterpreted statistics.** Numerical data are applied to unrelated populations that the numbers were never intended to represent.
     Example: More than 20 percent of people exercise daily and thus do not need fitness training.
   - **Overgeneralizations.** Examples and anecdotes are asserted as if they apply to all cases rather than a select few.
     Example: High school students do little work during their senior year and thus are overwhelmed at college.
   - **Questionable authority.** A testimonial suggests that people who are not experts actually do have authority in a certain area.
     Example: Dr. Lee, a university sociology professor, testified that the DNA reports were 100 percent accurate.

3. **Consistency fallacies: Does the support hold together, or does it fall apart and contradict itself?**
   - **Appeals to emotions.** Highly charged language is used for emotional manipulation.
     Example: Give money to our organization to help these children—these starving orphans—who are in desperate need of medical attention.
   - **Appeals to pity.** Pleas to support the underdog are made on behalf of a person or issue.
     Example: Please give me an A for the course because I need it to get into law school.
   - **Begging the question** or **circular reasoning.** Support for the conclusion merely restates the conclusion.
     Example: Drugs should not be legalized because it should be against the law to take illegal drugs.

- **Oversimplification.** An issue is reduced to two simple choices, without consideration of other alternatives or "gray areas" in between.
  Example: The choices are very simple in supporting our foreign-policy decision to send troops. You are either for America or against it.
- **Slippery slope.** Objections to an issue are raised because unless dealt with, it will lead to greater evil and disastrous consequences.
  Example: Support for assisting the suicide of a terminally ill patient will lead to the ultimate disposal of the marginally sick and elderly.

Signe Wilkerson/Cartoonists & Writers Syndicate

exercise 9.6   **Identifying Fallacies**

Identify the type of fallacy in each of the following statements by indicating *a, b,* or *c.*

_____b_____ 1. Hollywood movie stars and rock musicians are not experts on the environment and should not be dictating our environmental policy.

   a. testimonial
   b. *ad hominem*
   c. bandwagon

_____c_____ 2. Jennifer Lopez says, "I always wear evening gowns by this designer because the designer is the best."

   a. *ad hominem*
   b. misleading analogy
   c. testimonial

_____c_____ 3. The fight for equal rights is designed to force men out of jobs and encourage women to leave their young children alone at home.

    a. bandwagon
    b. questionable authority
    c. straw person

_____a_____ 4. People should give blood because it is important to give blood.

    a. begging the question
    b. appeal to pity
    c. appeal to emotions

_____c_____ 5. Prayer in the schools is like cereal for breakfast. They both get the morning off to a good start.

    a. circular reasoning
    b. appeal to emotions
    c. misleading analogy

_____a_____ 6. The advocate for re-zoning of the property concluded by saying, "George Washington was also concerned about land and freedom."

    a. transfer
    b. *ad hominem*
    c. straw person

_____b_____ 7. The explanation for the distribution of grades is simple. College students either study or they do not study.

    a. misinterpreted statistics
    b. oversimplification
    c. appeal to pity

_____b_____ 8. Your written agreement with my position will enable me to keep my job.

    a. misinterpreted statistics
    b. appeal to pity
    c. card stacking

_____a_____ 9. Everyone in the neighborhood has worked on the new park design and agreed to it. Now we need your signature of support.

    a. bandwagon
    b. appeal to emotions
    c. begging the question

_____c_____ 10. Democrats go to Washington to spend money with no regard for the hardworking taxpayer.

    a. circular reasoning
    b. bandwagon
    c. overgeneralization

_____a_____ 11. The suicide rate is highest over the Christmas holidays, which means that Thanksgiving is a safe and happy holiday.

    a. misinterpreted statistics
    b. card stacking
    c. questionable authority

_____b_____ 12. The workers' fingers were swollen and infected, insects walked on their exposed skin, and their red eyes begged for mercy and relief. We all must join their effort.

    a. oversimplification
    b. appeal to emotions
    c. overgeneralization

_____c_____ 13. Our minister, Dr. Johnson, assured the family that our cousin's cancer was a slow-growing one so that a brief delay in treatment would not be detrimental.

    a. transfer
    b. straw person
    c. questionable authority

_____b_____ 14. Crime in this city has been successfully addressed by increasing the number of police officers, seeking neighborhood support against drug dealers, and keeping teenagers off the streets at night. The city is to be commended.

    a. misleading analogy
    b. incomplete facts
    c. misinterpreted statistics

_____a_____ 15. A biology professor cannot possibly advise the swim coach on the placement of swimmers in the different races.

    a. *ad hominem*
    b. testimonial
    c. transfer

Determine Missing Support Arguments are written to persuade and thus include the proponent's version of the convincing reasons. Writers do not usually supply the reader with any more than one or two weak points that could be made by the other side. In analyzing an argument, remember to ask yourself, "What is left out?" Be an advocate for the opposing point of view, and guess at the evidence that would be presented. Decide if evidence was consciously omitted because of its adverse effect on the conclusion. For example, a businessperson arguing for an increased monthly service fee might neglect to mention how much of the cost reflects administrative overhead and profit.

Step 4: Evaluate the Argument

Important decisions are rarely made quickly or easily. A period of incubation is often needed for deliberating among alternatives. Allow yourself time to go over arguments, weighing the support and looking at the issues from different perspectives. Good critical thinkers are persistent in seeking solutions.

One researcher, Diane Halpern, expresses the difficulty of decision making by saying, "There is never just one war fought. Each side has its own version, and rarely do they agree."[2] As a reader, you are obligated to consider all factors carefully in seeking the truth. Halpern uses a picture of a table that represents the position on an issue and compares the legs of the table to four different degrees of support.

1. Unrelated reasons give no support.
2. A few weak reasons do not adequately support.
3. Many weak reasons can support.
4. Strong related reasons provide support.

Remember, in critical thinking there is no "I'm right, and you're wrong." There are, however, strong and weak arguments. Strong relevant, believable, and consistent reasons build a good argument.

exercise 9.7 Evaluating Your Own Decision Making

Now that you are familiar with the critical thinking process, analyze your own thinking in making the important recent decision of where to attend college. No college is perfect; many factors must be considered. The issue or conclusion is that you have decided to attend the college where you are now enrolled. List relevant reasons and/or evidence that supported your decision. Evaluate the strength of your reasoning. Are any of your reasons based on fallacies?

Position: My decision to attend this college was based on the following:

1. All answers will vary. Discuss in class. _____

_____

2. _____

_____

3. _____

_____

4. _____

_____

5. _____

_____

How would you evaluate your own critical thinking in making a choice among colleges? Perhaps you relied heavily on information from others. Were those sources credible?

_____

[2]Diane Halpern, *Thought and Knowledge*, 2nd ed. (Hillsdale, NJ: Lawrence Erlbaum, 1989), p. 191.

Inductive and Deductive Reasoning

In choosing a college, did you follow an inductive or deductive reasoning process? Did you collect extensive information on several colleges and then weigh the advantages and disadvantages of each? Those who follow an **inductive reasoning** process start by gathering data, and then, after considering all available material, they formulate a conclusion. Textbooks based on this plan give details first and lead you into the main idea or conclusion. They strive to put the parts into a logical whole and thus reason "up" from particular details to a broad generalization.

Deductive reasoning, on the other hand, follows the opposite pattern. With this type of reasoning, you start with the conclusion derived from a previous experience and apply it to a new situation. Perhaps your college choice is a family tradition; your parents are alumni, and you have always expected to attend. Perhaps you are attending the college closest to where you live. Although your thinking may have begun with the conclusion, you probably have since discovered many reasons why the college is right for you. When writers use a deductive pattern, they first give a general statement and then enumerate the reasons.

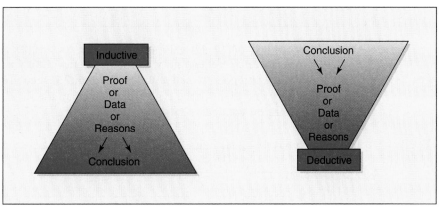

Helen R. Carr, San Antonio College

Despite the formal distinction between inductive and deductive reasoning, in real life we switch back and forth as we think. Our everyday observations lead to conclusions that we then reuse and modify to form new conclusions.

Applying the Four Steps of Critical Thinking

The following is an example of how the four-step format can be used to evaluate an argument. Read the argument, analyze it according to the directions for each step, and then read the explanation of how the critical thinking process was applied.

THE ARGUMENT: EXTRATERRESTRIAL LIFE

(1)Surely life exists elsewhere in the universe. (2)After all, most space scientists today admit the possibility that life has evolved on other planets. (3)Besides, other planets in our solar system are strikingly like Earth. (4)They revolve around the sun, they borrow light from the sun, and several are known to revolve on their axes, and to be subject to the same laws of gravitation as Earth. (5)What's more, aren't those who make light of extraterrestrial life soft-headed fundamentalists clinging to the foolish notion that life is unique to their planet?

Joel Rudinow and Vincent Barry,
Invitation to Critical Thinking, 3rd ed.

- **Step 1.** Identify the position on the issue. What is the topic of this argument, and what is the main point the writer is trying to convey? Although many ideas may be included, what is the central concern being discussed and supported? Record the number for the sentence that states the position on the issue.

  _____

- **Step 2.** Identify the support in the argument. What are the significant supporting details that support the position that is being argued? Record the numbers for supporting statements.

  _____

- **Step 3.** Evaluate the support. Examine each supporting assertion separately for relevance, believability, and consistency. Can you identify any as fallacies that are intended to sell a weak argument? List each sentence that expresses a fallacy and identify the type of fallacy. Then identify the type of supporting information you feel is missing.

  Fallacies: _____

  _____

  _____

  Missing support: _____

  _____

  _____

- **Step 4.** Evaluate the argument. What is your overall evaluation of the argument? Is the argument convincing? Does the argument provide good reasons and/or evidence for believing the thesis?

Explanation of the Four Steps

- **Step 1.** *Identify the position on the issue.* The position, assertion, thesis, main point, or conclusion is directly stated in the first sentence. Good critical thinkers would note, however, that "life" is not clearly defined as plant, animal, or human.
- **Step 2.** *Identify the support in the argument.* This argument contains three main premises or significant supporting details, in the following sentences:
    Sentence 2: Space scientists admit the possibility that life has evolved on other planets.
    Sentence 3: Other planets in our solar system are strikingly like Earth.

Sentence 5: Those who make light of extraterrestrial life are soft-headed fundamentalists clinging to the foolish notion that life is unique to this planet.

- **Step 3.** *Evaluate the support.* The first supporting detail, sentence 2, is a vague appeal to authority that does not reveal who "most space scientists" are. Do the scientists work for NASA? The second premise, sentence 3, is also vague and presented as a misleading comparison. Other planets may be round, but they have different temperatures and different atmospheres. The third supporting statement, sentence 5, is an oversimplified, personal attack on those who may not agree with the argument. Scientific support for this argument seems to be missing.

- **Step 4.** *Evaluate the argument.* This is not a good argument. There may be good reasons to believe that life exists on other planets, but this argument fails to provide them. The possibility of extraterrestrial life might be argued through statistics from astronomy and a specific definition of "life."

exercise 9.8   Applying the Four Steps to Different Arguments

Read the following three arguments, and apply the four-step format for evaluation. Using the sentence numbers, identify the position on the issue and the support. Then evaluate the argument.

ARGUMENT 1: CHILD CRIMINAL OFFENDERS

(1)Centuries ago, when there was little or no distinction between children and adults in daily life, children who committed crimes were treated exactly as adult offenders were treated. (2)More recently, they have been treated quite differently; they are given special consideration for first offenses, receive lighter sentences for second and subsequent offenses, and are placed in special reform schools and rehabilitation centers rather than in prisons. (3)But many people have begun to question the wisdom of that special consideration. (4)They reason that the crime in question, and not the criminal's age, should dictate the punishment. (5)Children who kill are either guilty of murder or not guilty.

—Adapted from Vincent Ryan Ruggiero,
The Art of Thinking, 7th ed.

- **Step 1.** Identify the position on the issue. ____4____
- **Step 2.** Identify the support in the argument. _1, 2, 3, 5_
- **Step 3.** Evaluate the support. Examine each supporting assertion for relevance, believability, and consistency. List each sentence that expresses a fallacy and identify the type of fallacy. Then identify the type of supporting information you feel is missing.

Fallacies: _1 and 2 are factual explanations. 3 is bandwagon. 5 is_
oversimplification.

Missing support: _Statistical data about actual criminal cases with children_

- **Step 4.** Evaluate the argument. What is your overall evaluation and why?

  The argument lacks evidence. It is supported only with weak opinions.

ARGUMENT 2: SCHOOL UNIFORMS

[1]A review of the evidence shows that a mandatory school uniform policy can be a solution to many high school learning and behavior problems. [2]Studies show that in schools recently implementing a mandatory uniform policy, academic achievement has gone up and discipline problems have decreased. [3]With the uniform policy, students are able to spend more time on their studies because they are not distracted by clothing choices. [4]In addition, students who learn to respect and follow a dress code will also learn to respect other institutional rules. [5]The principal of Taylor High School reported, "Our newly found success can be traced directly back to our uniform policy. The students enjoy and appreciate the opportunity to wear our school uniform." [6]In light of this evidence, one can only conclude that denying our students the opportunity for uniforms is denying them academic success.

—Joel Rudinow and Vincent E. Barry,
Invitation to Critical Thinking, 3rd ed.

- **Step 1.** Identify the position on the issue ___1___
- **Step 2.** Identify the support in the argument. ___2–5___
- **Step 3.** Evaluate the support. Examine each supporting assertion for relevance, believability, and consistency. List each sentence that expresses a fallacy and identify the type of fallacy. Then identify the type of supporting information you feel is missing.

  Fallacies: 2 is questionable authority because the studies are not explained. 3 and 4 are misleading analogies. 5 is questionable authority, and the quote is not proven. 6 appeals to emotions.

  Missing support: Statistical data are missing, as is feedback from students and parents.

- **Step 4.** Evaluate the argument. What is your overall evaluation and why?

  The argument lacks evidence. It is supported only with weak opinions. Uniforms may be good, but this doesn't prove it.

ARGUMENT 3: INVASION OF PRIVACY

(1) When you call 911 in an emergency, some police departments have a way of telling your telephone number and address without your saying a word. (2) The chief value of this, say the police, is that if the caller is unable to communicate for any reason, the dispatcher knows where to send help. (3) But don't be duped by such paternalistic explanations. (4) This technology is a despicable invasion of privacy, for callers may be unaware of the insidious device. (5) Even if they are, some persons who wish anonymity may be reluctant to call for emergency help. (6) Remember that the names of complainants and witnesses are recorded in many communities' criminal justice systems. (7) A fairer and more effective system seemingly would include an auxiliary number for 911 callers who wish anonymity.

—Joel Rudinow and Vincent E. Barry,
Invitation to Critical Thinking, 3rd ed.

- **Step 1.** Identify the position on the issue. _____7_____
- **Step 2.** Identify the support in the argument. _4, 5, 6_
- **Step 3.** Evaluate the support. Examine each supporting assertion for relevance, believability, and consistency. List each sentence that expresses a fallacy and identify the type of fallacy. Then identify the type of supporting information you feel is missing.

Fallacies: _4 is opinion and "despicable" is an emotional word. 5 might be true, but types of callers should be included. 6 is vague and appeals to emotions._

Missing support: _Statistics on fear of calling and why_

- **Step 4:** Evaluate the argument. What is your overall evaluation and why?
  Argument has merit because it calls for supplement, not overhaul.

ARGUMENT 4: BAN BOXING

(1) As a practicing physician, I am convinced that boxing should be banned. (2) First, boxing is a very visible example that violence is accepted behavior in our society—outside the ring as well as inside. (3) This sends the wrong message to America's youth. (4) Second, boxing is the only sport where the sole object is to injure the opponent. (5) Boxing, then, is morally offensive because its intent is to inflict brain injuries on another person. (6) Third, medical science can't take someone who has suffered repeated blows to the head and restore that person to normal function. (7) This causes many physicians to conclude that our society should ban boxing. (8) Boxing is

morally and medically offensive. [9]So as a physician, I believe boxing should be banned.

—Adapted from Robert E. McAfee,
"Regulation Won't Work: Ban Boxing,"
USA Today, December 20, 1990

- **Step 1.** Identify the position on the issue. <u>1 or 9</u>
- **Step 2.** Identify the support in the argument. <u>2–8</u>
- **Step 3.** Evaluate the support. Examine each supporting assertion for relevance, believability, and consistency. List each sentence that expresses a fallacy and identify the type of fallacy. Then identify the type of supporting information you feel is missing.

Fallacies: <u>2 could be interpreted as slippery slope. 3 is an overgeneralization and opinion. 4 is an oversimplication. 5 is slippery slope. 6 is factual. 7 is appeal to authority. 8 is opinion.</u>

Missing support: <u>Examples of long-term injuries from boxing</u>

- **Step 4.** Evaluate the argument. What is your overall evaluation and why?

<u>Argument is convincing from a medical point of view. It would be strengthened by specific examples and statistics related to injuries.</u>

ARGUMENT 5: DETECT ONLINE ROMANCE

[1]The following story is proof that surveillance software should be considered ethically correct. [2]The software is cheap. [3]Its legality has not been questioned. [4]It is available from a host of companies. [5]Computer spying woke me up to reality, as the story explains.

[6]"I'm not doing anything wrong, believe me," she'd said for weeks. But he didn't buy it. He'd read her e-mail, listened in on her phone conversations. He watched the chats, too. Fifty bucks bought him software to slip into the family computer and secretly record his wife's every move.

So it's 5 A.M., she's sleeping upstairs, he ventures onto the computer. He starts up the software and finds a series of black-and-white snapshots taken of the screen while she was online. She calls herself "rita_neb" and her every come-on, every flirtation, every misspelling, is saved. The correspondent is some guy in Nebraska, and the talk is not just flirting but, you know, graphic—and Greg Young begins to cry. His 22-year marriage is over.

—Bill Hancock, "Spying at Home:
A New Pastime to Detect Online Romance,"
Computers and Security, October 1, 2000

- **Step 1.** Identify the position on the issue. ___1___
- **Step 2.** Identify the support in the argument. _2, 3, 4, 5_
- **Step 3.** Evaluate the support. Examine each supporting assertion for relevance, believability, and consistency. List each sentence that expresses a fallacy and identify the type of fallacy. Then identify the type of supporting information you feel is missing.

Fallacies: _2, 3, and 4 are factual explanations. 5 is oversimplification._

_____

_____

Missing support: _This does not really speak to the ethics of spying, only the_

need.

_____

- **Step 4.** Evaluate the argument. What is your overall evaluation and why?

The story is emotional proof that spying revealed the truth to Greg, but it is

not rational proof that it is ethical. Should a child spy to get financial

information on parents or a parent spy on a child's e-mails to friends?

ARGUMENT 6: FILM VIOLENCE

[1]I walked out of the movie after a half hour. [2]It was either leave or throw up. [3]In an early scene, a wolf attacks two young men, killing one and badly slashing the other. [4]No gory detail is left to the imagination. [5]Yet, somehow, many people around me in the theater found the visual assault enjoyable as they laughed and laughed.

[6]Chicago film critic Roger Ebert reports that in viewing another film on two separate occasions, he observed both audiences laughing in scenes showing a woman beaten, raped, and cut up. [7]One respectable-looking man next to him kept murmuring, [8]"That'll teach her." [9]Ebert found that reaction frightening. Like any powerful experience, film viewing has the capacity to brutalize us. [10]No one should be permitted to poison the air the rest of us breathe. [11]Neither should a filmmaker have the right to poison the social climate.

—Adapted from Vincent Ryan Ruggiero,
The Art of Thinking, 7th ed.

- **Step 1.** Identify the position on the issue. ___11___
- **Step 2.** Identify the support in the argument. _5, 8, 9, 10_
- **Step 3.** Evaluate the support. Examine each supporting assertion for relevance, believability, and consistency. List each sentence that expresses a fallacy and identify the type of fallacy. Then identify the type of supporting information you feel is missing.

Fallacies: 1–5 is an anecdote to prove the case through opinion. 6–8 is an anecdote appealing to authority. 9 is an overgeneralization. 10 is an appeal to the emotions.

Missing support: Actual copycat crimes related to movie violence

- **Step 4.** Evaluate the argument. What is your overall evaluation and why?
  The argument is dramatic and exaggerated but perhaps too emotional to be persuasive.

Creative and Critical Thinking

A chapter on critical thinking would not be complete without an appeal for creative thinking. You might wonder, "Are critical thinking and creative thinking different?" Creative thinking refers to the ability to generate many possible solutions to a problem, whereas critical thinking refers to the examination of those solutions for the selection of the best of all possibilities. Both ways of thinking are essential for good problem solving.

Diane Halpern uses the following story to illustrate creative thinking:

> Many years ago when a person who owed money could be thrown into jail, a merchant in London had the misfortune to owe a huge sum to a money-lender. The money-lender, who was old and ugly, fancied the merchant's beautiful teenage daughter. He proposed a bargain. He said he would cancel the merchant's debt if he could have the girl instead.
>
> Both the merchant and his daughter were horrified at the proposal. So the cunning money-lender proposed that they let Providence decide the matter. He told them that he would put a black pebble and a white pebble into an empty money-bag and then the girl would have to pick out one of the pebbles. If she chose the black pebble, she would become his wife and her father's debt would be canceled. If she chose the white pebble, she would stay with her father and the debt would still be canceled. But if she refused to pick out a pebble, her father would be thrown into jail and she would starve.
>
> Reluctantly the merchant agreed. They were standing on a pebble-strewn path in the merchant's garden as they talked, and the money-lender stooped down to pick up two pebbles. As he picked up the pebbles the girl, sharp-eyed with fright, noticed that he picked up two black pebbles and put them into the money-bag. He then asked the girl to pick out the pebble that was to decide her fate and that of her father.

Diane Halpern,
Thought and Knowledge, 2nd ed.

If you were the girl, what would you do? Think creatively, and, without evaluating your thoughts, list at least five possible solutions. Next think critically to evaluate your list, and then circle your final choice.

1. _____

2. _____

3. _____

4. _____

5. _____

In discussing the possible solutions to the problem, Halpern talks about two kinds of creative thinking, vertical thinking and lateral thinking. **Vertical thinking** is a straightforward and logical way of thinking that would typically result in a solution like, "Call his hand and expose the money-lender as a crook." The disadvantage of this solution is that the merchant is still in debt, so the original problem has not been solved. **Lateral thinking,** on the other hand, is a way of thinking *around* a problem or even redefining the problem. DeBono suggests that a lateral thinker might redefine the problem from "What happens when I get the black pebble?"[3] to "How can I avoid the black pebble?" Using this new definition of the problem and other seemingly irrelevant information, a lateral thinker could come up with a winning solution. When the girl reaches into the bag, she should fumble and drop one of the stones on the "pebble-strewn path." The color of the pebble she dropped could then be determined by looking at the one left in the bag. Since the remaining pebble is black, the dropped one that is now mingled in the path must have been white. Any other admission would expose the money-lender as a crook. Probably the heroine thought of many alternatives, but thanks to her ability ultimately to generate a novel solution and evaluate its effectiveness, the daughter and the merchant lived happily free of debt.

DeBono defines vertical thinking as "digging the same hole deeper" and lateral thinking as "digging the hole somewhere else."[4] For example, after many years of researching a cure for smallpox, Dr. Edward Jenner stopped focusing on patients who were sick with the disease and instead began studying groups of people who never seemed to get the smallpox. Shortly thereafter, using this different perspective, Dr. Jenner discovered the clues that led him to the smallpox vaccine.

Creative and critical thinking enable us to see new relationships. We blend knowledge and see new similarities and differences, a new sequence of events, or a new solution for an old problem. We create new knowledge by using old learning differently.

---

[3]E. DeBono, *New Think: The Use of Lateral Thinking in the Generation of New Ideas* (New York: Basic Books, 1968), p. 195.

[4]E. DeBono, "Information Processing and New Ideas—Lateral and Vertical Thinking," in S. J. Parnes, R. B. Noller, and A. M. Biondi, eds., *Guide to Creative Action: Revised Edition of Creative Behavior Guidebook* (New York: Scribner's, 1977).

Summary *Points*

➤ **What is thinking?**

Thinking is an organized and controlled mental activity that helps you solve problems, make decisions, and understand ideas.

➤ **What is critical thinking?**

Thinking critically means deliberating in a purposeful, organized manner to assess the value of information, both old and new.

➤ **What are the characteristics of critical thinkers?**

Critical thinkers are flexible, persistent, and willing to plan and self-correct.

➤ **What are the barriers to critical thinking?**

Some people do not allow themselves to think critically because of their frame of reference or because of wishful thinking, hasty moral judgments, reliance on authority, and labels.

➤ **How do critical thinkers analyze an argument?**

Critical thinkers can use a four-step plan for analyzing an argument: (1) identify the position on the issue, (2) identify the support in the argument, (3) evaluate the support, and (4) evaluate the argument.

➤ **What is the difference between inductive and deductive reasoning?**

With inductive reasoning, the gathering of data precedes decision making; with deductive reasoning, the conclusion is arrived at first and is applied to a new situation.

➤ **What does creative thinking add to critical thinking?**

Creative thinking involves both vertical and lateral thinking.

selection 1 Essay

Contemporary *Focus*

Does personal appearance affect the way people are treated? If you like a person, does that affect your view of the person's attractiveness? Do attractive people have more advantages than their less attractive counterparts? If so, is this a form of discrimination that can be measured and proven?

The Beauty Premium

By Sarah Boyd
The Dominion Post (Wellington, New Zealand), June 4, 2005

The advantages of being attractive have long been explored and measured by psychologists, with various levels of precision. Ideas about what constitutes beauty differ, but there are general rules that appear to be cross-cultural about the wide appeal of symmetrical faces. Even three-month-old babies, according to several studies, prefer beautiful faces to plainer ones, and teachers favor better-looking kids.

Recent, though disputed, Canadian research suggests parents may even take better care of pretty children than they do of ugly ones. It studied how parents treated their children on trips to the supermarket and observed that less attractive children were allowed to wander farther and engage in potentially dangerous activities. Afterwards, they were less likely to be buckled into the car.

A much-quoted U.S. study by economist Daniel Hammermesh found plain people earned less than people with average looks, who earned less than the good looking. The penalty for plainness is 5–10 percent, and the effect is slightly stronger for men than for women.

COLLABORATE Collaborate on responses to the following questions:

➤ Do beautiful people get special treatment?

➤ Why do we think friends look better than strangers might judge them to look?

➤ If we willingly engage in discrimination according to looks, is this an issue worth worrying about? Why or why not?

Skill Development: Preview

Preview the next selection to predict its purpose and organization and to formulate your learning plan.

Activate Schema

Why are most politicians good looking?
Did looks help Arnold Schwarzenegger become governor of California?

Establish a Purpose for Reading

Recall a time when you might have discriminated against a person or people on the basis of appearance. Then reflect on whether you have been discriminated against because you were not nicely dressed. Do well-groomed customers receive better service from sales people and restaurant staff? Read the selection to discover how we subconsciously favor good looks.

Integrate Knowledge While Reading

Questions have been inserted in the margin to stimulate your thinking while reading. Remember to

Predict	Picture	Relate	Monitor	Correct

THE IMPORTANCE OF BEING BEAUTIFUL

Unlike many people, I was neither shocked nor surprised when the national Israeli TV network fired a competent female broadcaster because she was not beautiful. I received the news with aplomb because I had just finished extensive research into "person perception," an esoteric branch of psychology that examines the many ways
5 in which physical attractiveness—or lack of it—affects all aspects of your life.

Unless you're a 10—or close to it—most of you will respond to my findings with at least some feelings of frustration or perhaps disbelief. In a nutshell, you can't overestimate the importance of being beautiful. If you're beautiful, without effort you attract hordes of friends and lovers. You are given higher school grades than
10 your smarter—but less appealing—classmates. You compete successfully for jobs against men or women who are better qualified but less alluring. Promotions and pay raises come your way more easily. You are able to go into a bank or store and cash a check with far less hassle than a plain Jane or John. And these are only a few of the many advantages enjoyed by those with a ravishing face and body.

15 "We were surprised to find that beauty had such powerful effects," confessed Karen Dion, a University of Toronto social psychologist who does person perception research. "Our findings also go against the cultural grain. People like to think that success depends on talent, intelligence, and hard work." But the scientific evidence is undeniable.

20 In large part, the beautiful person can attribute his or her idyllic life to a puzzling phenomenon that social scientists have dubbed the "halo effect." It defies human reason, but if you resemble Jane Fonda or Paul Newman it's assumed that you're more generous, trustworthy, sociable, modest, sensitive, interesting, and sexually responsive than the rest of us. Conversely, if you're somewhat physically
25 unattractive, because of the "horns effect" you're stigmatized as being mean, sneaky, dishonest, antisocial, and a poor sport to boot.

The existence of the halo/horns effect has been established by several studies. One, by Dion, looked at perceptions of misbehavior in children. Dion provided 243 female university students with identical detailed accounts of the misbehavior of a
30 seven-year-old school child. She described how the youngster had pelted a sleeping

Is this all true? Is it fair?

Mark Mainz/Getty Images for Dressed to Kilt

Success in the modeling industry is based largely on physical attractiveness.

dog with sharp stones until its leg bled. As the animal limped away, yelping in pain, the child continued the barrage of stones. The 243 women were asked to assess the seriousness of the child's offense and to give their impression of the child's normal behavior. Clipped to half of the reports were photos of seven-year-old boys or girls
35 who had been rated "high" in physical attractiveness; the other half contained photos of youngsters of "low" attractiveness. "We found," said Dion, "that the opinions of the adults were markedly influenced by the appearance of the children."

One evaluator described the stone thrower, who in her report happened to be an angelic-looking little girl, in these glowing terms: "She appears to be a perfectly
40 charming little girl, well mannered and basically unselfish. She plays well with everyone, but, like everyone else, a bad day may occur. . . . Her cruelty need not be taken too seriously." For the same offense, a homely girl evoked this comment from another evaluator: "I think this child would be quite bratty and would be a problem to teachers. She'd probably try to pick a fight with other children. . . . She
45 would be a brat at home. All in all, she would be a real problem." The tendency throughout the 243 adult responses was to judge beautiful children as ordinarily well behaved and unlikely to engage in wanton cruelty in the future; the unbeautiful were viewed as being chronically antisocial, untrustworthy, and likely to commit similar transgressions again.

How might the halo or horn effect influence child development?

50   The same standards apply in judging adults. The beautiful are assumed inno-cent. John Jurens, a colorful private investigator, was once consulted by a small Toronto firm which employed 40 people. Ten thousand dollars' worth of merchan-dise had disappeared, and it was definitely an inside job. After an intensive investi-gation, which included the use of a lie detector, Jurens was certain he had caught
55 the thief. She was 24 years old and gorgeous—a lithe princess with high cheek-bones, green eyes and shining, long black hair. The employer dismissed Juren's proof with the comment, "You've made a mistake. It just can't be her." Jurens commented sadly, "A lot of people refuse to believe that beautiful can be bad."

    David Humphrey, a prominent Ontario criminal lawyer, observed, "If a beautiful
60 woman is on trial, you practically have to show the judge and jury a movie of her committing the crime in order to get a conviction." The halo and horns effect often plays an important role in sentencing by courts. After spending 17 days observing cases heard in an Ontario traffic court, Joan Finegan, a graduate psychology student at the University of Western Ontario, concluded that pleasant and neat-looking de-
65 fendants were fined an average of $6.31 less than those who were "messy."

CAREERS

If you're a good-looking male over six feet tall, don't worry about succeeding at your career.

    A study of university graduates by the *Wall Street Journal* revealed that well-proportioned wage earners who were six-foot-two or taller earned 12 percent more
70 than men under six feet. "For some reason," explained Ronald Burke, a York University psychologist and industrial consultant, "tall men are assumed to be dy-namic, decisive, and powerful. In other words, born leaders." A Toronto consultant for Drake Personnel, one of the largest employment agencies in Canada, recalled trying to find a sales manager for an industrial firm. He sent four highly qualified
75 candidates, only to have them all turned down. "The fifth guy I sent over was differ-ent," said the consultant. "He stood six-foot-four. He was promptly hired."

    The well-favored woman also has a distinct edge when it comes to getting a job she's after. "We send out three prospects to be interviewed, and it's almost always the most glamorous one that's hired," said Edith Geddes of the Personnel Centre, a
80 Toronto agency that specializes in female placements. "We sometimes feel bad be-cause the best qualified person is not chosen." Dr. Pam Ennis, a consultant to several large corporations, observed. "Look at the photos announcing promotions in the *Globe and Mail* business section. It's no accident that so many of the women hap-pen to be attractive and sexy-looking." Ennis, an elegant woman herself, attributes at
85 least part of her career success to good looks. Her photograph appears on the brochures she mails out to companies soliciting new clients. "About eight out of 10 company presidents give me an appointment," she said. "I'm sure that many of

How can you capitalize on this observation? → them are curious to see me in person. Beauty makes it easier to establish rapport."

OLD AGE

An elderly person's attractiveness influences the way in which he or she is treated in
90 nursing homes and hospitals. Doctors and nurses give better care to the beautiful ones.

    Lena Nordholm, an Australian behavioral scientist, presented 289 doctors, nurses, social workers, speech therapists, and physiotherapists with photos of eight attractive and unattractive men and women. They were asked to speculate about what kind of patients they would be. The good-lookers were judged to be more cooperative, better

95 motivated, and more likely to improve than their less attractive counterparts. Pam
Ennis, the consultant, commented, "Because the doctor feels that beautiful patients are
more likely to respond to his treatment, he'll give them more time and attention."

We like to think we have moved beyond the era when the most desirable
woman was the beauty queen, but we haven't. Every day we make assumptions
100 about the personality of the bank teller, the delivery man, or the waitress by their
looks. The way in which we attribute good and bad characteristics still has very little to do with fact. People seldom look beyond a pleasing façade, a superficial attractiveness. But the professors of person perception are not discouraged by this.
They want to educate us. Perhaps by arming us with the knowledge and awareness
105 of why we discriminate against the unattractive, we'll learn how to prevent this un-
witting bigotry. Just maybe, we can change human nature.

Should you fight this or use it?

(1,371 words)

—From Sidney Katz,
in *Motives for Writing*, 3rd ed., ed. Robert Miller

Recall

Stop to self-test, relate, and react.

Your instructor may choose to give you a true-false comprehension review.

Skill Development: Think Critically

Apply the four-step format for evaluating the argument. Use the perforations to
tear this page out for your instructor.

- **Step 1.** Identify the position on the issue. State the main point the author is
  arguing.

  Physical attractiveness affects success in many areas.

  _____

- **Step 2.** Identify the support in the argument. Make a lettered list of the major
  assertions of support.

  A. The beautiful attract more friends and lovers.

  B. The beautiful get better grades.

  C. The beautiful are more successful in the job market.

  D. The beautiful get promotions and pay raises more easily.

  E. The beautiful can cash checks with less hassle.

  F. The misbehavior of attractive children is judged less harshly than that of

  unattractive children.

  G. Physical attractiveness affects the perception of guilt.

H. Physical attractiveness affects sentencing in court.

I. Physical attractiveness affects medical treatment for the elderly.

• **Step 3.** Evaluate the support. Comment on weaknesses in relevance, believability, and consistency for the assertions you listed in step 2. Label the fallacies. What support do you feel is missing?

A–B: unproven generalization

C–D: proven from factual research studies

E: unproven generalization

F–I: proven with factual research studies

Data correlating IQ, talent, and hard work with success; data on Internet

success and looks

• **Step 4.** Evaluate the argument. What is your overall evaluation and why?

The results of the research studies seem to prove many instances of the

positive effects of physical attractiveness in personal success.

What is your opinion on the issue? Answers will vary.

Write About the Selection

How do you plan to use the ideas from this selection to your benefit and apply the author's documented awareness of discrimination according to looks?

Response Suggestion: Discuss this from two points of view: the way you manage yourself and the way you perceive and assess others.

Contemporary *Link*

Authors of both selections seek to prove their arguments by quantifying or measuring. Devise a research study of your own to prove or disprove the argument that attractive students get better grades than their smarter but less attractive counterparts. Design your study to account for different levels of ability. Also, consider the level of attractiveness and grades of a student who was previously known by the professor.

Check Your Comprehension

Answer the following questions about the selection:

1. Why do we like to believe that success depends on talent, intelligence, and hard work? To have more control of our destiny

2. How does the study of the misbehaving seven-year-old prove the existence of the halo/horns effect? For the same offense, cruelty was excused and not taken seriously in attractive children, while unattractive children were harshly judged to be morally corrupt.

3. What does the statement, "you get the top score" mean? On a scale of 1 through 10 for beauty, you rank the top score.

4. What evidence shows that the beautiful are treated differently in legal matters? The boss would not believe the guilt of the beautiful 24-year-old employee even with a lie detector test. Traffic fines averaged less for attractive defendants.

5. Why do you think tall men are assumed to be born leaders? Answers will vary.

6. What does the author mean by "Beauty makes it easier to establish rapport"? A sense of connection or bond is created by good looks, and that lets you in the door on a positive note.

7. For the elderly, why can looks be a life-and-death matter? Doctors can refuse treatment and medicine based on a patient's likelihood of recovery, which may be subconsciously based on looks.

Search the Net

Use a search engine such as Google, Yahoo, Ask.com, AltaVista, Excite, Dogpile, or Lycos to find out how our perception of beauty in art has changed over the years. Select and describe several differences in other centuries. For suggested Web sites and other research activities, go to http://www.ablongman.com/smith/.

selection 2 Essay

Contemporary *Focus*

What are the current health concerns about cell phones and cell towers? Would cell phones be on the market if they caused cancer or brain damage? With so many people relying on cell phones, the research on long-term health hazards should be extensive and reliable. How can users feel confident about product safety?

Mobile Phones Affect DNA

By John Blau, IDG News Service,
in *PC World,* December 21, 2004

Radio frequency radiation from mobile phones can damage DNA in laboratory conditions, European researchers say in a recent study.

The study, called REFLEX, which stands for Risk Evaluation of Potential Environmental Hazards from Low Energy Electromagnetic Field Exposure Using Sensitive in vitro Methods, was a four-year, $4 million-plus research project majority-funded by the European Union. Results of the research project, which ended in May, were published on the Internet earlier this month.

"We have proven that electromagnetic fields— in high and low frequencies—damage cells in individual cell systems," says Franz Adlkofer, executive director of the Munich-based Verum Foundation for Behavior and Environment, which coordinated the REFLEX research project. "But these results can't be readily transferred to human beings. Isolated cell systems are something entirely different from complete organisms."

If, however, similar findings are ever achieved in living organisms such as rats or mice, "then we have a big problem," Adlkofer says.

After being exposed to electromagnetic fields similar to those produced by mobile phones, the isolated cells showed a significant rise in single and double-strand DNA breaks, according to a summary of the final report. The cells were not always able to repair themselves.

Several brain-cancer suits have been filed against U.S. mobile phone companies, but judges have dismissed most of them for lack of scientific evidence.

COLLABORATE Collaborate on responses to the following questions:

➤ How often do you use a cell phone?

➤ What is the FDA's role in cell phone safety?

➤ Why are credentials important when judging research on cell phone safety?

Skill Development: Preview

Preview the next selection to predict its purpose and organization and to formulate your learning plan.

Activate Schema

Do you have any health concerns about using a cell phone?
Why should the government be involved in research on cell phone safety?

Establish a Purpose for Reading

What do you know about the safety and dangers of cell phone use? If you heard a negative report about cell phones, would you believe it? Would it affect your view or use of cell phones? Read this selection to discover the findings of one research study, and evaluate the argument for additional research.

Integrate Knowledge While Reading

Questions have been inserted in the margin to stimulate your thinking while reading. Remember to

Predict	Picture	Relate	Monitor	Correct

STUDY LINKS CELL PHONES TO BRAIN DAMAGE

The safety of cell phones has been called into question, again. This time the scientific community is paying very close attention.

Neurosurgeon Leif Salford and colleagues at Lund University in Sweden published data showing for the first time an unambiguous link between microwave radia-
5 tion emitted by GSM mobile phones (the most common type worldwide) and brain damage in rats. If Salford's results are confirmed by follow-up studies in the works at research facilities worldwide, including one run by the U.S. Air Force, the data could have serious implications for the one billion-plus people glued to their cell phones.

What are the human effects?

The findings have re-ignited a long-standing debate among scientists and cell
10 phone manufacturers over cell phone safety.

Many of the hundreds of studies performed during the past decade suggest cell phone use may cause a host of adverse effects, including headaches and memory loss. Other studies, however, have shown no such effects, and no scientific consensus exists about the effect of long-term, low-level radiation on the brain and other
15 organs. A comprehensive $12 million federal investigation of cell phone safety is currently under way but will take at least five years to complete.

Is the five-year study complete?

Meanwhile, the research world is scrambling to replicate Salford's surprising results. His team exposed 32 rats to 2 hours of microwave radiation from GSM cell phones. Researchers attached the phones to the sides of the rats' small cages using coax-
20 ial cables—allowing for intermittent direct exposure—and varied the intensity of radiation in each treatment group to reflect the range of exposures a human cell phone user might experience over the same time period. Fifty days after the 2-hour exposure, the rat brains showed significant blood vessel leakage, as well as areas of shrunken, damaged neurons. The higher the radiation exposure level, the more damage was apparent. The
25 controls, by contrast, showed little to no damage. If human brains are similarly affected, Salford says, the damage could produce measurable, long-term mental deficits.

How does this period compare with humans on phones?

The cell phone industry so far has been quick to dismiss the data, saying emissions from current mobiles fall well within the range of radiation levels the FCC

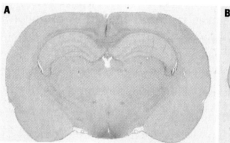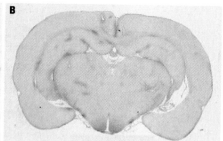

Researchers at Sweden's Lund University say these rat brain cross-sections show the first-ever evidence of brain damage from cell phone radiation. According to their research: **A,** normal rat brain. **B,** rat brain after cell phone exposure.

From "Nerve Cell Damage in Mammalian Brain after Exposure to microwaves from GSM Mobile Phones" by Leif G. Salford, Dept. of Neurosurgery; Arne E. Brun, Dept. of Neuropathology; Jacob L. Eberhardt, Dept. of Medical Radiation Physics; Lars Malmgren, Dept. of Applied Electronics and bertil R.R. Persson, Dept. of Medical Radiation Physics, Lund University, The Rausing Laboratory and Lund University Hospital, Lund, Sweden.

deems safe (body-tissue absorption rates of under 1.6 watts per kilogram). "Expert
30 reviews of studies done over the past 30 years have found no reason to believe that
there are any health hazards whatsoever," says Mays Swicord, scientific director of
Motorola's Electromagnetic Energy Programs. Dr. Marvin Ziskin, chair of the
Institute of Electrical and Electronics Engineer's Committee on Man and Radiation,
is similarly skeptical. "The levels of radiation they used seem way too low to be pro-
35 ducing the kinds of effects they're claiming."

How is Motorola biased?

Salford is the first to admit that it's too early to draw any conclusions, but con-
tends the unusual results deserve a closer look. "The cell phone is a marvelous invention; it has probably saved thousands of lives," he says. "But governments and suppliers should be supporting more autonomous research." Meanwhile, Salford advises
40 users to invest in hands-free headsets to reduce radiation exposure to the brain.

(489 words)

—From Elizabeth Svoboda,
Popular Science, February 2004

Recall

Stop to self-test, relate, and react.

Your instructor may choose to give you a true-false comprehension review.

Skill Development: Think Critically

Apply the four-step format for evaluating the argument. Use the perforations to tear this page out for your instructor.

- Identify the position on the issue.

  Governments and suppliers should support research on cell phone radiation because one study shows that it is dangerous to rats.

- Evaluate the following support for the argument:

  1. Salford linked radiation emitted by cell phones to brain damage in rats. Solid factual evidence is that the study was conducted properly and can be replicated.

- Identify the support in the argument:

  2. No scientific consensus exists concerning dangers. Opinion. If no consensus exists, some must feel dangers exist.

  3. Salford's 32 rats had 100 hours of radiation exposure, causing damage. Rats are very small. How does this amount compare with humans?

  4. The cell phone industry dismisses the data. Such dismissal is expected and thus casts a shadow on the numerous safety arguments.

  5. Use a hands-free headset. Emotional statement to promote fear

  6. What support do you feel is missing? The relationship between the amount of radiation the rats received and the amount humans normally get

- Evaluate the argument. What is your overall evaluation and why? _____ It certainly makes me want unbiased government research.

  What is your opinion? Answers will vary.

Write About the Selection

What factors operate against getting unbiased research on cell phone dangers? How does research on rats sometimes relate and sometimes not relate to humans?

Response Suggestion: Discuss the biases that might color the results found by different researchers.

Contemporary *Link*

What is your position on the health hazards of cell phones? What do you find lacking in the initial argument on cell phone safety? Describe the kind of report that you would like to see regarding cell phone safety. What research would be credible to you?

Check Your Comprehension

Answer the following questions about the selection.

1. What is meant by the phrase "unambiguous link" in Salford's research report? *Ambiguous* means that it is confusing or unclear, so this must be a clear link that cannot be attributed to other variables.

2. Why would a replication of Salford's study by the U.S. Air Force be considered more valuable than a replication by another scientist? The military is supposedly unbiased, has qualified researchers, and is not subject to manipulation by cell phone companies.

3. What are your questions about the 100 hours of radiation the rats received in Salford's experiment? Answers will vary.

4. What does the phrase "more autonomous research" mean? Researchers should have total freedom to find either positive or negative results and should not be driven by phone companies or special interest groups that only want positive findings.

5. Even if you wore a headset, if the cell phone were on your waist, do you think this would expose your body to radiation? Answers will vary.

6. What would you need to hear to convince you to not use your cell phone? Answers will vary.

Search the Net

Use a search engine such as Google, Yahoo, Ask. com, AltaVista, Excite, Dogpile, or Lycos to find the most recent research on the dangers of radiation from cell phones. Summarize your findings, and comment on the validity and relevance of the research. For suggested Web sites and other research activities, go to http://www. ablongman.com/smith/.

Contemporary *Focus*

Do you believe that boys and girls are brought up to express themselves differently? Are boys and girls rewarded differently at a young age? How is a typical male defined in American culture?

Boys' Perceptions of the Male Role

By Randolph H. Watts Jr. and L. DiAnne Borders
The Journal of Men's Studies, January 31, 2005

Participants for this study were a sample of high school aged boys currently enrolled in North Carolina public schools who were members of a local youth organization.

Participants robustly supported the gender role conflict theme of restricted affectionate behavior between men. Many of the participants said that they could not share their feelings of affection with their friends for fear of criticism. "You would never know if a guy liked another guy 'cause they would never talk about it," said one participant. If feelings were shared, "People would tease him or something." Another participant said, "I know that if I share with some of my friends, they just laugh in my face. And be like, 'Man, you're gay.' "

One participant articulated the reason why boys might fear expressing feelings to one another: "'Cause they've developed that unspoken code, you know. They know, if I do this to this guy, pat him on the back or something, some people might look at it in a different light and make some assumptions."

Some participants said that they simply did not have feelings of affection for male friends. "Well, yeah. I don't really have like . . . emotions for other guys. I mean . . . Or, yeah, friendship. But like, love? I don't love any guys!" Other participants were willing to share feelings of affection, but said they did so knowing that there would be retribution or ridicule. One boy, who claimed that he was pretty open about sharing his emotions, said that he would share his feelings with another boy: "And when I share with him, for example, he'll just laugh at me."

COLLABORATE Collaborate on responses to the following questions:

➤ Are boys taught not to show affection? If so, how?

➤ What purpose do fraternities serve in college?

➤ How do males bond?

Skill Development: Preview

Preview the next selection to predict its purpose and organization and to formulate your learning plan.

Activate Schema

What happy memories do you have of your childhood?
Who were the class bullies when you were in school?

Establish a Purpose for Reading

The author is making an argument about how boys become men. Read to understand his argument, weigh the support, and to determine your position on the issue.

Integrate Knowledge While Reading

Questions have been inserted in the margin to stimulate your thinking while reading. Remember to

Predict	Picture	Relate	Monitor	Correct

HOW BOYS BECOME MEN

Two nine-year-old boys, neighbors and friends, were walking home from school. The one in the bright blue windbreaker was laughing and swinging a heavy-looking book bag toward the head of his friend, who kept ducking and stepping back. "What's the matter?" asked the kid with the bag, whooshing it over his head. "You chicken?"

5   His friend stopped, stood still and braced himself. The bag slammed into the side of his face, the thump audible all the way across the street where I stood watching. The impact knocked him to the ground, where he lay mildly stunned for a second. Then he struggled up, rubbing the side of his head. "See?" he said proudly. "I'm no chicken."

Is this definition of manhood learned or genetically programmed?

10   No. A chicken would probably have had the sense to get out of the way. This boy was already well on the road to becoming a *man*, having learned one of the central ethics of his gender: Experience pain rather than show fear.

Women tend to see men as a giant problem in need of solution. They tell us that we're remote and uncommunicative, that we need to demonstrate less
15 machismo and more commitment, more humanity. But if you don't understand something about boys, you can't understand why men are the way we are, why we find it so difficult to make friends or to acknowledge our fears and problems.

Boys live in a world with its own Code of Conduct, a set of ruthless, unspoken, and unyielding rules:

20   Don't be a goody-goody.
Never rat. If your parents ask about bruises, shrug.
Never admit fear. Ride the roller coaster, join a fistfight, do what you have to do. Asking for help is for sissies.

Does this code of conduct cross cultural boundaries?

25   Empathy is for nerds. You can help your best buddy, under certain circumstances. Everyone else is on his own.
Never discuss anything of substance with anybody. Grunt, shrug, dump on teachers, laugh at wimps, talk about comic books. Anything else is risky.

Paul A. Souders/Corbis

A soccer game turns violent.

Boys are rewarded for throwing hard. Most other activities—reading, befriending girls, or just thinking—are considered weird. And if there's one thing boys don't
30 want to be, it's weird.

More than anything else, boys are supposed to learn how to handle themselves. I remember the bitter fifth-grade conflict I touched off by elbowing aside a bigger boy named Barry and seizing the cafeteria's last carton of chocolate milk. Teased for getting aced out by a wimp, he had to reclaim his place in the pack. Our fistfight, at
35 recess, ended with my knees buckling and my lip bleeding while my friends, sympathetic but out of range, watched resignedly.

When I got home, my mother took one look at my swollen face and screamed. I wouldn't tell her anything, but when my father got home I cracked and confessed, pleading with them to do nothing. Instead, they called Barry's parents, who re-
40 stricted his television for a week.

The following morning, Barry and six of his pals stepped out from behind a stand of trees. "It's the rat," said Barry.

I bled a little more. *Rat* was scrawled in crayon across my desk.

They were waiting for me after school for a number of afternoons to follow. I
45 tried varying my routes and avoiding bushes and hedges. It usually didn't work.

I was as ashamed for telling as I was frightened. "You did ask for it," said my best friend. Frontier Justice has nothing on Boy Justice.

In panic, I appealed to a cousin who was several years older. He followed me home from school, and when Barry's gang surrounded me, he came barreling toward
50 us. "Stay away from my cousin," he shouted, "or I'll kill you."

After they were gone, however, my cousin could barely stop laughing. "You were afraid of *them*?" he howled. "They barely came up to my waist."

Men remember receiving little mercy as boys; maybe that's why it's sometimes difficult for them to show any.

55 "I know lots of men who had happy childhoods, but none who have happy memories of the way other boys treated them," says a friend. "It's a macho marathon from third grade up, when you start butting each other in the stomach."

Is there an age at which male friendships do change and become more supportive?

"The thing is," adds another friend, "you learn early on to hide what you feel. It's never safe to say 'I'm scared.' My girlfriend asks me why I don't talk more about 60 what I'm feeling. I've gotten better at it, but it will *never* come naturally."

You don't need to be a shrink to see how the lessons boys learn affect their behavior as men. Men are being asked, more and more, to show sensitivity, but they dread the very word. They struggle to build their increasingly uncertain work lives but will deny they're in trouble. They want love, affection, and support but don't 65 know how to ask for them. They hide their weaknesses and fears from all, even those they care for. They've learned to be wary of intervening when they see others in trouble. They often still balk at being stigmatized as weird.

Some men get shocked into sensitivity—when they lose their jobs, their wives, or their lovers. Others learn it through a strong marriage, or through their 70 own children.

It may be a long while, however, before male culture evolves to the point that boys can learn more from one another than how to hit curve balls. Last month, walking my dog past the playground near my house, I saw three boys encircling a fourth, laughing and pushing him. He was skinny and rumpled, and he looked 75 frightened. One boy knelt behind him while another pushed him from the front, a trick familiar to any former boy. He fell backward.

When the others ran off, he brushed the dirt off his elbows and walked toward the swings. His eyes were moist and he was struggling for control.

"Hi," I said through the chain-link fence. "How ya doing?"

80 "Fine," he said quickly, kicking his legs out and beginning his swing.

(995 words)

—Jon Katz,
Reprinted by permission of SLL/Sterling Lord Literistic, Inc.
Copyright 1993 by Jon Katz. Originally published in *Glamour*.

Recall

Stop to self-test, relate, and react.

Your instructor may choose to give you a true-false comprehension review.

Skill Development: Think Critically

Apply the four-step format for evaluating the argument. Use the perforations to tear out this page for your instructor.

- **Step 1.** Identify the position on the issue. State the main point the author is arguing.

  Boys grow up learning a ruthless code of conduct that affects their behavior
  as men.

- **Step 2.** Identify the support in the argument. Make lettered lists of the major assertions of support.

  I. Boys grow up under a ruthless code of conduct that includes the following:

   A. Boys will experience pain rather than show fear.

   B. Boys should not be goody-goody.

   C. Boys should never rat.

   D. Boys should never admit fear or ask for help.

   E. Boys should not show empathy.

   F. Boys should not discuss matters of importance with anyone.

   G. Boys are supposed to learn how to handle themselves.

  II. As a consequence of the code of conduct, men exhibit the following behaviors:

   A. Men have trouble being sensitive.

   B. Men do not know how to ask for love, affection, and support.

   C. Men hide their weaknesses even from those they love.

   D. Men are slow to intervene when others are in trouble.

- **Step 3.** Evaluate the support. Comment on weaknesses in relevance, believability, and consistency for the assertions you listed in step 2. Label the fallacies. What support do you feel is missing?

  A–G: unproven generalizations. The argument is missing support; there is no statistical data.

- **Step 4.** Evaluate the argument. What is your overall evaluation and why?

  The argument is based on observation, reflection, anecdotes, and humor. While it is entertaining and logical, all support for the argument seems to be opinion rather than fact. No research studies or statistics are cited.

  What is your opinion on the issue? Answers will vary.

Write About the Selection

How might men get shocked into sensitivity through loss or marriage or children? Can this happen to women also?

Response Suggestion: Discuss an example of this kind of shock. What kind of sensitivity resulted?

Contemporary *Link*

If boys are indeed taught and rewarded differently, how is this later reflected in parenthood when affection is part of nurturing? How do boys learn to become good fathers? What cultural biases operate against fatherhood?

selection **3**

Check Your Comprehension

Inference   <u>c</u>   1. What is the best statement of the main idea of this selection?

    a. It is more difficult for boys than for girls to learn how to become responsible and fair-minded adults.

    b. Boys in today's world face a set of unspoken rules that put them in conflict with their parents.

    c. Boys grow up learning a code of conduct that affects adult male behavior.

    d. Boys in today's world are much more likely to break the unspoken rules because the rules limit their personal growth.

Inference   <u>c</u>   2. In telling the story of the two nine-year-old boys, the narrator is trying to explain

    a. what it is like to walk home from school with a friend.

    b. that courage is not easy to explain to school-age children.

    c. the kind of experiences that make boys into less sensitive men.

    d. why boys often behave with violence toward one another.

Inference   <u>b</u>   3. When the narrator mentions the "central ethics of his gender," he is referring to

    a. traditions of justice and honor for men.

    b. fundamental rules of male behavior.

    c. assessments of male moral character.

    d. rules that govern his own adult life.

Inference   <u>b</u>   4. The narrator indicates that the "Code of Conduct" is a set of rules that

    a. fathers teach to their sons.

    b. are unwritten yet understood.

    c. teach leadership and commitment.

    d. are emphasized by teachers.

Detail   <u>a</u>   5. According to the narrator, one of the worst things a boy can do is be

    a. different.

    b. uncommunicative.

    c. aggressive.

    d. friendly.

Inference   <u>c</u>   6. The narrator tells the story about himself in fifth grade primarily to illustrate that

    a. he had been an unusually fearful boy.

    b. his cousin liked protecting him from other boys.

    c. he had violated the Code of Conduct and suffered the consequences.

    d. his school had a lot of boys who picked on him.

Inference _____c_____ 7. The narrator says "I was as ashamed for telling as I was frightened" to illustrate that he

    a. grew tired of getting beaten up by classmates.
    b. thought his parents would get mad at him.
    c. felt pressure to live by the Code of Conduct.
    d. knew he had started it all by elbowing Barry.

Inference _____a_____ 8. The narrator uses the phrase "macho marathon" to suggest that the way boys treat each other in school

    a. seems to be never-ending.
    b. is physically exhausting.
    c. feels like a kind of workout.
    d. is ultimately channeled into organizational sports.

Detail _____b_____ 9. According to the author, men are most likely to

    a. readily admit when they are in trouble.
    b. hide weaknesses.
    c. intervene when others are in trouble.
    d. communicate feelings.

Inference _____c_____ 10. The story the narrator tells at the end, about the four boys on the playground, seems meant to show that the

    a. narrator had been shocked into sensitivity.
    b. narrator feels that male culture is evolving.
    c. boys of today are like boys have always been.
    d. boys who were playing were not really hurt.

Answer the following with *T* (true) or *F* (false).

Inference _____F_____ 11. The author concludes that men who learn not to fear pain as they are growing up build strong moral character in the process.

Inference _____F_____ 12. The narrator realized that the best solution was for Barry's father to be contacted about the fight.

Inference _____T_____ 13. The selection suggests that men dislike talking about their feelings because they learned not to talk about feelings when they were boys.

Detail _____F_____ 14. According to the author, although progress is slow, male culture is clearly evolving and becoming generally more sensitive.

Inference _____T_____ 15. The word "Fine" in the last line of the selection indicates that the young boy understands the "central ethic of his gender."

Search the Net

Use a search engine such as Google, Yahoo, Ask.com, Excite, Dogpile, or Lycos to find more information about the ways both boys and girls are taught their gender roles. How are these messages relayed to them, how do these messages differ, and are the messages only harmful or can they be beneficial as well? For suggested Web sites and other research activities, go to http://www.ablongman.com/smith/.

Vocabulary *Booster*

Lights, Camera, Action!

| **Roots** | *luc, lum*: "light" | *photo*: "light" |
| | *act, ag*: "to do" | |

Words with *luc, lum:* "light"

Mexican Christmas lanterns called *luminarias*—bags with sand and a lit candle inside—line streets and driveways not only in the Southwest but all over America at Christmas.

- *lucid:* clear; glowing with light; easily understood; sane

  The patient's statements were not *lucid* when she was brought into the psychiatric treatment center.

- *luminescence:* the giving off of light without heat

  A fluorescent light bulb or tube is a *luminescent* fixture that gives off light but remains cool when the mercury vapor inside the tube is acted upon by electrons.

- *luminous:* radiating or reflecting light; well-lighted; shining; enlightened

  Due to neon lighting on most of the buildings, Las Vegas is one of the most *luminous* cities in the United States at night.

- *luminary:* a celestial body; a person who is a shining example in a profession

  Muhammad Ali is still a *luminary* in the boxing world.

- *illuminate:* to supply with light; light up; to make lucid or clarify

  Let me *illuminate* the facts for you before you take misinformed action.

- *elucidate:* to make lucid or clear; explain

  Mario had to successfully *elucidate* details about his new invention to investors in order to get funding.

- *translucent:* allowing light to pass through without being transparent

  The Martinez family chose a *translucent* frosted glass that would provide privacy for the renovated bathroom.

Words with *photo:* "light"

The wrinkles and discolored skin on Brooke's face and hands were signs of *photoaging* from spending years in the sun without sunscreen protection.

- *photogenic:* having features that look attractive in a photograph

  The supermodel was extremely *photogenic,* and she could also act.

- *photography:* a process of producing images on sensitized surfaces by the chemical action of light or other forms of radiant energy

  Sensitized film in a camera receiving sunlight or flash lighting by opening the camera's aperture or eye is a form of *photography.*

- *photogrammetry:* the process of making surveys and maps through the use of aerial photographs

  The surveying firm had its own small airplane for taking aerial photos to use in the *photogrammetry* project for the National Park Service.

- *photosensitivity:* quality of being photosensitive; abnormal sensitivity of the skin to ultraviolet light

  Some prescription drugs can cause *photosensitivity,* requiring avoidance of the sun or use of a sunscreen.

- *telephoto lens:* a camera lens that produces a large image of distant or small objects

  George's *telephoto lens* made it possible to get close-up pictures of the inaccessible waterfall.

- *photocopy:* a duplicate of a document or print made on specialized copying equipment

  Xerox, the name of the first and most well-known *photocopy* machine manufacturer, is the word commonly used to mean "copy."

Words with *act, ag:* "to do"

The *actors* and *actresses* were waiting offstage for their cues to go onstage during Act Three of the play.

- *act:* anything done, being done, or to be done; a formal decision, law, or statute; a main division of a play

  A clown performing a magic *act* entertained the children at the six-year-old's birthday party.

- *activate:* to make active; to place a military unit on active status

  Before using her new credit card, Sheila *activated* it by calling a telephone number to notify the company that she received the card.

- *activism:* the practice of achieving political or other goals through actions of protest or demonstration

  During the 1960s, *activism* was used to protest the Vietnam War and civil rights injustices in the United States.

- *agent:* a representative working on behalf of another

  Toby's *agent* promised to get him a film role before the end of the year.

- *agency:* an organization that provides a particular service; the place of business of an agent

  The FBI is an *agency* of the U.S. government.

- *agenda:* a list or outline of things to be done or matters to be acted or voted upon

  A vote for a new accounting firm to represent the company was on the *agenda* for the annual stockholders' meeting.

- *acting:* serving as a temporary substitute during another's absence; the art of performing in plays, films, etc.

  While the city mayor was out on maternity leave, one of the council members served as *acting* mayor.

REVIEW

Part I

Indicate whether the following statements are true (*T*) or false (*F*):

___T___ 1. If you enjoy working with figures, a position as an Internal Revenue *agent* might be a job to consider.

___T___ 2. When she began to date another man, her boyfriend considered her behavior an *act* of betrayal.

___T___ 3. Some home security systems are *activated* by movement.

___T___ 4. Your local township surely has an *agency* devoted to helping the homeless find shelter.

___F___ 5. *Photogenic* students do not look attractive in most pictures.

___F___ 6. A *telephoto lens* is used to reduce the size of the object being photographed.

___T___ 7. When high-ranking executives leave their positions, companies ordinarily appoint someone to serve as an *acting* authority until a suitable replacement can be found.

___F___ 8. The word *photocopy* is a synonym for the word *plagiarize.*

___T___ 9. Someone who has just experienced a trauma might not be totally *lucid.*

___F___ 10. People in the business of nature *photography* probably have little interest in the outdoors.

Part II

Choose an antonym from the boxed list for each of the words below.

activism	photoaging	illuminate	photosensitivity
agent	luminous	activate	luminary

11. unknown _____luminary_____

12. reacting to dark _____photosensitivity_____

13. positive effects of sun on skin _____photoaging_____

14. adversary _____agent_____

15. apathy _____activism_____

16. turn off _____activate_____

17. dull _____luminous_____

18. to darken _____illuminate_____

10 Graphic Illustrations

- What do graphics do?
- What is a diagram?
- What does a table do?
- What is most helpful on a typical map?
- What does a pie graph represent?
- How do you read a bar graph?
- What is a line graph?
- What information does a flowchart convey?

Rafal Olbinski. *Castles Around the Baltic*, 1997. Acrylic on canvas. 32 x 22 inches.

What Graphics Do

If a picture is worth a thousand words, a graphic illustration is worth at least several pages of facts and figures. Graphics express complex interrelationships in simplified form. Instead of plodding through repetitious data, you can glance at a chart, a map, or a graph and immediately see how everything fits together as well as how one part compares with another. Instead of reading several lengthy paragraphs and trying to visualize comparisons, you can study an organized design. The graphic illustration is a logically constructed aid for understanding many small bits of information.

Graphic illustrations are generally used for the following reasons:

1. **To condense.** Pages of repetitious, detailed information can be organized into one explanatory design.
2. **To clarify.** Processes and interrelationships can be more clearly defined through visual representations.
3. **To convince.** Developing trends and gross inequities can be forcefully dramatized.

Reader's *Tip* —— How to Read Graphic Material

- **Read the title to get an overview.** What is it about?
- **Look for footnotes and read introductory material.**
  Identify the who, where, and how.
  How and when were the data collected?
  Who collected the data?
  How many persons were included in the survey?
  Do the researchers seem to have been objective or biased?
  Taking all this information into account, does the study seem valid?
- **Read the labels.**
  What do the vertical columns and the horizontal rows represent?
  Are the numbers in thousands or millions?
  What does the legend represent?
- **Notice the trends and find the extremes.**
  What are the highest and lowest rates?
  What is the average rate?
  How do the extremes compare with the total?
  What is the percentage of increase or decrease?
- **Draw conclusions and formulate future exam questions.**
  What does the information mean?
  What purpose does the information serve?
  What wasn't included?
  What else is there to know about the subject?

There are five kinds of graphic illustrations: (1) diagrams, (2) tables, (3) maps, (4) graphs, and (5) flowcharts. All are used in textbooks, and the choice of which is best to use depends on the type of material presented. This chapter contains explanations and exercises for the five types of graphic illustrations. Read the explanations, study the illustrations, and respond to the questions as instructed. The Reader's Tip gets you started by summarizing how to read graphics to get the most information from them.

Diagrams

A **diagram** is an outline drawing or picture of an object or a process. It shows the labeled parts of a complicated form, such as the muscles of the human body, the organizational makeup of a company's management and production teams, or the flow of nutrients in a natural ecological system.

exercise 10.1 **Diagrams**

The diagrams display the major structures of the human ear. Refer to the diagram to respond to the following statements with *T* (true), *F* (false), or *CT* (can't tell).

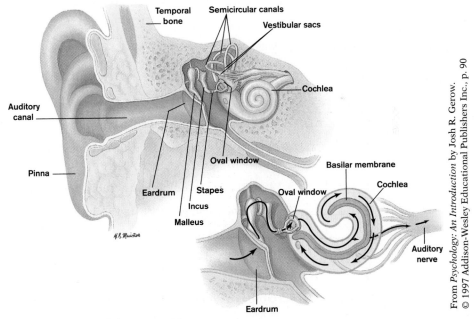

Major Structures of the Human Ear

From *Psychology: An Introduction* by Josh R. Gerow. © 1997 Addison-Wesley Educational Publishers Inc., p. 90

_____T_____ 1. Sound enters the ear through the auditory canal.

_____F_____ 2. The cochlea can be seen by looking through the auditory canal.

_____T_____ 3. Sound travels through the cochlea to the auditory nerve.

____CT____ 4. Most hearing problems result from damage to the eardrum.

____F____ 5. The nerves in the pinna conduct sound directly to the oval window.

____T____ 6. The basilar membrane is a part of the cochlea.

____T____ 7. The malleus, incus, and stapes are positioned to transmit sound from the eardrum to the oval window.

____F____ 8. According to the diagram, the semicircular canals contain the basilar membrane.

____CT____ 9. If punctured, the eardrum cannot be adequately repaired.

____T____ 10. The cochlea could be described as snail-like in appearance.

11. The purpose of each diagram is _to show the arrangement of the parts of the inner and outer ear._

Tables

A **table** is a listing of facts and figures in columns and rows for quick and easy reference. The information in the columns and rows is usually labeled in two different directions. First read the title for the topic and then read the footnotes to judge the source. Determine what each column represents and how they interact.

exercise 10.2 **Tables**

Refer to the table shown on page 537 to respond to the following statements with *T* (true), *F* (false), or *CT* (can't tell).

____T____ 1. Of the salad greens listed, a cup of watercress has the fewest calories.

____T____ 2. A cup of chicory has over three times as much vitamin A as a cup of spinach.

____F____ 3. Arugula has three times as much vitamin A as iceberg lettuce.

____T____ 4. All of the salad greens listed contain calcium and potassium.

____T____ 5. Of the salad greens listed, chicory is highest in all categories.

____CT____ 6. Iceberg lettuce is the most popular salad green served in the United States.

____F____ 7. Of the salad greens listed, iceberg lettuce is the lowest in all categories.

____T____ 8. Much of the calcium in spinach is not available for use in the body.

____F____ 9. For those who do not like chicory, red cabbage is the next best salad green choice for potassium.

10. The purpose of this chart is _to list the nutritional value of a variety of salad greens._

ADDING MORE SALADS TO YOUR DIET

Salads add variety to your diet and balance out the average American's meat-and-potatoes diet. Use this information to choose healthful salad greens and toppings for your salad.

NUTRITIONAL COMPARISON OF SALAD GREEN SERVINGS

Salad Green	Calories	Vitamin A (IU)	Vitamin C (mg)	Potassium (mg)	Calcium (mg)
Arugula (rocket, roquette)	5	480	3	74	32
Butterhead lettuce (Boston, Bibb)	7	534	4	141	18
Cabbage, red	19	28	40	144	36
Chicory	41	7,200	43	756	180
Endive	8	1,025	3	157	26
Fennel	27	117	10	360	43
Iceberg lettuce	7	182	2	87	10
Leaf lettuce	10	1,064	10	148	38
Romaine lettuce	8	1,456	13	162	20
Spinach	7	2,015	8	167	30*
Watercress	4	1,598	15	112	41

Note: Serving size is one cup; IU = International Units, mg = milligrams

*Much not available to body for use

Source: Rebecca Donatelle, *Access to Health*, 8th ed.

Maps

Traditional **maps,** such as road maps and atlas maps, show the location of cities, waterways, sites, and roads, as well as the differences in the physical terrain of specified areas. A modern use of the map as a visual aid is to highlight special characteristics or population distributions of a particular area. For example, a map of the United States might highlight all states with gun control laws in red and all states without gun control laws in blue.

Begin reading a map by noting the title and source. The legend of a map, which usually appears in a corner box, explains the meanings of symbols and shading.

exercise 10.3 ## Maps

Read the following passage about national exports and state economies. Then use the legend on the map shown on page 538 to help you respond to the subsequent statements with *T* (true), *F* (false), or *CT* (can't tell).

STATE ECONOMIES

All states are affected by the global economy, but some states are more dependent on it. Exports are a larger fraction of their economies. For example, the state of Washington, with its aerospace, fishing, and logging industries, depends most heavily on trade with other countries. Exports account for nearly 20 percent of Washington State's economy.

Most of the top exporting states are located on the nation's borders, which gives them easier access to other countries. For example, the state of Washington abuts Canada, and its seaports are a departure point for goods destined for Asia.

Thomas E. Patterson, *We the People: A Concise Introduction to American Politics,* 5th ed., p. 561 (2004). Reprinted by permission of The McGraw-Hill Companies.

_____T_____ 1. The western states bordering the Pacific Ocean are all among the highest exporters in the nation.

_____F_____ 2. Each island state exports more than 5 percent of its total economy.

_____F_____ 3. Each state bordering the Atlantic Ocean exports 3 percent or more of its total economy.

_____CT_____ 4. Nevada does not export more than 5 percent of its total economy because gambling is legal in Nevada.

_____F_____ 5. Each state bordering Canada exports 3 percent or more of its total economy.

_____T_____ 6. Each state bordering Mexico exports 3 percent or more of its total economy.

_____CT_____ 7. Florida and Maine export the same dollar amount of goods.

_____T_____ 8. Only 18 states export more than 5 percent of their total economies.

_____T_____ 9. Although the map shows they export the same percentage, California and Arizona could differ on the actual dollar amounts exported because their total state economies could be different.

_____F_____ 10. Tennessee and Kentucky are higher exporters than New York and Pennsylvania.

11. The purpose of the map is to compare states according to export level, which is defined as a percentage of the state's total economy, and to show each as a member of a high, intermediate, or low group.

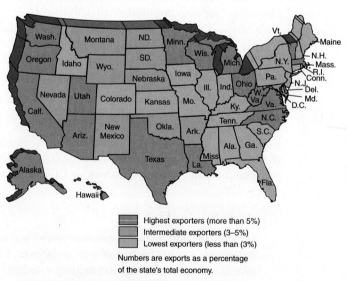

Highest exporters (more than 5%)
Intermediate exporters (3–5%)
Lowest exporters (less than (3%)

Numbers are exports as a percentage
of the state's total economy.

National Exports and State Economies

Source: *U.S. Census Bureau,* in Thomas E. Patterson, *We the People: A Concise Introduction to American Politics,* 5th ed., p. 561 (2004). Reprinted by permission of The McGraw-Hill Companies.

exercise 10.4   **Geographic Review**

Use the map below to test your knowledge of world geography.

CITIZENS OF THE WORLD SHOW LITTLE KNOWLEDGE OF GEOGRAPHY

In the spring of 1988, twelve thousand people in ten nations were asked to identify sixteen places on the following world map. The average citizen in the United States could identify barely more than half. Believe it or not, 14 percent of Americans tested could not even find their own country on the map. Despite years of fighting in Vietnam, 68 percent could not locate this Southeast Asian country. Such lack of basic geographic knowledge is quite common throughout the world. Here is the average score for each of the ten countries in which the test was administered.

Country	Average Score	Country	Average Score
Sweden	11.6	United States	8.6
West Germany	11.2	Britain	8.5
Japan	9.7	Italy	7.6
France	9.3	Mexico	7.4
Canada	9.2	Former Soviet Union	7.4

How would you do? To take the test, match the numbers on the map to the places listed.

—Robert L. Lineberry et al.,
Government in America

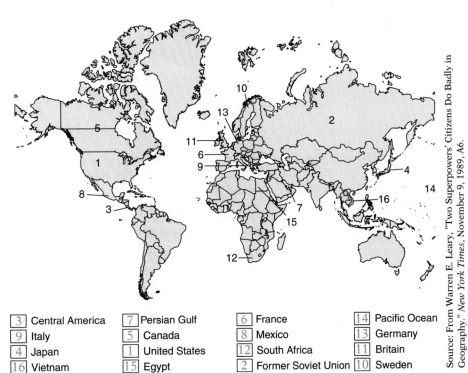

3 Central America	7 Persian Gulf	6 France	14 Pacific Ocean
9 Italy	5 Canada	8 Mexico	13 Germany
4 Japan	1 United States	12 South Africa	11 Britain
16 Vietnam	15 Egypt	2 Former Soviet Union	10 Sweden

Source: From Warren E. Leary, "Two Superpowers' Citizens Do Badly in Geography." *New York Times*, November 9, 1989, A6.

Pie Graphs

A **pie graph** is a circle divided into wedge-shaped slices. The complete pie or circle represents a total, or 100 percent. Each slice is a percentage or fraction of that whole. Budgets, such as the annual expenditure of the federal or state governments, are frequently illustrated by pie graphs.

exercise 10.5   **Pie Graphs**

Refer to the pie graphs shown here to respond to the following statements with *T* (true), *F* (false), or *CT* (can't tell). Note that the figures are percentages rather than actual numbers.

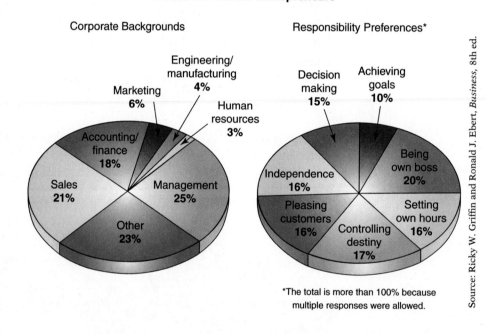

Profiles of Women Entrepreneurs

Source: Ricky W. Griffin and Ronald J. Ebert, *Business*, 8th ed.

_____T_____   1. Women who have been in management are more likely to be entrepreneurs than women who have been in other fields, such as teaching and nursing.

_____T_____   2. According to the graph, women with managerial experience make up the largest segment of entrepreneurs.

_____CT_____ 3. Female entrepreneurs with corporate backgrounds in management and sales are more likely to be successful than those who were employed in human resources and marketing. _____

The percentages do not measure success.

_____T_____   4. Women entrepreneurs rate being their own boss twice as important to them as the achievement of goals.

___F___ 5. Women entrepreneurs value making decisions slightly more than their ability to control their own destiny at work.

___T___ 6. There are over three times as many female entrepreneurs from accounting/finance backgrounds as there are from engineering/manufacturing fields.

7. The purpose of the pie graphs is to <u>show the corporate backgrounds of women entrepreneurs and to show what they like about running their own businesses.</u>

Bar Graphs

A **bar graph** is a series of horizontal or vertical bars in which the length of each bar represents a particular amount or number of what is being discussed. A series of different items can be quickly compared by noting the different bar lengths.

exercise 10.6 | **Bar Graphs**

Refer to the bar graph shown on page 542 to respond to the following statements with *T* (true), *F* (false), or *CT* (can't tell)

___F___ 1. No more than seven professions and technical fields are listed in which women make up the majority of workers.

___T___ 2. Fewer than one-third of computer systems analysts are women.

___T___ 3. College teachers are more likely to be male than female.

___T___ 4. The fields of social work and vocational/educational counseling have approximately the same percentage of male workers.

___CT___ 5. More females are accountants than are auditors.

___CT___ 6. According to the graph, the actual number of female elementary school teachers is greater than the number of female health technicians.

___F___ 7. Women make up only one-quarter of the workers who are natural scientists.

___T___ 8. A greater percentage of men teach in high school than teach elementary students.

___T___ 9. Men make up a lower percentage of workers in the field of nursing than in any other profession listed.

___T___ 10. Of the total workers in the field, the percent of women who are medical doctors exceeds the percent who are dentists.

11. The purpose of the bar graph is <u>to show the percentages of women employees in particular professions and technical fields.</u>

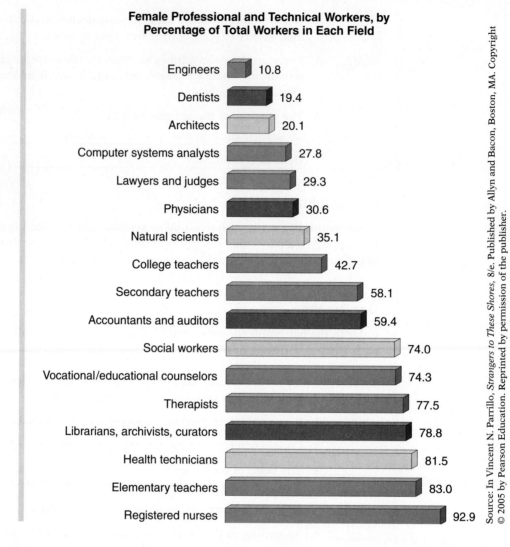

Female Professional and Technical Workers, by Percentage of Total Workers in Each Field

Engineers 10.8
Dentists 19.4
Architects 20.1
Computer systems analysts 27.8
Lawyers and judges 29.3
Physicians 30.6
Natural scientists 35.1
College teachers 42.7
Secondary teachers 58.1
Accountants and auditors 59.4
Social workers 74.0
Vocational/educational counselors 74.3
Therapists 77.5
Librarians, archivists, curators 78.8
Health technicians 81.5
Elementary teachers 83.0
Registered nurses 92.9

Source: In Vincent N. Parrillo, *Strangers to These Shores*, 8/e. Published by Allyn and Bacon, Boston, MA. Copyright © 2005 by Pearson Education. Reprinted by permission of the publisher.

Cumulative Bar Graphs

Both bar graphs and line graphs can be designed to show cumulative effects in which all the lines or segments add up to the top line or total amount. Rather than having multiple bars or lines, the groups are stacked on top of each other to dramatically show differences. The bar graph shown here illustrates a cumulative effect.

exercise 10.7   **Cumulative Bar Graphs**

Refer to the cumulative bar graph on page 543 to respond to the following statements with *T* (true), *F* (false), or *CT* (can't tell).

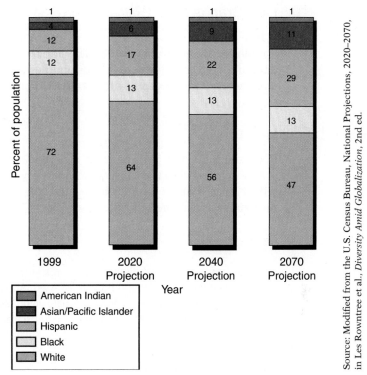

Source: Modified from the U.S. Census Bureau, National Projections, 2020–2070, in Les Rowntree et al., *Diversity Amid Globalization*, 2nd ed.

Projected U.S. Ethnic Composition, 1999 to 2070

_____F_____ 1. From 1999 to 2070, the percentage of the population of American Indians is expected to shrink.

_____T_____ 2. In each projected year, the percentage of the population that is white decreases.

_____F_____ 3. From 1999 to 2070, the percentage of Hispanics in the population more than triples.

_____F_____ 4. The black percentage of the population decreases between 2020 and 2070.

_____T_____ 5. Asian/Pacific Islanders as a percentage of the total population increase at a higher rate than blacks from 1999 to 2070.

_____CT_____ 6. The number of African Americans in the population is not projected to increase from 2020 to 2070.

_____T_____ 7. In 2070, whites and Asian/Pacific Islanders are projected to comprise more than half the population.

8. The purpose of the bar graph is to project the percentage of five ethnic groups in the composition of the total United States population until 2070.

Line Graphs

A **line graph** is a continuous curve or frequency distribution in which numbers are plotted in an unbroken line. The horizontal scale measures one aspect of the data and the vertical line measures another aspect. As the data fluctuate, the line will change direction and, with extreme differences, will become very jagged.

exercise 10.8 | **Line Graphs**

Read the following passage from a psychology text, and then examine the line graph to respond to the subsequent questions with *T* (true), *F* (false), or *CT* (can't tell). Notice that the graph's horizontal axis indicates age, and the vertical axis measures the average self-esteem score on a 5-point scale.

SELF-ESTEEM

In a cross-sectional study of self-esteem a large, diverse sample of 326,641 individuals between the ages of 9 and 90 was assessed. About two-thirds of the participants were from the United States. The individuals were asked to respond to the item, "I have high self-esteem," on the following 5-point scale:

—Adapted from John W. Santrock, *Life-Span Development*, 9th ed.

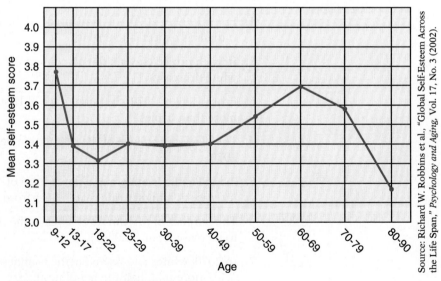

Self-Esteem Across the Life Span

Source: Richard W. Robbins et al., "Global Self-Esteem Across the Life Span," *Psychology and Aging*, Vol. 17, No. 3 (2002).

_____T_____ 1. Teenagers report lower self-esteem than do adults in their sixties.

_____T_____ 2. The decline in self-esteem measures from the ages of 9–12 to 13–17 is slightly less than the drop from the ages of 70–79 to 80–90.

___F___ 3. According to the graph, the two groups with the highest self-esteem ratings are adults of ages 60–69 and those of ages 70–79.

___T___ 4. Self-esteem measures show little variation from the ages of 23 to 49.

___CT___ 5. Self-esteem ratings increase after graduation from college because students have proved to themselves that they are capable of obtaining a degree and getting a job.

___T___ 6. Adult self-esteem ratings peak at ages 60–69.

___T___ 7. Self-esteem rises at approximately the same rate from the years 40–49 to 50–59 as it does from the years 50–59 to 60–69.

___T___ 8. On average, self-esteem ratings for all groups were more positive than negative.

9. The purpose of the line graph is _to show how various groups differed_ _in terms of self-esteem ratings._

Flowcharts

A **flowchart** shows the sequence of a set of elements and the relationships among them. Flowcharts were first used in computer programming. Key ideas are stated in boxes, and supporting ideas are linked by arrows. In the flowchart shown on page 546, arrows point toward a progression of steps required for a bill to become a law in the United States.

exercise 10.9 **Flowcharts**

Bills introduced in the U.S. House of Representatives or Senate follow a specific path before being passed into laws. Refer to the flowchart on page 546 to respond to the following statements with *T* (true), *F* (false), or *CT* (can't tell).

___F___ 1. If a bill is introduced in the Senate, the chart indicates that it can be debated in the House before it is passed in the Senate.

___T___ 2. After both the House and Senate vote on a bill, it goes to the Conference Committee.

___T___ 3. The House has a Rules Committee action stage that the Senate does not have.

___T___ 4. The president can veto and override a bill that has been passed and approved by both the House and Senate.

___F___ 5. Full Senate debate on a bill occurs before the full committee report.

___CT___ 6. If a bill has solid support from both the House and Senate, the president usually signs the bill into law.

7. The purpose of the flowchart is _to show the steps necessary for a bill_ _to become law._

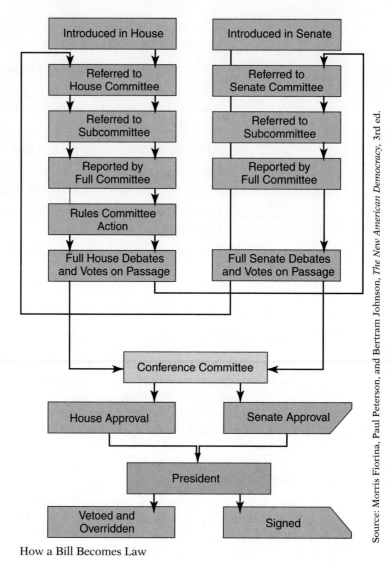

How a Bill Becomes Law

Source: Morris Fiorina, Paul Peterson, and Bertram Johnson, *The New American Democracy*, 3rd ed.

Summary *Points*

➤ **What do graphics do?**
Graphic illustrations condense, clarify, and convince. They express complex interrelationships in simplified form.

➤ **What is a diagram?**
A diagram is an outline drawing or picture of an object or a process with labeled parts.

➤ **What does a table do?**
A table lists facts and figures in columns for quick and easy reference. You must determine what the columns represent and how they interact.

➤ **What is most helpful on a typical map?**
The legend on a map of a geographic area explains the symbols and shading used to convey information.

➤ **What does a pie graph represent?**
A pie graph depicts a total, or 100 percent, divided into wedge-shaped slices.

➤ **How do you read a bar graph?**
You must determine what the length of each horizontal or vertical bar represents.

➤ **What is a line graph?**
A line graph represents a frequency distribution. To read a point on the continuous line, you must identify what the horizontal and vertical scales measure.

➤ **What information does a flowchart convey?**
A flowchart provides a diagram of the relationship and sequence of events of a group of elements. Key ideas usually appear in boxes, and arrows are used to connect the elements.

selection
1

selection 1 Economics

Contemporary *Focus*

In 1956 Prince Rainier of Monaco married Philadelphia film star Grace Kelly and made her a princess. The fifteen hundred reporters covering the wedding gave Monaco instant jet-set fame. What is the fascination of this tiny principality of 32,000 citizens, less than one square mile in area and breathtakingly perched above the French Riviera, overlooking the Mediterranean Sea?

Monaco Cleans Up Its Act

By Sarah Maxwell
Business Traveller, March 1, 2006

Monaco, once dubbed by Somerset Maugham as a "sunny place for shady people," is taking a gamble. To persuade the world it is more than a tax-free playground for rich eccentrics and racing drivers, the principality is pursuing an enthusiastic marketing campaign. From now on, it's out with the playboy elite and in with high-end business travel, whether for meetings, incentives, conferences or exhibitions.

Monaco has always attracted wealthy, image-conscious Europeans, who visited for the glamorous casinos, Grand Prix and exclusive shopping streets. But 9/11 brought a sharp reduction in American visitors keen to glimpse the fairytale home of the late Princess Grace Kelly (Prince Albert's mother). Their absence is noticeable. Visitors in 2004 were 17 percent lower than in 2000 and overall hotel occupancy stood at 58 percent.

Monaco is keen to encourage its visitors to stay for longer, but here it may struggle. Once you have marveled at the rows of sparkling yachts in Fontvieille, wandered through the magnificent gaming hall of the Monte Carlo Casino and hung around outside the Royal Palace for the changing of the guard, you've seen most of the best bits. Monte Carlo still has a Disneyland-for-the-rich quality about it; so much so that if you stay too long it feels as though you might begin to leak money. Just breathing the air on Casino Square feels expensive.

 Collaborate on responses to the following questions:

➤ Why is Monaco tax free?

➤ Why do tourists visit Monaco?

➤ Who rules Monaco now?

Skill Development: Preview

Preview the next selection to predict its purpose and organization and to formulate your learning plan.

Activate Schema

Why might tourism be down in Monaco?
Does the new ruler of Monaco have a family?

Establish a Purpose for Reading

The economy of the tiny principality of Monaco is unique. Read to learn how the citizens and the government make money to support themselves.

Increase Word Knowledge

What do you know about these words?

fitfully	sovereignty	reigning	succeeded	suffrage
engendered	solicited	constrained	haven	sever

Your instructor may give a true-false vocabulary review before or after reading.

Integrate Knowledge While Reading

Questions have been inserted in the margin to stimulate your thinking while reading. Remember to:

Predict	Picture	Relate	Monitor	Correct

THE PRINCIPALITY OF MONACO

Located on the Mediterranean Sea, surrounded on three sides by southeastern France, the tiny Principality of Monaco dates from the Middle Ages. Since the end of the thirteenth century, Monaco has been ruled by the Grimaldi Family. Its independence, although tolerated somewhat fitfully by the French for centuries, was
5 formally guaranteed by the Second Empire in 1861. After World War I, the French renewed their guarantee but imposed several major restrictions on Monaco's sovereignty—under the terms of a 1918 treaty, Monaco agreed to adopt no domestic and foreign policies that would be contrary to French political, economic, and military interests. A year later, the House of Grimaldi signed another treaty with the French,
10 which granted France the right to incorporate the principality should the reigning prince die without an heir.

Was Monaco once part of France?

In 1911, Prince Albert approved the country's first Constitution. His successor, Prince Louis II, reigned from 1922 until his death in 1949, at which time he was succeeded by his grandson, Prince Rainier III. In 1962, Prince Rainier approved a
15 new Constitution, which, among other things, granted universal suffrage, guaranteed the rights of association and trade unionism, abolished the death penalty, and provided for a more equal distribution of legislative power between the monarchy and the popularly elected National Council. This Constitution closely followed trends in France.

DEVELOPMENT

20 Prince Rainier has overseen a very successful diversification of Monaco's economy during his rule. No longer is the principality viewed solely as a tourist spot, though that sector of the economy continues to be important.

Monaco rates high in civil liberties and political rights. With no defense forces of its own, the principality relies on France to guarantee its security. Monaco's for-
25 eign relations are for the most part directed from Paris.

Monaco is the second smallest independent state in the world (after Vatican City). In essence, Monaco has been a one-party state since 1962, when its two largest political parties, the National Union of Independents and the National Democratic Entente, merged to form the National and Democratic Union (UND). The UND
30 represents political interests most closely aligned with the policies of Prince Rainier.

What makes Monaco a state, not a country?

THE ECONOMY

Prior to World War II, Monaco's economy depended almost exclusively on two related industries: tourism and gambling. Revenues from the famous Monte Carlo
Casino alone constituted more than 90 percent of the government's revenues.
Meanwhile, the absence of income and estate taxes attracted wealthy foreigners
35 wishing to avoid taxation elsewhere. By the time Prince Rainier came to power,
however, the liabilities of Monaco's one-dimensional economy and the international
reputation it had engendered were becoming painfully obvious. The European
tourist trade had become increasingly competitive, and France's growing impatience
with what it had come to view as the parasite on its southern flank threatened seri-
40 ous damage to French–Monégasque relations.

What made France view Monaco as a "parasite"?

Prince Rainier launched a successful campaign to diversify the principality's
economy. Since the late 1950s, Monaco has actively solicited light-manufacturing
industries from abroad. It now produces and exports a number of products, including electronic components, automotive parts, pharmaceuticals, and beauty prod-
45 ucts. By 1986, more than 25 percent of its total workforce were employed in the industrial sector. In recent years, Monaco has also experienced rapid growth in some
service industries, such as banking and commercial exchanges. Tourism still accounts for an estimated one quarter of Monaco's total income; however, the state
has also taken steps to diversify and stabilize this sector. While Monaco still has no
50 income or estate tax, casino receipts probably account for less than 4 percent of
government revenues. Most government revenues are now generated by value-
added taxes on goods and services, including hotels and industry. The government's
budget is thought to be in surplus as a result.

Why would a diverse economy be important to Monaco?

Though impressive to date, the economic transformation of Monaco has been
55 heavily influenced, if not constrained, by the French. The French government's concern over lost tax revenues in the early 1960s forced Monaco to accede to the French
demand that all corporations conducting less than 25 percent of their business in the
principality come under the French financial system. Today, French citizens with
fewer than five years' residence in Monaco are taxed at French rates. Monaco is com-
60 pletely integrated into the French monetary system and is therefore subject to extensive regulation and controls from Paris; this has clearly delayed the development of
offshore banking in the principality. Monaco also participates in the European Union
market system through its customs union with France. Thus, Monaco's economic future will continue to depend quite heavily on decisions made in Paris.

Describe the relationship between France and Monaco.

65 Late in 2000, the French government claimed that Monaco had joined the likes of
Andorra and Liechtenstein as a tax haven. Capital flight to Monaco could be costing

Prince Albert and his sisters, Princess Stephanie (left) and Princess Caroline (right) attend a Red Cross benefit in Monaco.

the French government a great deal in taxes, and Paris demanded banking reforms. Prince Rainier rejected the charges and threatened to sever the dynastic tie to France.

TODAY'S LEADERSHIP

In 2005 Prince Rainier died after a long illness. His only son, Prince Albert, took the
70 throne at age 47. Albert was unmarried and childless. Prince Albert acknowledges having an illegitimate son, but that son cannot rule. If Albert dies without a legitimate heir, Princess Caroline, will ascend.

Prince Albert has a passion for sports, especially winter sports. He represented his country on the Olympic four-man bobsled team at Calgary in 1988 and in Salt
75 Lake City in 2002. In the spring of 2006, Albert left the glamorous Mediterranean principality for a trek to the frozen North Pole. He and his team of seven made the frozen 57-mile journey to raise awareness of the dangers of global warming.

From his office overlooking moored yachts in the Mediterranean, Prince Albert takes pride in conducting the business of the principality. He speaks perfect English
80 with an American accent as taught by his mother, Grace Kelly, an American film star of the 1950s who tragically was killed in an automobile crash in 1982. Economic development is a major goal for Prince Albert. He wants to attract non-polluting industries to his tiny kingdom of 1.95 square kilometers, which also happens to be the most densely populated country in the world.

(1,015 words)

—E. Gene Frankland,
Global Studies: Europe 8e. Copyright © 2004 by The McGraw-Hill
Companies, Inc. All rights reserved. Reprinted by permission of
McGraw-Hill Contemporary Learning Series. The last three
paragraphs of this selection were written by Brenda D. Smith.

Recall

Stop to self-test, relate, and react.

Your instructor may choose to give you a true-false comprehension review.

Write About the Selection

What kind of economic conflict exists between Monaco and France? What steps have been taken to alleviate this conflict?

Response Suggestion: Write about the conflict from two points of view: that of Monaco and that of France.

Contemporary *Link*

If you were Prince Albert, what would be your ten-year economic plan for Monaco? What would be your priorities for fueling the economy? List five economic goals, and explain the significance of each.

Skill Development: Graphics

Refer to the designated graphic below, and answer the following items with *T* (true), *F* (false), or *CT* (can't tell).

Private Employment in Monaco

Of the total Monaco employment of 44,000 in 2005, the private sector employed 40,000 while the public sector employed 4,000. The pie graph shows the distribution per activity sector for private employment.

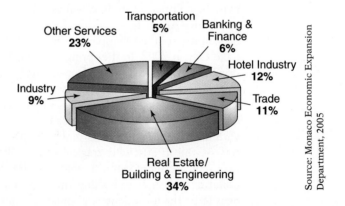

Source: Monaco Economic Expansion Department, 2005

_____T_____   1. In Monaco, more than three times the people are employed in the real estate/building and engineering sector than in the industry sector.

_____T_____   2. Gambling at the Grand Casino is not included as a specified sector on this graphic report.

_____T_____   3. The trade sector and the hotel industry sector employ about the same number of people.

_____CT_____   4. The trade sector and the hotel industry sector produce about the same amount of money for Monaco.

_____CT_____   5. The transportation sector is small because Monaco is a small country.

Check Your Comprehension

After reading the selection, answer the following questions with *a, b, c,* or *d.* To help you analyze your strengths and weaknesses, the question types are indicated.

Main Idea ____d____ 1. Which is the best statement of the main idea of this selection?

 a. Monaco is the leading politically independent principality in the world today.
 b. Monaco has been ruled by the Grimaldi family for over 700 years, and the latest ruler from that family is Prince Albert.
 c. Monaco is a small principality noted for its positive achievements in civil liberties and political rights.
 d. Monaco is an independent principality with close ties to France and a recently diversified economy.

Inference ____b____ 2. In the opening paragraph, the author's primary purpose is to provide

 a. a portrait of the Grimaldi family.
 b. facts relating to Monaco's sovereignty.
 c. facts about the citizens of Monaco.
 d. economic information about Monaco.

Detail ____a____ 3. It was only during the reign of Prince Rainier that all citizens of Monaco were finally allowed to

 a. vote in elections.
 b. be pardoned for crimes.
 c. own property.
 d. serve in the military.

Inference ____a____ 4. The reader can conclude that the National and Democratic Union Party (UND) is

 a. typically in agreement with the country's leadership.
 b. a powerful force in European economic policy.
 c. a leader in the fight for international human rights.
 d. active in reducing immigration into Monaco.

Detail ____d____ 5. The author indicates that the majority of Monaco's revenues come from

 a. gambling by tourists.
 b. the sale of electronic components.
 c. personal income taxes.
 d. taxes on goods and services.

Inference   _____a_____ 6. The reader can conclude that the disagreements between the governments of France and Monaco stem mainly from the French concern over

   a. loss of tax money.
   b. tourism competition.
   c. illegal gambling.
   d. the Grimaldi family.

Detail   _____d_____ 7. According to the passage, casino revenue in Monaco dropped from 90 percent of the government's revenue to about

   a. 50 percent.
   b. 25 percent.
   c. 20 percent.
   d. 4 percent.

Detail   _____b_____ 8. A corporation located in Monaco today must pay taxes to France if

   a. the company conducts only half its business in Monaco.
   b. the company conducts 20 percent of its business in Monaco.
   c. the company has been in Monaco less than 10 years.
   d. the company conducts 25 percent of its business in Monaco.

Detail   _____d_____ 9. Believing that Monaco was being used as a tax haven,

   a. Monaco became more independent from France politically.
   b. Monaco expanded its economy into goods and services.
   c. Prince Rainier severed all diplomatic relationships with France.
   d. France demanded new banking laws in order to recoup the lost taxes.

Inference   _____d_____ 10. The reader can conclude that Prince Albert of Monaco is very concerned with

   a. achieving independence from France.
   b. severely limiting tourism in Monaco.
   c. making Monaco a popular democracy.
   d. improving the global environment.

Answer the following with *T* (true) or *F* (false).

Detail   _____T_____ 11. If a foreign country threatened to invade Monaco, Monaco would first look to France for protection.

Detail   _____F_____ 12. France's disagreements with Monaco have primarily to do with different thoughts on social policy issues.

Detail   _____F_____ 13. Monaco is a completely sovereign nation, with no constraints limiting its autonomy.

Detail   _____T_____ 14. Vatican City is the smallest independent state in the world.

Detail   _____T_____ 15. A French citizen must live in Monaco more than five years to escape French taxes.

Build Your Vocabulary

According to the way the italicized word is used in the selection, indicate *a, b, c,* or *d* for the word or phrase that gives the best definition. The number in parentheses indicates the line of the passage in which the word is located.

___d___ 1. "tolerated somewhat *fitfully*" (4)
   a. peacefully
   b. cautiously
   c. boldly
   d. irregularly

___b___ 6. "reputation it had *engendered*" (37)
   a. destroyed
   b. created
   c. supported
   d. favored

___b___ 2. "Monaco's *sovereignty*" (6)
   a. conquest
   b. independence
   c. boundaries
   d. land

___a___ 7. "had actively *solicited*" (42)
   a. recruited
   b. purchased
   c. discouraged
   d. redirected

___a___ 3. "the *reigning* prince" (10)
   a. governing
   b. oldest
   c. youngest
   d. foreign

___a___ 8. "if not *constrained* by the French" (55)
   a. controlled
   b. ignored
   c. broadened
   d. lessened

___a___ 4. "*succeeded* by his grandson" (14)
   a. followed
   b. overthrown
   c. acknowledged
   d. assisted

___c___ 9. "tax *haven*"(66)
   a. economy
   b. market
   c. shelter
   d. increase

___d___ 5. "granted universal *suffrage*" (15)
   a. minimum wage
   b. land ownership
   c. civil rights
   d. voting rights

___c___ 10. "to *sever* the dynastic tie" (68)
   a. increase
   b. lengthen
   c. cut
   d. ignore

Search the Net

Use a search engine such as Google, Yahoo, Ask.com, Excite, Dogpile, or Lycos to find more information about why Monaco would want to diversify its economy. What would be the benefit of developing other industries besides tourism and gambling? For suggested Web sites and other research activities, go to http://www. ablongman.com/smith/.

selection 2 Science

Contemporary *Focus*

San Francisco lies on the San Andreas Fault and is expected to have another major earthquake. Although new buildings are constructed to withstand tremors, older homes, built above garages or shopfronts, have little structural support. Part of the city is built on reclaimed land that was under water fifty years ago; this land would turn to quicksand during an earthquake. What can be done to avert a major disaster and save the city of San Francisco?

Shock Tactic That Could Save a City

By Peter Sheridan
The Express, UK, April 18, 2006

Exactly 100 years ago an enormous earthquake flattened San Francisco and killed thousands. Today, as scientists fear another one is set to do the same, they're ready to take an extraordinary gamble—by blowing up the San Andreas fault.

The 1906 San Francisco earthquake remains one of America's greatest disasters—and a repeat of it is guaranteed. "The question isn't if, but when," says Jeffrey Mount, director of the Watershed Centre at the University of California in Davis, who predicts that the consequences of the inevitable 21st-century San Francisco earthquake will be "diabolical."

Diabolical possibilities perhaps call for diabolical measures. Drilling holes along the San Andreas fault, stuffing them with explosives and then blowing them up certainly doesn't seem like the work of sanity. Yet a small group of scientists believe that while they can't stop the next seismic tremor any more than King Canute could hold back the waves, this may be how they will be able to predict where it will cause the most damage.

An estimated 1,500 people in the city would be killed by falling buildings and fires, and in the Bay Area about 6,000 would die. Thousands would be injured, and almost 360,000 would be made homeless. Nearly 40 percent of private buildings could be destroyed because the majority were built before anti-earthquake building codes of the seventies came in.

COLLABORATE Collaborate on responses to the following questions:

➤ Why do people live in San Francisco if an earthquake is predicted?

➤ How would blowing up the fault with explosives ever be a viable consideration?

➤ What are earthquake building codes?

Skill Development: Preview

Preview the next selection to predict its purpose and organization and to formulate your learning plan.

Activate Schema

Have you ever felt an earthquake? What happened?
Why is fire a hazard after an earthquake?

Establish a Purpose for Reading

Rather than the earth opening up and swallowing people, as in the movies, the reality of an earthquake is different, but just as frighteningly destructive. Read to learn what happens as the result of an earthquake. What causes the destruction?

Increase Word Knowledge

What do you know about these words?

topple	debris	sediment	eliminated	triggered
loess	displacement	subsidence	unsettling	precede

Your instructor may give a true-false vocabulary review before or after reading.

Integrate Knowledge While Reading

Questions have been inserted in the margin to stimulate your thinking while reading. Remember to

Predict	Picture	Relate	Monitor	Correct

EFFECTS OF EARTHQUAKES

Ground motion is the trembling and shaking of the land that can cause buildings to vibrate. During small quakes, windows and walls may crack from such vibration. In a very large quake the ground motion may be visible. It can be strong enough to topple large structures such as bridges and office and apartment buildings. Most
5 people injured or killed in an earthquake are hit by falling debris from buildings. Because proper building construction can greatly reduce the dangers, building codes need to be both strict and strictly enforced in earthquake-prone areas. Much of the damage and loss of life in recent Turkey, El Savador, and India earthquakes were due to poorly constructed buildings that did not meet building codes. As we
10 have seen, the location of buildings also needs to be controlled. Buildings built on soft-sediment are damaged more than buildings on hard rock.

Why are buildings on soft sediment more vulnerable?

Fire is a particularly serious problem just after an earthquake because of broken gas and water mains and fallen electrical wires. Although fire was the cause of most of the damage to San Francisco in 1906, changes in building construction and im-
15 proved fire-fighting methods have reduced (but not eliminated) the fire danger to modern cities. The stubborn Marina district fires in San Francisco in 1989 attest to modern dangers of broken gas and water mains.

AP Photo

An Indonesian woman surveys the wreckage of her home after a devastating earthquake shook the region.

Landslides can be triggered by the shaking of the ground. The 1959 Madison Canyon landslide in Montana was triggered by a nearby quake of magnitude 7.7.
20 Landslides and subsidence caused extensive damage in downtown and suburban Anchorage during the 1964 Alaskan quake (magnitude 8.6). The 1970 Peruvian earthquake (magnitude 7.75) set off thousands of landslides in the steep Andes Mountains, burying more than 17,000 people. In 1920 in China over 100,000 people living in hollowed-out caves in cliffs of loess were killed when a quake collapsed
25 the cliffs. The 2001 El Salvador quake resulted in nearly 500 landslides, the largest of which occurred in Santa Tecla where 1,200 people were missing after tons of soil and rock fell on a neighborhood.

What is loess?

A special type of ground failure caused by earthquakes is liquefaction. This occurs when a water-saturated soil or sediment turns from a solid to a liquid as a re-
30 sult of earthquake shaking. Liquefaction may occur several minutes after an earthquake, causing buildings to sink and underground tanks to float as once-solid sediment flows like water. Liquefaction was responsible for much of the damage in the 1989 Loma Prieta quake and contributed to the damage in the 1906 San Francisco, the 1964 Alaska, the 1995 Kobe, Japan, and the 2001 Puget Sound,
35 Washington, and Gujarat, India quakes.

Permanent displacement of the land surface may be the result of movement along a fault. Rocks can move vertically, those on one side of a fault rising while those on the other side drop. Rocks can also move horizontally, those on one side of a fault sliding past those on the other side. Diagonal movement with both vertical
40 and horizontal components can also occur during a single quake. Such movement can affect huge areas, although the displacement in a single earthquake seldom exceeds 8 meters. The trace of a fault on Earth's surface may appear as a low cliff, called a scarp, or as a closed tear in the ground. In rare instances small cracks open during a quake (but not to the extent that Hollywood films often portray). Ground
45 displacement during quakes can tear apart buildings, roads, and pipelines that cross faults. Sudden subsidence of land near the sea can cause flooding and drownings.

Why is development allowed along faults?

Aftershocks are small earthquakes that follow the main shock. Although aftershocks are smaller than the main quake, they can cause considerable damage, particularly to structures previously weakened by the powerful main shock. A long period
50 of aftershocks can be extremely unsettling to people who have lived through the main shock. Foreshocks are small quakes that precede a main shock. They are usually less common and less damaging than aftershocks but can sometimes be used to help predict large quakes (although not all large quakes have foreshocks).

Make a list of effects.

(678 words)

—From Diane H. Carlson, Charles C. Plummer, and David McGeary,
Physical Geology: Earth Revealed, 6th Edition. Copyright © 2006 by
The McGraw-Hill Companies, Inc. Reproduced with permission.

Recall

Stop to self-test, relate, and react.

Your instructor may choose to give you a true-false comprehension review.

Write About the Selection

What are the effects of an earthquake? List and explain how damage occurs.
  Response Suggestion: Focus on three major types of damage. Give an explanation and an example of each.

Contemporary *Link*

What precautions can people who live in earthquake-threatened areas realistically take? How vulnerable is your area? How would you prepare if you lived in San Francisco?

Skill Development: Graphics

Refer to the designated graphic on page 560 and answer the following items with *T* (true) or *F* (false).

_____ F _____   1. The total number of earthquakes reported in 2001 was greater than that reported in 2000.

_____ T _____   2. The only deaths reported from U.S. earthquakes in the listed years occurred in 2003.

_____ T _____   3. The total number of earthquakes in the U.S. based on the graphic for 2006 was 891.

_____ F _____   4. In 2005 the largest number of U.S. earthquakes had a magnitude of 3.0 to 3.9.

_____ T _____   5. In the years listed in the report, Alaska had over half of the earthquakes that were 7.0 or higher.

NUMBER OF EARTHQUAKES IN THE UNITED STATES FOR 2000–2006 LOCATED BY THE US GEOLOGICAL SURVEY NATIONAL EARTHQUAKE INFORMATION CENTER							
Magnitude	**2000**	**2001**	**2002**	**2003**	**2004**	**2005**	**2006**
8.0 to 9.9	0	0	0	0	0	0	0
7.0 to 7.9	0	1	1	2	0	1	0
6.0 to 6.9	10	5	5	7	2	4	1
5.0 to 5.9	60	45	70	54	25	49	13
4.0 to 4.9	287	294	538	541	284	345	107
3.0 to 3.9	913	834	1525	1303	1362	1471	377
2.0 to 2.9	657	646	1228	704	1336	1738	380
1.0 to 1.9	0	2	2	2	1	2	4
0.1 to 0.9	0	0	0	0	0	0	1
No Magnitude	415	434	507	333	540	73	8
Total	2342	2261	3876	2946	3550	3683	891
Estimated Deaths	0	0	0	2	0	0	0

Red values indicate the earthquakes occurred in Alaska.

Source: United States Geological Survey as of June 2, 2006

Check Your Comprehension

After reading the selection, answer the following questions with *a, b, c,* or *d.* To help you analyze your strengths and weaknesses, the question types are indicated.

Inference _____d_____ 1. Which is the best statement of the main idea of this selection?

    a. Earthquakes cause many types of dangerous ground motion.
    b. Earthquakes may change a city landscape permanently.
    c. Earthquakes are most dangerous when landslides occur.
    d. Earthquakes can cause damage in many different ways.

Detail _____c_____ 2. The author indicates that of all the types of ground failure caused by earthquakes, the one that is least likely to occur is a

    a. closed tear.
    b. scarp.
    c. surface crack.
    d. landslide.

Inference _____c_____ 3. The author's main purpose in discussing fires and landslides is to show that

    a. fires and landslides that usually follow earthquakes can cause many thousands of deaths.
    b. fires and landslides are more likely to kill people than liquefaction is.

c. problems caused by earthquakes can be deadlier than the actual earthquakes themselves.

d. problems that are created by earthquakes can destroy whole neighborhoods or cities.

Inference _____b_____ 4. The author refers to liquefaction as a ground failure because during liquefaction the ground

a. is noticeably torn.
b. changes consistency.
c. moves horizontally.
d. becomes heated.

Inference _____b_____ 5. The reader can conclude that the word *fault*, when used to discuss an earthquake, refers to

a. a building code error.
b. a crack in the earth.
c. damage to a building.
d. deaths from a quake.

Inference _____a_____ 6. The reader can infer that a *scarp* is created by rocks that move

a. vertically from a fault.
b. horizontally along a surface.
c. diagonally into buildings.
d. slowly over large areas.

Detail _____c_____ 7. According to the passage, during earthquakes the structures that would predictably receive the least damage are those that are built on

a. sediment.
b. soil.
c. rock.
d. loess.

Detail _____a_____ 8. The selection indicates that, compared to aftershocks, earthquake foreshocks are less

a. damaging.
b. noisy.
c. predictable.
d. unsettling.

Inference _____d_____ 9. The purpose of this selection is to

a. warn people of the dangers of earthquakes and explain precautions.
b. argue for preventive building code enforcement for earthquakes.
c. record the worldwide damage caused by earthquakes since 1906.
d. explain how damage results from earthquakes.

Inference _____d_____ 10. The reader can reasonably infer that the ground motion referred to in the selection's first sentence is the result of

a. falling debris.
b. collapsing buildings.
c. liquefaction of some types of soil.
d. movement of rocks underground.

Answer the following with *T* (true) or *F* (false).

Detail _____F_____ 11. Most earthquake deaths are caused by a type of ground failure called liquefaction.

Detail _____T_____ 12. Earthquake aftershocks tend to be more dangerous than earthquake foreshocks because of previously weakened structures.

Detail _____F_____ 13. The author feels that the way that Hollywood movies depict earthquakes is fairly accurate.

Detail _____T_____ 14. Of all the effects of earthquakes described in this selection, the greatest loss of human life was caused by landslides in China occurring after earthquakes.

Detail _____F_____ 15. With the improvements in modern building techniques, fire is no longer a dangerous by-product of earthquakes.

Build Your Vocabulary

According to the way the italicized word was used in the selection, indicate *a, b, c,* or *d* for the word or phrase that gives the best definition. The number in parentheses indicates the line of the passage in which the word is located.

_____c_____ 1. "*topple* large structures" (4)
    a. build
    b. view
    c. collapse
    d. survive

_____a_____ 2. "falling *debris*" (5)
    a. fragments
    b. windows
    c. rain
    d. snow

_____b_____ 3. "soft-*sediment*" (11)
    a. concrete
    b. residue
    c. cotton
    d. wood

_____c_____ 4. "but not *eliminated*" (15)
    a. established
    b. started
    c. abolished
    d. escaped

_____a_____ 5. "can be *triggered*" (18)
    a. started
    b. stopped
    c. targeted
    d. measured

_____a_____ 6. "cliffs of *loess*" (24)
    a. clay
    b. sand
    c. minerals
    d. gravel

_____d_____ 7. "Permanent *displacement*" (36)
    a. distress
    b. distance
    c. disposal
    d. dislocation

_____c_____ 8. "Sudden *subsidence* of land" (46)
    a. swelling
    b. swaying
    c. sinking
    d. shrinking

selection **2**

_____b_____ 9. "extremely *unsettling*" (50)
     a. calming
     b. disturbing
     c. powerful
     d. lucky

_____a_____ 10. "*precede* a main shock" (51)
     a. go before
     b. go after
     c. follow
     d. stop

Search the Net

Use a search engine such as Google, Yahoo, Ask.com, Excite, Dogpile, or Lycos to find more information about the relationship between the earth's plates and earthquakes and volcanoes. Locate maps that show the land formations caused by plate tectonics. For suggested Web sites and other research activities, go to http://www.ablongman.com/smith/.

| selection 3 | Sociology |

selection 3

Contemporary *Focus*

Research shows that each Minnesotan now produces 1.16 tons of garbage every year, which is almost twice the amount of 15 years ago. By 2050 Africa's population will more than double to almost two billion. What are the effects on the environment of growing consumption in industrialized nations and surging population in poor nations?

Water Crisis Will Worsen Plight

The East African, March 28, 2006

Right now, Africa is facing a serious water shortage. The statistics are grim. Two out of every three people in the world will be facing water shortages by 2025, according to a report entitled "Running on Empty." Just over 1 billion people today have no access to safe drinking water, and 2.5 billion have no basic sanitation.

Consumption of water rose six-fold between 1990 and 1995, more than twice the population growth. While the United Kingdom and other prosperous nations of the world can cope with dwindling water supplies owing to efficient water management, poorer countries, especially from Africa, are already suffering massively, making it pretty hard to escape the ravages of drought and poverty.

This crisis is caused partly by the depletion of forest cover and unprecedented encroachment on the environment. Furthermore, supplies of water have been stretched to the limit due to rising populations, rising agricultural use, poor management and the effects of global warming.

With the current water scarcity, the poor of Africa cannot have the full enjoyment of the right to water. Yet it is estimated that about $100 billion is spent each year on bottled water.

COLLABORATE Collaborate on responses to the following questions:

➤ Why is Africa particularly vulnerable to a water shortage?

➤ What is the source for water in your city?

➤ What are the politics of water in arid areas such as Los Angeles and Las Vegas?

Skill Development: Preview

Preview the next selection to predict its purpose and organization and to formulate your learning plan.

Activate Schema

Where is the waste in your city dumped?
Who uses the highest percentage of water in your region?

Why do people in poor nations have more children than people of industrialized nations?

Establish a Purpose for Reading

Humans are damaging nature with waste and overconsumption, as well as depleting natural resources. Read to learn how humans are changing the planet.

Increase Word Knowledge

What do you know about these words?

migration	deficit	predictable	surging	affluent
abundance	disposable	decompose	arid	finite

Your instructor may give a true-false vocabulary review before or after reading.

Integrate Knowledge While Reading

Questions have been inserted in the margin to stimulate your thinking while reading. Remember to

Predict	Picture	Relate	Monitor	Correct

TECHNOLOGY AND THE ENVIRONMENT

Grandma Macionis, we always used to say, never threw anything away. Born in Lithuania—the "old country"—she grew up in a poor village, an experience that shaped her life even after she came to the United States as a young woman.

5 Her birthday was an amusing occasion for the rest of the family. After opening a present, she would carefully put aside the box, refold the wrapping paper, and roll up the ribbon; all this meant as much to her as the gift itself. Probably more, because Grandma never wore the new clothes given to her, and she was never known to go shopping for herself. Her kitchen knives were worn down from decades of sharpening, and every piece of furniture she ever bought stayed with her to the end 10 of her life (I still eat at the same table she had in her kitchen seventy-five years ago).

Why did Grandma Macionis save everything?

As curious as Grandma Macionis was to her grandchildren, she was a product of her culture. A century ago, there was little "trash." Grandma Macionis never thought of herself as an environmentalist. But she was: She lived simply, using few resources and creating almost no solid waste.

THE RISING POWER OF TECHNOLOGY

15 Our earliest ancestors—hunters and gatherers—had only simple technology, so they had a very little effect on the environment. Nature ruled much of their way of life: They lived according to the migration of animals, the changing of the seasons, and natural events such as fires, floods, and droughts.

Paul Marcus/Studio SPM, Inc.

The painting, *Day Dreaming*, by Paul Marcus depicts the pollution and environmental damage from unrestricted factories.

When the Industrial Revolution replaced muscle power with combustion en-
20 gines that burn fossil fuels (coal and, later, oil), societies began changing the environment much more, by consuming energy resources and by releasing pollutants
into the atmosphere. As a result of technological power, humans have brought more
change to this planet in the last two centuries than over the last billion years. The
typical adult in the United States consumes about one hundred times more energy
25 each year than the average person in the world's poorest nations.

What were the effects of the Industrial Revolution?

THE ENVIRONMENTAL DEFICIT

A short look at human history teaches an important lesson: By using more powerful
technology to improve living standards, people put the lives of future generations at
risk. The evidence is mounting that we are running up an **environmental deficit,**
profound and long-term harm to the environment caused by humanity's focus on short-
30 *term material affluence.*

How are we harming the environment?

POPULATION INCREASE

Consider that, 2,000 years ago the entire world's population was about 300 million—
about the population of the United States today.

Once humans developed industrial technology, higher living standards and improved medical treatments sharply decreased the death rates in Western Europe.
35 The predictable result was a sharp upward spike in world population. By 1800,
global population had soared to 1 billion.

Most experts predict that the world population will reach 8 to 9 billion people
by 2050. The most rapid population growth is occurring in the poorest regions of
the world. In 2003, the world's population was about 6.3 billion. Although the rate
40 of increase is slowing, we are adding 80 million people to the world's total each
year (218,000 every day).

Rapid population growth makes the problem of poverty worse. This is because a surging population offsets any increase in productivity so that living standards stay the same. If a society's population doubles, doubling its productivity
45 amounts to no gain al all. But poverty also makes environmental problems worse.
Because they are preoccupied with survival, poor people have little choice but to
consume whatever resources are at hand, without thinking about long-term environmental consequences.

How would rising populations in industrial societies impact the environment?

Now imagine the consequences of rising population and advancing technology
50 *together*. That is, what would happen if poor societies suddenly industrialized? An
affluent India, for example, would suddenly be a nation with more than 1 billion
additional cars on its streets. What effect would that have on the world's oil reserves
and global air quality?

Simply put, if people around the world lived at the level of material abundance
55 the people in the United States take for granted, the natural environment would
soon collapse even if birth rates were to drop. From an environmentalist point of
view, our planet suffers from economic underdevelopment in some regions and economic overdevelopment in others.

SOLID WASTE: THE DISPOSABLE SOCIETY

One environmental problem is waste—or, more precisely, too much of it. The aver-
60 age person in the United States discards about five pounds of paper, metal, plastic,
and other disposable materials daily; over a lifetime, that comes to 50 tons.

The problem of solid waste stems from a simple fact: The United States is a
disposable society. Not only is this country materially rich, but its people value convenience. As a result, we consume more products than any nation on Earth, and
65 many of these products come with excessive packaging. The most familiar case is
the cardboard, plastic, and Styrofoam containers that we buy with our fast food and
throw away within minutes.

Compare our disposable society to Grandma Macionis' times.

We like to say that we "throw things away." But the two-thirds of our solid waste
that is not burned or recycled never really "goes away." Rather, it ends up in landfills.
70 These dumping grounds are a threat to the natural environment for several reasons.

First, the sheer volume of discarded material is filling up landfills all across
the country. Already the United States is shipping trash to other countries to be
discarded. Second, the material in landfills contributes to water pollution.
Although the laws in most localities now regulate what can go in a landfill, the
75 Environmental Protection Agency has identified 30,000 dump sites across the
United States containing hazardous materials that are polluting water both above
and below the ground. Third, what goes into landfills all too often stays there,
sometimes for centuries. Tens of millions of tires, diapers, and plastic utensils do
not readily decompose and will be an unwelcome environmental burden for gen-
80 erations to come.

INADEQUATE WATER SUPPLY

In much of North America and Asia, people look to rivers rather than rainfall for
their water, making supply a problem. In some U.S. regions, the main source is
groundwater, water underground that supplies wells and springs. In many regions,
the supply is running low. For example, the Ogallala aquifer runs below ground
85 across seven states from South Dakota to Texas; it is now being pumped so rapidly
that some experts fear it could run dry within several decades.

How can we work together with other cities, states, and countries to preserve local and world water supplies?

Nowhere is water supply a bigger problem than in the Middle East. In Egypt, an arid region of the world, people depend on the Nile River for most of their water. But because of population increases, Egyptians make do with one-sixth as much
90 water per person as they did in 1900. Experts project that the supply may shrink by half again by 2015. Throughout the Middle East and Africa, where populations are rising rapidly, experts predict that as many as 1 billion people may lack necessary water by 2030.

In light of such developments, we must face the reality that water is a finite re-
95 source. Greater conservation of water by individuals (the average person consumes 10 million gallons in a lifetime) is part of the answer. However, individuals in households around the world account for just 10 percent of all water use. We need to curb consumption by industry, which is responsible for 25 percent of global water use, and by farming, which consumes nearly two-thirds of the total for irrigation.

(1,233 words)

—From John J. Macionis,
Social Problems, 2nd ed.

Recall

Stop to self-test, relate, and react.

Your instructor may choose to give you a true-false comprehension review.

Write About the Selection

How are humans changing the planet, and what are the consequences?

Response Suggestion: Focus on one major change, such as population growth or waste disposal. How does it affect us now? How might it affect us fifty years from now?

Contemporary *Link*

Will water become the oil of tomorrow? If so, who will get rich, and who will pay the price? Describe a worldwide scenario in which water demands a price equivalent to that of oil. How would this change our lives?

Skill Development: Graphics

Refer to the global map on page 569 and answer the following items with *T* (true) or *F* (false).

_____F_____ 1. Africa has the largest number of countries of any continent with very high water consumption in comparison to the natural supply.

_____F_____ 2. North America has the lowest consumption of water as a percentage of the natural supply of any continent.

_____T_____ 3. The water consumption as a percentage of the natural supply is higher in India than it is in Mexico.

_____T_____ 4. Argentina and Australia both have a similarly low water consumption as a percentage of their natural supply.

_____T_____ 5. Both Brazil and Indonesia contain tropical rain forests.

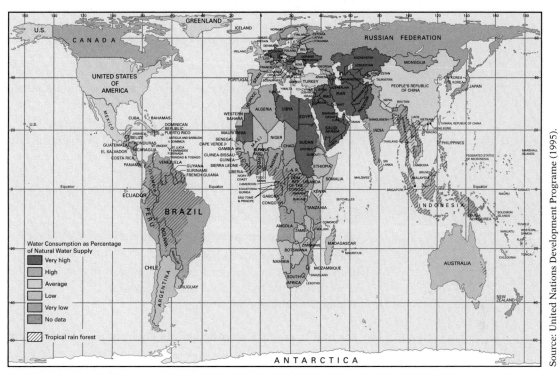

Source: United Nations Development Programme (1995).

Global Map Water Consumption around the World
This map shows each country's water consumption in relation to available resources. Nations near the equator consume only a tiny share of their available resources and do not face fresh water shortages. Northern Africa and the Middle East are a different story, however, with dense populations drawing on very limited water resources. As a result, in Libya, Egypt, Saudi Arabia, and other countries there is a serious problem of too little fresh water, especially for the poor.

selection 3

Check Your Comprehension

After reading the selection, answer the following questions with *a, b, c,* or *d.* To help you analyze your strengths and weaknesses, the question types are indicated.

Main Idea   ___d___   1. Which is the best statement of the main idea of this selection?

    a. Social problems cause poverty and suffering around the world today.
    b. Advances in technology are destined to worsen rather than solve environmental problems.
    c. The environment is suffering from overpopulation and poverty.
    d. Several factors contribute to the environmental problems we face today.

Inference   ___c___   2. The reader can conclude that the story about Grandma Macionis is used to introduce this selection because the author

    a. feels that Grandma Macionis was ecologically aware.
    b. needs to provide an example of how social problems originate.
    c. sees Grandma Macionis as someone from whom humans today could learn.
    d. feels Grandma Macionis was careful in spending her money.

Detail   ___b___   3. The author indicates that our very earliest ancestors did not appreciably alter their environment because they

    a. rejected the use of technology.
    b. lived simply in cooperation with nature.
    c. were affected by fires, floods, and droughts.
    d. migrated during the seasons.

Inference   ___a___   4. The author implies that the world's environmental deficit is in direct proportion to

    a. the material demands of humanity and population growth.
    b. technological research.
    c. the dreams of future generations.
    d. toxicity of pollutants.

Detail   ___a___   5. The author says that the "spike in world population" in the years leading up to 1800 was predictable because

    a. there were great advances in medicine.
    b. the world's population was fairly small.
    c. there were no major wars taking place.
    d. productivity was growing rapidly.

Detail   ___b___   6. The author claims that those who live in poverty

    a. seek to destroy the environment.
    b. damage the environment out of necessity.
    c. take little from the environment.
    d. consider long-term consequences.

selection 3

Inference _____c_____ 7. The author indicates that from an environmentalist perspective, world economic development is not

    a. fair.
    b. efficient.
    c. balanced.
    d. obvious.

Detail _____d_____ 8. The author describes the United States as a *disposable society* because it is a society that

    a. attempts unsuccessfully to recycle.
    b. sends waste to foreign countries.
    c. is regulated by the Environmental Protection Agency.
    d. values convenience over ecological concerns.

Inference _____b_____ 9. When the author says that the materials our society throws away don't actually go away, he means that they do not

    a. get recycled.
    b. fully disappear without a trace.
    c. get burned.
    d. go to landfills.

Inference _____c_____ 10. In the section "Inadequate Water Supply," the author observes that the world's future water supply problems will be mainly caused by

    a. a lack of rain.
    b. used-up aquifers.
    c. rising populations.
    d. pollutants in rivers.

Answer the following with *T* (true) or *F* (false).

Detail _____T_____ 11. Most of the world's water is used for agricultural purposes.

Detail _____T_____ 12. The more industrially advanced an economy, the more likely its industries are to cause pollution.

Detail _____F_____ 13. If a society's population doubles, its productivity automatically doubles.

Detail _____F_____ 14. Unlike the Nile River, the Ogallala aquifer runs underground and thus is not endangered by overconsumption.

Detail _____T_____ 15. Two-thirds of our solid waste goes into landfills, therefore it does not "go away."

selection 3

Build Your Vocabulary

According to the way the italicized word was used in the selection, indicate *a*, *b*, *c*, or *d* for the word or phrase that gives the best definition. The number in parentheses indicates the line of the passage in which the word is located.

____d____ 1. "*migration* of animals" (17)
    a. reproduction
    b. courtship
    c. breeding
    d. movement

____a____ 6. "material *abundance*" (54)
    a. prosperity
    b. misfortune
    c. consequence
    d. development

____a____ 2. "environmental *deficit*" (28)
    a. shortage
    b. technology
    c. condition
    d. design

____b____ 7. "*disposable* society" (63)
    a. collecting
    b. throw-away
    c. consumer
    d. expensive

____b____ 3. "*predictable* result" (35)
    a. disappointing
    b. anticipated
    c. wonderful
    d. scientific

____b____ 8. "readily *decompose*" (79)
    a. sell
    b. break down
    c. multiply
    d. survive

____c____ 4. "*surging* population" (43)
    a. poverty-stricken
    b. lively
    c. increasing
    d. shrinking

____d____ 9. "*arid* region" (88)
    a. wet
    b. mountainous
    c. historical
    d. dry

____b____ 5. "*affluent* India" (51)
    a. industrial
    b. wealthy
    c. technologically advanced
    d. growing quickly

____b____ 10. "*finite* resource" (94)
    a. knowledgeable
    b. limited
    c. expensive
    d. endless

Search the Net

Use a search engine such as Google, Yahoo, Ask.com, Excite, Dogpile, or Lycos to find information about environmental issues such as global warming and the shrinking water supply. Find the factors that contribute the most to both of these environmental challenges and search for suggested solutions to fixing these problems. For suggested Web sites and other research activities, go to http://www. ablongman.com/smith/.

Vocabulary Booster

Play It Again, Sam

Prefix	**Root**
re-: "back, again"	*lud, lus:* "to play"

Words with *re-:* "back, again"

Although Humphrey Bogart never said the line "Play it again, Sam" in the movie *Casablanca*, it has been *repeatedly* attributed to his character, Rick.

- *reconcile:* to cause to become friendly or peaceable again; to cause one to accept something not desired

  The purpose of the peace conference was to get the opposing sides to *reconcile* their differences and find a way to coexist in the region.

- *reconstruct:* to build again; to create again in the mind from available information

  The witness to the auto accident was asked by the police officer to *reconstruct* from memory the events leading up to the crash.

- *recriminate:* to bring a countercharge against an accuser

  Melissa feared that legally accusing her ex-husband of being an unfit father would cause him to *recriminate* against her as an unfit mother.

- *refrain:* to keep oneself from doing something

  I had to *refrain* from laughing when the professor walked into class wearing bedroom slippers.

- *regress:* to revert to an earlier or less advanced state

  The paralyzed patient had been making progress in physical therapy, but suddenly she *regressed* to being unable to walk a single step.

- *reiterate:* to say or do repeatedly

  The infomercial *reiterated* the cleaning product's claims until I became annoyed at hearing over and over how white my shirts could be.

- *rejuvenate:* to make young again; to make new again

  The facial product line was promoted as being able to *rejuvenate* a user's skin by reducing wrinkles and uneven skin tones within two weeks with a money back guarantee.

- *renege:* to go back on one's word

  Daniel had to *renege* on his promise to drive his friends to the football game after his father refused to lend him the car.

- *repel:* to push away by force; to fail to mix with; to resist absorption; to cause distaste in

  Oil and water do not mix; rather, they *repel* each other.

- *repercussion:* an effect of some previous action; recoil after impact; reverberation

  Excessive running on pavement can have serious *repercussions* on your health, such as wearing out the knee joints from the constant impact.

- *retract:* to withdraw a statement or opinion as inaccurate; to withdraw a promise

  Celebrities often sue magazines or newspapers asking for *retractions* of inaccurate statements printed about them.

- *revenge:* to inflict pain or harm in return for a wrong received; to get even or get satisfaction

  Cindy's *revenge* for Sonia's lies was not inviting Sonia to the best party of the year.

Words with *lud, lus:* "to play"

The *prelude* or introductory piece of music to an opera is called an overture.

- *ludicrous:* causing laughter because of absurdity; ridiculous

  Darren looked *ludicrous* in the extremely short haircut that made his ears stick out.

- *allude:* to refer casually or indirectly to

  He will *allude* to his days as a football star whenever the guys start discussing sports.

- *allusion:* a casual or passing reference to something, either direct or implied

  A casual *allusion* to Shakespeare would be to call him the Bard.

- *interlude:* any intermediate performance or entertainment, such as between the acts of a play

  The instrumental *interlude* between the verses of the song had a melancholy sound.

- *delude:* to mislead the mind or judgment of

  Jonathan felt silly when he realized the two con artists who tricked him out of his money had *deluded* him.

- *elude:* to avoid capture; to escape perception or comprehension of

  The reason for her popularity *eludes* me; I just don't get it.

- *illusion*: an unreal or misleading appearance or image

  Faux finishes like marbleizing a column with paint create an inexpensive *illusion* in home decorating.

REVIEW

Part I

Indicate whether the italicized words are used correctly (*C*) or incorrectly (*I*) in the following sentences:

C 1. Realizing that he had provided inaccurate information during his testimony, the defendant wished to *retract* his statement.

I 2. The host continued to *repel* the guests and thus strengthen their friendship.

I 3. A brief *interlude* was held before the concert began.

C 4. Detectives attempt to *reconstruct* the scene of a crime in order to solve it.

C 5. Self-tanning skin products create the *illusion* of a natural glow, without the accompanying sun damage.

C 6. The couple planned a month in the sun together in order to *rejuvenate* their relationship.

I 7. Her carefully chosen, tasteful outfit allowed the woman to *elude* others that she was an upstanding member of society.

C 8. The persistent toddler *repeatedly* asked his mother for items at his eye level in the grocery store.

C 9. The test monitor had to *reiterate* directions that had already been given.

C 10. Some say that the best form of *revenge* is a life well-lived.

Part II

Indicate whether the following statements are true (*T*) or false (*F*):

T 11. People sometimes *delude* themselves into believing things that are not true.

T 12. A sign of growing up is learning that all actions have *repercussions*, whether positive or negative.

T 13. To discourage the young man from asking her out, she could *allude* to the fact that her boyfriend will be visiting during the upcoming weekend.

F 14. The orchestra played a brief *prelude* at the concert's conclusion.

_____T_____ 15. Her father's attempts to dance were made all the more *ludicrous* by his total lack of rhythm.

_____T_____ 16. The boys knew their mother would not *renege* on her threat to withdraw privileges in exchange for poor behavior.

_____F_____ 17. By remaining silent, she thought she could avoid *recriminating* herself.

_____T_____ 18. Prior to offering counsel for divorce, family law attorneys are trained to encourage a couple to *reconcile*, if at all possible.

_____T_____ 19. Knowing her nephew might be sensitive about his appearance, she encouraged his cousins to *refrain* from commenting.

_____T_____ 20. To *regress* could be considered the opposite of making progress.

11 Rate Flexibility

- What is your reading rate?
- How fast should you read?
- How do faster readers maintain a better reading rate?
- What are some techniques for faster reading?
- What happens during regression?
- Why skim?
- What is scanning?

Will Bullas, *The Red and White Fleet*, 2004. Watercolor, 32 x 22 inches.

Why Is Reading Rate Important?

Professors of college reading are far more concerned with comprehension than with a student's rate of reading. They would say that students should not attempt to "speed read" textbooks, and they would be right.

However, when students are asked what they would like to change about their reading, most will say, "I read too slowly. I would like to improve my reading speed." Whether or not this perception is accurate, rate is definitely a concern of college students. Whether you are reading a magazine or a textbook, reading 150 words per minute takes twice as long as reading 300 words per minute. Understanding the factors that contribute to rate can both quell anxiety and help increase reading efficiency.

What Is Your Reading Rate?

How many words do you read on the average each minute? To find out, read the following selection at your usual reading rate, just as you would have read it before you started thinking about speed. Time your reading of the selection so that you can calculate your rate. Read carefully enough to answer the ten comprehension questions that follow the selection.

exercise 11.1   Assessing Rate

Time your reading of this selection so that you can compute your words-per-minute rate. To make the calculations easier, try to begin reading on the exact minute, with zero seconds. Record your starting and finishing times in minutes and seconds, and then determine your rate from the rate chart at the end of the passage. Answer the ten questions that follow, and determine your comprehension rate by calculating the percentage of correct answers. Remember, read the selection at your normal rate.

Starting time: _____ minutes _____ seconds

SEA LIONS

"Hey, you guys, hurry up? They're gonna feed the seals!" No visit to the zoo or the circus would be complete without the playful antics of the trained "seal." However, the noisy animal that barks enthusiastically while balancing a ball on its nose is not really a seal at all. In reality, it is a small species of sea lion.

Like all mammals, sea lions are air breathers. Nevertheless, they spend most of their lives in the ocean and are skilled and graceful swimmers. Two species live off the Pacific coast of North America. The California sea lion is the smaller and more southerly. This is the circus "seal." An adult male may measure over seven feet in length and weigh more than 500 pounds. Females are considerably smaller, with a length of six feet and a weight of 200 pounds.

The larger northern, or Steller, sea lion lives off the Alaskan shore in summer and off the California coast in winter. Bulls may weigh over a ton and reach a length of more than eleven feet. Cows weigh some 750 pounds and are about nine feet long.

The northern sea lion is generally not as noisy as the California sea lion, but it can bellow loudly when it wants to make its presence known.

At one time, sea lions were hunted almost to extinction for their hides, meat, and oil. Eskimos even stored the valuable oil in pouches made from the sea lion's stomach. Today, sea lions are protected by law, but many fall prey to their natural enemies, the shark and the killer whale. Sea lions are often disliked and sometimes killed by fishermen who accuse them of eating valuable fish and damaging nets. For the most part, the accusations are untrue. The northern sea lion eats mostly "trash fish," which are of little commercial value. The California sea lion prefers squid. Although sea lions do eat salmon, they also eat lampreys, a snakelike parasitic fish that devours salmon in great numbers. By controlling the lamprey population, the sea lion probably saves more salmon than it eats.

Sea lions come ashore in early summer to give birth and to mate. First to arrive are the bulls, which immediately stake out individual territories along the beach. The cows follow and soon give birth to the single pup that each has been carrying since the previous summer. The newborn pup has about a dozen teeth. Its big blue eyes are open from birth and will turn brown after a few weeks.

The pup is born into a tumultuous world of huge, bellowing adults, and it must mature quickly to avoid being trampled by the teeming mob around it. It can move about within an hour, and can be seen scrambling nimbly among its elders within a few days. It doubles its weight in the first month or two. The quick weight gain is largely attributable to the extremely rich milk of the sea lion mother. Low in water and high in protein, the milk is almost 50 percent fat, whereas cow's milk is about 4 percent fat. Zookeepers have found it difficult to provide sea lion pups with adequate nourishment in the absence of the mother. At Marineland of the Pacific, an orphaned pup was successfully raised on a diet of whipping cream, liquefied mackerel muscle, calcium caseinate, and a multivitamin syrup. Not a very delectable-sounding menu, perhaps, but the pup loved it.

Throw a human infant into the ocean and it would drown. So would a sea lion baby. The only mammals that are known to swim from birth are whales and manatees. Although it will spend most of its twenty-year life in the ocean, the sea lion pup is at first terrified of water. The mother must spend about two months teaching it to swim.

Mating is no quiet affair among the sea lions. Almost immediately after the birth of the pups the huge bulls begin to wage bloody battles, trying to keep control of their harems of about a dozen cows. Using their long canine teeth as weapons, they fight with great ferocity for possession of the females. Fighting and mating consume so much of the bulls' time and energy during this period that little time is left for sleeping or eating.

At the end of the summer, the sea lions return to the ocean. The bulls, thin and scarred after a busy breeding season, regain their lost weight with several months of active feeding. As the weather grows colder, the huge northern sea lions begin their southward migration, leaving deserted the northern beaches which in warm weather were covered with their massive dark bodies.

The sea lion has to adapt to a considerable range of climate conditions. Its thick blubber and rapid metabolism are assets in the cold northern waters. But the California sea lion ranges as far south as the Galapagos Islands off the coast of South America. How does it adapt to a hot and dry environment?

The most important thing that the sea lion does to stay cool is to sleep in the daytime and take care of business during the cooler night hours. Sea lions in warm climates spend a great deal of time sleeping on the wet sand. Their bodies are designed in such a way that a large surface of the torso comes in contact with the cool ground when the animal lies down. About 10 percent of body heat can be lost in this way. Furthermore, the animal produces nearly 25 percent less heat while it sleeps than it does when awake and active.

Unfortunately, none of the sea lion's cooling mechanisms are highly effective. Ultimately, the animal relies on immersion in the ocean to keep itself cool.

—Victor A. Greulach and Vincent J. Chiappetta,
Biology

958 words

Finishing time: _____ minutes _____ seconds

Reading time in seconds: _____

Words per minute: _____

Time (Min.)	Words per Minute	Time (Min.)	Words per Minute
3:00	319	5:10	185
3:10	303	5:20	180
3:20	287	5:30	174
3:30	274	5:40	169
3:40	261	5:50	164
3:50	250	6:00	160
4:00	240	6:10	155
4:10	230	6:20	151
4:20	221	6:30	147
4:30	213	6:40	144
4:40	205	6:50	140
4:50	198	7:00	137
5:00	190		

Mark each statement with *T* (true) or *F* (false).

____F____ 1. The author focuses mainly on the sea lion's insatiable appetite for high-protein food.

____F____ 2. The larger northern sea lion is the circus "seal."

____T____ 3. Sea lions eat lampreys, which eat salmon.

____T____ 4. Sea lions both give birth and get pregnant in the summer.

____T____ 5. Sea lion milk contains a higher percentage of fat than cow's milk.

____F____ 6. Baby sea lions, like whales and manatees, are natural swimmers.

____T____ 7. Male sea lions mate with more than one female.

_____F_____ 8. The cool ground provides the sea lion with a greater release of body heat than the ocean water.

_____F_____ 9. In warm climates sea lions sleep more at night than during the day.

_____F_____ 10. Sea lions are able to stay under water because they have gills.

Comprehension rate (percentage of correct answers) _____%

How Fast Should You Read?

Reading specialists say that the average adult reading speed on relatively easy material is approximately 250 words per minute at 70 percent comprehension. The rate for college students tends to be a little higher, averaging about 300 words per minute on the same type of material with 70 percent comprehension. However, these figures are misleading for a number of reasons.

Anyone who says to you, "My reading rate is 500 words per minute" is not telling the whole story. The question that immediately comes to mind is, "Is that the rate for reading the newspaper or for a physics textbook?" For an efficient reader, no one reading rate serves for all purposes or for all materials. Efficient readers demonstrate their flexibility by varying their rate according to their own purpose for reading or according to their prior knowledge of the material being read.

Rate Variations and Prior Knowledge

One reason textbooks usually require slower reading than newspapers is that the sentences are longer, the language is more formal, the vocabulary and ideas are new, and prior knowledge may be limited. If you already have a lot of knowledge on a topic, you can usually read about it at a faster rate than if you are exploring a totally new subject. For example, a student who has some experience in the field of advertising will probably be able to work through the advertising chapter in a business textbook at a faster rate compared with a chapter on a less familiar topic, like supply-side economics. The student might need to slow to a crawl at the beginning of the economics chapter to understand the new concepts, but as the new ideas become more familiar, he or she might be able to read at a faster rate toward the end of the chapter.

The "difficulty level" of a textbook is primarily measured according to a student's schemata of the subject. Another measure combines the length of the sentences and the number of syllables in the words. The longer sentences and words indicate a more difficult level of reading. Freshman textbooks vary greatly in difficulty from field to field and from book to book. Some are written at levels as high as the sixteenth-grade level (senior in college), whereas others may be at the eleventh- or twelfth-grade level. Even within a single textbook, the levels vary from one section or paragraph to another. Unfamiliar technical vocabulary can bring a reader to a complete stop. Complex sentences are more difficult to read than simple, concise statements. Sometimes the difficulty is caused by the complexity of the ideas expressed and sometimes, perhaps unnecessarily, by the formality of the author's writing style.

Before starting on the first word and moving automatically on to the second, third, and fourth at the same pace, take a minute to ask yourself, "Why am I reading this material?" and, based on your answer, vary your speed according to your purpose. Do you want 100 percent, 70 percent, or 50 percent comprehension? In other words, figure out what you want to know when you finish and read accordingly. If you are studying for an examination, you probably need to read slowly and carefully, taking time to monitor your comprehension as you progress. Because 100 percent comprehension is not always your goal, be willing to switch gears and move faster over low-priority material even though you may sacrifice a few details. If you are reading only to get an overview or to verify a particular detail, read as rapidly as possible to achieve your specific purpose.

Techniques for Faster Reading

Concentrate

Fast readers, like fast race-car drivers, concentrate on what they are doing; they try to think quickly while they take in the important aspects of the course before them. Although we use our eyes, we actually read with our minds. If our attention is veering off course, we lose some of that cutting-edge quickness necessary for success. Slow readers tend to become bored because ideas are coming too slowly to keep their minds alert. Fast readers are curious to learn, mentally alert, and motivated to achieve.

Distractions that interfere with concentration, as mentioned in Chapter 1, fall into two categories: external and internal. External distractions, the physical happenings around you, are fairly easy to control with a little assertiveness. You can turn the television off or get up and go to another room. You can ask people not to interrupt or choose a place to read where interruptions will be minimal. Through prior planning, you can set yourself up for success and create a physical environment over which you have control.

Internal distractions, the irrelevant ideas that pop into your head while reading, are more difficult to control. As mentioned in Chapter 1, a to-do list will help. Write down your nagging concerns as a reminder for action. Spend less time worrying and more time doing, and you will clear your head for success. Visualize as you read so that you will become wrapped up in the material.

Stop Regressing

During your initial reading of material, have you ever realized halfway down the page that you have no idea what you have read? Your eyes were engaged, but your mind was wandering. Do you ever go back and reread sentences or paragraphs? Were you rereading because the material was difficult to understand, because you were tired and not concentrating, or because you were daydreaming? This type of rereading is called **regression.**

Regression can be a crutch that allows you to make up for wasted time. If this is a problem for you, analyze when and why you are regressing. If you discern that your regression is due to distracting thoughts, start denying yourself the privilege in order to break the habit. Admit, "OK, I missed that paragraph because I was thinking of something else. I shouldn't do that now, because I've got to keep studying and start paying close attention." One effective strategy is to schedule a special time with yourself to deal with those internal distractions. Tell yourself, for example, "I'll give myself a chance to think about that stuff for 15 minutes after lunch—I'll take a 15-minute 'me break.'"

Rereading because you did not understand is a legitimate correction strategy used by good readers who monitor their own comprehension. Rereading because your mind was asleep is a waste of time and a habit of many slow readers.

Daydreaming is a habit caused by lack of involvement with the material. Be demanding on yourself and expect 100 percent attention to the task. Visualize the incoming ideas, and relate the new material to what you already know. Don't just read the words; think the ideas.

Expand Fixations

Your eyes must stop in order to read. These stops, called **fixations,** last a fraction of a second. On the average, 5 to 10 percent of reading time is spent on fixations. Thus, reading more than one word per fixation will reduce your total reading time.

Research on vision shows that the eye is able to see about one-half inch on either side of a fixation point. This means that a reader can see two or possibly three words per fixation. To illustrate, read the following phrase:

in the car

Did you make three fixations, two, or one? Now read the following word:

entertainment

You can read this word automatically with one fixation. As a beginning reader, however, you probably stopped for each syllable for a total of four fixations. If you can read *entertainment,* which has 13 letters, with one fixation, you can certainly read the 8-letter phrase *in the car* with only one fixation.

Use your peripheral vision on either side of the fixation point to help you read two or three words per fixation. In expanding your fixations, take in phrases or thought units that seem to go together automatically. To illustrate, the following sentence has been grouped into thought units with fixation points:

After lunch,   I studied   in the library   at a table.
•   •   •   •

By expanding your fixations, the sentence can easily be read with four fixations rather than ten and thus reduce your total reading time.

Monitor Subvocalization

Subvocalization is the little voice in your head that reads for you. Some experts say that subvocalization is necessary for difficult material, and others say that fast readers are totally visual and do not need to hear the words. Good college readers will probably experience some of both. With easy reading tasks you may find yourself speeding up to the point that you are not hearing every word, particularly the unimportant "filler" phrases. However, with more difficult textbook readings, your inner voice may speak every word. The voice seems to add another sensory dimension to help you comprehend. Because experts say that the inner voice can read up to about 400 words per minute, many college students can make a considerable improvement in speed while still experiencing the inner voice.

Vocalizers, on the other hand, move their lips while reading to pronounce each word. This is an immature habit that should be stopped. Putting a slip of paper or a pencil in your mouth while reading will alert you to lip movement and inspire you to stop.

Preview

Size up your reading assignment before you get started. If it is a chapter, glance through the pages and read the subheadings. Look at the pictures and notice the italicized words and boldface print. Make predictions about what you think the chapter will cover. Activate your schema, or prior knowledge, on the subject. Pull out your mental computer chip and prepare to bring something to the printed page.

Use Your Pen as a Pacer

The technique of using your pen or fingers as a pacer means pointing under the words in a smooth, flowing motion, moving back and forth from line to line. Although as a child you were probably told never to point to words, it is a very effective technique for improving reading speed. The technique seems to have several benefits. After you overcome the initial distraction, the physical act of pointing tends to improve concentration by drawing your attention directly to the words. The forward motion of your pen tends to keep you from regressing because rereading would interrupt your established rhythm. By pulling your eyes down the page, the pen movement helps set a rapid, steady pace for reading and tends to shift you out of word-by-word reading and move you automatically into phrase reading. Obviously, you cannot read a whole book using your pen as a pacer, but you can start out with this technique. Later, if you feel yourself slowing down, use your pen again to get back on track.

The technique is demonstrated in the following passage. Your pen moves in a Z pattern from one side of the column to the other. Because you are trying to read several words at each fixation, your pen does not have to go to the extreme end of either side of the column.

> Rapid reading requires quick thinking
> and intense concentration. The reader
> must be alert and aggressive. Being
> interested in the subject helps improve speed.

As you begin to read faster and become more proficient with the Z pattern, you will notice the corners starting to round into an S. The Z pattern is turning into a more relaxed S swirl. When you get to the point of using the S swirl, you will be reading for ideas and not reading every word. You are reading actively and aggressively, with good concentration. Use the Z pattern until you find your pen or hand movement has automatically turned into an S. The following illustration compares the two patterns.

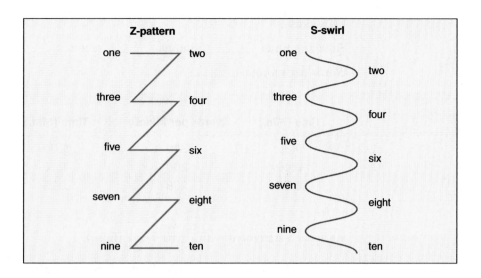

Push and Pace

Be alert and aggressive, and try to read faster. Sit up straight and attack the text. Get uncomfortable and force yourself to hurry. Changing old habits is difficult. You will never read faster unless you try to read faster.

Set goals and pace yourself. Count the number of pages in your homework assignments, and estimate according to your reading rate how many pages you can read in 30 minutes. Use a paper clip or a sticky note to mark the page you are trying to reach. Push yourself to achieve your goal.

exercise 11.2 | **Pacing**

Predict organization: Is the following passage organized by time order or classification? <u>Time order</u>

COCA-COLA

Although not as important as textiles or tobacco in 1900, a soft drink developed by an Atlanta pharmacist, Dr. John Pemberton, eventually became the most renowned southern product in the world. Pemberton developed the drink—a mixture of oils, caffeine, coca leaves, and cola nuts—in his backyard in an effort to find a good-tasting cure for headaches. He called his concoction Coca-Cola. It was not an overnight success, and Pemberton, short of cash, sold the rights to it to another Atlantan, Asa Candler, in 1889. Candler tinkered with the formula to improve the taste and marketed the product heavily. By the mid-1890s, Coca-Cola enjoyed a national market. Southerners were such heavy consumers that the Georgia Baptist Association felt compelled to warn its members "the more you drink, the more you want to drink. We fear great harm will grow out of this sooner or later, to our young people in particular." The Baptists may have been onto something, as Coca-Cola's original formula did, in fact, include chemically active coca leaves.

—David Goldfield et al.,
The American Journey, 3rd ed.

171 words

Finishing time: _____ minutes _____ seconds

Words per minute: _____

Time (Min.)	Words per Minute	Time (Min.)	Words per Minute
0:30	346	1:00	173
0:40	260	1:10	94
0:50	208	1:20	86

Mark each statement with *T* (true) or *F* (false).

___T___ 1. Coca-Cola was initially developed by a southern pharmacist to soothe ordinary headaches.

___F___ 2. Dr. Pemberton made a fortune from his soft drink once it became a nationally marketed product.

exercise 11.3   **Pacing**

Predict organization: Is it simple listing or description? _Description_____

SPAM

Anybody with an e-mail address gets it—spam, or unsolicited e-mail. Several spam items invite you to apply for very inexpensive life insurance. "John" offers you an opportunity to earn $50,000 with only a $20 investment. How about getting a university diploma without studying or going to class? Though most of us would prefer not to be spammed, it's as difficult to rid the public Internet of spam as it is to rid our mail boxes of junk mail. Just like at home, we must sort through the spam to find our legitimate e-mail. Also, people are concerned that spam is taking up valuable bandwidth on the Internet, stressing the information capacity of the Net.

Let's dispel the myth that the term, *spam*, was derived from the SPAM luncheon meat made by Hormel Foods. Actually, the derivation of spam can be traced back to an old Monty Python comedy routine where Vikings howled "spam spam spam spam" to drown out other conversations. Similarly, spam tends to overwhelm people's e-mail boxes, making important messages difficult to find.

Spammers get your e-mail address through a variety of sources. It is difficult to track how you turn up on somebody's spam list. One thing is for sure, spam costs you more to receive than it does for it to be sent. Consider the fact that millions of spam messages are sent each day to AOL users. The result is that these users must spend up to 10 cumulative person-years simply deleting these unwanted messages.

—Larry Long and Nancy Long,
Computers, 11th ed.

251 words

Finishing time: _____ minutes _____ seconds

Words per minute: _____

Time (Min.)	Words per Minute	Time (Min.)	Words per Minute
0:30	502	1:10	215
0:40	377	1:20	188
0:50	301	1:30	167
1:00	251	1:40	151

Mark each statement with *T* (true) or *F* (false).

_____F_____ 1. According to the authors, spam does not stress the information capacity of the Internet.

_____F_____ 2. According to the authors, spam received its name from the Hormel Foods product.

exercise 11.4 **Pacing**

Predict organization: Is the following passage organized by description or time order? Description _____

JEFFERSON AS PRESIDENT

Jefferson had no desire to surround himself with pomp and ceremony. The excessive formality of the Washington and Adams administrations had been distasteful to him. From the moment of his election, he played down the ceremonial aspects of the presidency. He asked that he be notified of his election by mail rather than by a committee, and he would have preferred to have taken the oath at Charlottesville, near Monticello, his home, rather than at Washington. After the inauguration, he returned to his boardinghouse on foot and took dinner in his usual seat at the common table.

In the White House he often wore a frayed coat and carpet slippers, even to receive the representatives of foreign powers when they arrived, resplendent with silk ribbons and a sense of their own importance, to present their credentials. At social affairs he paid little heed to the status and seniority of his guests. When dinner was announced, he offered his arm to whichever lady he was talking to at the moment and placed her at his right; other guests were free to sit wherever they found an empty chair. During business hours congressmen, friends, foreign officials, and plain citizens coming to call took their turn in the order of their arrival. "The principle of society with us," Jefferson explained, "is the equal rights of all . . . Nobody shall be above you, nor you above anybody."

—Mark C. Carnes and John A. Garraty,
The American Nation: A History of the United States, 12th ed.,
Vol 1.: To 1877

235 words

Finishing time: _____ minutes _____ seconds

Words per minute: _____

Time (Min.)	Words per Minute	Time (Min.)	Words per Minute
0:30	470	1:00	235
0:40	353	1:10	201
0:50	282	1:20	176

Mark each statement with *T* (true) or *F* (false).

___F___ 1. Jefferson's presidency relied heavily on ceremony and formality during social events.

___F___ 2. Jefferson only dressed to impress when he was meeting foreign dignitaries.

exercise 11.5 **Pacing**

Before reading the following passage, use the title and any clues in the passage to predict organization: Is it definition or generalization and example? _____

Generalization and example

TAKING A BITE OUT OF CRIME WITH PIZZA

Uncollectable debts are a recurring problem, and a financial drain, for most U.S. businesses. Consumers hold more than 53 million past-due credit-card accounts totaling $36 billion, and each year they write bad checks for even more. In attempting to recover lost monies, companies resort to measures such as hiring credit collection agencies and filing charges with district attorney's offices for prosecution. Collection agents track down offenders, sometimes using threatening calls and bullying tactics to recover overdue debt payments. With all these methods, though, retailers still typically write off up to 5 percent of sales in bad debts.

Skillful, non-paying debtors can be elusive and untraceable by changing residences, phone numbers, and checking accounts. Surprisingly, however, even the most elusive debtors are succumbing to a new weapon: the pizza. David Coplen, budget director of Missouri's Office of State Courts, has found out pizza delivery lists are one of the best sources for locating people. He plans to use that information for tracking down those who owe fines or fees and making them pay. "When you call to order a pizza, you usually give them your correct name, your correct address, and your correct phone number," says Coplen. Dallas-based ACS Inc., a data-mining firm, will comb through pizza companies' databases for names to be matched against lists of delinquent Missouri debtors. In return, for every $1 of a court fee it collects, ACS may add a surcharge of up to 20 percent onto the debt owed. Coplen states that in addition to bringing money into the state, the new arrangement will remind people that when they are fined, they are accountable for paying up.

—Ricky W. Griffin and Ronald J. Ebert,
Business, 8th ed.

272 words

Finishing time: _____ minutes _____ seconds

Words per minute: _____

Time (Min.)	Words per Minute	Time (Min.)	Words per Minute
0:30	543	1:10	233
0:40	408	1:20	204
0:50	326	1:30	181
1:00	272	1:40	163

Mark each statement with *T* (true) or *F* (false).

___T___ 1. Pizza delivery lists are valuable in locating correct and current addresses for many non-paying debtors.

___F___ 2. ACS Inc. has created a business based on recovering bad checks written to pizza restaurants.

Skimming

Skimming is a technique of selectively reading for the main idea. Because it involves processing material at rates of around 900 words per minute, it is not defined by some experts as reading. Skimming involves skipping words, sentences, paragraphs, and even pages. It is a method of quickly overviewing material to answer the question, "What is this about?"

Skimming and previewing are very similar in that both involve getting an overview. Previewing sets the stage for later careful reading, whereas skimming is a substitute for a complete reading. Skimming is useful for material that you want to know about but don't have the time to read. For example, you might want to skim some supplemental articles that have been placed on reserve in the library because your professor expects you only to understand the main idea of each article and a complete reading would be unnecessary. Or you may want to pick up a book and just "get the idea" but not read it completely. Skimming is a useful tool. The technique is presented in the Reader's Tip on page 590.

Reader's *Tip* ────── Techniques for Skimming
──

- Read the title and subheadings as well as words in italics and bold-face print to get an idea of what the material is about.
- Try to get an insight into the organization of the material, as discussed in Chapter 5, to help you anticipate where the important points will be located. Look for certain organizational patterns and understand their functions:

  Simple listing: explains items of equal value.

  Definition: defines a term and gives examples to help the reader understand the term.

  Time order or sequence: presents items in chronological order.

  Comparison-contrast: compares similarities and differences of items.

  Description: explains characteristics of an item.

  Cause and effect: shows how one item has produced another.

  Addition: provides more information.

  Classification: divides items into groups or categories.

  Generalization and example: explains with examples to illustrate.

  Location or spatial order: identifies the whereabouts of objects.

  Summary: condenses major points.
- If the first paragraph is introductory, read it. If not, skip to a paragraph that seems to introduce the topic.
- Move rapidly, letting your eyes float over the words. Try to grasp the main ideas and the significant supporting details.
- Notice first sentences in paragraphs, and read them if they seem to be summary statements.
- Skip words that seem to have little meaning, like *a, an,* and *the.*
- Skip sentences or sections that seem to contain the following:

  Familiar ideas

  Unnecessary details

  Superfluous examples

  Restatements or unneeded summaries

  Material irrelevant to your purpose
- If the last paragraph of a section is a summary, read it if you need to check your understanding.

Scanning

Because **scanning** is a process of searching for a single bit of information, it is more of a locating skill than a reading skill (see the following Reader's Tip). A common use of scanning is looking up a number in a telephone book. When scanning for information, you are not trying to understand the meaning of the material; instead you are merely trying to pinpoint a specific detail. For example, you might find that after reading a chapter on pricing in your marketing textbook, you cannot recall the definition of *price lining*. To locate the information, you would not reread the entire chapter but scan it to find the term *price lining* and then review the definition. This same scanning technique works well when you use a glossary or an index or when you do research on the Internet.

Reader's *Tip* ——— Techniques for Scanning

- Figure out the organization of the material. Get an overview of which section will probably contain the information you are looking for.
- Know specifically what you are looking for. Decide on a key expression that will signal your information, but be ready to switch to a related idea if that doesn't work.
- Repeat the phrase and hold the image in your mind. Concentrate on the image so that you will recognize it when it comes into view.
- Move quickly and aggressively. Remember, you are scanning, not reading.
- Verify through careful reading. After locating your information, read carefully to make sure you have really found it.

Researchers use a combination of skimming and scanning. If you are working on a research paper on paranoia, you might have a list of 30 books and articles to read. A complete reading of each reference is probably unnecessary. Instead, you can scan to locate the information relevant to your topic and skim to get the main idea.

Summary *Points*

➤ **What is your reading rate?**

Your individual reading rate can be calculated if you know your total reading time and the total number of words read during that time.

➤ **How fast should you read?**

The average adult reading speed on relatively easy material is approximately 250 words per minute at 70 percent comprehension.

➤ **How do faster readers maintain a better reading rate?**

Faster readers concentrate, are curious to learn, stay mentally alert, and are motivated to achieve.

➤ **What are some techniques for faster reading?**

Before reading, make predictions, anticipate organization, and activate schemata. Using the pen as a pacer is an important technique that can improve both concentration and rate.

➤ **What happens during regression?**

With regression, you must go back and reread material because of inattention. Regression thus wastes time.

➤ **Why skim?**

Skimming is a technique that allows you to get a quick overview of the material.

➤ **What is scanning?**

Scanning is the process of searching for a single bit of information.

Foreign Terms

- *bon vivant:* a lover of good living; a gourmet

  While living in Paris with plenty of money, he enjoyed the lifestyle of a *bon vivant*.

- *avant-garde:* advance guard, pioneers, offbeat

  The radical ideas of the sociology professor may be too *avant-garde* for the conservative freshmen.

- *carte blanche:* "white paper," unlimited authority, blanket permission

  The new company gave her *carte blanche* to entertain the top three customers at the convention.

- *magnum opus:* great work

  After seven years of work, the novel was recognized as the author's *magnum opus*.

- *de rigueur:* strict etiquette, very formal, in good taste at the moment

  A jacket and necktie are *de rigueur* for the occasion.

- *déjà vu:* already seen

  The feeling of *déjà vu* became more intense as the same people seemed to be saying the same things as in 1997.

- *double entendre:* allowing two interpretations with one usually being off color

  As soon as the sentence was uttered, the speaker realized the *double entendre* and laughed knowingly.

- *faux pas:* "false step," or mistake

  I realized the *faux pas* when I saw my friends giggling in the background.

- *joie de vivre:* "joy for living"

  The guide's *joie de vivre* was contagious, making the trip enjoyable for us all.

- *esprit de corps:* group spirit of pride

  Through shared experiences, the marines build a strong *esprit de corps*.

- *coup d'état:* sudden stroke that overturns the government

  The foreign diplomats sought to leave before the predicted *coup d'état*.

- *raison d'être:* "reason for being," justification

  For the last three years, raising my child has been my *raison d'être*.

- *potpourri:* mixture

  A *potpourri* of ideas was presented for the group to consider.

- *nouveau riche:* newly rich, suggesting poor taste

  Have you seen the pillow that says, "Better to be *nouveau riche* than not rich at all"?

- *nom de plume:* pen name, pseudonym

  Samuel Clemens used Mark Twain as his *nom de plume.*

- *junta:* group of political plotters

  By gaining control of the military, the *junta* overthrew the existing government.

- *sotto voce:* "under the voice," whisper

  The criticism was overheard even though it was said *sotto voce.*

- *vendetta:* blood feud

  Because of the assault, the gang continued the *vendetta.*

- *alfresco:* "in the fresh air," outdoors

  During the summer months, the restaurant offered *alfresco* dining.

- *fait accompli:* finished action

  Submit your comments to the dean before the decision becomes a *fait accompli.*

REVIEW

Part I

Indicate whether the following sentences are true (*T*) or false (*F*):

_____T_____ 1. If you fail to discuss grades with your instructor before final conferences, the mark you receive is most likely a *fait accompli.*

_____F_____ 2. During the cold winter months, many restaurant patrons enjoy dining *alfresco.*

_____F_____ 3. *Avant-garde* forms of art are considered old-fashioned.

_____T_____ 4. One who is a *bon vivant* could be said to enjoy the good life.

_____T_____ 5. Being color blind, her boyfriend failed to realize that combining red shorts with an orange shirt could be a serious fashion *faux pas.*

_____F_____ 6. His *raison d'être* for failing to notify us of his late arrival was that his cell phone had no remaining minutes.

_____F_____ 7. A person with great *joie de vivre* would likely be an unpleasant companion.

_____F_____ 8. A *coup d'état* is not likely to occur in a country with an unstable government.

_____T_____ 9. The graduate student considered her doctoral thesis to be her *magnum opus.*

_____T_____ 10. A novelist may write books using a *nom de plume.*

_____F_____ 11. Tourists in Italy may observe the sights and scenes of Venice while riding in a *vendetta*.

_____F_____ 12. A *junta* does not desire political power.

Part II

Choose the word from the boxed list that means the opposite of the words below.

nouveau riche	sotto voce	de rigueur	déjà vu
esprit de corps	double entendre	carte blanche	potpourri

13. casual _____de rigueur_____

14. low morale _____esprit de corps_____

15. restricted power _____carte blanche_____

16. not seen before _____déjà vu_____

17. single meaning _____double entendre_____

18. loudly _____sotto voce_____

19. one variety _____potpourri_____

20. chronically poor _____nouveau riche_____

12 Test Taking

- Can being testwise improve your score?
- How should you prepare before a test?
- What should you notice during a test?
- What strategies should you use to read a comprehension passage?
- What are the major question types?
- What hints help with multiple-choice items?
- How do you answer an essay question?

Victor Bregeda, *Transformation.*

Can Being Testwise Improve Your Score?

Are you preparing for a midterm or another important exam? Is it a multiple-choice or essay test? Can test-taking tricks help you get a higher score?

Research shows that gimmicks, such as schemes involving length of responses or the likelihood of *b* or *c* being the right answer, don't work.[1]

However, insight into the testing experience can help. High scores depend on preparation, both mental and physical.

The purpose of this chapter is to help you gain points by being aware. You can improve your score by understanding how tests are constructed and what is needed for maximum performance. Study the following and do everything you can both mentally and physically to gain an edge.

Strategies for Mental and Physical Preparation

Before Taking a Test

Get Plenty of Sleep the Night Before. How alert can you be with inadequate sleep? Would you want a surgeon operating on you if he had slept only a few hours the night before? The mental alertness you derive from a good night's sleep can add as much as six points to your score and mean the difference between passing or failing. Why gamble by staying up late? Prioritize tasks and budget your time during the day so you can go to bed on time.

Arrive Five or Ten Minutes Early and Get Settled. If you run into class flustered at the last second, you will spend the first five minutes of the test calming yourself rather than getting immediately to work. Avoid unnecessary stress by arriving for the test early. Find a seat, get settled with pen or pencil and paper, and relax with a classmate by making small talk.

Know What to Expect on the Test. Ask beforehand if the test will be essay or multiple choice so that you can anticipate the format when you study. Both stress main ideas, and research shows that one is not easier than the other.[2]

Have Confidence in Your Abilities. Achieve self-confidence by being well prepared. Be optimistic, and approach the test with a positive mental attitude. Lack of preparation breeds anxiety, but positive testing experiences tend to breed confidence. Don't miss quizzes; research shows that students who have frequent quizzes during a course tend to do better on the final exam.[3]

---

[1]W. G. Brozo, R. V. Schmelzer, and H. A. Spires, "A Study of Test-Wiseness Clues in College and University Teacher-Made Tests with Implications for Academic Assistance Centers," *College Reading and Learning Assistance*, Technical Report 84–01 (ERIC 1984), ED 240928.

[2]P. M. Clark, "Examination Performance and Examination Set," in D. M. Wark, ed., *Fifth Yearbook of the North Central Reading Association* (Minneapolis: Central Reading Association, 1968), pp. 114–22.

[3]M. L. Fitch, A. J. Drucker, and J. A. Norton, "Frequent Testing as a Motivating Factor in Large Lecture Classes," *Journal of Educational Psychology* 42 (1951): 1–20.

Know How the Test Will Be Scored. If the test has several sections, be very clear on how many points can be earned from each section so you can prioritize your time and effort. Determine if some items are worth more points than others. Find out if there is a penalty for guessing and, if so, what it is. Because most test scores are based on answering all the questions, you are usually better off guessing than leaving items unanswered. Research shows that educated guessing can add points to your score.[4]

Plan Your Attack. At least a week before the test, take an inventory of what you need to do and make plans to achieve your goals. Preparation can make a difference for both standardized tests and with content area exams. The Reader's Tip lists the elements of a sound test preparation strategy.

Reader's *Tip* ── Preparing for a Test

Professors report that students gain awareness before content area exams by writing truthful answers to questions like the following:

- **How will the test look?** How many parts will the test have? What kinds of questions will be asked? How will points be counted?
- **What material will be covered?** What textbook pages will the test cover? What lecture notes will be included? Will outside reading be significant?
- **How will you study?** Have you made a checklist or study guide? Have you read all the material? Will you study notes or annotations from your textbook? Will you write down answers to potential essay questions? Will you include time to study with a classmate?
- **When will you study?** What is your schedule the week before the test? How long will you need to study? How much of the material do you plan to cover each day? What are your projected study hours?
- **What grade are you honestly working to achieve?** Are you willing to work for an A, or are you actually trying to earn a B or C?

During the Test

Concentrate. Tune out internal and external distractions and focus your attention on the test. Visualize and integrate old and new knowledge as you work. Read with curiosity and an eagerness to learn something new. Predict, picture, relate, monitor, and use correction strategies. If you become anxious or distracted, close your eyes and take a few deep breaths to relax and get yourself back on track.

On a teacher-made test, you may have a few thoughts that you want to jot down immediately on the back of the test so you don't forget them. Do so, and proceed with confidence.

---

[4]R. C. Preston, "Ability of Students to Identify Correct Responses Before Reading," *Journal of Educational Research* 58 (1964): 181–83.

Read and Follow Directions. Find out what to do and then do it. On a multiple-choice test, perhaps more than one answer is needed. Perhaps on an essay exam you are to respond to only three of five questions.

Schedule Your Time. Wear a watch and use it. When you receive your copy of the test, look it over, size up the task, and allocate your time. Determine the number of sections to be covered, and organize your time accordingly. As you work through the test, periodically check to see if you are meeting your time goals.

On teacher-made tests, the number of points for each item may vary. Do the easy items first, but spend the most time on the items that will yield the most points.

Work Rapidly. Every minute counts. Do not waste the time that you may need later by pondering at length over an especially difficult item. Mark the item with a check or a dot and move on to the rest of the test. If you have a few minutes at the end of the test, return to the marked items for further study.

Think. Use knowledge, logic, and common sense in responding to the items. Be aggressive and alert in moving through the test.

If you are unsure, use a process of elimination to narrow down the options. Double-check your paper to make sure you have answered every item.

Ignore Students Who Finish Early. Early departures draw attention and can create anxiety for those still working, but reassure yourself with the knowledge that students who finish early do not necessarily make the highest scores. Rapid workers do not necessarily work more accurately. If you have time, carefully review test items that you found yourself answering with less confidence. If your reassessment leads you to another response, change your answer to agree with your new thoughts. Research shows that scores can be improved by making such changes.[5]

After the Test

Analyze Your Preparation. Question yourself after the test, and learn from the experience. Did you study the right material? Do you wish you had spent more time studying any particular topic? Were you mentally and physically alert enough to function at your full capacity?

Analyze the Test. Decide if the test was what you expected. If not, what was unexpected? Did the professor describe the test accurately or were there a few surprises? Why were you surprised? Use your memory of the test to predict the patterns of future tests.

Analyze Your Performance. Most standardized tests are not returned, but you do receive scores and subscores. What do these scores tell you about your strengths and weaknesses? What can you do to improve?

---

[5]F. K. Berrien, "Are Scores Increased on Objective Tests by Changing the Initial Decision?" *Journal of Educational Psychology* 31 (1940): 64–67.

Content area exams are usually returned and reviewed in class. Ask questions about your errors. Find out why any weak responses did not receive full credit. Look for patterns of strengths and weaknesses in planning for the next test.

Meet with your professor if you are confused or disappointed and ask for suggestions for improvement. Find out if tutorial sessions or study groups are available for you to join. Ask to see an A paper. Formulate a plan with your professor for improved performance on the next test.

Strategies for Standardized Reading Tests

Read to Comprehend the Passage as a Whole

Students often ask, "Should I read the questions first and then read the passage?" Although the answer to this is subject to some debate, most reading experts would not recommend this practice.

The reasoning behind reading the passage first and then answering the questions is convincingly logical. Examining the questions first burdens the reader with a confusing collection of key words and phrases. Rather than reading to comprehend the author's message, you must instead search for many bits of information. Reading becomes fragmented and lacks focus; and few people are capable of reading with five or six purposes in mind. Not only is the reading-of-questions-first method confusing, but because it is detail oriented, it does not prepare you for more general questions concerning the main idea and implied meanings.

Read to understand the passage as a whole. If you understand the central theme or main idea, the rest of the ideas fall into place. The central theme may have several divisions that are developed in the different paragraphs. Attempt to understand what each paragraph contributes to the central theme. Don't fret over details, other than understanding how they contribute to the central theme. If you find later that a minor detail is needed to answer a question, you can quickly use a key word to locate and reread for accuracy the sentence in which it appears.

Anticipate What Is Coming Next

Most test passages are untitled and thus offer no initial clue for content. Before reading, glance at the passage for a repeated word, name, or date. In other words, look for any quick clue to let you know whether the passage is about Queen Victoria, pit bulls, or chromosome reproduction.

Do not rush through the first sentence. The first sentence further activates your schema and sets the stage for what is to come. In some cases, the first sentence might give an overview or even state the central theme. In other cases, it might simply pique your curiosity or stimulate your imagination. You might begin to guess what will come next and how it will be stated.

Read Rapidly, but Don't Allow Yourself to Feel Rushed

Use your pen as a pacer to direct your attention both mentally and physically to the printed page. Using your pen will help you focus your attention, particularly at the times during the test when you feel more rushed.

Be aware of the times when you might feel rushed and uneasy. Such feelings tend to be with you at the beginning of a test when you have not yet begun to concentrate—during those unsettled moments just before you become mentally involved with the work. In the middle of the test, you might feel anxious again if you look at your watch and discover you are only half finished and half your time is gone (which is where you should be). Toward the end of the test, when the first person finishes, you will again feel rushed if you have not finished. Check your time, keep your cool, and use your pen as a pacer. Continue working with control and confidence.

Read to Learn and Enjoy

Reading a passage to answer five or six questions is reading with an artificial purpose. Usually you read to learn and enjoy, not for the sole purpose of quickly answering questions. However, most test passages can be fairly interesting to a receptive reader. Use the thinking strategies of a good reader to become involved in the material. Picture what you read, and relate the ideas to what you already know.

Self-Test for the Main Idea

Pull it together before pulling it apart. At the end of a passage, self-test for the main idea. This is a final monitoring step that should be seen as part of the reading process. Take perhaps 10 or 15 seconds to pinpoint the focus of the passage and to review the point that the author is trying to make. Again, if you understand the main point, the rest of the passage will fall into place.

Read the passage on the next page and pretend it is part of a reading comprehension test. Read it using the suggestions just discussed. Note the handwritten reminders to make you aware of a few aspects of your thinking.

Certainly your reading of the passage contained many more thoughts than those indicated on the page. The gossip at the beginning of the passage humanizes the empress and makes it easier for the reader to relate emotionally to the historic figure. Did you anticipate Peter's downfall and Catherine's subsequent relationships? Did you note the shift from gossip to accomplishments, both national and international? The shift signals the alert reader to a change in style, purpose, and structure.

Before proceeding to the questions that follow a passage, take a few seconds to regroup and think about what you have read. Self-test by pulling the material together before you tear it apart. Think about the focus of the passage, and then proceed to the questions.

Recognizing the Major Question Types

Learn to recognize the types of questions asked on reading comprehension tests. Although the phraseology might vary slightly, most tests will include one or more questions on main idea, details, inference, purpose, and vocabulary.

Main Idea

Main-idea questions test your ability to find the central theme, central focus, gist, controlling idea, main point, or thesis. These terms are largely interchangeable in

No title, so glance for key words. Dates? Names?

Practice Passage A

Great image

In January 1744 a coach from Berlin bumped its way eastward over ditches and mud toward Russia. It carried Sophia, a young German princess, on a bridal journey. At the Russian border she was met with pomp, appropriate for one chosen to be married to Peter, heir to the Russian throne. The wedding was celebrated in August 1745 with gaiety and ceremony. *Why wait 1½ years?*

Surprise!

Will he be tsar?

What is she planning?

Did she kill him?

For Sophia the marriage was anything but happy because the seventeen-year-old heir was "physically less than a man and mentally little more than a child." The "moronic booby" played with dolls and toy soldiers in his leisure time. He neglected his wife and was constantly in a drunken stupor. Moreover, Peter was strongly pro-German and made no secret of his contempt for the Russian people, intensifying the unhappiness of his ambitious young wife. This dreary period lasted for seventeen years, but Sophia used the time wisely. She set about "russifying" herself. She mastered the Russian language and avidly embraced the Russian faith; on joining the Orthodox church, she was renamed Catherine. She devoted herself to study, reading widely the works of Montesquieu, Voltaire, and other Western intellectuals. *What is that? How?*

Ironic, since she's not Russian

When Peter became tsar in January 1762, Catherine immediately began plotting his downfall. Supported by the army, she seized power in July 1762 and tacitly consented to Peter's murder. It was announced that he died of "hemorrhoidal colic." Quickly taking over the conduct of governmental affairs, Catherine reveled in her new power. For the next thirty-four years the Russian people were dazzled by their ruler's political skill and cunning and her superb conduct of tortuous diplomacy. Perhaps even more, they were intrigued by gossip concerning her private life. *What gossip? Lovers?*

Unusual term

Did she kill them?

Long before she became empress, Catherine was involved with a number of male favorites referred to as her house pets. At first her affairs were clandestine, but soon she displayed her lovers as French kings paraded their mistresses. Once a young man was chosen, he was showered with lavish gifts; when the empress tired of him, he was given a lavish going-away present.

Now moving from personal info to accomplishments

Double check years—not long

So, she did little toward human progress

Catherine is usually regarded as an enlightened despot. She formed the Imperial Academy of Art, began the first college of pharmacy, and imported foreign physicians. Her interest in architecture led to the construction of a number of fine palaces, villas, and public buildings and the first part of the Hermitage in Saint Petersburg. Attracted to Western culture, she carried on correspondence with the French *philosophes* and sought their flattery by seeming to champion liberal causes. The empress played especially on Voltaire's vanity, sending him copious praise about his literary endeavors. In turn this *philosophe* became her most ardent admirer. Yet while Catherine discussed liberty and equality before the law, her liberalism and dalliance with the Enlightenment was largely a pose—eloquent in theory, lacking in practice. The lot of serfs actually worsened, leading to a bloody uprising in 1773. This revolt brought an end to all talk of reform. And after the French Revolution, strict censorship was imposed. *Changes to foreign policy accomplishments*

In her conduct of foreign policy, the empress was ruthless and successful. She annexed a large part of Poland and, realizing that Turkey was in decline, waged two wars against this ailing power. As a result of force and diplomacy, Russian frontiers reached the Black Sea, the Caspian, and the Baltic. Well could this shrewd practitioner of power tell her adopted people, "I came to Russia a poor girl. Russia has dowered me richly, but I have paid her back with Azov, the Crimea, and Poland." *What was the point?*

T. Walter Wallbank et al.,
Civilization Past and Present

asking the reader to identify the main point of the passage. Main-idea items are stated in any of the following forms:

> The best statement of the main idea is . . .
> The best title for this passage is . . .
> The author is primarily concerned with . . .
> The central theme of the passage is . . .

Incorrect responses to main idea items tend to fall into two categories. Some responses will be too general and express more ideas than are actually included in the passage. Other incorrect items will be details within the passage that support the main idea. The details might be interesting and grab your attention, but they do not describe the central focus of the passage. If you are having difficulty with the main idea, reread the first and last sentences of the passage. Sometimes, though not always, one of the two sentences will give you an overview or focus.

The following main idea items apply to Practice Passage A on Catherine the Great.

EXAMPLE   Read the following main idea items. The italicized parenthetical remarks reflect the thinking involved in judging a correct or incorrect response.

_____   Which is the best statement of the main idea of this passage?

    a. Peter lost his country through ignorance and drink. (*Important detail, but focus is on her.*)
    b. Gossip of Catherine's affairs intrigued the Russian people. (*Very interesting, but a detail.*)
    c. Progress for the Russian people was slow to come. (*Too broad and general, or not really covered.*)
    d. Catherine came to Russia as a poor girl but emerged as a powerful empress and a shrewd politician. (*Yes, sounds great.*)

_____   The best title for this passage is

    a. Catherine Changes Her Name. (*Detail.*)
    b. Peter Against Catherine. (*Only part of the story, so detail.*)
    c. Catherine the Great, Empress of Russia. (*Sounds best.*)
    d. Success of Women in Russia. (*Too broad—this is only about one woman.*)

Details

Detail questions check your ability to locate and understand explicitly stated material. Frequently, such items can be answered correctly without a thorough understanding of the passage. To find the answer to such an item, note a key word in the question and then scan the passage for the word or a synonym. When you locate the term, reread the sentence to double-check your answer. Lead-ins for detail questions fall into the following patterns:

The author states that . . .
According to the author . . .
According to the passage . . .
All of the following are true except . . .
A person, term, or place is . . .

Incorrect answers to detail questions tend to be false statements. Sometimes the test maker will trick the unsophisticated reader by using a pompous or catchy phrase from the passage as a **distractor**—a word that is meant to divert your attention away from the correct response. The phrase might indeed appear in the passage and sound authoritative, but on close inspection, it means nothing.

EXAMPLE Read the following detail question on Catherine the Great, and note the remarks in parentheses:

_____ Catherine changed all the following *except* (*look for the only false item as the answer*)

    a. her religion. (*True, she joined the Orthodox church.*)
    b. her name. (*True, from Sophia to Catherine.*)
    c. Russia's borders. (*True, she gained seaports.*)
    d. the poverty of the serfs. (*The serfs were worse off but still in poverty, so this is the best answer.*)

Implied Meaning

Questions concerning implied meaning test your ability to look beyond what is directly stated and your understanding of the suggested meaning.

Items testing implied meaning deal with the writer's attitudes, feelings, or the motivation of characters. They may come in the form of sarcastic comments, snide remarks, favorable and unfavorable descriptions, and a host of other hints and clues. Lead-ins for such items include the following:

The author believes (or feels or implies) . . .
It can be inferred from the passage . . .
The passage or author suggests . . .
It can be concluded from the passage that . . .

To answer inference items correctly, look for clues to help you develop logical assumptions. Base your conclusions on what is known and what is suggested. Incorrect inference items tend to be false statements.

EXAMPLE Study the following inference question. The parenthetical italicized remarks reflect the thought process involved in selecting the correct answer.

_____ The author implies that Catherine

 a. did not practice the enlightenment she professed. (*Yes, "eloquent in theory but lacking practice."*)
 b. preferred French over Russian architecture. (*Not suggested.*)
 c. took Voltaire as her lover. (*Not suggested.*)
 d. came to Russia knowing her marriage would be unhappy. (*Not suggested.*)

Purpose

The purpose of a reading passage is not usually stated; it is implied. In a sense, the purpose is part of the main idea; you probably need to understand the main idea to understand the purpose. Generally, however, reading comprehension tests include three basic types of passages, and each type tends to dictate its own purpose. Study the following three types.

1. Factual
   Identification: gives the facts about science, history, or other subjects.
   Strategy: if complex, do not try to understand each detail before going to the questions. Remember, you can look back.
   Example: textbook.
   Purposes: to inform, to explain, to describe, or to enlighten.

2. Opinion
   Identification: puts forth a particular point of view.
   Strategy: the author states opinions and then refutes them. Sort out the opinions of the author and the opinions of the opposition.
   Example: newspaper editorial.
   Purposes: to argue, to persuade, to condemn, or to ridicule.

3. Fiction
   Identification: tells a story.
   Strategy: read slowly to understand the motivation and interrelationships of characters.
   Example: novel or short story
   Purposes: to entertain, narrate, describe, or shock.

EXAMPLE Read the following test item, and identify the purpose:

_____ The purpose of the passage on Catherine is

 a. to argue. (*No side is taken.*)
 b. to explain. (*Yes, because it is factual material.*)
 c. to condemn. (*Not judgmental.*)
 d. to persuade. (*No opinion is pushed.*)

Vocabulary

Vocabulary items test your general word knowledge as well as your ability to use context to figure out word meaning. The typical form for vocabulary items on reading comprehension tests is as follows:

As used in the passage, the best definition of _____ is _____ .

Note that both word knowledge and context are necessary for a correct response. The item is qualified by "As used in the passage," so you must go back and reread the sentence (context) in which the word appears to be sure you are not misled by multiple meanings. To illustrate, the word *pool* means *a body of water* as well as *a group of people* as in *the shrinking pool of job applicants*. As a test taker, you would need to double-check the context to see which meaning appears in your test passage. In addition, if you knew only one definition of the word *pool,* rereading the sentence would perhaps suggest the alternate meaning to you and help you answer the item correctly.

EXAMPLE   Read the following vocabulary test item, and note the reader's thought process in the parenthetical statements:

_____   As used in the passage, the best definition of *dreary* (see the second paragraph) is

a. sad. (*Yes, unhappiness is used in the previous sentence.*)
b. commonplace. (*Possible, but not right in the sentence.*)
c. stupid. (*Not right in the sentence.*)
d. neglected. (*True, but not the definition of the word.*)

Strategies for Multiple-Choice Items

Consider All Alternatives Before Choosing an Answer

Read all the options. Do not rush to record an answer without considering all the alternatives. Be careful, not careless, in considering each option. Multiple-choice test items usually ask for the best choice for an answer, rather than any choice that is reasonable.

EXAMPLE   Choose the best answer.

_____   Peter was most likely called a "moronic booby" because

a. he neglected Catherine.
b. he drank too much.
c. he disliked German customs.
d. he played with dolls and toys.

EXPLANATION Although the first three answers are true and reasonable, the last answer seems to be most directly related to that particular name.

Anticipate the Answer and Look for Something Close to It

As you read the beginning of a multiple-choice item, anticipate what you would write for a correct response. Develop an answer in your mind before you read the options, and then look for a response that corroborates your thinking.

EXAMPLE Before choosing from among *a*, *b*, *c*, and *d*, try to anticipate the correct response. Note the reader's thought process in italics.

_____ The author suggests that Catherine probably converted to the Russian Orthodox church because . . . *she wanted to rule the country and wanted the people to think of her as Russian, rather than German.*

a. she was a very religious person.
b. Peter wanted her to convert.
c. she was no longer in Germany.
d. she wanted to appear thoroughly Russian to the Russian people.

EXPLANATION The last answer most closely matches the kind of answer you were anticipating.

Avoid Answers with 100 Percent Words

All and *never* mean 100 percent, without exceptions. A response containing either word is seldom correct. Rarely can a statement be so definitely inclusive or exclusive. Here are some other 100 percent words to avoid:

no	none	only	every	always	must

EXAMPLE Answer the following with *true* or *false:*

_____ Catherine the Great was beloved by all the Russian people.

EXPLANATION *All* means 100 percent and thus is too inclusive. Surely one or two Russians did not like Catherine, so the answer must be *false.*

Consider Answers with Qualifying Words

Words like *sometimes* and *seldom* suggest frequency but do not go so far as to say *all* or *none.* Such qualifying words can mean more than *none* and less than *all.* By being so indefinite, the words are difficult to dispute. Therefore, qualifiers are more likely to be included in a correct response. Here are some other qualifiers:

few	much	often	may
many	some	perhaps	generally

EXAMPLE Answer the following with *true* or *false:*

_____ Catherine was beloved by many of the Russian people.

EXPLANATION The statement is difficult to dispute, given Catherine's popularity. An uprising against her occurred, but it was put down, and she maintained the support of many of the Russian people. Thus, the answer would be *true.*

Choose the Intended Answer Without Overanalyzing

Try to follow logically the thinking of the test writer rather than overanalyzing minute points. Don't make the question harder than it is. Use your common sense and answer what you think was intended.

EXAMPLE   Answer the following with *true* or *false:*

_____   Catherine was responsible for Peter's murder.

EXPLANATION This is false in that Catherine did not personally murder Peter. On the other hand, she did "tacitly consent" to his murder, which suggests responsibility. After seizing power, it was certainly in her best interest to get rid of Peter permanently. Perhaps without Catherine, Peter would still be playing with his toys, so the intended answer is *true.*

True Statements Must Be True Without Exception

A statement is either totally true or it is incorrect. Adding an incorrect *and, but,* or *because* phrase to a true statement makes the statement false and thus an unacceptable answer. If a statement is half true and half false, mark it *false.*

EXAMPLE   Answer the following with *true* or *false:*

_____   Catherine was an enlightened despot who did her best to improve the
            lot of all her people.

EXPLANATION It is true that Catherine was considered an enlightened despot, but she did very little to improve the lot of the serfs. In fact, conditions for the serfs worsened. The statement is half true and half false, so it must be answered *false.*

If Two Options Are Synonymous, Eliminate Both

If *both* is not a possible answer and two possible answers say basically the same thing, then neither can be correct. Eliminate the two and spend your time on the others.

EXAMPLE   Choose the correct answer, watching for synonyms.

_____   The purpose of this passage is

            a. to argue.
            b. to persuade.
            c. to inform.
            d. to entertain.

EXPLANATION Because *argue* and *persuade* are basically synonymous, you can eliminate both and move to the other options.

Study Similar Options to Determine the Differences

If two similar options appear, frequently one of them will be correct. Study the options to see the subtle difference intended by the test maker.

EXAMPLE   Choose the correct answer, noticing options that are similar.

_____   Catherine was

     a. unpopular during her reign.
     b. beloved by all of the Russian people.
     c. beloved by many of the Russian people.
     d. considered selfish and arrogant by the Russians.

EXPLANATION   The first and last answers are untrue. Close inspection shows that the 100 percent *all* is the difference between the second and third answers that makes the second answer untrue. Thus, the third answer with the qualifying word is the correct response.

Use Logical Reasoning If Two Answers Are Correct

Some tests include the options *all of the above* and *none of the above*. If you see that two of the options are correct and you are unsure about a third choice, then *all of the above* would be a logical response.

EXAMPLE   Choose the best answer. Be alert to the possibility that two options are actually correct.

_____   Catherine started

     a. the Imperial Academy of Art.
     b. the first college of pharmacy.
     c. the Hermitage.
     d. all of the above.

EXPLANATION   If you remembered that Catherine started the first two but were not sure about the Hermitage, *all of the above* would be your logical option because you know that two of the above *are* correct.

Look Suspiciously at Directly Quoted Pompous Phrases

In searching for distractors, test makers sometimes quote a pompous phrase from the passage that doesn't make much sense. Students read the phrase and think, "Oh, yes, I saw that in the passage. It sounds good, so it must be right." Beware of such repetitions and make sure they make sense before choosing them.

EXAMPLE Choose the answer that makes the most sense.

_____ In her country, Catherine enacted

     a. few of the progressive ideas she championed.
     b. the liberalism of the Enlightenment.
     c. laws for liberty and equality.
     d. the liberal areas of the philosophers.

EXPLANATION The first response is correct because Catherine talked about progress but did little about it. The other three answers sound impressive and are quoted from the text but are totally incorrect.

Simplify Double Negatives by Canceling Out Both

Double negatives are confusing to unravel and time consuming to think through. Simplify a double negative statement by first canceling out both negatives. Then reread the statement without the confusion of the two negatives, and decide on the accuracy of the statement.

EXAMPLE Answer the following with _true_ or _false_, being alert for double negatives:

_____ Catherine's view of herself was not that of an unenlightened ruler.

EXPLANATION Cancel out the two negatives, the _not_ and the _un_ in the word _unenlightened_. Reread the sentence without the negatives and decide on its accuracy: Catherine's view of herself was that of an enlightened ruler. The statement is correct, so the answer is _true_.

Use Can't-Tell Responses If Clues Are Insufficient

Mark an item _can't tell_ only if you are not given clues on which to base an assumption. In other words, there is no evidence to indicate the statement is either true or false.

EXAMPLE Use _true_, _false_, or _can't tell_ to describe the following item:

_____ Catherine the Great had no children.

EXPLANATION From the information in this passage, which is the information on which your reading test is based, you do not have any clues to indicate whether she did or did not have children. Thus, the answer must be _can't tell_.

Validate True Responses on "All the Following Except"

In this type of question, you must recognize several responses as correct and find the one that is incorrect. Corroborate each response and, by the process of elimination, find the one that does not fit.

Note Oversights on Hastily Constructed Tests

Reading tests developed by professional test writers are usually well-constructed and do not contain obvious clues to the correct answers. However, some teacher-made tests are hastily constructed and contain errors in test making that can help a student find the correct answer. Do not, however, rely on these flaws to make a big difference in your score because they should not occur in a well-constructed test.

Grammar. Eliminate responses that do not have subject-verb agreement. The tense of the verb as well as modifiers such as *a* or *an* can also give clues to the correct response.

EXAMPLE   Choose the correct answer to the following, paying attention to grammar:

_____   Because of his described habits, it is possible that Peter was an

        a. hemophiliac.
        b. alcoholic.
        c. Catholic.
        d. barbarian.

EXPLANATION   The *an* suggests an answer that starts with a vowel. Thus *alcoholic* is the only possibility.

Clues from Other Parts of the Test. If a test has been hastily constructed, information in one part of the test might help you with an uncertain answer.

EXAMPLE   Select the word that completes the following sentence correctly. Keep in mind the question you answered in the previous example.

_____   Not only was Peter childlike and neglectful, but he was also frequently

        a. abusive.
        b. drunk.
        c. dangerous.
        d. out of the country.

EXPLANATION   The previous question gives this answer away by stating that he was possibly an alcoholic.

Length. On poorly constructed tests, longer answers are correct more frequently.

EXAMPLE   Identify the option that completes the following sentence correctly:

_____   The word *cunning* used in describing Catherine suggests that she was

a. evil.
b. dishonest.
c. untrustworthy.
d. crafty and sly in managing affairs.

EXPLANATION   In an effort to be totally correct without question, the test maker has made the last answer so complete that its length gives it away.

Absurd Ideas and Emotional Words. Avoid distractors with absurd ideas or emotional words. The test maker probably got tired of thinking of distractors and in a moment of weakness included nonsense.

EXAMPLE   Choose the answer that makes the most sense.

_____   As used in the passage, the term *house pets* refers to

a. Peter's toys.
b. Catherine's favorite lovers.
c. the dogs and cats in the palace.
d. trained seals that performed for the empress.

EXPLANATION   Yes, the test maker has, indeed, become weary. The question itself has very little depth, and the last two answers are particularly flippant.

exercise 12.1   ## Reading with Understanding

The following selection is a passage from a reading comprehension test. Use what you have learned to read with understanding, and then answer the questions.

> Wolfgang Amadeus Mozart (1756–1791), one of the most amazing child prodigies in history, was born in Salzburg, Austria. By the age of six, he could play the harpsichord and violin, improvise fugues, write minuets, and read music perfectly at first sight. At age eight, he wrote a symphony; at eleven, an oratorio; at twelve, an opera.
>
> Mozart's father, Leopold, a court musician, was eager to show him off. Between the ages of six and fifteen Mozart was continually on tour; he played for Empress Maria Theresa in Vienna, Louis XV at Versailles, George III in London, and innumerable aristocrats. On his trips to Italy he was able to master the current operatic style, which he later put to superb use.
>
> When he was fifteen, Mozart returned to Salzburg—then ruled by a prince-archbishop. The archbishop was a tyrant who did not appreciate Mozart's music and refused to grant him more than a subordinate seat in the court orchestra. With his father's help, Mozart tried repeatedly but unsuccessfully over the next decade to find a position elsewhere.
>
> Ironically, and tragically, Mozart won more acclaim as a boy wonder than as an adult musician. Having begun his professional life as an international celebrity, he could not tolerate being treated like a servant; he became insubordinate when the

archbishop forbade him to give concerts or to perform at the houses of the aristocracy, and his relationship with his patron went from bad to worse. Moreover, his complete dependence on his father had given him little opportunity to develop initiative; and a contemporary observed that he was "too good-natured, not active enough, too easily taken in, too little concerned with the means that may lead him to good fortune."

When he was twenty-five, Mozart could stand it no more: he broke away from provincial Salzburg and became a freelance musician in Vienna. His first few years there were very successful. His German Opera *The Abduction from the Seraglio* (1782) was acclaimed; concerts of his own music were attended by the emperor and nobility; his compositions were published; pupils paid him high fees; and he formed a friendship with Haydn, who told Mozart's father, "Your son is the greatest composer that I know; he has taste and, what is more, the most profound knowledge of composition." In 1786 came his opera *The Marriage of Figaro*. Vienna loved it, and Prague was even more enthusiastic; "They talk of nothing but *Figaro*," Mozart joyfully wrote. This success led an opera company in Prague to commission *Don Giovanni* the next year.

Although *Don Giovanni* was a triumph in Prague, its dark qualities and dissonance did not appeal to the Viennese, and Mozart's popularity in Vienna began to decline. Vienna was a fickle city in any case, and it found Mozart's music complicated and hard to follow. His pupils dwindled; the elite snubbed his concerts.

During the last year of his life—1791—Mozart was more successful. He received a commission for a comic opera, *The Magic Flute*, and while working on it was visited by a mysterious stranger who carried an anonymous letter commissioning a requiem, a mass for the dead. As Mozart's health grew worse, he came to believe that the requiem was for himself and rushed to finish it while on his deathbed. (In fact, the stranger was the servant of a nobleman who intended to claim the requiem as his own composition.) *The Magic Flute* was premiered to resounding praise in Vienna, but its success came too late. Mozart died shortly before his thirty-sixth birthday, leaving the Requiem unfinished. (It was completed by his friend and pupil Franz Süssmayer.)

—Roger Kamien,
Music: An Appreciation, Fifth Brief Edition. Copyright © 2006 by
The McGraw-Hill Companies, Inc. Reproduced with permission.

Identify each question type, and answer with *a, b, c,* or *d*. In the right-hand column, explain what is wrong with the incorrect distractors.

_____a_____ 1. What is the best statement of the main idea of this passage?

(Question type ____Main Idea____)   (Explain errors)

a. Although Mozart was recognized as a gifted child musician, success during his adult years was more difficult to maintain.   ____Correct____

b. Mozart was a musical genius at age six.   ____Too narrow____

c. Mozart entertained the emperor and nobility as a freelance musician in Vienna.   ____Detail____

d. Mozart's father was the driving force behind his career in music.   ____Detail____ ___d___ 2. The best title for this passage is

(Question type ___Main Idea___)   **(Explain errors)**

a. Wolfgang: Boy Genius of Salzburg.   _Too narrow, detail_

b. The Music of Salzburg and Vienna.   _Too broad_

c. Mozart Dies at Thirty-six.   _Detail_

d. Mozart in Search of Musical Success.   _Correct_

___d___ 3. Mozart's father

(Question type ___Detail___)   **(Explain errors)**

a. was also a child prodigy.   _Not stated_

b. was a tyrant.   _Incorrect_

c. moved to Vienna with Mozart.   _Incorrect_

d. remained involved with his son's musical   _Correct_
career from childhood to adulthood.

___c___ 4. The author suggests all of the following *except:*

(Question type ___Implied Meaning___)   **(Explain errors)**

a. The audiences of Vienna were forever   _Correct, because false_
loyal to favored composers.

b. Mozart was paid to write *The Magic Flute*.   _True_

c. *The Magic Flute* was the last opera Mozart   _True_
completed.

d. The Requiem was not stolen from Mozart   _True_
and claimed by the nobleman.

___d___ 5. As used in the passage, the best definition of *subordinate* is

(Question type ___Vocabulary___)   **(Explain errors)**

a. remote.   _Incorrect_

b. beginning.   _Incorrect_

c. complimentary.   _Incorrect_

d. of lower rank.   _Correct_

___b___ 6. The author's purpose is to

(Question type ___Purpose___)   **(Explain errors)**

a. condemn.   _Does not condemn_

b. inform.   _Correct_

c. argue.   _No side taken_

d. persuade.   _Does not persuade_

Strategies for Content Area Exams

Almost all professors would say that the number one strategy for scoring high on content area exams is to study the material. Although this advice is certainly on target, there are other suggestions that can help you gain an edge.

Multiple-Choice Items

Multiple-choice, true-false, or matching items on content area exams are written to evaluate factual knowledge, conceptual comprehension, and application skill. *Factual questions* tap your knowledge of names, definitions, dates, events, and theories. *Conceptual comprehension* questions evaluate your ability to see relationships, notice similarities and differences, and combine information from different parts of a chapter. *Application questions* provide the opportunity to generalize from a theory to a real-life illustration; these are particularly popular in psychology and sociology.

To study for a multiple-choice test, make lists of key terms, facts, and concepts. Quiz yourself on recognition and general knowledge. Make connections and be sure you know similarities and differences. Finally, invent scenarios that depict principles and concepts.

EXAMPLE   The following is an example of an application question from psychology:

_____   An illustration of obsessive-compulsive behavior is

    a. Maria goes to the movies most Friday nights.
    b. Leon washes his hands more than a hundred times a day.
    c. Pepe wants to buy a car.
    d. Sue eats more fish than red meat.

EXPLANATION   The second response is obviously correct, but such questions can be tricky if you have not prepared for them. Use your own knowledge, plus the previous suggestions for multiple-choice tests, to separate answers from distractors.

Short-Answer Items

Professors ask short-answer questions because they want you to use your own words to describe or identify. For such questions, be sure that you understand exactly what the professor is asking you to say. You do not want to waste time writing more than is needed, but on the other hand, you do not want to lose points for not writing enough. Study for short-answer items by making lists and self-testing, just as you do when studying for multiple-choice items. For history exams, especially, be prepared to identify who, what, when, where, and why.

Essay Questions

Essay answers demand more effort and energy from the test taker than multiple-choice items. On a multiple-choice test, all the correct answers are before you. On an essay exam, however, the only thing in front of you is a question and a blank sheet of paper. This blank sheet can be intimidating to many students. Your job is to recall appropriate ideas, organize them under the central theme designated in the question, and create a response in your own words. The following suggestions can help you respond effectively.

Translate the Question. Frequently, an essay "question" is not a question at all but a statement that you are asked to support. When you see this type of question on a test, your first step is to read it and then reread it to be sure you understand it. Next, reword it into a question. Even if you begin with a question, translate it into your own words. Simplify the question into terms you can understand. Break the question into its parts.

Convert the translated parts of the question into the approach that you will need to use to answer each part. Will you define, describe, explain, or compare? State what you will do to answer. In a sense, this is a behavioral statement.

EXAMPLE   The following example demonstrates the translation process.

- **Statement to support.** It is both appropriate and ironic to refer to Catherine as one of the great rulers of Russia.
- **Question.** Why is it both appropriate and ironic to refer to Catherine as one of the great rulers of Russia?
- **Translation:** The question has two parts:
  1. What did Catherine do that was great?
  2. What did she do that was the opposite of what you would expect (irony) of a great Russian ruler?
- **Response approach.** List what Catherine did that was great and then list what she did that was the opposite of what you would expect of a great Russian ruler. Relate her actions to the question. (See page 603.)

Answer the Question. Make sure your answer is a response to the question that is asked, rather than a summary of everything you know about a particular subject. Write with purpose so that the reader can understand your views and relate your points to the subject. Padding your answer by repeating the same idea or including irrelevant information is obvious to graders and seldom appreciated.

EXAMPLE   The following is an inappropriate answer to the question "Why is it both appropriate and ironic to refer to Catherine as one of the great rulers of Russia?"

> Catherine was born in Germany and came to Russia as a young girl to marry Peter. It was an unhappy marriage that lasted seventeen years. She . . .

EXPLANATION   This response does not answer the question; rather, it is a summary.

Organize Your Response. Do not write the first thing to pop into your head. Take a few minutes to brainstorm and jot down ideas. Number the ideas in the order that you wish to present them, and use the plan shown on the opposite page as your outline for writing.

In your first sentence, establish the purpose and direction of your response. Then list specific details that support, explain, prove, and develop your point. Reemphasize the points in a concluding sentence, and restate your purpose. Whenever possible, use numbers or subheadings to simplify your message for the reader. If time runs short, use an outline or a diagram to express your remaining ideas.

I. Appropriate	II. Ironic (opposite)
1. Acquired land	1. Not Russian
2. Art, medicine, buildings	2. Killed Peter
3. 34 years	3. Serfs very poor
4. Political skill & foreign diplomacy	4. Revolt against her

EXAMPLE   To answer the previous question, think about the selection on Catherine and jot down the ideas that you would include in a response.

Use an Appropriate Style. Your audience for this response is not your best friend but your learned professor who is giving you a grade. Be respectful. Do not use slang. Do not use phrases like "as you know," "like," or "well." They may be appropriate in conversation, but they are not appropriate in formal writing.

Avoid empty words and thoughts. Words like *good, interesting,* and *nice* say very little. Be more direct and descriptive in your writing.

State your thesis, supply proof, and use transitional phrases to tie your ideas together. Words like *first, second,* and *finally* help to organize enumerations. Terms like *however* and *on the other hand* show a shift in thought. Remember, you are pulling ideas together, so use phrases and words to help the reader see relationships.

EXAMPLE   Study the following response to the question for organization, transition, and style.

> Catherine was a very good ruler of Russia. She tried to be Russian but she was from Germany. Catherine was a good politician and got Russia seaports on the Baltic, Caspian, and Black Sea. She had many boyfriends and there was gossip about her. She did very little for the Serfs because they remained very poor for a long time. She built nice buildings and got doctors to help people. She was not as awesome as she pretended to be.

EXPLANATION   Notice the response's lack of organization, weak language, inappropriate phrases, and failure to use transitional words.

Be Aware of Appearance. Research has shown that, on the average, an essay written in a clear, legible hand receives a score that is one grade level higher than does the essay written somewhat illegibly.[6] Be particular about appearance and considerate of the reader. Proofread for correct grammar, punctuation, and spelling.

Predict and Practice. Predict possible essay items by using the table of contents and subheadings of your text to form questions. Practice brainstorming to answer these questions. Review old exams for an insight both into the questions and the kinds of answers that received good marks. Outline answers to possible exam questions. Do as much thinking as possible to prepare yourself to take the test before you sit down to begin writing. The Reader's Tip shows the range of demands you might encounter in essay exams for your courses.

Reader's Tip — Key Words in Essay Questions

The following key words of instruction appear in essay questions.

- **Compare:** List the similarities between things.
- **Contrast:** Note the differences between things.
- **Criticize:** State your opinion and stress the weaknesses.
- **Define:** State the meaning so that the term is understood, and use examples.
- **Describe:** State the characteristics so that the image is vivid.
- **Diagram:** Make a drawing that demonstrates relationships.
- **Discuss:** Define the issue and elaborate on the advantages and disadvantages.
- **Evaluate:** State positive and negative views and make a judgment.
- **Explain:** Show cause and effect and give reasons.
- **Illustrate:** Provide examples.
- **Interpret:** Explain your own understanding of a topic that includes your opinions.
- **Justify:** Give proof or reasons to support an opinion.
- **List:** Record a series of numbered items.
- **Outline:** Sketch out the main points with their significant supporting details.
- **Prove:** Use facts as evidence in support of an opinion.
- **Relate:** Connect items and show how one influences another.
- **Review:** Write an overview with a summary.
- **Summarize:** Retell the main points.
- **Trace:** Move sequentially from one event to another.

---

[6]H. W. James, "The Effect of Handwriting upon Grading," *English Journal* 16 (1927): 180–85.

View Your Response Objectively for Evaluation Points. Respond to get points. Some students feel that filling up the page deserves a passing grade. They do not understand how a whole page written on the subject of Catherine could receive no points.

Although essay exams seem totally subjective, they cannot be. Students need to know that a professor who gives an essay exam grades answers according to an objective scoring system. The professor examines the paper for certain relevant points that should be made. The student's grade reflects the quantity, quality, and clarity of these relevant points.

Unfortunately, essay exams are shrouded in mystery. Sometimes the hardest part of answering an item is to figure out what the professor wants. Ask yourself, "What do I need to say to get enough points to pass or to make an A?"

Do not add personal experiences or extraneous examples unless they are requested. You may be wasting your time by including information that will give you no points. Stick to the subject and the material. Demonstrate to the professor that you know the material by selectively using it in your response.

The professor scoring the response to the question about Catherine used the following checklist for evaluation:

Appropriate	Ironic
1. Acquired land	1. Not Russian
2. Art, medicine, buildings	2. Killed Peter
3. 34 years	3. Serfs very poor
4. Political skill and foreign diplomacy	4. Revolt against her

The professor determined that an A paper should contain all the items. To pass, a student should include five of the eight categories covered. Listing and explaining fewer than five would not produce enough points to pass. Naturally, the professor would expect clarity and elaboration in each category.

After the Test, Read an A Paper. Maybe the A paper will be yours. If so, share it with others. If not, ask to read an A paper so that you will have a model from which to learn. Ask your classmates or ask the professor. You can learn a lot from reading a good paper; you can see what you could have done.

When your professor returns a multiple-choice exam, you can reread items and analyze your mistakes to figure out what you did wrong. However, you cannot review essay exams so easily. You may get back a C paper with only a word or two of comment and never know what you should have done. Ideally, essay exams should be returned with an example of what would have been a perfect A response so that students can study and learn from a perfect model and not make the same mistakes on the next test, but this is seldom, if ever, done. Your best bet is to ask to see an A paper.

EXAMPLE   Study the following response to the previous question. The paper received an A.

> To call Catherine one of the great rulers of Russia is both appropriate and ironic. It is appropriate because she expanded the borders of Russia. Through her cunning, Russia annexed part of Poland and expanded the frontier to the Black, Caspian, and Baltic seas. Catherine professed to be enlightened and formed an art academy and a college of pharmacy, and she imported foreign physicians. She built many architecturally significant buildings, including the Hermitage. For thirty-four years she amazed the Russian people with her political skill and diplomacy.
>
> On the other hand, Catherine was not a great Russian, nor was she an enlightened leader of all the people. First, she was not Russian; she was German, but she had worked hard to "russify" herself during the early years of her unhappy marriage. Second, and ironically, she murdered the legitimate ruler of Russia. When she seized power, she made sure the tsar quickly died of "hemorrhoidal colic." Third, she did nothing to improve the lot of the poor serfs and after a bloody uprising in 1773, she became even more despotic. Yet, Catherine was an engaging character who, through her cunning and intellect, has become known to the world in history books as "Catherine the Great."

EXPLANATION Note the organization, logical thinking, and effective use of transitions in this response.

Locus of Control

Have you ever heard students say, "I do better when I don't study," or "No matter how much I study, I still get a C"? According to Julian Rotter, a learning theory psychologist who believes that people develop attitudes about control of their lives, such comments reflect an *external locus of control* regarding test taking.[7] People with an external locus of control, called "externalizers," feel that fate, luck, or other people control what happens to them. Because they feel they can do little to avoid what befalls them, they do not face matters directly and thus do not take responsibility for failure or credit for success.

On the other hand, people who have an *internal locus of control* feel that they, not "fate," have control over what happens to them. Such students might evaluate test performance by saying, "I didn't study enough" or "I should have spent more time organizing my essay response." "Internalizers" feel their rewards are due to their own actions, and they take steps to be sure they receive those rewards. When it comes to test taking, be an internalizer: Take responsibility, take control, and accept credit for your success.

---

[7]Julian Rotter, "External Control and Internal Control," *Psychology Today* 5, no. 1 (1971): 37–42.

Summary *Points*

> **Can being testwise improve your score?**
> Test taking is a serious part of the business of being a college student. Preparation and practice—being testwise—can lead to improved scores on both standardized reading tests and content area exams.

> **How should you prepare before a test?**
> Study according to the type of test you are taking. Plan your study times to avoid having to cram. Arrive rested and alert.

> **What should you notice during a test?**
> Read the directions, and keep up with the time.

> **What strategies should you use to read a comprehension passage?**
> Items on standardized reading tests tend to follow a predictable pattern and include five major question types. Learn to recognize these types and the skills needed for answering each.

> **What are the major question types?**
> They are (1) main idea, (2) details, (3) inference, (4) purpose, and (5) vocabulary.

> **What hints help with multiple-choice items?**
> Be careful, not careless; consider all options; notice key words; and use logical reasoning.

> **How do you answer an essay question?**
> Be sure you understand the question, brainstorm your response, organize your thoughts, and write in paragraphs with specific examples.

Appendix

ESL: Making Sense of Figurative Language and Idioms

What Is ESL?

How many languages can you speak? Are you a native English speaker who has learned Spanish, or are you a native Farsi speaker who has learned English? If you have acquired skill in a second or third language, you know that it takes many years and plenty of patience to master the intricacies of a language. Not only must you learn new words, but you must also learn new grammatical constructions. For example, the articles that are habitually used in English such as *a, an,* or *the* do not appear in Russian, Chinese, Japanese, Thai, or Farsi. In Spanish and Arabic, personal pronouns restate the subject, as in *My sister she goes to college.* In Spanish, Greek, French, Vietnamese, and Portuguese, "*to* words" are used rather than "*-ing* words," as in *I enjoy to play soccer.* These complexities, which are innately understood by native speakers, make direct translation from one language to another difficult. The English language, especially, has many unusual phrases and grammatical constructions that defy direct translation.

To assist students with these complexities, most colleges offer courses in ESL, which stands for English as a Second Language. These courses are designed to teach language skills to nonnative speakers of English. If you are an ESL student, you may have been recruited through an international exchange program with another college, you may be a newly arrived immigrant, or you may be a citizen with a bilingual background. You bring a multicultural perspective to classroom discussions and campus life that will broaden the insights of others. Not only are some obvious things like holidays different from those of others, but your sense of family life, work, and responsibility may also be different. Share your thoughts and ideas with native English speakers as they share the irregularities of the language with you.

What Is Figurative Language?

One aspect of the English language that defies direct translation and confuses nonnative speakers, and sometimes even native speakers, is figurative language. This is the manipulation of the language to create images, add interest, and draw comparisons by using figures of speech (see Chapter 7 on inference). The two most commonly used figures of speech are *similes* and *metaphors*.

Simile: a stated comparison using *like* or *as*

The baby swims like a duck.

Metaphor: an implied comparison

The baby is a duck in water.

Many figurative expressions are common in English. As in the previous metaphor, the *baby* is not actually a *baby duck*, but the implication is that *the baby swims very well*. However, neither direct translation nor a dictionary will unlock that meaning. When you encounter a figure of speech, look for clues within the sentence to help you guess the meaning.

Directions

The following practice exercises contain figurative language. Read each dialogue passage for meaning and then use the context clues to match the number of the boldfaced figure of speech with the letter of the appropriate definition. To narrow your choices, the answers to questions 1 through 5 can be found in choices a through e, and the answers to questions 6 through 10 can be found in choices f through j.

exercise 1

Jennifer: You're (1) **burning the midnight oil.** What's keeping you up so late?

Carmen: I've been working (2) **24/7** on this project for English class. Every time I think I have it (3) **all wrapped up,** I seem to (4) **run across** one problem or another.

Jennifer: What seems to be the major (5) **sticking point?**

Carmen: If only I knew. I can't seem to (6) **nail it down.** I just don't feel like I (7) **have a handle on** the assignment.

Jennifer: Have you thought of contacting your instructor? She just might (8) **point you in the right direction.** In fact, I think she's known for taking students (9) **under her wing.**

Carmen: That's a good idea. Maybe I'll go to her office and see if I can (10) **run this by her.**

_a_ 1. burning the midnight oil	a. working late
_d_ 2. 24/7	b. finished
_b_ 3. all wrapped up	c. find
_c_ 4. run across	d. night and day
_e_ 5. sticking point	e. problem
_h_ 6. nail it down	f. understand
_f_ 7. have a handle on	g. show you what to do
_g_ 8. point you in the right direction	h. figure it out
_j_ 9. under her wing	i. see what she thinks of it
_i_ 10. run this by her	j. give extra help

exercise 2

Thomas: Getting ready for this speech is (1) **murder.** I am (2) **sweating bullets** just thinking about having to stand up in front of (3) **everyone and his brother.** Do you think there's any way my professor would (4) **let me off the hook?**

Michael: (5) **When cows fly!** Thomas, we're all (6) **in the same boat.** No one in class is (7) **itching to** give a speech.

Thomas: Maybe we should (8) **lay our cards on the table** and tell her we're not all (9) **jumping up and down** to be the first to present.

Michael: I thought you wanted to pass this class. (10) **Look at the bright side.** This is the only presentation you have to make for the term.

c	1. murder	a. never
b	2. sweating bullets	b. nervous
d	3. everyone and his brother	c. very difficult
e	4. let me off the hook	d. lots of people
a	5. when cows fly	e. waive the requirement
g	6. in the same boat	f. wanting to
f	7. itching to	g. in a similar position
j	8. lay our cards on the table	h. excited
h	9. jumping up and down	i. see the positive
i	10. look at the bright side	j. tell the truth

exercise 3

Rodney: This car I bought is (1) **a lemon.** The gas gauge and speedometer seem to have (2) **given up the ghost.** Next time I buy a used car, I'm going to have a mechanic (3) **go over** it (4) **with a fine-tooth comb.**

Jamal: My brother is a mechanic. He is busy, but if you need (5) an **ace in the hole,** I'll ask him to help you. He is certainly (6) **on the up and up.**

Rodney: Great! I'm going to (7) **bite the bullet** and (8) **dump** this car. Imagine if I run out of gas on the highway or get a speeding ticket on a date. That wouldn't (9) **go over big** with the girl.

Jamal: Maybe you should (10) **have it out with** the guy who sold it to you.

c	1. a lemon	a. resource in reserve
e	2. given up the ghost	b. very carefully
d	3. go over	c. merchandise that is defective
b	4. with a fine-tooth comb	d. examine
a	5. ace in the hole	e. stopped working
i	6. on the up and up	f. accept the unpleasant reality

	f	7.	bite the bullet	g.	discuss the conflict
	h	8.	dump	h.	get rid of
	j	9.	go over big	i.	trustworthy
	g	10.	have it out with	j.	impress

What Are Common English Idioms?

An **idiom** is an expression with a special meaning that cannot be understood by directly translating each individual word. Because of years of exposure to the language, native speakers usually understand idioms. However, they are confusing if you are learning English as a second language.

Idioms are more common in spoken and informal language than in formal writing. In fact, most idiomatic expressions can usually be replaced by a single formal word. To add to the confusion, some idioms have more than one meaning, and many idioms are grammatically irregular.

EXAMPLE   What does the idiomatic expression *go over* mean in the following sentences?

(a) How did my speech *go over*?

(b) I want to **go over** the exam paper with the professor.

EXPLANATION In both sentences, the use of the idiom is informal. A more formal version of each would be the following:

(a) How was my speech *received* by the audience?

(b) I want to *review* the exam paper with the professor.

Notice the grammatical irregularity in the first sentence. *Over* is not followed by a noun (the name of a person, place, or thing) as a preposition (a connecting word, like *in*, *out*, and *at*) normally would be according to the rules of grammar. Instead, *over* becomes part of the verb phrase (words showing action). Thus, the translation requires a change in wording, whereas the second use of the idiom is grammatically correct and can be directly translated by the single word *review*.

No one will argue that understanding idioms is easy. If you go to a bookstore, you will see that entire books have been written about categorizing, recognizing, and translating thousands of them. To help clear up the confusion, some books group idioms according to families like root words, and others categorize them according to grammatical constructions. Either way, understanding idiomatic expressions depends more on using context clues to figure out meaning and familiarity with the informal, spoken language than with learning rules.

In the following practice exercises, use the context clues within each sentence to write the meaning of the boldfaced idiom in the blank provided.

Reader's *Tip* ──── Categorizing Idioms ────

Idioms are sometimes categorized into the following groups:

- Word families: grouping around a similar individual word
  Down as in *step down, take down, pipe down, narrow down, nail down, run down, tear down, knock down, let down, die down, cut down*, etc.

- Verb + preposition: action word plus a connecting word
  Hammer away means persist, *stand for* means represent, and *roll back* means reduce.

- Preposition + noun: connecting word plus the name of a person, place, or thing
  On foot means walking, *by heart* means memorized, and *off guard* means surprised.

- Verb + adjective: action word plus a descriptive word
  Think twice means consider carefully, *hang loose* means be calm, and *play fair* means deal equally.

- Pairs of nouns: two words naming a person, place, or thing
  Flesh and blood means kin, *part and parcel* means total, and *pins and needles* means nervous.

- Pairs of adjectives: two descriptive words
  Cut and dried means obvious, *fair and square* means honest, *short and sweet* means brief.

exercise 4

1. If you call Esmeralda at work, **cut to the chase** quickly because she is very busy creating the new product advertisements. <u>get to the point</u>

2. When Marcy stopped him in the hall, Jim was **in a rush** because his math class had already begun. <u>hurrying</u>

3. Tom hadn't been notified that the party was formal and he looked **out of place** in his jeans. <u>inappropriate</u>

4. Juanita had a **heart-to-heart** talk about boys and dating with her younger sister. <u>sincere</u>

5. His channel surfing and the constant clicking of the TV remote control are getting **on my nerves.** <u>irritating</u>

6. Miguel is going to backpack through Europe after he graduates, but it will have to be **on a shoestring** because he hasn't been able to save much money. cheaply

7. Denise didn't study for the exam she is taking; she decided to **wing it** and hope for the best. go on instinct and be unprepared

8. I can't **get over** how much my blind date last night looked like Brad Pitt. grow accustomed to

9. Rather than being timid about the new job, just **give it your best shot.** ____ try very hard

10. Being assigned to the new project at work will finally give me a chance to **pull out all the stops** and show them what I'm really worth. ____ do all I am capable of

exercise 5

1. I try to do my homework every night because I feel anxious if it starts to **pile up** and I get behind schedule. accumulate

2. I'm feeling **on top of the world** about my new laptop computer. happy

3. Sergio and I are **on the same wavelength** about how the club money should be spent. thinking similarly

4. Let's **put our heads together** and see if we can grill hamburgers without buying more charcoal. think

5. When you go on the job interview, don't **sell yourself short** by being too modest about your skills. underestimate or undervalue your abilities

6. After her husband's lung cancer, my aunt quit smoking **cold turkey.** ____ instantly, without smoking another single time

7. Melinda seemed to be **having a bad hair day,** so Tonya delayed mentioning that the concert tickets were twice the amount anticipated. in a bad mood

8. Mandy's little brother is too much of a **live wire** for me to babysit. ____ energetic, active person

9. We might as well go in and **face the music** for breaking Dad's tool that we weren't supposed to be using. accept the consequences

10. I don't know how Eduardo can afford to buy every electronic gadget that comes on the market and still **make ends meet.** pay his expenses

exercise 6

1. The city official gave an **in your face** answer to a taxpayer with a very legitimate question about an excessive water bill. <u>insulting</u>

2. Her mother must have **nerves of steel** to be able to stay in a house full of screaming children and still remain sane. <u>be very calm</u>

3. Wanda has been walking around in a daze with her **head in the clouds** ever since she started dating Jose. <u>happy and oblivious</u>

4. I've **had it** with Bill borrowing money and never paying it back. No more! <u>will no longer tolerate</u>

5. My little brother is **a pain in the neck** when he'd rather annoy my friends than stay in his room. <u>an aggravation</u>

6. Tina is **playing with fire** by accepting rides from total strangers. <u>living dangerously</u>

7. I just got paid, and I'm finally going to **shell out** for the new DVD player I've wanted to buy. <u>use money to purchase</u>

8. Without **a nest egg** for major expenses, senior citizens face financial difficulties trying to live solely on Social Security. <u>money saved</u>

9. Roberto was **flying high** after he got accepted at the college of his first choice. <u>happy</u>

10. The senator was in a **catch-22** situation on the environmental issue because half of the voters in her constituency were for the new dam and half were against it. <u>couldn't win by acting either way</u>

Glossary

acronym An abbreviation pronounced as a word and contrived to simplify a lengthy name and gain quick recognition for an organization or agency. For example, *UNICEF* is the acronym for the United Nations International Children's Emergency Fund.

addition A pattern of organization that provides more information about something that has already been explained.

ad hominem An argument in which the person is attacked rather than the issue.

analogy A comparison showing connections with and similarities to previous experiences.

annotating A method of using symbols and notations to highlight textbook material for future study.

antonym A word that means the opposite of another word.

appeals to emotions A critical thinking fallacy that uses highly charged language for emotional manipulation.

appeals to pity A critical thinking fallacy that pleas to support the underdog, the person or issue that needs your help.

argument Assertions that support a conclusion with the intention of persuading.

assertion A declarative statement.

attention Uninterrupted mental focus.

bandwagon A critical thinking fallacy that gives the idea that everybody is doing it and you will be left out if you do not quickly join the crowd.

bar graph An arrangement of horizontal or vertical bars in which the length of each represents an amount or number.

believability Support that is not suspicious but is believable.

bias An opinion or position on a subject recognized through facts slanted toward an author's personal beliefs.

bookmarking On the Internet, a save-the-site technique that lets you automatically return to the designated Web site with just one or two mouse clicks.

browser The software that searches to find information on the Internet.

cause and effect A pattern of organization in which one item is shown as having produced another.

chronological order A pattern of organization in which items are listed in time order or sequence.

circular reasoning A critical thinking fallacy that gives support for the conclusion that is merely a restatement of it.

classification A pattern of organization dividing information into a certain number of groups or categories. The divisions are then named, and the parts are explained.

cognitive psychology A body of knowledge that describes how the mind works or is believed to work.

comparison A pattern of organization that presents items according to similarities between or among them.

comparison-contrast A pattern of organization in which similarities and differences are presented.

concentration The focusing of full attention on a task.

conclusion Interpretation based on evidence and suggested meaning.

connotation The feeling associated with the definition of a word.

consistency Support that holds together and does not contradict itself.

context clues Hints within a sentence that help unlock the meaning of an unknown word.

contrast A pattern of organization that presents items according to differences between or among them.

Cornell Method A system of notetaking that involves writing sentence summaries on the right side of the page with key words and topics indicated on the left.

creative thinking Generating many possible solutions to a problem.

critical thinking Deliberating in a purposeful, organized manner to assess the value of information or argument.

cumulative bar graph A bar graph that shows a cumulative effect in which all the bar's segments add up to a total. Rather than having multiple bars or lines, the groups are stacked on top of each other to dramatically show differences.

databases Computer-based indexes to assist research. A single article may be listed under several topics and may appear in several different indexes.

deductive reasoning Thinking that starts with a previously learned conclusion and applies it to a new situation.

definition A pattern of organization devoted to defining an idea and further explaining it with examples.

denotation The dictionary definition of a word.

description A pattern of organization listing characteristics of a person, place, or thing, as in a simple listing.

details Information that supports, describes, and explains the main idea.

diagram A drawing of an object showing labeled parts.

distractor A response on a multiple-choice test that detracts the reader from the correct response.

domain name A name registered by a Web site owner.

domain type The category to which a Web site owner belongs; for example, *edu* is the domain type for colleges and universities.

download A method of transferring a file from the Internet to a particular computer.

emoticons In e-mail communication, symbols such as smiley faces :) used to represent emotions in a lighthearted way. They are not appropriate for formal correspondence but are frequently used in informal contexts.

etymology The study of word origins involving the tracing of words back to their earliest recorded appearance.

euphemism A substitution of a mild, indirect, or vague term for one that is considered harsh, blunt, or offensive.

external distractors Temptations of the physical world that divert the attention from a task.

fact A statement that can be proved true.

fallacy An inference that first appears reasonable but closer inspection proves it to be unrelated, unreliable, or illogical.

figurative language Words used to create images that take on a new meaning.

fixation A stop the eyes make while reading.

flowchart A diagram showing how ideas are related, with boxes and arrows indicating levels of importance and movement.

generalization A pattern of organization in which a general statement or conclusion is supported with specific examples.

habit A repetitious act almost unconsciously performed.

home page The entry point to a Web site through which other pages on the site can be reached.

homonyms Words with different meanings that are spelled and sound alike such as *bear* in "bear the burden" or "kill the bear."

humorous Comical, funny, or amusing.

hyperbole Exaggeration using figurative language to describe something as being more than it actually is.

hypertext links In Web technology, phrases that appear as bold blue or underlined text. Clicking on them will not only move you from one page to another within the Web site, but can also send you to other related Web sites. The words chosen and underlined as the link describe the information you are likely to find at that destination.

idiom A figurative expression that does not make literal sense but communicates a generally accepted meaning.

imagery Mental pictures created by figurative language.

implied meaning Suggested rather than directly stated meaning.

incomplete facts or **card stacking** A critical thinking fallacy that gives or leaves out factual details in order to misrepresent reality.

inductive reasoning Thinking based on the collection of data and the formulation of a conclusion based on it.

inference Subtle suggestions expressed without direct statement.

intent A reason or purpose for writing, which is usually to inform, persuade, or entertain.

internal distractions Concerns that come repeatedly to mind and disturb concentration.

Internet An electronic system of more than 25,000 computer networks using a common language that connects millions of users around the world. The Internet is the networked system that allows the World Wide Web to function.

irony A twist in meaning or a surprise ending that is the opposite of what is expected and may involve a humorous undertone.

knowledge network A cluster of knowledge about a subject; a schema.

lateral thinking A way of creatively thinking around a problem or redefining it to seek new solutions.

learning style A preference for a particular manner of presenting material to be learned.

line graph A frequency distribution in which the horizontal scale measures time and the vertical scale measures amount.

main idea A statement of the primary focus of the topic in a passage.

map A graphic designation or distribution.

mapping A method of graphically displaying material to show relationships and importance for later study.

metacognition Knowledge of how to read as well as the ability to regulate and direct the process.

metaphor A figure of speech that directly compares two unlike things (without using the words *like* or *as*).

misinterpreted statistics A critical thinking fallacy that improperly applies numerical data to unrelated populations that they were never intended to represent.

misleading analogy A critical thinking fallacy that gives a comparison of two things suggesting that they are similar when they are in fact distinctly different.

mnemonic A technique using images, numbers, rhymes, or letters to improve memory.

multiple intelligences The theory explained by Howard Gardner that there are eight different ways of being smart and some people develop certain intelligences to a greater extent than others.

multiple meanings The defining of a word in several ways. For example, the dictionary lists over thirty meanings for the word *run*.

note taking A method of writing down short phrases and summaries to record textbook material for future study.

opinion A statement of a personal view or judgment.

outlining A method of using indentations, Roman numerals, numbers, and letters to organize a topic for future study.

overgeneralizations Examples and anecdotes asserted to apply to all cases rather than a select few. *Example:* High school students do little work during their senior year and thus are overwhelmed at college.

oversimplification A critical thinking fallacy that reduces an issue to two simple choices, without consideration of other alternatives or "gray areas" in between.

overstatement Exaggeration using figurative language to describe something as being more than it actually is.

pattern of organization The structure or framework for presenting the details in a passage.

personification Attributing human characteristics to nonhuman things.

pie graph A circular graph divided into wedge-shaped segments to show portions totaling 100 percent.

point of view A position or opinion on a subject.

politically correct language Doublespeak that is used to hide unpleasant ideas in politics or social interaction.

prefix A group of letters added to the beginning of a word and causing a change of meaning.

premise The thesis or main point of an argument.

previewing A method of glancing over a reading passage to predict what the passage is about and thus assess your prior knowledge and needed skills.

prior knowledge Previous learning about a subject.

propaganda A systematic and deliberate attempt to persuade others to a particular doctrine or point of view and to undermine any opposition.

purpose A writer's underlying reason or intent for writing.

questionable authority A critical thinking fallacy that gives a testimonial suggesting authority from people who are not experts.

rate Reading pace calculated according to the number of words read in one minute.

reading between the lines The figurative phrase for suggested thought for the reader or listener.

recall Reviewing what was included and learned after reading a passage.

regression Rereading material because of a lack of understanding or concentration.

relevance The degree to which related material supports a topic or conclusion.

root The stem or basic part of a word; in English, roots are derived primarily from Latin and Greek.

sarcasm A tone or language that expresses biting humor, usually meaning the opposite of what is said, with the purpose of undermining or ridiculing someone.

scanning Searching reading material quickly to locate specific points of information.

schema A skeleton or network of knowledge about a subject.

simile A comparison of two things using the words *like* or *as*.

simple listing A pattern of organization that lists items in a series.

skimming A technique for selectively reading for the gist or main idea.

slippery slope A critical thinking fallacy that objects to something because it will lead to greater evil and disastrous consequences.

spatial order A pattern of organization that identifies the whereabouts of a place or object.

straw person A critical thinking fallacy that gives a setup in which a distorted or exaggerated form of the opponent's argument is introduced and knocked down as if to represent a totally weak opposition.

study system A plan for working through stages to read and learn textbook material.

subvocalization The inaudible inner voice that is part of the reading process.

suffix A group of letters added to the end of a word and causing a change in meaning as well as the way the word can be used in the sentence.

summary A concise statement of the main idea and significant supporting details.

synonym A word with the same meaning of another word.

table A listing of facts and figures in columns for quick reference.

testimonials A critical thinking fallacy that gives opinions of agreement from respected celebrities who are not actually experts.

thesis statement A sentence that states the author's main point.

thinking An organized and controlled mental activity that helps you solve problems, make decisions, and understand ideas.

time order A pattern of organization that presents items in the chronological order in which they occurred.

to do list A reminder list of activities that you need to accomplish.

tone A writer's attitude toward a subject.

topic sentence A sentence that condenses the thoughts and details of a passage into a general, all-inclusive statement of the author's message.

topic A word or phrase that labels the subject of a paragraph, reading passage, article, or book.

transfer A critical thinking fallacy that gives an association with a positively or negatively regarded person or thing in order to lend the same association to the argument (also guilt or virtue by association).

transition A signal word that connects the parts of a sentence and leads readers to anticipate a continuation or a change in the writer's thoughts.

transitional words Connecting words that signal the direction of the writer's thought or the pattern of organization.

understatement Figurative language that minimizes a point.

Uniform Resource Locator (URL) The address for finding a specific site on the World Wide Web, just as an address and zip code are required to mail a letter. A URL is similar to an e-mail address, except that it routes you to a source of information called a *Web page* or *Web site* rather than to the mailbox of an individual person.

verbal irony The use of words to express a meaning that is the opposite of what is said.

vertical thinking A straightforward and logical way of thinking that searches for a solution to the stated problem.

Web directory A type of search engine that organizes hypertext links into categories similar to the way in which libraries organize books into categories.

Web pages The formal presentation of information provided by individual people, businesses, educational institutions, or other organizations on the Internet.

World Wide Web (WWW) An electronic information network that is similar to an enormous library, with Web sites being like books and Web pages being like the pages in the books.

Credits

Ahmad, Adil. "Remembering a Civil Rights Hero," *The Dartmouth* via U-WIRE, April 12, 2004. Reprinted by permission of U-WIRE.

Alexie, Sherman. "Superman and Me," *The Los Angeles Times*, April 19, 1998. Copyright © 1997 Sherman Alexie. All rights reserved.

Anderson, Fiona. From "Obtain Professional Advice if You Win Big on the Lottery: People Can Make So Many Mistakes Going It Alone, Financial Adviser Says," *Vancouver Sun* (British Columbia), May 5, 2006, p. C5. Reprinted with permission.

Blau, John. From "Study: Mobile Phones Affect DNA." Reprinted by permission of IDG News Service, from *PC World*, December 21, 2004.

Bovée, Courtland L., John V. Thill, and Barbara E. Schatzman. From *Business in Action*, 2nd Edition, © 2004, pp. 91, 109–110. Reprinted by permission of Pearson Education, Inc., Upper Saddle River, NJ.

Boyd, Sarah. From "The Beauty Premium," *The Dominion Post*, June 4, 2005. Reprinted by permission of Fairfax Media, Wellington, New Zealand.

Brehm, Barbara. From *Stress Management: Increasing Your Stress Resistance*. Boston: Pearson Allyn and Bacon, 1998. Reprinted by permission of the author.

Byer, Curtis O. and Louis W. Shainberg. From *Living Well: Health in Your Hands*, 2nd Edition. Copyright © 1995 Jones and Bartlett Publishers, Sudbury, MA. www.jbpub.com. Reprinted with permission.

Capobianco, Jordan. From "Growing Up Is Taking Longer Than It Used To," *The Oracle* (University of South Florida), May 15, 2006. © 2006 The Oracle. Reprinted with permission.

Donatelle, Rebecca J. From *Access to Health*, 8th Edition. Copyright © 2004 by Pearson Education, Inc., publishing as Benjamin Cummings. Reprinted by permission of Pearson Education, Inc., Glenview, IL.

Dowd, Ann Reilly. From "What Makes Condi Run." Reprinted from the September–October 2005 issue of *AARP the Magazine*, a publication of AARP. Copyright 2005 AARP. All rights reserved. http://www.aarp-magazine.org/. 1-888-687-2227.

Fiorina, Morris P., Paul E. Peterson, and Bertram Johnson. From *The New American Democracy*, 3rd Edition. Published by Longman. Copyright © 2003 by Pearson Education, Inc. Reprinted by permission of Pearson Education, Inc., Glenview, IL.

Gerow, Josh R. From *Psychology: An Introduction*, Second Edition. Copyright © 1989 Scott, Foresman and Company. Reprinted by permission.

Greer, Charles R. and W. Richard Plunkett. From *Supervision: Diversity and Teams in the Workplace*, 10th Edition, © 2003, pp. 24–25, 359–360. Reprinted by permission of Pearson Education, Inc., Upper Saddle River, NJ.

Gregory, Paul R. Adapted from *Essentials of Economics*, 6th Ed. by Gregory, pp. 41, 66, 68. © 2005, 2002, 1999, 1996 Pearson Education Inc. Reproduced by permission of Pearson Education, Inc. All rights reserved.

Greulach, Victor A. and Vincent J. Chiappetta. From *Biology: The Science of Life*. Copyright © 1977 by Scott, Foresman and Company. Reprinted by permission of Pearson Education, Inc., Glenview, IL.

Griffin, Ricky W. and Ronald J. Ebert. *Business*, 8th Edition, © 2006, pp. 229, 89–90, 57, 102, 572. Reprinted by permission of Pearson Education, Inc., Upper Saddle River, NJ.

Hall, Dave. From "Inventors Hope for Slice of Pizza Box Business: Perforated Lid," *National Post* (Canada), March 23, 2006, p. SR7. Material reprinted with the express permission of: "National Post Company," a CanWest Partnership.

Harris, E. B. "E. B.'s View from the Cow Pasture: He's Been Sleeping in My Bed," *The Carolina Cattle Connection*, June 2003. Reprinted by permission of the author.

Heaney, Seamus. "Mid-Term Break" from *Opened Ground: Selected Poems 1966–1996* by Seamus Heaney. Copyright © 1998 by Seamus Heaney. Reprinted by permission of Farrar, Straus and Giroux, LLC., and Faber and Faber Ltd.

Hernández, Macarena del Rocío. "What I Did for Love" from *The Philadelphia Inquirer Magazine*, July 2, 2000. Copyright © 2000 by Macarena del Rocío Hernández. Reprinted by permission of the author.

Hughes, Langston. "A Dream Deferred – Harlem [2]," from *The Collected Poems of Langston Hughes* by Langston Hughes, copyright © 1994 by The Estate of Langston Hughes. Used by permission of Alfred A. Knopf, a division of Random House, Inc.

Hunter, Evan. "On the Sidewalk, Bleeding" from *Happy New Year, Herbie, and Other Stories* by Evan Hunter. New York: Simon & Schuster, 1963. Reprinted by permission of Gelfman Schneider Literary Agents, Inc., as agent for Hui Corp.

Kamien, Roger. From *Music: An Appreciation*, Fifth Brief Edition. Copyright © 2006 by The McGraw-Hill Companies, Inc. Reproduced with permission.

Katz, Sidney M. From "The Importance of Being Beautiful," originally appeared in *Today*, July 24, 1982. © 1982 by Sidney Katz.

Kishlansky, Mark, Patrick Geary, and Patricia O'Brien. From *Civilization in the West*, Sixth Edition. Published by Longman. Copyright © 2006 by Pearson Education, Inc. Reprinted by permission of Pearson Education, Inc., Glenview, IL.

Klucha, Joan. From "Dogs Who Leave Too Early Show Signs of Aggression," Special to the *North Shore News* (British Columbia), October 23, 2005, p. 66. Reprinted by permission of the author.

Long, Larry and Nancy Long, *Computers: Information Technology in Perspective*, 11th Edition, © 2004. Reprinted by permission of Pearson Education, Inc., Upper Saddle River, NJ.

Lutgens, Frederick K. and Edward J. Tarbuck, illustrated by Dennis Tasa. *The Atmosphere: An Introduction to Meteorology*, 9th Edition, © 2004, pp. 378, 444, 396, 195, 147. Reprinted by permission of Pearson Education, Inc., Upper Saddle River, NJ.

Macionis, John J. *Social Problems*, 2nd Edition, © 2005, pp. 136, 423–431. Adapted by permission of Pearson Education, Inc., Upper Saddle River, NJ.

Malcolm X. "Learning to Read," from *The Autobiography of Malcolm X* by Malcolm X and Alex Haley, copyright © 1964 by Alex Haley and Malcolm X. Copyright © 1965 by Alex Haley and Betty Shabazz. Used by permission of Random House, Inc.

Marinovich, Matt. From "Intelligence," *The Quarterly*. Reprinted by permission of the author.

Maxwell, Sarah. From "Raising the Stakes: Monaco Is Cleaning Up Its Act and Staking All Its Chips on a New Golden Era of Business Travel," *Business Traveller*, March 2006. Reprinted by permission of the publisher.

McAfee, Robert E. "Regulation Won't Work: Ban Boxing" as appeared in *USA Today*, December 20, 1990. Reprinted by permission of the author.

Milford, Maureen. From "Entrepreneur Draws Inspiration from Cosmetics Industry Pioneer," *The News Journal*, October 7, 2005, p. 10B. Copyright © 2005 The News Journal (Wilmington, DE). Reprinted with permission.

Monaco Economic Expansion Department. Graph, "Private employment in Monaco: distribution per activity sector, 2005." Reprinted by permission of Monaco Economic Expansion Department.

Morrell, Anna. From "ARRESTING Development," *Western Mail*, February 25, 2006, Features Section, p. 4. © Western Mail & Echo Ltd. 2006. Reprinted with permission.

Nash, Gary B. et al., eds. From *The American People: Creating a Nation and a Society*, Sixth Edition, Volume One: To 1877. Published by Longman. Copyright © 2004 by Pearson Education, Inc. Reprinted by permission of Pearson Education, Inc., Glenview, IL.

Phillips, Valerie. From "Drink and Be Wary? Reading between the Lines about Energy Boosting Beverages," *Deseret Morning News* (Salt Lake City), April 26, 2006. Copyright © 2006 by Deseret News Publishing Company. Reprinted by permission.

Pitt, Leonard. From *We Americans*. Copyright © 1987 Kendall/Hunt Publishing Company. Reprinted with permission.

Pronzini, Bill. "A Dip in the Poole." Copyright © 1970 by H.S.D. Publications, Inc. First published in *Alfred Hitchcock's Mystery Magazine*. Reprinted by permission of Bill Pronzini.

Pruitt, B. E. and Jane J. Stein. From *Decisions for Healthy Living*. San Francisco: Pearson Benjamin Cummings, 2004. Reprinted by permission of the authors.

Ramirez, Robert. "The Barrio" by Robert Ramirez, in *Models for Writers: Short Essays for Composition*, 8th Edition, by Alfred Rosa and Paul Eschholz. New York: Bedford/St. Martin's, 2003. Reprinted by permission of Robert Ramirez.

Reeve, Lloyd Eric. "Caged" from "Practical English," *Household Magazine*, March 2, 1960.

Robbins, Alexandra and Abby Wilner. From *Quarterlife Crisis* by Alexandra Robbins and Abby Wilner, copyright © 2001 by Alexandra Robbins & Abby Wilner. Used by permission of Jeremy P. Tarcher, an imprint of Penguin Group (USA) Inc.

Robins, Richard W. et al. From Figure 1 from "Global Self-Esteem Across the Life Span," *Psychology and Aging*, vol. 17, no. 3 (2002): 423-434. Copyright 2002 by the American Psychological Association, Inc. Adapted with permission.

Roseliep, Raymond. "campfire extinguished," from *Listen to Light: Haiku* by Raymond Roseliep. Ithaca, NY: Alembic Press, 1980, © 1980 by Raymond Roseliep, © 1985 by Daniel J. Rogers, by permission of Daniel J. Rogers.

Rowntree, Lester, Martin Lewis, Marie Price, and William Wyckoff, *Diversity Amid Globalization*, 2nd Edition, © 2003. Reprinted by permission of Pearson Education, Inc., Upper Saddle River, NJ.

Ruggiero, Vincent Ryan. From *The Art of Thinking*, 7th Edition. Published by Longman. Copyright © 2004 by Pearson Education, Inc. Reprinted by permission of Pearson Education, Inc., Glenview, IL.

Sheridan, Peter. From "Shock Tactic That Could Save a City," *The Express*, April 18, 2006. Reprinted by permission.

Sturgeon, Jeff. From "Snuffing Out Magazines," *The Roanoke Times* (Virginia), September 3, 2006. © McClatchy-Tribune Information Services. All Rights Reserved. Reprinted with permission.

Svoboda, Elizabeth. "A Swedish Study Links Mobile Phones to Brain Damage," *Popular Science*, February 2004. © 2004 POPULAR SCIENCE Magazine. Reprinted by permission of Time4 Media, Inc.

Tannen, Deborah. "Gender Gap in Cyberspace," by Deborah Tannen, *Newsweek*, May 16, 1994, copyright Deborah Tannen. Reprinted by permission.

Thompson, Janice and Melinda Manore. From *Nutrition: An Applied Approach*. Copyright © 2005 Pearson Education, Inc., publishing as Benjamin Cummings. Reprinted by permission of Pearson Education, Inc., Glenview, IL.

Vivian, John. From *The Media of Mass Communication*, 6e. Published by Allyn and Bacon, Boston, MA. Copyright © 2002 by Pearson Education. Reprinted by permission of the publisher.

Vonnegut, Jr., Kurt. From *Deadeye Dick*. New York: Delacorte Press/Seymour Lawrence, 1982.

Watkins, Billy. From "Kid Doesn't Want to Read? Skip Classics, Try Comics," *The Clarion-Ledger*, January 20, 2005, p. 1E. Reprinted by permission of The Clarion-Ledger, Jackson, Mississippi.

Watts, Randolph H., Jr. and L. DiAnne Borders. From "Boys' Perceptions of the Male Role: Understanding Gender Role Conflict in Adolescent Males," *The Journal of Men's Studies, 13*. Copyright © 2005 by The Men's Studies Press, L.L.C. Reprinted by permission.

Index of Concept Prep Terms

Index